As a busy pastor I am always on the lookout for excellent commentaries—and I can say with confidence that many of them are not very excellent! Fortunately, this one is. Cara has written an impressive commentary—deeply researched yet conversational in tone, theologically rich yet pastorally attuned—on one of the most important and difficult books of the Bible. From his discussion on the authorship of Hebrews, to the application of the Sabbath for today, to the supremacy of Christ over all things, Cara's work on Hebrews is exegetically careful (showing a broad knowledge of the interpretive tradition) and clearly laid out (with most of the technical material located in the footnotes). The result is a terrific exposition of Hebrews that can be used, with profit, by students, pastors, and scholars alike.

KEVIN DEYOUNG
Senior Pastor, Christ Covenant Church, Matthews, North Carolina;
Associate Professor of Systematic Theology, Reformed Theological Seminary, Charlotte, North Carolina

Robert Cara's commentary on Hebrews is marked by clear and convincing exegesis, theological depth, and practical relevance. Theologically he mines the wells of early church history and Reformation readings. Students, pastors, and all those desiring to learn from and teach Hebrews will profit from this excellent and accessible commentary.

THOMAS R. SCHREINER
James Buchanan Harrison Professor of New Testament Interpretation, Southern Baptist Theological Seminary, Louisville, Kentucky

The Epistle to the Hebrews is one of the most difficult and one of the most rewarding books in Scripture. We may be grateful to Robert J. Cara for a commentary that especially serves those tasked with preaching or teaching Hebrews. Cara's footnotes demonstrate a thorough acquaintance with the relevant literature (contemporary and historical), while his exposition provides readers with exegetically careful and theologically sound readings of the text. He provides readers with generous lines of application and with multiple ties between Hebrews and the creeds and confessions of the church. Highly recommended.

GUY P. WATERS
James M. Baird, Jr. Professor of New Testament,
Reformed Theological Seminary, Jackson, Mississippi

Here is a real treat: a commentary on Hebrews written from a consistently Reformed perspective, which interacts with both historical and contemporary scholarship. Cara has provided a timely, clear, and mature resource on Hebrews. Pastors and students of Hebrews will want this commentary on their shelves.

BRANDON D. CROWE
Professor of New Testament, Westminster Theological
Seminary, Philadelphia, Pennsylvania

Robert J. Cara's commentary on Hebrews provides great help for those preaching and teaching in the local church. The scope and depth of Dr. Cara's commentary bears great fruit in sermon preparation as he clearly and carefully lays out the substance of the text and exegetical options in a length befitting the preacher. This will be a key commentary for anyone studying or preaching through the book of Hebrews.

ROSS DURHAM
Pastor, Grace Hill Church, Hillsborough, North Carolina

Hebrews

A Mentor Commentary

Robert J. Cara

MENTOR

Copyright © Robert J. Cara 2024

Hardback ISBN 978-1-5271-1098-4
Ebook ISBN 978-1-5271-1142-4

10 9 8 7 6 5 4 3 2 1

Published in 2024
in the Mentor Imprint
by
Christian Focus Publications,
Geanies House, Fearn, Tain,
Ross-shire, IV20 1TW, Great Britain
www.christianfocus.com

Cover design by Daniel van Straaten

Printed and bound by Bell & Bain, Glasgow

All rights reserved. No part of this publication may be reproduced, stored in a retrieval system, or transmitted, in any form, by any means, electronic, mechanical, photocopying, recording or otherwise without the prior permission of the publisher or a licence permitting restricted copying. In the U.K. such licences are issued by the Copyright Licensing Agency, 4 Battlebridge Lane, London, SE1 2HX. www.cla.co.uk

To Crystal Cara Mitchell
&
Calvin Augustine Cara

Psalm 126:3

Contents

Abbreviations xi
Preface xvii

Introductory Matters 1

1. Prologue (1:1–4) 23

2. Son Superior to Angels (1:5–2:18) 41
   Son Superior to Angels—Scriptural Catena (1:5–14) 41
   Son Superior to Angels—Exhortation (2:1–4) 65
   Son Superior to Angels—Psalm 8 (2:5–9) 71
   Son Superior to Angels—Made Like His
   Brothers (2:10–18) 82

3. Son Superior to Moses (3:1–6) 99

4. Rest (3:7–4:13) 113
   Rest—Quote of Psalm 95 (3:7–11) 116
   Rest—Do Not Harden Your Hearts (3:12–19) 121
   Rest—God's and Ours (4:1–10) 128
   Rest—Word of God (4:11–13) 144

5. Sympathetic High Priest (4:14–5:10) 151
   Great High Priest (4:14–16) 152
   Did Not Exalt Himself (5:1–10) 161

6. Warning and Promise (5:11–6:20) 177
Milk and Solid Food (5:11–14) 178
Not Laying Again the Foundation (6:1–3) 186
Warning of Apostasy (6:4–8) 191
Better Things (6:9–12) 202
Promise (6:13–20) 209

7. Melchizedek (7:1–28) 223
Melchizedek in Non-Canonical Literature 224
Melchizedek and Abraham (7:1–10) 229
Change in Priesthood (7:11–19) 239
Surety and Intercessor (7:20–25) 248
Summary of Priesthoods: Law Versus Oath (7:26–28) .. 260

8. New Covenant in My Blood (8:1–10:18) 269
Platonic Influence? 270
OT Tabernacle Relates Both Forward and Upward 272
New Covenant: Earthly Priests Versus the
Heavenly Priest (8:1–6) 273
New Covenant: Jeremiah 31:31–34 (8:7–13) 283
First Covenant Tabernacle (9:1–10) 295

> *Excursus: Translation of* Θυμιατήριον *as
> 'Censer' in Hebrews 9:4* 300

The Blood of Christ (9:11–14) 315
Inauguration of Covenants by Death
and Blood (9:15–22) 327
Once to Die, Then Judgment (9:23–28) 339
Not Blood of Bulls and Goats (10:1–10) 346
Jeremiah 31 Again (10:11–18) 359

9. Exhortations Based on the Great Priest (10:19–39) 369
Three Exhortations (10:19–25) 370
Warning: No More Sacrifice for Sins (10:26–31) 382
Do Not Throw Away Your Confidence (10:32–39) 392

10. Heroes of Faith (11:1–40) 409
  Faith: Definition through Noah (11:1–7) 411
  Faith: Abraham through Joseph (11:8–22) 425
  Faith: Moses through Rahab (11:23–31) 443
  Faith: Rapid Summary (11:32–40) 458

11. Endurance (12:1–29) 471
  Endurance: Jesus and a Cloud of Witnesses (12:1–3) 471
  Endurance: Discipline (12:4–11) 480
  Endurance: Make Straight Paths (12:12–17) 492
  Endurance: Mount Zion and the Mediator (12:18–24) ..502
  Endurance: With Reverence and Awe (12:25–29) 511

12. Ending Exhortations and Closing (13:1–25) 523
  Ending Exhortations: First Group (13:1–6) 525
  Ending Exhortations: Second Group (13:7–17) 536
  Closing (13:18–25) 554

Bibliography 569

Scripture Index 601
Extra-Biblical Resources 611
Creeds and Confessions Index 613
Subject and Select Author Index 615

Abbreviations

AB	Anchor Bible
ABD	D. N. Freedman, ed., *The Anchor Bible Dictionary* (6 vols., 1992)
ACCS	Ancient Christian Commentary on Scripture
AH	Author of Hebrews
AnBib	Analecta Biblica
ANE	Ancient Near East
ANF	*Ante-Nicene Fathers* (10 vols.)
AOTC	Abingdon Old Testament Commentaries
Artap.	Artapanus
ASV	American Standard Version
AThR	*Anglican Theological Review*
b.	Babylonian Talmud tractate
BA	*Biblical Archaeologist*
2–4 Bar.	2–4 Baruch
Barn.	Epistle of Barnabas
BBR	*Bulletin for Biblical Research*
BDAG	W. Bauer, F. W. Danker, W. F. Arndt, and F. W. Gingrich, *A Greek-English Lexicon of the New Testament and Other Early Christian Literature* (3rd. ed., 2000)
BDF	F. Blass, A. Debruner, and F. W. Funk, *A Greek Grammar of the New Testament and Other Early Christian Literature* (1961)

Bib	Biblica
BSac	Bibliotheca Sacra
BSC	Bible Student's Commentary
BT	The Bible Translator
CBQ	Catholic Biblical Quarterly
CBQMS	Catholic Biblical Quarterly Monograph Series
CBR	Currents in Biblical Research
CD	Cairo Genizah copy of the Damascus Document
CEB	Common English Bible
1–2 Clem.	1–2 Clement
CSB17	Christian Standard Bible 2017
ConcC	Concordia Commentary
CTQ	Concordia Theological Quarterly
Denzinger[43]	H. Denzinger, Compendium of Creeds, Definitions, and Declarations on Matters of Faith and Morals, 43rd ed. (2012)
Did.	Didache
Diogn.	Epistle to Diognetus
DLNT	R. P. Martin and P. H. Davids, eds., Dictionary of the Later New Testament & Its Developments (1997)
DNTB	C. A. Evans and S. E. Porter, eds., Dictionary of New Testament Background (2000)
DPL	G. F. Hawthorne and R. P. Martin, eds., Dictionary of Paul and His Letters (1993)
DSS	Dead Sea Scrolls
Ebib	Etudes bibliques
ECC	Eerdmans Critical Commentary
EKKNT	Evangelisch-katholischerKommentarzum Neuen Testament
1–2 En.	1–2 Enoch
ESV	English Standard Version
ET	English Translation

ABBREVIATIONS   xiii

Ezek. Trag.	Ezekiel the Tragedian
GKC	*Gesenius' Hebrew Grammar*, ed. E. Kautzsch, trans. A. E. Cowley (2nd ed., 1910)
Gk. Apoc. Ezra	Greek Apocalypse of Ezra
HALOT	L. Koehler and W. Baumgartner, *The Hebrew and Aramaic Lexicon of the Old Testament* (2001)
HCSB	Holman Christian Standard Bible
ICC	International Critical Commentary
Ign. *Pol.*	Ignatius, *To Polycarp*
Ign. *Rom.*	Ignatius, *To the Romans*
Int	*Interpretation*
IVPNTC	Intervarsity Press New Testament Commentary
ISBE	G. W. Bromiley, ed., *The International Standard Bible Encyclopedia* (4 vols., 1979–1988)
JBL	*Journal of Biblical Literature*
JETS	*Journal of the Evangelical Theological Society*
JSNT	*Journal for the Study of the New Testament*
JSNTSup	Journal for the Study of the New Testament Supplement Series
JTS	*Journal of Theological Studies*
Jub.	Jubilees
KJV	King James Version
LAB	Liber antiquitatum biblicarum (Pseudo Philo)
LAE	Life of Adam and Eve
LCL	Loeb Classical Library
LEC	Library of Early Christianity
LEH	J. Lust, E. Eynikel, and K. Hauspie, eds. *Greek English Lexicon of the Septuagint* (1992, 1996)
Liv. Pro.	Lives of the Prophets
LNTS	The Library of New Testament Studies

LSJ	H. G. Liddell, R. Scott, H. S. Jones, *A Greek English Lexicon* (9th ed.,1996)
LXX	Septuagint
1–4 Macc.	1–4 Maccabees
Mart. Ascen. Isa.	Martyrdom and Ascension of Isaiah
m.	Mishnah tractate
MNTS	McMaster New Testament Studies
MT	Masoretic Text
NAB	New American Bible
NAC	New American Commentary
NASB	New American Standard Bible
NCB	New Century Bible Commentary
NHC	Nag Hammadi codices
NHNE	New Heavens and New Earth (final eschaton)
NICNT	New International Commentary on the New Testament
NICOT	New International Commentary on the Old Testament
NIDNTTE	M. Silva, ed., *New International Dictionary of New Testament Theology and Exegesis* (5 vols., 2014)
NIDOTTE	W. A. VanGemeren, ed., *New International Dictionary of Old Testament Theology & Exegesis* (5 vols., 1997)
NIGTC	New International Greek Testament Commentary
NIV	New International Version (2011)
NIV84	New International Version 1984
NJB	New Jerusalem Bible
NKJV	New King James Version
NLT	New Living Translation
NovT	*Novum Testamentum*
NovTSup	Supplements to Novum Testamentum
NTS	*New Testament Studies*
NTT	New Testament Theology

NRSV	New Revised Standard Version
NPNF	*Nicene and Post-Nicene Fathers* (Series 1, 14 vols.; Series 2, 14 vols.)
ns	new series
NT	New Testament
NTC	New Testament Commentary
NTL	New Testament Library
NTS	*New Testament Studies*
OT	Old Testament
OTL	Old Testament Library
OTP	*Old Testament Pseudepigrapha*, ed. J. H. Charlesworth (2 vols., 1983, 1985)
PRSt	*Perspectives in Religion Studies*
PTMS	Princeton Theological Monograph Series
PTR	*Princeton Theological Review*
Pss. Sol.	Psalms of Solomon
RF&P	*Reformed Faith & Practice* (Journal of Reformed Theological Seminary)
RSV	Revised Standard Version
SBLDS	Society of Biblical Literature Dissertation Series
SBLMS	Society of Biblical Literature Monograph Series
SBTJ	*Southern Baptist Theological Journal*
Sib. Or.	Sibylline Oracles
Sir.	Sirach (Ecclesiasticus)
SNTSMS	Society for New Testament Studies Monograph Series
SP	Sacra Pagina
Str-B	H. L. Strack and P. Billerbeck, *Kommentar zum Neuen Testament aus Talmud und Midrasch* (4 vols., 1922–1928)
t.	Tosefta tractate
T. Dan	Testament of Dan
T. Jud.	Testament of Judah

T. Levi	Testament of Levi
T. Mos.	Testament of Moses
T. Reu.	Testament of Reuben
TCGNT²	B. M. Metzger, *A Textual Commentary on the Greek New Testament*, 2nd ed. (1994)
TJ	*Trinity Journal*
Tob.	Tobit
TOTC	Tyndale Old Testament Commentaries
TWOT	R. L. Harris, G. L. Archer, Jr., B. K. Waltke, *Theological Wordbook of the Old Testament* (1980)
TynBul	*Tyndale Bulletin*
WBC	Word Biblical Commentary
WCF	Westminster Confession of Faith
Wis.	Wisdom of Solomon
WLC	Westminster Larger Catechism
WSC	Westminster Shorter Catechism
WTJ	*Westminster Theological Journal*
WUNT	Wissenschaftliche Untersuchungen zum Neuen Testament
ZNW	*Zeitschrift für die neutestamentliche Wissenschaft und die Kunde der älteren Kirche*

Preface

I am thankful to Christian Focus for asking me to write on the Letter to the Hebrews. To say that I enjoyed writing this commentary is a definite understatement. I love studying the Word of God directly and also interacting with what others, ancient and modern, have said about it. I trust that my effort aids the church and is to the glory of God (Ps. 115:1).

How would I describe this commentary on Hebrews relative to others? In a significant sense, it is typical of any modern academic commentary on Hebrews, whether critical or conservative. This commentary includes a close exegesis of each pericope, an explanation of important features of the Greek text, interaction with other modern commentators, hermeneutical discussions concerning the OT quotes, consideration of possible influences from Second Temple Judaism and Greco-Roman sources, too many footnotes (!), etc.

On the other hand, this commentary is not typical of many modern commentaries because I am committed to a high view of the Word of God and consider Reformed theology as the best, although not infallible, understanding of the Bible. Thus, this commentary is *aimed primarily at pastors and professors who have a high view of the Word of God and are in general agreement with Reformed theology.* Given this high view of the Word of God, the reader should understand that my analysis of everything in Hebrews is filtered through this reality—or at least that is my intention. This high view often affects specific exegetical decisions but also is a driving force to consider the theological implications of a specific text as God encourages us to make 'by good and necessary consequence' (WCF 1.6) connections from his word to his world.

My interests in and commitment to Reformed theology are reflected in the commentary in several ways. They are shown by my citation and use of many Reformed authors from the 1500s through to the present, both theologians and exegetes. Also, given Reformed theology's view of the church and common grace, I also cite many church fathers, non-Reformed believers, and modern critical commentators. As opposed to many modern commentaries, I find the 'pre-modern' exegetes and theologians to be valuable in my analysis of Hebrews, both at the exegetical level and for broader theological issues.

A specific personal interest of mine is creeds, confessions, and catechisms, primarily Reformed ones, but also Lutheran and Roman Catholic. Further, I am especially interested in the scriptural references used in these to buttress a theological assertion. Therefore, I often note when specific creeds reference various Hebrews texts.

The entire translation of Hebrews is mine. I intentionally made it fairly wooden to aid the reader to better understand the Greek text and/or some of my micro-exegetical decisions. I am assuming that the reader is also working with a major English translation while interacting with my commentary.

I appreciate that Christian Focus has allowed me to add a 'Reflections' after each subsection. I use these in different ways. Many of them are exhorting the reader and me to personal spiritual growth based on the great truths of the specific subsection. For others, it is an occasion to delve deeper into a theological topic related to the subsection. A few of them include a specific aspect related to me.

My teaching assistant at Reformed Theological Seminary, Mr. Benjamin P. Preiser, helped me by looking up many of my verse references outside of Hebrews, both biblical and non-canonical, to ensure they made 'sense'. Yes, some needed to be corrected.

I dedicate this book to my two children, Crystal Cara Mitchell and Calvin Augustine Cara. They were born sixteen and a half years apart. As my wife Jill says, 'We have two *only* children.' It is an inexpressible joy to parents to see their children walking with the Lord—and Jill and I have that joy! Yes, 'the Lord has done great things for us' (Ps. 126:3).

Robert J. Cara
Reformed Theological Seminary
Charlotte, North Carolina
December 2022

Introductory Matters

After finishing the commentary proper, that is, the exegetical sections covering Hebrews 1:1–13:25, and before writing this Introductory Matters section, I asked several of my colleagues at a faculty meeting as to their preferred length of introductions for commentaries. They all responded to the effect 'keep it shorter rather than longer'. Thus I will try.

Below I cover typical issues related to traditional 'introductory matters.' Since many of the exegetical aspects of these issues are also covered in the commentary proper, I am fairly brief and summative.

Theological issues, for example, covenant, two natures of Christ, hermeneutics, are not discussed here and are instead covered at various locations throughout the commentary proper. Similarly, background issues that may or may not affect exegesis such as Melchizedek in Second Temple Judaism (related to Hebrews 7) and 'discipline' (*paideia*) in Greco-Roman culture (related to Heb. 12:3–11) are discussed in the commentary proper at the appropriate locations.[1] Also note that the canonicity of Hebrews and God's being the ultimate author of Hebrews are simply assumed as a commentary is not the place for an in depth discussion on these two important topics.

---

1. I tried to keep extended discussions of each theological topic or background issue at one location in the commentary and refer the reader to that location when the topic comes up elsewhere in the commentary. Also, the subject index should help the reader to find various extended discussions.

Author, Addressees, and Date

So the reader knows where I am going as to author, addressees, and date: In brief, the author of Hebrews (AH) is someone from Paul's inner circle of pastoral ministers. He wrote a letter addressed to a predominantly Jewish-Christian local church that was near or in Rome. The letter was written after the death of Paul in the late AD 60s. None of this is explicit in Hebrews. Much of it is debated and has been throughout church history. As to how much of a difference one's view of author, addressees, and date makes for interpretation, see the discussion at the end of this section.

Author

Over the past several years, I am often asked, 'Who wrote Hebrews?' My standard response is, 'God.' If the enquirer persists as to the human author, I quote Origen, 'But who wrote the epistle, in truth, God [only] knows.'[2]

Formally, Hebrews is anonymous, that is, anonymous to us. The original addressees knew the AH and that the letter was from him (Heb. 13:19). Thus, for them, it was not anonymous.

What internal evidence does the letter reveal about the AH? We learn that he is a male.[3] He has some type of ministerial authority as he writes a 'word of exhortation' (Heb. 13:22). Based on his use of both 'I' and 'we', I take it that the AH is writing as the head of a group of ministers (Heb. 13:18–19). The AH has been at the congregation previously (Heb. 13:9), probably as a minister. He knows the congregation's past and current difficulties (Heb. 5:11–12; 10:32–35). He is connected to Timothy, calls him 'our brother', hopes to travel with him on his way to visit the congregation, and possibly they both ministered previously in the congregation at the same time (Heb. 13:23). The AH well knows the OT's implications relative to Christ. He often,

---

2. Origen as quoted by Eusebius, *Church History* 6.25.14 (*NPNF*², 1:273).

3. In Heb. 11:32, the participle translated 'recounting' or 'tell' (διηγούμενον) is *masculine* singular, and the grammatical antecedent is 'me'.

but not always, cites the OT using the LXX.[4] He writes in an elevated Greek style. The ending exhortations in Hebrews 13:1–17 are somewhat similar to those near the end of Pauline letters, and the closing in Hebrews 13:18–25 is very similar to a Pauline closing. The opening of Hebrews differs completely from Paul's. Finally and importantly for this discussion, the AH does not hear about 'salvation' directly from Christ, but from those who heard/saw the incarnated Christ (Heb. 2:3). That is, the AH was a 'second generation' Christian. For me, this 'second generation' conclusion confirms that Paul was not the author.

To summarize the internal evidence, the AH was a second-generation Christian minister who strongly grasped the connections between Christ and the OT. Hebrews exhibits an elevated Greek style and uses the LXX often. The AH traveled to churches and knew Timothy well. Thus, almost certainly, he also knew Paul well and was part of his inner circle of ministers.

As to author, what do we learn from the early church up through Augustine? Clement of Alexandria (AD 150–215) considers Hebrews to be written by Paul in the Hebrew language and then translated into Greek by Luke.[5] Tertullian

---

4. For this commentary, I assume that Rahlfs' text accurately reflects the existing LXX in the first century AD. I realize that this is not certain.

5. Clement of Alexandria as quoted by Eusebius, *Church History* 6.14.2–3 (*NPNF*[2], 1:261). Clement also notes that the name of Paul was not attached because the Jewish addressees were prejudicial against Paul. Possibly, it is implied that these are also the views of Clement's teacher, Pantaenus (died in AD 190) (*Church History* 6.13.2 [*NPNF*[2], 1:259]). Thomas Aquinas has a similar view — Paul wrote in an elevated Hebrew style as he knew Hebrew better than Greek. Then Luke translates 'this ornateness from Hebrew into Greek'. Paul did not include his name because his apostleship related to Gentiles and his name was 'odious to Jews' (*Commentary on the Epistle to the Hebrews*, trans. Chrysostom Baer [South Bend: St. Augustine, 2006], 7). For a modern argument agreeing to Luke as the author of Hebrews, although without the view that Luke translated a Hebrew original by Paul, see David L. Allen, *Lukan Authorship of Hebrews*, NAC Studies in Bible & Theology (Nashville, B&H Academic, 2010). Arguments for Luke would include his connection to Timothy and Paul (e.g., Acts 16:10; 20:4–5), his elevated Greek

(AD 160–225) tells us that Barnabas is the AH and notes the close connection between Barnabas and Paul.[6] As noted above, Origen (AD 185–254) comments that only God knows who wrote Hebrews, but he also says that many have said that Paul wrote it. According to Origen, the thoughts of Hebrews seem to be from Paul but the phraseology is from someone else.[7] Origen also comments that some have said that the author is Clement of Rome,[8] and others, that it is Luke.[9] The fragmentary Muratorian Canon (ca. AD 170–195?) names all thirteen of Paul's epistles and does not mention Hebrews.[10] Manuscript 𝔓[46] (ca. AD 200) includes Hebrews within a list of Pauline letters between Romans and 1 Corinthians.[11] Eusebius

---

style in Luke 1:1–4 and Acts 1:1–3, and being the 'author' of Acts 7 which has similarities to Hebrews.

6. Tertullian, *On Modesty* 20 (*ANF*, 4:97). Of modern commentators, Philip Edgecumbe Hughes gives a weak vote for Barnabas (*A Commentary on the Epistle to the Hebrews* [Grand Rapids: Eerdmans, 1977], 29). Arguments for Barnabas would include his connection to Paul (Acts 11:25; 13:2; 15:39?), he is a Hellenistic Jew ('from Cyprus,' Acts 4:36), he is a Levite (Acts 4:36), and the Epistle of Barnabas includes OT typology (e.g., Barn. 7:6–8; 10:2–3).

7. Matthew J. Thomas complains that some scholars only quote Origen's 'God only knows' statement and do not go on to mention that Origen strongly affirmed that Paul was the primary author of Hebrews and it is only the secondary hand that is in question. To buttress his point, Thomas includes Origen quotes from across his corpus ('Origen on Paul's Authorship of Hebrews,' *NTS* 65 [2019]: 598–609).

8. Arguments for Clement of Rome would include that 1 Clement has numerous quotes and allusions from Hebrews. The most well-known connection is 1 Clement 36. Also see 1 Clem. 5:2; 12:1; 17:1; 19:2; 27:2; 43:1; 55:3; 56:4; 61:3, and 64:1. Phil. 1:1 and 4:3 connect Clement to Paul and Timothy.

9. Origen as quoted by Eusebius, *Church History* 6.25.14 (*NPNF*[2], 1:273).

10. *ANF* 5:603. The extant copy is clearly partial. Hebrews is not mentioned in the Paul section, but it may have been included later in the original.

11. The majority of Greek manuscripts place Hebrews either (1) after 2 Thessalonians and before the pastorals and Philemon, apparently considering it the last book written to churches before the books written to individuals or (2) Hebrews is placed after Philemon, which placement is ambiguous as to the author. See Metzger, *TCGNT*[2], 591–92. Gregory Goswell uses the various placements of Hebrews in the canonical lists and

(AD 260–340) summarizes the church's view: Paul is the author but the church in Rome does not agree.[12] Athanasius (AD 276–393) includes Hebrews as one of the fourteen epistles of Paul in his canonical list.[13] The Third Synod of Carthage (AD 397) affirms Pauline authorship of Hebrews, although in a slightly ambiguous manner.[14] Chrysostom (AD 347–407) in his commentary affirms Pauline authorship.[15] Jerome (AD 342–420) affirms Pauline authorship, but notes that Hebrews, although being part of the canon, is not always included with the other Pauline letters in canonical lists.[16] Augustine (AD 354–430) at least at one point affirms Pauline authorship,[17] but elsewhere he comments that a few deny it without giving his view.[18]

To summarize the information from the early church, there were three basic views: (1) Paul was the author, (2) Hebrews was written by an associate of Paul who translated an original Pauline Hebrew-language document into Greek, and (3) Hebrews was written by an associate of Paul. (The associates of Paul being explicitly mentioned were Luke, Barnabas, and Clement of Rome.) By AD 400, the church as a whole had agreed to Pauline authorship whether in the form

---

manuscripts to show that the early church considered it at least closely related to Paul. He then concludes that the covenant theme in both Paul and Hebrews shows that 'Hebrews plays a significant role in helping to hold the writings of the NT together as a unified testimony that calls Jews and Gentiles to faith in Jesus Christ' ('Finding a Home for the Letter of Hebrews,' *JETS* 59 [2016]: 747–60, esp. 760).

12. Eusebius, *Church History* 3.3.5 (*NPNF*², 1:134).

13. Athanasius, *Letter 39* §5 (*NPNF*², 4:552).

14. 'The canonical writings are: ... the thirteen Epistles of Paul the apostle, one of the same to the Hebrews' (Heinrich Denzinger, *Compendium of Creeds, Definitions, and Declarations on Matters of Faith and Morals*, eds. Robert Fastiggi and Anne Englund Nash, 43rd ed. [San Francisco: Ignatius, 2012], §186).

15. Chrysostom, 'Homily on Hebrews, Argument' (*NPNF*¹, 14:363).

16. Jerome, *Letter 53* §8 (*NPNF*², 6:101).

17. Augustine, *On Christian Doctrine* 2.8 (*NPNF*¹, 2:539).

18. Augustine, *City of God* 16.22 (*NPNF*¹, 2:322).

of # 1 or # 2. Broadly speaking, the eastern church viewed Paul as the AH earlier than the western church.

The Reformation brought renewed interest to the authorship question. Luther suggested Apollos,[19] and many have subsequently agreed.[20] Calvin is against Pauline authorship and comments that it is 'probable that Luke or Clement is the author'.[21] Many also argued for Pauline authorship of the Greek, for example, John Owen.[22] (The argument that Hebrews is a translation of an earlier Hebrew-language document was dismissed.) Of the Reformation era creeds that listed the canonical books, they all agreed

---

19. In Luther's discussion of Gen. 48:20 and its connection to Heb. 11:21, he comments, 'The author of the Epistle to the Hebrews—whoever he is, whether Paul, or, as I think, Apollos' (*Lectures on Genesis: Chapters 45–50*, trans. Paul D. Pahl, vol. 8 of *Luther's Works*, ed. Jaroslav Pelikan [Saint Louis: Concordia, 1966], 178.) In Luther's earlier lectures on Hebrews, Apollos is not mentioned. Arguments for Apollos would include his connection to Paul and Timothy (1 Cor. 16:10–12; 1 Clem. 47:1–3), he is a Hellenistic Jew (Alexandria, Acts 18:24), and is an 'eloquent (λόγιος) man ... mighty in the Scriptures' (Acts 18:24). For those who see some level of connections to Philo, the arguments for Apollos are enhanced by the Alexandria homeland matching to Philo, and Philo's using λόγιος several times to refer to sophisticated Greek writers (e.g., Philo, *On the Posterity of Cain* 53, 162; *On the Life of Moses* 1.2; *On the Embassy to Gaius* 237).

20. So also, e.g., C. Spicq, *L'Épître aux Hébreux*, 2 vols., EBib (Paris: Gabalda, 1952–1953), 1:211–19; and R. C. H. Lenski, *The Interpretation of the Epistle to the Hebrews and the Epistle to James* (Minneapolis: Augsburg, 1966), 22–24.

21. John Calvin, *The Epistle of Paul the Apostle to the Hebrews and the First and Second Epistles of St Peter*, trans. William B. Johnson, eds. David W. and Thomas F. Torrance, Calvin's Commentaries 12 (Grand Rapids: Eerdmans, 1963), 1, 216.

22. John Owen, *An Exposition of the Epistle to the Hebrews*, vols. 17–23 of *The Works of John Owen*, ed. William H. Goold (Carlisle: Banner of Truth, 1991), 17:65–92, 102–05. One of Owen's important arguments is that 2 Pet. 3:15–16 is referring to Paul's authorship of Hebrews. This is based on the assumption that 1 and 2 Peter are written to a Jewish audience (17:83–87). Owen also argues strongly against there being a Hebrew language original that was then translated into Greek. William Gouge uses this same 2 Peter argument for Pauline authorship (*Commentary on Hebrews: Exegetical and Expository*, 2 vols. [Birmingham: AL: Solid Ground Christian, 2005 {1655}], 1:3–4).

that Hebrews was canonical, but they differed as to Pauline authorship. Those explicitly in favor of Pauline authorship include the Council of Trent (Canonical Scriptures section),[23] Belgic Confession 4, Second Helvetic Confession 16, Irish Articles 2, and Sandomierz Consensus 16.[24] Those listing Hebrews separately from the other Pauline epistles include the French Confession 3, Westminster Confession of Faith 1.2, and Second London Confession 1.2. Whitaker is typical of a Reformed view of the issue: 'That his epistle is canonical, we all concede in the fullest sense; but it is not equally clear that it was written by the apostle Paul.' Whitaker continues with an analogy about an author and his pen to make the point that the major issue is to listen to God who speaks through Hebrews, not which human author wrote it.

> If we read the words in some letter which we had gotten from some great man [divine author], and raised the question, what pen [human author] they were written with; it would surely be thought ridiculous that we should be curious not to know the author and understand his meaning, but discover what sort of pen it was [that he used].[25]

To summarize the views during the Reformation, the Roman Catholic Church affirmed Pauline authorship and the canonicity of Hebrews. Protestants both affirmed and doubted Pauline authorship; however, the canonicity of Hebrews was *not* in doubt.

Modern scholarship with few exceptions, both conservative

---

23. See Phillip Schaff, ed. *The Creeds of Christendom: With History and Critical Notes*, rev. David S. Schaff, 6th ed., 3 vols. (Grand Rapids: Baker, 1931), 2:81; or Denzinger43 §1503.

24. Sandomierz Consensus is a Polish and Lithuanian document written in AD 1570. See *Reformed Confessions of the 16th and 17th Centuries in English Translation*, compiled with introductions by James T. Dennison, Jr., 4 vols. (Grand Rapids: Reformation Heritage, 2008–2014), 3:213.

25. William Whitaker, *A Disputation on Holy Scripture Against the Papists, Especially Bellarmine and Stapleton*, trans. William Fitzgerald, Parker Society (Eugene, OR: Wipf & Stock, 2004 [1588]), 106, 108.

and critical, has functionally dismissed even considering Paul as the AH.[26] Although, virtually all do acknowledge that there is 'substantial contact with the Pauline tradition'.[27] However, in addition to Hebrews 2:3, the differences in Greek-language style, rhetorical features, and letter openings, along with the emphasis on Christ as priest confirms for the vast majority that Paul is not the author.[28] Who then is the AH? All affirm at a minimum he is a Jewish Christian familiar with the LXX. But beyond that, the vast majority simply conclude that no more can be known with any degree of certainty as to the author's name.[29] I agree but also want to stress that the AH is connected to Timothy and part of the inner Pauline circle of ministers.

What is the city of provenance, that is, from where did the AH write? The answer revolves around one's understanding of Hebrews 13:24, 'the ones from Italy greet you,' which is somewhat ambiguous. It could mean that the AH is in Italy as he writes, or, more likely from my perspective, the AH is writing from somewhere else to a congregation in Italy (for

---

26. Although Allen is against Pauline authorship, see his sympathetic treatment of the few modern scholars who argue for it (*Lukan Authorship of Hebrews*, 45–77).

27. M. Eugene Boring, *An Introduction to the New Testament: History, Literature, Theology* (Louisville, Westminster John Knox, 2012), 416. He includes as examples of Pauline connections broad Christological connections, including Christ's sacrificial death and heavenly intercessor, the term 'new covenant', the connection to Timothy, and the Pauline type ending.

28. I am not completely comfortable with some of these arguments because they assume that Paul could not adjust linguistic style or theological emphases depending on the circumstances. For me, it is Heb. 2:3 that is the ultimate confirmation of non-Pauline authorship.

29. So, e.g., F. F. Bruce, *The Epistle to the Hebrews*, 2nd ed., NICNT (Grand Rapids: Eerdmans, 1990), 20; William L. Lane, *Hebrews 1–8*, WBC 47a (Dallas: Word, 1991), xlix–li; James W. Thompson, *Hebrews*, Paideia (Grand Rapids: Baker Academic, 2008), 5–6; Luke Timothy Johnson, *Hebrews: A Commentary*, NTL (Louisville: Westminster John Knox, 2006) 13–46; and Thomas R. Schreiner, *Commentary on Hebrews*, Biblical Theology for Christian Proclamation (Nashville: Homan Reference, 2015), 4–5, 15.

details, see commentary at Heb. 13:24). For those who take the former view, Rome is usually considered the provenance, whether Paul is considered the author or not.[30] Given my view that Hebrews 13:24 does not relate to the provenance, I am completely agnostic as to the city from where the AH wrote.

Addressees

As noted above, Hebrews was written to a specific congregation. For the vast majority of interpretative history, the original addressees were considered to be Jewish Christians, whether living in Palestine or somewhere else in the Greco-Roman world. In the latter nineteenth century and into the twenty-first, there is a substantial minority that argue for the addressees being Gentile Christians, although the majority position still is Jewish Christians. My view is that the addressees were predominantly Jewish Christians living in or near Rome.

The view that the addressees were Jewish Christians also entails that they formerly attended a synagogue (or temple) and were influenced by their Jewish families and friends; that is, they were ethnically, culturally, and religiously Jewish. Of course, no matter where one was in the Greco-Roman world, even in Jerusalem, one would also be interacting with non-Jewish Greco-Roman influences. Another caveat to this view is that there were possibly some Gentile Christians in the congregation who had formerly attended a synagogue and were subject to similar influences. Hence, this view is more accurately stated as the *predominantly* Jewish Christian view.

I strongly favor the predominantly Jewish Christian view. Arguments for this view are fairly straightforward.[31] They

---

30. So, e.g., Aquinas, *Hebrews*, 310; Calvin, *Hebrews and 1 & 2 Peter*, 216; and David L. Allen, *Hebrews*, NAC 35 (Nashville: B&H, 2010), 48, 75.

31. Commentaries in the twentieth and twenty-first centuries favoring (predominantly) Jewish Christian addressees include Lenski, *Hebrews & James*, 12–13; Spicq, *Hébreux*, 1:220–52 (former Jewish priests); Bruce, *Hebrews*, 6; Hughes, *Hebrews*, 11–15; Simon J. Kistemaker, *Exposition of the Epistle to the Hebrews*, NTC (Grand Rapids: Baker, 1984), 17–18; Lane, *Hebrews 1–8*, liii–liv; Paul Ellingworth, *The Epistle to the Hebrews: A*

include: (1) The earliest extant manuscripts of the letter have the title, 'to the Hebrews' (πρὸς Ἑβραίους),[32] and the earliest explicit references to it by the church fathers also use this title.[33] Even though the title is almost certainly not part of the original manuscript, it is an important consideration. (2) The content of the book includes a significant emphasis on the OT Scriptures, priests, sacrifices, the tabernacle, and various OT persons. While this does not necessarily mean the congregants were Jewish Christians, it is a reasonable assumption. (3) Although the Jewish temple is not explicitly mentioned, many of the arguments concerning the tabernacle would also apply to the temple, especially considering that many stipulations in the Mosaic law apply to both. Given this, several texts in Hebrews make significantly more sense if the addressees were aware that temple sacrifices were continuing (e.g., Heb. 7:11; 8:4; 10:2–3, 26; 13:10). (4) The logic of Hebrews 10:26 turns on the congregants' not returning to a 'sacrifice for sins', which surely means a Jewish-temple sacrifice for sins. This would only be a temptation if the congregants were predominantly Jewish Christians. (5) The AH's 'insistence that the old covenant has been antiquated is expressed with a moral earnestness and driven home repeatedly in a manner which would be pointless if [the addressees] were not especially disposed to live under that covenant.'[34]

Commentary on the Greek Text, NIGTC (Grand Rapids: Eerdmans, 1993),23–29; Johnson, *Hebrews*, 33; Allen, *Hebrews*, 62 (former Jewish priests); Gareth Lee Cockerill, *The Epistle of Hebrews*, NICNT (Grand Rapids: Eerdmans, 2012), 20, 40; John W. Kleinig, ConcC (Saint Louis: Concordia Publishing House, 2017), 5; Schreiner, *Hebrews*, 7, 14; and Richard D. Phillips, *Hebrews*, Reformed Expository Commentary (Phillipsburg: P&R, 2006), 7.

32. For a listing of titles in early Greek and non-Greek manuscripts, see B. F. Westcott, *The Epistle to the Hebrews* (Grand Rapids: Eerdmans, 1980 [1892]), xxvii–xxx. The important manuscript 𝔓46 also has 'to the Hebrews' as a title.

33. E.g., Clement of Alexandria (AD 150–215), as quoted by Eusebius, *Church History* 6.14.4 (*NPNF*², 1:261). Possibly, it is implied that this is the view of Clement's teacher, Pantaenus, who died in AD 190 (*Church History* 6.13.2 [*NPNF*², 1:259]).

34. Bruce, *Hebrews*, 6.

The minority view that the addressees were not Jewish Christians per se gained prominence in the English-speaking world through Moffatt's 1924 commentary.[35] He argued that (1) Those that affixed the canonical title, although referring to Jewish Christians, 'had no idea of its original destination, otherwise they would have chose a local term' (e.g., 'to the Jerusalemites'). (2) The AH never mentions Jews nor Christians, nor refers to the temple[36] nor circumcision. (3) The AH's knowledge of the tabernacle and sacrifices is gained solely from the LXX. (4) The appeal to the LXX is 'cogent for Gentile Christians in the early church' as they would have 'accepted the LXX as their Bible.' I find these arguments unconvincing.

Where were the addressees located? The two most prominent options throughout church history have been Jerusalem or Rome. The Jerusalem option assumes the addressees were Jewish Christians and the somewhat ambiguous phrase 'the ones from Italy greet you' (Heb. 13:24) indicates those with the AH as he wrote *from* Rome.[37] With the discovery of the Dead Sea Scrolls and the supposed connections between them and Hebrews, the Jerusalem option gained, at least for a short time, more adherents.[38]

---

35. James Moffatt, *A Critical and Exegetical Commentary on the Epistle to the Hebrews*, ICC (Edinburgh: T. & T. Clark, 1979 [1924]), xv–xvii. Prior to Moffatt, in the late 1800s, several German authors favored the Gentile Christian view (see list of authors in Craig R. Koester, *Hebrews*, AB 36 [NY: Doubleday, 2001], 47 n. 101). Other commentaries favoring predominantly Gentile Christian addressees, or a significantly mixed group, or not specifically Jewish Christian include Ernst Käsemann, *The Wandering People of God: An Investigation of the Letter of Hebrews*, trans. Roy A. Harrisville and Irving L. Sandberg (Minneapolis: Augsburg, 1984 [1957]), 25; Thompson, *Hebrews*, 6–10; Koester, *Hebrews*, 48; and David A. deSilva, *Perseverance in Gratitude: A Socio-Rhetorical Commentary on the Epistle 'to the Hebrews'* (Grand Rapids: Eerdmans, 2000), 7.

36. The standard rebuttal as to why the temple is not mentioned by those who favor Jewish Christian addressees is that the AH 'goes back to first principles as the basis of his argument and this is better demonstrated from the tabernacle' (Donald Guthrie, *New Testament Introduction*, 3rd ed. [Downers Grove, IL: Inter-Varsity, 1971], 702).

37. So, e.g., Chrysostom, 'Homily on Hebrews, Argument' (*NPNF*[1], 14:364); Owen, *Hebrews*, 17:101; and Westcott, *Hebrews*, xl.

38. So, e.g., Hughes, *Hebrews*, 15.

As noted above, I understand 'the ones from Italy greet you' to refer to those with the AH as he wrote *to* a congregation in Italy, most likely near or in Rome. The majority of modern commentators, whether favoring the Jewish Christian view or not, affirm, whether weakly or strongly, a Roman destination.[39] In support of a Roman destination, in addition to the exegesis of Hebrews 13:24; commentators often note that 1 Clement, which certainly quotes and alludes to Hebrews (e.g., 1 Clem. 36), was written to the Corinthians from Rome in ca. AD 96.[40] In my view, the 1 Clement argument does not hold much weight. Other arguments for me that dovetail well with a Roman destination are (1) the persecution of Jews and Jewish Christians in Rome (see discussion below) and (2) Paul and his inner circle of ministers had many connections to Rome. However, my primary argument is my exegesis of Hebrews 13:24, and that exegesis does not have complete certainty.

Date

What is the latest date that Hebrews could have been written? Since portions of Hebrews are quoted and alluded to in 1 Clement, which was probably written in AD 96, Hebrews had to have been written before this date. So far all agree.

The major disagreement among modern commentators is whether Hebrews was written before or after the Jewish temple destruction in AD 70. Of course, if one agrees to Pauline authorship, then one concludes that Paul wrote Hebrews before the temple destruction because he died ca. AD 65. If one agrees that the addressees are Jewish Christians as I do, one is significantly more inclined to see a pre-AD-70 date because it is hard to believe that the AH would not have

---

39. So, e.g., Lenski, *Hebrews and James*, 15; Bruce, *Hebrews*, 13–14; Kistemaker, *Hebrews*, 17–18; Lane, *Hebrews 1–8*, lviii; Koester, *Hebrews*, 50; Alan C. Mitchell, *Hebrews*, SP 13 (Collegeville: Liturgical, 2007), 7; Cockerill, *Hebrews*, 40; Kleinig, *Hebrews*, 5; and Phillips, *Hebrews*, 8.

40. So, e.g., Lane, *Hebrews 1–8*, lviii.

used this destruction as at least a secondary argument that the OT pointed to a final priest and sacrificial victim, which is Christ.[41] Also, as noted above, Hebrews at points implies strongly that the temple is still standing. If the addressees are not Jewish Christians per se, a broader date from AD 60–90 is usually assumed.[42]

How does dating relate to a destination of Rome and the internal evidence about the addressees? In addition to being predominantly Jewish Christians, the internal evidence in Hebrews about the addressees reveals that due to their faith, some in the congregation suffered, including beatings, losing property, and being in prison (Heb. 10:32–34, 13:3). At least some of this involved magistrates as being thrown in prison implies. This suffering, as of the date of the letter, had not yet resulted in death (Heb. 12:4). Prior to the letter, the congregation had struggles that were more severe than they are as the AH writes (Heb. 13:32).

Several events occurred in Rome that may relate to the internal evidence. (1) The AD 49 Claudius edict due to the 'Chrestus' (Christ) disturbance among Jews led to an expulsion of at least some Jews and Jewish Christians from Rome (Acts 18:2). Claudius died in AD 54, after which Jews begin returning to Rome. (2) The great fire occurred in Rome in AD 64, and Nero subsequently persecuted Christians, including death as punishment, from AD 64 till his death in AD 68. (3) The death of Paul occurred under Nero, ca. AD 65.

I begin with the conclusion that Hebrews must have been written after Paul's death or otherwise he would have been mentioned in the closing. The Claudius edict would explain the loss of property. The Neronian persecution presents a

---

41. Virtually all commentators that see the addressees as Jewish Christians conclude a pre-AD-70 date, so, e.g., Bruce, *Hebrews*, 21; Hughes, *Hebrews*, 30–32; and Schreiner, *Hebrews*, 6.

42. So, e.g., Harold W. Attridge, *A Commentary on the Epistle to the Hebrews*, Hermeneia (Philadelphia: Fortress, 1989), 9; Thompson, *Hebrews*, 7; and Koester, *Hebrews*, 50. DeSilva is an example of one who sees the addressees as a mixed group but does see a pre-AD-70 date (*Hebrews*, 20).

possible difficulty. It does explain the suffering and beatings but seems to contradict Hebrews 12:4, which affirms that the congregants had not yet died for their faith. The death of Nero in AD 68 does appear to explain that the persecution was worse before the letter was written if it was written after his death. Therefore, the 'fly in the ointment' is how to coordinate the Neronian persecution with some congregants suffering persecution but not death. At least for me, two possibilities present themselves: (1) It just might have happened that there were no members of this congregation itself that were martyred even though the congregation was located in Rome proper. (2) The congregation was not located in Rome proper but near Rome and thus not as severely affected by the persecution in intensity or length. If option # 1 is assumed, then a date after Nero's death and before the temple destruction is probable, that is AD 68–69. If option # 2 is assumed, then the range could be slightly broader, that is, AD 65 to 69.

Implications of Author, Addressees, and Date Differences
Given the above uncertainty and debate, my reading through a vast array of commentaries, monographs, and articles somewhat surprisingly reveals that one's view of the author, addressees, and date does not affect the vast majority of exegetical decisions that need to be made. Yes, exegetical decisions do significantly differ among scholars; but in general, it is not because of these issues per se. Admittedly, sometimes it is due to these issues.

Why would one's view of author, addressees, and date not make that much of a difference? Because broadly considered, they do not differ that much in four major areas. (1) All agree that Hebrews was written by a Christian to addressees who were attending a Christian congregation. (2) All agree that whether or not the author and addressees were Jewish Christians or Gentile Christians or a mixed group, they had a high view of the OT (e.g., Heb. 12:5) and knew basic information about Christ (e.g., Heb. 7:14). (3) All agree that the author and addressees lived somewhere in the Greco-Roman world, whether, for example, in Jerusalem or Rome. Anyone in the Greco-Roman world that used the OT would at least be minimally aware, consciously or not, of both broad Greco-Roman views (e.g., Platonism, lax sexual values) and broad Jewish views (e.g., Apocalyptic Judaism, Pharisaical/Rabbinic Judaism, Philo). These views were probably reasonably well known by the author, and yes, probably not that well-defined in the minds of many congregants, but these ideas were 'in the air.' (4) All agree that Hebrews was written somewhere between AD 60 and 100, which is a very well-defined time frame. The major dating decision is whether Hebrews was written before or after the destruction of the Jewish temple in AD 70. Yes, this decision affects a few passages at the margins, but since the tabernacle, not the temple, is the focus in Hebrews, the exegetical implications relative to AD 70 are not that significant.

Above, I just made the argument that one's view of author, addressees, and date does not make as much exegetical difference as one might suppose. However, I was using 'author' in the sense of the human author. If the question concerns whether the Triune God is the ultimate author of Hebrews, that is, whether Hebrews is the written Word of God, then many more exegetical decisions are affected. For example, one with a high view of Scripture will *not* see it as an exegetical option that the AH misunderstood or misinterpreted an OT text in his many quotes and allusions of the OT. Why? It was the same ultimate author, God, who wrote both Hebrews and the quoted OT text. On the other hand, those with a 'critical' perspective would consider a misinterpretation a possibility, and many times conclude that the AH was wrong in his understanding of the OT text. To be clear, I have a high view of Scripture and all the implications this entails. However, as it is abundantly evidenced in the commentary proper, I still find it useful to both learn from and critique critical scholars.[43]

---

43. Even the atheist biblical scholar is made by God and lives in God's

Occasion and Purpose

What is the occasion that prompted the writing of this letter? Occasion may be driven by the author, the addressees, or some combination. Further, occasion and purpose are usually related.[44]

As noted above, I view the addressees as a predominantly Jewish-Christian congregation in or near Rome. They are experiencing some level of persecution. In addition, at least some of them are being tempted to return to a truncated form of Judaism, a Judaism denying the OT typology about a divine and human Messiah and thus also denying that Jesus Christ is in fact the mediator of the new covenant.

In the closing of Hebrews, the AH states that he will be coming to the congregation (Heb. 13:23). If Timothy arrives at where the AH is staying soon enough, the AH and Timothy will be traveling together. If not, the AH will come by himself. There is no mention of who will be delivering the letter ahead of the AH's arrival.

As most agree from the content of Hebrews, the primary purpose is to encourage and exhort the congregants to *persevere* in Christ and the Christian faith.[45] More specifically, the AH emphasizes Christ as both Son and High Priest (e.g., Heb. 3:6; 8:1). Christ is presented, at least partially, with these emphases because some in the congregation are tempted to return to a truncated Judaism. To put the purpose into a pithy saying: *Persevere in Christ, the Son and High Priest*.

Now allow me to put the occasion and purpose together, along with a few assumptions. I assume that knowledge of the

---

world; thus, he is able by common grace to provide at least some surface-level insights into the text of Hebrews.

44. Occasion and purpose may not necessarily be related. For example, consider a university student away from home. Her friend at university asks her if she has contacted her parents lately. This 'occasion' prompts her to telephone her parents. However, since her finances are running low, the primary 'purpose' of the phone call is to request money.

45. So also, e.g., Charles Hodge, *Exegetical Lectures and Sermons on the Epistle of Hebrews*, ed. and introduced by William VanDoodewaard (Carlisle: Banner of Truth, 2019) 3; and Lane, *Hebrews* 1–8, c.

difficulties (both material and spiritual) that the congregation was experiencing reached the AH. Out of concern for the congregation and cognizant of his ministerial duties, the AH is compelled to aid them, at least spiritually. He plans to write a letter to the congregation and then visit them at some point after the letter arrived. He does in fact write the letter. He terms it 'a word of exhortation' (Heb. 13:22), and we call it 'The Letter to the Hebrews.' I also assume that subsequent to the letter arriving, the AH does visit the congregation, either arriving with Timothy or with Timothy arriving later. I finally assume that the Holy Spirit used the combination of the letter and the AH and Timothy's visit to make a very positive impact on the congregants so that the vast majority do *persevere in Christ, the Son and High Priest.*

Genre: Homily Converted to a Letter?

Many see Hebrews, or at least 1:1–12:29, as originally an oral homily or sermon that was then put into written form.[46] Hebrews 13 or 13:18–25 was added afterwards to conform to a letter format. Arguments for the oral homily view include (1) Hebrews 1:1–4 is not a typical letter opening, (2) the elevated style is similar to oral Greco-Roman rhetoric, (3) Hebrews 9:5b and 11:32 indicate time constraints consistent with an oral presentation, (4) the expression 'word of exhortation' in Hebrews 13:22 is used in Acts 13:15 to refer to a sermon,[47] and (5) Hebrews 13:1–25 is a 'postscript'.

I am not convinced. I interpret Hebrews as a letter that was intentionally written for a specific congregation and includes exhortations, doctrine, greetings, etc., like any other NT letter.[48] That is, Hebrews is not an oral homily converted

---

46. So, e.g., Lane, *Hebrews* 1–8, lxix–lxxv; Thompson, *Hebrews*, 12; Koester, *Hebrews*, 81; Cockerill, *Hebrews*, 18; and Boring, *An Introduction to the New Testament*, 414–15.

47. The only difference in expressions is that Heb. 13:22 is definite (ὁ λόγος τῆς παρακλήσεως) and Acts 13:15 indefinite (λόγος παρακλήσεως), which is understandable given the two contexts.

48. There is a tendency by some to assume that a written document

into a written letter. Yes, Hebrews is a letter with elevated Greek style, whose opening is not typical of letters but whose closing is very typical. In response to the four points above: (1) 1 John is another canonical letter that does not have a typical letter opening. (2) The connection to classical oral Greco-Roman rhetoric is not clear because scholars who propose this disagree on exactly which specific type of Greco-Roman rhetoric is being used.[49] (3) Hebrews 9:5b and 11:32 do not necessarily refer to time in an oral sermon as similar expressions have been used in clearly written documents.[50] (4) The context of 'word of exhortation' in Hebrews 13:22 is explicitly referring to the *written* letter. (5) Hebrews 13 is not a 'postscript' but a typical letter closing that includes generic exhortations along with exhortations that are integrated with the rest of the letter.[51] Allow me one additional point: (6) Hebrews includes several very specific comments about the congregation (e.g., Heb. 10:32–34; 12:4). This argues against the letter being originally an oral homily—to whom or where was the homily first preached?

What difference does the above discussion make? Many commentators do not see classical oral Greco-Roman rhetoric influencing the AH in any significant way. They simply see Hebrews as a written homily or sermon with an elevated

---

with exhortations must have been derived from a homily since homilies by definition include exhortation sections. The remainder of the NT letters disproves this.

49. The three types of Greco-Roman rhetoric are typically identified as judicial, deliberative, and epideictic. See D. F. Watson for explanation of each and his summary of scholars' differing conclusions as to which one best fits Hebrews ('Rhetoric, Rhetorical Criticism,' *DLNT*, 1041–51, esp. 1041–43). DeSilva does not see any of the three fitting Hebrews but still sees Greco-Roman rhetoric as influencing the AH (*Hebrews*, 35–58). After surveying the various types of rhetoric, deSilva concludes, 'While arrangement appears to be derived largely from the form of the homily, its argumentative elements and strategies are largely informed by classical Greco-Roman rhetorical practice' (p. 58).

50. For references, see discussion at Heb. 11:32.

51. See further discussion at beginning of the Heb. 13:1–25 section.

Greek style.⁵² The resulting exegetical differences between this view and mine are very minimal. For those who do see classical oral Greco-Roman rhetoric as significant, I will have more exegetical differences, especially as to the overall outline of Hebrews.

Outline of Hebrews

In one sense, there is broad consensus as to the outline in that most agree to the delineation of many of the larger sections. For example, Hebrews 3:7–4:13 is a large section related to 'rest', and Hebrews 7:1–28 is a large section concerning Melchizedek. Also, all agree that there are many overlapping themes and repeated theological motifs throughout the sections. On the other hand, there is modest disagreement as to the logical connections between the sections and significant disagreement as to the overall rationale for the order of all the sections. All agree at a minimum that the logical connections and rationale for the order of the sections are not always clear, and thus the overall 'structure' is debated.

Beginning anew with Albert Vanhoye's 1963 work,⁵³ there have been many scholarly attempts to find the 'correct' outline using different grids, including chiastic structures, Greco-Roman rhetoric, narrative analysis, emphasis on the hortatory sections, emphasis on doctrinal themes (e.g., Jesus is superior than...), etc. After a useful taxonomy of many options, Joslin concludes, maybe with some understatement, 'After a summation of these eight influential proposals, one can see that there is little consensus regarding the structure of Hebrews.'⁵⁴

For many, the interest in finding the 'correct' outline of Hebrews is driven by the assumption that it will provide

---

52. So, e.g., Hughes, *Hebrews*, 592; and Schreiner, *Hebrews*, 10–11.

53. For English readers, see Albert Vanhoye, *Structure and Message of the Epistle of Hebrews*, Subsidia Biblica 12 (Rome: Editrice Pontificio Istituto Biblico, 1989).

54. Barry C. Joslin, 'Can Hebrews be Structured? An Assessment of Eight Approaches,' *CBR* 6 (2007): 99–129, esp. 122.

deeper exegetical insight into certain verses and illuminate the AH's true emphases. Fair enough as an initial goal for any book, but for Hebrews, I just do not see the outline yielding these benefits in any significant way.

Another complication concerning the outline is that all agree that the exhortation sections are important, but there is disagreement as to whether they are separate units and how to show this importance within the outline structure. For example, the first exhortation section is Hebrews 2:1–4, but it appears to be within the larger unit of 1:5–2:18 that emphasizes that the Son is superior to angels. On the other hand, Hebrews 10:19–39 is a large coherent unit that only has exhortations.

As to my outline, which the commentary proper follows, I have simply separated the larger sections into coherent grammatical units without initially connecting them logically together.[55] Following the presentation of this outline I have comments related to the exhortation sections and some logical connections between the larger grammatical units.

1:1–4	Prologue
1:5–2:18	Son Superior to Angels
3:1–6	Son Superior to Moses
3:7–4:13	Rest
4:14–5:10	Sympathetic High Priest
5:11–6:20	Warning and Promise
7:1–28	Melchizedek
8:1–10:18	New Covenant in My Blood
10:19–39	Exhortations Based on the Great Priest
11:1–40	Heroes of Faith
12:1–29	Endurance
13:1–25	Ending Exhortations and Closing

---

55. Within the commentary proper, at the beginning of each major section and subsection, I note the connections with other sections and offer a tentative rationale as to the order.

Introductory Matters

Although not shown in the outline, the exhortation sections are significant. They occur in 2:1–4; 3:7–4:13; 4:14–16; 5:11–6:12; 10:19–39; 12:1–13:17. Most of these emphasize perseverance/endurance, that is, a Christian is exhorted to persevere in Christ until the end of his life. (Hebrews 13:1–17 is the quasi-exception to this.) In my view, these exhortation sections at least partially, if not significantly, explain the choice of doctrinal topics. Note that my view of the purpose, 'Persevere in Christ, the Son and High Priest,' connects the exhortation sections to doctrine about Christ.

The main thrust of the letter concerning persevering in Christ is Hebrews 1:1–12:29. Following this is Hebrews 13:1–17 in which are 'practical' exhortations typical of many NT letters, although there are also several echoes from the 1:1–12:29. Finally, Hebrews 13:18–25 is a typical letter closing.

Hebrews 4:14–10:39 is some sort of broad multi-section unit that emphasizes Christ as the high priest, although in the middle of this broad unit is an exhortation section (Heb. 5:11–6:12).

Hebrews 8:1–10:18 is certainly a large section that is closely related to Hebrews 7, the Melchizedek chapter. Thus 7:1–10:18 is the theological core of the AH's argument concerning the person and work of Christ as high priest. Hebrews 7 emphasizes more the *person* of Christ as high priest, that is, the fact that he is the high priest, along with a justification of this. Hebrews 8:1–10:18 emphasizes more of the *work* of Christ as a high priest, including his work's connections to his priesthood, the OT tabernacle, and the new covenant, in addition to his work's significance for believers. Beginning at Hebrews 9:11 and continuing through 10:18, there is more of an emphasis on Christ's sacrifice per se. Hence, the related themes of blood, sacrifice, offering, and covenant are especially emphasized.

Hebrews 11 is a separate section based on the genre, content, and the ending inclusio (Heb. 11:39 with 11:1–2). The primary theme, although not the only theme, of Hebrews 11 is the persevering faith of the OT saints; a faith based on divine promises (or more specific commands), and a faith that results in commendable actions. The obvious implicit purpose of this theme is to exhort the congregants to imitate the OT saints appropriately. And in thus doing they strengthen their faith so as to persevere to the end of their lives, and thereby receive the full, promised eschatological benefits. Thus, Hebrews 11 is not an exhortation per se, but its purpose is clearly exhortative.

1.
Prologue
(1:1–4)

The book of Hebrews begins with a clear prologue (Heb. 1:1–4). This prologue is fairly short but theologically dense (Heb. 1:1–4).

The prologue to Hebrews is glorious. In fact, 'glorious' or any other word does not seem grand enough for this section of Scripture. In one sentence, the author of Hebrews (AH) informs us of the redemptive-historical reality of God's plan and core aspects of his Son's person (divine and human natures) and work (creator and redeemer). In addition, these central theological truths are presented with rhetorical flair (e.g., alliteration and parallels) and serve to introduce important themes to be discussed later in Hebrews (e.g., Son, new related to old, spoken word of God, high priest, sin, angels).

Although Hebrews is a letter, it does not begin with a traditional opening like most letters in the NT.[1] Instead, it begins with a theologically and rhetorically rich prologue.[2]

---

1. See earlier chapter, Introductory Matters.

2. For those who see the AH as having a closer connection to traditional Greco-Roman oral-rhetoric than I do, the term *exordium* is used instead of 'prologue' or 'introduction' for Heb. 1:1–4, e.g., Albert Vanhoye, *Structure and Message of the Epistle of Hebrews*, Subsidia Biblica 12 (Rome: Editrice Pontificio Istituto Biblico, 1989), 79; Andrew T. Lincoln, *Hebrews: A Guide* (London:

The only close parallel in the NT for a letter is 1 John 1:1–4. In non-letters, John 1:1–18 is similarly rich theologically and fairly rhetorical.³ Luke 1:1–4 is certainly rhetorically sophisticated. AH's unusual opening, as opposed to a traditional letter, adds to the impact of the prologue.

As to the grammatical/logical flow of the prologue, Hebrews 1:1–4 is one sentence. All agree that the primary grammatical clause is 'God ... spoke to us in the Son' (1:1–2).⁴ As to the logical order of the remaining six statements about Christ in 1:2–3, there is disagreement. My view is presented below.

Following the primary clause are two relative clauses with the grammatical subject being God the Father:

1:2b: whom [the Son] he [God] placed heir of all
1:2c: through whom [the Son] also he [God] made all ages

Hebrews 1:2b refers to the Son's ascension after his resurrection and 1:2c refers to the initial creation. Hence, 1:2b and 1:2c are presented in reverse historical order. This purposely contrasts for rhetorical effect with the four statements about the Son in Hebrews 1:3. These four statements in 1:3 have as their grammatical subject the Son and are in 'normal' historical order including the Son's essence in eternity past, his work in creation, his work on the cross, and his ascension.

T&T Clark/Continuum, 2006), 24; Harold W. Attridge, *A Commentary on the Epistle to the Hebrews*, Hermeneia (Philadelphia: Fortress, 1989), 19; and Alan C. Mitchell, *Hebrews*, SP 13 (Collegeville: Liturgical, 2007), 21, 35. Note, a few see the *exordium* as extending to 2:4, e.g., Craig R. Koester, *Hebrews*, AB 36 (NY: Doubleday, 2001), 174–75. D. F. Watson defines an *exordium* as 'an introduction that strives to make the audience attentive, well-disposed and receptive to the message' ('Rhetoric, Rhetorical Criticism,' *DLNT*, 1041–51, esp. 1042).

3. Although I do not agree to his 'levels of style' emphasis, Dan Nässelqvist sees Heb. 1:1–4 having a 'grand' style and John 1:1–18 having 'aspects of both plain and grand style' ('Stylistic Levels in Hebrews 1:1–4 and John 1:1–18,' *JSNT* 35 [2012]: 31–53, esp. 44, 50).

4. E.g., Luke Timothy Johnson, *Hebrews: A Commentary*, NTL (Louisville: Westminster John Knox, 2006), 63.

1:3a: who [Son] being the radiance of his [God's] glory and imprint of his [God's] substance
1:3b: and upholding all things by the word of his [Son's] power
1:3c: after [the Son's] making purifications of the sins
1:3d: He [Son] sat at the right hand of the Majesty on high

As opposed to my view, some explain the somewhat usual order by assuming that the AH is intentionally using a chiastic structure. For example, Ebert sees a A B C D C' B' A' structure with Hebrews 1:3a–b being the important center D.[5] Still others believe that the difference between Hebrews 1:2b–c and 1:3a–d is explained by viewing Hebrews 1:3a–d as a hymnic fragment not originally composed by AH.[6]

1:1–2a [*In*] *many parts and many ways, long ago, God, [after] speaking to the fathers by the prophets, in these last days spoke to us by [the] Son ...*

This opening to Hebrews has rhetorical flair in three ways. First, there is the double use of **many** (πολύς) in the opening words.[7] Second, the alliteration of the Greek letter π (English 'p') is used for five major words in the opening participial phrase.[8] Third, there is the wonderful parallel presented here in Greek order:

---

5. Daniel J. Ebert IV, 'The Chiastic Structure of the Prologue to Hebrews,' *TJ* 13 ns (1992): 163–79, esp. 168. William L. Lane sees an A B C C' B' A' pattern with C being 1:2c and C' being 1:3a–b (*Hebrews 1–8*, WBC 47a [Waco: Word, 1991], 6–7). The supposed exegetical impact of a chiastic structure is the importance of the center phrase.

6. Koester does not agree to this view, but gives a good explanation of it along with various authors who support it (*Hebrews*, 178–79).

7. Πολυμερῶς καὶ πολυτρόπως, 'many-parts and many-ways.' Note, these are the absolute first words of Hebrews; the Greek text has no 'in.'

8. Πολυμερῶς (many-parts), πολυτρόπως (many-ways), πάλαι (long-ago), πατράσιν (fathers), and προφήταις (prophets). David Allen Black states that alliteration with π occurs often in Hebrews. He references 1:1; 2:1–2, 10; 3:12; 9:26; 11:4; 12:11; 13:19 ('Hebrews 1:1–4: A Study in Discourse Analysis,' *WTJ* 49 [1987]: 175–94, esp. 189n27).

Long ago	God after speaking	to the fathers	by the prophets
in these last days	he spoke	to us	by the Son

In the OT, God spoke during **many parts**, which implies different times or sections or occasions throughout OT history.[9] This speaking in **many parts and many ways** is positive, but it is surpassed by the completeness and finality of the Son.[10] God's **speaking to the fathers by the prophets** is functionally the OT Scriptures.[11] The Son's coming is part of the **last days** as he inaugurates the final redemptive period that extends into the New Heavens and Earth.[12]

God **spoke to us by the Son**. As noted above, this is the primary grammatical clause of Hebrews 1:1–4. For the OT, God's **speaking ... by the prophets** is using **speaking** in a straight-forward way. However, the way God **spoke** by the Son is primarily through the Son's actions, although it does include both God's and the Son's words (e.g., Heb. 1:5, 2:12–13).[13] The theme of God speaking is significant

---

9. Hence, the translation 'times' is implied. So also John Owen, *An Exposition of the Epistle to the Hebrews*, vols. 17–23 of *The Works of John Owen*, ed. William H. Goold (Carlisle: Banner of Truth, 1991), 19:2; Simon J. Kistemaker, *Exposition of the Epistle to the Hebrews*, NTC (Grand Rapids: Baker, 1984), 26; and many major translations, e.g., KJV, NIV, ESV, CEB. BDAG prefers 'in various parts' (847).

10. Some see an implied 'fragmentary' aspect to the OT revelation, e.g., Philip Edgcumbe Hughes, *A Commentary on the Epistle to the Hebrews* (Grand Rapids: Eerdmans, 1977), 36. I disagree.

11. OT 'prophets' quoted in Hebrews include Moses (Heb. 1:6; 8:5); Nathan (Heb. 1:5), Isaiah (Heb. 2:13), Jeremiah (Heb. 8:8–12; 10:16–17), Habakkuk (Heb. 10:37–38), Haggai (Heb. 12:26), and David (Heb. 1:13; 2:6–8; 4:7; 10:5–7). Another angle is that Christ is seen to be a speaker in the OT (Heb. 2:12; 10:5–7).

12. For 'last days' used similarly in the NT, see Acts 2:17; 2 Tim. 3:1; 2 Pet. 3:3; cf. 1 Pet. 1:5, 20; 1 John 2:18; and Jude 18. At the word level, this expression (באחרית הימים, ἐπ' ἐσχάτου τῶν ἡμερῶν) is in the OT at Gen. 49:1; Num. 24:14; Deut. 4:30; Jer. 23:20; 49:39 (LXX 25:19); and Dan. 10:14.

13. The Greek preposition ἐν has a semantic range of instrumental use ('by') and locative/sphere ('in'). Hence, for **by** (ἐν) **the prophets**, the instrumental use is clearly used; for **by** (ἐν) **the Son**, a combination of

throughout the book of Hebrews and is highlighted in 1:5–13.¹⁴

Son and the priesthood of Christ are two important aspects of Christology in Hebrews, and the Son theme is introduced first.¹⁵ In the expression, **by the Son** (ἐν υἱῷ), there is no definite article in Greek, although it is clear to all that the definite Jesus is in mind as the Son. Most translations insert 'his' to show this definiteness.¹⁶ So why no article?¹⁷ Most likely the AH is including a *qualitative* aspect of the definite Son.¹⁸ That is, part

---

instrumental and sphere is used—God **spoke** by and in the actions of the person of the Son. Is Christ here called the Word of God? Not exactly, but it certainly dovetails with other passages that do (e.g., John 1:1). For a good overview of God's Word being more than words, see John M. Frame, *The Doctrine of the Word of God* (Phillipsburg: P&R, 2010), 63–81.

14. See Jonathan I. Griffiths, *Hebrews and Divine Speech*, LNTS 507 (London: T. & T. Clark, 2014). For a good general discussion of God being a speaking God, see John M. Frame, *The Doctrine of God* (Phillipsburg: P&R, 2002), 470-75. For a review of the Word of God throughout redemptive history, see Matthew Barrett, *God's Word Alone: The Authority of Scripture: What the Reformers Taught ... and Why It Still Matters*, Five Solas (Grand Rapids: Zondervan, 2016), 165–220.

15. Maybe slightly overstating the case, but Attridge notes that 'two elements which determine the whole christology of Hebrews [are] the status of Christ as the exalted Son and the sacrificial, priestly act by which he effected atonement for sin' (*Hebrews*, 36). Donald A. Hagner also sees Son and High Priest as the two most important, but further concludes that Son of God 'is clearly the central christological designation of Hebrews' ('The Son of God as Unique High Priest: The Christology of the Epistle of Hebrews,' in *Contours of Christology in the New Testament*, ed. Richard N. Longenecker, MNTS 7 [Grand Rapids: Eerdmans, 2005], 247–67, esp. 249).

16. E.g., 'his' in the Geneva Bible, KJV, NIV, NASB, ESV; although 'a' in RSV, NRSV, CEB.

17. An initial option that presents itself is that definite nouns often drop articles in prepositional phrases. However, this option is to be dismissed here as the parallel **by the prophets** (ἐν τοῖς προφήταις) does include the article. For a general discussion of articles dropping out of prepositional phrases, see BDF §255 and Daniel B. Wallace, *Greek Grammar Beyond the Basics: An Exegetical Syntax of the New Testament* (Grand Rapids: Zondervan, 1996), 247. For anarthrous 'son', see Heb. 5:8; 7:28; and 11:24.

18. In fact, Wallace uses this text as one of his prime examples of the qualitative aspect of an anarthrous noun (*Greek Grammar Beyond the Basics*,

of the emphasis is that God spoke by 'Son-ness' as opposed to speaking by prophets.[19] As Lane states well, 'The eternal, essential quality of Jesus' sonship qualified him to be the one through whom God uttered his final word.'[20]

The theology here is very profound. There is *continuity* between the OT and NT in that God has spoken in both. However, there also is *contrast* in that **in these last days**, God has spoken with finality in the Son.

The theme of contrast-within-continuity is another large theme in Hebrews that is introduced in Hebrews 1:1–2.[21] God's covenantal plan and Scriptures extend throughout redemptive history, and the plan includes a progressive escalation of God's presence and benefits. The Son has come and continues as the mediator of the 'new covenant' (Heb. 9:15). This dovetails well with the Reformed covenantal/redemptive-historical hermeneutic.[22]

244–45). For another discussion of quality and anarthrous nouns, see Maximillian Zerwick, *Biblical Greek: Illustrated by Examples*, trans. Joseph Smith (Rome: Scripta Pontificii Instituti Biblici, 1963), §§171–83.

19. So also Black, 'Hebrews 1:1–4: A Study in Discourse Analysis,' 183; and F. F. Bruce, *The Epistle to the Hebrews*, 2nd ed., NICNT (Grand Rapids: Eerdmans, 1990), 44n2.

20. William L. Lane, *Hebrews 1–8*, WBC 47a (Dallas: Word, 1991), 11.

21. Lincoln states, 'The exposition sections are all variations on the theme of the comparison between the previous stage of God's revelation to Israel and the final and superior stage of that revelation in Christ' (*Hebrews: A Guide*, 52). As examples of contrast-within-continuity, I. Howard Marshall notes that to understand the new covenant and Christ's priestly work, one needs to understand the continuity and discontinuity of these analogies from the OT. He also points out that the 'concept of faith' provides a 'strong element of continuity' (*New Testament Theology: Many Witnesses, One Gospel* [Downers Grove: InterVarsity, 2004], 611–13).

22. In a good, brief discussion, Richard B. Gaffin, Jr. uses Heb. 1:1–2 and the implications throughout Hebrews as 'provid[ing] explicit biblical warrant' for the 'redemptive-historical' hermeneutical approach to Scripture ('Systematic Theology and Hermeneutics,' in *Seeing Christ in All of Scripture: Hermeneutics at Westminster Theological Seminary*, ed. Peter A. Lillback [Philadelphia: Westminster Seminary Press, 2016], 39–51, esp. 44–49).

1:2b–3 *... whom he placed heir of all, through whom also he made all ages; who being [the] radiance of [his]²³ glory and imprint of his substance, and upholding all things by the word of his power, [after] making purification of the²⁴ sins, he sat at the right hand of the Majesty on high, ...*

As discussed above, the two phrases **whom he placed heir of all** and **through whom also he made all ages** both have God the Father as their grammatical subject and are in 'reverse' historical order. God **placed** the Son as **heir** or owner/inheritor **of all** things. Here, the AH is most likely speaking of this occurring at the Son's ascension/exaltation in his mediatorial Messianic role (cf. Heb. 1:3, 13; 2:8–9; 12:2; Pss. 2:8; 89:27; Rom. 4:13; 1 Cor. 15:28; Phil. 2:9–11).²⁵ That is, the Son was **placed** or publicly made the **heir** at his ascension with the full inheritance coming at the Second Coming. In the list of six phrases related to the Son, the exaltation is first as it signals the glorious accomplishment of his earthly work. The concepts of 'son' and **heir** are clearly related. Later in Hebrews, believers will also be deemed heirs who inherit salvation (Heb. 1:14; 6:11–12).

---

23. As do most translations, I take **his** (God the Father) following **substance** as distributive and thus to modify also **glory**.

24. Some Greek manuscripts have ἡμῶν, 'our.' Hence, the KJV translates as 'our sins'. Otherwise, all the Greek manuscripts have the definite article τῶν. However, most English translations do not include 'the' as the context makes it clear that the Son died for definite sins and there is no implied contrast to some other category of sins. As usual, my translation is purposely mechanical.

25. As to exaltation, so also Koester, *Hebrews*, 178; Hughes, *Hebrews*, 47; and C. Spicq, *L'Épître aux Hébreux*, 2 vols., EBib (Paris: Gabalda, 1952–1953), 2:5; contra James Moffatt who sees this as a 'pre-temporal act' (*A Critical and Exegetical Commentary on the Epistle to the Hebrews*, ICC [Edinburgh: T. & T. Clark, 1979 {1924}], 5). Calvin and Chrysostom see **heir** as only referring to Christ's human nature (John Calvin, T*he Epistle of Paul the Apostle to the Hebrews and the First and Second Epistles of St Peter*, trans. William B. Johnson, eds. David W. and Thomas F. Torrance, Calvin's Commentaries 12 [Grand Rapids: Eerdmans, 1963], 7; John Chrysostom, 'Homily 1 on Hebrews,' (*NPNF*¹, 14:366–69, esp. 367). Contra Calvin and Chrysostom, Owen sees Christ's exaltation related to his mediatorial role as a person in both natures (*Hebrews*, 19:40, 90).

Through (διά) the Son, God the Father **made all ages.**[26] The NT often connects God the Father and God the Son (and implied God the Holy Ghost) in the function of creator (e.g., John 1:3, 10; 1 Cor. 8:6; Col. 1:16–17; cf. Gen. 1:1–2). That is, the Trinity is the creator, not just God the Father.[27] Although the term may not be the best, the Son is 'instrumentally' involved in creation as the NT always uses an instrumental preposition to describe the relationship.[28] In context, declaring that the Son is the creator is looking to eternity past and affirming the Son's divinity. The creator-Son will be further discussed in 1:10–12 (cf. 13:8) and the creator-Father in 2:10; 3:4; 4:3–4; 9:26; and the creating word of God in Heb. 11:3.

Starting with **who being the radiance of his glory and imprint of his substance**, Hebrews 1:3 has four statements with the Son as the grammatical subject. As noted above, these four are in 'normal' historical order including the Son's essence in eternity past, his work in creation, his work on the cross, and his ascension.

The Son is the **radiance of** the Father's **glory**.[29] **Glory** has

---

26. My translation of **ages** is a mechanical translation of the plural of αἰών, which etymologically comes into English as 'aeon'. LSJ gives the default meaning as 'period of existence' (p. 45). The Greek word has a broad semantic range, even in Hebrews itself, from 'forever' (Heb. 1:8) to 'age' (Heb. 6:5) to 'world/universe' (Heb. 11:3). Clearly here it implies the whole universe (that has existed through all periods). In Heb. 1:3, the Geneva Bible and KJV translate as 'worlds', NIV as 'universe', and ESV and NASB as 'world'. See BDAG for more nuances (pp. 32–33).

27. 'It pleased God the Father, Son, and Holy Ghost, for the manifestation of the glory of his eternal power, wisdom, and goodness, in the beginning, to create or make of nothing, the world' (WCF 4.1). The Nicene Creed includes Christ as a creator, 'by whom all things were made.' For a very good discussion on 'The Creator is the Triune God', see Herman Bavinck, *Reformed Dogmatics*, ed. John Bolt, trans. John Vriend, 4 vols. (Grand Rapids: Baker Academic, 2003–2008 [2nd ed. 1906–1911]), 2:420–26.

28. John 1:3 διά; John 1:10 διά; 1 Cor. 8:6 διά; Col. 1:16–17 ἐν, διά; Heb. 1:2 διά.

29. 1 Clem. 36 has several direct connections to Heb. 1, including 'radiance of his majesty', 'much greater than angels as he inherited a more excellent name,' and quotes of Ps. 2:7–8 // Heb. 1:5; Ps. 104:4 // Heb. 1:7; and Ps. 110:1 // Heb. 1:13.

quite a broad semantic range in biblical literature, but here, as can be inferred from **radiance**, it is emphasizing, at least metaphorically, brilliant light. In Scripture, the Godhead is often metaphorically pictured in heaven as radiating brilliant, beautiful light (e.g., Pss. 36:9; 104:1–2; Isa. 60:1; Rev. 4:5; 21:23). In addition, often in theophanies, God appears as light to the humans witnessing the event (e.g., Exod. 16:7, 10; Deut. 5:24; Luke 9:29; Acts 9:3; 22:11; Rev. 21:24; cf. Matt 5:16; Luke 2:32; 2 Cor. 4:4, 6).[30] **Radiance** refers to light actively coming from a source.[31] The Lord Jesus Christ radiates the true glory of the Father in all his aspects, not just light. What a grand thought! Christ is the light of the world (John 8:12; 9:5; 12:46), and whoever has seen him has seen the Father (John 14:9). Calvin states, 'The radiance in the substance of God is so mighty that it hurts our eyes, until it shines on us in Christ.'[32] Kelly comments, 'Christ is not merely a reflection of God, but he is the true radiance of the eternal light. As we confess in the Nicene Creed, he is "light from light".'[33] All the glorious

---

30. BDAG lists as the first definition of **glory** (δόξα), 'condition of being bright or shining, brightness, splendor, radiance' (257, emphasis theirs). See excellent discussions in Silva, ed., 'δόξα,' *NIDNTTE*, 1:761–67; Frame, *Doctrine of God*, 592–95; Petrus Van Mastricht, *Theoretical-Practical Theology*, trans. Todd M. Rester, ed. Joel R. Beeke, 7 vols. (Grand Rapids: Reformation Heritage, 2018– [1698–1699]), 2:469–79; and Bavinck, *Reformed Dogmatics*, 2:252–55. 1 Clem. 36:2 quotes this phrase but interchanges 'majesty' from Heb. 1:4 for 'glory'.

31. **Radiance** (ἀπαύγασμα) could have a more passive meaning such as 'reflection'; however, virtually all interpret with the active 'radiance' or 'effulgence' meaning, e.g., BDAG, 99; LSJ, 181; Lane, *Hebrews 1–8*, 13; and Bruce, *Hebrews*, 48 n. 22; *contra* NJB and RSV. Wis. 7:26 possibly uses ἀπαύγασμα with more of a reflection sense, 'For she [wisdom] is a reflection/radiance of eternal light.'

32. Calvin, *Hebrews and 1 & 2 Peter*, 8. Chrysostom, 'Truly he [Christ] has led them to unapproachable light, to the very brightness itself' ('Homily 1 on Hebrews,' [*NPNF*[1], 14:367]).

33. Douglas F. Kelly, *The Beauty of Christ: A Trinitarian Vision*, vol. 2 of *Systematic Theology: Grounded in Holy Scripture and Understood in the Light of the Church* (Ross-shire: Christian Focus/Mentor, 2014), 169. Kelly notes that often in Scripture the beauty/light of creation is connected to inner-Trinitarian beauty, cf. Heb. 1:1–3; 2 Cor. 3:18; 4:6 (p. 30).

attributes of the Godhead exist in the Father, Son, and Holy Spirit. Using the metaphor of brilliant light, the AH moves his reader to first think upon the physical beauty and splendor of brilliant light (e.g., lightning flashes), which then moves the reader to consider the glorious attributes of the Godhead, and then finally the reader considers that these glorious divine attributes are shown in the person of the Lord Jesus Christ, who also suffered for us.[34]

Closely connected grammatically to **radiance of his glory** is the phrase **imprint of his substance** (ὑπόστασις, *hypostasis*).[35] More or less making the same point as the first phrase, the second phrase declares that the Son is the **imprint** or representation of the Father's **substance**. This phrase combines the ideas of a coin being imprinted from the original stamp with a son being an 'imprint' of his father. Again, this is another remarkable statement of high Christology as the divinity of Christ is affirmed.

Although **imprint of his substance** clearly refers to the divinity of Christ, there is quite a debate as to the exact meaning of ὑπόστασις, which I translate as **substance**.

Option 1: By using **substance**, I conclude that the Son has the same substance/nature/being/essence/*ousia* as the Father. That is, the Son's substance and the Father's substance are exactly the same and are one. The substance/being of the Son from all eternity has had the **imprint** of substance/being of the Father. The emphasis of **imprint** would be an *exactness*.[36] To quote the WSC 6, 'There are three persons in the Godhead ... the same in *substance*, equal inpower and glory' (italics mine).

---

34. Zwingli in his 1523 Short Christian Instruction §5 states, 'He [Christ] also embodies the beauty and image of **the father** according to Hebrews 1:3 and has let himself be so miserably spit on, mocked, and beaten for our sakes' (*Reformed Confessions of the 16th and 17th Centuries in English Translation*, ed. James T. Dennison, Jr., 4 vols. [Grand Rapids: Reformation Heritage, 2008–2014], 1:18).

35. **Who being** at the beginning of Heb. 1:3 grammatically applies to both phrases.

36. ESV translates as 'exact imprint'; NASB, 'exact representation'; Geneva Bible, 'ingraued forme.'

Prologue (1:1-4)

This option is supported by most modern exegetes and theologians.[37]

Option 2: This option concludes that ὑπόστασις should be translated here as person/subsistence/personal-properties/ hypostasis.[38] Hence, the text would be confirming that the *person* of Christ properly represents the *person* of the Father. The emphasis of **imprint** would be on a correct representation but not exactness. That is, the Son is not the Father, but the Son is the correct representation and image of the Father. This option has been well supported by the earlier Reformed tradition.[39] *Both options are theologically true; the question is, Which one is being advocated by Hebrews 1:3?*

In Hebrews, ὑπόστασις is used several ways: 'confidence' or 'assurance' in 3:14 and 'reality' in 11:5. There is an additional

---

37. E.g., Donald Macleod, *The Person of Christ*, Contours of Christian Theology (Downers Grove: InterVarsity, 1998), 80–86; John Webster, 'One Who is Son: Theological Reflections on the Exordium to the Epistle of Hebrews,' in *The Epistle to the Hebrews and Christian Theology*, ed. Richard Bauckham, Daniel R. Driver, Trevor A. Hart, and Nathan MacDonald (Grand Rapids: Eerdmans, 2009), 69–94, esp. 87–88; Hughes, *Hebrews*, 43; Kistemaker, *Hebrews*, 30; Paul Ellingworth, *The Epistle to the Hebrews: A Commentary on the Greek Text*, NIGTC (Grand Rapids: Eerdmans, 1993), 99–100; Thomas R. Schreiner, *Commentary on Hebrews*, Biblical Theology for Christian Proclamation (Nashville: Homan Reference, 2015), 57; and the Catechism of the Catholic Church §§241–42

38. The Geneva Bible and KJV translations of 'person' follows this option.

39. E.g., Calvin, *Hebrews and 1 & 2 Peter*, 8; *Institutes* 1.13.2; William Ames, *The Marrow of Theology* (Durham: Labyrinth, 1983 [1629]), 88; David Dickson, *Truth's Victory over Error: A Commentary on the Westminster Confession of Faith*, trans. and ed. John R. DeWitt (Carlisle: Banner of Truth, 2007 [1684]), 21–23; Owen, *Hebrews*, 19:85–95; Francis Turretin, *Institutes of Elenctic Theology*, trans. George Musgrave Giger, ed. James T. Dennison, Jr., 3 vols. (Phillipsburg: P&R, 1992–1997 [1679–1685], 1:254, 299; and Wilhelmus à Brakel, *The Christian's Reasonable Service*, trans. Bartel Elshout, ed. Joel R. Beeke, 4 vols. (Grand Rapids: Reformation Heritage, 1992–1995 [1702]), 1:141, 1:165. See discussion in Richard A. Muller, *Post-Reformation Reformed Dogmatics: The Rise and Development of Reformed Orthodoxy, ca. 1520 to ca. 1725*, 2nd ed., 4 vols. (Grand Rapids: Baker, 2003), 4:182–86, 233, 254–55. The Belgic Confession 8, 10 and Hungarian Szikszó Synod (1568) 10 interpret *hypostasis* in Heb. 1:3 as referring to person (for Szikszó Synod translation, see *Reformed Confessions of the 16th and 17th Centuries*, 3:150).

linguistic complication from Church history. The AD 325 Nicene Creed used *hypostasis* and *ousia* interchangeably to refer to 'being/essence' in the anathema section. However, by the AD 451 Chalcedon Creed, *hypostasis* was now a technical term for 'person' and *ousia* for 'being'.[40] Of course, just because Hebrews 1:3 uses *hypostasis* does not mean that the Chalcedon technical meaning of 'person' for *hypostasis* should apply to Hebrews.

As mentioned above, I conclude that *hypostasis* in Hebrews 1:3 refers to the Son and Father having the same **substance**/being. This is primarily based on (1) **imprint** having an 'exact' connotation, (2) better dovetails with **glory**,[41] and (3) the next phrase concerning creation/providence is more related to divine attributes that the Father and Son share (e.g., **power**).[42]

The second of the four statements with Son as the

---

40. For Greek and Latin texts for Nicene and Chalcedon Creeds, see Phillip Schaff, ed. *The Creeds of Christendom: With History and Critical Notes*, rev. David S. Schaff, 6th ed., 3 vols. (Grand Rapids: Baker, 1931), 2:60–62; or Heinrich Denzinger, *Compendium of Creeds, Definitions, and Declarations on Matters of Faith and Morals*, eds. Robert Fastiggi and Anne Englund Nash, 43rd ed. (San Francisco: Ignatius, 2012), §§125–26, 300–03.

41. That is, both **glory** and **substance** are referring to the being of the Father that is shared by the Son, thus making the same general point with the two phrases. So also Lane, *Hebrews 1–8*, 13. Geerhardus Vos disagrees. He sees **radiance of his glory** as referring to the Father's being that is shared by the Son, but the **imprint of his substance** refers to the Father's person. Hence, both the unity of being (first phrase) and distinction of persons (second phrase) are shown in these two phrases. 'Two images were chosen' because 'one image was not able to express these two truths at the same time' (*Reformed Dogmatics*, trans. and ed. Richard B. Gaffin, Jr., 5 vols. [Bellingham: Lexham, 2012–2016], 1:58–59).

42. The best argument against my view is well stated by Owen (*Hebrews*, 19:85–95, esp. 90). He sees the whole person of Christ in view (both human and divine natures, not just the divine nature). Given this, the comparison is between the Son's person and the Father's person. He complains that my view assumes that only Christ's divine nature is being considered. Hence, for Owen, if the whole person of Christ is being emphasized, then there cannot be an exact connection between the Father's divine nature and Christ's two natures.

grammatical subject is **upholding all things by the word of his** [the Son's] **power**. This expands upon the Son's being involved in initial creation as discussed above. The Son is also involved in continuing providence.[43] Many creeds cite Hebrews 1:3 to show God/Christ's continuing providence (e.g., Heidelberg Catechism 27, Belgic Confession 12, WCF 5.1, WLC 18, WSC 11). The expression **word** ($\acute{\rho}\tilde{\eta}\mu\alpha$) **of his power** is, of course, related to Genesis 1 where God 'speaks' creation into existence (cf. Ps. 33:6). Similar wording is used in Hebrews 11:3, 'the ages were prepared by the word ($\acute{\rho}\tilde{\eta}\mu\alpha$) of God.'

After noting the Son's being and his providential control of creation, the AH includes the Son's redemptive work in the statement **making purification of the sins**, which is the third statement with Son as the grammatical subject. It is the Son, not man, who atones for the elect's sins. The Son is *both* the priest and the sacrifice (Heb. 9:11–12), which according to Brown, is the 'germ [of] the leading argument for the superiority of Christianity to [an improperly truncated] Judaism.'[44] This juxtaposition of the Son as divine creator and his having died for sins is jarring—assuming one does not know the glorious redemptive story. The dying clearly reveals the human nature of the Son and foreshadows that emphasis in Hebrews 2:5–18. Having both the divine and human natures of the person of the Son emphasized in Hebrews 1:3 also foreshadows and explains the later emphasis on mediator (Heb. 8:6; 9:15; 12:22).[45]

The fourth and final statement of Hebrews 1:3 with Son

---

43. In Scripture, when God is referred to as the initial creator, it is implied that he also is active in continuing providence. For examples of explicit statements to this effect, see Ps. 104; Col. 1:16–17; and Rev. 4:11.

44. John Brown, *Hebrews*, Geneva (Carlisle: Banner of Truth, 1961 [1862]), 34.

45. Lincoln argues for the AH's Christology 'the key concept, though by no means the dominant title, ... [is] mediator.' This explains how both the divine and human natures exist 'side by side in this epistle ... both aspects of this portrayal have to be held together and taken equally seriously if the true nature of Christ as intermediary is to be appreciated' (*Hebrews: A Guide*, 85).

as the grammatical subject is **he sat at the right hand of the Majesty on high**. The exaltation of the Son is clearly stated here and elsewhere in Hebrews (1:13; 8:1; 10:12; 12:2). Of course, the sitting at the throne of God is understood metaphorically.[46] The expression **right hand** emphasizes the power of the Son. Calvin comments that in context this power shows that salvation is not temporary despite present appearances.[47] Putting the third and fourth statements together is the humiliation/exaltation scheme that often describes Christ in Hebrews and the NT (e.g., Luke 24:46; Acts 2:23–24; 5:30–31; Phil. 2:6–11; 2 Cor. 13:4; Heb. 2:7; 12:2; 1 Pet. 1:11; 4:13; WSC 27–28).[48] With this exaltation statement, the AH assumes the resurrection, but it is curious that resurrection is not explicit in Hebrews except for the benediction (Heb. 13:20–21).[49]

1:4 ... *[after] becoming so much better than the angels, he has inherited a name much superior in contrast to them.*

This verse is somewhat of a transition between Hebrews 1:1–3 and 1:5–14 as much of 1:5–14 relates explicitly to **angels**.[50] Why bring up **angels** here? Many see Hebrews 2:2 as the answer where angels are mediators of God's message (cf. Acts 7:53; Gal. 3:19).[51] Hence, both angels and prophets

---

46. For a good discussion, see Turretin, *Institutes of Elenctic Theology*, 2:369–73. This is not to deny, however, that Christ's body is currently in heaven.

47. Calvin, *Hebrews and 1 & 2 Peter*, 9.

48. Attridge argues that both the humiliation and exaltation of Christ are 'essential and Hebrews will develop each with equal insistence' (*Hebrews*, 47). Georg Strecker sees a larger pattern matching Phil. 2: preexistence (Phil. 2:6 // Heb. 1:1–3b; humiliation (Phil. 2:7 // Heb. 1:3c); exaltation (Phil. 2:9 // Heb. 1:3d–5); and parousia (Phil. 2:10–11 // Heb. 1:6–13) (*Theology of the New Testament*, trans. M. Eugene Boring [Louisville: Westminster John Knox, 2000], 610).

49. Thomas R. Schreiner argues that the resurrection is important to the AH and is implied often. See *New Testament Theology: Magnifying God in Christ* (Grand Rapids: Baker, 2008), 399–400.

50. So also Ellingworth, *Hebrews*, 103.

51. So, e.g., Lane, *Hebrews 1–8*, 17; Ellingworth, *Hebrews*, 104; and

were mediators of God's revelation. Hebrews 1:2 already declared the Son greater than prophets, and here, the Son is greater than the **angels**. Another option dovetailing with this is simply to see the 'internal logic of the Epistle's argument' as a lesser-to-greater argument.[52] The Son is greater than the prophets, angels, Moses, Joshua, and priests. It would be appropriate to include angels in this as they are presented in the OT as especially gifted beings. A final option, based on mirror reading, might be that in the congregation or in those influencing the congregation there is an unhealthy interest in angels and/or improper exaltation of angels that the AH is implicitly counteracting. In any event, it is clear that the AH exalts the Son above **angels**.

Similar to the last clause in Hebrews 1:3, **he has inherited** refers to the Son's exaltation. The Son receives his name in a more public way at the completion of his earthly mediatorial work.[53] The Greek verb for **inherited** is the cognate of 'heir' in Hebrews 1:2.[54] In some sense, this is an inclusio for the several wonderful statements about the Son. Of course, the Son was always **better**[55] **than the angels**, it is just at his exaltation this became more public.

Exactly what is the **name**? Apparently, it is 'Son' as this is the emphasis of the prologue and Hebrews 1:5–8.[56] Obviously,

---

Mitchell, *Hebrews*, 39. Of course, there may have been other angel issues related to the congregation that we do not know about.

52. John P. Meier, 'Symmetry and Theology in the Old Testament Citations of Heb. 1, 5–14,' *Bib* 66 (1985): 504–33, esp. 522.

53. So also Kistemaker, *Hebrews*, 32; and Owen, *Hebrews*, 19:125.

54. 'Heir' (κληρονόμος) and 'to inherit' (κληρονομέω). The English translation also uses cognates.

55. This is the first of thirteen times 'better' (κρείττων) is used in Hebrews (e.g., Heb. 8:6). It matches the pattern of contrast within continuity. The AH uses an unusual amount of comparatives. See Andreas J. Köstenberger, 'Jesus, the Mediator of a "Better Covenant": Comparatives in the Book of Hebrews,' *Faith & Mission* 21 (2004): 30–49, esp. his listing of all comparatives on pp. 40–42.

56. So also Bruce, *Hebrews*, 50–51; Koester, *Hebrews*, 182; and Mitchell, *Hebrews*, 39. Contra Johnson who prefers 'Lord/kyrios' (*Hebrews*, 73) and

the second person of the Trinity is the Son before his exaltation as Hebrews 1:2–3 and 5:8 show. Interestingly, 'Jesus' is not mentioned until Hebrews 2:9, and 'Christ' not until 3:6.

Reflections

As mentioned above, the prologue to Hebrews is glorious. If one assumes, as I do, that these four verses present the reality of Christ, my confidence to live for him increases. No matter the difficulties or attractions of this world, they are put into proper perspective by the Son, who is the creator and redeemer, the God-man, and the one humiliated and then exalted.

Although not especially emphasized by the flow of Hebrews 1:1–4, the Son is presented as prophet, priest, and king, which of course relates to the three major offices of the OT.[57] The *prophet* aspect is shown as God the Father 'spoke by the Son' and in comparison to the OT 'prophets' (Heb. 1:1–2). The *priest* aspect is related to 'making purification for sins' (Heb. 1:3) The *king* aspect is included in the Son's being 'heir of all things' (Heb. 1:2) and 'at the right hand of the Majesty on high' (Heb. 1:3).[58]

Eusebius (AD 260–340) discusses Christ's three offices in the context of a variety of quotes from Hebrews, including Hebrews 1. He notes that OT prophets, priests, and kings were anointed and were a 'type' of Christ, *the* anointed one, the 'only and true Christ.' He was the 'only High Priest of

---

Richard Bauckham, 'YHWH' ('The Divinity of Jesus Christ in the Epistle to the Hebrews,' in *The Epistle to the Hebrews and Christian Theology*, 15–36, esp. 20–22).

57. Hughes also notes the prophet-priest-king triad in Heb. 1:1–4 (*Hebrews*, 49). Calvin emphasizes these three offices of Christ (*Institutes* 2.15). Also see WSC 24–26, WLC 43–45, and Richard P. Belcher, Jr., *Prophet, Priest, and King: The Roles of Christ in the Bible and Our Roles Today* (Phillipsburg: P&R, 2016).

58. The Reformed tradition sees Christ functioning in his three offices as mediator in both his state of humiliation and his state of exaltation. See Louis Berkhof, *Systematic Theology*, 4th ed. (Grand Rapids: Eerdmans, 1941), 356; Turretin, *Institutes of Elenctic Theology*, 2:333; and WLC 42.

the whole [universe], the only King of all creation, and only Archprophet of the Father of the prophets.'[59]

The *Geneva Bible: 1602 Edition*'s summary of the whole book of Hebrews includes the three major offices. 'The drift and end of this epistle is to show that Jesus Christ is the Son of God, both God and man, is that true eternal & only *Prophet, King,* and high *Priest,* that was foreshadowed by the figures of the old law, and is now in deed exhibited of whom the whole Church ought to be *taught, governed, & sanctified.*'[60]

The Heidelberg Catechism 31–32 connects the three offices of Christ to the same three 'mini-offices' for Christians. (1) Prophet. Christ is 'our chief Prophet and Teacher, who fully reveals to us the secret counsel and will of God concerning our redemption.' We respond in faith to 'confess his name.' (2) Priest. Christ is 'our only High Priest, who by the one sacrifice of his body has redeemed us, and ever liveth to make intercession for us with the Father.' We respond by being 'a living sacrifice of thankfulness to him.' (3) King. Christ is 'our eternal King, who governs us by his Word and Spirit and defends and preserves us in the redemption obtained for us.' We respond to 'fight against sin and the devil in this life, and hereafter, in eternity to reign with him over all creatures.'

---

59. Eusebius, *Ecclesiastical History* 1.3.8–9, translation mine. He quotes from Ps. 2:7 // Heb. 1:5; Ps. 45:6–7 // Heb. 1:8–9; and Ps. 110:1, 3–4 // Heb. 1:13; 5:6; 7:17, 21 in the same section (1.3).

60. *The Geneva Bible: The Annotated New Testament 1602 Edition, With Introductory Essays*, ed. Gerald T. Sheppard (Cleveland: Pilgrim, 1989), folio 109, italics mine, English is slightly updated.

2.
Son Superior to Angels (1:5–2:18)

Following the prologue, the AH includes a fairly large section that I have entitled 'Son Superior to Angels' (Heb. 1:5–2:18). This section breaks down into four subsections, which are entitled: 'Son Superior to Angels—Scriptural Catena' (Heb. 1:5–14), 'Son Superior to Angels—Exhortation' (Heb. 2:1–4), 'Son Superior to Angels—Psalm 8' (Heb. 2:5–9), and 'Son Superior to Angels—Made Like His Brothers' (Heb. 2:10–18).

The prologue is clearly linked to the 'Son Superior to Angels' section by the 'angels' reference in Hebrews 1:4. However, in addition, there are several other connections noted in the immediate discussion below. As to why the emphasis on angels, see the discussion at Hebrews 1:4.

Son Superior to Angels—Scriptural Catena (1:5–14)

Hebrews 1:5–14 includes seven OT quotations: Psalms 2:7; 2 Samuel 7:14 // 1 Chronicles 17:13; Deuteronomy 32:43; Psalms 104:4; 45:6–7; 102:25–27; and 110:1. These are introduced and connected with minimal wording; hence, they are termed a 'chain' or *catena* (*catena* is Latin for 'chain').[1]

---

1. Other examples of *catenae* include Rom. 3:9–18; 1 Pet. 2:6–8; 4Q174 (Florilegium); and 4Q175 (Testimonia).

The *catena* proper begins with a rhetorical question (Heb. 1:5) and ends with a very similar rhetorical question (Heb. 1:13). Hebrews 1:14 is another rhetorical question following the *catena* that ends the section. Grammatically, the *catena* proper has just three sentences: Hebrews 1:5; 1:6–12; and 1:13.[2] This is then followed by the final and fourth sentence (Heb. 1:14).

This section is clearly justifying the statement in Hebrews 1:4 that the Son is superior to angels. In addition, however, these OT texts prove and expand upon various statements about the Son in Heb. 1:1–4, for example, the Son's divinity (Heb. 1:8), his being creator (Heb. 1:10–12), and his sitting at the right hand of God (Heb. 1:13).[3] Of course, these expansions further emphasize the fact that the Son is superior to angels. Because there are many connections between Hebrews 1:14 and 1:5–13, and many connections within 1:5–13 itself, there are various attempts to see a chiastic pattern for the whole chapter or for just for 1:5–13.[4] Although intriguing, I am not convinced by the chiastic options. However, I certainly agree that 1:5–13 is expanding upon statements about the Son in 1:1–4.

Another connection between the OT quotations and Hebrews 1:1–4 is that Hebrews 1:1 refers primarily to the OT and the prophets. Taking 'prophets' as meaning all of the OT writers, this *catena* is an evidence of that. Further, Hebrews 1:1 emphasized God 'speaking' and all the introductions to the citations in Hebrews 1:5–13 note that 'God says' as opposed to writes.[5]

---

2. So emphasized by Ellingworth, *Hebrews*, 108. However, defining a sentence is not an exact science.

3. So also Attridge, *Hebrews*, 50, 53.

4. E.g., for the whole chapter, so John P. Meier, 'Structure and Theology in Heb. 1, 1–14,' *Bib* 66 (1985): 168–89; and Victor Rhee, 'The Role of Chiasm for Understanding Christology in Hebrews 1:1–14,' *JBL* 131 (2012): 341–62, esp. 342. For Heb. 1:5–13, so Herbert W. Bateman IV, 'The First-Century Messianic Uses of the OT: Heb. 1:5–13 and 4QFlor 1.1–19,' *JETS* 38 (1995): 11–27, esp. 26; and Richard Bauckham, 'Monotheism and Christology in Hebrews 1,' in *Early Christianity in Context*, ed. John M. G. Barclay, JSNTSup 263 (NY: T&T Clark, 2004), 167–85, esp. 175–77.

5. Two different synonymous Greek verbs for speaking are used; 1:1, 2 (λαλέω); 1:5, 6, 7, 13 (λέγω).

1:5 *For to which of the angels did he ever say, 'You are my Son, today I have begotten you'? and again, 'I will be to him a father, and he shall be to me a son'?*

The AH begins his proof (**for**) that Christ is superior to the angels by concentrating on the 'name' that Christ receives, that is **Son**.[6] God refers to Christ as **Son**, and this is never said to angels. He quotes Psalm 2:7 and 2 Samuel 7:14 as positive proof that Christ is called 'Son'. This proof is put in the form of a rhetorical question. The expected answer is 'To none of the angels did God ever call even one a "Son".'

Is it true that an angel is never called 'Son' in the OT? Yes, it is true, but a nuanced answer is required. Several times angels are called 'sons of God' (Deut. 32:43 [LXX only]; Job 1:6; 2:1; 38:7; Ps. 29:1).[7] As is often noted by commentators, this is a collective term rather than an individual term.[8] In addition, the two texts cited in Hebrews are emphasizing the special relationship between God and his king and the name **Son** associated with this. No angel was viewed this way.[9]

The AH clearly interprets Psalm 2 as referring to Christ as do other NT texts (Acts 4:25–26; 13:33; Heb. 5:5; cf. Matt. 3:17; 17:5; Luke 3:22; Rev. 2:27; 12:5; 19:15).[10] Psalm 2 on the surface

---

6. Moffatt sees Heb. 1:5 answering the superior 'name' of Heb. 1:4, and Heb. 1:6–14 answering the general 'better than the angels' of Heb. 1:4 (*Hebrews*, 9).

7. Some include Gen. 6:1, 4; Deut. 32:8 (4Q37); and Ps. 82:1, 6. Sometimes the LXX translates 'sons of God' as 'angels of God'; see Job 1:6; 2:1; and 38:7 ('my angels'). In Dan. 3:25 (3:92 LXX), King Nebuchadnezzar sees a fourth figure in the fiery furnace whom he terms a 'son of god/gods' (Aramaic בר־אלהין; LXX ἀγγέλου θεοῦ; Theodotion υἱῷ θεου). Since this is a term that Nebuchadnezzar uses and ultimately may refer to Christ, this does not invalidate the AH's claim.

8. So, e.g., Bruce, *Hebrews*, 53; Ellingworth, *Hebrews*, 111; and Koester, *Hebrews*, 191.

9. So also Johnson, *Hebrews*, 77.

10. Others in Second Temple Judaism also interpreted Ps. 2 messianically, e.g., Pss. Sol. 17:23–24; and 4Q174 (Florilegium) I, 18–19. Rabbinic material rarely connects Ps. 2 to the messiah; however, b. Sukkah 52a does. Interestingly, Ps. 2:7–8 is quoted excepting 'the Lord said to me, "You are my Son."' 1 Clem. 36:4 quotes Heb. 1:5 // Ps. 2:7–8.

speaks of the triumph of the Lord's king over his enemies. Many interpret Psalm 2 as the anointing and coronation ceremony of the Davidic kings (2 Kgs. 11:12).[11] Following Acts 4:25, I see David as the author, and the psalm having strong connections to the Davidic covenant (2 Sam. 7:14), although that is not to say that this psalm could not have been used later in coronation ceremonies.[12] The comment in Psalm 2:8 that the king's reign will extend to the ends of the earth matches the forward looking aspect of the Davidic covenant and its typological, if not directly predictive, connection to Christ.[13]

The quote **you are my Son, today I have begotten you** (Ps. 2:7) in its Psalm 2 context is the Lord directly speaking to the king.[14] The emphasis by the AH falls on **you are my Son**. As opposed to angels, or to other Davidic kings, Jesus Christ is *the* **Son** of the Father.

How should **today** be interpreted? Given that the Son existed from eternity (Heb. 1:1–3), some throughout church history have interpreted **today** as an eternal concept—it was always today.[15] However, currently the majority interpret

---

11. So, e.g., Peter C. Craigie, *Psalms 1–50*, WBC 19 (Waco: Word, 1983), 64–65; Willem A. VanGemeren, 'Psalms,' in *The Expositor's Bible Commentary*, ed. Frank E. Gaebelein, 12 vols. (Grand Rapids: Zondervan, 1991), 5:1–880, esp. 5:64; Artur Weiser, *Psalms: A Commentary*, trans. Herbert Hartwell, OTL (Philadelphia: Westminster, 1962), 109; Tremper Longman III, *Psalms: An Introduction and Commentary*, vols. 15–16, TOTC (Downers Grove: IVP Academic, 2014), 59–60.

12. It is a common view to see Pss. 1 and 2 as the 'editor's two introductory psalms'; see Bruce K. Waltke, *An Old Testament Theology: An Exegetical, Canonical, and Thematic Approach* (Grand Rapids: Zondervan, 2007), 885.

13. See excellent discussion of Ps. 2 and its connection to Christ by Richard P. Belcher, Jr., *The Messiah and the Psalms: Preaching Christ from all the Psalms* (Ross-shire: Mentor, 2006), 122–29.

14. The Greek of **you are my Son, today I have begotten you** in Heb. 1:5 is an exact match to the LXX, which in turn is a word-for-word translation of the Hebrew.

15. So, e.g., Augustine, *On the Psalms*, Psalm 2 (*NPNF*[1], 8:3); *Enchiridion* 49 (*NPNF*[1], 3:253); and Brakel, *The Christian's Reasonable Service*, 1:158–60. Arguments from Hebrews that today would be eternal include the 'flexible'

today I have begotten you as referring to Christ's ascension/ exaltation, which is most probable.[16] If true, then this aspect of being a **Son** relates to Christ's mediatorial role, which dovetails well with the following quote (2 Sam. 7:14). Of course, the mediatorial role presupposes an eternal sonship.[17] How? This OT announcement by the Father to the Son of a future 'begetting' shows the Son's preexistence. Also, the mediatorial role itself requires that the Son be both *divine* and human to be a proper mediator of *God* and men.

The second quote comes from the influential 2 Samuel 7 // 1 Chronicles 17 passage that describes the inauguration of the Davidic covenant (cf. 2 Sam. 23:5; 1 Chr. 22:10; 28:6; 2 Chr. 1:8; Pss. 89:3–4; 132:11–12; Isa. 7:14; 9:6–7; 11:1; Jer. 23:5; 33:14–22; Ezek. 34:23–24; Mic. 5:2; Luke 1:32; Acts 2:30; Rom. 1:3–4).[18] David is concerned that the ark of God needs a

---

use of 'today' in Heb. 3:7–15; 4:7; and 13:8.

16. So, e.g., George H. Guthrie, 'Hebrews,' in *Commentary on the New Testament Use of the Old Testament*, ed. G. K. Beale and D. A. Carson (Grand Rapids: Baker, 2007), 919–95, esp. 928; Mitchell, *Hebrews*, 47; Lane, *Hebrews*, 26. Owen agrees that this text refers to Christ's exaltation, and he notes that there are several good options in addition to the exaltation without much difference. These options include the incarnation (Luke 1:35), baptism (Matt. 3:17), and resurrection (Rom. 1:4; Acts 13:33) (Owen, *Hebrews*, 19:136–37). R. B. Jamieson argues that Hebrews describes 'the Son who became Son', that is, the preexistent divine Son becomes the Son of the messianic office. That is, the name 'Son' is used intentionally in two interrelated ways. For Jamieson, Heb. 1:5 refers to the Son's receiving his name referring to his office at his enthronement (*The Paradox of Sonship: Christology in the Epistle to the Hebrews* [Downers Grove: IVP Academic, 2021], 17–20, 102–9). For a modern defense of 'today' referring to divine eternity, see Scott R. Swain, *The Trinity: An Introduction*, Short Studies in Systematic Theology (Wheaton: Crossway, 2020), 42 n. 5; and Bauckham, 'The Divinity of Jesus Christ in the Epistle to the Hebrews,' 34.

17. Turretin comments, 'Christ as Mediator can be said in a certain sense to have sat down at the right hand of God without flesh even before the incarnation; thus from the beginning of the world because he always was the head and King of the church who governed and defended it (Ps. 2:6; Heb. 13:8)' (*Institutes of Elenctic Theology*, 2:371).

18. For an extended discussion of the Davidic covenant, see O. Palmer Robertson, *The Christ of the Covenants* (Phillipsburg: Presbyterian and Reformed, 1980), 229–69.

'house' (temple) (2 Sam. 7:1–3). God tells Nathan to tell David that his son (Solomon) will build the 'house' (both temple and dynasty) and that David's throne and kingdom will be established forever (2 Sam. 7:4–17). After hearing Nathan's words, David prays thanking God for these covenantal promises (2 Sam. 7:18–24) and asking for the fulfillment of these promises (2 Sam. 7:25–29).

In context, **I will be to him a father, and he shall be to me a son** (2 Sam. 7:14 // 1 Chr. 17:13) refers superficially to Solomon as the **son** who will build the temple and continues the dynasty.[19] However, given the grand promises of an eternal throne and kingdom and the double use of 'house', the text clearly refers to a greater **Son** that is to come.[20] Further confirming this is that 2 Samuel 7:12 and Psalm 89:29 refer to David's seed (זרע, σπέρμα).[21] This 'seed' (σπέρμα) wording is explicitly applied to Christ in John 7:42; Acts 13:22–23; Romans 1:3; and 2 Timothy 2:8.

Given the above exegesis of Hebrews 1:5, the following are miscellaneous comments. (1) The AH uses an argument from silence—God nowhere called an angel 'son'.[22] Hence, though arguments from silence can be abused, one cannot argue they are always illegitimate. (2) There is a clear chiastic structure

---

19. Similar to the Ps. 2:7 quote, the Greek of **I will be to him a father, and he will be to me a son** in Heb. 1:5 is an exact match to the LXX of both 2 Sam. 7:14 and 1 Chr. 17:13, which in turn is a word-for-word translation of the Hebrew of 2 Sam. 7:14 and 1 Chr. 17:13.

20. So also 4Q174 (Florilegium) I, 10–14; cf. Sir. 47:11. Walter Brueggemann believes that the 2 Sam. 7:14 'enduring promise to David has placed messianism at the heart of both Judaism and Christianity.' He also notes that 'it goes without saying that this text does not intend to point to Jesus' (*First and Second Samuel*, Interpretation [Louisville: John Knox, 1990], 257–58). As to his second statement, I disagree. The divine author certainly intended this text to point to Jesus! For a good discussion of the several Davidic promises in 2 Samuel 7 // 1 Chronicles 17 and their NT connections, see Richard L. Pratt, *1 and 2 Chronicles* (Ross-shire: Mentor, 1998), 152–54.

21. For a discussion of the 'seed' in 2 Sam 7:12 and its connections to Christ, see C. F. Keil and F. Delitzsch, *Biblical Commentary on the Books of Samuel*, trans. James Martin, in *Commentary on the Old Testament in Ten Volumes* (Grand Rapids: Eerdmans, 1985), 2:2:346–49.

22. Other arguments from silence include Heb. 1:13 and 7:3.

with Son-Father-Father-Son in Heb. 1:5. What is the exegetical 'therefore'? Usually, those who put significant exegetical weight on the importance of chiastic structures argue that the middle term is being highlighted. In this case, the middle term is 'Father', which is clearly not being highlighted in this context as 'Son' is being highlighted. (3) At the word level, 'Father' as referring to God the Father is only used twice in Hebrews (1:5 and 12:9). Of course, God the Father is implied numerous times because of the use of 'Son'. I do not know what to make of this curious phenomenon. (4) The Hebrews 1:5 quote of 2 Samuel 7:14 emphasizes the unique 'Son'. Later in Hebrews, believers will be called 'sons' (e.g., Heb. 2:10). This Son/son connection is due to a believer's union with Christ. In a parallel way to this Son/son understanding, 2 Samuel 7:14 is (apparently) quoted in 2 Corinthians 6:18 and Revelation 21:7. In these two passages, 'son' is applied corporately to all believers based on their being in union with *the* Son.[23]

1:6 *And again, when he brings the firstborn into the universe, he says, 'And let all the angels of God worship him,'*

Because of some of the complications with the OT quote, **and let all the angels of God worship him**, I will deal with this first before exegeting Hebrews 1:6. The question is whether the quote is from Deuteronomy 32:43 or Psalm 97:7, with most scholars opting for Deuteronomy 32:43.[24] This concern is mostly driven by the fact that the MT of Deuteronomy 32:43 does not include this phrase, although the Dead Sea Scroll document 4Q44, the LXX, and Ode 2 do include it.

---

23. So also Philip Edgecumbe Hughes, *Paul's Second Epistle to the Corinthians: The English Text with Introduction, Exposition and Notes*, NICNT (Grand Rapids: Eerdmans, 1962), 257; and G. K. Beale, *The Book of Revelation: A Commentary on the Greek Text*, NIGTC (Grand Rapids: Eerdmans, 1999), 1058. In addition, possibly there is a connection to Heb. 8:10 // Jer. 31:33 ('I will be their God, and they shall be my people').

24. In favor of Deut. 32:43 are Moffatt, *Hebrews*, 11; Lane, *Hebrews 1–8*, 28; Hughes, *Hebrews*, 59; and David L. Allen, *Hebrews*, NAC 35 (Nashville: B&H, 2010), 175. In favor of Ps. 97:7 are most commentaries written before the DSS discoveries, e.g., Owen, *Hebrews*, 19:160–62. A modern commentary in favor of Ps. 97:7 is Mitchell, *Hebrews*, 48.

Below is a tabulation of the options including my very wooden translations.

Deut. 32:43 4Q44 (from Dead Sea Scrolls)
והשתחוו־לו כל־אלהים
And worship him, all gods

Deut. 32:43 MT
[No text]²⁵

Deut. 32:43 LXX
καὶ προσκυνησάτωσαν αὐτῷ πάντες υἱοὶ θεοῦ
And let all sons of God worship him

Deut. 32:43 Ode 2²⁶
καὶ προσκυνησάτωσαν αὐτῷ πάντες οἱ ἄγγελοι θεοῦ
And let all the angels of God worship him

Ps. 97:7 MT
השתחוו־לו כל־אלהים
Worship him, all gods

Ps. 97:7 (96:7) LXX
προσκυνήσατε αὐτῷ πάντες οἱ ἄγγελοι αὐτοῦ
Worship him, all the angels of him

Heb. 1:6
καὶ προσκυνησάτωσαν αὐτῷ πάντες ἄγγελοι θεοῦ
And let all angels of God worship him

Based upon the above tabulation, I believe that the original Hebrew text of Deuteronomy 32:43 included the phrase 'and

---

25. Many English translations follow the MT and do not include our clause, e.g., Geneva Bible, KJV, ASV, RSV, NASB, NIV, and HCSB. The ESV, NRSV, and CEB do include it.

26. Attached to the LXX Psalter are various odes that are 'psalms' from other portions of the OT. Ode 2 reproduces Deut. 32:1–43. See Alfred Ralphs, *Septuaginta*, ed. Robert Hanhart, rev. ed., 2 vols. (Stuttgart: Deutsche Bibelgesellschaft, 2006), 2:166–69. The Greek of Ode 2 for Deut. 32:43 matches the Greek of Justin Martyr, *Dialogue with Trypho* 30 (*ANF*, 1:264). See discussion in Simon Kistemaker, *The Psalm Citations in the Epistle of Hebrews* (Eugene: Wipf & Stock, 2010 [1961]), 20–23.

worship him, all gods' even though the MT does not include this phrase. Hence, this would be one of the rare instances in my view that the MT does not reflect the original Hebrew text.

Deuteronomy 32:43 is the last verse of the Song of Moses (Deut. 32:1–43). The Song is recorded just before Israel crosses the Jordan to enter the promised land.[27] I agree with most scholars that the AH is referring to Deuteronomy 32:43 and not Psalm 97:7.[28] The strongest argument for this is that the context of this Song (Deut. 31:30–32:47) matches many themes in Hebrews. For example, both are encouraging believers to continue to be steadfast in their commitment to the Lord despite coming difficulties, both emphasize inheritance, and both emphasize land (see especially Deut. 32:47).[29] A further argument is that Deuteronomy 32:35–36 is quoted in Hebrews 10:30.[30]

Although there are some interpretive questions as to *when* the angels worship Christ, the central point of this verse is clear. An additional proof that Christ is better than the angels is that the angels worshiped/will-worship Christ.

The introduction to the quotation is **and again, when he brings the firstborn into the universe, he says**. Most likely, due to the context, this is referring to the worship Christ receives at his exaltation as opposed to his incarnation and

---

27. There are two Songs of Moses. The first is Exod. 15:1–18 recorded right after Israel crossed the Red Sea.

28. As to the technicalities of the Greek of Heb. 1:6 relative to the Hebrew of Deut. 32:43, the Hebrew text has a (second person) imperative followed by a vocative. Heb. 1:6 understandably uses a third person imperative by which the vocative has become the grammatical subject of the imperative. Also, the Hebrew text clearly is using 'gods' to imply angels. Hence, the AH, no matter what Greek text he used or whether he translated the Hebrew himself, interpreted the Hebrew text accurately.

29. The best two arguments for Ps. 97:7 are that οἰκουμένη ('universe' or 'world') is in both Heb. 1:6 and Ps. 97:4 and Ps. 97 emphasizes God's rule and exaltation (Ps. 97:1, 9).

30. Other quotes of Deut. 32 in the NT are Deut. 32:4 // Rev. 15:3; Deut. 32:21 // Rom. 10:19; Deut. 32:35 // Rom. 12:19; and Deut. 32:43 // Rom. 15:10; also Deut. 32:39 // 4 Macc. 18:19.

second coming.³¹ The exaltation interpretation takes **again** as referring to another proof as opposed to understanding **again** to mean the second time God brought Christ into the world. Further the exaltation view emphasizes that **firstborn** has both an exaltation nuance (e.g., Ps. 89:27; Col. 1:15, 18) and an heir/inheritance aspect (e.g., Exod. 4:22; 13:2; Deut. 6:10; 21:16–17; 2 Chr. 21:3; Heb. 12:23) as opposed to simply another word for 'Son'.³² Finally, the exaltation view entails seeing **universe** as referring directly to or at least including the heavenly realm (cf. Heb. 2:5).³³

What is the hermeneutical logic by which the AH uses Deuteronomy 32:43 to apply **him** to Christ? One option for some scholars is simply to say that the AH arbitrarily takes the quote out of context³⁴—I reject this out of hand. Another option is to note that Deuteronomy 32:39–42 has God speaking in first person (all agree to this) and then assume that the AH viewed 32:43 as continuing in first person. Hence, it was God who was saying in first person **let all the angels of God worship him**. Given this, then **him** must be referring to someone other than God, that is, it refers to Christ.³⁵ I do not

---

31. Also in favor of exaltation, see Ellingworth, *Hebrews*, 117; Lane, *Hebrews 1–8*, 28; Koester, *Hebrews*, 192; and Schreiner, *Hebrews*, 66–69. For the incarnation view, see Chrysostom, 'Homily 3 on Hebrews' (*NPNF*¹, 14:375); Calvin, *Hebrews and 1 & 2 Peter*, 12; and Attridge, *Hebrews*, 56. For the second coming view, see Ernst Käsemann, *The Wandering People of God: An Investigation of the Letter of Hebrews*, trans. Roy A. Harrisville and Irving L. Sandberg (Minneapolis: Augsburg, 1984 [1957]), 112–14. In the Jewish document, Life of Adam and Eve, Satan tells Adam that Michael told all the angels that God instructs them to worship Adam because he is in the image of God. Satan and the evil angels refused (LAE 13–15).

32. The AH also uses the plural of 'firstborn' in Heb. 11:28 and 12:23.

33. Normally in Greek literature, 'universe' (οἰκουμένη) means the inhabited world (BDAG, 699–700). However, in Hebrews, it is only used in Heb. 1:6 and 2:5 with 2:5 clearly related to the coming age. This appears to be contrasted with 'world' (κόσμος) and its use in Heb. 4:3; 9:26; 10:5; 11:7, 38 which appears to refer always to this world/age.

34. So, e.g., Attridge, *Hebrews*, 57.

35. So Bauckham, 'Monotheism and Christology in Hebrews 1,' 179, esp. 179n28; and Allen, *Hebrews*, 175–76.

accept this because Deuteronomy 32:43 (and Ps. 97:7) clearly has Moses (the psalmist) speaking, not God.[36] Instead, the AH saw that Deuteronomy 32 emphasizes God's salvation of Israel as they are about to go into the promised land which parallels Christ's salvation of his people. Therefore, given his Trinitarian understanding, the AH identifies Christ with the OT God.[37] As to **he** (God) **says**, here it is not referring to God's speaking in the first person (as in Heb. 1:5), but to God's speaking in any Scripture as he is responsible for all Scripture (as in Heb. 1:7).[38]

1:7 *and, on-the-one-hand, concerning*[39] *the angels, he says, 'the one making his angels winds, and his ministers a flame of fire,'*

The AH shows that Hebrews 1:7 continues the catena by his use of **and** (καί). He also adds **on-the-one-hand** which is contrasting 1:7 with 1:8–9 (μὲν ... δέ).[40] That is, the contrast is between the **angels** and the 'Son' (1:8). More specifically, the explicit contrast is between the angels as **ministers**/servants of God and the Son's divine kingship ('your throne, O God,' 1:8). Yes, the angels are important and are special because they are God's **ministers**, but they pale in comparison to the Son who is the king and sovereign over all.

To make his point that **angels** are **ministers**/servants, the AH could have quoted many OT texts, but he quotes from

---

36. So John D. Currid, *A Study Commentary on Deuteronomy*, EP Study Commentary (Darlington: Evangelical Press, 2006), 512–13; and J. G. McConville, *Deuteronomy*, AOTC 5 (Downers Grove: InterVarsity, 2002), 459.

37. So also Kistemaker, *Hebrews*, 39; Hughes, *Hebrews*, 60; and Schreiner, *Hebrews*, 66.

38. Owen agrees, 'Whatever is spoken in the Scripture in his name, it is his speaking; and he continueth to speak it unto this day' (*Hebrews*, 19:160).

39. The preposition πρός is used in this catena to mean either 'to' (spoken to) or 'concerning' (spoken about). See BAGD, 873–75.

40. It is hard to show this in a translation unless one is overly mechanical like my translation. See translation discussion in Johnson, *Hebrews*, 79. The ESV dropped the 'and' at the beginning of Heb. 1:7 to better show the contrast between 1:7 and 1:8–9.

Psalm 104:4.[41] This psalm praises Yahweh as creator. In the Psalm 104:4 context, God is using his **angels/ministers** as instruments (**winds/flame of fire**) for accomplishing his providential control over creation.[42] Possibly, the AH chose Psalm 104 because the creation motif in Hebrews 1 and/or the later use of **ministers** and its cognates (Heb. 1:14; 8:2, 6; 9:21; 10:11; cf. Ps. 103:20–21).

1:8–9 *and-on-the-other-hand, concerning the Son [he says], 'Your throne, [O] God, is forever and ever, and the scepter of uprightness is the scepter of your*[43] *kingdom; you loved righteousness and you hated lawlessness; on account of this God, your God, anointed you [with]*[44] *oil of gladness more than*[45] *your companions,'*

Using **and-on-the-other hand**, Hebrews 1:8–9 refers to the **Son** and is in contrast to 'angels' in Hebrews 1:7. More

---

41. The Greek of Heb. 1:7 is very close to the LXX, excepting 'flaming fire' (LXX) compared with 'flame of fire' (Heb. 1:7). The LXX interprets/translates the Hebrew 'messengers' (מלאכי) as 'angels,' which is legitimate. Some, however, believe that the LXX (and thus Heb. 1:7) mistranslates the Hebrew which according to them should read that God makes the wind into messengers and the fire into ministers, that is, the text is not referring to actual angels/messengers (e.g., John Calvin, *Commentary on the Book of Psalms*, trans. James Anderson, Calvin's Commentaries [Grand Rapids: Baker, 1996], 6:1:143–47; Mitchell Dahood, *Psalms III: 101–150: Introduction, Translation, and Notes*, AB 17A [Garden City: Doubleday, 1970], 31; Moffatt, *Hebrews*, 104; and Lane, *Hebrews 1–8*, 28–29). I disagree. The LXX translation matches better to the Hebrew word order. The Targum matches the LXX. Ps. 103:20–21 (a companion psalm to 104) and Ps. 35:5 clearly see angels/messengers as literal. Just because Ps. 104:3 refers to inanimate objects, that does not mean that 104:4 must also, see Pss. 18:10 and 148:2. Agreeing that actual angels/messengers are intended by the Hebrew, so also Derek Kidner, *Psalms 73–150: A Commentary on Books III-V of the Psalms*, TOTC (Downers Grove: Inter-Varsity, 1975), 369; William S. Plumer, *Psalms: A Critical and Expository Commentary with Doctrinal and Practical Remarks* (Carlisle: Banner of Truth, 1975 [1867]), 922; Owen, *Hebrews*, 19:172–74; and Kistemaker, *Hebrews*, 41.

42. 1QH IX, 11 and 4 Ezra 8:22 also connect angels to winds. 1 Clem. 36:3 quotes Heb. 1:7 // Ps. 104:4.

43. Three Greek manuscripts have 'his'. This reading is rightly rejected by most. See Bruce M. Metzger, *TCGNT*², 592–93.

44. Following the LXX, **you** and **oil** are double accusatives of the verb **anointed**. Hence, **with** is implied. See BDAG, 1091.

45. 'More than' translates παρά which has a wide semantic range. See BDAG, 756–58, esp. §C.3.

specifically, as mentioned above, the primary contrast is between the **Son** as the divine king and the angels as 'ministers'. To show the kingship of Christ, the AH quotes from Psalm 45:6–7.[46] The kingship of Christ is shown by reference in the quote to **throne, scepter, kingdom,** and **anointed you with oil**.

Psalm 45 depicts a grand marriage ceremony between an ideal king and a beautiful queen.[47] This psalm is unusual in that (1) there are no other royal wedding psalms in the Psalter (although Song of Songs), (2) the author's comment about the importance of this psalm (Ps. 45:1) is also unique to the Psalter, and (3) using 'God' in an absolute way to refer to one individual (here, the king, Ps. 45:6) occurs nowhere else in the OT except to refer to the true God.[48]

The AH clearly interprets **O God** in Hebrews 1:8 as being addressed to Christ and an expression of Christ's divinity.[49]

---

46. The MT, LXX, and NT all agree with one very minor exception. The MT does not explicitly determine between 'scepter of uprightness' and 'scepter of your kingdom' as to which one is the subject and which one is the predicate nominative. The LXX by placement of an article chooses 'scepter of your kingdom' as the subject. The NT's textual history is mixed. Some manuscripts follow exactly the LXX. Others, which I have followed, choose 'scepter of uprightness' as the subject by placement of an article and add an 'and' before 'scepter of uprightness'. These differences are virtually irrelevant for interpretation.

47. Ps. 45 outline: Writer's comment (v. 1); Glory of the groom/king (vv. 2–9); Glory of the bride/queen (vv. 10–15); Remembrance of the king (vv. 16–17).

48. Concerning #3, many note this and conclude that divinity is intended even in the context of Ps. 45, making this a directly Divine-Messianic psalm. So, e.g., Irenaeus, *Against Heresies* 3.6 (*ANF*, 1:416–19); Owen, *Hebrews*, 19:181; and Brown, *Hebrews*, 55. Others agree that the king is addressed as 'God' but do not think that in the context of Ps. 45 this refers to divinity, although it is very suggestive typologically of an ideal Messiah (e.g., Delitzsch, *Psalms*, 5:2:83; Weiser, *Psalms*, 360, 363; Belcher, *The Messiah and the Psalms*, 129–35). Finally, others note that this is unusual, so much so in fact, that the Hebrew translation must be changed to avoid the king being addressed as 'God' (e.g., Craigie, *Psalms 1–50*, 336; and Longman, *Psalms*, 200).

49. That is, **O God** (ὁ θεός) is a nominative being used as a vocative. See BDF §147.3. Virtually all English translations take this as a vocative.

Virtually all agree to this whether or not they believe that Psalm 45:6 is making the same point.[50] My view is that Psalm 45 itself and specifically Psalm 45:6 is primarily presenting an idealized (divine) Messiah that secondarily would apply to kings in the Davidic line. The reference to the queen is primarily to be taken as referring to the OT/NT Church and secondarily to actual queens.[51]

Your throne, O God, is forever and ever is an amazing statement of Christ's eternal, divine kingship (2 Sam. 7:14; Pss. 72:7; 89:3–4; 132:11–12; 145:13; Isa. 9:7; Dan. 7:14; Mic. 4:7; 1 Cor. 15:24–27). This dovetails well with Christ's being creator, which demands both eternality and divinity (Heb. 1:2–3, 10–12) and his perpetual priesthood (Heb. 7:24). In addition to a throne, Christ has a second symbol of traditional kingship, a **scepter**. Genesis 49:10 connects a **scepter** to the Judah/Davidic/Messianic kingship (cf. Num. 24:17; Isa. 14:5; Zech. 10:11; 4Q252 V, 1–9; T. Jud. 24:1–6; Targum Ps. 45:2, 6; b. Shabbat 63a). As opposed to other kings, Christ's rule is/will-be in **uprightness**.[52]

While Hebrews 1:8 refers to Christ's eternal, divine kingship, Hebrews 1:9 appears to refer to the aspect of Christ's

---

Interestingly, exceptions are Wycliffe and Tyndale. Christ is called 'God' elsewhere in the NT in John 1:1, 18; 20:28; Rom. 9:5; 2 Thess. 1:12 (?); Titus 2:13; 2 Pet. 1:1; and 1 John 5:20.

50. So also Eusebius, *Ecclesiastical History* 1.3; Cyril of Jerusalem, *Catechetical Lectures* 11.15 (*NPNF*[2] 7:68); Chrysostom, 'Homily 3 on Hebrews' (*NPNF*[1], 14:376); Calvin, *Hebrews and 1 & 2 Peter*, 14; Owen, *Hebrews*, 19:181; Hughes, *Hebrews*, 63–64; Ellingworth, *Hebrews*, 122; Attridge, *Hebrews*, 58–59; Johnson, *Hebrews*, 80; Allen, *Hebrews*, 181; WLQ 10; Beza Confession 12 (*Reformed Confessions of the 16th and 17th Centuries in English Translation*, 2:259); and Debrecen Synod 3 (*Reformed Confessions of the 16th and 17th Centuries*, 3:75). Contra Mitchell, *Hebrews*, 54.

51. For marriage metaphors, see Deut. 31:16; Jer. 3:1; Hos. 1–3; Matt. 9:14–17; 22:1–14; Rom. 7:1–4; 2 Cor. 11:2; Eph. 5:27–32; Rev. 12:1; 19:6–8; 21:2; and 22:17. Justin Martyr quotes Ps. 45:6–11 and concludes based on the use of king and queen that 'those who believe in him [are] one soul, and one synagogue, and one church ... and as a daughter [Ps. 45:10] teaches us also to forget our old ancestral customs' (*Dialogue with Trypho* 63 [*ANF*, 1:229]).

52. Koester sees **scepter of uprightness** as intentionally referring to the situation of the original congregation. Christ will not abandon those who persevere and will punish the lawless (*Hebrews*, 202).

kingship related to his earthly work and exaltation. The primary argument is due to **on account of this** or 'therefore'. The **this** most likely references **you have loved righteousness and you have hated wickedness**, which most naturally refers to Christ's earthly obedience (Heb. 2:18; 3:2, 6; 4:15; 5:8–9; 7:26, 28; 9:14; 10:5–10; 12:3).[53]

As a result of Christ's earthly work, **God, your God, has anointed you**. Clearly, **your God** is God the Father, and **you**, Christ. There is a question about **God**. Some see this as another vocative addressing Christ paralleling verse 8; however, it is best to take it as referring to God the Father.[54] Hence, within Hebrews 1:8–9, Christ is addressed as **God** and God the Father is referred to as **God, your God**.[55] That is, as mediator, as the God-man with emphasis on his human nature, Christ's God is God the Father (Heb. 2:13; Ps. 22:1, 10; John 20:17). The Trinitarian implications just from these two verses are vast. Both Christ and God the Father are divine. Readers also see Christ in both his divine and human natures.[56]

Christ is **anointed** by God the Father. Israelite kings were anointed with **oil** (1 Sam. 10:1; 15:17; 2 Sam. 12:7; 2 Kgs. 9:3; Ps. 89:20). In fact, the Hebrew and Greek verbs 'to anoint' are related to the nouns 'messiah' and 'christ'. Hence, **anointed** is another clear allusion to Christ's kingship. The only question here is *when* this anointing occurs. Most, including me,

---

53. So also Brown, *Hebrews*, 58; Hughes, *Hebrews*, 65; and Schreiner, *Hebrews*, 73. Contra those who see this as simply part of Christ's eternal character, so Kistemaker, *Hebrews*, 43; and Victor Rhee, 'Christology in Hebrews 1:5–14: The Three Stages of Christ's Existence,' *JETS* 59 (2016): 717–29, esp. 725–26.

54. In favor of **God** being a vocative and referring to Christ are Ellingworth, *Hebrews*, 124; Koester, *Hebrews*, 195, 202; Johnson, *Hebrews*, 80, and the NLT ('O God'). In favor of **God** and **your God** both referring to God the Father are Owen, *Hebrews*, 185; Schreiner, *Hebrews*, 73; Guthrie, 'Hebrews,' 939; and virtually all English translations. Either way, within Heb. 1:8–9, both Christ and God the Father are referred to as God.

55. In the book of John, Christ is called 'God' (John 1:1, 18; 20:28) and also refers to God the Father as 'my God' (John 20:17).

56. If **anointed** implies the Holy Spirit, all three persons of the Trinity are involved.

conclude that it is at Christ's exaltation based on the general emphasis of Hebrews1 and the joy (**gladness**) referred to in Hebrews 12:2.[57]

Christ is anointed in a special way. It is **more than** his **companions**. Most likely these **companions** (μέτοχος) are other believers, as μέτοχος is used that way in Hebrews 3:1, 14 (although Heb. 6:4, 12:8) and fits well with Psalm 45:7 where it would refer to the king's friends.[58]

1:10–12 *and 'You, O Lord, in the beginning*[59] *founded the earth, and the heavens are the works of your hands; they will perish, but you remain; and all like a garment will grow old; and like a robe you will roll them up, and as a garment they will be changed; but you are the same, and your years will not fail.'*

Hebrews 1:10–12 is another text in Hebrews 1 with an astoundingly high view of the Lord Jesus Christ. The AH quotes Psalm 102:25–27 and indicates that the **Lord** referred to in this psalm is the Son. That the AH is still discussing the Son is clearly shown by the **and** (καί) at the beginning of Hebrews 1:10 that refers back to the beginning of Hebrews 1:8, 'concerning the Son he [God] says.'

If one just considers the quote as opposed to the whole psalm, the Son is given a divine name (**Lord**) and is considered the creator (**founded the earth**), eternal (**you remain, your years will not fail**), involved in the consummation (**you**

---

57. So also Owen, *Hebrews*, 186; Attridge, *Hebrews*, 60; and Koester, *Hebrews*, 195. Schreiner connects it to Christ's resurrection (*Hebrews*, 72).

58. So the majority, e.g., Koester, *Hebrews*, 195; Kistemaker, *Hebrews*, 44; Bruce, *Hebrews*, 61; Heidelberg Catechism 32. Contra a few who see it as angels due to Heb. 1:7, e.g., Lane, *Hebrews 1-8*, 30; Mitchell, *Hebrews*, 54; and Meier, 'Symmetry and Theology in the Old Testament Citations of Heb. 1,5–14,' 516.

59. The Greek for 'in the beginning' is κατ' ἀρχάς, which is only used elsewhere in Scripture in Pss. 102:25 and 119:152. The more common phrase is ἐν ἀρχῇ, which is in Gen. 1:1 and many other verses, e.g., John 1:1–2. The AH used κατ' ἀρχάς because the LXX of Ps. 102:25 used it. Despite not exactly matching Gen 1:1, the AH is probably invoking it.

will roll them up), and immutable (**you are the same**).⁶⁰ In context of Hebrews 1, the AH continues the contrast of the Son with angels. The specific aspects of the Son that are to be highlighted are not clear. Possibly, the AH is continuing aspects of Hebrews 1:7–8 such as the Son being given a divine name and considered eternal ('your throne, O God, is forever and ever'). He is certainly continuing broader themes from the chapter such as the creation theme (Heb. 1:2) and continuing providence through to the consummation (Heb. 1:3).⁶¹

Psalm 102 is an individual lament of physical exhaustion and distress (Ps. 102:1–11) that also has a community aspect (Ps. 102:16–22).⁶² Apparently, Jerusalem has been destroyed (Ps. 102:13–14).⁶³ Commentators differ as to whether the psalmist's lament is at least partially related to his individual sin or is the lament solely related to the effects of the destruction of Jerusalem.⁶⁴ In context of Psalm 102, the Psalm 102:25–27

---

60. Within a discussion of the divinity of Christ, Turretin uses Heb. 1:10–12 to show Christ is creator and immutable (*Institutes of Elenctic Theology*, 1:283, 287). The Debrecen Synod uses these verses to prove that 'Christ subsisted from eternity' and that 'Paul testifies to Him [Christ] as Jehovah, God' (*Reformed Confessions of the 16th and 17th Centuries*, 3:34, 75). To some degree, I am surprised as to the few creeds that reference these verses.

61. Guthrie sees the emphasis on the 'creation and consummation of the universe' (*Hebrews*, 939). Lane opts for the contrast between the Son's eternal and stable nature and the mutability of the angels (*Hebrews 1–8*, 30–31). Allen considers the emphasis to be on the Son's eschatological activities stressed in Heb. 1:11–12 (*Hebrews*, 182).

62. Ps. 102 outline: Hear my prayer (vv. 1–2); Individual difficulties (vv. 3–11); Have pity on Zion (vv. 12–17); Let Zion worship the Lord (vv. 18–22); Individual difficulties (vv. 23–24); You are the same (vv. 25–28).

63. Normally this psalm is seen as either exilic (e.g., VanGemeren, 'Psalms,' 644) or post-exilic (e.g., Samuel Terrien, *The Psalms: Strophic Structure and Theological Commentary*, ECC [Grand Rapids: Eerdmans, 2003], 699).

64. The key verses are Ps. 102:10, 23. In favor of including sin are Augustine, *On the Psalms*, Psalm 102 (NPNF¹, 8:498); VanGemeren, 'Psalms,' 646; and Terrien, *Psalms*, 698; contra Calvin, *Psalms*, 6:1:105–6; Plumer, *Psalms*, 905; and Kidner, *Psalms 73–150*, 360. The medieval Church considered Ps. 102 as one of the seven penitential psalms (the others are Pss. 6, 32, 38, 51, 130, 143). If Ps. 102 does not refer to the psalmist's specific

comments about the Lord are contrasted with the psalmist's concern that his days will be shortened (Ps. 102:23–24). The psalmist considers that even though his days may be short, his Lord is eternal and hence Israel and her children 'shall dwell secure' into the future (Ps. 102:28).

The AH, following the LXX, includes **you O Lord**.[65] At least in Hebrews, **you O Lord** is useful to immediately grasp who is the subject of the quote. In Psalm 102, 'Lord' is Yahweh (102:1, 12, 15, 16, 19). Hence, this is another verse in the NT where based on the OT reference, Christ is considered Yahweh.[66] It is also another proof of an assumed Trinitarian understanding of God.

Hebrews 1:10 concerns the initial creation. Interestingly, Hebrews 1:11–12a indicates that the existing heavens and earth **will perish**, be **rolled up**, and **will be changed**. A clothing metaphor is being used. Like clothes that eventually wear out, the created world will also degenerate until the consummation (cf. Isa. 50:9; 51:6). The garment will be **changed**, that is, replaced with another garment.[67] This does not give us that much information, but the comment that the heavens and earth **will be changed** indicates that complete annihilation of the current created world is *not* in view as there will still be a garment that continues, albeit a

---

sin, this is then improperly considered a penitential psalm. The rabbinic tradition included Ps. 102 in fasting rituals (m. Ta'anit 2:3).

65. The Hebrew of Ps. 102:25 does not have **you O Lord**, although it has a similar vocative in Ps. 102:12 that apparently the LXX paralleled. The AH slightly altered the LXX to move the you to the beginning of the quote, apparently for emphasis (LXX κατ' ἀρχὰς σύ κύριε; Heb. 1:10 σὺ κατ' ἀρχάς, κύριε). Other than this, there are only very minor differences between the MT, LXX, and Hebrews excepting **as a garment** being added in Heb. 1:12 in some manuscripts (see Metzger, *TCGNT*², 593).

66. For a good analysis and list of verses where Paul considers Christ as Yahweh based on OT usage, see L. W. Hurtado, 'Lord,' *DPL*, 560–69.

67. The Greek behind **changed** is ἀλλάσσω, and the Hebrew in Ps. 102:26 is חלף. Both of these words have the semantic range that includes both 'transform' and 'replace'. When used with a clothing context, they clearly mean 'replace' (e.g., Gen. 35:2).

new garment (cf. Heb. 12:27). Although there is disagreement as to the level of continuity between the current creation and the new heavens and earth, Hebrews 1:11–12 confirms that there is at least a minimum of continuity.[68]

In addition to being eternal, the Son is **the same**. In context of Psalm 102, this refers to the constancy of God's love toward believers and is supported by his constancy as creator/sustainer of his creation (cf. Ps. 90:1–2) . See further discussion at Hebrews 13:8, 'Jesus Christ is *the same* yesterday and today and forever.'

What is the hermeneutical logic for the AH using Psalm 102 to refer to the Son? Most likely it is simply a Trinitarian understanding that the divine nature of the Father, Son, and Holy Spirit is the same. Owen comments that Psalm 102 has a forward looking or 'prophetical' aspect because of the future redemption (v. 13), future calling of the Gentiles (vv. 15, 22), and future believers (v. 18).[69] Possibly, this contributed to considering the Son. Further, there are linguistic parallels between Psalm 104:5–6; Isaiah 50:9; 51:6, 16; 66:22; and Hebrews 1:10–12, although I do not know what to make of this.[70]

1:13 *And to which [one][71] of the angels has he ever said, 'Sit on my right [hand], until I make[72] your enemies a footstool for your feet'?*

Hebrews 1:13 begins a new subunit with δέ, which can be

---

68. Bavinck is at pains to point out that this wearing out of creation is not a 'destruction of substance' (*Reformed Dogmatics* 4:717). Vos comments that the Reformed view is that 'the substance of the presently existing world will be preserved but [also] will be restored, purified in glory' (*Reformed Dogmatics* 5:308).

69. Owen, *Hebrews*, 19:197.

70. Another option that I do not accept is that, based on the LXX mistranslating Ps. 102:23, the AH took Ps. 102:25–27 as the Father directly addressing the Son. So Allen, *Hebrews*, 182; and Ellingworth, *Hebrews*, 126.

71. Τίνα is a singular interrogative pronoun, hence 'which one'.

72. Τίθημι here takes the double accusative and is therefore translated 'make'. BDAG categorizes this under 'to cause to undergo a change in experience/condition' (p. 1004, §5).

translated **and** or 'but'; the **and** probably has the connotation of the next logical point, and the 'but' relates to the subject not being the Son but the angels.[73] The final of the seven quotations in the catena is Psalm 110:1,[74] which highlights the Son's power. The rhetorical question harkens back to the similar rhetorical question for the first quotation in the catena (Heb. 1:5). The reference to the Son's sitting looks back to Hebrews 1:3, and the reference to power and feet points forward to Hebrews 2:8 // Psalm 8:6. Aspects of Psalm 110:1 and 110:4 will be discussed later in Hebrews (5:6, 10; 6:20; 7:3, 11, 17, 21; 8:1; 10:12–13; 12:2).

The AH rhetorically asks **to which one of the angels has [God the Father] ever said** the words of Psalm 110:1. The AH is presupposing the introductory words of Psalm 110:1, 'The Lord [God the Father] said to my Lord [God the Son].' The answer to the rhetorical question is 'not to any of the angels, only the Son.' This is another argument from silence in that no angel is ever addressed this way in Scripture; therefore, no angel is given this power nor sits at the right hand of God.

Psalm 110:1 is directly quoted and alluded to often in the NT.[75] It has three 'individuals': the psalmist, Yahweh, and Adoni/Adonai. All agree that the NT writers uniformly take

---

73. Zerwick says, 'The particle δέ nearly always implies some sort of contrast, but is sometimes also used with "progressive" or "explanatory" force' (*Biblical Greek* §467).

74. The LXX and Heb. 1:13 match exactly. The LXX is a mechanical translation of the MT, excepting the MT has 'right' in 'at my right' pointed as a singular (לימיני) and the LXX/Heb. 1:13 has 'right' in 'at my right' as a plural (ἐκ δεξιῶν μου). However, in all other places in Hebrews where 'at the right' is included, the singular with a different preposition is used (ἐν δεξιᾷ).

75. Full quotes in the NT: Matt. 22:44; Mark 12:36; Luke 20:42–43; Acts 2:34–35; 1 Cor. 15:25 (?); Heb. 1:13; cf. 1 Clement 34:5; Barn. 12:5. Partial quotes/allusions: Matt. 26:64; Mark 14:62; 16:19; Luke 22:69; Rom. 8:34; Eph. 1:20; Heb. 1:3; 8:1; 10:12–13. The standard critical studies of Ps. 110 in the NT include David M. Hay, *Glory at the Right Hand: Psalm 110 in Early Christianity*, SBLMS 18 (Atlanta: SBL, 1989) and Martin Hengel, *Studies in Early Christology* (Edinburgh: T&T Clark, 1995), 119–226, concerning Hebrews, 145–48, 221–22.

the psalmist as David prophesying about a conversation between Yahweh/LORD/God-the-Father and Adoni/Lord/God-the-Son.[76]

The metaphorical **sit at my right hand** is clearly a statement of power and ruling.[77] To sit at the king's right hand is the ultimate place of honor. Given the context of Psalm 110, the Son's being at the Father's **right hand** indicates that the Son will also be involved in the ruling with the Father (matches also to 1 Cor. 15:24–28).

One of the Father and Son's activities will be to crush the Son's **enemies**. In the immediate context of Hebrews 1, nothing is said of **enemies**. Hebrews 2:14–15 speaks of the enemy, the devil; Hebrews 11:35–38 speaks of human enemies in the history of God's people; Hebrews 10:32–34 and 13:13–14 speak of those against the congregation in their day.[78] What an encouraging statement! Christ has ascended and is at the **right hand**. In fact, this was prophesied in the OT. Now

---

76. While acknowledging that this is how the NT writers take Ps. 110:1, critical scholars usually assume that the psalmist is a court poet, Yahweh is Yahweh, and Adoni is a human Israelite king (e.g., Leslie C. Allen, *Psalms 101–150*, WBC 21 [Waco: Word, 1983], 86). Other critical scholars see the superscription as a later addition referring to David as the psalmist (although not actually written by David) and thus the psalm has an eschatological focus with Adoni being messianic (e.g., Weiser, *Psalms*, 692). See Belcher for a good discussion of how one's assumption of the original setting affects one's interpretation (*The Messiah and the Psalms*, 143–47). Ancient Judaism's interpretation of Ps. 110 is not clear. Mark 12:35 implies that some Jews took Ps. 110 messianically. The Targums interpret Ps. 110:1 as David talking about himself as Adoni as does b. Sanhedrin 38b. Justin Martyr notes that some Jews understood Adoni as Hezekiah (*Dialogue with Trypho* 33 [*ANF* 1:211]). Abraham is considered Adoni in b. Sanhedrin 108b and b. Nedarim 32b because of the connection between Gen. 14 and Ps. 110:4. Hughes and Strack-Billerbeck surmise that Jewish interpretation moved away from a messianic view as Christianity grew (*Hebrews*, 70; Str-B, 4:452–60).

77. WLC 54 and Heidelberg Catechism 50 connect 'seated at the right hand' with power and ruling. See G. C. Berkouwer's similar discussion (*The Work of Christ*, Studies in Dogmatics [Grand Rapids: Eerdmans, 1965], 223–34).

78. The enemies in Heb. 10:13 are not defined.

and certainly in the future, all **enemies** of believers will be defeated. Intriguingly, Hebrews 8:1–2 will connect the Son's being at the **right hand** with his priestly work as opposed to here where his kingly work is emphasized.

Footstool for your feet is the metaphor of a defeated enemy. The **footstool** is low and the enemy has been humiliated. In the ANE, kings were often pictured sitting on a throne with a footstool.[79] Possibly, the **footstool** metaphor also includes a victorious king putting his foot on the neck of the vanquished vassal (Josh. 10:24; 1 Kgs. 5:3; cf. Isa. 51:23).[80]

The word **until** (עַד, ἕως) is flexible in both Hebrew and Greek.[81] Linguistically, it may mean that the Son will be at the right hand only till the time of the defeat of the enemies. Then the Son is no longer at the right hand. On the other hand, **until** sometimes has the meaning that the activity continues even when the condition is met (e.g., Gen. 28:15; Ps. 123:2; Dan. 1:2; Matt. 28:20). That is, the Son continues at the right hand even after the defeat of the enemies.[82] Supporting the latter view is Hebrews 1:8, which has already declared that the Son's throne will be forever. However, Owen, after a linguistic discussion of the **until** options, wants to say that there is some sense that aspects of the Son's kingdom will end and some that will never end. The 'economical kingdom of Christ over the church, and all things in order unto the protection and salvation thereof, the immediate ends of it will cease.'[83]

---

79. For a picture of a relief of King Darius, see *ISBE*, 2:333.

80. For pictures of ANE kings putting their feet on vassal kings, see *ISBE*, 2:332, 2:453.

81. See *HALOT*, 786–87 and BDAG, 422–24. These discussions could be better.

82. In favor of this view with linguistic discussion, see Turretin, *Institutes of Elenctic Theology*, 2:492–93; and Brown, *Hebrews*, 68–69. *Contra* Ellingworth, *Hebrews*, 131.

83. Owen, *Hebrews*, 19:231–34, quote is on 19:232–33. Similar to Owen and in the midst of anti-Arian arguments, see Gregory of Nazianzus, 'Fourth Theological Oration,' 4–5 (*NPNF²*, 7:310–11).

1:14 *Are they not all ministering spirits being sent for service on account of those who are going to inherit salvation?*

Hebrews 1:14 is tied to Hebrews 1:13 and is a rhetorical question that expects an affirmative answer.[84] Yes, angels are **being sent out for service**. This is as opposed to the Son who rules at the right hand of God the Father and sends the angels.[85] Thus, this further confirms that the substance of Psalm 110:1 was never spoken to angels. In addition to directly relating to Hebrews 1:13, Hebrews 1:14 is also ending the catena section (Heb. 1:5–14) and its characterization of the angels could be contrasted with all of the aspects of the Son mentioned in Hebrews 1:5–6; 8–13.[86] In Hebrews 1:14, the discussion of angels and their **ministering** directly recalls Hebrews 1:7.[87] Hebrews 1:14 also looks forward to Hebrews 2:1–4 with the mention of believers' **salvation**.

Could it not be objected that the Son did minister and serve? In fact, in Hebrews 8:2, 6, using the same cognate, the Son is said to be a 'minister' and have a 'ministry' (cf. Mark 10:45). Calvin correctly notes that the Son's ministry 'was not of his nature, but of his voluntary self-emptying.'[88] For the angels, their nature was and is to serve.

The 'angels' of Hebrews 1:13 are termed **ministering spirits**. Apparently, due to Psalm 103:20–21 and Psalm 104:4 // Hebrews 1:7, **ministering** and its cognates are applied to angels in Hebrews and in other Jewish texts (Philo, *On the*

---

84. Grammatically, an affirmative answer is required because the question has begun with the negative particle οὐχί. See BDF §427; and Nigel Turner, *Syntax*, vol. 3 of *A Grammar of New Testament Greek* (Edinburgh: T&T Clark, 1963), 282–83.

85. Brown argues for a double contrast: (1) Son is ruler; angels are servants; (2) Son sits; angels are sent forth (*Hebrews*, 70).

86. Emphasizing the connection to Heb. 1:5–13 are Ellingworth, *Hebrews*, 132; Mitchell, *Hebrews*, 54; and Allen, *Hebrews*, 185.

87. 'Ministers' (λειτουργός) in Heb. 1:7 is a cognate of **ministering** in Heb. 1:14 (λειτουργικός).

88. Calvin, *Hebrews and 1 & 2 Peter*, 16. Owen makes similar comments (*Hebrews*, 19:238, 241).

Virtues 73–74; Mekilta Pisha 14; Mekilta Beshallah 3, 7; Mekilta Shirata 1; cf. T. Levi 3:1–10). In Scripture, **spirits** refers occasionally to good beings/'angels' (e.g., Heb. 12:9) and often to evil beings (e.g., Matt. 10:1; Acts 8:7; 1 Tim. 4:1). The term **spirits** is used for angels because it is 'in contrast to a being that can be perceived by the physical senses'.[89]

The angels are to serve **those who are going to inherit salvation**. That is, one of the callings of angels is to serve believers.[90] In one sense, this is wonderfully shocking. The reader is not prepared for this comment. In Hebrews 1:7, angels are described in a general way as aiding God in his providential control, but here the reader finds that they specifically aid believers (cf. Ps. 91:11–12). Also, the tenor of Hebrews 1 has been 'negative' toward the angels because of the context of their comparison with the Son; but here in these last words of Hebrews 1:14, a decidedly positive comment is made about them. No details are given here as to exactly what angels do to aid believers, although see Hebrews 2:2; 12:22; and 13:2. Hebrews 1:14 is a standard reference in various Christian creeds when referring to angels.[91] This verse reminds us that ultimate reality includes other beings in addition to humans and God.

Each word (and its cognates) in the three-word Greek expression **going to inherit salvation** are used often in Hebrews.[92] **Salvation** in context here is a full-orbed

---

89. BDAG, 833, §4.

90. John M. Frame summarizes the callings of angels as (1) 'bringing God's word,' (2) 'fighting God's battles,' and (3) 'ministering to God's people' (*Systematic Theology: An Introduction to Christian Belief* [Phillipsburg: P&R, 2013], 773). For a good summary of angels, see Berkhof, *Systematic Theology*, 141–49.

91. See Second Helvetic Confession 7, Belgic Confession 7, French Confession 7, WCF 12, WLC 19, Beza's Confession 2.2 (*Reformed Confessions of the 16th and 17th Centuries*, 2:243), Sandomierz Consensus 7 (*Reformed Confessions of the 16th and 17th Centuries*, 3:189), and Catechism of the Catholic Church §331.

92. **Going** or 'about to' or 'coming'(μέλλω), Heb. 1:14; 2:5; 6:5; 8:5; 10:1, 27; 11:8, 20; 13:14; **inherit** (κληρονομέω) and cognates, Heb. 1:2, 4, 14; 6:12, 17;

eschatological salvation that includes our justification, sanctification, and final glorification in the new heavens and earth.[93]

Reflections

Hebrews 1:5–14 informs us that Jesus is the 'Son' (1:5), 'God' (1:8), and 'Lord' (1:10). Jesus is to be worshiped (1:6), is anointed by God (1:9), is on his throne at the right hand of God (1:8, 13), sends out angels to help us (1:13–14), exists for ever (1:11–12), will be involved in the consummation of this world (1:12), and finally, Jesus is the creator (1:10).

The truth that the Lord Jesus Christ is the Creator, along with the Father and Holy Ghost, is explicitly taught in several places in the NT (John 1:3, 10; 1 Cor. 8:6; Col. 1:16–17; Heb. 1:2–3, 10–12). Hebrews 1:10–12 // Psalm 102:25–27 has gripped me since my seminary days in the late 1980s. The idea that the AH would read Psalm 102 and conclude that the divine being discussed in that psalm is Christ expanded my truncated view of Christ. In addition to being the Redeemer, he is also the Creator.

Believers (and angels, Heb. 1:6) are to worship Christ and be thankful for his work. Believers are to worship Christ as the Redeemer, *but also worship him as the Creator* (see Rev. 4:11 referring to the Triune Creator). In the Nicene Creed, Christians confess that their belief in 'one Lord Jesus Christ … by whom all things were made.'

Son Superior to Angels—Exhortation (2:1–4)

Hebrews 2:1–4 is two sentences. The main point and first sentence is 2:1. Believers are to pay close attention to the things of the Son so that they do not drift in their faith. Hebrews 2:2–4 is the second sentence and supports 2:1. This

---

9:15; 11:7, 8, 9; 12:17; **salvation** (σωτηρία) and cognates, Heb. 1:14; 2:3, 10; 5:7, 9; 6:9; 9:28 (*bis*); 11:7.

93. All agree to the eschatological emphasis, e.g., Moffatt, *Hebrews*, 16; and Schreiner, *Hebrews*, 77, 498–99.

is a lesser-to-greater argument put in the form of a rhetorical question. Since there was punishment for those in the OT covenant community, how much greater will be the loss of salvation and resultant punishment for those in the NT covenant community, when this salvation was confirmed to us because it was spoken of by the Son, attested to us by believers who had heard Christ, and those believers were attested by God with various miracles?

What are the connections to chapter one? Hebrews 1 presented the Son as grand in many ways. Therefore, he is the pinnacle of salvation of which there is nothing greater. This connection primarily relates to Hebrews 2:1. But Hebrews 1 also emphasizes the movement from the OT to the NT, the Son is greater than the OT prophets (Heb. 1:1–2) and the angels (Heb. 1:5–14). As the Son is greater than angels, so also the NT revelation of him and by him is greater than the OT revelation that included angels as intermediaries. This connection relates to Hebrews 2:2–4.

Hebrews 2:1–4 is the first of several exhortation sections (3:7–4:13; 4:14–16; 5:11–6:12; 10:19–39; 12:1–13:17). In scholarship, portions of these exhortation passages are also called the 'warning' passages with the high water mark of theological difficulties being 6:4–6. See my extended discussion there dovetailing warnings with Reformed theology. In brief, as all agree, warnings are *primarily* intended to encourage all toward a greater love of God.[94]

2:1 *On account of this,*[95] *it is necessary [that] we pay much more attention to the things that were heard, lest we drift away.*
What does **on account of this** refer back to in chapter 1? I take

---

94. Koester, 'Warnings are not designed to rob people of hope, but to steer them away from danger in order to preserve them so that they persevere and inherit what has been promised to them' (*Hebrews*, 209).

95. As opposed to the more common 'therefore' (οὖν), **on account of this** (διὰ τοῦτο) is used. Steven E. Runge concludes that generally these two have significant overlap with διὰ τοῦτο having a 'narrower *causal* constraint' (*Discourse Grammar of the Greek New Testament: A Practical Introduction for Teaching and Exegesis* [Peabody: Hendrickson, 2010], 49, emphasis his).

the grandness of the Son to primarily refer to Hebrews 2:1 and the relative superiority of the Son over the OT prophets and angels to be in view for Hebrews 2:2–4.

Because the Son is the pinnacle of God's salvation plan (Heb. 1:2), **it is necessary** that the readers **pay much more attention** to guard their souls against the neglect of the Son. The expression **to the things that were heard** in substance surely relates to the full glory of the Son. More specifically, it probably refers to the general preaching of the early church that the AH and the congregation (**we**) would have heard, which coordinates with the AH's presentation of the Son in Hebrews and what God 'spoke'.[96]

The positive **pay attention** is paralleled by the negative **lest we drift away**. Here, the concern is not an abrupt turning away from Christianity, but a slow drifting.[97] My view, as with many others, would be a slow drifting back toward what is now a truncated Judaism. Most likely, the AH is using a nautical metaphor.[98] In non-biblical Greek, **drift away** (παραρρέω) is often related to water (cf. LXX Isa. 44:4), and **pay attention** (προσέχω), with its base meaning of 'hold to', is occasionally used to 'bring a ship into port'.[99] The metaphor would be that one is in a boat on a river and has missed the port (salvation) and is floating downstream away from the port. Due to **drift away**, it appears here that the danger is not a sudden turning away from Christ, but a gradual drifting from him.[100]

---

96. Owen connects it to preaching (*Hebrews*, 19:261) and Hughes to God's final word about the Son (Heb. 1:2) (*Hebrews*, 72). Possibly, the AH is intentionally using heard as the correlation with 'spoke' from Heb. 1:1–2.

97. So also Koester, *Hebrews*, 206, 208.

98. So also Koester, *Hebrews*, 205; and Owen, *Hebrews*, 19:259. *Contra* Spicq, *Hébreux*, 2:25; and Ellingworth, *Hebrews*, 137. Cf. the 'anchor' metaphor in Heb. 6:19.

99. LSJ, 1322, 1512.

100. O. Palmer Robertson, picking up on the water metaphor, well says, 'Just as you might be towed away imperceptibly from the ocean's shore by a receding tide, so the distance between yourself and Christ may increase without your ever noticing the change' (*God's People in the Wilderness: The*

2:2–3a *For if the word spoken through angels was firm and every transgression and disobedience*[101] *received a just reward, how shall we escape [if we] neglect*[102] *such a great salvation,*

The **word spoken through angels** refers to the Mosaic law given by God in which God used angels, at least partially, as intermediators to deliver the law.[103] Since this was God's word, it was **firm**[104] (βέβαιος) and certain. Of course the Mosaic law had gracious aspects, but it also included a potentially negative **reward** for **every** infraction if one did not have a saving God.

How shall we escape? Using a lesser-to-greater rhetorical argument, the AH presses that because the OT law had sure punishments, will not there also be more certain punishment for those who neglect the grandness of the Son and his superiority to the OT angels and prophets?[105] The AH makes similar arguments in Hebrews 10:28–31 and 12:25.[106]

Church in Hebrews [Ross-shire: Mentor, 2009], 121).

101. Some see in the expression **every transgression and disobedience** (πᾶσα παράβασις καὶ παρακοὴ) the AH intentionally using π for alliteration (e.g., Turner, *Syntax*, 107; Lane, *Hebrews 1–8*, 34–35).

102. The adverbial participle ἀμελήσαντες is clearly conditional. Ernest DeWitt Burton uses it as his number one example of a conditional adverbial participle (*Syntax of the Moods and Tenses in New Testament Greek*, 3rd ed. [Eugene: Wipf and Stock, 2003 {1900}], §436).

103. For angels used by God in association with the law, see Acts 7:53; Gal. 3:19; Deut. 33:2 (LXX); Ps. 68:17; Jub. 1:29; Mekilta Bahodesh 9; Philo, *On the Life of Abraham* 115; Josephus, *Jewish Antiquities* 15:136; b. Shabbat 88a; cf. T. Dan 6:2; Jub. 2:1; and Philo, *On Dreams* 1:143, 148.

104. **Firm** (βέβαιος) is also used relative to God's word in Rom. 4:16 and 2 Pet. 1:19 (in 2 Pet. 1:19 βέβαιος is in its comparative form βεβαιότερον). The verb form βεβαιόω ('confirmed') is in Heb. 3:3b.

105. Calvin notes the implicit lesser-to-greater argument and comments, 'If the Law, which was given by angels, was not to be lightly accepted, and transgression of it was visited with heavy penalties, what will happen, he asks, to those who despise the Gospel which has the Son of God as its Author and which was confirmed by so many miracles?' (*Hebrews and 1 & 2 Peter*, 18). For an explicit lesser-to-greater argument, see Heb. 9:13–14.

106. WLC 151 notes that the heinousness of sins is increased if specifically 'against Christ, and his grace.' Heb. 2:2–3 and 12:25 are referenced.

Negatively, in 'these last days' (Heb. 1:2) the punishment is more sure. Positively, the solution is **such a great salvation**. This **salvation**, as in Hebrews 1:14, is a full-orbed salvation including justification, sanctification, and glorification. Due to the context of non-believers' receiving a negative **reward**, the emphasis here is probably toward glorification, that is, eschatological salvation.[107] Yes, this salvation is **great** and is centered on the Son. 'To whom [else] shall we go?' (John 6:68).

2:3b–4 *which, after first being spoken by the Lord, was confirmed to us by those who heard, while God witnessed with [them] by signs and wonders,*[108] *and various miracles, and distributed [gifts] of the Holy Spirit according to his will?*

In Greek, the relative pronoun **which** clearly connects to 'salvation' (both are feminine singulars). These verses continue the rhetorical question about neglecting the reality of this 'great salvation.' How can one do that because in addition to its being great, its truth has been **confirmed**? To summarize: This salvation was preached by Jesus; those who heard Jesus confirmed this salvation to us; and further confirming was that God was involved with those who heard Jesus by distributing various miraculous gifts to them.

The message about our salvation was **spoken by the Lord** (Heb. 1:1; 2:12–13, Mark 1:14; Luke 4:18–21). Although the emphasis in Hebrews is clearly on the kingly and priestly work of the Son, he is also presented as the prophet (see Reflections following Heb. 1:1–4).

---

107. As opposed to my interpretation, which is fairly common, some interpret **salvation** here as not the reality of salvation, but the message about salvation. That is, **salvation** is here used as a 'metonymy'—the effects (actual salvation) are substituted for the cause (message about salvation). This is based on Heb. 2:3b that clearly relates to the message of salvation. So Calvin, *Hebrews and 1 & 2 Peter*, 19; Owen, *Hebrews*, 19:278; and Ellingworth, *Hebrews*, 139.

108. By use of the commas, **signs and wonders** is shown as a unit. Instead of a simple καί for **and**, τε καί shows a 'close or logical affinity' (Turner, *Syntax*, 339; also see A. T. Robertson, *A Grammar of the Greek New Testament in the Light of Historical Research*, 4th ed. [Nashville: Broadman, 1934], 1179; and BDAG 993, §2.c). The options related to τε καί explain the different uses of 'and' and 'also' in the Tyndale, Geneva Bible, and KJV translations.

The work of the Son in our salvation and his message about it **w[ere] confirmed to us by those who heard** and saw the Son in his incarnate state before and after his resurrection (1 Cor. 15:3–8). The AH and the original congregation are included in the **us**. The Apostles and others through (primarily) preaching and through writings **confirmed to us** this great salvation.[109] The AH and many in his congregation actually **heard** eyewitnesses vouch for their hearing and seeing Jesus. As noted in the Introductory Matters chapter concerning the authorship of Hebrews, this verse confirms for most that Paul was not the author of Hebrews. The AH says that he had not **heard** the Son, but Paul says that he did (1 Cor. 15:8; Gal. 1:1).[110] On the other hand, related to canonicity, the AH is one who interacted with **those who heard**, and this would certainly include Apostles. Given that, the book of Hebrews is 'apostolic' through this connection.[111]

The veracity of those who actually heard and saw Jesus was further **confirmed** because **God witnessed with them**. God gave **signs and wonders and various miracles** to confirm their message (Acts 2:22; 2 Cor. 12:12). I take **distributed gifts of the Holy Spirit** to refer to miraculous charismatic gifts.[112] The expression **according to his will** refers to God the Father's will and most likely refers to all of the miraculous gifts mentioned. This text has the *possible* implication that the miraculous gifts had ceased with those who actually heard the incarnate Jesus.[113]

---

109. In Greek and in English, **confirmed** is a cognate of 'firm' in Heb. 2:2.

110. Calvin cites this verse as proof of non-Pauline authorship (*Hebrews and 1 & 2 Peter*, 20). Owen defends Pauline authorship. He argues that us is general and does not necessarily include every individual. Also, Paul was not with Jesus during the first part of Jesus' ministry (*Hebrews*, 19:280).

111. So also Michael J. Kruger, *Canon Revisited: Establishing the Origins and Authority of the New Testament Books* (Wheaton: Crossway, 2012), 182–83.

112. I take **of the Holy Spirit** as an objective genitive. That is, for this passage, the Holy Spirit is the gift that is distributed; he is not the one distributing the gifts. So also Bruce, *Hebrews*, 69n7; and Attridge, *Hebrews*, 68n67; *contra* BDAG, 633.

113. So also Allen, *Hebrews*, 197–200. For Wayne Grudem's argument

Reflections

'Such a great salvation' or the older translation, 'so great salvation (KJV),' is the famous phrase from this section.[114] One's sense of how great this salvation is partially depends on one's sense of the need of salvation. Preeminently, the depth of my sin, both its legal ramifications and its distortion of my thinking and acting, is great. Also, the world I live in is distorted. Hence, I see my salvation as great given the great depth of my sin. I am thankful that I have been justified, am being sanctified, and will be living with Christ and his saints forever with a perfected body and soul in a perfected world.

One's sense of the greatness of salvation also depends on one's view of the Savior. I am thrilled to put my trust in the Son, 'the great high priest' (Heb. 4:14; 10:21) and 'the great shepherd of the sheep' (Heb. 12:20).[115]

May the reader and I, through the power of the Holy Spirit, see our salvation and Savior as great. Yes, 'such a great salvation.'

Son Superior to Angels—Psalm 8 (2:5–9)

Hebrews 2:5–9 is a coherent section that is closely connected to 2:10–18. Several of the themes in 2:5–9 such as angels, suffering, Christ's humanity, and substitutionary death are clearly picked up in 2:10–18.[116]

Briefly, Hebrews 2:5–9 begins with the AH noting that God did *not* subject all things to angels (2:5). Then Psalm 8:4–6 is

---

to the contrary, see *Systematic Theology: An Introduction to Biblical Doctrine* (Grand Rapids: Zondervan, 1994), 361–68, esp. 367.

114. Alan M. Stibbs' devotional commentary uses this phrase as its title (*So Great Salvation: The Meaning and Message of the Letter to the Hebrews* [Exeter: Paternoster, 1970]).

115. Within Hebrews, several Greek words are translated 'great' by the standard English translations; Heb. 2:3 τηλικοῦτος; Heb. 4:14; 10:21, 35; 13:20 μέγας; Heb. 7:4 πηλίκος; and Heb.12:1 τοσοῦτος.

116. Although I do not completely agree, Ellingworth sees the angel comments in Heb. 2:5 and 2:16 as the 'structural framework' and 2:17–18 as transitional verses to the theme of high priest (*Hebrews*, 143).

quoted that speaks of 'man' as having all things in subjection to him (2:6–8a). Based on the logic of Psalm 8, Jesus *does have* all things in subjection to him (2:9). Hence, the implied conclusion is that Jesus is better than angels. So far, all commentators agree. However, there is significant disagreement among commentators as to the AH's interpretation of Psalm 8. This then explicitly affects the interpretation of 'him' in Hebrews 2:8b and implicitly relates to the logical connection, if any, of Hebrews 2:5–9 to the previous paragraphs. Although at some level, this disagreement in the end is more of a 'tempest in a teapot' as both interpretations conclude that Jesus *is* related to Psalm 8 and all things *are* in subjection to him.

So what is the disagreement? In Hebrews 2:9, all commentators agree that the AH argues that Jesus is better than angels because all things have been subjected to Jesus and not subjected to angels. Further, all commentators agree that this conclusion comes somehow from the citation of Psalm 8:4–6 // Hebrews 2:6–8a. The disagreement is over the logic by which the AH gets from Psalm 8 to the conclusion about Jesus. More specifically, does the AH understand 'man' in Psalm 8:4 // Hebrews 2:6 to be mankind in general (anthropological interpretation) or to be already interpreted as Jesus (Christological interpretation)? This then directly affects the interpretation of 'him' in 2:8b as to the proper implication of not seeing everything in subjection to 'him'. Or to say it another way, the anthropological view sees mankind in general being referenced in Hebrews 2:6–8, including the two references to 'him' in 2:8 following the quote. Thus, Jesus is not referred to until Hebrews 2:9. The Christological view sees Jesus solely being referenced throughout Hebrews 2:6–9.

For clarity, allow me to restate the two interpretations in their most standard forms. Anthropological: 'Man' in Psalm 8:4 and Hebrews 2:6 both refer to mankind. But all things had not truly been in subjection to mankind/'him' (Heb. 2:8b). However, Jesus himself and all those connected to him will rule and thus the mankind aspect of Psalm 8 is fulfilled. As

Westcott says, '[Psalm 8 is not] directly Messianic; but as expressing the true destiny of man it finds its accomplishment in the Son of Man and *only through Him in man*.'[117] This then proves the point that as part of mankind, Jesus is better than angels because of the ruling.[118]

Christological: The AH quotes Psalm 8:4 in Hebrews 2:6 having already concluded that 'man' in Psalm 8 refers to Jesus. That is, the logic by which the AH concluded 'man' in Psalm 8:4 is Jesus is not explicitly discussed; it is assumed. AH simply notes that we do not see all things in subjection to Jesus (Heb. 2:8b). This dovetails well with Hebrews 1:13 // Psalm 110:1 ('Sit at my right hand *until* I make your enemies a footstool'). Everything *is* in subjection to Jesus *now* properly understood ('at my right hand'), but we just do not *fully* see it here ('until'). We will fully see it and experience it when 'all your enemies' are defeated at the second coming.[119]

As will be evident in my exegesis below, I will argue for

---

117. Westcott, *Hebrews*, 42, italics mine.

118. In addition to Westcott, those in favor of an anthropological interpretation include Brown, *Hebrews*, 86, 96–97; Moffatt, *Hebrews*, 23; Kistemaker, *Psalm Citations*, 105 and *Hebrews*, 66; Barnabas Lindars, *The Theology of the Letter to the Hebrews*, NTT (Cambridge: CUP, 1991), 39–40; Richard N. Longenecker, *Biblical Exegesis in the Apostolic Period*, Biblical and Theological Classics Library (Carlisle, UK: Paternoster, 1995), 181; and Craig Blomberg, 'Better Things in this Case: The Superiority of Today's New International Version in Hebrews,' *BT* 55 (2004): 310–18, esp. 312. The anthropological interpretation is also seen in Bible versions that explicitly translate 'man' and 'son of man' in Heb. 2:6–8 as plurals such as 'mankind' or 'human beings' (NIV, NLT, NRSV, CEB, NJB).

119. Those in favor of the Christological interpretation include Chrysostom, 'Homily 4 on Hebrews' (*NPNF*^{1}, 14:383); Aquinas, *Hebrews*, 54–58; Owen, *Hebrews*, 19:338–42, 363; Wilhelm Bousset, *Kyrios Christos: A History of the Belief in Christ from the Beginnings of Christianity to Irenaeus*, trans. John E. Steely (Waco: Baylor University Press, 2013 [1913]), 110; Hughes, *Hebrews*, 85–87; Attridge, *Hebrews*, 72; Ellingworth, *Hebrews*, 150–52; Formula of Concord, Solid Declaration, 8; and George H. Guthrie and Russell D. Quinn, 'A Discourse Analysis of the Use of Psalm 8:4–6 in Hebrews 2:5–9,' *JETS* 49 (2006): 235–46, esp. 238–46. Of course, there are those who favor a 'both/and' option, e.g., Koester, *Hebrews*, 215, 221; Allen, *Hebrews*, 208; and Schreiner, *Hebrews*, 87n81.

the Christological interpretation and assume this for other exegetical decisions in Hebrews 2:5–9.

2:5 *For it was not to angels that he subjected the coming universe,*[120] *concerning which we are speaking.*

The **he** refers to God the Father. God the Father did *not* put **angels** in control. Ultimately, God the Father put God the Son in control. Thus, this is another aspect of the Son being greater than angels.

For (γάρ)[121] in the Christological interpretation relates back to the Son's ascension in Hebrews 1:13 (seeing Heb. 2:1–4 as somewhat of a parenthesis). Hence, another obvious implication of the Son's ascension is that angels are not in control.

In addition to the Psalm 110:1 // Hebrews 1:13 ascension argument, the AH will also use Psalm 8 to make the point that Jesus is in control. He does this by using the verb **subjected** (ὑποτάσσω) in Hebrews 2:5. This verb is also in the Psalm 8 quote (Ps. 8:6 // Heb. 2:8a). And then is used again twice in Hebrews 2:8b.

The **coming universe** refers to the inaugurated kingdom at the Son's ascension and extends through to his Second Coming and/or through to the New Heavens and Earth.[122] As will be discussed below at Hebrews 2:8, **coming** here assumes a 'now/not-yet' eschatology—the kingdom has *now* begun but has *not yet* been consummated. The verb **coming**

---

120. See discussion of **universe** at Heb. 1:6.

121. The conjunction γάρ is normally used to indicate cause or reason ('for'); so my translation above. However, sometimes it is much weaker and is simply used to indicate a transition ('now'); so the NRSV; NLT; Moffatt, *Hebrews*, 21; and Mitchell, *Hebrews*, 64. For a good brief discussion of γάρ, see Richard A. Young, *Intermediate New Testament Greek: A Linguistic and Exegetical Approach* (B&H: Nashville, 1994),182–83.

122. The vast majority of commentators agree that the **coming universe** begins at the Son's ascension (e.g., Brown, *Hebrews*, 89; Hughes, *Hebrews*, 82; Attridge, *Hebrews*, 70; and Allen, *Hebrews*, 203). Chrysostom and Aquinas disagree. They see this from Christ's perspective in eternity 'past' and conclude that the initial creation of the world is the **coming universe** ('Homily 4 on Hebrews' [*NPNF*[1], 14:382]; and *Hebrews*, 54; respectively).

(μέλλω, translated variously as 'going to,' 'about to') is used in several theologically charged verses relating to eschatological realities (Heb. 1:14; 6:5; 10:1; 11:8; 13:14).

2:6–8a *And somewhere someone testified, saying, 'What is man that you remember him, or son of man that you are concerned for him? You lowered him for a little [while] in contrast to the angels; you crowned him with glory and with honor; you subjected all things under his feet.'*

The AH quotes Psalm 8:4–6. He introduces this quote with **somewhere someone testified**. The verb **testified**, although unique in the NT to introduce a quote, is appropriate to introduce Scripture as it usually has a serious, solemn sense.[123] What is initially jarring is the wording **somewhere someone** (πού τις). This is especially true as one would assume that Psalm 8 was well known and the superscription assigns it to David. Is there evidence that this was a common idiom to introduce Scripture outside of the NT? Not particularly.[124] The **somewhere** is similar to Hebrews 4:4 and may indicate a text that is commonly known.[125] The use of **someone** is consistent with the AH's emphasis on God being the author of Scripture (e.g., Heb. 3:7) in that he only explicitly names the human author when needed for the argument (so Heb. 4:7).[126] In addition, possibly the AH did not explicitly mention God as author because the Psalm 8 quote is from a human perspective. In sum, divine authorship so overrides human authorship that the human author can be referred to simply as **someone** even when it is David.

---

123. Cf. Acts 20:24; 23:11; 1 Thess. 4:6; 1 Tim. 5:21.

124. Philo does use this exact expression once to introduce a quote of Gen. 20:12 (*On Drunkenness* 61). In two other places he uses 'somewhere' (πού) in introducing Ps. 101:1 and Exod. 23:20 (*That God is Unchangeable* 74, *On Agriculture* 51, respectively, also cf. *On Planting* 90).

125. Attridge notes '[It] probably reflects a common homiletic practice, whereby the expositor does not dwell on what is commonly known or presupposed' (*Hebrews*, 70–71).

126. So also Hughes, *Hebrews*, 83; and Allen, *Hebrews*, 204.

Psalm 8 is a glorious psalm. David begins and ends the psalm noting God's majestic name (Ps. 8:1, 9). God is praised for his creation of the heavens and stars (Ps. 8:1b, 3). This greatness then prompts the rhetorical question as to why God is concerned with seemingly insignificant 'man' (Ps. 8:4, cf. Pss. 90:5–6; 144:3; Job 7:17; 25:6).[127] This amazement at God's concern for 'man' is especially acute in that God has 'crowned him' and given him dominion over 'all things', including various animals (Ps. 8:5–8). Psalm 8:2 breaks the flow between 8:1b and 8:3.[128] David admits that God has foes; however, these will be overcome by praises coming from the 'mouth of babes.'

Psalm 8 contains clear allusions to Genesis 1–2 with the creation motif, the use of 'man',[129] and dominion theology. Although this psalm has clear allusions to Adam, verse 2 confirms that the psalm at some level refers more broadly to humans rather than simply to Adam. In fact, Christ quotes Psalm 8:2 in Matthew 21:16 where he is cleansing the temple and performing healings. Children were praising Christ in contradistinction to the chief priests and scribes. Christ interpreted those children as the 'babes' of Psalm 8:2, and the chief priests and scribes as the 'foes' of Psalm 8:2.[130] Hence, the Psalm refers to events post-Adam.

In my view, God intended that each psalm in various ways refers to *both* Christ and Christians. In some psalms, Christ

---

127. Interestingly, Rabbinic literature sometimes has the angels' quoting Ps. 8:4 as they ask God why he cares about Adam soon after he was created (t. Sotah 6:5; b. Sanhedrin 38b).

128. As Longman says, 'verse 2 takes an unexpected turn' (*Psalms*, 80).

129. In Ps. 8:4 for 'man,' the Hebrew uses both אנוש and אדם. The LXX uses ἄνθρωπος twice.

130. By implication, Christ was putting himself in the position of God as the one being praised! See discussion in Belcher, *The Messiah and the Psalms*, 160–62. Interestingly in the Tosefta, one Rabbi uses Ps. 8:2 as proof that even infants rejoiced and sang just after God defeated the Egyptians at the red sea (t. Sotah 6:4). Another Rabbi disagrees and connects Ps. 8:2 only to Isaac's telling Abraham about the ram (t. Sotah 6:5).

is primary and Christians are secondary. In other psalms, the reverse is true.[131] At the 'Christian' level, Psalm 8 is about humans as Matthew 21:16 confirms. Hence, at one level, 'man' and 'son of man' are collectives to refer to mankind. However, this psalm is also about Christ being *the* 'man' and *the* 'son of man' (e.g., Heb. 2:9; 1 Cor. 15:27; Eph. 1:22). Although I view Psalm 8 itself as referring at some level to both Christ and Christians, I will argue below at Hebrews 2:8b–9 and in the Reflections section that the AH intended only the Christological sense of Psalm 8 here.

Concerning the quote per se, in general, the LXX is a straightforward translation of the Hebrew for Psalm 8:4–6, and Hebrews 2:6–8a matches the LXX. However, there are a few complications.[132] The first is that Psalm 8:6a, 'you have given him dominion over the works of your hands,' is deleted by the AH.[133] There is no obvious rationale for this, but also, there is no problem in the deletion. Possibly, the AH assumed that immediately going to the parallel following clause, **you subjected all things under his feet** (Ps. 2:6b // Heb. 2:8a), made the point more forcefully in his rhetorical context. Except for this deletion, the AH follows the LXX exactly.

Another complication has to do with the clause **you**

---

131. For one aspect of this argument, see Robert J. Cara, 'Psalms Applied to Both Christ and Christians: Psalms 8, 22, 34, 118 and Romans 15:3 // Psalm 69:9,' in *Redeeming the Life of the Mind: Essays in Honor of Vern Poythress*, ed. Wayne Grudem, John Frame, and John Hughes (Wheaton: Crossway, 2017), 97–111, esp. 103–5.

132. A quasi-complication is that the Hebrew verbs 'to crown' (Ps. 8:5, עטר) and 'to give dominion' (Ps. 8:6, משל) are in the imperfect tense, which would normally be translated as English present tenses. However, the LXX saw these as conceptually past tenses and translated these verbs as aorists (Greek past tense). Given the poetical nature of the context, the major English translations also see these Hebrew verbs as conceptually past tenses, agreeing with the LXX. The only exception to this is the NASB.

133. However, several ancient Greek manuscripts do include Ps. 8:6a at the end of Heb. 2:7. The KJV, Geneva Bible, and the NASB include this in Heb. 2:7. The UBS committee preferred the shorter reading as it assumed that a scribe expanded Heb. 2:7 matching the LXX. See discussion in Metzger, *TCGNT*[2], 593–94.

lowered him for a little while in contrast to the angels (Ps. 8:5a // Heb. 2:7a), which actually has two issues. The first issue relates to the Hebrew word אלהים (*Elohim*), which is translated by the LXX and AH as **angels**.

Most often אלהים is properly translated as 'God', although occasionally it is used as 'gods' or 'angels' or 'heavenly beings' (cf. Gen. 6:2?; Exod. 12:12; 20:3; Pss. 82:6; 86:8; 1QM XII, 4–5, XV, 4; 11QMelch II, 25).[134] In the Psalm 8 context, the translation 'angels' is best as the author is making a surprising point, and there is nothing surprising about concluding that man is lower than God.[135]

The second issue relates to **little**. Both the Hebrew and Greek words are equally ambiguous (מעט, βραχύ τι). With no context, possible meanings include (1) short in time, (2) short in distance, or (3) being slightly lower in quality, degree, or dignity. As all commentators agree, the AH understood **little** in sense of time as he applies this to the time of Christ's humiliation (hence, my translation **little while**).[136]

2:8b–9 *For in 'subjecting to him all things,' he left nothing not in subjection to him. But now we do not yet see all things being in subjection to him. But we see Jesus, the one 'lowered for a little [while] in contrast to the angels,' on account of the suffering of death [is the one] 'being crowned with glory and honor' so that by [the] grace of God he might taste death for everyone.*

The AH re-refers to Psalm 8, **for in 'subjecting to him all things,'** and concludes that this shows that God the Father

---

134. See *HALOT*, 53.

135. The Hebrew Targum also translated as angels. In favor of the angels translation in the Ps. 8 context, Owen, *Hebrews*, 19:321, 327; Moffat, *Hebrews*, 22; ESV ('heavenly beings'); KJV; and NIV. Against angels and in favor of 'God,' Longman, *Psalms*, 81; Craigie, *Psalms 1–50*, 108; Geneva Bible; ASV; RSV; and CEB.

136. Not all commentators agree that *in the context of Psalm 8* the translation should be **little while**. This is especially true if 'God' as opposed to **angels** is assumed. The translation would then be 'you made him little less [quality] than God' (e.g., Craigie, *Psalms 1–50*, 105, 108; and Geneva Bible).

left nothing not in subjection to him (Son). Thus the AH proves that the Son is greater than angels because all things, including angels but excluding God the Father, are subject to him (1 Cor. 15:27).

One possible objection to this argument is that **we do not yet see all things being in subjection to him** in this current world, especially given the distress some in the congregation were experiencing. The AH solves this by first noting that the Son is truly on his throne and Christians do **see**[137] **Jesus.**[138] That is, there is a true sense that the Son is reigning now and there will be a more complete sense at the second coming.[139] The second aspect of the solution is to show that the humiliation and exaltation of the Son matches to Psalm 8, proving the exaltation as true because God's word said it was. The Son's humiliation is shown by his being **'lowered for a little [while] in contrast to the angels'** and his exaltation by **'being crowned with glory and honor.'**[140]

Although not completely clear, **on account of the suffering**

---

137. Here, the AH uses two different, but common, verbs for 'see' (ὁράω, βλέπω). In general Greek literature, these verbs are fairly synonymous. Both these verbs are used several times in Hebrews, and I cannot 'see' (!) any difference.

138. This is the first time **Jesus** is used in Hebrews. Often when the AH uses **Jesus**, he rhetorically inserts it later in the sentence for emphasis (Heb. 2:9; 3:1; 6:20; 7:2; 10:19 (?); 12:2, 24; 13:20). This rhetorical feature is hard to show in English translations and is not shown in mine. For example, the ESV and CEB have tried to include this.

139. See Alexander E. Stewart, 'The Temporary Messianic Kingdom in Second Temple Judaism and the Delay of the Parousia: Psalm 110:1 and the Development of Early Christian Inaugurated Eschatology,' *JETS* 59 (2016): 255–70, esp. 267–68; and Donald G. Bloesch, *Jesus Christ: Savior & Lord*, Christian Foundations (Downers Grove: InterVarsity, 1997), 212–13. Robert L. Brawley connects the unseen aspect in Heb. 2:8 to Heb. 11:1 ('Discourse Structure and the Unseen in Hebrews 2:8 and 11:1: A Neglected Aspect of the Context,' *CBQ* 55 [1993]: 81–98).

140. Some believe that these two phrases in the original Ps. 8 context are parallel positive-statements and do *not* describe a humiliation/exaltation scheme (e.g., Calvin, *Psalms*, 4:2:103–4; Koester, *Hebrews*, 222). I disagree. See discussions above concerning 'while' and 'God'/'angels.'

of death, while alluding backwards to being **lowered**, is primarily giving the cause for the Son's being exalted (**'being crowned with glory and honor'**).[141]

The final purpose clause, **so that by the grace**[142] **of God he might taste death for everyone**, adds a slightly different angle to the Son's death. The phrase, **on account of the suffering of death**, relates the Son's death to *his* exaltation, while this purpose clause relates the Son's death to the *elect's* benefit and ultimate exaltation.[143] This then anticipates the next section, Hebrews 2:10–18.

The expression **taste death** clearly refers to the Son's actual death and probably adds a *bitterness* aspect to it (cf. Matt. 16:28; 20:22; Mark 9:1; 10:38–39; Luke 9:27; 14:24; John 8:52; Isa. 51:17; 4 Ezra 6:26). Although most disagree, Chrysostom connected this to the shortness of the Son's death experience—he *only* tasted it for three days, he did not fully swallow it.[144]

For whom did the Son die?—**for everyone**. Does this mean everyone without exception, or is it qualified in context? As the subsequent context will show, **everyone** is synonymous with 'bringing many sons to glory', 'sanctified,' 'brothers,' and 'seed of Abraham' (Heb. 2:10–11, 16). That is, the Son died for the elect.[145]

---

141. So also Brown, *Hebrews*, 99; Hughes, *Hebrews*, 88; and Schreiner, *Hebrews*, 90.

142. Some manuscripts have 'without God' (χωρίς θεοῦ) as opposed to 'by the grace of God' (χάριτι θεοῦ). All English translations use 'by the grace of God' and Metzger gives the latter reading an 'A' rating (*TCGNT*², 594). However, the 'without God' reading and its theological implications were hotly debated in the patristic period. See Hughes, *Hebrews*, 94–97 and Paul A. Hartog, 'The Text of Hebrews 2:9 in Its Patristic Reception,' *BSac* 171 (2014): 52–71.

143. So also Hughes, *Hebrews*, 90.

144. Chrysostom, 'Homily 4 on Hebrews' (*NPNF*¹, 14:383).

145. So also the *Geneva Bible: 1602 Edition*, 'all the faithful' (folio 110); Bremen Consensus, Death of Christ § 6 (*Reformed Confessions of the 16th and 17th Centuries*, 3:664); Schreiner, *Hebrews*, 91; John Owen, *The Death of Death in the Death of Christ* (Carlisle: Banner of Truth, 1959), 237–38; and Turretin,

Reflections

The Son, to whom 'everything is in subjection', is a man, yes, the God-man. Although anticipated by several aspects in Hebrews 1, the blatant designation of the Son here in Hebrews 2:5–9 as a 'man,' a 'son of man,' and one who 'tasted death' still warms the hearts of Christians. Look what the second person of the Trinity did for believers; among other things, he took on human nature! The AH will present more on the Son's human nature in the following section (Heb. 2:10–18).

What was the 'theological logic(s)' that drove the AH to be convinced that Psalm 8 was ultimately referring to the Son, given that in a secondary sense it did refer to mankind in general? The more confidence we have in the AH's logic, the more confidence we have in God's word and its proclamation of the God-man.

We cannot be sure of all of AH's 'logics', but allow me to offer several biblical logics. (1) The AH understood it as a historical fact that (a) the Son was both divine and human and (b) that the Son was humiliated and then exalted. (2) Psalm 110:1 and Psalm 8:6 connect the Davidic Messiah with 'man' in subjecting all things. This combination of verses is noted three times in the NT (Heb. 1:13; 2:8; 1 Cor. 15:24–27; Eph. 1:20–22). (3) The humiliation / exaltation scheme is included in Psalm 8:5. (4) The Son is the second Adam (Rom. 5:12–21; 1 Cor 15:21–22, 42–49), and Psalm 8 has intentional allusions to the first Adam reigning (Gen. 1:28). (5) Mankind in the Garden and currently in this sinful world was/is not reigning in an absolute sense; hence, Psalm 8 must be speaking of *the* man. (6) The expression 'son of man' often refers to the Son (e.g., Dan. 7:13; Matt. 8:20; Mark 10:45; Luke 19:10; John 3:13–14; Acts 7:56; Rev. 1:13; 14:14). (7) All the Psalms exhibit both Christological and anthropological senses.

Institutes of Elenctic Theology, 2:472.

Son Superior to Angels—Made Like His Brothers
(2:10–18)

Hebrews 2:10–18 is an amazing section of Scripture as it deepens our understanding of the incarnation of the Lord Jesus Christ. In addition to the requirement of being divine, the second person of the Trinity had to become *man* to be the savior.[146] Primarily, he had to become man (1) to represent and identify with his people and (2) to die (the divine nature cannot die). This pericope of Scripture has been a focal point of many classic discussions of the incarnation and two natures of Christ and is virtually always referenced in the Christological sections of creeds.[147]

Hebrews 2:10–18 expands upon the end of Hebrews 2:9, 'by the grace of God he might taste death for everyone.' The flow of Hebrews 2:10–18 appears to be a thesis, then three OT quotes to prove a portion of the thesis, followed by two restatements/expansions of the thesis separated by a parenthesis.[148] The thesis is Hebrews 2:10–11. The Father determined that for Christ to be a savior, he must suffer and be connected to his 'sons'. Then in Hebrews 2:12–13 three OT quotes (Ps. 22:22; Isa. 8:17; Isa. 8:18) are used to confirm that Christ is closely

---

146. L. W. Hurtado notes, 'Striking is the author's [AH] dual emphasis upon Christ as exalted divine Son and as full partaker in the human nature of those he redeems to God. This dialectic is particularly profound in Hebrews 1–2' ('Christology,' *DLNT*, 170–84, esp. 173).

147. E.g., Athanasius, *On the Incarnation* 10 (*NPNF*², 4:41–42); Gregory of Nazianzus, 'Fourth Theological Oration, 6' (*NPNF*², 7:311–12); Ambrose, *Of the Christian Faith* 3.11 (*NPNF*², 10:254–55); Calvin, *Institutes* 2.13.1–2; Formula of Concord, Epitome 1; Belgic Confession 18; Heidelberg Catechism 36, 40; French Confession 14; Second Helvetic Confession 11; Emden Examination of Faith 14 (*Reformed Confessions of the 16th and 17th Centuries*, 2:47); WCF 8; WLC 39, 48, 52, 85; and WSC 22, 25.

148. Scholars are not unified on the 'flow' of this pericope. My outline is probably closest to Koester, *Hebrews*, 234–35. *Contra* me, Lane sees the pericope as a 'homiletical midrash' using the three quotes. 'Brothers' from Ps. 22:22 relates to Heb. 2:11, 17; 'trust' from Isa. 8:17 relates to Heb. 2:17; and 'children' from Isa. 8:18 relates to Heb. 2:14–15 (Lane, *Hebrews 1–8*, 52–53).

connected to his sons and God the Father. Hebrews 2:14–15 restates with more specificity Hebrews 2:10–11. Christ must be human like his sons and his suffering involves death to destroy death. Then there is a parenthesis; Christ's work is related to the 'seed of Abraham' and not to angels (Heb. 2:16). Following the parenthesis, there is another restatement of the thesis with additional information. Christ's being human prepares him to be a high priest (Heb. 2:17–18).

2:10–11 *For it was fitting to him, on account of whom are all things and through whom are all things, in bringing many sons to glory to perfect the leader of their salvation through sufferings. For even*[149] *the one sanctifying and those being sanctified [are] all from one, on account of which cause he is not ashamed to call them brothers,…*

It was not that Christ's sufferings were a second best option or out of the control of God the Father; no, **it was fitting to him**, the Father, to effect this plan. The Father is none other than the one **on account of whom are all things and through whom are all things.**[150] As Aquinas puts it, God is both the 'efficient' cause (**through whom**) and the 'final' cause (**on account of whom**) of all things.[151] Since everything is done by God and for the will/purpose of God, then the sufferings of Christ are certainly an aspect of the Father's plan — a most glorious aspect.

God the Father is **bringing many sons to glory.**[152] For the

---

149. I translated τε in τε γὰρ as 'even'. Τε γὰρ occurs in the NT only in Rom. 1:26; 7:7; 14:8; 2 Cor. 10:8; and Heb. 2:11. Τε appears to have the sense of 'even' in some of these texts.

150. For God as creator in Hebrews, see Schreiner, *Hebrews*, 435–37. Verses of interest are Heb. 1:2; 2:10; 3:4; 4:3–4; 9:26; and 11:3.

151. Aquinas, *Hebrews*, 63. He goes on to say that all things 'exist for the sake of communicating his goodness' (p. 63).

152. Virtually all commentators agree with me that the participle **bringing** (ἀγαγόντα, accusative) refers to the Father even though the surface-level grammar might indicate that it refers to **leader**. That is, on the surface, the accusative **bringing** matches better to the accusative **leader** and not to the dative **him** (Father). The proper response to justify the common view is that the accusative **bringing** is the implied 'subject' of the infinite **to**

first time in Hebrews, Christians are referred to as simply **sons**. This has some punch as Christ has been *the* Son. Also, believers will be brought to **glory**, that is the new heavens and new earth. This **glory** at some level parallels Christ's glory (Heb. 1:3; 2:9; 13:21).

Christ is called the **leader** (ἀρχηγός[153]) of the sons. This title for Christ is used in Acts 3:15; 5:31; and Hebrews 12:2. In the LXX ἀρχηγός refers to heads of tribes, leaders of households, military leaders, and leading women (Lam. 2:20). Here in Hebrews 2:10, it is variously translated in English Bibles as 'Lorde' (Tyndale), 'Prince' (Geneva Bible), 'Captain' (KJV), 'author' (NASB), 'pioneer' (NIV, RSV, CEB), and 'founder' (ESV).[154]

The two expressions **leader of their salvation** and **the one sanctifying and those being sanctified** at the same time show both the similarities and differences between Christ and the sons.[155] Christ leads the sons to salvation and sanctifies (Heb. 10:10, 14; 13:12) them; but he himself does not need salvation nor sanctification.[156]

---

perfect. So also, e.g., Attridge, *Hebrews*, 82; and Lane, *Hebrews 1–8*, 56; *contra* Käsemann, *The Wandering People of God*, 143. Why is the **bringing** an *aorist* participle? One guess is that it is an ingressive aorist emphasizing that the action has started without indicating an ending. So Koester, *Hebrews*, 227; and Kleinig, *Hebrews*, 119. See BDF §318.1, although this is not discussing participles explicitly.

153. The etymology is ἀρχή (beginning, ruler) plus ἄγω (I lead, bring). Of course, etymology is not necessarily meaning.

154. Secular usage also includes all these translations, see LSJ, 252. Heb. 5:8–9 also has both 'to suffer' and 'to perfect' in its context and designates Christ as 'source'/ 'cause'/'author' (αἴτιος) 'of salvation.' For a good broad discussion, see J. Julius Scott, Jr., '*ARCHĒGOS* in the Salvation History of the Epistle to the Hebrews,' *JETS* 29 (1986): 47–54. Geerhardus Vos argues strongly that 'leader' is the best translation throughout Hebrews based on the background idea that a priest's 'leadership [is] based on identification with those who are led' ('The Priesthood of Christ in the Epistle to the Hebrews' [first article] *PTR* 5 [1907]: 423–47, esp. 433–34).

155. Chrysostom has a very good discussion of this, 'Homily 4 on Hebrews' (*NPNF*[1], 14:384).

156. For a discussion of the verb 'to sanctify,' see Heb. 10:10.

The main grammatical structure of Hebrews 2:10 is that **it is fitting for** the Father ... **to perfect** Christ ... **through sufferings**. The concept of **to perfect** and its importance in Hebrews is discussed more fully at Hebrews 5:9. Here it refers to making Christ *fit for his service* as a **leader** and **one who sanctifies**. It does *not* refer to Christ's growing in ethical/moral ways.[157]

Christ and the sons are **all from one**. Yes, they are different, but here the obvious emphasis is that they are united. **One** is not further defined.[158] Since it is theologically true that there are multiple ways that Christ and his sons are 'one', various understandings have developed. One primary option is that Christ and the sons have one *human nature*.[159] The other primary option is that Christ and the sons have one *origin/source/Father*.[160] I opt for one *human nature* based on the general emphasis of the pericope (Heb. 2:14a and 2:17a) and a much stronger connection to the following clause.

Given that Christ and the sons are one, **on account of which cause he is not ashamed to call them brothers**. Now the **sons** are called **brothers** (cf. Rom. 8:29). It is not just that Christ is the **leader** and **the one who sanctifies**; but given the same human nature, Christ and the sons are **brothers**. 'When [Christ] clothed himself with flesh, he clothed himself with brotherhood.'[161] Christ was **not ashamed** implies that there

---

157. Moisés Silva well notes that 'the modern reader ... naturally associates *perfection* with moral and ethical qualities'. This then 'complicate[s] matters' as to our understanding ('Perfection and Eschatology in Hebrews,' *WTJ* 39 [1976]: 60–71, esp. 60, emphasis his).

158. In fact, in form **one** (ἑνὸς) could be either masculine or neuter.

159. So, e.g., Owen, *Hebrews*, 19:418; Calvin, *Hebrews and 1 & 2 Peter*, 26; *Geneva Bible 1602 Edition*, folio 110; Hughes, *Hebrews*, 105; Kistemaker, *Hebrews*, 71; NIV, NJB. James Swetnam argues for a subset of this option. The oneness is that Christ's *trust* in Heb. 2:13a matches to the *trust* that the seed of Abraham have (Heb. 2:16) ("Ἐξ ἑνὸς in Hebrews 2,11,' *Bib* 88 [2007]: 517-25).

160. So, e.g., Aquinas, *Hebrews*, 64; Lane, *Hebrews 1–8*, 58; Attridge, *Hebrews*, 88–89; NASB, NAB, NLT, RSV, ESV, CEB.

161. Chrysostom, 'Homily 4 on Hebrews' (*NPNF*[1], 14:384).

was/is a gap between Christ and his people.[162] He is the *God-man*; we are men and women. He was sinless; we are not sinless brothers and sisters. But still Christ chose to be our brother.

2:12–13 ... *saying, 'I will announce your name to my brothers; in the midst of the church, I will sing [hymns] to you'; and again, 'I will have trust in him'; and again, 'Behold, I and the children whom God gave me.'*

The AH quotes three OT verses, Psalm 22:22; Isaiah 8:17;[163] and Isaiah 8:18, that show (1) that the Son truly does have brothers and (2) the close connections among the Father, the Son, and the Son's brothers. The three quotes all have Christ speaking in the first person, which coordinates with the end of Hebrews 2:11, 'he is not ashamed to call them brothers.' In the first quote, Christ is directly speaking to the Father. In the following two, Christ is speaking about the Father.

The first quote is from Psalm 22:22, **'I will announce your name to my brothers; in the midst of the church, I will sing hymns to you.'**[164] Psalm 22 is written by David and includes two movements. The first, 22:1–21, is an individual lament. The second, 22:22–31, includes praise and thanksgiving in the midst of the congregation. The NT writers clearly took Psalm 22 as Christological.[165] The lament concerned Christ

---

162. 'These words plainly intimate that it was an act of condescension to call them brethren' (Brown, *Hebrews*, 116).

163. Similar wording is in the LXX at 2 Sam. 2:3 and Isa. 12:2; cf. Ps. 18:2.

164. The LXX is a straightforward translation of the Hebrew. The AH only changes one word from the LXX, and it is simply a synonym change from 'to tell' (διηγέομαι, also in Heb. 11:32) to 'to announce' (ἀπαγγέλλω). Points of interest include that the common verb 'to praise' (הלל), which is translated by several Greek verbs, is here translated by 'to sing hymns' (ὑμνέω). The weighty word 'assembly' (קהל) is translated by 'church' (ἐκκλησία).

165. Ps. 22:1 // Matt. 27:46; Mark 15:34. Ps. 22:8 // Matt. 27:43. Ps. 22:13b // 1 Pet. 5:8. Ps. 22:18 // Matt. 27:35; Mark 15:24; Luke 23:34; John 19:24. Ps. 22:22 // Heb. 2:12. Except the 1 Pet. 5:8 quote which is applied to believers, all quotes are applied to Christ. For my discussion of Ps. 22 relative to the quotes in the NT, see Cara, 'Psalms Applied to Both Christ and Christians:

and his life of suffering, and the praise related to his praise within his church.[166] The AH quotes from the first verse of the praise section (Ps. 22:22).

The key point in the quote for the AH is **brothers**. Christ, speaking in the first person, calls other believers **brothers**. Hence, the point from Hebrews 2:10 is proven. The **brothers** are further qualified as those in the **church** or 'congregation' or 'assembly'. The AH is also showing that Christ is a 'leader' (Heb. 2:10) in that he leads the **church** in praising and **sing[ing] hymns to** the Father (**your name, you**). Intriguingly, as this epistle was/is read in a worship service, the congregation is being reminded that Christ is spiritually in her midst and leading her in worship (cf. Heb. 13:15).[167]

Before getting to the second (Isa. 8:17) and the third (Isa. 8:18) quotes, some background on this section of Isaiah is useful. In context of Isaiah 7–8, Isaiah has just fruitlessly warned the people of Judah and King Ahaz not to appeal to Assyria to save them from the Syria-Israel coalition.[168]

Psalms 8, 22, 34, 118 and Romans 15:3 // Psalm 69:9,' 106–07. Ps. 22:22 is quoted and applied to Christ in Barn. 6:16.

166. Note the similar praise within the congregation in Ps. 40:9–10 in a psalm that the AH also takes as Christological (Ps. 40:6–8 // Heb. 10:5–7).

167. Michael LeFebvre, 'When you sing the Psalms, you are actually singing the songs of Jesus, with Jesus as your song leader' (*Singing the Songs of Jesus: Revisiting the Psalms* [Ross-Shire: Christian Focus, 2010], 50, emphasis removed). Calvin has similar comments; Christ is the 'chief Conductor of our hymns' (*Hebrews and 1 & 2 Peter*, 27). Kleinig argues that the AH intentionally presents Christ as a 'second David, a royal praise singer. Just as David established the choir to sing the Lord's song in the Divine Service at the temple in Jerusalem [see 1 Chr. 6:31–32], so Jesus now leads the congregation as his choir in an assembly that is both earthly and heavenly, local and universal' (*Hebrews*, 135).

168. The historical background relates to the rise of powerful Assyria. Syria and Israel have joined together to defend themselves against Assyria (735 BC). They want Judah to join them, but Judah refuses. Then Syria and Israel plan to attack Judah (734–33 BC). Ahaz, the king of Judah, an evil king, considers appealing to Assyria for help, and Isaiah strongly urges Ahaz instead to trust God (Isa. 7:1–8:10). Israel and Syria do attack. Ahaz appeals to Assyria, which minimally helps in the short run, although he had

However, after judgment for their subsequent appeal to Assyria, Isaiah sees hope. God tells Isaiah to record his statements among his 'disciples' (Isa. 8:16). Isaiah proclaims his trust in God despite the current and upcoming difficulties (Isa. 8:17). Isaiah understands that he and his given 'children' are signs that God will accomplish his purposes (Isa. 8:18).[169]

What may have prompted the AH to see Isaiah 8:17–18 as messianic? There are multiple NT messianic quotes related to Isaiah 6–9, including Isaiah 8:14 (see Rom. 9:33 and 1 Pet. 2:8). More specifically, Isaiah and his small remnant proclaimed their trust in God no matter the difficult circumstances.[170] This matches to Christ and his remnant.[171] Finally, possibly the 'hiding his [God's] face' in Isaiah 8:17b connects to Psalm 22:1, 24.

---

become an Assyrian vassal. Then Assyria destroys both Syria and Israel, with Israel falling in 722 BC. Assyria eventually invades Judah and reaches all the way to Jerusalem in 701 BC and is miraculously defeated there. See 2 Kgs. 15:27–31; 16:1–20; 2 Chron 28; Isa. 7–8; 36–37; and John Bright, *A History of Israel*, 3rd ed. (Philadelphia: Westminster, 1981), 269–88, 291–92.

169. Most likely, the 'children' are Isaiah's biological children (Isa. 7:3; 8:1, 3) as opposed to his 'disciples' in Isa. 8:16 because of the emphasis on signs (so J. Ridderbos, *Isaiah*, trans. John Vriend, BSC [Grand Rapids: Regency/Zondervan, 1985], 98; and F. Delitzsch, *Isaiah*, trans. James Martin, 2 vols. [Grand Rapids: Eerdmans, 1986], 1:238). However, at some level the 'disciples' are secondarily included as their faith in God's/Isaiah's message are also signs. For this more inclusive view, see John Calvin, *Commentary on the Book of the Prophet Isaiah*, trans. William Pringle, 4 vols., Calvin's Commentaries (Grand Rapids: Baker, 1996), 1:283–86; and Edward J. Young, *The Book of Isaiah: The English Text, with Introduction, Exposition, and Notes*, 3 vols., NICOT (Grand Rapids: Eerdmans, 1965–1972), 1:315–17.

170. At the beginning of Isa. 8:17, the LXX inserts 'and he will say.' The implication being that Isaiah was speaking about someone else and putting the other's comments into the first person. Hence, some commentators believe that the AH understood the 'I' of Isa. 8:17–18 as not referring to Isaiah himself but must be referring to a future person, that is Christ (Moffatt, *Hebrews*, 33; Ellingworth, Hebrews, 169). I am not convinced.

171. Geerhardus Vos emphasizes the remnant idea as the driving factor here in the typology. He sees Isaiah himself as the beginning of the 'church within a church, the idea of the invisible church' (*The Teaching of the Epistle to the Hebrews* [Phillipsburg: Presbyterian and Reformed, 1956], 61, emphasis his).

What is the AH's point(s) with his second (**and again**) quote, **'I will have trust in him'** (Isa. 8:17c // Heb. 2:13a)?[172] Christ is like his brothers in that he has **trust** in the Father (**him**) like they do. Christ also exhibited that **trust** during difficult times and is an example ('leader') to believers to continue their trust in the Father (cf. Heb. 12:2–3). The explicit statement of Christ's **trust** is again emphasizing his human nature, almost shockingly so.

The third quote (**and again**) is **'Behold, I and the children whom God gave me'** (Isa. 8:18a // Heb. 2:13b).[173] The use of **children** here reinforces the close connection of (1) Christ to his people and (2) the Father (**God**) to Christ and the **children**. The use of **children**, as opposed to **brothers**, further adds to the sense that Christ is the 'leader' (cf. Isa. 53:10). The expression **whom God gave me** is reminiscent of John 6:37 and reinforces that there is always a remnant of God's people (OT and NT) connected to Christ.[174]

For the second and third quotes, the AH puts Isaiah's words into the mouth of Christ. The NT writers assumed that aspects of OT saints were typological of Christ partially because they assumed that God was in complete control of history. Here, the great prophet Isaiah, who had difficult times, is typological of Christ in his trust and his being connected to a remnant of believers.[175] Christ, by his identification with Isaiah, is again

---

172. The Hebrew at the end of 8:17, וְקִוֵּיתִי־לוֹ, is more mechanically translated as 'I will wait upon him' with 'wait' (קוה) in the sense of 'hope,' 'trust,' and 'being persuaded'. This Hebrew expression is used often in Isaiah in a similar way (Isa. 25:9; 26:8; 30:18; 33:2; 40:31; 49:23; 51:3; 60:9) with a variety of LXX translations. Given this, the Isa. 8:17 future perfect periphrastic translation of πεποιθὼς ἔσομαι ('I will have trust') by the LXX is reasonable. The AH follows the LXX wording except for reversing πεποιθὼς ἔσομαι and adding ἐγώ, both of which do not conceptually change the LXX translation.

173. The Hebrew and LXX texts match except that the Hebrew has 'Lord' (יהוה) and the LXX 'God' (θεός). The AH followed the LXX exactly.

174. In addition to this connection, C. J. A. Hickling notes multiple connections between the Gospel of John and Heb. 2:10–18 ('John and Hebrews: The Background of Hebrews 2:10–18,' *NTS* 29 [1983]: 112–16).

175. See Brian Pate, 'Who is Speaking? The Use of Isaiah 8:17–18 in

shown in Hebrews to have a prophetic ministry. For Christians reading the Scriptures, this text is another reminder that we should be reading the OT prophets looking for Christ, not simply the prophets' pronouncements about Christ and his kingdom, but in addition, the prophets' personal actions and statements about themselves.

2:14–15 *Since therefore the children have shared in blood and flesh, he also likewise partook of the same [things] in order through death*[176]*to destroy the one having power of death, that is, the devil, and to release these, as many as through all of life*[177] *by fear of death were subject to slavery.*

As noted above, Hebrews 2:14–15 restates the thesis, Hebrews 2:10–11, but with more specificity. Christ's humanity involves an actual body to match his sons' bodies and his suffering involves death to destroy death. The **therefore** only looks back generally to Hebrews 2:10–13 with the verbal connection being 'children' in Hebrews 2:13. The main grammatical structure of Hebrews 2:14–15 is that Christ **partook of the same things in order through death [1] to destroy ... the one having power of death ... and [2] to release these**, the children.

To re-emphasize that Christ is connected to his people, the AH points out that **since therefore the children have shared in blood and flesh, he also likewise partook of the same things**. The AH is explicit here about Christ's human nature. Christ had/has **blood and flesh**, that is, **the same things**.[178] In

---

Hebrews 2:13 as a Case Study for Applying the Speech of Key OT Figures to Christ,' *JETS* 59 (2016): 731–45.

176. 'Death' here and in the following phrase both have the article, which is common in Greek. In English, the definite article is often dropped, as in my translation and virtually all other English translations.

177. The expression διὰ παντὸς τοῦ ζῆν is woodenly translated 'through all [things] to live'.

178. All early Greek manuscripts have the order 'blood and flesh'. Some very late manuscripts, including Stephanus' edition (1550), have the reverse. The order 'blood and flesh' is also in Eph. 6:12. I see no importance to the order.

context, obviously the **blood and flesh** relate to the **children**, who **have shared in blood and flesh**, but also relates to **through death**, as Christ had to be human to die (cf. Heb. 9:12–14; 10:19–20). That Christ **partook** implies a choice by him that further implies pre-existence before the incarnation.[179]

The expression **through death** harkens back to Hebrews 2:9. It applies to both verbs **to destroy** and **to release** and is the instrument that accomplishes both.

Of course, there are many purposes for which Christ became human. The AH indicates here two purposes. The first is **to destroy the one having power of death, that is, the devil** (cf. Heb. 11:28). In what sense does the **devil**, that is Satan, possess the **power of death**? This **power** relates initially to the Garden events (Gen. 3) where Satan encouraged Adam and Eve to rebel against God.[180] It works itself through sin into many facets of this evil age (cf. 2 Cor. 4:4; Gal. 1:4; Eph. 2:2; Col. 1:13; 1 John 3:12; 5:19; Rev. 12:9; 11:15). Although Satan is not completely powerless yet, Christ **through death** has irreversibly **destroy[ed]** Satan's power, which will be completely destroyed at the consummation (Heb. 10:11–14; 1 John 3:8). Of course, never in any age was Satan's **power of death** absolute over God's (Job 1–2; Zech. 3:1–2).[181]

Christ's victory to **destroy** Satan and his power evokes

---

179. So also Brown, *Hebrews*, 123; and Hughes, *Hebrews*, 111.

180. As compared with the OT, there are many Second Temple Judaism and Rabbinic references to Satan and his power. For a good, brief summary of Second Temple Judaism references, see D. G. Reid, 'Satan, Devil,' *DPL*, 862–67, esp. 862–63. For examples specifically related to the Garden, Wis. 1:13–14 and 2:21–24 explicitly blame Satan for bringing death into the world. 'God created man for incorruption ... but through the devil's envy death entered the world' (Wis. 2:23–24). In Life of Adam and Eve 12–17, Satan tells Adam that he deceived Eve because previously Michael required Satan to honor/worship Adam, which Satan refused to do. In t. Sotah 4:17, Satan 'wanted to slay Adam and to marry Eve'. Satan is called the 'angel of death' in Mekilta Bahodesh 9 and b. Baba Batra 16a.

181. For an excellent discussion of 'Messiah's victory over Satan, the accuser,' see Kelly, *The Beauty of Christ*, 67–70; 401–02.

Genesis 3:15 where the seed of Eve will bruise Satan's head (cf. Rom. 16:20). Satan caused man to fall, but by a man, the God-man, Satan will again fall—but with no Covenant of Grace to save him.[182] Although not explicitly stated, another reason Christ had to be **blood and flesh** is to fulfill Genesis 3:15 that Eve's *human* seed would overcome Satan.

The second purpose for which Christ died is **to release these, as many as through all of life by fear of death were subject to slavery.** The negative side was to defeat Satan; the positive side is to **release** believers from the **fear of death**. The AH assumes that all of humanity outside of Christ is, or at least should be, in **fear of death**, which is a form of **slavery**.[183] However, because of Christ's death for believers, they are **release[d]** from this **fear**, and of course, also from the reality of negative consequences at death, or as John Owen wonderfully put it in his book title, *The Death of Death in the Death of Christ*.[184] Death and its final triumph has been killed by Christ. Once seeing our true end in the new heavens and new earth, Chrysostom commented about this verse, 'Let us stand then nobly, laughing death to scorn.'[185]

---

182. Augustine, 'It belonged also to the justice and goodness of the Creator, that the devil should be conquered by the same rational creature which he rejoiced to have conquered, and by one that came from that same race which, by the corruption of its origin through one, he held altogether' (*On the Trinity* 13.17 [*NPNF*[1] 3:180]). See discussion in Brakel, *The Christian's Reasonable Service*, 1:451–52. Note that the Heidelberg Catechism 1 and WLC 52 both reference Heb. 2:14 related to being delivered from the power of the devil.

183. At first glance, one might guess that the verb **to release** (ἀπαλλάσσω) would be often used with a **slavery** metaphor. However, it is not so. See LSJ, 176.

184. Get the copy with Packer's essay, John Owen, *The Death of Death in the Death of Christ: with an Introductory Essay by J. I. Packer* (Carlisle: Banner of Truth, 1959 [1648]).

185. 'Homily 4 on Hebrews' (*NPNF*[1], 14:385). See Calvin's discussion noting that Christ also had to conquer this fear as he went to the cross (*Institutes* 2.16.11).

2:16 *For surely he*[186] *does not take hold of angels, but he takes hold of [the] seed of Abraham.*

For surely gives the sense of a parenthesis in the argument, and the content indicates such.[187] **Angels** are brought back into the argument. They have not been mentioned since Hebrews 2:9. Here they are used as a foil compared to believers, **the seed of Abraham**. The comparison is used to heighten the sense of what Christ has done for believers as mentioned in Hebrews 2:14–15. Christ has taken on human flesh, died, defeated death and the devil; and he has *only* done this for believers, not **angels**.

The **seed of Abraham** refers to all true believers, both OT and NT.[188] This provides yet another synonym for whom Christ died in Hebrews 2:10–18: 'sons,' 'those being sanctified,' 'brothers,' 'children,' 'people,' and 'those being tempted.'

I translated the Greek verb ἐπιλαμβάνομαι as **takes hold of**, which is a minimalistic translation. Overwhelmingly, this verb is used simply at the literal level, e.g., Genesis 5:26; Judges 16:21; Matthew 14:31; Acts 9:27; and Hebrews 8:9. The few metaphorical uses include Jeremiah 44:23 (LXX 51:23); Sirach 4:11; Luke 20:20; and 1 Timothy 6:12.[189] As shown by my above exegesis, I interpret **takes hold of** in the sense of taking hold to *aid* the **seed of Abraham**. Possibly the metaphor

---

186. Michael E. Gudorf interprets the 'he' as 'it', referring back to the 'fear of death'. Hence, he translates the verse as 'For it (the fear of death) clearly does not seize angels, but it does indeed take hold of the seed of Abraham.' He bases this off Greco-Roman sources where one seizes something that one fears ('Through a Classical Lens: Hebrews 2:16,' *JBL* 119 [2000]: 105–8, esp. 108). This is a very idiosyncratic interpretation.

187. So also Moffatt, *Hebrews*, 36; Lane, *Hebrews 1–8*, 63; Attridge, *Hebrews*, 94. *Contra* Vanhoye who sees Heb. 2:16 as a conclusion to the section (*Structure and Message of the Epistle of Hebrews*, 24).

188. Based on Gen. 17:9, the exact expression **seed of Abraham** is found here and in 2 Chr. 20:7; Ps. 105:6; Isa. 41:8; Jer. 33:26; John 8:33, 37; Rom. 9:7; 11:1; Gal. 3:29 (3 Macc. 6:3; Pss. Sol. 9:9; 18:3); cf. Gen 22:17; Rom. 4:13, 16; Gal. 3:16; Heb. 11:11, 18.

189. BDAG, 374; LSJ, 642; Silva, ed., 'λαμβάνω,' *NIDNTTE*, 3:79–85, esp. 83.

is related to 'Christ' being the 'leader' from Hebrews 2:10 and bringing believers along.[190] Whether the 'leader' angle is included or not, the vast majority of modern translations and commentaries opt for my 'aid' interpretation, usually translating as 'help'.[191]

In church history, a more common interpretation was that Christ **takes hold of** *human nature* as opposed to angelic nature.[192] Of course, it is theologically true that Christ does this, as has been clearly shown in Hebrews 2:14 and most likely also in Hebrews 2:11. It is also true that one way Christ helps believers is by taking on their nature. However, arguments against the 'nature' interpretation here are (1) the present tense of the verb does not match the initial incarnation (see past tense in Heb. 2:14, 'partook') and (2) interpreting **seed of Abraham** as the nature of *Christ* denies that the text indicates that Christ grasps believers themselves.[193]

2:17–18 *Wherefore*[194] *he had to be made like his brothers according to all [things]*[195] *in order that he might become a merciful and faithful*

---

190. So also Attridge, *Hebrews*, 94.

191. So , e.g., NKJV, NASB, NIV, NRSV, ESV, CEB, Brown, *Hebrews*, 131; Bruce, *Hebrews*, 87, 78n56; Koester, *Hebrews*, 232. Note, the verb βοηθέω in Heb. 2:18, commonly translated 'help', is a different word.

192. So, e.g., Tyndale, Geneva Bible, KJV, Chrysostom, 'Homily 5 on Hebrews' (**NPNF**[1], 14:389); Ambrose, *Of the Christian Faith* 3.11 (*NPNF*[2], 10:255); Aquinas, *Hebrews*, 71; Owen, *Hebrews*, 19:455–58; Brakel, *The Christian's Reasonable Service*, 504–5; Hughes, *Hebrews*, 118; WSC 22; WLC 39.

193. For a longer discussion rejecting the 'nature' interpretation, some of which I disagree, see Ellingworth, *Hebrews*, 176–77.

194. Greek is ὅθεν. Sometimes it is translated 'from whence'. In addition, it probably originally made an implication based on an antecedent *place* or what happened at an antecedent *place* (e.g., 1 John 2:18); thus, it would often be translated '*wherefore*'. But it also came to be used more generically as 'for which reason', or 'therefore' unrelated to *place*—just like 'wherefore' did in English. See LSJ, 1200; and Robertson, *A Grammar of the Greek New Testament*, 300. The AH uses ὅθεν more than any other NT writer (2:17; 7:25; 8:3; 9:18; 11:19). For consistency and for the reader to get a feel for the AH's language, I will translate ὅθεν as 'wherefore' throughout this commentary. The older standard translations also use 'wherefore' (Tyndale, Geneva Bible, KJV).

195. I take πάντα as an accusative plural neuter and thus translate as 'all

high priest [concerning] the [things] toward God, to propitiate the sins of the people. For by which he himself has suffered being tempted, he is able to help those being tempted.

Hebrews 2:17–18 is the third statement more or less making the same point as Hebrews 2:10–11 and 2:14–15—Christ became human for the salvation of his people. However, Hebrews 2:17–18 adds for the first time that Christ is a **high priest**, which ends this long section (Heb. 1:5–2:18) and prepares for the next sections.

The expression **he had to be made like his brothers according to all things** by itself is a grand statement of Christ's humanity.[196] The contrast between Christ's divinity and supremacy in Hebrews 1:5–14 and this statement is breathtaking, as it has been also in Hebrews 2:10–11 and 2:14–15. From the general context of Hebrews 2:10–18, the **all things** includes primarily his human body and undergoing suffering. Of course, Hebrews 4:15 qualifies the **all things** by adding 'without sin.'

In the immediate context of this verse, the reason for Christ's humanity is to qualify him to be a **high priest**. An OT high priest represents his people, and is a mediator between God and his fellow Israelites. The theme of **high priest** will dominate large portions of the book (see discussion at Hebrews 4:15), and 'mediator' will also be included (Heb. 8:6; 9:15; 12:24; cf. Heb. 5:1). Christ as **high priest** is qualified as a **merciful and faithful** one. The adjective **merciful** (ἐλεήμων) is only used in the NT here and in the beatitudes (Matt. 5:7); however, it has special prominence in the OT due to its translation of 'gracious' (חנון) in the important description of God Almighty in Exodus 34:6 and all the verses related to this verse (e.g., Neh. 9:17; 2 Chr. 30:9; Pss. 86:15; 145:8; Joel 2:13).

---

things'. In form, it could also be an accusative singular masculine and be translated as 'every way'.

196. G. C. Berkouwer comments about Christ's humanity, 'One can characterize his entire life with the words: "It behooved him in all things to be made like unto his brethren" (Heb. 2:17)' (*The Person of Christ*, trans. John Vriend, Studies in Dogmatics [Grand Rapids: Eerdmans, 1954], 209).

This word, **merciful**, whether intentional or not by the AH, beautifully brings together the divine and human natures of Christ. The adjective **faithful** is picked up in Hebrews 3:2.[197]

The job of the OT priest **concern[s] the things toward God**.[198] More specifically here, Christ's work as **high priest** was **to propitiate the sins of the people**. As I interpret it, the implied object of the verb **propitiate** (ἱλάσκομαι) or 'appease' is the Father. The phrase **the sins of the people** is an accusative of respect. That is, Christ by his death propitiated/appeased the Father in respect to the sins of the people.[199] The necessity of Christ's death for the sins of the people and the OT cultic context both implicitly argue that the wrath of God must be propitiated.

Given the death and suffering of Christ (**for**), he endured these situations that were, among other things, occasions for his **being tempted**. In an understanding manner (**by which**), Christ **is able to help those being tempted**. (For a discussion on **tempted**, see Heb. 4:15.) In addition to dying for our sins, Christ also **help[s]** believers as they are tempted in a multitude

---

197. Although I do not agree, Vanhoye sees **merciful and faithful** as intentional to the outline of Hebrews; **faithful** relates to Heb. 3:4–14 and **merciful** to Heb. 4:15–5:10 (*Structure and Message of the Epistle to the Hebrews*, 24–26; so also Lane, *Hebrews* 1–8, 64–65).

198. This exact expression, τὰ πρὸς τὸν θεόν, is also in Heb. 5:1 and Rom. 15:17. See also Exod. 4:16; 18:19; and Deut. 31:27. After evaluating numerous examples of this phrase in Greek literature, Andrie du Toit concludes that in Hebrews the phrase means 'cultic service before God' ('Τὰ πρὸς τὸν θεόν in Romans and Hebrews: Towards Understanding an Enigmatic Phrase,' *ZNW* 101 [2010]: 241–51, esp. 249).

199. So also Owen, *Hebrews*, 19:474–77; Hughes, *Hebrews*, 121, 121 nn. 122, 123; and Simon J. Kistemaker, 'Atonement in Hebrews,' in *The Glory of the Atonement: Biblical, Historical & Practical Perspectives: Essays in Honor of Roger Nicole*, ed. Charles E. Hill and Frank A. James III (Downers Grove: InterVarsity, 2004): 163–75, esp. 165–67. Others disagree and see only expiation (removal of sin), e.g., Attridge, *Hebrews*, 96 n. 192; and Bruce, *Hebrews*, 78–79n59. Still others see both propitiation and expiation, e.g., Koester, *Hebrews*, 233. Concerning the accusative of respect, see Wallace, *Greek Grammar Beyond the Basics*, 203–4. Concerning the NT scholarly battle over propitiation and expiation, see Roger R. Nicole, 'C. H. Dodd and the Doctrine of Propitiation,' *WTJ* 17 (1955): 117–57.

of ways. In the context of the book, this particular aspect of Christ's work is highlighted as the AH encourages the readers to 'hold fast our confession' (Heb. 4:14) and not be tempted to let go of Christ.

Reflections
I offer two quotes from the fourth century AD to encourage us to love Christ even more.

The Nicene Creed (AD 325) has the wonderful line, 'who [Christ] for us and for our salvation came down from heaven and was incarnate.' Why did Christ become and remain man? The Creed answers, 'for us and for our salvation.'

Gregory of Nazianzus (AD 330–390) was arguing against those who believed Christ had a human body, but not a human mind/soul (Apollinarianism). He concluded correctly that Christ must have a human mind/soul 'for that which [Christ] has not assumed he has not healed.'[200] That is, Christ had to become *fully* human to save his brothers, who are fully human. Although Gregory did not explicitly say in context, I assume that he was significantly influenced by 'he had to be made like his brothers according to all things' (Heb. 2:17).

---

200. Gregory of Nazianzus, *Epistle 101* (*NPNF*[2], 7:440). WLC 37 affirms that Christ has a 'body' and a 'reasonable [rational] soul', which opposes Apollinarianism.

3.
Son Superior to Moses (3:1–6)

Hebrews 3:1–6 is clearly a coherent section. It indicates that Christ, the Son, is superior to Moses. The AH connects this section backwards. In the previous much-longer section, Hebrews 1:5–2:18, he also argued that the Son is superior, but to angels. In addition, the phrase 'faithful high priest' in Hebrews 2:17 is related to Hebrews 3:1–2. In this section, the AH also looks forward. The theme of 'high priest' will be emphasized in Hebrews 4:14–5:11. Also, Hebrews 3:6 ends with an implicit imperative to 'hold fast'; this could easily be taken as the theme of Hebrews 3:7–4:13.[1]

At first glance, one may wonder why it is necessary to show that the Son is superior to Moses since it has already been shown that the Son is superior to angels. Are not angels above Moses? Well, yes and no. Yes, angels are certainly above humans in several senses, and Hebrews 2:5–9 discusses this. But no, one could argue that Moses is in some ways above angels because God gave the law to him and angels were only intermediaries (Exod. 34; Acts 7:38, 53; Gal 3:19; Heb. 2:2).[2]

---

1. Lane calls Heb. 3:6b a 'hinge-passage' (*Hebrews 1–8*, 72). Moffatt goes further; he separates Heb. 3:6b from 3:1–6a and connects it explicitly with 3:7–19 (*Hebrews*, 43–44).

2. So also Kistemaker, *Hebrews*, 83.

Clearly, during the Second Temple Period, Moses was highly esteemed and maybe too highly esteemed (e.g., Testament of Moses; Philo's Life of Moses; Sir. 45:1–5; Josephus, *Against Apion*, 2:168; John 5:45). However, it does not appear that the AH assumes his readers have an incorrect estimation of Moses. In fact, the AH refers to Moses by name eleven times with no negative comments.[3] So why is the Moses section after the angels section? My best *guess* is that since the AH is interested in the pattern of the Son both having continuity with the OT and being decidedly better than the OT (i.e., contrast within continuity), he uses Moses here to enforce that pattern. Hence, his later discussions of the limitations of Moses' writings and covenant will be in the context of a positive attitude toward Moses and his being 'faithful' (Heb. 3:2, 5).

In Hebrews, the author tends to include both clear doctrinal sections and hortatory sections. However, Hebrews 3:1–6 is a mixture.[4] Hebrews 3:2b–6a is the Moses/Son comparison that begins in an explicit hortatory manner 'consider the apostle and high priest' (Heb. 3:1) and ends with an implicit imperative to 'hold fast' (Heb. 3:6).

My outline of the pericope is as follows:[5]

1–2a: Consider Jesus who was faithful
2b: Similar to Moses who was also faithful
3a: But Jesus has more glory than Moses
3b–4: More glory as a builder of a house than the house itself
5–6a: And Jesus was more faithful as a son over a house than a servant in it
6b: We are the house if we hold fast

---

3. For an in depth discussion of Moses in Hebrews, see Mary Rose D'Angelo, *Moses in the Letter of Hebrews*, SBLDS 42 (Missoula: Scholars, 1979).

4. Theodoret of Cyrrhus, 'He mingles exhortation with the comparison' (Erik M. Heen and Philip D. W. Krey, eds., *Hebrews*, ACCS NT 10 [Downers Grove: InterVarsity, 2005], 51).

5. Commentators generally agree to the same outline excepting whether to consider Heb 3:4 a parenthesis or not. For a detailed discussion of the options, see Lane, *Hebrews 1–8*, 71–74.

As will be discussed below, the AH clearly alludes to Numbers 12:7 in Hebrews 3:2 and virtually quotes it in Hebrews 3:5. Although I am not convinced, in addition to Numbers 12:7, other OT texts have been suggested as being intentional allusions by the AH. These include Zechariah 6:12–15, 1 Samuel 2:35; and 1 Chronicles 17:14.[6]

3:1–2a *Wherefore, holy brothers, companions of a heavenly calling, consider the apostle and high priest of our confession, Jesus*[7]*; who was faithful to the one who appointed him ...*

The AH uses **wherefore** probably to connect back to 'faithful high priest' in Hebrews 2:17, or less likely, to connect back to the broad comparison of the Son's superiority over angels and now over Moses. The readers are addressed as **holy brothers, companions of a heavenly calling**.[8] Interestingly, the terms **brothers** and **companions** include Jesus in Hebrews 2:9, 11–12, 17; but here, they do not.

The imperative **consider ... Jesus** is the main grammatical clause of Hebrews 3:1–6.[9] The reader is to think deeply about Jesus and the aspects concerning him discussed in this pericope. This then should aid the reader to 'hold fast' (Heb. 3:6b). Aquinas notes that since Jesus is greater than Moses, then Jesus 'ought to be more effectively obeyed' than Moses.[10] This argument would have significant weight with first-century readers who have a high view of Moses but are wavering about Jesus.

Jesus is termed **the apostle and high priest**. The AH will discuss **high priest** in more detail in Hebrews 4:14–5:10. Concerning **apostle**, this is the only place in the NT where

---

6. Zech. 6:12–15, e.g., Hughes, *Hebrews*, 132; both 1 Sam. 2:35 and 1 Chr. 17:14, e.g., D'Angelo, *Moses in the Letter of Hebrews*, 71–92.

7. The 1550 Stephanus Greek text has 'Christ' before Jesus. This is reflected in the Geneva Bible and KJV.

8. The vocative *brothers* is also used in Heb. 3:12; 10:19; and 13:22.

9. The verb *consider* (κατανοέω) is also used in Heb. 10:24 as an imperative (hortatory subjunctive). It is not used elsewhere in Hebrews.

10. Aquinas, *Hebrews*, 75.

Jesus is so designated. At a minimum, **apostle** (ἀπόστολος) means 'the sent one.' Elsewhere, using the cognate verb form (ἀποστέλλω), the NT clearly states that Jesus is the one sent from the Father (e.g., John 3:34; 6:29; 1 John 4:9; cf. Exod. 3:12; Isa. 48:16).

How does being the **apostle**, 'the sent one,' relate to the context of Hebrews 3:1? There is only one article for the two titles. This implies that the AH considers **apostle** and **high priest** as one, coherent unit.[11] Does this simply mean that Jesus is the especially 'sent' **high priest**? My view is 'yes', but others add another aspect. All agree that the Greco-Roman use of ἀπόστολος and later Rabbinic use of שליח ('the sent one') may be for envoy or ambassador.[12] Some then argue based on this that the AH is emphasizing Jesus' proclamation.[13] Others also agree that **apostle** implies proclamation based on previous context in Hebrews (Heb. 1:2; 2:12)[14] or based on Moses being a prophet (Deut. 18:15–19; Acts 3:22–26; Heb. 3:5).[15] The 'proclamation' view would argue that the one article is summarizing Jesus based on his word (**apostle**) and work (**high priest**). As stated above, I prefer simply to see **apostle** here in context emphasizing that Jesus is the especially 'sent' high priest to do the will of God the Father.[16] This is based on (1) the one article that ties **apostle** to **high priest** closely together and (2) no clear rationale to emphasize Jesus as a proclaimer/prophet in this context.

The expression **our confession** grammatically relates to

---

11. For an excellent discussion of one article for two substantives connected by καί, see Wallace, *Greek Grammar Beyond the Basics: An Exegetical Syntax of the New Testament*, 270–90.

12. The noun ἀπόστολος is not in the LXX, and שליח is not in the Hebrew Bible (cf. Ezra 7:14; Dan. 5:24).

13. So Spicq, *Hébreux*, 2:64–65.

14. So Lane, *Hebrews 1–8*, 75.

15. So Allen, *Hebrews*, 239. James Swetnam argues the 'proclamation' view based on seeing the OT high priest proclaiming thanksgivings to God as part of the sacrificial ceremony ('ὁ ἀπόστολος in Hebrews 3,1,' Bib 89 [2008]: 252–62).

16. So also Hughes, *Hebrews*, 127–28.

the apostle and high priest. Primarily **confession** refers to the content of our faith about Jesus, and secondarily it refers to the activity of actually professing it. **Confession** is also used in two other key verses in Hebrews, 4:14 and 10:23, which both also have connections to Hebrews 3:6. See further discussion below in the Reflections section.

The specific emphasis concerning Jesus in Hebrews 3:1–2a is that he was **faithful** to God the Father, which will be expanded in Hebrews 3:5–6a. Jesus did and is doing the covenantal work he was supposed to do. This **faithful** aspect also ties back to Hebrews 2:17 where Jesus is referred to as a 'merciful and faithful high priest' and to Hebrews 2:13 where Jesus has 'trust' in God the Father. Many see this connected to Jesus' being the 'leader and perfecter of faith' in Hebrews 12:2, although I do not.

The one who appointed him refers to God the Father appointing Jesus. **Appointed** is a translation of ποιέω, which is very often translated as 'made'. The **appointed** translation is favored by all modern scholars and modern translations and also older translations such as the Geneva Bible and KJV (but not Tyndale). The **appointed** translation is justified by its use in 1 Samuel 12:6; Mark 3:14; and Acts 2:36. In church history, this verse was often translated as 'made', with the idea of created. The heretical Arians used this as a proof text that Jesus' divine nature was created, and thus Jesus was not fully divine, nor equal to the Father. The orthodox responded that the text referred to the creation of Jesus' human nature.[17]

Jesus' being **faithful** to the work that the Father **appointed** to him dovetails well with the Reformed concept of the covenant of redemption. God the Son was **faithful** to perform the agreed upon requirements of the covenant of redemption made in eternity 'past' with God the Father and the Holy Spirit.[18]

---

17. See Chrysostom, 'Homily 5 on Hebrews' (*NPNF*[1], 14:390); Athanasius, *Four Discourses Against the Arians* 2.14 (*NPNF*[2], 4:348–54); Ambrose, *Of the Christian Faith* 3.11 (*NPNF*[2], 10:254–55); and Aquinas, *Hebrews*, 78.

18. Arthur W. Pink argues from Heb. 3:2 that Jesus' being **faithful** 'presupposes a trust; that is, a pledge that a certain thing shall be done in

3:2b *... as also Moses [was faithful] in his whole house.*

Hebrews 3:2b–6a will make three statements. The first, Hebrews 3:2b, will favorably compare Jesus to Moses. The remaining two, Hebrews 3:3–4 and 3:5–6a, will show that Jesus is superior to Moses.

The emphasis in Hebrews 3:1–2a is that Jesus was 'faithful' to the Father in his work. Similarly, **Moses was faithful** in his work. The life of Moses and his faithfulness is simply assumed.

The wording **in his whole house** parallels Hebrews 3:5 and comes from Numbers 12:7. See discussion at Hebrews 3:5.

Whose **house** is it? The Greek has **his** (αὐτοῦ). To whom does this refer? Three options in context are Moses, Jesus, and God the Father. However, **his** clearly refers to God the Father as it most naturally refers back to the 'the one who appointed' in Hebrews 3:2a and matches the 'my' of Numbers 12:7.[19]

What is the **house**? As does the OT, the AH plays off the variously-related literal and metaphorical understandings of house. They include: 'house' refers to a physical home and a physical temple; 'house' refers to a 'household' or individual family (e.g., Heb. 11:7) or paternal family (e.g., Heb. 8:8), that is, those that live in the house (a metonymy); and finally, 'house' refers to the true people of God (e.g., Heb. 10:21). In this verse, **house** ultimately refers to the OT church that Moses' actions and writings greatly influenced. It is further noted that based on the subsequent logic of Hebrews 3:5–6a, the AH is also emphasizing here that Moses was **in** and part of the **house**.

3:3–4 *For this one has been counted worthy of more glory than Moses, in as much as the one who builds it has more honor than the*

---

accordance with the directions given him' (*The Divine Covenants* [Grand Rapids: Baker, 1973], 20). For a classic description of the covenant of redemption, see *The Sum of Saving Knowledge* 2.1–3, which is conveniently found in *Westminster Confession of Faith* (Glasgow: Free Presbyterian Publications, 1994), 321–43, esp. 324. For more discussion, see Heb. 7:20–22.

19. Several English translations insert 'God's,' e.g., NIV, ESV, NRSV, CEB. The NASB uses 'His.'

house[20] *[itself]. For every house is built by someone, but the one who builds all [things] is God.*

Moses had significant glory, especially considering the glory shining from his face from his meeting with God (Exod. 34:29–35; 2 Cor. 3:7, 13). But **this one,** Jesus, **has been counted worthy of more glory than Moses.** In the Greek text, **more** is emphasized.[21] One aspect of the **more glory** is an analogy between the **one who builds** a house and **the house itself.** This analogy works on two levels. The surface level is that the architect/contractor who designs and constructs the house is worthy of **more honor** than the physical house itself. The deeper level is that Jesus is the **one who builds** the house, the people of God, and Moses is only a part of the **house itself.**[22] Calvin notes that although Jesus as our brother is part of the house, here he is portrayed as our Lord.[23] In fact as the **one who builds,** Jesus' divine nature and pre-incarnate existence is emphasized. Jesus built the **house** that contains *both* the OT and NT people of God.

The translation for Hebrews 3:4 is straightforward, **For every house is built by someone, but the one who builds all things is God.** All agree that the Hebrews 3:4a is proverbial about a physical house. However, there is disagreement on the interpretation of Hebrews 3:4b, especially how it relates to Hebrews 3:3.

If one takes **God** to refer to God the Son (cf. Heb. 1:8), one

---

20. Most, including me, take the Greek τοῦ οἴκου as a genitive of comparison. Hence, the translation is '*than* the house'. For a discussion of genitives of comparison, see Wallace, *Greek Grammar Beyond the Basics,* 110–12.

21. **More** (πλείονος) is the first word in Heb. 3:3 even though it is describing **glory,** which is the fourth word in the sentence. The second use of **more** in Heb. 3:3 is not grammatically emphasized.

22. Commentators in agreement that the builder is Jesus include Aquinas, *Hebrews,* 78 (with reference to Prov. 9:1); Owen, *Hebrews,* 19:532–33; Hughes, *Hebrews,* 132 (with reference to Zech. 6:12–13); Ellingworth, *Hebrews,* 205; and Schreiner, *Hebrews,* 115.

23. Calvin, *Hebrews and 1 & 2 Peter,* 35.

usually also takes **all things** to refer to all things relative to the **house**, the people of God. This option then well connects Hebrews 3:3 and 3:4 because in both Jesus is the **one who builds** and his divine nature is enforced.[24]

If one takes **God** to refer to God the Father, **all things** refers to all of creation.[25] For this option, the relationship between 3:4 and 3:3 produces several sub-options. Sub-option (a): Jesus' glory in being over a house is greater than Moses in the same way that God the Father's glory in building the universe is greater than the creation itself.[26] Sub-option (b): Since God the Father is the builder of everything there is a connection and unity between him and God the Son's building of the church.[27] Sub-option (b) is my view. My primary justification is that Hebrews 1:2–3 indicate that the Father and Son are both involved in creation. Hence, Hebrews 3:4 reinforces that since God the Father is over the **house** as the divine creator is over everything, God the Son who is connected to God the Father in creator activities, is also divinely over and the divine builder of the **house**.[28]

3:5–6a *And, on-the-one-hand,*[29] *Moses was faithful in his whole house as a servant for a testimony of the things that were to be*

---

24. This is Owen's view. He also has an excellent discussion of various other options (*Hebrews*, 19:533–56).

25. Belgic Confession 12 references Heb. 3:4 as referring to creation. In context, this is referring to the Father creating by the Son.

26. So Lane, *Hebrews 1–8*, 77.

27. So Kistemaker, *Hebrews*, 86.

28. An additional justification to this view is to connect the Father and the Messiah as interrelated builders of the **house** to the Davidic covenant. There are many verbal connections between 2 Samuel 7 // 1 Chronicles 17 and 1 Samuel 2:35 with the wording in Hebrews 3:1–6 (cf. Heb. 1:5). See D'Angelo, *Moses in the Letter of Hebrews*, 65–93; and Guthrie, 'Hebrews,' 919–95, esp. 952. I do not believe that the AH was intentionally alluding to the Davidic covenant here because (1) Moses is primarily in view and (2) Jesus' divine nature related to his being creator adequately explains Hebrews 3:4 and its relationship to Hebrews 3:3.

29. My translation of **on-the-one-hand** and **but-on-the-other-hand** reflects the μὲν ... δέ construction.

spoken [later]; but-on-the-other-hand, Christ [is faithful] as a son over his house;

And (καί) connects back to Hebrews 3:3–4 and refers to the second aspect of Jesus' being superior to Moses.[30] The continuity between **Moses** and **Christ** is that both were **faithful**, which reintroduces that theme from Hebrews 3:2.[31] The contrast that shows the superiority of Christ has two elements: (1) Christ is a **son**, and Moses was a **servant**; (2) Christ is **over** the house, and Moses was **in** and part of it.

The expression **Moses was faithful in his** (the Father's) **house as a servant** is virtually a quote from Numbers 12:7. In context of Numbers 12, Miriam and Aaron have questioned Moses' choice of his Cushite wife and whether God speaks through Moses in a special way. God himself defends Moses including that he is greater than other prophets because God does not speak to Moses in dreams but directly. God is quoted saying, 'Not so with my servant Moses, he is faithful in all my house.'[32] In using Numbers 12:7, the AH chooses to refer to a direct quote by God that praises Moses compared to Miriam, Aaron, and prophets.[33] The AH has a very high view of Moses!

Of course, Moses was **faithful** in many things,[34] but here the AH intriguingly notes Moses' faithfulness relative to foreshadowing about Christ. Moses' speaking, writings,

---

30. So also Moffat, *Hebrews*, 43.

31. This is the first time **Christ** is used in Hebrews.

32. In the Hebrew text, the words 'all' (כל) and 'servant' (עבד) are standard. The LXX uses slightly unusual words to translate, ὅλος and θεράπων, respectively. The AH used these LXX words here and nowhere else in Hebrews (ὅλος is used also in Heb. 3:2), which further confirms his intentional use of Num. 12:7. The change by the AH from 'my' (in both the Hebrew and LXX) to **his** is easily explained by noting that Num. 12:7 is a direct quote from God and Hebrews 3:5 is referring to the incident.

33. In an argument among the Rabbis as to whether Moses sinned in Num. 11:23, Simeon ben Yohai argues Moses did not sin and uses Num. 12:7 as proof of Moses' impeccable character (t. Sotah 6:7).

34. The OT presents Moses as having mediatorial role(s). Christ is explicitly said to be a mediator in Hebrews 8:6; 9:15; and 12:24. In Hebrews, Moses is implicitly viewed as a mediator (Heb. 3:3–5; 9:19–20).

and the tabernacle itself were all **a testimony of the things that were to be spoken later** about Christ and by Christ (cf. Heb. 1:1–2; 8:5; 9:9, 23; 10:1; Acts 7:44). The theme of contrast-within-continuity is well shown here.

Given the AH's high view of Moses, this magnifies Christ even more. **Christ is faithful as a son over his** (Father's) **house.** As noted above, **Christ** exceeds Moses because he is (1) a **son** and (2) **over** the house (also Heb. 10:21). In one significant sense, Christ *is* a servant. But here his kingly office with respect to the Church is shown by his being a **son over** the **house.**[35]

Similar to Hebrews 3:2b, the NT Greek text has **his** (αὐτοῦ) in reference to **house**. Does **his** refer to God the Father or God the Son as both are involved in building the **house** (Heb. 3:3–4)? I opt for God the Father because of (1) the 'my' of 'my house' in Numbers 12:7 most likely refers to God the Father and (2) Hebrews 10:21 'a great priest over the house of God' strongly implies that Christ is over the house of God the Father.[36]

3:6b ... *whose house we are if indeed we hold fast the confidence and the boast of the hope.*[37]

Believers are the **house** of the Father (cf. Heb. 10:21; Gal. 6:10; Eph. 2:19; 1 Pet. 2:5). They are to have **confidence**, that is, boldness in their belief and actions relative to Christ.[38] Also, believers are to have the **boast of the hope**. Here **hope** is

---

35. So also Owen, *Hebrews*, 19:557.

36. Several older English translations explicitly refer to God the Son, e.g., Geneva Bible, KJV, and Douay-Rheims. Several newer translations explicitly refer to God the Father, e.g., RSV, NIV, ESV, and CEB.

37. Several major Greek manuscripts add 'firm until the end'. This is reflected in the KJV. Metzger argues that this phrase is not original because it is 'probable' that it is an 'interpolation from Hebrews 3:14' (*TCGNT*², 595).

38. **Confidence** (παρρησία) is also in Hebrews 4:16; 10:19; and 10:35. The Roman Catholic tradition in the liturgy encourages the congregants to say the Lord's prayer with 'confidence' (παρρησία). The Catechism of the Catholic Church defines παρρησία as 'straightforward simplicity, filial trust, joyous assurance, humble boldness, the certainty of being loved' (§2778).

not the act of hoping, but the content of the hope about Christ including the 'end game' of our faith, the New Heavens and Earth.[39] They are to **boast** in the best sense of the word, both inwardly and occasionally publicly.

Believers are part of the church **if indeed we hold fast**.[40] **If** could be used as a *condition* or as a *description* (i.e., statement of fact).[41] As a *condition*, the AH would be saying that some are currently believers but would no longer be believers if they did not hold fast to their faith. That is, holding fast is a true condition or cause that results in their continuing in the **house**.[42] This seems to deny that Christ and the Father are the infallible builders of the true **house** unless one simply assumes that the **house** does not include specific individuals.[43] As a *description*, the AH would be saying that for one to be denominated or accurately 'described' as being part of the **house** now, one would by definition **hold fast** till the end. Or to say it simply, true believers persevere to the end. This 'description' view assumes that the AH realizes that (1) some in the visible church are not truly part of the **house** now

---

39. Schreiner agrees about content of **hope** (*Hebrews*, 119). **Hope** is an objective genitive.

40. **Hold fast** (κατέχω) is also used in Hebrews 3:14 and 10:23.

41. I am using Owen's terms (*Hebrews*, 19:560–62). In more modern technical terms, 'condition' would match to if-cause-then-effect, and 'description' would match to 'if-evidence-then-inference.' An example of the latter would be, 'If you pick up those barbells, you are strong.' Picking up the barbells did not make or 'cause' you to be strong, it was the 'inference' from the fact or 'evidence' of your strength that you picked them up. See Wallace's discussion of various types of 'if' clauses, *Greek Grammar Beyond the Basics*, 682–83. Buist M. Fanning argues that Hebrews 3:6b and 3:14 are 'evidence to inference' grammatical structures. See his excellent article for NT examples of this type of construction ('A Classical Reformed View,' in *Four Views on the Warning Passages in Hebrews*, ed. Herbert W. Bateman IV [Grand Rapids: Kregel Academic & Professional, 2007], 172–219, esp. 206–16).

42. So many in the broad Arminian and Roman Catholic traditions, e.g., deSilva, *Hebrews*, 140n13, 150–51; and Johnson, *Hebrews*, 110.

43. Allen states, 'The author addressed the community as a whole ("*we* are his house") and did not speak in an individual manner' (*Hebrews*, 248–49, emphasis his).

as some will not hold on to the end, and (2) that one aid to preserve true believers is to warn them. The *description* view is my view.[44]

For the true believer, the **if indeed we hold fast** description is implicitly an imperative, which conceptually connects to the explicit imperative 'consider' in Hebrews 3:1. To **hold fast** is the warning that we need, and using that warning, the AH is confident that true believers will persevere to the end. May all readers of this commentary **hold fast** and so prove true that they are part of the glorious **house** now and forever more.

Reflections

We are to 'consider' Jesus of our *'confession'* (Heb. 3:1). As mentioned above, our 'confession' primarily refers to the content of our faith about Jesus, and secondarily it refers to the activity of actually professing it. This well matches 'holding fast the confidence and boast of hope' (Heb. 3:6). This 'confidence' or boldness in belief (and actions) and content of 'hope' also relate to the content of faith and our occasionally proclaiming it to others. All that to say, having a 'confession' about Jesus and thinking upon it is an aid to our loving him more and our final perseverance. Also there should be a joy or 'boast' in our confession.

In context of Hebrews 3:1–6, what would this 'confession' involve? Jesus is 'the apostle and high priest', 'faithful' to the work that the Father 'appointed to him', the divine 'one who builds' the OT and NT church, 'over' the church, 'Son,' and having 'more glory than Moses.'

Through the ages, the church has developed corporate confessions and creeds. These confessions have some level of authority, similar to the authority that teachers and elders have in the church. To be clear, confessions do *not* have ultimate authority and are *not* infallible—this is true only

---

[44]. So also Owen, *Hebrews*, 19:561–62; Brown, *Hebrews*, 168; Bruce, *Hebrews*, 94; Fanning, 'A Classical Reformed View,' 206–7; Schreiner, *Hebrews*, 119 and Andrew J. Wilson, 'Hebrews 3:6B and 3:14 Revisited,' *TynBul* 62 (2011): 247–67, esp. 258–62.

of the Bible. Further, these confessions are useful only in as much as they accurate summarize the Word of God.[45] To say it another way, the Bible is the ultimate standard and (good!) confessions/creeds/catechisms are secondary standards.[46]

There are many uses of corporate creeds.[47] At least two uses are suggested by Hebrews 3:1–6. Confessions should be used to aid Christians in thinking about Jesus (and other issues) to increase their personal sanctification.[48] Also, confessions should be used as a tool for publicly professing our faith within worship services ('*our* confession,' Heb. 3:1).

Related to Jesus' being the 'one who builds' the church and is 'over' the church, 'consider,' meditate, and 'boast' upon the following first thesis from the Ten Theses of Berne (AD 1528): 'The holy catholic church, whose sole head is Christ, has been begotten from the Word of God, in which also it continues, nor does it listen to the voice of any stranger.'[49] Amen and Amen.

---

45. See Second Helvetic Confession 2.

46. For a recent well-nuanced discussion of *sola Scriptura* as being compatible with the use of creeds in a '*ministerial* role,' see Barrett, *God's Word Alone: The Authority of Scripture: What the Reformers Taught ... and Why It Still Matters*, 23 (emphasis his), 45–75.

47. For two classic 19th-century Presbyterian statements, see Samuel Miller, *The Utility and Importance of Creeds and Confessions* (Princeton: Borrenstein, 1824); and James Bannerman, *The Church of Christ: A Treatise on the Nature, Powers, Ordinances, Discipline, and Government of the Christian Church* (Carlisle: Banner of Truth, 2015 [1869], 291–338. Carl R. Trueman argues that the Bible requires that the church develop some type of creeds (summaries of the Bible) to be able to evaluate church members and teachers (*The Creedal Imperative* [Wheaton: Crossway, 2012], 66–80).

48. B. B. Warfield discusses various options for what seminary students should read for their personal spiritual growth. He covers and broadly recommends many types of literature. However, he concludes, 'But I have reserved for the last mention a class of religious literature which, for my own part, I esteem the very highest of all for spiritual impression. I refer to the great Creeds of the Church. He who wishes to grow strong in his religious life, let him, I say, next to the Bible, feed himself on the great Creeds of the Church' ('Spiritual Culture in the Seminary,' in *Selected Shorter Writings of Benjamin B. Warfield*, ed. John E. Meeter, 2 vols. [Phillipsburg: P&R, 1970, 1973], 2:468–96, esp. 492).

49. *Reformed Confessions of the 16th and 17th Centuries*, 1:41.

4.
Rest
(3:7–4:13)

Hebrews 3:7–4:13 is clearly one large unit related to Psalm 95:7–11. This large unit begins with a quote of Psalm 95:7–11 // Hebrews 3:7–11 and then continues with three subunits expositing various aspects of the Psalm. The subunits are Hebrews 3:12–19; 4:1–10; and 4:11–13.[1]

The large unit is clearly tied back to Hebrews 3:6b where the readers are encouraged to 'hold fast' to Christ. Conceptually, this is linked to Hebrews 3:7–4:13 as it also encourages the readers to persevere in the Gospel. Directly following this large unit, in Hebrews 4:14–16, several key words from 3:1–6 will reappear ('high priest,' 'hold fast,' 'confession,' 'confidence'). The connections of the pericopes directly before and after Hebrews 3:7–4:13 further confirm it is a coherent unit.

How does Hebrews 3:7–4:13 fit into the whole of Hebrews? It is one of the exhortation ('warning') passages that also includes 2:1–4; 4:14–16; 5:11–6:12; 10:19–39; and 12:1–13:17.

Before getting to the commentary proper, I alert the reader to three issues related to Hebrews 3:7–4:13: (1) the AH's intriguing dual hermeneutical-use of Psalm 95, (2) the AH's

---

1. So also Vanhoye, *Structure and Message of the Epistle of Hebrews*, 83–86. However, Vanhoye more closely ties 3:1–6 to 3:7–4:13 than I do. Also, he puts 4:11 with 4:1–10, and has 4:12–13 as a subunit.

use of the redemptive-historical timeline, and (3) the debated meaning of 'rest'.

Intriguingly, the AH uses Psalm 95 hermeneutically in two ways.[2] First, he uses it as a moral example or what is termed, 'exemplary exegesis.' The disobedience of the Israelites in the wilderness is a negative 'example' for what his readers should not do. They should not turn their hearts away from God like the wilderness generation did. Second, the AH sees the 'rest' in Psalm 95 as typologically related to the 'rest' connected to heaven. In sum, for the NT believer, Psalm 95 has both *exemplary* aspects and *typological* aspects.[3] These aspects will be fleshed out below in the commentary proper.

Another interesting hermeneutical angle in Hebrews 3:7–4:13 is the AH's use of the redemptive-historical timeline of Scripture. Including us as modern readers, six points on the line can be discerned. Here I will name the six. The AH's use of the timeline and implications for us will be made in the commentary proper. The six are as follows: (1) God's resting on the seventh day (Gen. 2), which is related, at least partially, to creation in the past; (2) Moses and the wilderness generation (1450 BC); (3) David's writing of Psalm 95 (1000 BC); (4) the AH and his readers (AD 65); (5) modern readers (XXI AD); and (6) New Heavens and New Earth (future eternity).

The AH wants his readers to enter the true 'rest'. The meaning of 'rest' in Hebrews 3:7–4:11 has been debated by scholars for centuries. I will present here a brief summary of the three basic views so that my readers do not have to wait until the key verses of Hebrews 4:3 and 4:9–10 to understand the options more fully and critically evaluate my view as I present it in the commentary proper.

There are three basic scholarly views concerning 'rest'

---

2. So also Owen, *Hebrews*, 20:5.

3. Leonhard Goppelt more-or-less combines these two for 3:1–4:13. See his section entitled 'God's Rule over Israel as a Type that Warns and Strengthens the Church' (*Typos: The Typological Interpretation of the Old Testament in the New*, trans. Donald H. Madvig [Eugene: Wipf and Stock, 2002 {1939}], 170–75, esp. 170]).

in Hebrews (not in the whole Bible). (1) 'Rest' is obtained upon initially putting one's faith in Christ, that is, is a *present* (*'existential'*) *reality* for the NT believer. Many times, this is combined with the view that the rest will continue into heaven, but the emphasis is on the present rest. This view often sees the believer's resting from 'works' (Heb. 4:10) as meaning the believer has stopped attempting to merit salvation by works. Hebrews 4:3 is stressed.[4]

(2) Although 'rest' begins upon putting one's faith in Christ in this life (Heb. 4:3), the *main emphasis is on the 'location' of the future heavenly rest,* where the believer will have existential rest (Heb. 4:9–10). The believer's resting from 'works' refers to the good works of this life and/or resting from the difficulties of this life, but some also include resting from sinful works. This view argues that it does take into account both Hebrews 4:3 and 4:9–10 and the now/not-yet structure of NT eschatology.[5]

---

4. So, e.g., Calvin, *Hebrews and 1 & 2 Peter*, 47–49; David Dickson, *A Short Explanation of the Epistle to the Hebrews* (Birmingham, AL: Solid Ground Christian, 2005 [1635]), 20–21; Owen, *Hebrews*, 20:254–58, 326–33 (although Owen does not see 'works' as the attempt to justify oneself); Kistemaker, *Hebrews*, 107–14; Ray C. Stedman, *Hebrews*, IVPNTC (Downers Grove: InterVarsity, 1992), 56–59; and Kleinig, *Hebrews*, 217–18. Cf. Matt. 11:28–30.

5. So, e.g., Turretin, *Institutes of Elenctic Theology*, 2:78–79, includes sinful works; Brown, *Hebrews*, 208, includes sinful works; William Gouge, *Commentary on Hebrews: Exegetical and Expository*, 2 vols. (Birmingham: AL: Solid Ground Christian, 2005 [1655]), 1:292, 299, 316–18; C. K. Barrett, 'The Eschatology of the Epistle of Hebrews,' in *The Background of the New Testament and Its Theology*, ed. W D. Davies and D. Daube (Cambridge, CUP, 1956), 363–93, esp. 372–73; Moffatt, *Hebrews*, 51–53; Attridge, *Hebrews*, 126–28; Lane, *Hebrews 1–8*, 99–102; A. T. Lincoln, 'Sabbath, Rest, and Eschatology in the New Testament,' in *From Sabbath to Lord's Day: A Biblical, Historical, and Theological Investigation*, ed. D. A. Carson (Eugene: Wipf and Stock, 1999), 197–220, esp. 210–13, includes sinful works; Herold Weiss, 'Sabbatismos in the Epistle of Hebrews,' *CBQ* 58 (1996): 674–89, esp. 685–87; Allen, *Hebrews*, 293; Mitchell, *Hebrews*, 96; Phillips, *Hebrews*, 125–26; and Schreiner, *Hebrews*, 136–38. The Gnostic tract Gospel of Truth has a significant emphasis on 'rest' that includes an existential aspect in this life along with a future location of rest (see Judith Hoch Wray, *Rest as a Theological Metaphor in the Epistle of Hebrews and the Gospel of Truth: Early Christian Homiletics of Rest*, SBLDS 166 [Atlanta: Scholars Press, 1998] 95–140).

(3) 'Rest' is a *location, solely future and eschatological*. It is a heavenly rest that is primarily a location, but it provides existential rest. The believer's resting from 'works' refers to good works in this life and/or resting from difficulties in this life. This view argues that the overall contextual point of Hebrews 3:7–4:11 concerning perseverance, the typology of wilderness and promised land, the summarizing verses of Hebrews 4:9–10, and the 'sabbath-rest' related to God (Heb. 4:4, 9) all argue for a solely future rest. This view includes that Hebrews 4:3, properly understood, does not refer to the present.[6] This third understanding of 'rest' is my view. Detailed exegesis and defense of this will be provided below.

Rest—Quote of Psalm 95 (3:7–11)

Hebrews 3:7–11 includes an introductory comment (Heb. 3:7a) and a quote of Psalm 95:7d–11 (Heb. 3:7b–11).

3:7a *So then,[7] just as the Holy Spirit says,*

So then clearly refers back to the encouragement and warning from Hebrews 3:6b to 'hold fast' to Christ and persevere to the end as this shows that one is part of 'God's house.' Because this is true that believers need to persevere, **so**

---

6. So, e.g., Brakel, *The Christian's Reasonable Service*, 3:176–78; Bruce, *Hebrews*, 110; Koester, *Hebrews*, 286; Richard B. Gaffin, Jr., 'A Sabbath Rest Still Awaits the People of God,' in *Pressing toward the Mark: Essays Commemorating Fifty Years of the Orthodox Presbyterian Church*, ed. Charles G. Dennison and Richard C. Gamble (Philadelphia: Committee for the Historian of the Orthodox Presbyterian Church, 1986), 33–51, esp. 41–43; John M. Frame, *The Doctrine of the Christian Life* (Phillipsburg: P&R, 2008), 558–60; Jon Laansma, 'I Will Give You Rest': *The Rest Motif in the New Testament with Special Reference to Mt 11 and Heb 3-4*, WUNT 2:98 [Tübingen: Mohr Siebeck, 1997], 277–83; Ellingworth, *Hebrews*, 246; G. K. Beale, *A New Testament Biblical Theology: The Unfolding of the Old Testament in the New* (Grand Rapids: Baker Academic, 2011), 782–89; and Gareth Lee Cockerill, *The Epistle of Hebrews*, NICNT (Grand Rapids: Eerdmans, 2012), 63–64, 197–200, 210. Cf. Rev. 14:13; 4 Ezra 7:75; 8:52; Barn. 15:3–9; 2 Clem. 5:5; 6:7; m. Tamid 7:4.

7. Here for the first of nine times, the AH uses the inferential conjunction διό. For purposes of consistency, I will translate διό as 'so then', οὖν as 'therefore', and ὅθεν as 'wherefore'.

then Psalm 95:7d–11 was written to make the same point.[8] Of course, Psalm 95 uses a negative example to make the point.

Later in Hebrews 4:7, the AH refers to David as the author of Psalm 95. But here the **Holy Spirit** is the author in the sense of divine inspiration (cf. Heb. 9:8; 10:15–17; m. Sotah 9:6).[9] Another angle of interest here is that a large part of the quote (Ps. 95:8–11) is actually a quote of God speaking, and further within this quote, God quotes himself . Hence, we have several levels of authorship at least for Psalm 95:8–11, God (the Father or Godhead) at two levels, the **Holy Spirit**, and David. Finally, in Hebrews 4:12, Psalm 95 is clearly included in the general 'word of God' reference. All this shows Trinitarian and deity assumptions about the **Holy Spirit**.[10]

In addition to the **Holy Spirit's** original authorship of Psalm 95, based on the present tense of **says** and 'today', there is also a dynamic manner in which the **Holy Spirit** speaks through the Scripture as a believer reads the Scripture.[11]

3:7b–11 *'Today, if you hear his voice, "Do not harden your hearts as in the provocation on the day of testing in the wilderness, where your fathers tested me*[12] *with trial and saw my works for forty years. So then I was grieved with that*[13] *generation and said, '"They always*

---

8. Some see an additional connection to Heb. 3:1–6 based on the Son-greater-than-Moses comparison. If Moses' generation was punished for not persevering, how much more so will those who deny Christ. So Owen, *Hebrews*, 20:3; Bruce, *Hebrews*, 99; and Schreiner, *Hebrews*, 121.

9. So also Bruce, *Hebrews*, 95 n. 23. Martin Emmrich disagrees. He sees the **Holy Spirit** here being referenced as to original authorship. Heb. 3:7; 9:8; and 10:15–17 refer to the Holy Spirit's prophetic role in 'revealing of interpretative secrets' about Christ to the NT community ('Pneuma in Hebrews: Prophet and Interpreter,' *WTJ* 63 [2002]: 55–71, esp. 71).

10. So also Schreiner, *Hebrews*, 121.

11. Hence, the emphasis on 'word and Spirit' in the Westminster Standards, e.g., WCF 1.5, 8.8, WLC 43, WSC 24, 89.

12. Some ancient manuscripts do not have 'me' (με), although I believe it is the original reading. It is explicitly included in the Hebrew but not in the LXX. If not original, it is clearly implied.

13. Some manuscripts have 'this', and some 'that'. The Hebrew has neither, and the LXX 'that'. Peter E. Enns sees 'this' as the original

stray in [their] heart; and they did not know my ways.'" As[14] *I swore in my wrath, '" They shall not*[15] *enter my rest.'"'"*

Hebrews 3:7b–11 is a quote of Psalm 95:7d–11.[16] Psalm 95 is an invitation to worship God (Ps. 95:1, 2, 6).[17] The first part (Ps. 95:1–7c) is joyous, and praises God as king over both creation and redemption. However, the second part (Ps. 95:7d–11), which the AH quotes, is a warning to worshipers.[18] Simply being outwardly connected to the covenant community is not enough. One must love God from the **heart** and follow his **ways**.

---

reading and an intentional change of the LXX by the AH to make the point that his audience is the 'generation with which God is ultimately concerned' ('Creation and Re-Creation: Psalm 95 and its Interpretation in Hebrews 3:1-4:13,' *WTJ* 55 [1993]: 255–80, esp. 276).

14. **As** (ὡς) here has meaning of 'so that' (BDAG, 1105).

15. An explicit 'not' is missing in the Hebrew and LXX of Ps. 95:11 // Heb. 3:11. Hebrew has an odd construction for oaths where 'if' (אִם) acts as a strong negative, e.g., Num. 14:23, Ps. 89:35. The 'if' is probably short hand for the oath formula 'Let me not be God if they should enter.' See GKC §149; and P. Joüon and T. Muraoka, *A Grammar of Biblical Hebrew*, 2nd ed., Subsidia Biblica 27 (Rome: G&BP, 2016), §165a, d. The LXX and the AH follow this and simply translate with the Greek 'if' (εἰ), which in this context would also be a strong negative. See T. Muraoka, *A Syntax of Septuagint Greek* (Leuven: Peeters, 2016), 766; and Turner, *Syntax*, 333.

16. There are minimal differences between the Hebrew text and the LXX of Ps. 95:7d–11; none of which results in a change of meaning. However, in Ps. 95:8, there is an interesting translation question for מריבה ('Meribah' or 'provocation') and מסה ('Massah' or 'testing'). The Hebrew could be taken as either a proper noun (e.g., Geneva, NIV, ESV) or as a rhetorical 'the provocation' and 'the testing' (e.g., KJV). The LXX has the rhetorical option, as does the Targum and the NT. The AH quotes the LXX very closely with only one minor change. The AH inserted a 'so' after 'forty years'. This resulted in 'forty years' being taken with 'my works'. In the Hebrew (although not the MT) and LXX, it is ambiguous as whether 'forty years' grammatically goes with 'my works' or with 'I was grieved'. Of course, conceptually, this does not matter as both are related to the forty years in the wilderness.

17. In various Christian liturgical traditions, Ps. 95 has been used for the morning service.

18. Kidner quips, '[The Psalm's] austere conclusion balances the exuberant opening' (*Psalms 73-150*, 343).

David warns his audience with the use of negative example(s) of Israel's disobedience in the **wilderness**. Although not completely clear, David is probably especially referring to three situations: the two incidents at Meribah/Massah where Israel tests God as to the provision of water (Exod. 17:1–7, Num. 20:1–13) [19] and the grumbling of Israel at the spies' report (Num. 13:25–14:38).[20] David quotes God's oath that those disobedient Israelites **shall not enter my rest**.[21] With this, David is exhorting his audience not to imitate their **fathers** by only outwardly being connected to the covenant community's God. Instead, love him fully.

Surprisingly, Psalm 95:11 uses **rest** where one would expect 'land'. There are two interesting aspects to this. First, clearly God's **wrath** upon the first wilderness generation is that the vast majority will not enter the physical land of Canaan (e.g., Num. 14:22–23); however, instead of explicitly using 'land', David uses **rest**. There will be rest for Israel upon entering the promised land—the difficult journey is finished and they will partake of the land of milk and honey. On the other hand, this parallel of land/rest is not so unusual as several times the OT relates 'land' and 'rest' (Gen. 49:15; Deut. 12:9–10; Josh. 1:13; 21:43–44;1 Kgs. 8:56; Ps. 132:14). The second interesting aspect is that David and his readers are

---

19. There are two similar incidents. The first is Exod. 17:1–7 where Moses strikes the rock to provide water for the complaining Israelites who are testing God. The second is Num. 20:1–13 where again Israel is complaining and testing God about the lack of water. Moses is instructed by God to speak to the rock, but instead he strikes it. Cf. Num. 20:24; 27:14; 32:7–13; Deut. 1:19–35; 32:51; 33:8; Pss. 78:40–42; 81:7; 106:24–26, 32–33; Neh. 9:15–17; CD 3:6–9; 4 Ezra 7:106.

20. There are several linguistic parallels between Ps. 95 and Num. 14:20–23, 28–30.

21. Rabbis disagreed as to whether this Ps. 95 oath related to the wilderness generation not entering the land or not entering the world to come. Arguments in favor of restricting the wrath to only the physical land was that (1) **today** implies that tomorrow some Jews could do more works to merit entering the world to come and (2) also **today** implies that tomorrow God can retract his oath (t. Sanhedrin 13:10–12).

actually in the land of Canaan as he implores them that **today** they may enter God's **rest**. Hence, David is clearly using **rest** to mean more than physical land (cf. Heb. 4:7). The promised land for David was typological of something greater than simply physical rest in Canaan.[22]

See the next three subunits for the AH's use of Psalm 95:7d–11.

Reflections

The AH introduces the quote of Psalm 95 with 'the Holy Spirit says' (Heb. 3:7). Among other audiences, the Holy Spirit was speaking to the AH's NT audience. Referring to this introduction, Aquinas noted, 'For the Spirit Himself alleges that the words of the Old Testament are for the sake of the New.'[23]

Long after Psalm 95 was written, the Triune God in the person of the Holy Spirit speaks to present believers through Psalm 95 as well as all of Scripture. Traditional Christians have always had this 'high' view of Scripture. It is verses like Hebrews 3:7 that confirm this view.

What an authoritative word Christians have! The Holy Spirit himself speaks! This should embolden us to resist the world's calling to follow 'experts' that intentionally contradict the Bible.

'Jesus was just a man.'

'No,' we respond, 'the *Holy Spirit* says he was/is also the eternal "Son of God"' (Heb. 4:14).

'Don't base your life on a god that does not exist.'

'Should I believe you or the *Holy Spirit* who says that there is a "living God"' (Heb. 3:12)?

---

22. In the OT, 'rest' is also used in conjunction with God's temple/sanctuary (e.g., Ps. 132:8; 1 Kgs. 8:56; Isa. 66:1; Targum Ps. 95:11; cf. Exod. 33:14). Probably also seeing a broader use of **rest**, some Rabbis interpreted **today, if you will obey his voice** (Ps. 95:7) as hastening the coming of the Messiah (b. Sanhedrin 98a) and the **forty years** (Ps. 95:10) as the length of time of the Messiah (b. Sanhedrin 99a).

23. Aquinas, *Hebrews*, 82.

'You don't actually believe that blood is required for forgiveness; after all, you live in the twenty-first century.'

'Well, I understand your comment, but almighty God through the *Holy Spirit* says, "without the shedding of blood there is no forgiveness" (Heb. 9:22). I intend no disrespect, but the *Holy Spirit* speaking through the Scripture, not you, is the ultimate authority.'

Rest—Do Not Harden Your Hearts (3:12–19)

The AH quotes Psalm 95:7d–11 // Hebrews 3:7b–11 and follows this with three subunits related to the quote. The first subunit is Hebrews 3:12–19. This subunit may be further subdivided into (1) a negative and a positive exhortation about one's heart (Heb. 3:12–13); (2) a parenthesis concerning Christ and perseverance (Heb. 3:14); and (3) wilderness examples as exhortations about one's heart (Heb. 3:15–19).

3:12–13 *See[24] [to it], brothers, lest there be in any of you an evil heart of unbelief, which is[25] to depart from the living God, but exhort one another every day while it is called 'today' in order that none of you are hardened by the deception of sin.*

Given that David warned his audience, 'do not harden your hearts' (Heb. 3:8), using the example of the wilderness generation, the AH similarly warns and exhorts his. First, he uses a 'negative' exhortation. **See to it**, that is, make sure that you and those in the congregation do not have **an evil heart of unbelief**.

As occurs often in Scripture, the **heart** is here related to **evil** (e.g., 1 Sam. 17:28; Ps. 140:2; Prov. 26:23; Jer. 3:17;

---

24. The imperative 'see' (βλέπετε) is a mechanical translation (also in Heb. 12:25 as an imperative). The sense is more 'watch out'. Note that this subunit ends with a slightly different nuance of 'see' in Hebrews 3:19.

25. I am taking the construction ἐν τῷ ἀποστῆναι to be a contemporaneous infinitive that metaphorically becomes an epexegetical clause (i.e., 'while at the same time' becomes 'that is the same as'. So also BDF §404.3; and Lane, *Hebrews*, 82. Wallace does not agree and sees this as an unusual result clause (*Greek Grammar Beyond the Basics*, 593n12).

16:12; Matt. 15:19). The **heart** is also related to **unbelief** (cf. Num. 14:11), which will be further emphasized in Hebrews 3:19.[26] In Hebrews 3:12, **unbelief** is not a minor wavering of assurance, but a full rebellion that is defined as **to depart from the living God**. This 'heart' departure in the Hebrews' context results initially in one going through the motions at Christian worship and continues toward a cessation of attendance or attending only a Jewish synagogue. The verb **to depart** (ἀποστῆναι) is etymologically related to the theological term 'apostasy'. Apostasy is the falling away or departing from the covenant community, which matches this use of the verb in Hebrews 3:12.

After the above negative exhortation, the AH gives a positive exhortation to protect against apostasy, **exhort one another every day**. Although the AH will later reference leaders who teach (Heb. 13:7), here he enjoins all the congregation to care about others by encouraging each other often (**every day**!) to trust Christ (cf. Heb. 10:24–25). Thus, correctly so, Hebrews 3:13 is often referenced in Christian literature as to the duties and benefits of *all* Christians to spiritually help and be helped by each other—it is not just the minister's role.[27]

The AH references the word **today** from Psalm 95:7d (Heb. 3:7b) in his phrase **while it is called 'today.'** By doing this, the AH adds another 'logic' to continue to encourage others so they will not commit apostasy. The logic is that, excepting death, it is never too late to truly call upon the Lord (cf. Isa. 49:8; John 9:4; 12:35; 2 Cor. 6:2). The AH notices that David said, 'today if you hear his voice.' That implies that anytime one hears God's voice in any form—worship service, Bible reading, a friend's statement about Christ—one is able to heed the warning and trust Christ. The notes in the Geneva Bible well comment, 'He [AH] shows by this word

---

26. WLC 105 includes 'unbelief' as a sin forbidden by the first commandment and references Heb. 3:12.

27. E.g., Turretin, *Institutes of Elenctic Theology*, 3:220; London Baptist Confession 27.2; Frame, *Systematic Theology*, 1039.

"today" that we must not neglect the occasion while we have it: for that word is not to be restrained to David's time, but it comprehends all that time wherein God calls us.'[28]

The phrase **hardened by the deception of sin** is related to the Psalm 95 quote 'do not harden your hearts' (Ps. 95:8 // Heb. 3:8). Note the use of **harden** in both, and that **deception of sin** parallels 'hearts'. Thus, in Hebrews 3:12–13, **sin**, **evil**, and **unbelief** are connected to the **heart** of an unbeliever.

3:14 *For we have become partakers of Christ if indeed we firmly hold fast the beginning of [our] assurance*[29] *until the end.*

This verse is a parenthesis of sorts within Hebrews 3:12–19 because 3:15–19 will pick up again the 3:12–13 theme of not hardening one's heart.[30] The **for** marks that Hebrews 3:14 will make explicit the implicit thought of Hebrews 3:12–13—to be explicit, one's belief is related to Christ and a true believer will persevere.

Should μέτοχοι be understood as **partakers** or 'companions'?[31] If **partakers** or 'those who share in', which is my view, this would relate to a believer's union-with-Christ through faith and all the resultant benefits, similar to Paul's 'in Christ' and 'head'/'body' statements and John's 'vine'/'branch' statements.[32] If 'companions', this would not

---

28. *Geneva Bible: 1602 Edition*, folio 110, updated spelling mine. Also see the heartwarming final chapter in the Bohemian Confession (AD 1573) 20 entitled 'Of the Time of Grace,' which references Heb. 3:13 (*Reformed Confessions of the 16th and 17th Centuries*, 386–389). The Catechism of the Catholic Church connects 'Today' to anytime the mass is offered (§1165).

29. I chose to translate ὑπόστασις as the believer's subjective **assurance** in Christ (e.g., KJV, NASB, NIV, ESV) as opposed to the objective 'reality' or 'substance' of Christ himself (e.g., Tyndale, Geneva, NAB).

30. So also Brown, *Hebrews*, 186; Moffat, *Hebrews*, 48; and Attridge, *Hebrews*, 117.

31. I take μέτοχοι as **partakers** or the sharing-in idea in Heb. 3:14; 6:4; and 12:8; 'companions' in Heb. 1:9 and 3:1.

32. So also Chrysostom, 'Homily 6 on Hebrews' (*NPNF*[1], 14:394); Owen, *Hebrews*, 143; Bruce, *Hebrews*, 101; Attridge, *Hebrews*, 118; Geneva Bible, KJV, NIV, and ESV. An additional twist on this view is to see this connected to the sacraments, so Aquinas, *Hebrews*, 89; and Hughes, *Hebrews*, 150.

be as strong a statement, but it would emphasize the many 'inheritance' benefits of being Christ's friend (e.g., Heb. 9:15).[33] The translation **partakers** best connects to the belief emphasis of Heb. 3:12, and as I will show below, better matches to the 'house' parallel of Heb. 3:6b.

Note the parallel between Hebrews 3:6b and 3:14:

> 3:6b whose Father's house we are
>
> 3:14 **we have become partakers of Christ**
>
> 3:6b if indeed we hold fast the confidence and the boast of the hope
>
> 3:14 **if indeed we firmly hold fast the beginning of our assurance until the end**

The union-with-Christ theme of **partakers of Christ** is reasonably paralleled by believers' being the 'Father's house.' There is an intimate connection to God in both. The 'if' clauses are quite parallel. Both have the verb **hold fast**, and both are emphasizing that a true believer's faith ('confidence'// **assurance**) will persevere **until the end**. As in Hebrews 3:6, the **if** clause should be interpreted as a *description* of a true Christian—that is, a true Christian is defined by one who perseveres.[34] The **if** here is *not* the *condition* to continue as a true Christian—that is, a true Christian stops being a Christian when he does not persevere. See extended discussion at 3:6.

3:15 *While it is said, 'Today if you hear my voice, do not harden your hearts as in the provocation.'*

Focusing on **while it is said**, Calvin notes, 'God never makes an end of speaking.'[35]

---

33. So also Spicq, *Hébreux*, 2:77; Koester, *Hebrews*, 260; NAB, NRSV, and CEB.

34. The Formula of Concord, Solid Declaration 4 quotes Heb. 3:14 to disprove the 'false Epicurean delusion' that a Christian cannot lose his salvation no matter his sin. That is, **if** is a condition. On the other hand, the section balances this comment by also noting that admonitions to good works should be done 'without obscuring the doctrine of faith and teaching of justification'.

35. Calvin, *Hebrews and 1& 2 Peter*, 42.

With Hebrews 3:14 as a parenthesis, 3:15 reconnects back to 3:13 by re-introducing the quote from Psalm 95:8 // Hebrews 3:8. Hence, **today if you hear my voice** connects to the 'today' of 3:13, and **do not harden your hearts** connects to 'none of you are hardened by the deception of sin' of 3:13.

Hebrews 3:15 also looks forward. **As in the provocation** sets up Hebrews 3:16–18 and its use of the wilderness generation as negative examples.

3:16–18 *For who having heard provoked? But was it not all those who came out of Egypt by Moses? And with whom he was grieved for forty years? Was it not those having sinned, of whom the corpses fell in the wilderness? And to whom did he swear to not enter his rest, but to those having disobeyed?*

As noted above, David is probably especially referring to three incidents in the wilderness (Exod. 17:1–7; Num. 13:25–14:38; 20:1–13), and generally, so is the AH.[36]

In Hebrews 3:16–18, the AH exhibits an elevated writing style. Concerning the wilderness generation, he uses a series of three parallel questions and gives his answers as rhetorical questions. His intention is (1) to eliminate possible excuses from those who cling to the false assurance of simply being outwardly connected to a covenant community and (2) to enforce the gravity of their situation. Paul similarly uses the wilderness generation as an example to dissuade those from using the sacraments as false assurance (1 Cor. 10:1–13).

In addition to seeing God's actions, the wilderness generation also **heard** God's voice, either directly or through Moses (cf. Heb. 4:2). David's generation also **heard** (Heb. 3:7), and the AH's readers have **heard** (e.g., Heb. 1:1–2; 4:2). Yet, the wilderness generation **provoked** God.[37] This generation is

---

36. Laansma concludes that the AH used linguistic and conceptual ideas primarily from Num. 14 for Hebrews 3:7–4:11 ('*I Will Give You Rest*', 262–64).

37. The verb **provoked** (παραπικραίνω) is the cognate of the noun 'provocation' (παραπικρασμός, Ps. 95:8; Heb. 3:8, 15). The verb is also used in

also described as **all those who came out of Egypt by Moses**. Obviously, the AH is speaking generally as not all without exception **provoked** God (e.g., Num. 14:30–31; Jer. 31:2).

The wilderness generation also **grieved** God for **forty years** (Heb. 3:9). They were **those having sinned**, which parallels the AH's comment to his readers not to be 'hardened by the deception of sin' (Heb. 3:13). The wording of **the corpses fell in the wilderness** comes from Numbers 14:29, 32 (cf. 1 Cor. 10:5) and is a grim reminder to the readers of the gravity of apostasy.

Paralleling the climax of Psalm 95:11 // Hebrews 3:11, the AH's final rhetorical question is, **To whom did he** (God) **swear to not enter his rest**? **Rest** for the wilderness generation is Canaan, but the AH is using it typologically, as is David, to mean more than that. The wilderness generation is here described as **those having disobeyed**.[38]

3:19 *And [so][39] we see that they were unable to enter on account of unbelief.*

The AH is clearly summarizing in Hebrews 3:19, which concludes 3:15–19. In addition, with the use of **see** and **unbelief**, Hebrews 3:19 connects back to 3:12 and concludes the larger subunit of 3:12–19.

Although the AH uses many words to describe the wilderness generation, here he summarizes them as having **unbelief** (also in Num 14:11, cf. Jude 5). The wilderness

---

Ps. 106:7 in a similar context.

38. The verb **disobeyed** (ἀπειθέω) is used in Deut. 1:26 related to the wilderness generation. Also related to the wilderness generation is the substantival adjective cognate ('disobedient one,' ἀπειθής) in Num. 20:10. Within Hebrews, the verb is used here and in Heb. 11:31. The noun 'disobedience' (ἀπείθεια) is used in Heb. 4:6, 11. Matthew D. Jensen argues the minority view that this word group throughout the NT is more properly translated as 'unpersuaded', which is closer to the actual etymology (α ['not'] plus πείθω ['to persuade']) ('Some Unpersuasive Glosses: The Meaning of ἀπείθεια, ἀπειθέω, ἀπειθής in the New Testament,' *JBL* 138 [2019]: 391–412).

39. As in English, the conjunction 'and' (καί) may be used in the sense of a conclusion, thus **and so** (BDF §442.2).

generation included those who disbelieved temporarily (e.g., Num. 20:12) and those who disbelieved in a full apostasy sense. Both groups did not make it to Canaan. The AH applies this failure to reach the earthly promised land to his readers as a warning for them to ensure they will reach the true, heavenly, promised land (cf. Jude 5).[40]

The AH is obviously stressing that his readers should not have **unbelief**. Pink succinctly summarizes the AH's view, 'We are saved by faith; we are lost through unbelief.'[41] Given all the sins that the wilderness generation did, the summarizing sin is **unbelief**. That is, **unbelief** in *Almighty God*, and even more, unbelief in the God who has made a gracious covenant with his people (e.g., land promises of Abrahamic covenant, Gen. 12:1; 15:18; Heb. 11:9).[42] It is to whom this **unbelief** is directed that explains the extreme level of heinousness of this sin.

Reflections

Although the AH uses positive examples from the OT in Hebrews, here in Hebrews 3:7–4:13 he uses the wilderness generation as a negative example.[43] This example is sobering, and the language of 'corpses' (Heb. 3:17) is graphic.

God has designed *all* of the Bible for Christians' edification,

---

40. So also Schreiner, 'The earthly failure of the Israelites is analogous to and typological of the eternal judgment the readers face if they fall away' (*Hebrews*, 131 n. 181).

41. Arthur W. Pink, *An Exposition of Hebrews* (Grand Rapids: Baker, 1954), 186.

42. See J. van Genderen and W. H. Velema for a discussion of whether sin is more (1) fundamentally breaking of God's covenant, (2) unbelief, or (3) disobedience. They conclude that all three are related, but breaking God's covenant is the more fundamental sin (*Concise Reformed Dogmatics*, trans. Gerrit Bilkes and Ed M. van der Mass [Phillipsburg, P&R, 2008], 393–401). The Westminster Standards explicitly connect sin to violating God's law (WCF 6.6, WSC 14, WLC 24) but also note that the first sin was in the context of God's covenant of works (WCF 6.1, 7.2, WSC 12, WLC 20–21). In addition, 'justifying faith' is emphasized (WLC 72).

43. See O. Palmer Robertson's insightful chapter, 'A New People of the Wilderness—The Tension of Life in the Wilderness' in his *God's People in the Wilderness*, 65–80.

among other things. Hence, the corporate Church and we as individuals need negative examples. These warnings are good for us.

God has graced us with all his benefits upon our faith in Christ. Even our faith is a gift. So why these warnings and admonitions, even graphic ones? Does this speak against the doctrine of perseverance? Bavinck, speaking in concert with the Reformed tradition, comments:

> [The admonitions and threats] are rather the way in which God himself confirms his promise and gift through believers. They are the means by which perseverance in life is realized ... It is precisely God's will, by admonition and warning, morally to lead believers to heavenly blessedness and by the grace of the Holy Spirit to prompt them willingly to persevere in faith and love.'[44]

Oh Lord, warn us; if need be, warn us often.

Rest—God's and Ours (4:1–10)

Recall the discussion at the beginning of this commentary chapter concerning the three scholarly views of 'rest'. I am arguing for God's 'rest' being a location that is solely future and eschatological (heavenly). In that location, the believer will have existential rest.

Hebrews 4:1–10 breaks down into two sections that overlap with each section having tight reasoning (note five uses of 'for', two of 'therefore', and one of 'then'). At points this parallels Hebrews 3:12–19, but it does add arguments concerning God's resting on the seventh day of creation, an argument based on Joshua, and that believers will rest from their 'works as God did from his.'

---

44. Bavinck, *Reformed Dogmatics*, 4:267. For significantly more discussion on this topic, see comments at Hebrews 6:4–8.

4:1–2 *Therefore, let us fear, while [the] promise is still open*[45] *to enter into his rest, lest some of you seem to fall short. For indeed we have received good news just as also those, but the word of the hearing*[46] *did not benefit those who upon hearing had not united*[47] *with faith.*

Somewhat paralleling the beginning of Hebrews 3:12 ('see to it, brothers'), the AH again exhorts the readers, and himself, to be concerned about their spiritual state with **let us fear**. He is using **fear** in the sense of 'appropriately concerned given the consequences.' The readers are warned not to **fall short**, that is, make sure you arrive at the future heavenly **rest**. How would the AH know they **f[e]ll short** if the rest is future? Although the rest is future, current unbelief is a sign that some **seem to fall short**.

Positively, the AH notes that no matter the past in his readers' individual lives or in redemptive history, **the promise is still open to enter his** (God's) **rest**. This **promise** as a promise *per se* exists during the AH's lifetime, but also as any promise, its fulfilment is directed toward the future. Here that future element is the future heavenly rest.[48]

Hebrews 4:2 begins with **for indeed** as the AH gives a proof that his readers ought to have appropriate **fear**. Both **we** and those in the wilderness heard the **good news**, that is, both are in the same situation. But only **hearing** this did not **benefit** the wilderness generation because their **hearing** was not in **faith**

---

45. I translated καταλείπω as **still open** following BDAG (521, §4). This participial phrase is a genitive absolute.

46. The **word of the hearing** (ἀκοή) is a report or message. The noun **hearing** is an obvious cognate with the participle **hearing** (ἀκούω) in the same verse.

47. Manuscripts are split between the participle **united** being an accusative plural (thus antecedent **those**) or a nominative singular (thus antecedent **word**). I prefer the accusative plural; however, the overall point is the same no matter the manuscript. Metzger also opts for the accusative plural arguing it 'best explains the origin of the other' readings (*TCGNT*², 595).

48. The term **promise** (ἐπαγγελία) is first used here in Hebrews and will become important later, especially related to the Abrahamic promises (see discussion at Heb. 6:11).

(cf. Heb. 3:12, 19, Rom. 10:17). Hence, the AH argues to **let us fear** to ensure that we have **faith**.[49]

The verb translated **we have received good news** is the passive of the verb often translated elsewhere in the NT as 'to preach the gospel' (e.g., Acts 14:7; Rom. 1:15; 1 Cor. 1:17; 1 Pet. 4:6).[50] In the Hebrews 4:2 (and 4:6) context, the **good news** is related to the **promise**.[51] This refers to both the promised typological rest of Canaan and the promised heavenly rest. Ultimately, this 'gospel' is related to Christ's work and is an aspect of his benefits given to believers (cf. Heb. 3:6, 14; 4:14, Gal. 3:8).

4:3a *For we who believed are entering the rest, just as he has said, 'As I swore in my wrath, "They shall not enter my rest"';*

Since the wilderness generation indicates that one does *not* obtain rest because of unbelief, the AH now proves (**for**) that those who have faith *do* enter. To show this, he first states his thesis that those with faith will enter and then proves it by a quote from Psalm 95:11 (Heb. 3:11).[52] The quote/proof is an argument 'from the opposite'.[53] If God does *not* allow those *without* faith to enter, that indicates that he *does* allow those *with* faith (**who believed**) to enter. Lane insightfully comments that the AH has made a 'tactical shift' from 'warning' to 'a basis of hope and encouragement.'[54]

Does the phrase **we who believed are entering** (εἰσέρχομαι)

---

49. The Westminster Standards properly use Heb. 4:2 as a reference to prove that the **word** must be combined with **faith** to be effective (WCF 21.5, WSC 90, WLC 160).

50. In Hebrews 4:2, the construction is a periphrastic perfect passive (ἐσμεν εὐηγγελισμένοι); cf. Hebrews 4:6. As opposed to εὐαγγελίζομαι referring to the 'Gospel' *per se* about the death and resurrection of Christ, it has a broader use of a 'joyful annunciation' being made to both the wilderness generation and the AH's readers (Brown, *Hebrews*, 203).

51. So also Aquinas, *Hebrews*, 93; Attridge, *Hebrews*, 124–25; Ellingworth, *Hebrews*, 241; and Laansma, *'I Will Give You Rest'*, 278–79.

52. So also Owen, *Hebrews*, 20:254.

53. Calvin, *Hebrews and 1 & 2 Peter*, 47.

54. Lane, *Hebrews 1–8*, 99.

the rest refer to (1) a present rest, (2) a present rest that has a future heavenly component, or (3) a solely future heavenly rest? As noted previously, I opt for the third.⁵⁵ The primary argument for the option #1 is this verse, which is based on the present tense of **are entering**. For option #2, it combines the present tense here and the future of Hebrews 4:8–9. This is connected to the now/not-yet eschatology of the NT.⁵⁶ Concerning the present-tense argument, yes, **are entering** in the present tense could be taken as occurring in present time.⁵⁷ However, because of the future connotation of the semantic nature of 'to enter' and other similar verbs, they often are used in solely a future sense (e.g., Matt. 11:3; John 4:21; 8:14; 1 Cor. 16:5b).⁵⁸ This is similar to English. One might say, 'we who believe in Christ are entering heaven.'⁵⁹ Due to context, 'are entering' clearly means the future.

---

55. For a list of scholars with various views, see the beginning of this chapter in the commentary.

56. So, e.g., Lincoln, 'Sabbath, Rest, and Eschatology in the New Testament,' 211–12; and Weiss, '*Sabbatismos* in the Epistle to the Hebrews,' 685.

57. Schreiner, who opts for an aspect of present rest here, nevertheless warns against making that decision based on the 'significance of the present tense' (*Hebrews*, 136).

58. See BDF section 'The futuristic use of the present' (§323). BDF note that 'ἔρχομαι figures strongly in this usage'. Wallace comments about futuristic presents, 'Most instances involve verbs whose lexical meaning involves anticipation (such as ἔρχομαι, -βαίνω, προεύομαι, etc.). This usage is relatively common' (*Greek Grammar Beyond the Basics*, 535–36). Ellingworth takes the present usage as a rhetorical 'emphatic equivalent of the future tense' (*Hebrews*, 246). Cockerill argues for a 'true continuous present', that is, 'we are entering' but have not actually entered (*Hebrews*, 205). I wonder if there is also an aspect of a gnomic or proverbial present (Wallace, *Greek Grammar Beyond the Basics*, 523–25) — it is a truism that those who believe until the end enter the rest. One problem for the present time view is that most commentators see the entering as having both a present and future aspect. Where does the future aspect come from if one has presently entered? Mitchell solves this by seeing the present tense as having an 'ingressive sense' that 'indicates a present state that will be completed in the future' (*Hebrews*, 97).

59. The English expression 'going to' is technically a present but is clearly used for the future, e.g., 'I am going to study tomorrow.' 'Going to' is interestingly a parallel to the Greek verb translated as 'enter', εἰσέρχομαι. This is more mechanically translated as 'I go to/into'.

What about the now/not-yet eschatology argument? Well, yes, in the NT and in Hebrews there is an aspect of the benefits of salvation now (e.g., Heb. 10:17–18) and future benefits (Heb. 10:13). However, that does not necessarily mean that **rest** here so defined also has this. As Gaffin forcefully points out,

> The entire passage rests on the assumption which is never spelled out: Israel in the wilderness and believers under the new covenant are in analogous situations ... In the NT as well as OT times God's people are pilgrims and travelers; now as then, they are a people "on the way."

Hence, in Hebrews 3:7–4:13, '"today" is the time of the wilderness sojourn' where a believer's faith is emphasized. **Rest** 'stands in pointed contrast to the believer's present circumstances.'[60] See further discussion at Hebrews 4:9–10.

4:3b–5 *although [his] works were finished from the foundation of [the] world, for it*[61] *has said somewhere*[62] *concerning the seventh [day] thus, 'And God rested on the seventh day from all his works.' And again in this [passage], 'They shall not enter my rest.'*

First, some general comments about the Genesis 2:2b quote, **And God rested on the seventh day from all his works.**[63] This

---

60. Gaffin, 'A Sabbath Rest Still Awaits the People of God,' 37–38. So also Robertson, *God's People in the Wilderness*, 66.

61. The perfect verb εἴρηκεν in Heb. 4:3a and 4:4 could be translated as it **has said** or 'he has said'. In 4:3a, 'he' is fairly obvious as it precedes a direct quote by God within Ps. 95. In 4:4, it is preferred because it relates to the Scripture and the passive is used in Heb. 4:7. So also Bruce, *Hebrews*, 107. Of course, there is not much difference between the two as the AH (and I!) considers all of the Bible to be written by God, and Heb. 3:7 prefaced Ps. 95:7–11 with 'the Holy Spirit says'.

62. For **somewhere**, see discussion at Heb. 2:6.

63. The Hebrew matches the LXX except for works being plural in the LXX and a singular collective in the Hebrew. The NT matches the LXX except that the explanatory **God** and **on** have been added. Both of these words are in Gen. 2:2a. As will become important in Heb. 4:9, note that the Hebrew verb for rest/cease is שָׁבַת, a clear cognate of Sabbath (שַׁבָּת). This cannot be seen if one is only at the Greek/LXX level.

comes from the end of the important Genesis 1:1–2:3 passage. God created the world in six days and then rests on the seventh. In addition, God blesses the seventh day and makes it holy (Gen. 2:3). The seventh day (Sabbath), holy, and rest are all also included in the important fourth commandment (Exod. 20:8–11). Confusingly to an English reader, there are two major verbs in Hebrew properly translated 'to rest' (שָׁבַת in Gen. 2:2, 3, and נוח in Exod. 20:11). There are two cognate nouns related to these two verbs, the noun 'sabbath' (שַׁבָּת in Exod. 20:8, 10, 11) and the noun 'rest' (מנוחה in Ps. 95:11). The LXX uses a variety of verbs to translate the two Hebrew verbs, although καταπαύω is used in both Genesis 2:2, 3 and Exodus 20:11 in the LXX and Hebrews 4:4, 7, 10. Further the verb καταπαύω ('to rest') has the obvious connection to the noun κατάπαυσις ('rest') in the Greek of Psalm 95:11 and Hebrews 3:7–4:13. These linguistic factors add to the connection between Genesis 2:1–3 and Psalm 95:11 and will also come into play with 'Sabbath-rest' in Hebrews 4:9.

The connection between Hebrews 4:3b–5 and 4:3a is not clear. I take the concessive **although** to explain the oddity of the connection between God's rest that has already occurred and believers' rest that is future (Heb. 4:10). Hence, the **my** of **my rest** in Hebrews 4:3a is explained in 4:3b–5. That is, **although** God has rested, there is still a future heavenly rest for believers that is connected to God's past, present, and future rest.

To prove (**for**) that God's **works were finished from the foundation of the world** (i.e., God rested in the past), the AH quotes Genesis 2:2b, **God rested on the seventh day from all his works**. This is straightforward. Then, to confirm that this post-creational rest is connected to the rest that God will provide for believers, he quotes **again** from Psalm 95:11 with his emphasis on explaining *my* (God's) **rest**. Yes, believers will rest, but it is properly called *my* **rest** because it is related to God's. Also, God will provide the location and his presence will provide existential rest for the believer. In addition, although the AH will not discuss it here, he will connect God's creational **works** to believers' works in Hebrews 4:10.

Connecting the future rest of believers to God's post-creation rest is another confirmation that there was something more to the promised land than simply earthly land. God worked in earthly creation and then apparently had a heavenly rest. Analogously, believers will work on earth and then experience God's place of heavenly rest. The AH will elaborate on this in Hebrews 4:9–10, as will I.

4:6–7 *Since therefore it remains for some to enter it, and the ones who formerly received good news did not enter on account of disobedience, again he appoints a day, 'today,' saying by David after long time, just as it has been said before, 'Today, if you hear his voice, do not harden your hearts.'*

With **since therefore**, the AH is here re-summarizing and resuming the argument from Hebrews 4:1–2 after the minor digression of 4:3–5.[64]

To re-summarize: The promise **to enter it** (the rest) still stands. And yes, some **who formerly received the good news** (Heb. 4:2) were barred from Canaan because of **disobedience** (Heb. 3:18; 4:11). Following (**again**) this promise of Canaan, at the time of **David**, which is a **long time** after the wilderness event, God (**he**) **appoints** that every **day** is **'today'** to turn in faith to God (Heb. 3:13). The AH previously quoted (**it has been said before**) the OT text that includes **today** to make his point (Ps. 95:7–8 // Heb. 3:7–8; Heb. 3:15).[65]

The purpose of this re-summarizing is to resume the argument to advance to another major point at Hebrews 4:9–10. However, before he gets there, he comments on Joshua.

---

64. So also Ellingworth, *Hebrews*, 250.

65. As opposed to Heb. 3:8 and 3:15, the AH does not include 'as in the rebellion'.

4:8 *For if Joshua gave them rest, he would not have spoken*[66] *concerning another day after these.*

The AH is going to add another argument to prove (**for**) that God's future rest is still available to those who believe. He uses a contrary-to-fact conditional logic.[67] **If Joshua gave them rest**, then there was *no* need for God/David later to mention another rest. However, since in fact *it is not true* that **Joshua gave them rest**, then there *was* a need for David to mention another rest.

To put it in a more straightforward logic, yes, it looks plausible that **Joshua**, who survived the wilderness and brought Israel into Canaan, gave Israel rest (Num. 32:12–13; Josh. 1:1–3; 21:44; 22:4).[68] But the fact that God/David later in redemptive history mentions rest proves that **Joshua** in fact did *not* give them rest. In addition, this shows that although the earthly Canaan provided aspects of rest (Josh. 21:44; 22:4), this was not the eschatological/heavenly rest that Psalm 95 and the AH are speaking about.

Given that **Joshua** is referring primarily to Joshua son of Nun from the OT, did the AH consciously intend his readers to consider implicitly that **Joshua** is typologically related to Jesus Christ?[69] Many answer 'yes'.[70] The surface positive evidence

---

66. It is not clear why the apodosis (then clause) has the imperfect. *Possibly* this is used (as opposed to an aorist) to indicate the continual implications of Ps. 95 to all generations. Hence, I have translated as an English perfect, as have all major translations.

67. The grammar follows the classic contrary-to-fact (second class) conditional-clause format. For slightly different views of contrary-to-fact conditional clauses, see Zerwick, *Biblical Greek*, §§313–14; and Wallace, *Greek Grammar Beyond the Basics*, 689, 694–96. Hebrews has three other contrary-to-fact conditional clauses, Heb. 8:4, 7; 11:15 (7:11?) (BDF §360).

68. Owen (*Hebrews*, 20:319) and Hughes (*Hebrews*, 160) also see the AH refuting the possible objection that Joshua gave Israel rest.

69. Hebrews 13:5 is related to Joshua. There the AH uses him as an exemplar for promises God makes to all believers.

70. So Justin Martyr, *Dialogue with Trypho* 113 (*ANF*, 1:255–56); *Geneva Bible: 1602* Edition, folio 111; Bruce, *Hebrews*, 109; Attridge, *Hebrews*, 130; Allen, *Hebrews*, 280; Schreiner, *Hebrews*, 143; Richard Ounsworth, *Joshua*

is that in both Greek and Hebrew the name 'Joshua' // 'Jesus' is the same name (יהושע, Ἰησοῦς).⁷¹ This would at a minimum make a Greek reader pause as he read Ἰησοῦς—is Jesus Christ or Jesus son of Nun intended? Also, Joshua did lead Israel to some level of rest in Canaan. In addition, some argue that the use of Jesus as 'leader' (ἀρχηγός) in Hebrews 2:10 parallels Joshua as one of the twelve leader-spies (ἀρχηγός) in Numbers 13:2–3.⁷² Finally some interpret Hebrews 4:10 as referring to Christ, which would buttress the Joshua typology here (see discussion at Heb. 4:10).⁷³ First off, I do not agree in substance with the last two arguments. Also, it is hard to believe that the AH who frequently is explicit about typological connections intended to be implicit here. Hence, I do not believe that the AH intended the readers to connect Joshua to Jesus. However, my view of *divine* authorship leads me to conclude that *God* intended believing readers to secondarily consider Joshua as typological of Christ at many points in Scripture, including here. This matches God's intended general Scriptural pattern of presenting various redemptive-historical figures as typological of Christ (Luke 24:27, 44). Or to say it another way, the intention of the human author of Scripture does not exhaust the intention of the divine author of Scripture.⁷⁴

Typology in the New Testament, WUNT 2/328 (Tübingen: Mohr Siebeck, 2012), 55–97; and Bryan J. Whitfield, 'The Three Joshuas of Hebrews 3 and 4,' *Perspectives in Religious Studies* 37 (2010): 21–35. Whitfield sees the AH referring to Joshua from Numbers, Joshua the high priest (Zech. 3:1), and Jesus as Joshua. Cf. Sir. 46:1–8; Barn. 6:9.

71. It is simply an English translation decision to use 'Joshua' in the OT. In the NT, 'Jesus' is used when referring to Jesus Christ and 'Joshua' in three places when not referring to Christ (Luke 3:3 [not Joshua son of Nun]; Acts 7:45; Heb. 4:8). The KJV does not follow this pattern; it has 'Jose' in Luke 3:29, and 'Jesus' in Acts 7:45 and Heb. 4:8.

72. So, e.g., Whitfield, 'The Three Joshuas of Hebrews 3 and 4,' 23–24.

73. So, e.g., Nicholas J. Moore, 'Jesus as "The One who Entered his Rest": The Christological Reading of Hebrews 4:10,' *JSNT* 36 (2014): 383–400, esp. 391–92.

74. For a defense of this view, see Robert J. Cara, 'The Use of the Old Testament in the New Testament: Trusting the New Testament's Hermeneutics,' in *A Biblical-Theological Introduction to the New Testament: The Gospel Realized*, ed. Michael J. Kruger (Wheaton; Crossway, 2016),

4:9–10 *So then a Sabbath-rest remains for the people of God. For the one who has entered his rest also himself rested from his works as God [did] from his.*

With **so then** in Hebrews 4:9, the AH is concluding his argument from Hebrews 4:6a that a rest **remains** (same 'to remain' verb), which is really more broadly concluding his argument from Hebrews 4:1. Hebrews 4:10 explains (**for**) in more detail the **Sabbath-rest** connection.

Throughout Hebrews 3:11–4:11, the Greek for the noun 'rest' is κατάπαυσις. In 4:9, however, the AH uses a different term for the same reality, σαββατισμός, translated **Sabbath-rest**,[75] possibly a term he made up.[76] The nature of this rest is analogous to the best aspects of OT Sabbath rests.[77] It brings to mind worship, praise, meals, celebrations, resting from traditional labors, etc.[78] Also with the use of **Sabbath-rest**, the

---

593–602; and Vern Sheridan Poythress, 'Divine Meaning of Scripture,' *WTJ* 48 (1986): 241–79.

75. Normally, when a μος (σμος for ιζω verbs) ending is attached to a verb to make it a noun, thus a name is given to the action resulting from the verb (similar to a 'tion' ending in English, e.g., creation, purification, construction). See J. H. Moulton and W. F. Howard, *Accidence and Word-Formation*, vol. 2 of *A Grammar of New Testament Greek* (Edinburgh: T&T Clark, 1929), 350–51; and Bruce M. Metzger, *Lexical Aids for Students of New Testament Greek*, new edition (Princeton: Theological Book Agency, 1995), 42–43. If this holds true here, then (σ)μος added to the verb σαββατίζω ('to keep the Sabbath') would result in a Sabbath-type action, which would be a Sabbath-type resting. Kleinig suggests the translation, 'Sabbath celebration,' especially given how the verb σαββατίζω is used in the LXX (e.g., Exod. 16:30; Lev. 23:32; 2 Macc. 6:6) (*Hebrews*, 205).

76. This is the only use of this word in the LXX and NT. Spicq argues it is a *neologism* (*Hébreux*, 2:83–84), and Attridge responds that it is not (*Hebrews*, 131n103). The argument revolves around a textual difficulty in Plutarch.

77. *Contra* Käsemann who connects it to a Gnostic background (*The Wandering People of God*, 87–96).

78. Lev. 23:1–44 connects Sabbath, rest from work, holy convocation, and festivals. Jubilees 50:9–10 strongly connects Sabbath, worship, and festivals. Philo connects 'sacred seventh day' to a 'festival' and 'birthday' (*On the Life of Moses* 2:209–10). Ps. 92's superscription is a 'Song for the Sabbath'. M. Tamid 7:4, while noting the various psalms sung by the Levites in the temple, quotes the superscription and concludes that Ps. 92 is 'a song for the world to come, for the day which is wholly Sabbath rest for eternity'

Genesis 2:2b quote in Hebrews 4:4 is brought back into play. This expands the understanding to connect it to a rest in the heavenly presence of God, and indeed, a rest in covenantal *fellowship* with the Triune God (Heb. 8:10). Intriguingly, both God's creation activity and his redemptive activity are brought together by combining the creation related rest from Genesis 2:2b and the Psalm 95:11 redemptive rest.[79]

As mentioned at the beginning of this commentary chapter, I hold that the **rest** is a future heavenly and eternal one, and this is consistent throughout Hebrews 3:7–4:11. **Sabbath-rest** confirms this as it clearly connects the believers' rest to God's post-creation rest, which is implied to be heavenly and timeless.[80] I interpret **rest** in 4:10 (and throughout this section) as more related to the location of the rest, but includes the quality. **Sabbath-rest**, on the other hand, is emphasizing the quality, but does include the location and time.[81] Laansma concludes that **Sabbath-rest** is 'life for the people of God in God's resting place [that] will be an eternal, festive Sabbath celebration.'[82]

In my view, does this **Sabbath-rest** begin upon a believer's death or at the beginning of the new heavens and new earth (NHNE)? The AH is not clear. Considering the whole Bible

---

(trans. Jacob Neusner, *The Mishnah: A New Translation* [New Haven: Yale University Press, 1988]). The Mekilta also connects Ps. 92 to an eternal Sabbath and adds that the Sabbath holiness of the present world is similar to the holiness in the eternal Sabbath (Shabbata 1). Cf. Heb. 12:22.

79. Enns especially emphasizes this ('Creation and Re-Creation: Psalm 95 and its Interpretation in Hebrews 3:1–4:13,' esp. 278–80).

80. For those who agree, see the list of authors in the footnote at the beginning of this commentary chapter. Several who believe in both a present and future rest in Hebrews 3:7–4:13 do see **Sabbath-rest** as only referring to an eschatological heavenly rest, e.g., Hughes, *Hebrews*, 161; and Lane, *Hebrews 1–8*, 102. For a discussion of Canaan as a type of the future eschatological inheritance, see Patrick Fairbairn, *The Typology of Scripture*, 2 vols. (Grand Rapids: Zondervan, n.d.), 2:3–4. Also see 1:418–20, where he includes a partial 'rest' now.

81. With a slightly different view, Ellingworth sees **Sabbath-rest** as 'temporal' and rest as 'spatial' (*Hebrews*, 255).

82. Laansma, '*I Will Give You Rest*', 277.

there is a sense of rest now for the believer upon putting one's faith in Christ (Matt. 11:29[83]; cf. Exod. 33:14; 1 Kgs. 8:56).[84] Also, when a believer, whether in the OT or NT, dies there is a glorious ushering into the presence of God, which most certainly is restful and heavenly. However, I perceive that the AH is speaking of the ultimate future NHNE in his use of **Sabbath-rest**. The end of Hebrews 4:13 implies the future judgment, which dovetails with this. Hebrews 2:8; 6:2; 9:28; 10:36; 11:10, 16, 19, 35, 40; and 13:14 also hint at the NHNE.[85]

The exact expression **people of God** is fairly rare in Scripture (Judg. 20:2; 2 Sam. 14:13; Heb. 11:25; LXX only 1 Sam.14:45; Esth. 10:3); however, it is easily understood because it is shorthand for the 'covenant formula' of 'I will be your God and you shall be my people.'[86] The covenant formula is found later in Hebrews within the Jeremiah new covenant quote (Heb. 8:10). Note that both OT and NT covenant communities are referred to as the **people of God** in Hebrews (Heb. 4:9; 8:10; 11:25).

My translation above for Hebrews 4:10 is very wooden. Allow me to expand upon it with inserted brackets. **For** [it is a general truth that[87]] **the one** [any believer from the people of God] **who entered** [in the future] **his** [God's] **rest also himself**

---

83. The verb 'to rest' in Matt. 11:28 is ἀναπαύω, which differs from καταπαύω in Hebrews, although it is a cognate (cf. Jer. 6:16).

84. Augustine uses 'rest' this way in the famous opening of his *Confessions*, 'Thou hast formed us for Thyself, and our hearts are restless till they find rest in Thee (1.1 [*NPNF*¹, 1:45]). Interestingly, he ends another of his famous books, *The City of God*, with a reference to the eternal rest following allusions to Hebrews 4:9–10: 'God shall rest as on the seventh day, when He shall give us ... rest in Himself.... The seventh day shall be our Sabbath, which shall be brought to a close, not by an evening, but by the Lord's day, as an eighth and eternal day, consecrated by the resurrection of Christ, and prefiguring the eternal repose not only of the spirit, but also of the body. There we shall rest and see, see and love, love and praise. This is what shall be in the end without end' (22.30 [*NPNF*¹, 2:511]).

85. For further discussion on this question, see Bruce, *Hebrews*, 110.

86. So also Mitchell, *Hebrews*, 99.

87. I take the aorist verb **rested** (καταπαύω) as a gnomic aorist. So also Ellingworth, *Hebrews*, 256. For discussion of gnomic aorists, see BDF §333.

[the believer] **rested from his** [believer's] **works as God did from his** [God's works].

A few commentators take **the one who has entered** as referring to Christ;[88] however, I disagree primarily based on (1) the overall context, which is referring to believers getting to the rest and (2) the AH did not explicitly name Christ.[89] Many modern English translations are explicitly against the Christological view by their translation of 'whoever,' or 'anyone,' or 'those' (e.g., NAB, RSV, NIV, NJB, NLT, NRSV, CSB17).

The believer will **rest from his works as God did from his**. Obviously, the **works** of the believer and God's creational works are related. As Scripture shows, God's resting from his creational works does not prevent him from subsequently working in other ways (John 5:17). In fact, Psalm 95:9 // Hebrews 3:9 refers to God's 'works' in the wilderness. Therefore God's rest referred to in Genesis 2:2 and Hebrews 4:10 must refer to a specific type of work that God rested from, that is, the creational works are in some sense special types of works that cannot be repeated.[90] In addition, there is the idea that God worked in this world and apparently then rested in heaven.

In what sense does the believer **rest from his works**?[91] Some in the Reformed tradition have seen these works as *evil*

---

88. So, e.g., Owen, *Hebrews*, 20:332; deSilva, *Perseverance in Gratitude*, 167–68; Whitfield, 'The Three Joshuas of Hebrews 3 and 4,' 26–27; Moore, 'Jesus as "The One who Entered his Rest": The Christological Reading of Hebrews 4:10,' 383–400. Attridge sees it referring to both believers and Christ (*Hebrews*, 131–32). Owen's arguments assume: (1) Works attributed to believers would only be evil works, and the context is certainly good works as they are related to God's works; hence, the works must be the good works of Christ (20:331–33). (2) Typology may only be related to Christ, thus not land as heaven; hence, rest must refer to Christ (20:257–58).

89. Ellingworth, who is against the Christological reading, well summarizes the arguments in favor of the Christological reading. He then gives his response to each one (*Hebrews*, 255–57).

90. Aquinas, *Summa Theologiae* 1a.73.2.

91. The AH uses 'works' for both 'dead works' (Heb. 6:1; 9:14) and good 'works' (Heb. 4:10; 6:10; 10:24).

works and/or works improperly done to achieve justification.[92] This view dovetails with the assumption that the **rest** begins in this life upon putting one's trust in Christ. This is *probably* the view of Heidelberg Catechism 103 (related to the fourth commandment), which connects 'rest from my evil works' to 'begin in this life the everlasting Sabbath.' However, nothing from Hebrews 3:7–4:13 is referenced for Heidelberg Catechism 103.[93]

With the majority of commentators, I see the believer's

---

92. So, e.g., William Farel's Summary 28 (*Reformed Confessions of the 16th and 17th Centuries*, 1:81); Calvin, *Hebrews and 1 & 2 Peter*, 48–49; *Geneva Bible: 1602 Edition*, folio 111; Dickson, *Hebrews*, 21; Large Emden Catechism 37–40 (*Reformed Confessions of the 16th and 17th Centuries*, 1:598); and Kistemaker, *Hebrews*, 103, 111, 114. In the broadly Reformed camp, Lincoln, 'Sabbath, Rest, and Eschatology in the New Testament,' 213; also the Lutheran Kleinig, *Hebrews*, 217–18. T. Levi 18:9 connects a future priest and resting from evil deeds in him.

93. Only Isa. 66:23 is referenced. I found one edition of the Heidelberg Catechism 103 that does reference Hebrews 4:9–11, e.g., Christian Reformed Church version approved by the 1975 Synod. In his commentary, Ursinus, the primary author of the Heidelberg Catechism, does not reference Hebrews 3:7–4:13 related to this question. He does refer to an 'internal Sabbath' that includes a 'rest from sin' and also refers to a current Sabbath that is 'a true rest from the labors and miseries of this life' (*The Commentary of Dr. Zacharias Ursinus on the Heidelberg Catechism*, trans. G. W. Williard [Phillipsburg: Presbyterian and Reformed, 1985 {1852 reprint of 1591 original}], 557–71, esp. 562–63). However, in Ursinus' Larger Catechism 189 he clearly connects God's stoppage of work on the seventh day with 'rest from their works, that is, their sins'(cf. Smaller Catechism 89 and Geneva Catechism 172–77 [*Reformed Confessions of the 16th and 17th Centuries*, 1:491]). (For translation of Ursinus' Smaller Catechism and Larger Catechism, see Lyle D. Bierma with et al., *An Introduction to the Heidelberg Catechism: Sources, History and Theology: With a Translation of the Smaller and Larger Catechisms of Zacharias Ursinus*, Texts and Studies in Reformation and Post-Reformation Thought [Grand Rapids: Baker, 2005], 141–223). This reasonably confirms the connection to Hebrews 4:10. Otto Thelemann gives several references for 'cease from my evil works' but none of them are from Hebrews; however, he does reference Hebrews 4:9, 11 for 'the eternal Sabbath [that] will be found in the life beyond, when we shall be free from all sin, and from all the troubles and miseries of the present life' (*An Aid to the Heidelberg Catechism*, trans. M. Peters [Grand Rapids: Douma, 1959 {1892}], 375). Again, not clear, at least to me, as to his understanding of 'evil works' in Heidelberg Catechism 103 related to Hebrews.

works as good works.⁹⁴ The connection to God's works argues that these must be good works (cf. Heb. 10:26). Although, these works many times are done in the midst of this life's difficulties (e.g., Heb. 10:32–34); they are often 'toil'. This dovetails well with the saints in heaven who 'rest (ἀναπαύω) from their labors' (Rev. 14:13). Gaffin calls these works '*desert-works*, the works of believers in the present wilderness, that is, a *non*-rest situation.'⁹⁵ Possibly, these difficult works allude typologically to God's covenantal promises to Noah of reducing the 'toil' of work (Gen. 5:29).⁹⁶

So how are God's works and the believer's works connected? God rested from a certain type of works—creation works; the believer rests from a certain type of works—works in this life that are mostly difficult. Neither ceases activity; the type of works changes.⁹⁷ Commenting on the believers' rest related to Hebrews 4:9–10, Bavinck says, 'Though their work on earth is finished, this does not alter the fact that they still have other works to do in heaven.'⁹⁸ There is also an analogy between God's working on earth and then apparently resting in heaven that parallels believers' working on earth and then having a heavenly rest with God. In sum, the believer's future work will be in God's heavenly location, which will be all that God promised. It will be so joyful that it can be properly termed **rest**.

---

94. So also, e.g., Aquinas, *Hebrews*, 98; Hughes, *Hebrews*, 161–62; Bruce, *Hebrews*, 109; Cockerill, *Hebrews*, 211–12; Schreiner, *Hebrews*, 145–46; and Beale, *A New Testament Biblical Theology*, 787. In addition, all those who interpret this verse Christologically also see **works** as good works.

95. Gaffin, 'A Sabbath Rest Still Awaits the People of God,' 45, emphasis his.

96. Suggested to me by J. Ligon Duncan III in a personal conversation.

97. The OT Sabbath analogy is apt. Israel ceased from certain types of labor on the Sabbath, not from all activities. John Murray makes the same point (*Principles of Conduct: Aspects of Biblical Ethics* [Grand Rapids: Eerdmans, 1957], 33).

98. Bavinck, *Reformed Dogmatics*, 4:642. Also see his interesting reflections on heavenly activities (4:729–30).

Reflections

Although not all agree that the 'rest' is entirely future as I do, the vast majority of theologians and commentators agree that at least part of the 'rest' is future. For me, this future aspect, whether in whole or part, argues for the continuity of the Christian Sabbath as still typological of the future 'Sabbath-rest.'[99] Of course, the argument is strengthened if the 'Sabbath-rest' is solely future.[100] The continuity of the Sabbath sign (cf. Exod. 31:13; Ezek. 20:12) is even further strengthened upon seeing the Sabbath as a 'creation ordinance' in Genesis 2:2–3.[101]

Given that the Sabbath is a sign of our glorious future, how should this affect our Sunday (Sabbath) experience? As a start, just realizing that Sunday is supposed to be a pattern of our future 'Sabbath-rest' should motivate many of us to stop and enjoy the benefits of an average Sunday. Most go to a local church, which includes fellowship with other believers and various worship activities. In addition, most have a day off from their traditional employment. These are wonderful benefits that foreshadow many of the benefits of the future 'rest.' Christians do and need to appreciate even more these benefits.

Many, me included, could probably improve the festive

---

99. *Contra* Lincoln, 'Sabbath, Rest, and Eschatology in the New Testament,' 214–17; Stedman, *Hebrews*, 58; and Schreiner, *Hebrews*, 144n198. Agreeing with my view, James Ussher responds to the argument that Christ's death takes away the fourth commandment, '[The Sabbath] is constantly and perpetually to be observed, and never to cease 'till it be perfectly consummated in the Heavenly Sabbath, Heb. 4:9–10' (*The Body of Divinity: Or, The Sum and Substance of Christian Religion*, ed. Michael Nevarr [Birmingham, AL: Solid Ground Christian, 2007 {1648}], 219).

100. So also, e.g., Brakel, *The Christian's Reasonable Service*, 3:176–78; Gaffin, 'A Sabbath Rest Still Awaits the People of God,' 47–48; and Frame, *The Doctrine of the Christian Life*, 528–74, esp. 558–60.

101. So also, e.g., Roger T. Beckwith and Wilfrid Scott, *The Christian Sunday: A Biblical and Historical Study* (Grand Rapids: Baker, 1980), 2–12, 43–47 (these sections were written by Beckwith); Turretin, *Institutes of Elenctic Theology*, 2:78–83; Murray, *Principles of Conduct*, 30–35; and Geerhardus Vos, *Biblical Theology: Old and New Testaments* (Carlisle: Banner of Truth, 1975 [1948]), 139–43.

aspect of the Sabbath. How could we enhance the joy and celebration of the day more? Let us be more creative in thinking about this.

A large aspect of the Sabbath-rest is that we are joining God's ('my') rest. This emphasizes the covenantal fellowship and relationship we have with God. Personally thinking/praying through the Bible and reading Christian 'devotional' literature often enhances our relationship with the Triune God. Sunday is a good day to emphasize this.

Another aspect of the Sabbath-rest is that it reminds us that the Triune God is both creator and redeemer (Gen. 2:2; Exod. 20:11; Deut. 5:15). We do not simply worship him and enjoy him as redeemer, but as both creator and redeemer. Sunday is a day to enjoy both aspects of our God.

Finally, I am reminded of Kline's comment related to Genesis 2:2–3. After noting that 'the Sabbath is set apart as sacred to the Creator' and 'witnesses to God's ultimate proprietorship of the land and to his lordship over the total life of man,' Kline concludes that 'observance of the Sabbath by man is thus a confession that Yahweh is his Lord and Lord of all lords.'[102] May we proudly remind ourselves and indicate to our neighbors as we set Sunday apart that we proclaim by our actions that Christ is Lord of all!

Rest—Word of God (4:11–13)

Hebrews 4:11–13 ends the large unit of 3:7–4:13.[103] With 4:11, the AH restates the implication of the entire argument—one ought to enter the rest and not fail due to disobedience. In 4:12–13, he focusses on the warning portion of 4:11 and gives two similar reasons for the warnings—God's word and God himself will know if one is disobedient.

---

102. Meredith Kline, *Kingdom Prologue* (np: Kline, 1989), 25.

103. Some connect Hebrews 4:11 to 4:1–10 and see 4:12–13 as a separate subunit, although a unit tightly connected to both 4:11 and the larger unit of Hebrews 3:7–4:11; e.g., Cockerill, *Hebrews*, 2:14–15.

4:11 *Therefore, let us strive to enter that rest in order that someone may not fall by the same example of disobedience.*

Given the argument in Hebrews 4:6–10 that a rest does remain, or more specifically 4:9–10, the obvious implication (**therefore**) is that one ought to enter it. Also, picking up from the remainder of Hebrews 3:7–4:5 that God will punish disobedience, not entering has the result of punishment. Hence, the AH's exhortation is stated both positively, **enter that rest**, and negatively, **not fall**.

Hebrews 4:11 reuses words and concepts from Hebrews 3:7–4:10. The exhortation **let us strive**[104] parallels Hebrews 4:1, 'let us fear.' **That rest** refers back to the future heavenly **rest**. The words **fall** and **disobedience** are repeated words/ cognates, of Heb. 3:17 and 3:18; 4:6, respectively.

The wilderness failings (Num. 26:65) are here explicitly termed an **example** (ὑπόδειγμα).[105] Obviously, this is a negative example. Do *not* do what the wilderness generation did ('provoked,' 'sinned,' 'unbelief,' **disobedience**) because the same result will occur. Paul uses the same wilderness events and also terms them as examples, although with different Greek words (1 Cor. 10:6, 11).[106] The AH will later use a slew of positive examples in Hebrews 11. Hermeneutically, it is clear that the AH practices 'exemplary exegesis' (see discussion at the beginning of this commentary chapter).

---

104. The verb **let us strive** (σπουδάζω) might be a word play with **rest** because it has at the literal level the sense of motion or speed, which could be translated as 'make haste' (LSJ, 1630). Hence, the word play would be to make **haste** (motion) in order **to enter the rest** (no motion). Note NJB translation, 'let us press forward, then, to enter this place of rest.' The grammatically closest NT example for σπουδάζω here is 2 Tim. 4:9 as that also includes a cognate of to enter as the following infinitive.

105. In Hebrews, ὑπόδειγμα is also used in 8:5 and 9:23, where it has the meaning of 'copy' or 'pattern'. In the rest of the NT, it is used three times with the clear meaning of 'example', both to be imitated (John 13:15; Jas. 5:10) and not imitated (2 Pet. 2:6). See 1 Clement 5:1 for use of ὑπόδειγμα referring to both good and bad examples (noted by Attridge, *Hebrews*, 132n117). Cf. 1 Clem. 6:1; 46:1; 55:1; 63:1.

106. 1 Cor. 10:6, τύπος; 1 Cor. 10:11, τυπικῶς.

4:12 *For the word of God is living; and effective; and sharper than any two-edged sword; and piercing to the division of soul and spirit, of joints and marrows; and a discerner*[107] *of thoughts and intents of the heart;*

Hebrews 4:12–13 has a rhetorical excellence to it (see below). Yes, it is grammatically and logically related to Hebrews 4:11, but the rhetorical aspect and its ending of a long unit give these verses more of an intentionally broader application.

Primarily related to the warning given in Hebrews 4:11b, the AH gives the reason (**for**) it. The **word of God** knows truly the **intents of the heart**, that is, whether one is a believer or not. Apparently, the emphasis is on those who might be only outwardly part of the covenant community and not true believers, similar to the emphasis of David in Psalm 95 to his community. The intent of the warning is to encourage all to be serious about their faith *now* with the end result of entering the 'rest'.

The broader sense would include the positive aspect of Hebrews 4:11a. God's active word will aid the believer in comforting and exhorting him to get to the final 'rest'. Hence, God's word relates to and has an effect upon believers, temporarily unbelievers, and even ultimately unrepentant unbelievers (cf. John 16:8–11; 2 Cor. 2:14–16; Isa. 55:10–11).

The expression **word of God** here refers to God's speaking his message; the readers are hearing him 'today' through the 'Holy Spirit' (Heb. 3:7, 15; cf. 1:1–2, 5; 2:3, 3:7; 4:2; 5:6, 12; 7:28; 8:5, 13; 10:15–16; 11:3; 12:25–26; 13:7, 22).[108] Further, God's message includes the quotes of the OT (in context Ps. 95:7b–11; Gen. 2:2b) and the NT redemptive-historical realities (Heb. 1:2) that are mediated through the Christian message/preaching.[109] This view of preaching as the mediated

---

107. I take the adjective κριτικός ('discerning,' 'judging,' 'critical') as a substantival adjective; so also KJV.

108. That is, **word of God** is a subjective genitive; so also Ellingworth, *Hebrews*, 260; and Schreiner, *Hebrews*, 146.

109. For a discussion of the Reformed view of Scripture as the *immediate* word of God and preaching as the *mediate* word of God, see Muller, *Post-*

word of God matches Heb. 13:7a, 'Remember your leaders, those who spoke to you the word of God' (cf. Heb. 13:22).

Although a decidedly minority position since the Reformation, some have taken **word of God** to be Christ, the second person of the Trinity.[110] This is primarily based on the Johannine usage (e.g., John 1:1; Rev. 19:13) and an assumed personification of **word of God** in Hebrews 4:12 (cf. Wis. 8:15–16). This fails to convince as (1) the AH is clear when he refers to Christ and (2) a robust view of God's speaking better explains the active **word** rather than a literal personification.

The rhetorical aspect of Hebrews 4:12 is shown by five parallel aspects of what the **word of God** is. The first, **living** (cf. Acts 7:38; 1 Pet. 1:23), is put in the emphatic position by being the first word of the Greek sentence. God is 'living' (Heb. 3:12); hence, his word is **living** as it interacts with men.[111] Similar to **living**, the second aspect is that God's word is **effective** or active. God's word is **effective** no matter with whom it interacts, for good or for ultimate judgment.[112] In

---

Reformation Reformed Dogmatics, 2:204–5. Note the distinction between the 'written word of God' and the 'preached word' in WCF 1.2, WSC 89, and WLC 155, cf. Second Helvetic Confession 1. The Theodore Beza Confession 28; the Confession of Tarcal and Torda 4:28; the Somerset Confession 19; and the Waldensian Confession 4 all connect preaching, the Holy Spirit, and Heb. 4:12 (*Reformed Confessions of the 16th and 17th Centuries*, 2:280; 2:703; 4:450; and 4:501, respectively). As I say it, the preached word of God is the word of God as it is properly derivative of the written word of God. See my discussion of 1 Thess. 2:13 (Robert J. Cara, *1 & 2 Thessalonians*, EP Study Commentary [Webster, NY: EP, 2009], 70–75).

110. So Athanasius, *Four Discourses against the Arians* 2.72 (*NPNF*², 4:387); Aquinas, *Hebrews*, 100; Owen, *Hebrews*, 353; James Swetnam, 'Jesus as Λόγος in Hebrews 4,12–13,' *Bib* 62 (1981): 214–24. Allen considers this a reasonable option (*Hebrews*, 284–88).

111. Emphasizing the interaction with men, so also Calvin *Hebrews*, 52; and *Geneva Bible: 1602 Edition*, folio 111. Emphasizing God is living as his word is, so also Schreiner, *Hebrews*, 146.

112. Speaking about the Scriptures' 'light and power to convince and convert sinners, to comfort and build up believers unto salvation,' WLC 4 references Heb. 4:12. The Westminster Directory for the Publick Worship of God in the 'Of the Preaching of the Word' section paraphrases Heb. 4:12

human-to-human interaction, the human that is speaking can fallibly 'read' the listener when he speaks and often can change the behavior of the listener. Similarly, God the speaker through his living **Word** infallibly 'reads' our hearts and is **effective** for our good or negative judgment.

The third aspect of God's word is that it is **sharper than any two-edged sword**. Some take this as referring to judgment and the utter destruction of unrepentant men.[113] However, I prefer to see it, anticipating the remainder of the verse, as such a sharp **sword** that it penetrates into the inner thoughts of man. **Piercing to the division of soul and spirit, of joints and marrows** is the fourth aspect, which is closely related to the third. The sharpness can divide what is metaphorically not divisible.[114]

The fifth aspect, **discerner of thoughts and intents of the heart**, with the first, **living**, are the primary emphases. God's word can read and affect the heart (e.g., 1 Cor. 14:24–25). It knows the heart and can awaken in man thoughts that result in good, or convict man's heart so that repentance occurs, or

---

in a discussion encouraging the preacher to apply with 'special use' the 'general doctrine' of the biblical text so that the hearers 'may feel the word of God to be quick and powerful, and a discerner of the thought and intents of the heart.'

113. So, e.g., Brown, *Hebrews*, 215–18, citing Isa. 49:2; Rev. 1:16; 2:12, 16; 19:15, 21 (cf. Num. 14:43). Augustine saw the **two-edged** as 'the two testaments', that is, the OT and the NT (*City of God* 20.21 [*NPNF*[1], 2:441]).

114. Some who hold a trichotomy position take **soul** and **spirit** as literally two entities within man, usually citing 1 Thess. 5:23, Heb. 4:12, and Gen. 2:7, so e.g., Henry Clarence Thiessen, *Introductory Lectures in Systematic Theology* (Grand Rapids: Eerdmans, 1949), 226–28; and Aquinas, *Hebrews*, 102. For a response to this, see Hughes, *Hebrews*, 165; Grudem, *Systematic Theology*, 477–82; and Cara, *1 & 2 Thessalonians*, 162–63. John Murray, a dichotomist, although not seeing a 'fast line of distinction', does in general view **spirit** as the 'principle of life as derived from God and returning to him on the event of death', and **soul** as the 'animating entity as life constituted in a body, and finds its prototype in Genesis 2:7' ('Trichotomy,' in *Collected Writings of John Murray*, 4 vols. [Carlisle: Banner of Truth, 1976–1982], 2:23–33, esp. 2:32). Older Reformed commentaries tended not to see two different entities, but different aspects of man's inner being, **soul** related to affections and **spirit** to mind (so e.g., Calvin, *Hebrews and 1 & 2 Peter*, 52; Owen, *Hebrews*, 360; *Geneva Bible: 1602 Edition*, folio 111). Catechism of the Catholic Church §367 has a dichotomist view.

convict man's heart so that no resulting repentance occurs in man and furthers God's judgment. Calvin noted about confessing our sins that, since through the word, God is a 'discerner of hearts, the one cognizant of all thoughts, let us hasten to pour out our hearts before him.'[115]

4:13 *and there is no creature unseen before him, and all things are naked and have been exposed*[116] *to his eyes, to whom the account [is given] by us.*

Pressing the point that one's thoughts will truly be known, the AH deftly moves from the 'word of God' to God himself (**him, his, whom**).[117] He states essentially the same thing twice: first negatively, **there is no creature unseen before him**, and then positively, **all things are naked and have been exposed to his eyes**. His emphasis is on the 'now'. Since God sees your heart now, ought you not stop trying to 'fake it' and turn to him? The AH ends by noting that at the future judgment, you must give an **account**; hence, be serious now. There is another word play with this ending. *Our* **account**/'word' (λόγος) is the final Greek word of 4:13 that is contrasted with the 'word (λόγος) of *God*' that is near the beginning of 4:12.[118]

---

115. Calvin, *Institutes* 3.4.9.

116. The Greek word behind the verb **exposed** (τραχηλίζω) occurs only here in biblical Greek. At the literal level, it is obviously related to neck (τράχηλος) and has several meanings in different non-biblical contexts (including the cognate ἐκτραχηλίζω). What is the intended metaphor here, if in fact it is not a 'dead metaphor'? One option is of a wrestler who grabs the neck to subdue the opponent (so Allen, *Hebrews*, 289). Or it may mean to grab by the neck to cut open an animal, as with a sacrificial animal (so Attridge, *Hebrews*, 136). Either way, the literal option results in a metaphorical translation for a passive related to **exposed** or 'laid bare'. See LSJ, 1811. Note that 1 Clem. 63:1 includes 'example' (ὑπόδειγμα) and 'neck' (τράχηλος) in same context; 'to such examples, bow the neck and take up the place of obedience' (my translation). Again, this shows some sort of exposure.

117. *Contra* Erich Grässer who connects **eyes** to the 'word of God' as opposed to God himself (*An die Hebräer*, 3 vols., EKKNT 17 [Zurich: Benziger, 1990–1997], 1:239).

118. Λόγος has many meanings in the NT. It means **account** (a summarizing 'word' given in an accounting or judgment situation) in Heb. 4:13; 13:17; Matt. 12:36; 18:23; 25:19; Luke 16:2; Rom. 14:12; and 1 Pet. 4:5. Attridge

God is omniscient. He knows and sees all things. This fundamental reality is stated numerous times in Scripture (e.g., 1 Chr. 28:9; Job 28:24; Pss. 33:13; 40:20–21; Ezek. 8:12; Luke 16:15; Rev. 20:12; cf. WLC 106). Hebrews 4:13 is often referenced in creeds to this effect (e.g., WCF 2.2, WLC 7; Catechism of the Catholic Church §303; Swiss Brethren Confession of Hesse 2). For the believer, at our best, this is a wonderfully comforting truth; for the non-believer, the consequences are disastrous if there is no repentance. Glory be, grace is promised in the next verse. There is a 'great high priest' (Heb. 4:14).

Reflections

The 'word of God is living and effective' (Heb. 4:12). Although this statement is primarily in a negative context, as I argued above, there is an intentionally broader, and more positive, application.

For the Christian, we understand that it is not simply that we are changing by applying the truths of Scripture to ourselves. Yes, from our perspective that is true. But the Christian also acknowledges that it is the almighty Triune God in the person of the Holy Spirit who uses Scripture in a special way to change us.[119] In fact, God has told us that Scripture is 'living and effective.'

Christians believe that reading/studying the Scripture and hearing the Scripture preached are life changing both in the comprehensive sense and in the details. Multitudes of believers through the ages attest to this. May the reader and I be motivated by Hebrews 4:12 to be even more attentive, and when we are changed by Scripture, acknowledge that it was the *living* word of the *living* God that changed us.

---

comments, '[the AH] delights in the subtle manipulation of language in shifting the meaning of λόγος' (*Hebrews*, 136).

119. Concepts here partially from Charles Hodge, *Systematic Theology*, 3 vols. (Grand Rapids: Eerdmans, 1982 [1871–1873], 3:476). Cf. Canons of Dort 3/4.11–13.

5.
Sympathetic High Priest (4:14–5:10)

Hebrews 4:14–10:39 is a large section that emphasizes the priesthood of Christ, with an intermixing of doctrinal and hortatory sections.[1] This large section may be subdivided into five subsections: 4:14–5:10; 5:11–6:20; 7:1–28; 8:1–10:18; and 10:19–39.

Within this large section, the hortatory pericopes include 4:14–16; 5:11–6:12; and 10:19–39. As all note, there are clear verbal and conceptual parallels between the opening hortatory pericope (4:14–16) and the beginning (10:19–23) of the ending one (10:19–39). See the comparison below:

4:14	'therefore having'
10:19	'therefore having'
4:14	'great high priest'
10:21	'great priest'
4:14	'let us hold firm (κρατέω) the confession'
10:23	'let us hold fast (κατέχω) the confession of hope'

---

1. Not all completely agree, e.g., Vanhoye sees Heb. 5:11–10:39 as the large unit (*Structure and Message of Epistle of Hebrews*, 79) and Cockerill 4:14–10:18 (*Hebrews*, 218–20).

4:16	'let us approach with confidence the throne of grace'
10:19	'having confidence for the entrance into the Holy of Holies'
10:22	'let us approach with a true heart in full assurance of faith'

Hebrews 4:14–5:10 is clearly composed of two smaller sections, 4:14–16 and 5:1–10. The first resumes the discussion of the priesthood of Christ making explicit hortatory connections. The sympathetic and mediatorial aspects of Christ's priesthood are stressed. The second expands upon these aspects noting the contrast-within-continuity between Christ and Aaronic high priests.

Great High Priest (4:14–16)

Hebrews 4:14–16 emphasizes Christ's priesthood and is the beginning of the large section of 4:14–10:39 that also emphasizes that priesthood. Within Hebrews 4:14–16, 4:14 is the more overarching statement about Christ's priesthood, and 4:15–16 stresses the sympathetic nature of Christ our mediator.[2]

4:14 *Therefore, having a great high priest who has passed through the heavens, Jesus, the Son of God, let us hold firm the confession.*

The **therefore** is somewhat weak and primarily is resuming the previous comments in Hebrews 2:17–3:1 concerning Christ being a high priest, tempted, and helping those tempted,[3] and possibly the 'Son' comment in Hebrews 3:6. Hence, **having a great high priest** is restated as the premise and **let us hold firm** is the inference. Obviously, the **let us hold firm**

---

2. So also Owen, *Hebrews*, 20:391; and Cockerill, *Hebrews*, 225.

3. So also Ellingworth, *Hebrews*, 265; and Attridge (*Hebrews*, 138). Concerning a resumptive **therefore** (οὖν), BAGD defines as 'to resume a subject once more after an interruption' (736). Runge suggests using 'thus' for the resumptive sense (*Discourse Grammar of the Greek New Testament*, 47). Tyndale translated as 'seynge [seeing] then', which the Geneva Bible and KJV followed. The ESV translates as 'since then', which works well.

continues the emphasis of perseverance to the final rest from Hebrews 3:7–4:13.

The addition of **great** (μέγας) to **high priest** (ἀρχιερεύς) only occurs here in the Bible (cf. Heb. 10:21).[4] It is emphasizing Christ's superiority to the Aaronic priesthood.[5] Christ is called **Jesus, the Son of God**. What a grand name-title?! **Jesus** emphasizes his humanity, and **Son** *of God*, in this context, his divinity (cf. Heb. 1:2–3, 8; 3:6, 5:5, 7:3).[6] Also note that this grand name-title is coupled with **great high priest**. Reminiscent of Hebrews 1:2–3, the Sonship and priesthood of Christ are here brought together in the most explicit way. This serves to connect the previous 'Son' discussions in Hebrews to the upcoming emphasis on priesthood. Also, this verse connects Christ's two natures to the priesthood, which is logical since a priest is a mediator (WLC 40). Given the mediator aspect, this then anticipates later covenant discussions (e.g., Heb. 7:22; 8:8; 12:24).

An aspect of Christ's current exalted status is that he **has passed through the heavens** of this world to arrive where God

---

4. Although often translated as 'high priest' in English Bibles, the OT Hebrew is 'great priest' (הכהן הגדול, ὁ ἱερεὺς ὁ μέγας). Actually, the Greek 'high priest' (ἀρχιερεύς) is rare in the OT. It only occurs three times in the canonical OT (Lev. 4:3; Josh. 22:13; 24:33; cf. 1 Chr. 27:5), although often in the non-canonical portions of the LXX. In the NT, ἀρχιερεύς in the plural is often translated as 'chief priests' when it clearly does not refer to the single high priest but a group of leading priests (e.g., Matt. 2:4; Mark 11:18; John 18:35; Acts 4:23; cf. Ezra 8:29). The expression 'great high priest' does occur three times in Philo (*On Dreams* 1:214, 219; 2:183), although more often he uses 'great priest' (e.g., *On Dreams* 2:231; *On the Life of Moses* 1:313; *On the Embassy to Gaius* 306). Intriguingly, Josephus quotes Caius Julius Caesar referring to himself as 'high priest' (ἀρχιερεύς) in the midst of several other titles (*Jewish Antiquities* 14:190).

5. Referencing Heb. 4:14, Lattanzio Ragnoni (Italian Reformer) refers to Christ as '*Summus Pontifex*'—Supreme High Priest (*Reformed Confessions of the 16th and 17th Centuries*, 2:171).

6. So also Aquinas, *Hebrews*, 107; Hughes, *Hebrews*, 170; and Cockerill, *Hebrews*, 224. The expression **Son of God** is used four times in Hebrews, 4:14; 6:6; 7:3; and 10:29. Hence, in Hebrews, Christ is called both 'son of man', referring to his human nature, and **Son of God**, referring to his divine nature.

the Father is. Primarily, this phrase refers to Christ's ascension (Acts 1:9–10; Heb. 1:3; Heidelberg Catechism 46). However, in a secondary way, the AH is making an allusion to the OT high priest's activities on the Day of Atonement (Lev. 16). The high priest passed through the tabernacle/temple and its veil once a year to be in the presence of God at the mercy-seat (throne).[7] This secondary aspect is confirmed by Hebrews 6:19; 8:2; 9:11, 24; 10:19–20 and the general parallel, as shown at the beginning of this chapter, between 4:14–16 and 10:19–23.

The first person imperative, **let us hold firm**[8] **the confession**, is the inference from having **Jesus, the Son of God** as our **great high priest**. Where else and to whom is one to go (cf. John 6:68)?

4:15 *For we do not have a high priest not being able to sympathize with our weaknesses, but [we have] one having been tempted according to all [things] according to [the] likeness*[9] *[of us, yet] without sin.*

For (γάρ) is here used to strengthen the incentive to 'hold firm the confession' from the previous verse.[10] Possibly, the AH perceived that the grandeur of Christ as the 'Son of God' would hinder some readers from appreciating his priestly mediatorial role.[11] They could relate to a human priest

---

7. So also Owen, *Hebrews*, 20:395; Brown, *Hebrews*, 227; Hughes, *Hebrews*, 170; Koester, *Hebrews*, 282; and Kleinig, *Hebrews*, 225.

8. **Let us hold firm** (κρατῶμεν) is a Greek hortatory subjunctive. This verb is also used in Heb. 6:18. The synonym 'hold fast' (κατέχω) is used in Heb. 3:6, 14; and 10:23.

9. Obviously, this is a wooden translation. The expression **according to the likeness** is also used in Heb. 7:15. In both Gen. 1:11 and 1:12, it is used in conjunction with 'kind', 'according to kind and according to likeness,' to interpret the one Hebrew phrase 'according to its kind'. Often the expression **according to the likeness** takes a genitive following **likeness**; hence, I added **of us**. The ESV more smoothly adds 'as we are'. See genitive examples in LSJ, 1225.

10. Runge comments about γάρ, 'The information introduced does not advance the discourse but adds background information that strengthens or supports what precedes' (*Discourse Grammar of the Greek New Testament*, 52).

11. So also Lane, *Hebrews 1–8*, 107, 114; and Schreiner, *Hebrews*, 153.

but possibly not to the 'great high priest.' Hence, the AH discusses one aspect of Christ's priesthood in this verse—his sympathetic concern for his people enhanced by his experiential understanding of their difficulties.[12]

In the clause, **we do *not* have a high priest *not* being able to sympathize with our weaknesses**, a double negative is used. This adds emphasis to the resulting positive affirmation that we *do* have a high priest *able* to sympathize.[13] Further his sympathy is not just intellectual, but experiential. As Aquinas notes, Christ 'knows our misery through experience, which, as God, he knew from eternity through simple knowledge.'[14]

The combination of **weaknesses** and **tempted according to all things according to the likeness of us** would *on the surface* imply that **weaknesses** include difficulties due to cold, hunger, disease, temptations, jealousy, internal and resulting outward sin, mental confusion, embarrassed by the Gospel, sinfully afraid, etc. Note that 'weakness' of human high priests in Hebrews 5:2 is related to their sin in 5:3. However, because the context also includes **yet without sin**, it is certain that **weaknesses** related to Christ do *not* include any sin or mental confusion, but they relate to numerous difficulties in this life whereby one would be **tempted** to sin and not perform God's will.[15] These would primarily be external difficulties, but could include (internal) physical 'common infirmities' such as having a cold.[16] In Christ's case, there was an emphasis on his suffering from external difficulties.

---

12. Vos comments, 'It was as temptation that the weaknesses entered into the Saviour's experience, and it is as temptation that they draw forth His sympathy. The readers are assured that His pity goes out towards them as tempted, as potential sinners' ('The Priesthood of Christ in the Epistle to the Hebrews,' *PTR* 5 [1907]: 423–47, 579–604, esp. 583).

13. So also Owen, *Hebrews*, 20:417; Brown, *Hebrews*, 231; Spicq, *Hébreux*, 2:03; and Cockerill, *Hebrews*, 225. This is termed 'litotes'. See somewhat similar construction at Heb. 6:10; cf. Heb 9:7.

14. Aquinas, *Hebrews*, 108.

15. Ellingworth states, '[Heb.] 5:2 suggests that the author is thinking, not of physical weakness, but of intellectual and moral weakness which leads to failure to do God's will' (*Hebrews*, 268).

16. The expression 'common infirmities' is used in WCF 8.2 and WLC 52.

Given Christ's person, how could he be tempted? Owen well notes two aspects of temptations. Some temptations are in principle sin as they precede from the sin within us; that is, 'men are tempted to sin by sin, to actual sin by habitual sin, to outward sin by indwelling sin, Jas. 1:14–15.' In other situations, temptations come upon one from outside circumstances (or internal common infirmities) to entice one to sin.[17] These are only sin if one acts on that temptation. It is this second aspect of temptation that came upon Christ. 'None of them [temptations] in the least degree [had] any effect in him or upon him.'[18] The orthodox Reformed tradition, following the historical Christian tradition, has made two general points about Christ's temptability. First, Christ had no indwelling sin.[19] Second, Christ's temptations were real.[20] Pertaining to the more abstract question of whether Christ was in principle capable of sinning, the Reformed tradition has consistently held that the person Christ was not able to sin in these temptations because of the union of his divine and human natures ('impeccability' view).[21]

---

17. E.g., assume one finds a wallet with lots of money in it. The outside circumstance 'tempted' the finder not to return the wallet and simply take the money.

18. Owen, *Hebrews*, 20:427.

19. The traditional view also includes that the Son of God assumed an *un*fallen human nature from Mary, stressing the importance of Luke 1:35. Unfortunately, in the last two centuries, some have argued for the assumption of a fallen nature. For a recent discussion upholding the traditional view with an emphasis on Hebrews, see Michael Allen, 'Christ,' in *Companion to the Doctrine of Sin*, ed. Keith Johnson and David Lauber (Edinburgh: Bloomsbury T&T Clark, 2016), 451–66, esp. 458–64.

20. See good discussion by Kelly, *Systematic Theology*, 2:248–49.

21. So Bavinck, *Reformed Dogmatics*, 3:314–16; Berkhof, *Systematic Theology*, 318–19, 324; Berkouwer, *The Person of Christ*, 239–70; Macleod, *The Person of Christ*, 222–29; Robert L. Dabney, *Systematic Theology* (Carlisle: Banner of Truth 1985 [1878]), 470–73; William G. T. Shedd, *Dogmatic Theology*, ed. Alan W. Gomes, 3rd ed. (Phillipsburg: P&R, 2003 [1888–1894]), 659–71; James Oliver Buswell, *A Systematic Theology of the Christian Religion*, 2 vols. (Grand Rapids: Zondervan, 1962), 2:61; and Robert Letham, *Systematic Theology* (Wheaton: Crossway, 2019), 520–26. Augustine held the impeccability view (*Enchiridion* 36 [*NPNF*[1], 3:250]). B. B. Warfield comments: 'In the case of our Lord's person, the human nature remains truly human while yet it can never

One might object, if Christ did not sin, does this not reduce believers' connection to him? In a word: No. One answer to this is to note that sin in fact causes separation, not solidarity. Does one feel more connected to one's spouse the more sinful they are? Another objection, does not misery like company? But is this a Christian view of the comfort afforded by company when one has sinned? Better to have compassion from one who has gone through the same difficulties but has come out on the other side without sin. This person will not fail as a friend.[22] Final objection, the comment is often heard, 'To err is human,' and thus Christ is not human if he does not sin. No, man was not originally made sinful. In fact, for pre-fall Adam, for Christ existentially, and for believers post-death there is no sin. Of course, there are other reasons that Christ's sinfulness would cause problems for our connection to him—a significant one is that he could not be our Savior!

In context, the immediate use of **without sin** is to deny that Christ's temptations resulted in sin. However, this grand expression has a creedal and broad sense to it because the AH has no need to justify it. He simply assumes it.[23] This creedal sense is confirmed by the many NT statements affirming Christ's sinlessness (e.g., Luke 23:4; John 7:18; 2 Cor. 5:21; 1 Pet. 1:19; 1 John 3:5).[24] The broadness of **without sin** is

---

fall into sin or error because it can never act out of relation with the Divine nature into conjunction with which it has been brought' ('The Biblical Idea of Inspiration,' in *The Inspiration and Authority of the Bible*, ed. Samuel G. Craig [Phillipsburg: Presbyterian and Reformed, 1948], 131–66, esp. 162). Surprisingly, Charles Hodge is an outlier here. While strongly affirming that Christ did not sin, he argues that if Christ 'was a true man, he must have been capable of sinning'(*Systematic Theology*, 2:457). For a summary of a variety of non-Reformed views, see Allen, *Hebrews*, 309–13.

22. Several ideas in this paragraph were obtained from Albert Vanhoye, *Old Testament Priests and the New Priest*, trans. J. Bernard Orchard (Petersham, MA: St. Bede's, 1986), 112–16; and John Murray, 'The Heavenly, Priestly Activity of Christ,' in *Collected Writings of John Murray*, 4 vols. (Carlisle: Banner of Truth, 1979–1982), 1:44–58, esp. 50–51.

23. Attridge comments, 'Christ's sinlessness is not a quality for which Hebrews need justification; it is assumed and affirmed as virtually self-evident' (*Hebrews*, 140–41).

24. Vague ideas of a sinless high priest did exist in the Second Temple

confirmed by the previous verse as it refers to Christ as 'Jesus, the Son of God' and as the 'great high priest.' In addition, the argument of Hebrews will unfold to necessitate a sinless priest (Heb. 7:25) and a sinless sacrifice (e.g., Heb. 9:13–14).[25] Hence, **without sin** is certainly intended as a broad and absolute statement that has a creedal sense to it.

Given the creedal sense, it is no surprise that the expression **according to all things according to the likeness of us, yet without sin** is used in numerous Christian creeds (with smoother English!).[26] It becomes one of the standard phrases to describe Christ's human nature; Christ as man was/is in all things like us yet without sin. This phrase is used virtually word for word in the famous Council of Chalcedon (AD 451) that dealt with the two natures of Christ.[27]

4:16 *Therefore, let us approach[28] with confidence the throne of grace in order that we might receive mercy and we might find grace for well-timed help.*

---

period. Philo views the Logos as related (somehow?) to an undefiled high priest (*On Flight and Finding* 108–12, cf. *On the Special Laws* 1.230). T. Levi. 18:9 refers to a future priesthood period during which sin will cease. Psalms of Solomon 17:32–36 includes a future 'Lord Messiah' who will be free from sin. See R. A. Stewart, 'The Sinless High-Priest,' *NTS* 14 (1967): 126–35.

25. In a controversial article, Ronald Williamson argues that **without sin** only relates to the climax of Christ's life. Christ was a sinner for most of his life but was finally prepared or perfected or ceremonially pure to be the proper priest as he went to the cross and his subsequent intercession. Only at that point did he become a priest with no sin ('Hebrews 4:15 and the Sinlessness of Jesus,' *ExpTim* 86 [1974]: 4–8). Lindars has the same view (*The Theology of the Letter to the Hebrews*, 63 n. 53). For a point-by-point rebuttal of Williamson, see David Peterson, *Hebrews and Perfection: An Examination of the Concept of Perfection in the 'Epistle to the Hebrews'* (Cambridge: Cambridge University Press, 1982), 188–90.

26. E.g., Council of Chalcedon, Second Helvetic Confession 11.6, French Confession 14, Belgic Confession 18, Heidelberg Catechism 35, Thirty-Nine Articles 15; WCF 8.2, WSC 22, WLC 37, Catechism of the Catholic Catechism §612.

27. Chalcedon: κατὰ πάντα ὅμοιον ἡμῖν χωρὶς ἁμαρτίας; Heb. 4:15: κατὰ πάντα καθ' ὁμοιότητα χωρὶς ἁμαρτίας. Greek for Chalcedon from Schaff, *Creeds of Christendom*, 2:62 or Denzinger[43] §301.

28. **Let us approach** (προσερχώμεθα) is a Greek hortatory subjunctive.

The sympathetic aspect of Christ's priesthood does double duty. In Hebrews 4:15, it is used to strengthen the incentive to 'hold firm the confession' of 4:14. In Hebrews 4:16, the sympathetic Christ is used as the grounds (**therefore**) to make an appeal to **approach with confidence the throne of grace**.

This **approach** refers to prayers.[29] Yes, in the OT, God had compassion on and listened to the prayers of his covenant people. But how much more now, that there is a sympathetic great high priest who has experienced the difficulties of his people in his human nature, should God's people come to him **with confidence**.[30]

The Greek verb for **approach** (προσέρχομαι) is used to translate the Hebrew verb (קרב) that is often used in the OT in priestly settings (e.g., Lev. 9:7; 21:21) and in settings where the people of God 'approach' him (Lev. 9:5). In these texts, 'approach' has a theologically charged meaning. In other texts in the OT, the verb is used in more mundane non-theologically charged situations. In Hebrews, 'approach' is clearly used in 'priestly/theological-charged' contexts in Hebrews 7:25; 10:1; and 10:22; although it is less clear in Hebrews 11:6; 12:18; and 12:22. Given the context of priesthood here, there is a strong allusion to a priestly/theologically-charged **approach**.[31]

The wonderful phrase **throne of grace** combines the power of God to answer our prayers (**throne**) and the compassion to help us with our petitions (**grace**). Note that here and elsewhere in Hebrews, a kingly metaphor (**throne**) is included with a priestly implied tabernacle metaphor (e.g., Heb. 1:3, 5:5–6; 8:1–2).[32] Related to the tabernacle is the Ark of the

---

29. See excellent discussion in John M. Scholer, *Proleptic Priests: Priesthood in the Epistle of Hebrews*, JSNTSup 49 (Sheffield: Sheffield Academic Press, 1991), 106–09.

30. In comparing the 'liberties' that NT believers have to OT ones, WCF 20.1 notes that NT believers have '*greater* boldness of access to the throne of grace' (emphasis mine).

31. So also Owen, *Hebrews*, 20:429; Attridge, *Hebrews*, 141; and Kleinig, *Hebrews*, 226–27.

32. For OT combinations of king and tabernacle/temple, see Pss. 11:4;

Covenant. In the OT, the Ark of the Covenant and/or the mercy-seat on top of the Ark are occasionally referred to as God's throne or the footstool of his throne.[33] In Scripture, both the kingly throne and Ark of the Covenant emphasize God's presence; hence, the two metaphors of kingly throne and priestly tabernacle dovetail well here, although, I prefer to see the kingly **throne** as primary and the tabernacle throne as secondary in this context.[34] Further, I conclude that God the Father with Christ at his right hand is on the **throne** based on the 'right hand' language in Hebrews (1:3, 13; 8:1; 10:12; 12:2; although 1:8).[35]

The purpose of these prayers is that **we might receive mercy and we might find grace for well-timed help**.[36] What are the problems for which the readers need **help**? From the context of the entire book, it is preeminently **help** to continue to persevere in the faith. However, the **help** also applies to other problems mentioned in Hebrews related to the readers. They include being in prison, being mistreated, temptations to adultery, temptations with money, public reproach, and loss of property (Heb. 10:33–34; 12:12–16; 13:3–5), not to mention their problems that may parallel those associated with the OT saints (11:11, 24–27 , 35–38).

In the Greek, there is an obvious chiastic structure: (A) **we-might-receive**, (B) **mercy**, (B') **grace**, (A') **we-might-find**. This brings emphasis to this compound clause and confirms that **mercy** and **grace** are, in this context, synonyms.[37] Grammatically, the prepositional phrase **for well-timed help**

18:7; 29:9; Isa. 6:1; Ezek. 43:6–7; Zech. 6:13; Rev. 7:15; and 16:17.

33. E.g., 1 Sam 4:4; 2 Sam 6:2; 2 Kgs 19:15; 1 Chr. 28:2; Pss. 99:5; 132:7; Ezek. 43:6–7. For an excellent article on the Ark from a conservative perspective, see W. Lotz, M. G. Kyle, and C. E. Armerding, 'Ark of the Covenant,' *ISBE*, 1:291–94.

34. So also Ellingworth, *Hebrews*, 270.

35. So also Bruce, *Hebrews*, 116.

36. Cognates of **help** are used in Hebrews 2:18 and 13:6.

37. So also Ellingworth, *Hebrews*, 270.

could go with **we might find grace** or the full compound clause **we might receive mercy and we might find grace**. Given the chiasm, it applies to the latter.

Reflections
The Lord Jesus Christ sympathizes with believers. He understands our situation; he has been in our shoes; he has been tempted like we have been ... 'yet without sin.' What a priest we have! He, almighty God, took on a human nature for many reasons, but one is to sympathize with believers.

Further, as a believer, I realize that the Lord Jesus Christ sympathizes with *me* (Gal. 2:20b). I know my wife loves me very much and sympathizes with my difficulties. However, 'there is no creature, either in heaven or on the earth, who loves [me] more than Jesus Christ ... If so, should [I] seek for another mediator?' (Belgic Confession 24). Knowing Christ's sympathy for *me* should drive *me* to the 'throne of Grace' through the only mediator between God and men, the man Christ Jesus (1 Tim. 2:5).

Did Not Exalt Himself (5:1–10)

Hebrews 5:1–10 connects back to Hebrews 4:14–16 as it continues the theme of Christ as a sympathetic high priest. However, it is also clearly its own unit. It compares and contrasts aspects of OT high priests (Heb. 5:1–4) with Christ (Heb. 5:5–10).

Many see a chiastic structure for Hebrews 5:1–10, although they do not agree on the structure exactly.[38] I agree that the chiastic pattern of sympathy (5:2–3), divine call (5:4), divine

---

38. Bruce has sympathy (5:1–3), divine call (5:4), divine call (5:5–6), sympathy (5:7–10) (*Hebrews*, 118, 123). Ellingworth has each of the two sections having their own chiastic structures, although he admits the details are not clear: divine call (5:1), sympathy (5:2–3), divine call (5:4), divine call (5:5–6), sympathy (5:7–9), divine call (5:10) (*Hebrews*, 271). Lane is more sure of his outline. He proposes old office of high priest (5:1), solidarity (5:2–3), humility (5:4), humility (5:5–6), solidarity (5:7–8), new office of high priest (5:9–10) (*Hebrews*, 111).

call (5:5–6), sympathy (5:7–8) loosely exists. However, I am not convinced that the opening (5:1) and closing statements (5:9–10) are intentionally part of the pattern. Also, 5:7–10 is one, complicated unit that further loosens any tight chiastic structure as its main grammatical emphasis is not sympathy per se but that Christ learned obedience to effect salvation (5:8–9).

Not surprisingly, since this is the beginning of the explicit comparisons between OT high priests and the priesthood of Christ, several themes in Hebrews 5:1–10 are again brought up later in 7:1–10:18 where the argument is expanded. These repeated themes include being appointed (7:20, 28; 8:3), offering gifts and sacrifices for sins (8:3; 9:9; 10:3, 12), priests (not Christ) offer sacrifices for their own sins because of weakness (7:26, 28), and Christ's similarity to Melchizedek using Psalm 110:4 (7:1–28).

5:1 *For every high priest being taken from men is appointed on behalf of men [concerning] the [things] toward God in order that he may offer gifts and sacrifices for sins,*

In Hebrews 5:1–4, the AH does not give all the attributes of a high priest; at a minimum he gives those that relate to his following arguments about Christ. Knowing a comparison is coming, any reader in this subsection is encouraged to make the contrasts-within-continuity between Christ and the high priests even though the AH does not make them all explicit.

For (γάρ) relates Hebrews 5:1–10 back to 4:14–16, although it is not a tight connection. In general, it is giving both the ground and additional explanatory information as to Christ's being a great high priest with somewhat of an emphasis on his sympathy.

The AH notes that the successive high priests were **taken from men** (cf. Exod. 28:1; Lev. 21:10; Num. 8:6). **Taken**, as well as **appointed**, is anticipating Hebrews 5:4 where it is explicitly stated that God called the high priests.[39] **From men**

---

39. It is also true that the 'law appoints' the high priest (Heb. 7:22), but

at one level states the obvious about the high priests, but it has added emphasis as one thinks about Christ's humanity and his sympathy for us. Owen comments that **taken from** *men* is a 'great ground of consolation unto believers'.[40]

The high priests were **appointed on behalf of men concerning the things toward God**.[41] In the OT, priests in general were mediators **on behalf of** *men* relative to the **things toward** *God*. However, the **high priest** was especially so, as demonstrated on the Day of Atonement (Lev. 16). Although not saying explicitly here, the AH is clearly anticipating his discussion of Christ as a mediator (Heb. 7:22; 8:6; cf. 1 Tim. 2:5). The **high priest** is a *man* who mediates between God and man; Christ is the better mediator because he is the *God/man* who mediates between God and man.

The **and** (τε καὶ) in the expression **gifts and sacrifices** ties these two nouns closely together as a unit.[42] Probably **gifts and sacrifices** is an overarching phrase covering all types of OT offerings (e.g., peace offerings, sin offerings, Day of Atonement) without specifically distinguishing them. The context in Hebrews emphasizes those offerings more specifically related to sin/trespass offerings (cf. Ezek. 45:15–17).[43]

5:2–3 *being able to deal gently with the ones being ignorant and those straying since also he himself is surrounded in weakness. And on account of it, he had to offer [sacrifices] concerning sins, just as concerning the people, thus also concerning himself.*

In Hebrews 5:1, the emphasis was on the implied similarities

---

that is not the point here.

40. Owen, *Hebrews*, 20:447.

41. **Concerning the things toward God** (τὰ πρὸς τὸν θεόν) is the same Greek expression as Heb. 2:17 and Rom. 15:17.

42. See discussion of τε καὶ in the expression 'signs and wonders' at Heb. 2:3b–4.

43. Hence, the prepositional phrase **for sins** most likely relates to both **gifts** and **sacrifices**, not just **sacrifices**. So also Attridge, *Hebrews*, 143; and Ellingworth, *Hebrews*, 274–75.

between high priests and Christ, they were both 'taken from men', 'appointed,' mediators, and 'offer gifts and sacrifices for sins.' Hebrews 5:2–3 moves with subtlety to include the implied differences between Christ and the high priests.

Grammatically, Hebrews 5:2 is a participial phrase with no explicit marker of how it relates to 5:1.[44] However, it is clearly providing more of an explanation as to the incentive and capacity the high priest has to act 'on behalf of men.' This is connected back to Christ's sympathy in Hebrews 4:15 and connected forward to his implied sympathy in 5:7–8.

The high priest is **able to deal gently**. The verb translated **deal gently** (μετριοπαθέω) is only used here in the NT and LXX. As is clear from the word itself, there is an element of 'moderating' (μετριο) in this word.[45] There is most likely an intentional distinction between Christ's more complete 'sympathiz[ing]' (συμπαθέω) in Hebrews 4:15 and the high priest's **deal[ing] gently**.[46]

The expression **the ones being ignorant and those straying** refers to both sins of ignorance and sins of commission (cf. Lev. 16:21).[47] The verb **straying** is often used as in the context of wrongful wandering (Ps. 95:10 // Heb. 3:9; Ps. 119:110, 176; Isa. 53:6; 1 Pet. 2:25).

One incentive (**since**) for the high priest to **deal gently** is that **also he himself is surrounded in weakness**. As in Hebrews 4:15, **weakness** includes the difficulties in life such as hunger, cold, temptation, but here as opposed to Christ in 4:15, it also includes personal sinful/moral failures as is clear from 5:3. Owen argues that the natural, non-moral **weakness** aspect relates to the high priest's appropriate compassion

---

44. Most English translations for smoothness convert the participial phrase into a complete sentence or clause, e.g., KJV, NASB, and ESV.

45. LSJ, 1122.

46. So also Schreiner, *Hebrews*, 158; and Attridge, *Hebrews*, 144; *contra* Calvin, *Hebrews and 1 & 2 Peter*, 60.

47. Note that one article covers both substantival participles; hence, the expression is considered one unit. Also see discussion at Heb. 9:7.

(Heb. 5:1–2a), and the moral **weakness** of the high priest, which is not part of the appropriate compassion, is taken up in Hebrews 5:3.[48]

In the expression **on account of it**, **it** grammatically refers to **weakness**.[49] Given the sinful/moral aspects of **weakness**, the high priest in addition to offering sacrifices for the sins of the people, **he had to offer sacrifices ... also concerning** *himself*. This sacrifice for the sins of the high priest is clearly set out in the OT (Lev. 9:7; 16:6, 11; 17, 24; cf. Lev. 4:3–12) and Rabbinic literature (m. Yoma 3:8; 4:2; 6:2; t. Kippurim 2:1).

Hebrews 5:2 notes a minor difference between the Christ and the high priests—Christ has a more complete sympathy. In 5:3, the reader cannot help but notice the implied major difference—Christ did *not* sin and the high priests do (Heb. 7:26–27).

5:4 *And no one takes the honor for himself but [takes it] when being called by God just as even Aaron [was].*

Adumbrated in Hebrews 5:1, another aspect of a high priest is that he does not **take the honor for himself**, that is, he does not choose to be the high priest (cf. Num. 18:8; 1 Chr. 13:10; 23:13). Instead, he is **called by God**.[50] This was required of all high priests, but especially (**even**) **Aaron**, the first high priest (Exod. 28:1; Num. 3:10).[51] Interestingly, **Aaron** the person is only here in Hebrews, and his name is mentioned only two other times (Heb. 7:11; 9:4).[52] The AH will take up the matter

---

48. Owen, *Hebrews*, 20:460–61.

49. **It** (αυτὴν) is singular feminine as is **weakness**. Some Greek manuscripts have the feminine singular 'this' (ταυτὴν), which would also refer to **weakness**.

50. Josephus also notes that God chose Aaron and gave him 'honor'. In context, Josephus also lavishes significant praise on Aaron as being 'most righteous' (*Antiquities of the Jews*, 3:188–92).

51. So also Ellingworth, *Hebrews*, 280; *contra* Owen who sees only Aaron with this type of call (*Hebrews*, 20:478).

52. In the remainder of the NT, his name appears only in Luke 1:5 and Acts 7:40. See the great ode to Aaron in Sir. 45:6–22. T. Kippurim says, 'It is the religious requirement of the high priest to be greater than his brethren

of Christ's calling immediately in the next two verses, and then again in Hebrews 5:10 (also in 7:20–21).

Calvin well comments that the principle—one should not **take the honor for himself** but should be **called by God**—applies to all church officers.[53] Many creeds reference Hebrews 5:4 on this point in discussions of church officers.[54]

5:5–6 *Thus also Christ did not glorify himself to become a high priest, but the one who said to him, 'you are my Son, today I have begotten you'; just as also in another [place] he says, 'You are a priest forever according to the order of Melchizedek';*

Hebrews 5:1–4 includes at least two qualifications for OT high priests: sympathy (5:2–3) and being called (5:4). Hebrews 5:5–10 gives qualifications for Christ's being a high priest. The first is that he was called (5:5–6), which clearly parallels 5:4. The second includes sympathy but is broader than that (5:7–10). In any event, it loosely parallels 5:2–3.

The successive Aaronic high priests were chosen by God (Heb. 5:4). The AH asserts that this aspect of the OT Aaronic priesthood should match (**thus also**) to Christ. That is, **Christ did not glorify himself to become a high priest**, instead he was also appointed by God the Father (**the one who said**) just as the Aaronic priests were. The NT elsewhere confirms that Christ did not seek his own glory (e.g., John 8:50; Rom. 15:3; Phil. 2:6).

To confirm that Christ was appointed by God and not by himself, the AH quotes from Psalms 2:7 and 110:4. Psalm 2:7

---

in beauty, strength, wealth, wisdom, and good looks' (1:6).

53. Calvin, *Hebrews and 1 & 2 Peter*, 61. He also stresses that this principle applies to church *offices*. 'No form of government is to be drawn up in the Church by human judgment, but that men must wait for the command of God.'

54. E.g., Belgic Confession 31, Geneva Confession 4 (*Reformed Confessions of the 16th and 17th Centuries*, 2:100), Debrecen Synod 18 (*Reformed Confessions of the 16th and 17th Centuries*, 3:111), French Confession 31, WCF 17.4, 23.3, WLC 158, 176, Catechism of the Catholic Church §1578; WCF 8.3 relates to Christ. The Apostolic Constitutions makes the same point but cites Heb. 5:5–6 (2.27 [*ANF*, 7:410]).

was previously quoted in Hebrews 1:5.[55] For Psalm 110:4, here is the first of three times (Heb. 5:6; 7:17, 21; cf. 6:20) that Psalm 110:4 will be quoted in Hebrews, although Psalm 110:1 has been previously quoted in Hebrews 1:13 (cf. Heb. 1:3; 8:1; 10:12).[56] Interestingly, the AH here combines the first and last OT quotes of his catena in Hebrews 1:5–13.

Exactly what in the quotes shows that **Christ did not glorify himself**? In Psalm 2:7, it is that God the Father said to the **Son** that '**I have begotten you**.' That is, Christ was publicly declared (**begotten**) to be the **Son**; he did not declare himself to be the **Son**. In Psalm 110:4, God the Father declared to Christ, '**You are a priest forever;**' similarly, Christ did not declare himself to be a **high priest**. Note that both quotes involve direct speech from God the Father to God the Son and are in the form of promises, or solemn speech, or a covenant-oath.[57]

Intriguingly, although the AH's point is to confirm that Christ did not declare himself to be a **high priest**, the first quote relates to his being a **Son**. It is only the second quote that explicitly includes **priest**. Why might this be? **Son** and **priest**

---

55. The Greek for the Ps. 2:7 quote in Heb. 5:5 is an exact match to the Greek for the same quote in Heb. 1:5, which is an exact match to the LXX, which in turn is a word-for-word translation of the Hebrew. For a detailed explanation of Ps. 2:7 and Ps. 2, see discussion at Heb. 1:5.

56. The Greek for the Ps. 110:4 quote in Heb. 5:6 (and 7:17) matches the LXX excepting the elimination of the 'to be' verb εἶ, which is simply implied in Heb. 5:6. The Heb. 5:6 (and 7:17) quote is a word-for-word translation of the Hebrew (the Hebrew also has an implied 'to be' verb). For background on Ps. 110, see discussion at Heb. 1:13.

57. This is a strong argument for what Reformed theologians call the covenant of redemption—an agreement in eternity past among the Trinitarian persons. The eternal Father-Son relationship grounds these eternal promises that are also made within redemptive history (so also J. V. Fesko, *The Trinity and the Covenant of Redemption* [Ross-shire: Mentor, 2016], 94. Also related to Heb. 5:5–6, see the good discussion by Scott R. Swain, 'Covenant of Redemption,' in *Christian Dogmatics: Reformed Theology for the Church Catholic*, ed. Michael Allen and Scott R. Swain (Grand Rapids: Baker, 2016), 107–25, esp. 118–22. See further discussion at Heb. 7:20–22.

combine two major themes about Christ within Hebrews—the **Son** aspect of Christ is emphasized in Hebrews 1:1–3:6, and the **priest** aspect, from Hebrews 4:14–10:18. The AH wants to show by use of both major titles that Christ truly did not call himself. In addition, the use of **Son** prepares for a portion of the argument in Hebrews 5:8. Further, although the AH has already endeavored to show the kingship of Christ (**Son**), to this point in Hebrews he has only asserted that Christ is a **high priest**. He has not yet explained how this combination of kingship and priesthood matches with the OT's having *at some level* separate priests and kings (e.g., 2 Chr. 26:16–21, but Zech. 6:13).[58] Here is the double importance of Psalm 110: (1) it clearly combines the kingship of Christ (Ps. 110:1) with the priesthood of Christ (Ps. 110:4),[59] and (2) it adds the key point that Christ's physical lineage does not need to be from Levi to be a high priest; there is another priestly line, **according to the order of Melchizedek**.[60]

A major point in the book of Hebrews is that Christ is a **priest according to the order of Melchizedek**; however, this point is not expanded upon in 5:5–10. The emphasis in this section is that Christ has been *appointed* as a **high priest**,[61] not how this relates or does not relate to a Levitical priesthood.

---

58. In the Testament of Levi, confusingly there are three future priests, one is 'from Judah a king will arise and shall found a new priesthood in accord with the gentile model and for all nations' (8:11–14 [*OTP* 1:791]). The DSS community looked forward to two Messiahs, one from Aaron and one from Israel (1QS IX, 11). While at meals together, the Priest ate first after his blessing (the Messiah of Aaron?), then the Messiah of Israel ate, and then the entire community (1QSa II, 20–21).

59. Why did the AH use Ps. 2:7 instead of Ps. 110:1 here to make his point about the king-priest? In addition to the above arguments, possibly because both Ps. 2:7 and 110:4 quotes use explicitly the second person (**you are**) and Ps. 110:1 only implies it (suggestion by Guthrie, 'Hebrews,' 960).

60. For a discussion of the unfolding argument within Hebrews using Ps. 110 and especially Heb. 5:5–6, see Jared Compton, *Psalm 110 and the Logic of Hebrews*, LNTS 537 (London: T&T Clark, 2015), 70–76.

61. The AH takes **priest** in the Ps. 110:4 quote to be the **high priest** (Heb. 5:5, 10). Clearly, he is assuming that the Ps. 110:4 priesthood is unique to Christ due to **forever**.

The AH (intentionally?) leaves the congregation to ponder the **Melchizedek** implications, which he will subsequently discuss in detail in Hebrews 7.

When did Christ become a high priest? See discussion in the Reflections section below.

5:7–8 *who in the days of his flesh, having offered petitions and supplications with loud crying and tears to the one who is able to save him out of death and having been heard because of [his] reverence, although being a Son,*[62] *he learned obedience from the [things] which*[63] *he suffered,*

Hebrews 5:7–10 is one grammatical unit with two main (finite) verbs.[64] The grammatical emphasis is that Christ *learned* obedience (5:8) and *became* the source of eternal salvation (5:9). Each of these main verbs has two participles that modify them. 'Learned' is modified by 'having offered' and 'having been heard.' 'Became' is modified by 'having been perfected' and 'having been designated'.

Hebrews 5:7 begins with the subject of 5:7–10, **who in the days of his flesh**. **Who** obviously refers to Christ from 5:5. As all agree, **flesh** here refers to Christ's time upon the earth, and the term **flesh** is used in the sense of 'weak and fragile nature' (cf. 1 Cor. 15:50).[65] (The AH is not arguing that Christ's human nature ceased upon exaltation.[66]) This **flesh** emphasis conceptually parallels the previous 'weakness' comments

---

62. With no definite article, the emphasis is on the quality of Sonship. Cockerill suggests that a better translation would be 'Although being One who is Son' (*Hebrews*, 247).

63. The expression ἀφ' ὧν is apparently shorthand for ἀπὸ τούτων ἅ. So BDAG, 785.

64. Technically, because of the initial relative pronoun **who** that refers back to 'Christ' in Heb. 5:5, 5:7–10 is a subset of a long sentence that begins at 5:5.

65. Quote from notes in the *Geneva Bible: 1602 Edition*, folio 111.

66. So also, e.g., Aquinas, *Hebrews*, 114; and Owen, *Hebrews*, 20:498. Bruce notes that this is so because the AH's emphasis about a currently exalted, sympathetic high priest would not hold otherwise (*Hebrews*, 126).

about Christ (Heb. 4:15) and about the Aaronic high priests (Heb. 5:2). Thus, the AH implicitly makes the point that Christ has the experiential qualifications to sympathize with his people, as does the comment that his prayers were **loud crying and tears**. As with many previous statements in Hebrews, the clarity and boldness of this affirmation of the human nature of Christ is stunning.[67]

Concerning the expression, **having offered petitions and supplications with loud crying and tears**, the participle **having** *offered* is the same verb (προσφέρω) used in Hebrews 5:1, '*offer* gifts and sacrifices'; and 5:3, '*offer* sacrifices concerning sins, just as concerning the people, thus also concerning himself.' Clearly Hebrews 5:1 and 5:3 refer to priestly offerings.[68] Hence, these prayers are included, at least in part, in Christ's priestly work.[69] These prayers would have included prayers for others, and for himself as the sacrificial offering (cf. Heb. 13:15).[70] Some of Christ's prayers were with **loud crying and tears** (cf. Ps. 22:24). Many of Christ's anguished prayers and weeping for others occurred significantly before the cross event (e.g., Mark 1:35; Matt. 14:23; Luke 13:34; John 11:35). However, the Gospels also record that Christ prayed with intensity for himself (which would result in benefits to others) as *the* impending priestly self-sacrifice approached. This prayer in Gethsemane is well known to the church and probably was also to the AH and his congregation (Matt. 26:36–44 // Mark 14:32–39 // Luke 22:39–45; cf. Matt. 27:46; Luke 23:46; John 17:1–26).

---

67. So much so that Chrysostom comments on Heb. 5:7 concerning heretical groups that denied the humanity of Christ, 'Let the heretics be ashamed ... Seest thou that this is spoken concerning the Incarnation?' ('Homily 8 on Hebrews' [*NPNF*[1], 14:404]).

68. The LXX also uses προσφέρω often for presenting ('to offer' or 'to bring') various ritual offerings to God, e.g., Exod. 32:6; Lev. 1:13; 2:1; 3:6; 16:9, and Num. 3:4.

69. So also Brown, *Hebrews*, 253; Lane, *Hebrews*, 119; Johnson, *Hebrews*, 146; and Kleinig, *Hebrews*, 252; *contra* Attridge, *Hebrews*, 149.

70. Some see these prayers as only related to Christ and not for others, e.g., Koester, *Hebrews*, 288.

Christ's prayers are to God the Father, who is given the epithet, **one who is able to save him** (Christ) **out of death** (cf. Job 5:20; Pss. 33:19; 109:31; Hos. 13:14; Jas. 4:12). Obviously, Christ did die on the cross. Hence, this prayer relates to 'through and out of death'.[71] That is, Christ prayed for his resurrection **out of** the realm of **death**.

Christ's prayers were **heard**, that is, they were answered. Why? — **because of his** (Christ's) **reverence**.[72] God's answering prayers of righteous believers is certainly a theme throughout the Bible (e.g., Ps. 34:15; Prov. 15:29; Jas. 5:16).[73] In context, the AH is also alluding to the difference between Christ and the Aaronic priesthood; Christ was 'without sin' (Heb. 4:15) as opposed to Aaronic high priests who sacrificed partially for their 'own sins' (Heb. 5:3). This enhances even more the **reverence** of Christ and that his prayers would be **heard**.

Although being a Son, he learned obedience from the things which he suffered (Heb. 5:8). This is another amazing statement in Hebrews (cf. Phil. 2:6–8; Rom. 5:19).[74] The

---

71. Vos, 'The Priesthood of Christ in the Epistle of Hebrews,' 585. Thus I translated ἐκ θανάτου not ambiguously as 'from death', but more specifically, **out of death**. For a good explanation of this view, see Attridge, *Hebrews*, 150. *Contra* those who see Christ asking to be saved from the fear of the actual death experience, e.g., Owen, *Hebrews*, 20:509–10; and Brown, *Hebrews*, 256.

72. Many older translations and commentaries, but not all, translate ἀπὸ τῆς εὐλαβείας as 'from fear', implying anxious fear, e.g., KJV; and Calvin, *Hebrews and 1 & 2 Peter*, 65. This is a reasonable translation, However, most understand it today as **because of reverence** or 'godly fear'. In Greek literature, εὐλαβεία has a broad semantic range and includes the meanings of 'over-caution,' 'timidity,' '[anxious] fear,' 'reverence,' 'godly fear,' and 'piety' (LSJ, 720). The argument for **reverence** is that εὐλαβεία and its cognate elsewhere in Hebrews (11:7; 12:28) clearly mean **reverence**. Once given this, then ἀπό is interpreted as having a causal meaning (**because**) instead of 'from', even if **because** is not the statistically most prominent meaning (BDF §210.1). For a good explanation of options and implications along with the conclusion that **because of reverence** is correct, see Hughes, *Hebrews*, 184–86.

73. Attridge adds to this that there was 'a pattern delineating the ideal prayer of a pious man as that was understood in Hellenistic Judaism' ('"Heard Because of His Reverence" [Heb 5:7],' *JBL* 98 [1979]: 90–93, esp. 90).

74. Gregory of Nazianzus comments on this verse, 'Bearing all me and mine in Himself, that in Himself He may exhaust the bad, as fire does

concessive **although** indicates that this type of **Son**, the eternal **Son**, would *not* have been expected to learn obedience because learning obedience is normally required for those who are disobedient (cf. Heb. 12:3–11).[75] In fact, the eternal **Son** as he came into the world pledged to do God's will (Heb. 10:5–9) and he was 'without sin' (Heb. 4:15). Therefore, in what sense did Christ *learn* **obedience**? He **learned obedience** *existentially* or *experientially* as a fully human person with all the difficulties that encumber the human existence (cf. Luke 2:52).[76] Before the incarnation, Christ was obedient to his promises in the covenant of redemption. As part of his mediatorial (God-man) role, Christ in his human nature **learned obedience** existentially. This obedience is related to his qualifications to be a high priest and the merit by which believers are justified.

There are multiple ways that Christ was obedient, but he especially learned **from the things which he suffered**. Preeminently, this suffering of both body and soul certainly refers to the passion events and death of Christ, but it also includes all the suffering and humiliation throughout his life.[77] Further, this suffering includes the humiliation of Christ's simply becoming a human, given his exalted state before the incarnation—**although a Son**.[78] All of these sufferings contributed to aspects of Christ's **obedience**.

---

wax, or as the sun does the mists of earth' ('Fourth Theological Oration,' 6 (*NPNF*², 7:311).

75. Due to the similarities of sound, the combination of the verbs for learning (μαθ-) and suffering (παθ-) are often used in Greek literature. Sometimes the point is that suffering for one's own wrongs positively results in learning. Of course, this is not the point here. For a good list of citations, see Koester, *Hebrews*, 290.

76. So also Aquinas, *Hebrews*, 116; Owen, *Hebrews*, 20:524; Moffatt, *Hebrews*, 66; Vos, 'The Priesthood of Christ in the Epistle to the Hebrews,' 585; Koester, *Hebrews*, 290; Allen, *Hebrews*, 322; and Schreiner, *Hebrews*, 164.

77. So also Cockerill, *Hebrews*, 248; cf. Heidelberg Catechism 37. *Contra* Owen who wants to restrict the suffering mentioned here to Christ's passion (*Hebrews*, 20:523).

78. WSC 27.

5:9–10 *and, having been perfected, he became the source of eternal salvation to all those who obey him, having been designated by God a high priest according to the order of Melchizedek.*

In what sense was Christ **perfected** (τελειόω, Heb. 2:10; 5:9; 7:28)?[79] Does this relate to believers' being perfected (τελειόω, Heb. 7:19; 10:14; 11:40; 12:23; cf. 7:11)?[80] The concept of perfection in Hebrews has generated a fair amount of scholarly attention.[81]

First, some linguistic background: As cognates in Greek, the verb 'to perfect' (τελειόω) is related to the noun 'end'/'goal' (τέλος). Hence, with no specific context, the verb 'to perfect' could broadly and generically mean 'to complete/finish' or 'to be perfect', or 'to reach the end' or 'to accomplish the goal.' The context then 'fine tunes' the meaning. The LXX uses the verb with two basic meanings; one is the just-mentioned broad meaning that is fine tuned in context (e.g., 2 Sam. 22:26; 2 Chr. 8:16; Neh. 6:16; Sir. 50:19). The second meaning has a much more specific technical use. It relates to the consecration/ordination of OT priests and their appurtenances (e.g., Exod. 29:9, 29; Lev. 4:5; 16:32; 21:10; Num. 3:3). For example, in Exodus 29:9, the ESV translates as, 'Thus you shall *ordain* Aaron and his sons'; the KJV, 'Thou shalt *consecrate* Aaron and his sons.'[82] In the Hebrew, an idiom is used for 'to ordain/consecrate,' which mechanically translates as 'to fulfill the hand' (מלא יד). The LXX translates as 'to perfect (τελειόω) the hands.' Obviously, the LXX is using τελειόω with the very specific meaning of 'to ordain' or 'to consecrate'—that is, to set apart in a priestly context for God's special use.[83]

---

79. Other cognates in Hebrews are perfect/complete/mature (τέλειος, 5:14; 9:11); maturity/perfection (τελειότης, 6:1; τελείωσις, 7:11); perfecter (τελειωτής, 12:2); and end/goal (τέλος, 3:14; 6:8, 11; 7:3).

80. For extended discussion of believers' perfection, see commentary at Heb. 7:11.

81. See, e.g., Silva, 'Perfection and Eschatology in Hebrews,'; Silva ed., *NIDNTTE*, 4:472–77; Peterson, *Hebrews and Perfection*; Scholer, *Proleptic Priests*; and Allen, *Hebrews*, 324–26; and deSilva, *Hebrews*, 194–204.

82. In Lev. 16:32, the ESV translates as 'consecrate'.

83. The Geneva Bible translates as 'to consecrate' in Heb. 2:10; 5:9; and 7:28.

In Hebrews 5:9–10, the participial phrase **having been perfected** looks back to 'he learned obedience from the things he suffered' (Heb. 5:8) and looks forward to **became the source of eternal salvation ... having been designated by God a high priest**. Hence, here and in Hebrews 7:28, the priestly context is strong, although less so in 2:10. Is the AH using this special LXX meaning of 'to consecrate' at least partially when referring to Christ's **having been perfected**? For me, given the priestly context of the Hebrews, I conclude that at least partially the concept of being consecrated or being set apart as a priest is in view.[84] Of course, Christ's being set apart is connected to his priestly qualifications, which do include his 'having learned obedience'.[85] Hence, the more generic use of τελειόω as 'to perfect' is a good translation, maybe something like 'to perfect for priestly service' would be best in the passages that relate to Christ. How this relates to believers will be discussed at Hebrews 7:11.

Christ **became the source of eternal salvation**. Source probably has some overlap with Christ as 'leader' (Heb. 2:10; 12:2) because Hebrews 5:8–9 has linguistic and conceptual overlap with Hebrews 2:10, 'to perfect the leader of their salvation through sufferings.'

Hebrews 5:1–10 closes with **having been designated by God a high priest according to the order of Melchizedek**. This reinforces several points of the passage; Christ does provide **eternal salvation**, he has been **designated by God** for this task, and he is a **high priest according to the order of Melchizedek**.

---

84. So also Silva, 'Perfection and Eschatology in Hebrews,' 61; Allen, *Hebrews*, 325; and Beale, *A New Testament Biblical Theology*, 737–38; *contra* Peterson, *Hebrews and Perfection*, 29. Calvin prefers 'sanctified', which is more focused on qualifications (*Hebrews and 1 & 2 Peter*, 66). From my perspective, much of the discussion about τελειόω really revolves around when Christ became a priest. Usually, one's view of that determines much of one's conclusions concerning τελειόω.

85. Here I agree with Peterson who prefers a 'vocational' understanding of τελειόω, that is, during Christ's life he is being further equipped and further qualified to be a high priest (*Hebrews and Perfection*, 70–71, 96–103).

Reflections

According to Hebrews, when did Christ's mediatorial priesthood begin? The Christian churches that have the Westminster Standards as their subordinate standards confess that Christ had/has the office of priest during both his state of humiliation and his state of exaltation (WSC 23, WLC 42). However, some understand that Christ's priesthood in Hebrews did not begin until his exaltation.[86] This would then deny, at least in the book of Hebrews, the biblical book most concerned with Christ's priesthood, that Christ was priest during his state of humiliation.

An argument that Christ's priesthood began at his exaltation could be and has been made from Hebrews 5:5–6 and 4:14–16. Psalm 2:7 // Hebrews 5:5 is related to Christ's being Son at his exaltation. Psalm 110:4 // Hebrews 5:6 declares Christ's priesthood. This then matches the emphasis on Christ's interceding for us from heaven (Heb. 4:14–16). Hence, as the argument goes, Christ did not become the high priest until his exaltation.

---

86. So historic Socinian view; and Käsemann, *The Wandering People of God*, 223. For additional references, see lists in Attridge, *Hebrews*, 146n120; and Peterson, *Hebrews and Perfection*, 191–95. David M. Moffitt influentially (and wrongly) argues that Christ does not begin his priesthood until his resurrection and it is only in the heavenly sanctuary that Christ's sacrifice is presented to God (*Atonement and the Logic of Resurrection in the Epistle of Hebrews*, NovTSup 141 [Leiden: Brill, 2011]; and 'Jesus' Heavenly Sacrifice in Early Christian Reception of Hebrews: A Survey,' *JTS* 68 [2017]: 46–71.). Several of Moffitt's articles have been conveniently gathered in his *Rethinking the Atonement: New Perspectives on Jesus's Death, Resurrection, and Ascension* (Grand Rapids: Baker, 2022). For explanations, sources, and critiques of the historic Socinian view, see Benjamin J. Ribbens, 'Ascension and Atonement: The Significance of Post-Reformation, Reformed Responses to Socinians for Contemporary Atonement Debates in Hebrews,' *WTJ* 80 (2018): 1–23; Owen, *Hebrews*, 22:272–77, 298; Turretin, *Institutes of Elenctic Theology*, 2:403–06; and A. A. Hodge, *Outlines of Theology* (London: Banner of Truth, 1972 [1879]), 106–7. For an excellent article affirming Christ's priestly work both on earth and heaven, including interactions with Moffitt, see Brandon D. Crowe, 'Son and Priest, Then and Now: Christology and Redemptive History in Hebrews in light of the History of Interpretation,' *WTJ* 84 (2022): 19–38. For a helpful five-fold categorization of all views related to this question, see R. B. Jamieson, 'When and Where Did Jesus Offer Himself? A Taxonomy of Recent Scholarship on Hebrews,' *CurBR* 15 (2017): 338–68, esp. 342–54.

Before giving my view, here are some of the complications: Christ's offices of prophet, priest, and king are not always neatly separated. Christ's divine nature existed from eternity 'past', and his divine and human natures exist from his conception to eternity 'future'. The mediatorial (as God-man) role of Christ has its seeds in eternity past (covenant of redemption) and at some level is related to OT saints. Although there are difficulties in distinguishing Christ's work and qualifications as a *priest* and his work and qualifications as a *sacrifice* for sins, there must be significant overlap.

I do strongly affirm that Christ was/is the mediatorial priest in both his state of humiliation and his state of exaltation. I believe that Christ became a priest at his conception (Heb. 10:5–9);[87] he accomplished priestly acts with his various prayers throughout his life (Heb. 5:7);[88] his prime priestly act was the sacrificing of himself on the cross (7:26–27; 9:11–14, 23–28; 10:10; 13:12),[89] and his priestly work continues now as he intercedes for us (Heb. 4:14–16; 8:1–2).

In his 'high priestly prayer', Christ as a priest said concerning his disciples, '*I am praying for them*' (John 17:9) and *I do not ask for these only, but also for those who will believe in me through their word* (John 17:20). Oh, thank God! Christ prayed/prays for us in his states of humiliation and exaltation.

---

87. Calvin argues that Christ's 'birth included his priesthood'. The announcement in Heb. 5:6 was only 'the testimony the Father gave Him among men' (*Hebrews*, 62). Compton notes that the AH 'has placed it [Ps. 40:6–8] on the messiah's lips as he comes into the world (Heb. 10:5) and, thus, *prior* to his death … This runs contrary to Moffitt's claim that messiah's offering took place *after* his deliverance/resurrection' (*Psalm 110 and the Logic of Hebrews*, 150, 150n231; emphasis his; the Moffitt reference is *Atonement and the Logic of Resurrection in the Epistle of Hebrews*, 240–57).

88. So also, e.g., Johnson (*Hebrews*, 145–46); and Scholer, *Proleptic Priests*, 86–87, 197.

89. Cockerill notes that the 'analogy with the Day of Atonement sacrifice (9:11–14) … requires him to be High Priest before his self-offering' (*Hebrews*, 239). Vos argues that once it is settled that Christ's heavenly priestly activity 'rests on the preceding sacrifice' that is 'propitiatory', the technical question as to when Christ's priesthood began is of 'secondary importance' ('The Priesthood of Christ in the Epistle to the Hebrews,' 595).

6.
Warning and Promise
(5:11–6:20)

Hebrews 5:11–6:20 is one of five subsections of Hebrews 4:14–10:39.[1] The previous section ended with a comment connecting Christ to Melchizedek (Heb. 5:10). Hebrews 7 will emphasize in detail this connection. Hebrews 5:11–6:20 is a necessary interlude to encourage the readers to take seriously the teaching of Hebrews 7 about Christ and his Melchizedekian priesthood, which then in turn prepares for Christ's priestly work more specifically described in Hebrews 8:1–10:18. Note that Hebrews 5:11–6:20 opens ('concerning this') and closes referring to Melchizedek.

Hebrews 5:11–6:20 is primarily an exhortation passage and may further be subdivided.[2] Hebrews 5:11–6:12 includes a very severe warning. Hebrews 6:13–20 is positive encouragement related to God's 'promise' and 'oath.'[3]

---

1. The five subsections are 4:14–5:10; 5:11–6:20; 7:1–28; 8:1–10:18; and 10:19–39.

2. Exhortation passages in Hebrews are 3:7–4:13; 4:14–16; 5:11–6:12; 10:19–39; 12:1–13:17.

3. So also Vanhoye, *Structure and Message of the Epistle of Hebrews*, 87–88; and Attridge, *Hebrews*, 156. *Contra* Schreiner who agrees that Heb. 5:11–6:20 is the large section but prefers to see 5:11–6:8 as a warning subsection and 6:8–20 as an 'assurance and comfort' subsection (*Hebrews*, 167). Admittedly, Heb. 6:9–12 is somewhat of a transition passage.

Hebrews 5:11–6:12 begins and ends with comments related to the readers being exhorted not to be 'sluggish'. Further, the cohesiveness of this section is shown by the final verses (Heb. 6:11–12) being the primary point of the passage. Although, 6:9–12 is somewhat of a transition paragraph as it moves from warning to a mixture of assurance and exhortation in light of the warning.[4] The promise passage, Hebrews 6:13–20, picks up on the 'promises' mentioned in 6:12 and continues the aspects of assurance alluded to 6:9–12.

For purposes of this commentary, I will simply separate Hebrews 5:11–6:20 into five paragraphs: 5:11–14; 6:1–3; 6:4–8; 6:9–12; 6:13–20. Not all agree concerning the exact outline of this section, with 6:9–12 usually being the difficulty; however, all agree to these five paragraphs as some type of sub-units.

Milk and Solid Food (5:11–14)

Hebrews 5:11–14 is the beginning of the 5:11–6:12 exhortation section. The initial complaint is that the congregation, at least some of them, have been 'sluggish' in their concern to grow in the things related to Christ. To explain and rhetorically to motivate the 'sluggish', the AH uses the analogy of infants who need milk compared to mature adults who eat solid food. Obviously, the intent of this paragraph is to motivate the 'sluggish' to grow in their Christian understanding and practical outworking of the faith.

5:11–12a *Concerning which,[5] the word by us [is] extensive and*

---

4. Schreiner agrees that Heb. 5:11–6:20 is the large section but prefers to see 5:11–6:8 as a warning subsection and 6:9–20 as an 'assurance and comfort' subsection (*Hebrews*, 168). Schreiner matches to Cockerill who argues for 'shame (5:11–6:3), warning (6:4–8), consolation (6:9–12), and assurance (6:13–20)' (*Hebrews*, 252).

5. In form, οὗ can be either masculine or neuter, with the translations of either 'whom' or 'which,' respectively. Both would refer to the end of Heb. 5:10. 'Whom' relates directly to Melchizedek, and **which** to Christ as high priest related to Melchizedek. Both of these options are functionally the same.

difficult to say, since you have become sluggish in hearing. For indeed, [although] you ought to be teachers on account of time, you have need again [that] someone[6] teach you the basic principles of the oracles of God.

Concerning which relates directly back to the comment that Christ's priesthood is related to Melchizedek's (Heb. 5:10). The AH (**us**[7]) admits that his **word** or message about this is (1) **extensive**, that is, he has many things to say about it and (2) **difficult** (cf. 2 Pet. 3:16).[8] The extensiveness and difficulty are not simply due to the fault of the congregation, but are also related to the subject itself, Christ's priesthood and many of the OT connections (Heb. 7:1–10:18).[9] Of course, the AH believes one should be able to understand the message with some explanation as he will do beginning at Hebrews 7:1.

However, the AH's main point is not the inherent difficulty of the subject material, but that the difficulty is significantly increased **since you have become sluggish in hearing**. **Sluggish** is an adjective that is only used here and Heb. 6:12 in the NT. In general Greek, it is a negative term that with no context could also be translated as 'slothful'.[10] When applied to this context with **hearing**, it implies *morally* lazy to learn. Many Bible translations use 'dull', following Tyndale's 1526 Bible translation.[11] The AH does not refer to low *natural*

---

6. As most Bible translations do, I am taking τινα as the 'subject' of the infinitive 'to teach' (i.e., accusative, singular, masculine) as opposed to an interrogative pronoun that would result in 'what are the basic principles' (nominative, plural, neuter). The Douay-Rheims version opts for the interrogative pronoun.

7. As here, the AH sometimes uses 'we' (Heb. 2:1, 3; 3:1 (?); 5:11; 6:9; 13:18), and sometimes he uses 'I' (11:32; 13:19, 22, 23). See further discussion at Heb. 13:18–19.

8. As I interpret the Geek grammar of Heb. 5:11: **word** is the subject; there is an implied 'to be' verb; **extensive** and **difficult** are predicate adjectives; and **to say** is an epexegetical infinitive modifying **difficult**.

9. So also Owen, *Hebrews*, 20:547; and Ellingworth, *Hebrews*, 300.

10. LSJ, 1186.

11. 'You are slow to learn' (NIV); 'you have become too lazy to understand' (CSB17); 'you have been lazy and you haven't been listening' (CEB).

intelligence. He is pointing out a spiritual problem that results in **sluggish**/lazy behavior toward learning about Christ. The readers need to be exhorted about Christ, and this includes their being concerned to understand better his priesthood and its implications.

The AH's primary argument here is: Some in the congregation are **sluggish** in that **although** they have been Christians for long enough **time** to have become themselves **teachers** of others, in fact, they **need again** to be taught **the basic principles of the oracles of God**. The AH is using **teachers** in a generic sense—a more mature Christian should reasonably be able to instruct a less mature Christian—not in the sense of the ecclesiastical office of teacher (cf. Heb. 13:7).[12]

What is behind the expression **the basic principles of the oracles of God**? In the LXX, the expression **oracles** (λόγιον) **of God**/Lord often refers in a special way to the word(s) of God (Num. 24:4, 16; Pss. 12:6; 18:30; 105:19; 107:11; 119:82 [many times in Psalm 119]; 138:2; Isa. 5:24; 28:13; 30:27). In the NT, **oracles** (λόγιον) is used in Acts 7:38; Romans 3:2, and 1 Peter 4:11 and here. It always refers to God's special words. In Hebrews 5:12, it most likely refers to the OT Scriptures plus Christ speaking in the NT through his servants (cf. Heb. 1:2), that is, functionally, both the OT and the NT. But what are the **basic principles**?[13] There is no explicit explanation here, but in Hebrews 6:1–2 there are several examples. Possibly, the **basic principles** are the understanding that in principle Christ is the fulfillment of the OT.[14] Beyond that is the more

---

12. So also Hughes, *Hebrews*, 190; Attridge, *Hebrews*, 12; and Schreiner, *Hebrews*, 12; *contra* Owen, *Hebrews*, 20:567–68; he does qualify that not all in the congregation had the duty to become official teachers.

13. The Greek word behind **principles** is στοιχεῖον. Philo in a context of comparing sophisticated and unsophisticated learning uses στοιχεῖον to refer to vowels as the rudiments of learning, similar to our 'learning the A, B, C's' (*On the Preliminary Studies* 148–50). In Gal. 4:3, 9; Col. 2:8, 20, στοιχεῖον is used as evil principles. In 2 Pet. 3:10, 12, it refers to physical aspects of the earth.

14. Chrysostom thought the **basic principles** were related to Christ's human nature ('Homily 8 on Hebrews,' [*NPNF*[1], 14:405]). Aquinas, after

advanced understanding of the working out of many details of that principle; that is, the multiple ways Christ is the fulfillment of the OT and the many implications for one's life. Again possibly, the AH is making the point that some of the readers are flirting with the notion that Christ is not really the fulfillment of the OT, that is, maybe some are tempted to go back to Judaism or to a pagan religion, and along with this, their love for Christ and practical Christian virtues are waning.

5:12b *And you have become [such as] having need of milk and not solid food.*

Grammatically, this is the second (**and**) clause related to the 'for' in 5:12a. The readers' being 'sluggish' is shown by (1) 'you need again someone to teach you' and (2) **you have become such as having need of milk**. Although, Hebrews 5:12b is not really adding additional information, it is adding the **milk** metaphor that results in rhetorical punch to buttress his first point.

Having need of milk in context is not a compliment![15] Here the use of **milk** and **solid food** is obviously taken from a newborn baby's literally needing **milk** and not being able to eat **solid food**, which is then metaphorically applied to learning. **Milk** represents the educational level of an immature child and the inability to understand complex teaching. **Solid food** is for the mature learner. Of course literally, adults also drink **milk** in addition to **solid food**, but this is not the point of the metaphor. The AH is assuming that one understands that he is really comparing **milk** *only* with **solid food** plus **milk**. (See below 5:13–14 for a discussion of the **milk** metaphor outside of Hebrews.)

---

noting the difficult subjects already discussed in Hebrews, saw them as including the Trinity, two natures of Christ, and the decalogue. However, these were simply stated and were 'not explained or studied thoroughly' (*Hebrews*, 118–20, esp. 120).

15. The *Geneva Bible: 1602 Edition* curtly notes that this is 'an example of Apostolike chiding' (folio 111, original spelling retained).

With the use of **you *have* become** here and in Hebrews 5:11, the impression is given that some in the congregation have digressed in their spiritual walk. They were at some previous point beyond only **milk**, but now, at least metaphorically, they again require a significant amount of it.

5:13–14 *For everyone who partakes milk [is] inexperienced in the word righteousness, for he is an infant; but solid food is for the mature, who, on account of practice, have the senses being trained to discern good and evil.*

In Hebrews 5:13–14, the AH will further explain (**for**) the metaphor by adding some literal Christian-life details. Also note that he moves grammatically to a proverbial third person (**everyone who**) as opposed to the 'you' of 5:12. This has the effect of softening the direct accusation.[16] Further, it makes each reader ask himself whether he is an **infant** or a **mature** person (similar to how parables work). The intent is for those readers who identify themselves as an **infant** to be convicted, then repent and be motivated to move toward Christian maturity.

The Greek word for **mature** (τέλειος) is a cognate to the perfection word group, which has a special emphasis in Hebrews (see extended discussion at Heb. 5:9 and 10:14). On the surface, here the special emphasis does not appear to be explicitly in play because **mature** (τέλειος) is often contrasted in Greek literature with **infant**. However, it does dovetail nicely with the special emphasis.

Interestingly, the **solid food** metaphor incorporates athletic-training language to explain the **mature** person's behavior. The participle **being trained** (γυμνάζω) is a clear cognate to the Greek gymnasiums; however, it may be approaching a 'dead metaphor' in context.[17]

---

16. So also Ellingworth, *Hebrews*, 305; and Cockerill, *Hebrews*, 258. Ellingworth compares this to a similar move in Heb. 6:4–8 (*Hebrews*, 305).

17. An English example of a dead metaphor is the 'eye of a needle'. Virtually no current English speakers relate the small circular portion of a

How do the **infant** and **mature** Christian compare? The AH makes the same antithetical parallel point about each with different words. The **infant** is **inexperienced**. This is the antithesis to the **mature** person who by **practice** has his **senses being trained**. The **infant** is not familiar enough with the **word of righteousness** (i.e., word *about* righteousness, objective genitive). This is the antithesis to the **mature** person having the ability **to discern good and evil**.[18]

Given the above parallel, the **word of righteousness** and **to discern good and evil** relate to the same aspects of the mature Christian faith—centered on Christ that results in the many doctrinal and practical implications. This is contrasted with and/or built upon the 'basic principles of the oracles of God' (Heb. 5:12).

The **milk** metaphor in Scripture and in Greek non-canonical texts is used in a variety of ways.[19] The following includes various points of interest. The OT usage is dominated by the phrase 'a land flowing with milk and honey' (e.g., Exod. 3:20; Lev. 20:24; Num. 14:8; Deut. 27:3; Josh. 5:6; Jer. 32:22; Ezek. 20:6). Obviously, 'milk' here is a good thing as this referred to the land of Canaan and typologically to the NHNE. Interestingly, the AH discusses this promised land (of rest) in Hebrews 3:7–4:13, but no mention is made of this positive 'milk'. The author of the Epistle of Barnabas uses the OT 'milk and honey' and connects it the Christian life.[20] He claims that a literal child (παιδίον, not **infant** [νήπιος]) is normally nourished first with honey, then by

---

needle to a human eye. Although not as 'dead' as 'eye of a needle', similarly, γυμνάζω may have come to mean generic training or practice without any allusion to the athletic analogy, unless the context hinted at it.

18. Chrysostom comments that a baby is not able **to discern good and evil** even of food because 'oftentimes at least it puts dirt in its mouth' ('Homily 8 on Hebrews' [*NPNF*[1], 14:406]).

19. For general overviews of the literal and metaphorical use, see C. S. Keener, 'Milk,' *DNTB*, 707–9; and M. J. Wilkins, 'Milk, Solid Food,' *DLNT*, 736–38.

20. Tertullian describes the typical baptism ceremony. Immediately after being baptized, the new Christian is given 'to taste' a 'mixture of milk and honey' as if 'new-born children' (*On Crown* 3 [*ANF* 3:94]). I assume this relates to the OT 'milk and honey'.

milk.²¹ This then matches to faith first (honey) and then the 'word' (milk) (Barn. 6:8–19, esp. 6:17).

In 1 Peter 2:2, 'milk' for babies is used positively as spiritual nourishment for all Christians. The connection is the baby's 'strong and instinctive longing for a mother's milk'.²² The milk is related to the word of God (1 Pet. 1:22–25) and Christians should crave it.

Similar to Hebrews 5:11–14, 1 Corinthians 3:2 and various Greek wisdom/philosophical texts use milk to represent the immature person and food for the mature person. In 1 Corinthians 3:2, Paul connects 'infants' and 'milk' to immature Christians who are still involved in improper intra-church arguments. They are not yet mature Christians who could be taught with 'food'.²³ (Paul also uses 'milk' in 1 Cor. 9:7, but this is unrelated to 1 Cor. 3:2.)

Philo is an example of a Greek writer who often uses 'milk,' 'infant,' 'mature,' 'food,' and 'to train,' to make the point that one needs to progress in understanding.²⁴ He compares the 'milk'/'infant' of learning to 'encyclical sciences' (e.g., mathematics, grammar) and 'food' / 'mature'-person to higher level philosophy and/or various virtues.²⁵ For example,

> Do you not see that our bodies do not use solid and costly food before they have first, in their age of infancy, use such as had no variety, and consisted merely of milk? And, in the same way, think also that infantine food is prepared for the soul, namely the encyclical sciences, and the contemplations which are directed to each of them; but the more perfect [mature] food, namely the virtues, is prepared for those who are really full-grown men.²⁶

---

21. I am confused here as to the honey first and then milk.

22. J. Ramsey Michaels, *1 Peter*, WBC 49 (Waco: Word, 1988), 86.

23. A different Greek word is used for 'food': βρῶμα in 1 Cor. 3:2 and τροφή in Heb. 5:12, 14.

24. See *On Agriculture* 9; *On the Life of Abraham* 29; *On the Preliminary Studies* 19; *On Flight and Finding* 124; *On Dreams* 2.10; *That Every Good Person is Free* 111, 160.

25. E.g., *On Agriculture* 9; and *That Every Good Person is Free* 160.

26. Philo, *On the Preliminary Studies* 19, translation C. D. Yonge.

Here and elsewhere with the milk metaphor, Philo's word-level similarities are quite striking to the AH, but the conceptual-level is not. This simply shows that the AH is capable of and willing to use a common metaphor known in the Greco-Roman world and apply it to the Christian life (cf. Acts 17:28; Titus 1:12; 1 Cor. 3:2).

Reflections

Hebrews 5:12–14 acknowledges that a new Christian is at the 'milk' level and over time a Christian should progress to 'solid food.' The Westminster Standards reference these verses, among others, when making three straight-forward implications.

First, 'faith is different in degrees, weak and strong' (WCF 14.2). At one level this is stating the obvious, but it is a good reminder that the Bible presents the Christian life realistically. Not all Christians are at the same level of love for Christ, understanding of doctrine, and practical Christian living.

Second, in a discussion of how justification and sanctification differ, the point is first made that all Christians are blessed by God with both justification and sanctification. However, although justification is the same for all Christians, sanctification 'is neither equal in all, nor is this life perfect in any, but growing up to perfection' (WLC 77). In a discussion of the differences among Christians relative to sanctification, it is good to be reminded that (1) the imputed righteousness of Christ levels the playing field and (2) those Christians who are advanced in sanctification are still not perfect in this life.

Third, for the one teaching others, the differences in sanctification of those being taught should be taken into account. Teachers and preachers should be 'applying themselves to the necessities and capacities of the hearers' (WLC 159).[27] 'Necessities' covers a lot, but it does include a

---

27. The references for this quote all use the metaphor of food related to learning (1 Cor. 3:2; Heb. 5:12–14; Luke 12:42).

strong exhortation when needed (cf. Gal. 1:6–10; Heb. 12:7). The 'capacities' includes realizing that not all have the same understanding of the Bible, some need to be fed 'milk' and others 'solid food.' Of course, in most situations, the teacher is providing both 'milk' and 'solid food' in the same meal/context.

Not Laying Again the Foundation (6:1–3)

In Hebrews 5:11–14, the AH rhetorically states that some of the readers are 'sluggish' and 'infant(s)' with the obvious *implied* goal of having them grow in their Christian faith. Hebrews 6:1–3 is making the same point, but here the point is *explicitly* made: 'let us go on to maturity' and build further upon the initial 'foundation'.

The 'foundation' of the Christian life is described with six items that are in three pairs. The first and third pairs are straightforward; the second pair—'baptisms'/washings and 'laying on of hands'—has been debated throughout the history of Christianity.

6:1a–b *So then, let us leave[28] the basic word about[29] Christ [and] let us go on to maturity, not laying again a foundation ...*

By his use of **so then**, the AH shows those in the congregation that he realizes they are not stuck with always being 'sluggish' and 'infant(s)' as described in Hebrews 5:11–14. He now

---

28. **Let us leave** is my translation for the Greek participle ἀφέντες. I interpret this participle as an 'attendant circumstance' participle, which means it takes on the imperatival force from the main verb **let us go on** (similar construction in Heb. 12:1), although the main verb still has greater imperatival force. There is not an English grammatical equivalent to show two levels of imperatival force. My translation is reflected in, e.g., NIV, ESV, and CEB. Translating as a simple adverbial participle is KJV and NASB. For a good discussion of attendant circumstance participles, see Wallace, *Greek Grammar Beyond the Basics*, 640–45.

29. As virtually all commentators do, I take τοῦ Χριστοῦ as an objective genitive ('word about Christ') as opposed to a subjective genitive (word spoken by Christ). Attridge is an exception (*Hebrews*, 162).

explicitly encourages them to grow in their Christian doctrine and practice, that is, to move toward being Christians with an expected level of **maturity**.[30] He does this with a softer tone as he, at least grammatically, includes himself (**us**) among those who need to **go on to maturity**.[31] Of course, all Christians have room for **maturity** in some areas of their life, and the AH is alluding to this; however, his main point is for the readers to move beyond their current stunted-growth.

The expression **the basic word** (i.e., doctrine) **about Christ** (i.e., Christianity) is functionally equivalent to the 'basic principles of the oracles of God' in Hebrews 5:12. Both of these expressions emphasize doctrine, but Christian practice is also related to **maturity** as shown by the first of the following six foundational items ('repentance from dead works'). To **leave** does not mean to totally abandon the **basic word**, but do not be *only* a '**basic-word** Christian.' This understanding is clear from the **foundation** metaphor.[32] One does not abandon the **foundation** when constructing the remainder of the house, but builds upon it.[33] However, to lay **again** a second **foundation** is improper, a house only needs one **foundation**.

---

30. The Greek for **maturity** is τελειότης, which is a cognate of the 'perfection' word group in Hebrews. See discussion at Heb. 5:9 and 7:11. Here, however, τελειότης does not have the more typical sense of eschatological/new-covenant perfection as prominent elsewhere in Hebrews (*contra* Craig Allen Hill, 'The Use of Perfection Language in Hebrews 5:14 and 6:1 and the Contextual Interpretation of 5:11–6:3,' *JETS* 57 [2014]: 727–42).

31. So also, e.g., Moffatt (*Hebrews*, 73) and Hughes (*Hebrews*, 194). *Contra* Brown who sees the AH as considering himself as the teacher and the readers as the pupils, not that the AH needed **maturity** himself (*Hebrews*, 275).

32. Several times Philo also uses both **basic** (αρχή) and **foundation** (θεμέλιος) in the same context as parallel concepts, see *Allegorical Interpretation* 3:113; *Who is the Heir* 116; *On the Preliminary Studies* 146; and *On the Special Laws* 2:110.

33. Chrysostom has the wonderful analogy of a boy learning his letters (i.e., A, B, Cs). The boy cannot go on to read literature while forgetting his letters; similarly a Christian cannot advance in the Christian life while forgetting the foundational truths ('Homily 9 on Hebrews,' [*NPNF*[1], 14:409]).

6:1c–2 ... *of repentance from dead works and faith toward God, teaching*[34] *of baptisms and laying on of hands, and resurrection of [the] dead and eternal judgment.*

The AH lists six items in three pairs that form the 'foundation':

repentance from dead works / faith toward God
teaching of baptisms / laying on of hands
resurrection of the dead / eternal judgment

As noted above, the first pair and the third pair are fairly straightforward. As most agree, the first pair, **repentance from dead works and faith toward God**, refers to one's initial coming to Christ.[35] The expression **dead works** means sinful works done by an unregenerate person (cf. Heb. 9:14; 4 Ezra 7:119). Certainly, a Christian is to have **faith** throughout his life (e.g., Hebrews 11); however, here it relates to one's initial coming to **God**/Christ.

The third pair, **resurrection of the dead and eternal judgment**, clearly refers to the end of the age. **Judgment** would not necessarily be punishment, but would be God's either positive (by grace) judgment or negative judgment about humans. This **judgment** is **eternal** in the sense that it cannot be changed.

What about the second pair, **teaching of baptisms and laying on of hands**? There is significant disagreement here. First of all, I do not see these three pairs as the full-orbed summary of the foundation of the Christian life. For example, there is no explicit mention of Christ, or God as

---

34. A few important manuscripts have **teaching** in the accusative (διδαχὴν) as opposed to the genitive (διδαχῆς). This has the effect of making **teaching** an appositive with **foundation**, which results in items three through six all being prefaced with the word **teaching**. Lane chooses the accusative and concludes that items three through six are all 'catechetical instruction' built upon repentance and faith (*Hebrews 1–8*, 130, 132, 140). *Contra* Lane, Metzger gives an 'A' rating to the genitive (*TCGNT*[2], 596). My translation and exegesis assume the genitive.

35. So also Calvin, *Hebrews and 1 & 2 Peter*, 71; Brown, *Hebrews*, 277; Hughes, *Hebrews*, 197; and Koester, *Hebrews*, 304. Cf. Heb. 9:14.

creator, the Scriptures, etc. Instead, the Christian life is quickly summarized by noting the obvious *beginning* (first pair, **repentance, faith**) and the great events of the *end* of the age (third pair, **resurrection, judgment**). The second pair (**baptisms, laying on of hands**) is a further explanation of the first pair, that is, it is a parenthesis between the first and third pairs.[36]

Concerning **teaching of baptisms** and/or washings,[37] virtually everyone agrees that this refers to or includes Christian baptism due to the connection to **repentance** and **faith** and/or Christian baptism being a foundational aspect of Church membership.[38] But how does one explain the plural? Options include: (1) Some had improperly thought that multiple baptisms were proper with this teaching showing that there was only one correct baptism.[39] (2) Proper Christian teaching on water baptism would also include baptism by fire (purification of the Spirit) and by blood (Rom. 6:3 and martyrdom).[40] (3) Plural people are baptized.[41] (4) The teaching about Christian baptism by distinguishing it from

---

36. Although not an airtight argument for my view, it is noted that the second pair does not have a conjunction (neither τέ nor καί) connecting it to the first pair and there is a conjunction connecting the third pair to the first/second. Those who also see the second pair as some sort of parenthesis include Calvin, *Hebrews and 1 & 2 Peter*, 72–73; and Owen, *Hebrews* 21:18. Others functionally see it that way if they interpret the second pair as related to Christian baptism (e.g., Koester, *Hebrews*, 305; Schreiner, *Hebrews*, 176–77; and Kleinig, *Hebrews*, 276). Those explicitly against seeing a parenthesis include Brown, *Hebrews*, 279 and those who interpret **teaching** as being in the accusative.

37. The Greek is βαπτισμός, which could be translated as 'washing' (Mark 7:4, 8 [some manuscripts]; Heb. 9:10) or as more specifically, Christian baptism (Col. 2:12 [some manuscripts]). Although not in Hebrews, also in the NT is βάπτισμα, which often refers to John the Baptist's baptism (e.g., Matt. 21:25; Acts 1:22), but does also include Christian baptism (Rom. 6:4; Eph. 4:5; 1 Pet. 3:21; cf. Luke 12:50).

38. Belgic Confession 34 references Heb. 6:2 to show that one is to only be baptized once, that is, baptism is part of the one foundation.

39. Chrysostom, 'Homily 9 on Hebrews,' (*NPNF*[1], 14:410).

40. Aquinas, *Hebrews*, 125. Owen, interestingly, says this is the second best option (*Hebrews*, 21:56–57).

41. Owen, *Hebrews*, 21:57.

John the Baptist's baptism, OT washings, and/or first-century Jewish washing-rituals.[42] The fourth option is the best.

How is **laying on of hands** related to **baptisms**? Aquinas sees the **laying on of hands** as the later sacrament of confirmation for those who were baptized as an infant.[43] Most connect this more directly to baptism by seeing the **laying on of hands** as part of the baptism ceremony and that it symbolizes the gift of the Holy Spirit, that is, water and Spirit are combined (cf. Ezek. 36:25–27; John 3:5; Acts 8:17; 19:5–6; Titus 3:5).[44] Although the connection between water, Spirit, and baptism is strong in the NT, the connection with **laying on of hands** is less so. Hence, I suggest that the **laying on of hands** refers to ministerial ordination (e.g., Num. 8:10; Acts 6:6; 13:3; 1 Tim. 4:14; 5:22). It is connected to baptism in that an ordained minister would be performing the baptism.[45]

6:3 *And we will do this, if indeed God permits.*

This refers back to 'let us go on to maturity' from Hebrews 6:1. The AH further encourages the congregation by the comment **we will do this**. Interestingly, he inserts the qualifier, **if indeed God permits**. It is not unusual for Bible writers to insert this type of phrase when making statements about future plans (e.g., Acts 18:21; 1 Cor. 4:19; 16:7; Jas. 4:13–17).[46] What may have prompted its inclusion here

---

42. This is the most common solution, e.g., Moffatt, *Hebrews*, 75; Hughes, *Hebrews*, 199–202; and Schreiner, *Hebrews*, 176.

43. Aquinas, *Hebrews*, 125. Calvin has a similar confirmation view, although without the Roman Catholic sacramental theology. He mentions that 'this passage also tends towards the approval of paedo-baptism' (*Hebrews and 1 and 2 Peter*, 73).

44. So, e.g., Owen, *Hebrews*, 21:59–60; Bruce, *Hebrews*, 142; and Mitchell, *Hebrews*, 120. There are references in church history that appear to combine **baptism** and **laying on of hands** in the same ceremony, but they do not clearly do so, at least to me. See Tertullian, *On the Resurrection of the Flesh* 8 (*ANF*, 3:551); *On Baptism* 18 (*ANF*, 3:677); and *Epistles of Cyprian* 73.6–7 (*ANF*, 5:388)

45. Interestingly, Timothy is mentioned in Heb. 13:23, and it is he who is ordained in 1 Tim. 4:14 using the same expression, **laying on of hands**.

46. The Bohemian Confession 20 (1535) references Heb. 6:3 to note that

beyond the fact that the AH made a future plan? Possibly, he is conscious of time constraints as events in his location may prevent him from finishing the letter (cf. Heb. 11:32). Or maybe it is a broader reminder that any spiritual growth is ultimately done in accordance with God's providential will.

Reflections
As noted above, the specific rationale for inserting 'if indeed God permits' in the context of Hebrews 6:3 is not clear. It is true, however, that any statement about our future plans ought to have this or a similar qualifier. Of course, we do not need to *say* or *write* it every time, but we ought to at least *think* it.

In the past, many formal invitations in the western world would add '*DV*' somewhere on the invitation. *DV* stands for the Latin *Deo volente*, 'God willing.' That is, the wedding will take place on such and such a date, God willing. Since these were formal invitations, the thoughts about God were formalized on the invitation.

Although less so now, I still occasionally receive e-mails from ministers that include *DV* about a plan for a future event. I used to include *DV* in my e-mails; however, to avoid confusion, I do now sometimes use 'Lord willing' as opposed to *DV*.

Warning of Apostasy (6:4–8)

Hebrews 6:4–8 is clearly divided between the explicit warning (6:4–6) and the agricultural metaphor related to the warning (6:7–8).[47]

This explicit warning passage has caused debates down through church history, and those debates continue today. The text indicates there are a type of people who at some

---

for any living non-Christian there is still time to repent, 'if God permits' (*Reformed Confessions of the 16th and 17th Centuries*, 1:338). 1 Cor. 16:7 and Heb. 6:3 use the same verb (ἐπιτρέπω), although 1 Cor. 16:7 uses the aorist subjunctive and Heb. 6:3, the present subjunctive.

47. Note the many parallel concepts in Heb. 3:6, 12; 10:26–31; and 12:25–29.

point were associated with the church and then 'fell away'; it is now impossible for these people to repent. Questions related to this include: Are these people true believers? Can true believers lose their salvation? What does 'fell away' mean and is it irrevocable? Is this simply a hypothetical situation?

To orient the reader to various major options before getting to the details of my exegesis, a brief summary of four major views is presented without presenting the justifications for each view.[48] There are more views than the four listed. Note that 'apostasy' is usually defined as a complete abandonment of Christ and his church by a baptized person. As a subset of that, *irrevocable* apostasy further includes that the apostate person will never truly return to Christ and his church. My view is the first option below.

Option 1: Traditional Reformed.[49] This view assumes that a true believer will persevere in Christ until the end. The people referred to in Hebrews 6:4–6 are not true believers but are non-believers associated with the visible church. 'Fell away' refers to irrevocable apostasy.

Option 2: Minority Reformed.[50] This view assumes that

---

48. Allen has an excellent discussion of five views. Some of his five overlap with mine (*Hebrews*, 370–77).

49. So, e.g., Calvin, *Hebrews and 1 & 2 Peter*, 74–77; Owen, *Hebrews*, 21:69–91; Brown, *Hebrews*, 283–96; Hughes, *Hebrews*, 206–12; Bruce, *Hebrews*, 144; Turretin, *Institutes of Elenctic Theology*, 2:587–93; Brakel, *The Christian's Reasonable Service*, 4:288–92; WCF 10.4; WLC 68; Vos, *Reformed Dogmatics*, 4:107, 222–26; Berkhof, *Systematic Theology*, 549; Roger Nicole, 'Some Comments on Hebrews 6:4–6 and the Doctrine of the Perseverance of God with the Saints,' in *Current Issues in Biblical and Patristic Interpretation: Studies in Honor of Merrill C. Tenney Presented by His Former Students*, ed. Gerald F. Hawthorne (Grand Rapids: Eerdmans, 1975), 355–64; Wayne Grudem, 'Perseverance of the Saints: A Case Study from Hebrews 6:4–6 and the Other Warning Passages in Hebrews,' in *The Grace of God, The Bondage of the Will*, ed. Thomas R. Schreiner and Bruce A. Ware, 2 vols. (Grand Rapids: Baker, 1995), 1:133–82; and Fanning, 'A Classical Reformed View.'

50. So, e.g., G. C. Berkouwer, *Faith and Perseverance*, trans. Robert D. Knudsen, Studies in Dogmatics (Grand Rapids: Eerdmans, 1958), 120; Loraine Boettner, *The Reformed Doctrine of Predestination* (Phillipsburg: Presbyterian and Reformed, 1932), 195–96; Shedd, *Dogmatic Theology*, 805n13; and Schreiner, *Hebrews*, 480–91.

a true believer will persevere in Christ until the end. 'Fell away' refers to irrevocable apostasy. The people referred to in Hebrews 6:4–6 *are* true believers; however, God uses these warnings as a means to ensure that none of them fall. Hence, true believers never actually become apostates.

Option 3: No Second Baptism.[51] Most in this view assume that it is possible for a true believer not to persevere in Christ. Some of the people referred to in Hebrews 6:4–6 are true believers who have abandoned Christ and his church. 'Fell away' does not refer to irrevocable apostasy. To what then does 'it is impossible ... to renew them again to repentance' refer? — to a denial of a second baptism. Hence, a true believer who fell from the faith could be restored to the faith; however, he could not be baptized a second time. This is primarily an early and medieval church view that probably came to prominence with the Novatian controversy. Many in the church abandoned her under threat of execution by the Roman emperor Decius in AD 250–251. Following this persecution, Bishop Novatian said that those who abandoned the church ('lapsed' Christians) could not ever be restored again (taking 'fell away' as irrevocable apostasy). Cyprian argued that they could be restored, but not re-baptized.[52]

Option 4: Traditional Arminian and Trent/Post-Trent Roman Catholic.[53] This view assumes that it is possible for a true believer not to persevere in Christ. The people referred to in Hebrews 6:4–6 are true believers who have abandoned Christ

---

51. So, e.g., Chrysostom, 'Homily 9 on Hebrews,' (*NPNF*[1], 14:410); Ambrose, *Concerning Repentance* 2.2.6–12; and Aquinas, *Hebrews*, 128.

52. Cyprian, *Epistle 40, 43, 48* (*ANF*, 5:319, 321–22, 325–26); Eusebius, *Ecclesiastical History*, 6.42–43; 7.7–8; *A Treatise Against the Heretic Novatian by an Anonymous Bishop* (*ANF*, 5:657–63). So also Aquinas, *Summa Theologiae* 3a.84.10 (*Ad Primum* 1).

53. So, e.g., Moffatt, *Hebrews*, 76–79; Scot McKnight, 'The Warning Passages of Hebrews: A Formal Analysis and Theological Conclusions,' *TJ* 13 (1992): 21–59; Grant R. Osborne, 'A Classical Arminian View,' in *Four Views of the Warning Passages in Hebrews*, 86–128; Cockerill, *Hebrews*, 273–77; and Catechism of the Catholic Church §§598, 655, 679; cf. Council of Trent, Decree on Justification, chs. 12–15.

and his church. 'Fell away' refers to irrevocable apostasy here. Scholars in this camp also strongly believe that one can regain salvation. Hence, a true believer may become an apostate, but not necessarily irrevocably apostate.[54]

6:4–6a *For [it is] impossible [for] those who once were enlightened, and tasted the heavenly gift, and became partakers of the Holy Spirit, and tasted the good word of God and powers of the coming age, and [then] fell away to renew [them] again to repentance,*

Hebrews 6:4–6 is one sentence. The main grammatical part of the sentence is **it is impossible ... to renew them again to repentance**. The group discussed (**them**) is designated by five Greek participles, **those enlightened**, **tasted**, **became partakers**, **tasted**, and **fell away**.[55] The pronouns in Hebrews 4:4–8 are all third person. This is different than those in 6:1–3 and 6:9–12 that are first and second person.

The exact nuance of the opening **for** is not clear. It probably gives the general reason that any visible church ought to be concerned about true 'maturity' (Heb. 6:1).[56] The consequences for those who move to irrevocable apostasy are devastating.

With no context, the first four participial phrases could reasonably be used to describe true believers. However, several factors lead me to see this group as not true believers. (1) The emphasis elsewhere in Hebrews on the assurance of the believer to persevere based on the faithfulness of God in Christ the high priest needs to be taken into account

---

54. Allen complains that 'most contemporary Arminians are inconsistent in their treatment of Heb. 6:6 where renewal to repentance is said to be "impossible"' (*Hebrews*, 371 n. 396). Roger Nicole, from a Reformed perspective, calls this a 'happy inconsistency' ('Some Comments on Hebrews 6:4–6,' 357).

55. These five substantival participle phrases are all related to the one article τούς, which is in the accusative because they are the 'subject' of the infinitive **to renew**. In the minority, Schreiner argues that the fifth participle, **fell away**, is a conditional participle, that is, '*if* one fell away' (*Hebrews*, 188).

56. So also Owen, *Hebrews*, 21:72. Others connect directly to 'if God permits' in Heb. 6:3 (e.g., Moffatt, *Hebrews*, 76; Lane, *Hebrews 1–8*, 141) with differing rationales for doing so.

(e.g., Heb. 2:17–18; 6:10, 13–20; 7:25; 8:12; 9:15; 10:14).[57] (2) The change of pronouns to third person appears to be 'purposely vague'.[58] This encourages those in the congregation to see this group as generally different from themselves. (3) The comment that 'better things, that is, having salvation' (Heb. 6:9) is strong evidence that the group are *not* considered as having salvation. (4) Those that fell in the OT typological wilderness situation described in Hebrews 3:7–19 fits very well with the group described in Hebrews 6:4–6. Both groups experienced as part of the visible covenant community amazing things and also neither persevered.[59] (5) Hebrews 6:7–8 includes the same land that received the same rain but with two different results. (6) The parable of the sower includes 'soils' that initially appeared to be good but time showed they were not (Matt. 13:1–23 // Mark 4:1–20 // Luke 8:4–15). (7) The broad biblical teaching that the church may be categorized as visible (includes both believers and non-believers) and invisible (only believers) (Rom. 9:6; 1 Cor. 11:19; 1 John 2:19; Rev. 3:1; WCF 25.1–2). (8) The broad biblical teaching that every true believer will persevere (e.g., John 10:28–29). Once given these factors, a more careful look at these four participial phrases confirms that the language is appropriate for those who are not true believers but were only visible members of a covenant community.[60]

Those enlightened refers to those who at some level understand the Christian gospel and have been instructed (cf. Eph. 1:18; Heb. 10:32).[61] Those who **tasted the heavenly**

---

57. Fanning well emphasizes this ('A Classical Reformed View,' 197–99); similarly, Nicole, 'Some Comments on Hebrews 6:4–6,' 358–59.

58. Kistemaker, *Hebrews*, 161.

59. So also Dave Mathewson, 'Reading Heb 6:4–6 in Light of the Old Testament,' *WTJ* 61 (1999): 209–25.

60. For an excellent defense of these four not referring to true believers, see Grudem, 'Perseverance of the Saints,' 141–48.

61. Many in the early and medieval church tie **enlightened** to baptism based on Rom. 6:3–4 and Titus 3:5, e.g., Justin Martyr, *The First Apology* 61 (*ANF*, 1:182); Ambrose, *Concerning Repentance* 2.1.6–12 (*NPNF*[2], 10:345–46); and Aquinas, *Hebrews*, 128. So also Catechism of the Catholic Church §1216.

gift are those who have experienced aspects of God's blessings but not the full salvation. **Tasted** is an ambiguous word and does not itself require a conclusion of full salvation (cf. Heb. 2:9; Matt. 27:34). Possibly this is an allusion to the manna in the wilderness (Exod. 16:35). **Partakers of the Holy Spirit** refers to those who 'may have some common operations of the Spirit' (WCF 10.4; cf. Matt. 7:22–23; 13:20–21) and also may have benefited from others in the church who had the gift of the Holy Spirit. The final of the four is **tasted the good word of God and powers of the coming age**.[62] Again, the ambiguous **tasted** is involved. These visible members sat under the preaching of the **good word of God**.[63] Possibly, they experienced some level of conviction of sin. The context of the church included signs and wonders that were a foreshadowing of the **powers of the coming age** (cf. Heb. 2:4), not to mention Christ's second coming. This group experienced significant spiritual blessings, but in the end, they never put saving trust in Christ. I see this group not simply as nominal church attenders, but those who to a significant degree had tasted the bountiful fruits of Christ's blessings.[64]

The fifth participle is **fell away**. The vast majority of modern commentators of all stripes interpret this as irrevocable apostasy (cf. Mark 3:28–29; 1 John 5:16; Rom. 11:11; Heb. 3:12;

---

62. The AH uses **tasted** twice in Heb. 6:4–5 but changes the case of the direct object; in Heb. 6:4, the object is in the genitive and in 6:5, the accusative. Normally, if the direct object of **taste** is in the genitive, the idea would be that only a part of the object is tasted (partitive genitive). This makes sense in Heb. 6:4. If the direct object is in the accusative, one would expect that the whole object is tasted/eaten (holistic genitive). This does *not* make sense in Heb. 6:5. Why then the change? I conclude that it is simply a stylistic variation (so also Kistemaker, *Hebrews*, 163). For a general grammatical discussion, see BDF §169; and BDAG, 195.

63. Matthew McAffee argues that the **good word** is an 'equivalency' for the OT covenantal blessings based primarily on Josh. 21:45 and 23:15 and confirmed by 'blessing' in Heb. 6:7 ('Covenant and the Warnings of Hebrews: The Blessing and the Curse,' *JETS* 57 [2014]: 537–53, esp. 538–44, 548).

64. So also Brown, *Hebrews*, 290.

12:17).⁶⁵ This is the only place **fell away** (παραπίπτω) is used in the NT. In the LXX in Ezekiel, it is consistently used in contexts of apparent irrevocable apostasy (Ezek. 14:13; 15:8; 18:24; 20:27; 22:4).⁶⁶ The argument for the concept of irrevocable apostasy here is not solely based on the word **fell away**, but also on the context of an **impossible** future **repentance** and the two participles in Hebrews 6:6b.

It is impossible ... to renew them again to repentance. Other usage in Hebrews (6:18; 10:4; 11:6) confirms that **impossible** is a very strong word. The subject of who causes it to be or why it is **impossible** for this group to repent is not explicit. Ultimately, it must include God's providence and his justice, but it also probably includes the proximate reason that those in this group do not want to repent.⁶⁷ **Repentance** here means true repentance of a believer upon first coming to Christ (cf. Heb. 6:1). Obviously, this group first had a non-saving repentance experience and it is now **impossible** for them to have a true saving **repentance**. The adverb **again** in **to renew them again to repentance** is used based on the two similar, but not exactly the same, types of repentances.

---

65. So, e.g., Calvin, *Hebrews and 1 & 2 Peter*, 75; Owen, *Hebrews*, 21:86–91; Moffat, *Hebrews*, 79; Hughes, *Hebrews*, 206; Ellingworth, *Hebrews*, 323; Attridge, *Hebrews*, 171; Koester, *Hebrews*, 312, 319; Cockerill, *Hebrews*, 273; Johnson, *Hebrews*, 161; and Lindars, *The Theology of the Letter of Hebrews*, 68–71. A significant exception to this would be those who see **fell away** as referring to some type of punishment short of losing one's salvation. Allen is the best representative. He sees the punishment as 'loss of rewards' partially in this life and partially in the eschaton (cf. 1 Cor. 3:13–15; Rom. 14:10–12; 2 Cor. 5:10) (*Hebrews*, 359–63, 370, 377, 380–93).

66. So also Schreiner, *Hebrews*, 187. Παραπίπτω is also use in Esth. 6:10; Wis. 6:9; 12:2; these contexts are not necessarily apostasy. Although not emphasized, the concept for irrevocable apostasy is in Philo, *Allegorical Interpretation* 3:213; and *On Flight and Finding* 84; and in Rabbinic literature, m. Abot 5:13; and b. Sanhedrin 107b.

67. Calvin, 'The author of Hebrews does not say that pardon is refused if they turn to the Lord, but he utterly denies that they can rise to repentance, because they have been stricken by God's just judgment with eternal blindness on account of their ungratefulness' (*Institutes* 3.3.24).

6:6b *[because] those are recrucifying for themselves the Son of God and making an example [of him].*

Hebrews 6:6b has two Greek participles (**recrucifying** and **making-an-example**[68]) that modify 'it is impossible ... to renew them again to repentance.' The participles modify by giving the cause as to why it is impossible.[69]

The meaning of the phrase **recrucifying for themselves the Son of God** is not completely clear. Possibly it refers to the need to crucify Christ a second time in order to have forgiveness. This would be against the refrain in Hebrews that Christ died once (e.g., Heb. 9:12; 10:10) and indicate that his first death was not good enough.[70] Or more likely, the phrase notes that in their apostasy, they were and will be continually insulting and mocking Christ similar to the mob at Christ's crucifixion that shouted 'crucify him' (Mark 15:13).[71] That is, they are with enjoyment *metaphorically* **recrucifying** Christ. This second interpretation better dovetails with **making an example of him**, which is in context a negative example.

Allow me to summarize my exegesis of Hebrews 6:4–6 and add an implication related to true believers. In the book of Hebrews, the AH is addressing members of a visible church that he is encouraging to persevere in Christ. He indicates that the majority of the group are true believers but realizes that not all are. In 6:4–6, as opposed to 6:1–3 and 6:9–12, the AH indicates that it is possible for some to have a serious engagement with spiritual things but not be truly converted. Further, he indicates that some of these may turn away from the faith and irrevocably apostatize. Of course, for true believers, this warning *secondarily* affects them even though

---

68. Both of these words only occur here in the NT.

69. So also Hughes, *Hebrews*, 213; Bruce, *Hebrews*, 149; and Ellingworth, *Hebrews*, 324. A 'causal participle' is quite common in the NT, see Wallace, *Greek Grammar Beyond the Basics*, 631. The present tense of the participles implies the continuing state of the irrevocable apostasy (so also Hughes, *Hebrews*, 218n68; and Attridge, *Hebrews*, 172).

70. So Ellingworth, *Hebrews*, 324.

71. So Hughes, *Hebrews*, 218; and Attridge, *Hebrews*, 171.

it is primarily a statement about non-believers in the visible church and irrevocable apostasy.[72] It is a warning that is used by God to encourage true believers to examine themselves as to their commitment to Christ. The stakes for not being a true believer are very high. Thus this warning is one of the means God uses to ensure that true believers persevere.[73]

6:7–8 *For the land that drank the rain that often comes upon it and produces vegetation useful to those on account of whom indeed it is cultivated receives blessing from God, but [the land that] bears thorns and thistles [is] worthless and near [to being] cursed, which the end [is to be] burned.*

Hebrews 6:7–8 is one sentence with one subject, **the land that drank the rain that often comes upon it**. There are two scenarios related to different portions of the same **land that drank the rain**: (1) a portion **produces** good **vegetation ... receives blessing from God**, and (2) a portion **bears thorns and thistles ... which the end is to be burned**. Interestingly, the illustration begins with the positive scenario and then the negative; this is the inverse of Hebrews 6:4–6 (negative) and 6:9–12 (positive).

Agricultural realities and metaphors are often used in the Bible to describe God's relationship to his covenant people (e.g., Gen. 2:8; Ps. 1:3; Isa. 5:1–7; Luke 20:9–18; John 15:1–11; Rom. 11:11–24). In Hebrews 6:7–8, some see the reference to **rain**, **land**, **blessing**, and **cursed** as making an intentional connection to Deuteronomy (e.g., Deut. 11:8–17; 27:15–26;

---

72. 'And as it hath pleased God, by the preaching of the gospel, to begin this work of grace in us, so he preserves, continues, and perfects it by the hearing and reading of his Word, by meditation thereon, and by the exhortations, *threatenings*, and promises thereof, as well as by the use of Sacraments' (Canons of Dort 5.15 [emphasis mine]).

73. Augustine sees all true believers as elect and having the gift of perseverance. However, he also argues that God 'mingles' some in the visible church who do *not* persevere as an aid to the true believers who have a 'temptation' to 'security,' i.e., they are complacent (*On the Gift of Perseverance* 19 [*NPNF*[1], 5:532]).

28:2, 12; 29:23–27).[74] The phrase **thorns and thistles** matches exactly to the LXX in Genesis 3:18, which is related to the cursing of the ground in the Garden.[75] My sense is that the AH wants the reader to see a strong allusion of **thorns and thistles** to Genesis 3:18[76] and a more general connection of **blessing** and **cursed** to OT covenant blessings and curses (as opposed to specifically in Deuteronomy).

For indicates that this agricultural illustration is explanatory of the visible church.[77] It includes both those who will persevere and receive the eschatological **blessing** and those who will not persevere and be eschatologically **cursed**. The expression **near to being cursed** does not mean there is still time to repent; it means the cursed end is inevitable as confirmed by the same use of **near** in Hebrews 8:13.[78]

Based on the context of Hebrews, the **rain** probably represents God's word both in the sense of the OT Scriptures and apostolic preaching (Heb. 1:1–2; 4:7–11; 6:1–2, 13–14; cf. Deut. 32:2; Isa. 55:10–11).[79] **Land** clearly represents those in the visible church. **Vegetation** (cf. Gen. 1:11) is positive and the evidence of those persevering, and the phrase **thorns and thistles** (cf. Gen. 3:18) is very negative and the ultimate evidence of one not persevering. **Which** in the phrase **which is to be burned** clearly (in Greek) refers to the **land**,[80] or at

---

74. So Guthrie, 'Hebrews,' 963–64. Mathewson sees a 'clear allusion to Deut. 11:11 in Heb. 6:7' ('Heb 6:4–6 in Light of the Old Testament,' 221).

75. This phrase also matches exactly to Hos. 10:8, which relates to the cursing of Samaria's worship structures.

76. So also Hughes, *Hebrews*, 223. Hughes also notes Gen. 1:11 (**vegetation**); 2:5, 9 to make the connection stronger. Philo in reference to Gen. 3:18 interprets the **thorns and thistles** as an 'unreasonable impulse' (ἡ ἄλογος ὁρμὴ) in the soul (*Allegorical Interpretation* 3:248).

77. So also Owen, *Hebrews*, 21:91. *Contra* Moffatt who sees **for** as giving the reason it is impossible to repent again (*Hebrews*, 76).

78. So also Attridge, *Hebrews*, 173; and Hughes, *Hebrews*, 223–24.

79. So also Chrysostom, 'Homily 10 on Hebrews,' (*NPNF*[1], 414); Aquinas, *Hebrews*, 130; and Owen, *Hebrews*, 21:98; and Brown, *Hebrews*, 298.

80. The relative pronoun ἧς (**which**, singular and feminine) refers back to γῆ (**land**, singular and feminine).

least that portion to be destroyed. **Blessing of God** and **to be burned** represent the final eschatological realities.

Reflections

The AH, with the agricultural metaphor in Hebrews 6:7–8, ultimately sees two groups existing at any time in the visible church, one that ultimately perseveres and one that does not. Hebrews 6:4–6 notes that there is a category of people who, after having significant involvement in the church, leave the church and explicitly deny Christ. The AH states that this group will become irrevocably apostate. Hence, the AH is warning those currently in the visible church to continue on in maturity in the Christian faith because the possible consequences of not doing so are dire. The traditional Reformed view (Option 1 above) considers that those who become irrevocably apostate were not true believers in the first place.

One of the difficulties of Hebrews 6:4–8 is whether those who leave the church, termed apostates, are all irrevocably apostate. This difficulty exists for the traditional Arminian view: Are there any apostates who lose their salvation and turn away from Christ but are then able to turn back to Christ? And this difficulty also exists for the traditional Calvinistic view: Are there any apostates who leave the church who were not true Christians in the first place but are then able to turn to Christ? The difficulty is greater for the Arminian view, especially if scholars use this as a primary passage to argue that believers can lose their salvation,[81] but the difficulty still exists for the Calvinistic view. Hebrews 6:4–8 does not appear to address this question.

Part of the answer, at least for me, is that the group in Hebrews 6:4–6 appears to have more than a nominalistic engagement with the church. They to a significant degree taste the bountiful fruits of Christ's blessings, without being

---

81. That is, the more one emphasizes that Heb. 6:4–6 is *the* key passage to prove believers can lose their salvation, the more one would (at least logically) move toward affirming that all those who lose their salvation have irrevocably lost it. However, Arminians do not affirm this.

true believers. This hints toward more types of people being in the visible church than just true believers and irrevocable apostates; there are also nominalistic church attenders. Hence, in addition, there may be other types of apostates who are not irrevocably apostate.

The more complete answer for the traditional Reformed view (and others) to the above difficulty is simply to note that the Bible emphasizes God's mercy and presents many examples in many different types of scenarios of individuals (and groups) being forgiven following some level of fading from the faith.[82] In addition to this, if an apostate is truly moved to repentance and faith, then it is God who must have initiated this (cf. Rom. 8:28; Eph. 1:10–11; 2 Tim. 1:9–10; WCF 10).

In sum, Christians realize that temporary apostasy and irrevocable apostasy exist. Also, they realize that only God knows if irrevocable apostasy has occurred in a specific person. Hence, Christians should occasionally sound the general warning at the corporate level in the visible church that irrevocable apostasy is a reality. Further, Christians should tell their apostate acquaintances that if they truly repent and put their faith in Christ, the gracious Lord of mercy and his church will receive them with open arms.

Better Things (6:9–12)

Hebrews 6:9–12 ends the 5:11–6:12 exhortation passage. This is shown by the use of 'sluggish' in 5:11 and 6:12, and by the ending of Hebrews 6:11–12 that nicely summarizes the point of 5:11–6:12. However, Hebrews 6:9–12 is also somewhat of a transition passage between the exhortation passage (Heb. 5:11–6:12) and the promise passage (Heb. 6:13–20) because it includes a mixture of exhortation and assurance/promise.

---

82. E.g., Adam (Gen. 3:15); 2 Sam. 12:1–15; Ps. 51; Jer. 31:31–33; Luke 15:11–32; 22:31–34; 1 Cor. 5:5 with 2 Cor. 2:6–7; Rev. 3:19.

6:9 *But we*[83] *have been persuaded concerning you, beloved, of better things, that is,*[84] *having salvation, though thus we are speaking.*

After the dire warning of Hebrews 6:4–6, 8, the AH makes a very encouraging statement that he **has been persuaded** that the vast majority in this visible church (**you**) are true believers (cf. Heb. 10:39; Rom. 15:14).[85] He will give his evidence of this in the next verse. Here is the only time he refers to them as **beloved**, adding to the warmth of this verse.

Though thus we are speaking relates back to the negative comments in Hebrews 6:4–8. Normally, one would expect this phrase at the beginning of the verse, but **we have been persuaded** has been put there to emphasize the encouragement with the abrupt transition.[86]

Better things, that is, having salvation is both a comparison (***better* things**) and in opposition (**having salvation**).[87] Compared to the surface level of Christianity described in Hebrews 6:4–5, the readers are **better**. Compared to the irrevocable apostasy (Heb. 6:6) and the eschatological end (Heb. 6:8), the readers' **salvation** is a complete opposite. **Salvation** here includes the initial (justification) and continuing (sanctification) aspects based on the comparison to those in Hebrews 6:4–5 and the present-tense **having**, but it also includes the eschatological aspect (glorification) based on Hebrews 6:8.

---

83. The editorial/rhetorical 'we' is often used in Greco-Roman and biblical letters instead of the first person singular. However, at least in some cases, the AH intends his ministerial circle. See discussion at Heb. 13:18–19.

84. Καί is epexegetical (**that is**). So also Moffatt, *Hebrews*, 83; and Lane, *Hebrews 1–8*, 133. For a general discussion of the epexegetical καί, see BDAG, 495 (1.c); and BDF §442.9.

85. WLC 144 references Heb. 6:9 and 1 Cor. 13:7 for an implication of the ninth commandment, 'a charitable esteem of our neighbours.'

86. Several English translations put this phrase first as expected in normal English/Greek order, e.g., RSV, NIV, ESV, and CSB17.

87. So also Owen, *Hebrews*, 154–55.

6:10 *For God is not unjust to neglect your work and the love that*[88] *you showed to his name, having served the saints and serving [them].*

Here the AH gives his logic (**for**) for his conclusion in Hebrews 6:9 that the vast majority of the readers are not those described in Hebrews 6:4–6. The logic is two-fold: (1) God justly fulfills his covenantal promises of gracious rewards, and (2) the readers have evidenced their true faith and love for God by the service they have done and are doing toward other Christians.

The AH adds some rhetorical punch with the phrase **God is *not un*just**. This phrase is an example of ironic understatement using two negatives to make the positive point, God is *very* just, that is, the ironic understatement results in making the point with greater emphasis.[89]

The clause **God is not unjust to neglect your work** ultimately refers to God fulfilling his covenantal promises to reward believers with many benefits, emphasizing the reward of the NHNE.[90] That these rewards are ultimately gracious and non-meritorious is confirmed in context by 'faith' and 'inheriting the promises' in Hebrews 6:12 and the 'oath' discussion in Hebrews 6:17–18. Yes, in a *very* qualified sense God is indebted to us.[91] Calvin explains, '[God] has made

---

88. **That** (ἧς) grammatical refers to **love** (ἀγάπης). One would expect the genitive ἧς to be in the accusative as the direct object of **show**; however, it is in the genitive due to 'attraction' with ἀγάπης.

89. This is termed 'litotes' (cf. Heb. 4:15; Rom. 1:16a).

90. Concerning rewards, the Heidelberg Catechism 63 succinctly remarks, 'The reward comes not of merit, but of grace'; similarly WCF 16.6, which references Heb. 6:10. See my discussion of rewards related to justification in Robert J. Cara, *Cracking the Foundation of the New Perspective on Paul: Covenantal Nomism versus Reformed Covenantal Theology*, Reformed Exegetical and Doctrinal Studies (Ross-shire: Mentor, 2017), 53–56. Also see discussion at Heb. 10:35.

91. Hebrews 6:10 was commonly part of the justification battleground between sixteenth and seventeenth century Reformation and Roman Catholic scholars because it was explicitly quoted by Trent theologians to prove that a believer's good works are 'meritorious' (Council of Trent, Decree on Justification, ch. 16; cf. canon 32).

himself our debtor not by receiving anything from us, but by fully promising us all things.'[92]

The **work** that the AH is commending is their **having served the saints and serving them**.[93] He mentions both their past service and present service. As to the specifics of the service, this is probably a broad statement (cf. Heb. 13:1), but it certainly would include their aid to those in prison (Heb. 10:32–34; 11:3). Christians are referred to as **saints** or 'holy ones' here and in 13:24 (cf. 3:1).[94] Often in Scripture, Christians are commended for their special love and good works toward other Christians (e.g., John 13:35; 1 John 3:14; 2 Thess. 1:3; Col. 1:4). Of course, when not in a church context, individual Christians are encouraged to have appropriate concern for non-Christians also (e.g., Luke 10:25–37; Gal. 6:10; 1 Thess. 5:15).

It is not clear whether the **love** is directed toward other Christians or toward God the Father (**his**).[95] Either way, all the **work** they did demonstrated (**showed**) a concern for **his name**, that is, their **work** of service to other Christians was ultimately directed toward and motivated by their understanding of God the Father.

---

92. Calvin, *Hebrews and 1–2 Peter*, 79, also see his *Institutes* 3.18.7. After noting Heb. 6:10, Brakel comments, 'It is also righteous for God to recompense his heirs, not *because of*, but *upon* their good works. This he had promised, and it is righteous to keep one's promise' (*The Christian's Reasonable Service*, 2:370, italics his). See similar discussions in Owen, *Hebrews*, 21:160–62; and Vos, *Reformed Dogmatics*, 4:171–72.

93. The verb is διακονέω and could be translated as 'ministering' (e.g., Geneva, KJV) or 'serving-as-deacon' (e.g., 1 Tim. 3:10). It is the cognate of 'deacon' (διάκονος) (e.g., Phil. 1:1).

94. Grammatically, **saints** is a substantival adjective from 'holy' (ἅγιος). This adjective is also used in Hebrews attributively in *Holy* Spirit (e.g., Heb. 2:4; 6:4) and numerous times substantively for the earthly and heavenly sanctuaries ('holy place') (e.g., Heb. 8:2; 9:24).

95. Some Greek manuscripts have 'work and *labor* of **love**' (see KJV). If this was the original text, then **love** would clearly be directed toward other Christians.

6:11-12 *And we desire each of you to show the same earnestness toward full assurance of hope until the end in order that you may not be sluggish but be imitators of those who through faith and patience inherit the promises.*

Although clearly connected (**and**, δέ) to Hebrews 6:9-10, 6:11-12 is also somewhat of a summary of the entire 5:11-6:12 exhortation section as it includes the concluding encouragement toward **full assurance** and not being **sluggish** (Heb. 5:11). The expression **those who through faith and patience inherit the promises** connects (1) directly forward to Hebrews 6:13-20 through 'promise to Abraham' (6:13) and 'heirs of the promise' (6:17) and (2) distantly forward to the 'faith' chapter, Hebrews 11.

The AH has concern (**we desire**) for everyone (**each of you**) in the congregation. He wants them all **to show the same earnestness** of the good works and love for God that he mentioned in the previous verse. Further he wants them to demonstrate this **until the end** of their Christian walk.

One advantage of this **earnestness** is that it aids in providing **full assurance of hope**. As most do, I take **full assurance** (πληροφορία) as the subjective, internal assurance or certainty of current and future salvation.[96] The contrary position is to translate as 'fulfillment' or 'realization' meaning one's hope in the NHNE will be completed at the end, the eschaton.[97] In support of my view, πληροφορία is not in the LXX but is used elsewhere three times in the NT and clearly refers to 'certainty' or 'full assurance' (Heb. 10:22; 1 Thess. 1:5; Col. 2:2).

Hope has significant overlap with **faith** (cf. Heb. 11:1). **Hope**

---

96. So also, e.g., BDAG, 827; LSJ, 1419; Owen, *Hebrews*, 21:193; Hughes, *Hebrews*, 228; Geneva; KJV; RSV; NASB; NIV84; ESV; CSB17; WCF 18.2; WLC 80. This view usually also involves taking **until the end** as referring more specifically to **to show**.

97. So, e.g., Lane, *Hebrews 1-8*, 130, 144; Johnson, *Hebrews*, 167; NAB; NIV; and NLT. This view usually also involves taking **until the end** as referring only to **hope**. Schreiner sees πληροφορία as including both nuances (*Hebrews*, 195).

is related to one's current trust or **faith** in the Triune God and his promised blessings, but it emphasizes one aspect of that trust in God's blessings—getting to the NHNE. As I term it, **hope** is a 'now/not-yet word.' **Hope** is something one has 'now', but it is a now trust oriented toward the future ('not yet'). It is structurally the same as the word 'inheritance' (**inherit the promises**). One has the promise (or is designated in a will as an heir) of the inheritance 'now', but the realization of that promise is future ('not yet'). Hence, **full assurance of hope** is the subjective certainty that one has now about the future.[98]

As one's past and present **earnestness** of good works aids one's present **full assurance of hope**, one's **full assurance of hope** further aids (**in order that**) one in continuing in the Christian life. Yes, it is circular, or better, it is an upward spiral. The Christian life is here described both negatively, **not be sluggish**,[99] and positively, **be imitators of those who through faith and patience inherit the promises**.

Concerning **imitators**, this is another instance in Hebrews where Christians are to grow from the example of others, either negative (Heb. 4:11) or positive (Heb. 11; 13:7) examples.[100] **Those who ... inherit the promises** are not directly named.[101] Clearly it includes Abraham as he is discussed in the next section. Further, it includes all those mentioned in Hebrews 11 (cf. Heb. 11:39). Finally, it includes NT believers (e.g., Heb. 13:7; cf. Heb. 1:14). Of the many things to imitate, the AH emphasizes their examples of **faith and patience**, which directly relates to his exhortation to persevere in the

---

98. Bavinck notes the variety of emphases that different biblical authors have in their description of faith. He comments that, as all NT writers do, the AH has Christ as the objective side to faith; but the AH also 'looks at faith much more from its subjective than from its objective side' (*Reformed Dogmatics*, 4:107).

99. For **sluggish**, see discussion at Heb. 5:11.

100. The noun **imitators** (μιμητής) only occurs here in Hebrews. Paul uses it in 1 Cor. 4:16; 11:1; Eph. 5:1; 1 Thess. 1:6; and 2:14. The verb cognate of **imitators** (μιμέομαι) is in Heb. 13:7; 2 Thess. 3:7, 9; and 3 John 1:11.

101. For **inherit the promises**, see discussion at Heb. 6:13 and 6:17.

Christian life. One could almost say that the combination of **faith and patience** is a definition of **hope**. Interestingly, the triad of **faith, hope,** and 'love' is included in Hebrews 6:10–12 and 10:22–24.[102]

Reflections

In Hebrews 6:11, the phrase 'full assurance of hope' is used. The AH wants the readers to move toward this 'full assurance.' As there is weak and strong faith, there is weak and strong/full assurance.[103]

In context of Hebrews 6:9–12, this 'full assurance' is based on God's character ('God is not unjust,' Heb. 6:10) and his actions (his 'promises' and his fulfilling those promises for saints of the past, Heb. 6:12). But also, this 'full assurance' is based on realizing that God has changed us as we recognize our concern for God and some of our (imperfect) good works (Heb. 6:10–11). Of course, the basis of God's character and action is the foundation for and more sure than the basis of our own concern for God and our good works. But both are important.

WCF 18 is a chapter entitled, 'Assurance of Grace and Salvation.' More specifically, WCF 18.2 (and WLC 80) gives three grounds of assurance. These three grounds are very similar to the Canons of Dort 5.9–10, which addresses assurance within the section, 'Of the Perseverance of the Saints.' My summary of these grounds is: (1) faith in the Bible's divine promises of salvation, (2) our inward evidence of love of God and desire (with some results) to perform

---

102. For more discussion on the triad, see Reflections section following Heb. 10:19–25.

103. The Reformed tradition has differed as to what level of assurance, if any, is necessarily tied to true faith. Part of the differences are semantic. For example, are there levels of assurance? Heidelberg Catechism 21 and Calvin (e.g., *Institutes* 3.2.15) emphasize assurance necessarily tied to faith. The Westminster Standards do not. WCF 18.3 states, 'This infallible assurance doth not so belong to the essence of faith, but that a true believer may wait long, and conflict with many difficulties before he be partaker of it.' Also see the Canons of Dort that emphasizes 'various degrees' (1.12; similarly 5.9).

good works, and (3) inward testimony of the Holy Spirit (e.g., Rom. 8:15–16). Again, I view the first ground as the primary one. Hebrews 6:9–12 clearly matches to #1 and #2.

May God through the Holy Spirit use Hebrews 6:9–12 itself and the implications of it to move us toward 'full assurance' and/or sustain our current 'full assurance.'

Promise (6:13–20)

Hebrews 6:13–20 ends the fairly lengthy 5:11–6:20 section on a positive note. It consists of two fairly-long Greek sentences, 6:13–15 and 6:16–20. The first concerns God's promise and oath to Abraham from Genesis 22:16–17 and Abraham's patience. The second expands upon the implications of God's making an oath that results in more encouragement for the congregants to have hope; and it ends connecting Christ's work to this hope using the metaphors of an anchor and the holy of holies, along with a reference to Melchizedek.

Within Hebrews 5:11–6:20, 6:13–20 is clearly its own subunit. Hebrews 6:12 ends with 'be imitators of those who through faith and patience inherit the promises.' Hebrews 6:13 then uses Abraham as the prime example of one to imitate. Hebrews 6:20 ends this subunit and the long 5:11–6:20 section by connecting Christ to Melchizedek, which then explicitly connects back to 5:10, the verse before this long section, and also prepares the reader for the important Melchizedek discussion in Hebrews 7.

Before getting to the exegesis, I present here some OT background on Abraham[104] and on the OT terms 'promise,' 'swear,' and 'oath.' The AH refers to Abraham explicitly in four contexts (Heb. 2:16; 6:13–15; 7:1–10; 11:8–19) and implicitly in one context (Heb. 13:2).[105] To state the obvious, the Abrahamic

---

104. This paragraph and the next follow closely to my article, Robert J. Cara, 'Covenant in Hebrews,' in *Covenant Theology: Biblical, Theological, and Historical Perspectives*, ed. Guy P. Waters, J. Nicholas Reid, and John R. Muether (Wheaton: Crossway, 2020), 247–66, esp. 251–52.

105. For discussions on Abraham in Hebrews, see Cara, 'Covenant

covenant is prominent in the OT and plays a significant role in the AH's theology.[106]

Key OT covenantal events are the calling of Abram to go to Canaan and his being a blessing to many (Gen. 12:1–4); the explicit making of a covenant (smoking pot) and a promise of giving of the land to Abram's seed (Gen. 15:12–21); an everlasting covenant between God and Abraham and his seed, a covenant of circumcision, and promise to be a father of many nations (Gen. 17:1–14); and Abraham's offering up of Isaac and God's oath to bless Abraham and his seed (Gen. 22:1–19).

Although in Hebrews the noun 'promise' (ἐπαγγελία) and the verb 'to promise' (ἐπαγγέλλομαι) are prominent, these Greek words are very rare in the LXX and there is no real equivalent for them in the Hebrew OT either.[107] In certain OT contexts where God speaks about future blessings, the NT simply terms these 'promises' (e.g., Gen. 12:7 with Acts 7:5 and Gal. 3:16; Exod. 20:12 with Eph. 6:2; Gen. 22:17 with Heb. 6:13). In fact, the expression 'promised land' comes from Hebrews 11:9, not the OT.

The verb 'to swear' (נשבע, ὀμνύω) is very prominent in the OT; the noun 'oath' (שבועה, ὅρκος) is less so.[108] The verb 'to swear' implies, whether stated or not, that an oath is taken. In man-to-man situations, one's swearing of an oath would involve two aspects. First, either a statement of a present or

---

in Hebrews,' 251–54; J. Swetnam, *Jesus and Isaac: A Study of the Epistle of Hebrews in the Light of the Aqedah*, AnBib 94 (Rome: Biblical Institute, 1981); Susanne Lehne, *The New Covenant in Hebrews*, JSNTSup 44 (Sheffield: Sheffield Academic Press, 1990), 19–22; and N. Calvert-Koyzis, 'Abraham,' *DLNT*, 1–6, esp. 2–4.

106. Prominent other NT discussions include Acts 7; Rom. 4; and Gal. 3.

107. In the 'Protestant' LXX, they occur only four times (Esth. 4:7; Ps. 55:9; Prov. 13:12; Amos 9:6). When English OT translations use 'promise', the Hebrew has simply God's 'word' (דבר, אמרה, e.g., 1 Kgs. 8:20, Ps. 119:58) or God 'says' (אמר, Exod. 3:17).

108. See T. W. Cartledge, 'שבע,' *NIDOTTE*, 4:32–34; and Silva, ed., 'ὀμνύω,' *NIDNTTE*, 3:492–98.

past fact as, for example, a witness in a legal case ('assertory oath,' e.g., Exod. 22:10–11) or a statement to carry out a future action ('promissory oath,' e.g., Gen. 21:22–23). Secondly, the one swearing also includes as part of his statement that he swears by a 'higher' person, usually God, implying that the 'higher' person will punish (curse) him if he has sworn falsely (assertory oath) or if he does not fulfill his promise (promissory oath) (e.g., Gen. 31:50; 1 Sam. 20:13). Although both of the above aspects are included in the terminology of swearing an oath, in Hebrews 6:13–17, the AH will understandably separate the above two aspects. He will term the statement to carry out a future action as the 'promise', and he will term the calling on a 'higher' person as 'to swear'/'oath.'

OT covenants between God and man are often subsequently referred to with the language that God swore (by an oath) (e.g., Gen. 24:7; 26:3; Deut. 1:8; 7:8–9, 12; 8:18; 29:12–14; Ps. 89:3; Luke 1:72–73; Acts 2:30).[109] But by whom does God swear in covenants? In several texts it is explicit that God swears by himself (Exod. 32:13; Amos 6:8; Isa. 45:23; cf. Gen. 15:7–21; Exod. 6:8; Num. 14:28; Deut. 32:40; Jer. 34:15–20; 46:18; T. Mos. 3:9), and therefore, implicit

---

109. Dennis J. McCarthy especially emphasizes that oaths are connected to OT covenants, paralleling ANE treaties. He lists Gen. 21:22–24, 27, 31; 26:26–30; Josh. 9:15; Neh. 6:18 with Gen. 14:13 (*Treaty and Covenant*, new ed., AnBib 21a [Rome: Biblical Institute, 1981], 43, 185, 253, 253n18). Meredith G. Kline also connects oaths to covenant with a special emphasis on the implications of circumcision as an 'oath-curse' and its connection to Christ's being cursed (*By Oath Consigned: A Reinterpretation of the Covenant Signs of Circumcision and Baptism* [Grand Rapids: Eerdmans, 1968], 14–16, 41–49). Robertson, picking up on the 'cutting' terminology associated with covenants (e.g., Gen. 15:18; 26:28) with covenantal cutting-of-animal ceremonies (e.g., Gen. 15:10; Jer. 34:18–20), concludes that all covenants have a 'bond-in-blood' character that stands for the 'potential curse-factor in the covenant' (*The Christ of the Covenants*, 7–12). The Rabbinic document Mekilta Pisha 18 in exegeting the comment that God swore to the fathers in Exod. 13:11 asks, In what texts did God 'swear' to the fathers? The answer is Gen. 15:18 for Abraham, Gen. 26:3 for Isaac, and Gen. 28:13 for Jacob. Note that in neither Gen. 15:18 nor Gen. 28:13 is the wording of 'swear' or 'oath' used. Therefore, it is assumed that covenants involve swearing an oath.

in all covenants is that he swears by himself. It is amazing that God would swear to curse himself if he does not uphold his covenant.

In chapter 7:20–21, 28, the AH will again discuss the importance of oaths. The discussion there relates oaths to Psalm 110:4 and Christ's priesthood.

6:13–14 *For when*[110] *promising to Abraham, since he had by no one greater to swear, God swore by himself, saying 'Surely I will indeed*[111] *bless you and indeed multiply you';*

For clearly relates the phrase **promising to Abraham** directly to the 'promises' in the previous verse (Heb. 6:12). There the AH exhorts the readers not to be 'sluggish' but to be 'imitators' of others who had 'inherited the promises.' He will then use **Abraham** as an example of one to be imitated. Another connection is Hebrews 6:11 with the 'assurance of hope'; both 'hope' and the concept of assurance are stressed in 6:12–20.

---

110. The participle **promising** is aorist as is the finite verb **swore**. Hence, the temporal aspect of the participle would normally be translated 'after' (e.g., Heb. 6:15) but often could be **when** (so also BDF §339; and Wallace, *Greek Grammar Beyond the Basics*, 624–25). As do the major English translations and most commentators, I translated as **when** because the oath and the promise are considered one composite event both here and in Gen. 22:16–17. Kistemaker disagrees and takes the aorist as referring to all previous promises to Abraham (*Hebrews*, 172). Similarly, Ellingworth sees all previous promises to Abraham as a unit contained in **promising** and the oath as the climax (*Hebrews*, 335).

111. I have included **indeed** to account for the Greek LXX and NT construction of a cognate participle connected to the corresponding finite verb (εὐλογῶν εὐλογήσω and πληθύνων πληθυνῶ) that is translating the Hebrew cognate infinitive absolute connected to the corresponding finite verb, which occurs in Gen. 22:17. The NT only uses this construction in quotations from the LXX involving this Hebrew cognate-infinitive-absolute-plus-corresponding-finite-verb construction; see Matt. 13:14, Acts 7:34, and Heb. 6:14. For a discussion of NT use, see BDF §422; for LXX, see Muraoka, *A Syntax of Septuagint Greek*, 383–85. The Geneva Bible has 'abundantly bless' and 'marvelously multiply' (spelling modernized). The KJV simply mechanically translates the participles, 'blessing I will bless' and 'multiplying I will multiply.'

Hebrews 6:13–14 is directly related to Genesis 22:16–17, where God swears an oath reiterating the covenantal promises to Abraham. This swearing follows the climax of the narrative where Abraham is about to sacrifice Isaac but instead God provides a ram.[112] The AH will again refer to this Isaac incident in Hebrews 11:17–19. Although God made many overlapping covenantal promises to Abraham (Gen. 12:2–3, 7; 13:14–17; 15:5–7, 13–16, 18–21; 17:2–14, 19; 21:12; 22:15–18; cf. Gen. 24:7), why did the AH use Genesis 22:16–17 here? It certainly gave the 'greatest evidence of [Abraham's] faith',[113] but it may have also been because of the explicitness of God's declaring an oath by himself.

When promising to Abraham refers to the quote from Genesis 22:17, **surely I will indeed bless you and indeed multiply you**. But the AH's interest at this point is more in the oath that accompanied the promise. He comments **since he had by no one greater to swear, God swore by himself**. In Genesis 22:16, God introduces his discourse with 'by myself I have sworn', which the AH appropriately adjusts to third person to match his sentence structure, **God swore by himself**. And the AH's interest is not simply that God made an oath. His interest is in the oddity that as opposed to normal man-to-man oaths where one swears by God, God **had by no one greater to swear** and had to ground his oath by calling upon **himself** as the one to inflict the implied curse of nonfulfillment.[114] The AH will return to this topic in Hebrews 6:16–18.

The comment that God **had by no one greater to swear** reminds us that when God speaks, there is no higher authority by which to authenticate his word. This concept

---

112. The events of Gen. 22:1–19 are often referred to as the *Aqedah*, which is Hebrew for the 'binding' (implied of Isaac) coming from the verb 'to bind' (עָקַד) in Gen. 22:9.

113. Owen, *Hebrews*, 21:223.

114. In several places Philo also notes the oddity of God swearing by himself (*Allegorical Interpretation* 3:203–08; *On the Sacrifices of Cain and Abel* 91–97; *On the Life of Abraham* 273).

then relates to Scripture as a whole. Ultimately, one cannot have a higher authority than God's speaking in Scripture in order to authenticate that the Scripture was written by God. That is, neither the church, nor archaeology, nor scholarship are the final attestation that Scripture is the Word of God. Yes, these may be secondary evidences, but the final confirmation is God himself speaking in Scripture. This objective reality is then confirmed by the inward testimony of the Holy Spirit. In sum, because it is written by God, Scripture is self-attesting ('autopistic').[115]

The quoted portion of Genesis 22:17 in Hebrews 6:14 matches very well to the Hebrew and the LXX.[116] The only intentional difference is that the AH substitutes **you** for 'your seed' in the expression 'multiply your seed.' Although the connection between Abraham and his seed is inherent, most likely this change is done to emphasize the connection to Abraham himself (**you**) and Isaac, which matches more directly to Hebrews 6:15.[117] The connection to Abraham's broader seed will be emphasized shortly in Hebrews 6:16–20.

In addition to being his God, two of God's primary promises

---

115. See WCF 1.4–5 for a wonderfully balanced and rhetorically satisfying statement of this concept. See John Murray for an important article defending WCF 1.4–5 ('The Attestation of Scripture,' in *The Infallible Word*, ed. Paul Woolley, 3rd rev. ed. [Philadelphia: Presbyterian and Reformed, 1967], 1–54. Kruger uses this concept in his multifaceted defense of the traditional NT canon of Scripture (*Canon Revisited*, 88–122). Cornelius Van Til especially emphasizes this concept in apologetics (*The Defense of the Faith*, 3rd ed. [Philadelphia: Presbyterian and Reformed, 1967], 105–14, 258; and Greg L. Bahnsen, *Van Til's Apologetic* [Phillipsburg: P&R, 1998], 194–203). Often this concept is associated with the term, 'autopistic' (mechanically translated as 'self-faithful' but meaning 'self-authenticating' or 'self-attesting'); see, for example, Calvin, *Institutes* 1.7.1–5, esp. 1.7.5 ; and Bavinck, *Reformed Dogmatics*, 1:452–59.

116. Although murky due to text critical difficulties, the LXX Gen. 22:17 and Heb. 6:14 have two slightly different expressions for **surely**, ἦ μήν and εἰ μήν, respectively. There is no semantic difference between these two (so LSJ, 1127).

117. So also Guthrie, but he adds an additional 'stylistic' reason in that the two clauses both end with **you** ('Hebrews,' 966).

to Abraham in the OT are land and the people of God. The quoted phrase **surely I will indeed bless you and indeed multiply you** obviously emphasizes the Abraham/Isaac (people of God) aspect. This quote is not the full quote from Genesis 22:17; the AH has dropped an oblique reference to land. This makes sense given the land aspects were discussed in Hebrews 3:7–4:13 and will be in Hebrews 11:8–10, 16.

6:15 *and thus, after being patient, he obtained the promise.*

Hebrews 6:12 exhorts the readers to imitate others 'who through faith and patience inherit the promises'. This verse picks up on 'patience' and 'promise'.

Abraham was given the initial promise of a people when he was seventy-five years old (Gen. 12:2–4). However, it was not until Abraham was one-hundred years old that Isaac was born (Gen. 17:17; 21:5). The age of Isaac at the time of Genesis 22 is not given. Assuming Isaac was ten, God's promise in Genesis 22:17 would have been thirty-five years after the initial promise. Hence, Abraham's life was characterized by the comment **after being patient**.

Concerning **he obtained the promise**, **promise** is being taken in the sense that he was given *what/who* was promised, not simply he was given a promise. Of course, Isaac is the aspect of the promise that is referred to here, and more specifically, it is Isaac post the Genesis 22 events, as opposed to his birth.[118]

Later the AH will state that Abraham and other OT saints *did not* receive the promises (Heb. 11:13, 39), but he will also state that they *did* (Heb. 11:9, 33). Obviously, the AH is able to distinguish between partially realized (proximate) promises (Heb. 6:15; 11:9, 33) and full eschatological-NHNE promises (e.g., Heb. 4:1; 10:18, 36; 11:39). This is consistent with the reality of the ever expanding Abrahamic covenant.

Thus ... he obtained the promise. Thus here combines two

---

118. So also Bruce, *Hebrews*, 153; and Koester, *Hebrews*, 326.

interrelated reasons for this.[119] First, based on the immediate context of Hebrews 6:13–14 and the emphasis to follow in 6:16–20, it was God's faithfulness to his own promise that was the reason for Isaac. Second, based on **after being patient** and Hebrews 6:12, it was Abraham's continued 'faith and patience' that was responsible for Isaac. Of course, because God is the God of mysterious providence, both of these can be true. The obvious implication for the readers is that God's faithfulness and Abraham's example of receiving his proximate promise should encourage them in their perseverance of the eschatological promise.

6:16–17 *For men swear by the greater, and an oath for confirmation [is] an end of every dispute among them; by which [means] God, willing to show more [clearly] to the heirs of the promise the immutability of his will, pledged by an oath...*

Hebrews 6:16–20 is one sentence. The AH uses **for** because he is giving the reason why God swore by himself instead of simply declaring a promise without swearing an oath. This harkens back to Hebrews 6:13.

Initially, he begins with a truism for a man-to-man situation, **men swear by the greater, and an oath for confirmation is an end of every dispute among them**. He states the standard OT and first-century Greco-Roman and Jewish[120] cultural point that in certain serious situations a statement's truth is given more weight when one swears an oath. Also, the thing or one

---

119. Schreiner sees Heb. 6:15 as somewhat of an 'interupt[ion] of the flow of the argument' because one would have expected the **thus** clause only to emphasize the 'inviolability of God's word' and not emphasize the response of Abraham (*Hebrews*, 200).

120. Oath discussions are common in Second Temple Jewish literature, e.g., m. Shevu'ot; Josephus, *Jewish War* 2.135–42; 1QS V, 1–10. This would not prove that a fair proportion of the original readers were ethnically Jewish, but it would at least be consistent with this view. Note, there is here no complaint of the excessive and casuistic use of oaths as in Matt. 5:33–37; 23:16–22; and Jas. 5:12. Given the flow of the argument, there would be no need to since the point is to show that God used positively the normal man-to-man practice of swearing by oaths.

by whom one swears is 'higher' (**greater**), usually some god (or the God). (This is analogous to today's placing one's hand on the Bible for court testimony.[121]) Of course, one could still lie, but this serious **oath for confirmation** of the truth of a statement *should* **end** the **dispute**.[122]

Using the same **means** as a man-to-man oath (**by which means**), **God ... pledged by an oath**,[123] that is, Gen 22:16–17.[124] The Greek verb (μεσιτεύω) translated by me as **pledged** occurs only here in the entire NT and LXX.[125] The important cognate

---

121. For example, the North Carolina General Statutes (as of August 2018), Chapter 11 on Oaths, opens with, 'Whereas, lawful oaths for the discovery of truth and establishing right are necessary and highly conducive to the important end of good government; and being most solemn appeals to Almighty God, as the omniscient witness of truth and the just omnipotent avenger of falsehood, and whereas, lawful affirmations for the discovery of truth and establishing right are necessary and highly conducive to the important end of good government, therefore, such oaths and affirmations ought to be taken and administered with the utmost solemnity' (§11-1). Further, although exceptions are allowed, judges shall 'require the party to be sworn to lay his hand upon the Holy Scriptures, in token of his engagement to speak the truth and in further token that, if he should swerve from the truth, he may be justly deprived of all the blessings of that holy book and made liable to that vengeance which he has imprecated on his own head' (§11-2). The required oath in a criminal trial is as follows: Do 'you swear that the evidence you shall give to the court and jury in this action between the State and A.B. shall be the truth, the whole truth, and nothing but the truth; so help you, God'? (§11-11).

122. Should Christians swear oaths? This verse is properly cited to confirm that it is proper (e.g., Heidelberg Catechism 101, WCF 22.2, London Confession [1646] 50). The Reformed tradition argues that Matt. 5:33–37 and Jas. 5:12 (cf. Matt. 23:16–22) refer to restrictions on excessive and casuistic oath taking (e.g., Owen, *Hebrews*, 21:247–51; and Calvin, *Institutes*, 2.8.26).

123. The concept of God's swearing an oath is in Heb. 3:11, 18; 4:3; 6:13, 17; 7:20–21, 28. There are two Greek nouns translated as 'oath'; ὅρκος in Heb. 6:16–17, and ὁρκωμοσία in Heb. 7:20 (*bis*), 21, 28.

124. A few commentators see this **oath** as related to the one made with Christ in Heb. 7:20–22 // Ps. 110:4, e.g., Brown, *Hebrews*, 317.

125. Other options include 'confirmed' (KJV, NIV), 'interposed' (RSV, NASB), 'guaranteed' (ESV, CEB). LSJ surprisingly recommend 'act as arbiter or mediator' for Heb. 6:17. Other general options by LSJ include 'negotiate,' 'pledge,' and 'mortgage' (1106). BADG recommends 'guarantee' for Heb. 6:17 (634).

noun, 'mediator' (μεσίτης), occurs later in Hebrews 9:15 and 12:24 where Christ is the 'mediator of a new covenant'. However, apparently the meaning of the verb does not exactly include here the idea of mediation.[126]

God made the **oath** because he wanted **to show more clearly**[127] ... **the immutability of his will**. God's inviolable **oath** is logically related to the **immutability of his will**.[128] In context, this **will** is referring to the complete fulfillment of the Abrahamic covenant to the **heirs of the promise**.[129] By using **heirs**, note the plural, the AH is again confirming that the Abrahamic **promise** is more than just to Abraham/Isaac. It relates to all those who have faith in God (cf. 'seed of Abraham,' Heb. 2:16).

Was not God's promise without an oath good enough? It should have been, but due to the frailties of man, God mercifully accommodated himself.[130]

6:18 ... *in order that, through two immutable things, in which*[131] *[it is] impossible [for] God to lie, we, those who fled for refuge, might have a strong encouragement*[132] *to hold firm the hope set before [us];*

---

126. *Possibly*, the idea of mediator could relate to the **oath** itself being the mediator.

127. I take the adverb **more clearly** (περισσότερον) to modify **to show** (so also NKJV, ESV, RSV, NIV; Cockerill, *Hebrews*, 287), although grammatically, it could modify **willing** (so KJV, NASB).

128. In Reformed categories, **will** here refers to God's 'secret' will, as opposed to his 'revealed' will (Deut. 29:29). For more on this distinction, see Berkhof, *Systematic Theology*, 77–78. The WCF 3.1 cites Heb. 6:17 in relation to 'God from all eternity did, by the most wise and holy counsel of his own will, freely and unchangeably ordain whatsoever comes to pass.'

129. Aquinas, 'Whenever the Lord swears something under an oath it is a prophecy of predestination, which is indicative of the divine counsel and this promise is utterly immutable' (*Hebrews*, 138).

130. So most commentators, e.g., Chrysostom, 'Homily 11 on Hebrews,' *NPNF*[1], 14:419; Calvin, *Hebrews and 1 & 2 Peter*, 17; *Geneva Bible: 1602 Edition*, folio 111; Hughes, *Hebrews*, 230; Kistemaker, *Hebrews*, 174; and Koester, *Hebrews*, 327. So also Philo, *On the Sacrifices of Cain and Abel* 94.

131. **Which** is plural in Greek (οἷς) confirming that the impossibility of God's lying relates to the **two immutable things**.

132. The noun used here παράκλησις and the cognate verb παρακαλέω have a range/continuum of meaning in the NT from a softer 'comfort'/'consolation'

The **two immutable things** are (1) God's Abrahamic promise and (2) God's oath concerning the promise.[133] To even add another factor, since the promise and oath are God's words, **it is impossible for God to lie** (cf. Num. 23:19; 1 Sam. 15:29; Titus 1:2).[134] Given the emphasis on **immutable** here and the previous verse, this impossibility of lying is ultimately connected to God's attribute of unchangeableness (Mal. 3:6; Jas. 1:17).[135]

The oath and the promise are designed by God to be a **strong encouragement** for believers (**we**) to **hold firm the hope set before [them]**. The **hope** is the subjective confidence they have now about their persevering to the objective future NHNE. This amazing reality for true believers that God's promise, oath, immutable will, and non-lying character will ensure their entry to the heavenlies is quite a **strong encouragement**.[136] The congregants are given the epithet, **those who fled for refuge**. Apparently, this refers to their having **fled** metaphorically from their pre-Christian state to the **refuge** of Christ and his church.[137]

---

to a middling 'encouragement' to a harsher 'exhortation'. Several times in Hebrews, the meaning is more clearly 'exhortation' (e.g., 3:13; 12:5); however, here it is probably a middling **encouragement**. So also Ellingworth, *Hebrews*, 18; and Attridge, *Hebrews*, 182. Owen instead opts for 'comfort' (*Hebrews*, 21:275). Note that the entire letter of Hebrews is termed a 'word of παράκλησις' (13:22).

133. So virtually all commentators, e.g., Chrysostom, 'Homily 11 on Hebrews,' *NPNF*[1], 14:418; Aquinas, *Hebrews*, 135; Owen, *Hebrews*, 21:271; Bruce, *Hebrews*, 18; Hughes, *Hebrews*, 233; Attridge, *Hebrews*, 181; Koester, *Hebrews*, 328; Cockerill, *Hebrews*, 288; and Schreiner, *Hebrews*, 202. Johnson is an exception. He gives several possibilities: (1) promise and oath; (2) Ps. 110:1 and 110:4; and (3) God's speech and God's action of exalting Jesus (*Hebrews*, 171).

134. The AH uses **impossible** (ἀδύνατος) in several emphatic texts (Heb. 6:4; 10:4; 11:6).

135. So also Schreiner, *Hebrews*, 202–03. In exegeting Exod. 32:13, R. Eleazar connects God's swearing by himself to God's living forever, which in turn means that the oath will last forever (b. Berakhot 32a). Clement comments in language very similar to Heb. 6:18, 'For nothing is impossible with God except to lie' (1 Clement 27:2).

136. For creedal references of Heb. 6:17–18 for election and assurance, see Canons of Dort 1.14 and WCF 18.2.

137. Spicq sees the congregation as literal exiles and refugees (*Hébreux*, 2:163).

6:19–20 *which we have as an anchor of the soul, sure and firm, and entering to the inside of the veil, where a forerunner entered for us, Jesus, according to the order of Melchizedek has become a high priest forever.*

Which clearly refers to 'hope' from the previous verse.[138] The assurance of this hope of reaching the 'now' heavenlies and the subsequent NHNE is metaphorically (technically, a simile) compared to an **anchor**.[139] As one would expect, an **anchor** evokes thoughts of stability.[140] Hence, the **anchor**/'hope'[141] is **sure and firm**. The reason for the stability is the previously mentioned 'two unchangeable things' (Heb. 6:18).

The AH now adds another wrinkle to increase our assurance by combining two metaphors.[142] The **anchor**/'hope' is **inside of the veil**, that is, it is in the holy of holies (Exod. 26:31–35; Lev. 16:2).[143] The holy of holies here represents the heavenly presence of God (Heb. 9:24).[144] The pay-off to increase our assurance is that Christ as **forerunner** has already **entered** into the **veil**/heavenlies **for us**. His being a **forerunner** is not simply that he went first, but that he is out front leading his group to a destination (**for us**). Hence, **forerunner** is similar to Christ's designation as the 'leader of their salvation' (Heb. 2:10) and 'leader and perfecter of our faith' (Heb. 12:2).[145] There are

---

138. Both are feminine singular in Greek.

139. There is no OT reference to an anchor. In the NT, **anchor** is used four times, literally three times, 27:29, 30, 40; and once metaphorically, Heb. 6:19. A literal anchor is strongly implied in Acts 27:13 and possibly implied in Mark 6:53.

140. Many Greco-Roman sources also used 'anchor' metaphorically for stability. See list of references in Koester, *Hebrews*, 329.

141. Since **hope**, **anchor**, **sure**, **firm**, and **entering** are all feminine singular in Greek, it is difficult to be dogmatic as to when the AH is referring to **hope** or to the metaphor of **anchor**. I prefer simply to combine them.

142. Some see two separate metaphors, e.g., Cockerill, *Hebrews*, 291.

143. For an explanation of this view, see Daniel M. Gurtner, 'LXX Syntax and the Identity of the NT Veil,' *NovT* 47 (2005): 344–53.

144. So also Schreiner, *Hebrews*, 203–4.

145. The cognate verb of **forerunner**, 'to run,' is in Heb. 12:1.

aspects of a union-with-Christ theology here.¹⁴⁶ If the **anchor** metaphor is to be pressed, a human anchor is unseen down in the sea and the Christian's **anchor** is unseen up in heaven.¹⁴⁷

Finally, another wrinkle related to the one above. The holy of holies (**inside the veil**) is not simply a metaphor for the heavenly presence of God, but it is also the location where only the OT high priest goes once-per-year to make the day-of-atonement sacrifice (Lev. 16). **Jesus** is not simply the **forerunner**, he is also *the* **high priest** who will make the once-for-all atonement. This **high priest** comment and the associated **according to the order of Melchizedek** harkens back to Hebrews 5:11 and prepares the reader for Hebrews 7:1–10:18. Note that the AH has reversed the order of the wording of Psalm 110:4 to end on **has become a high priest forever** (cf. Heb. 5:6; 7:17).¹⁴⁸ This is for rhetorical flourish.

In sum of Hebrews 6:16–20 and factors that provide 'strong encouragement', these are God's 'promise,' 'oath,' 'immutability of his will,' 'impossible for God to lie,' Jesus is the **forerunner**, and Jesus is the **high priest forever**. Amen!

Reflections

The anchor was a very common early symbol in Christian catacombs from AD 100 to 300. In the catacombs, the drawn/

---

146. Speaking of Christ visibly going up to heaven, WLC 53 only references Heb. 6:20 for 'forty days after his resurrection, he, in our nature, and as our head.' I assume that 'as our head' is connected to **forerunner**. Similarly, referencing Eph. 4:10; John 14:2, 3; and Heb. 6:20, the Confession of the English Congregation in Geneva 3 comments that at his resurrection Christ would 'take possession for us in His kingdom' (*Reformed Confessions of the 16th and 17th Centuries*, 2:98).

147. So Calvin, *Hebrews and 1 & 2 Peter*, 86; *Geneva Bible: 1602 Edition*, folio 111; Owen, *Hebrews*, 21:283; and Kistemaker, *Hebrews*, 177. *Contra* Ellingworth who sees the AH using 'restraint' with the metaphor (*Hebrews*, 346), also Bruce, *Hebrews*, 154–55.

148. Concerning *when* Christ became a **high priest**, see my discussion in the Reflections section following Heb. 5:10. Concerning **forever**, which I take as including eternity 'past,' see discussion at Heb. 7:16.

carved anchor would look similar to the standard anchor symbols one sees today. These anchors would normally have a curved bottom with two arms, a crossbar stock (although sometimes missing), and a ring at the top of the shaft (for the rope).[149] It makes sense to have the anchor as a symbol for a dead loved one because Hebrews 6:18–19 connects it to the hope/assurance of reaching the Christian's heavenly home.

Somewhat surprisingly, given the starting point in the catacombs, the anchor lost favor (as far as archaeology can detect) as a common symbol of Christianity around AD 300. With the victory of Constantine in AD 312 and his penchant for the cross, the cross then became *the* standard Christian symbol. In fact, it is very difficult to find any Church father discussing the anchor symbol as a symbol per se, as opposed to simply the metaphorical use.[150]

Although not intended by the AH, the anchor symbol with the crossbar stock also made the standard anchor symbol look like a cross. This combination of hope and Christ's cross proved to be too good so that the anchor symbol eventually became popular again in Christian art.

Although I am personally very uninformed about modern anchors and boats, the Christian anchor symbol resonates with me. Every time I see on TV a large ship that drops its huge anchor, I cannot help but to think of the assurance of the Christian hope and this Hebrews 6:12–20 passage. God's covenantal 'promise' and 'oath' are 'two immutable things' along with the work of Christ as our 'forerunner' and 'high priest' that give Christians 'strong encouragement' that we will be in the heavenly presence of our Triune God. Yes, our 'hope' is as 'sure and firm' as a huge 'anchor'.

---

149. See reproduced drawings in Charles A. Kennedy, 'Early Christians and The Anchor,' *BA* 38 (1975): 115–24, esp. 117–18.

150. Clement of Alexandria (AD ca. 150–ca. 215) is the rare case often cited. He is discussing what type of symbol to have on a signet ring. He recommends a dove, fish, boat, lyre, or a ship's anchor. However, he does not connect the anchor to Heb. 6:18 but to Seleucus, a successor to Alexander the Great. But in any case, do not put the faces of idols/gods on a Christian's signet ring. See *The Instructor* 3.11 (*ANF*, 2:285).

7.
Melchizedek
(7:1–28)

Although the AH has previously mentioned Melchizedek (Heb. 5:6 // Ps. 110:4; 5:10; 6:20), Hebrews 7 is his sustained discussion of the typology of Melchizedek related to Christ. Melchizedek is a mysterious figure in the OT and is only mentioned twice (Gen. 14:18–20 and Ps. 110:4). The AH uses both of these OT texts in Hebrews 7 to demonstrate that Christ is truly *the* high priest, emphasizing that Christ's priesthood is better than the Levitical/Aaronic priesthood.[1]

Hebrews 7:1–28 is one of five subsections of Hebrews 4:14–10:39.[2] Hebrews 7 is closely related to 8:1–10:18, which together, they form the theological core of the AH's argument concerning the person and work of Christ as high priest. Interestingly, both of the two previous subsections, Hebrews 4:14–5:10 and 5:11–6:20, end with a reference to Melchizedek (Heb. 5:10 and 6:20). As noted above, Hebrews 5:11–6:20 is the necessary interlude between the section-ending comment about Melchizedek in

---

1. Alan Kam-Yau Chan argues that in addition to Gen. 14 and Ps. 110 influencing Heb. 7, the AH is also influenced by 1 Sam. 7 (sonship) and Num. 22–24 (kingship) in Hebrews 7 (*Melchizedek Passages in the Bible: A Case Study for Inner-Biblical and Inter-Biblical Interpretation* [Berlin: De Gruyter Open, 2016], 197).

2. The five subsections are Heb. 4:14–5:10; 5:11–6:20; 7:1–28; 8:1–10:18; and 10:19–39.

Hebrews 5:10 and the sustained discussion in Hebrews 7. The interlude encourages the readers to take seriously the teaching of Hebrews 7 about Melchizedek despite the difficulties of the doctrine (Heb. 5:11; 6:1). The comment about Melchizedek in Hebrews 6:20 ends the interlude and prepares the readers for the glorious discussion of Christ based on the intriguing typology of Melchizedek.

Hebrews 7:1–28 is one integrated argument concerning Melchizedek related to Christ. For purposes of this commentary, I will subdivide Hebrews 7 into four units: 7:1–10; 7:11–19; 7:20–25; and 7:26–28.[3]

Melchizedek in Non-Canonical Literature

Both the DSS (Jewish documents from 150 BC to AD 68) and the Nag Hammadi Library (Coptic 'Christian' gnostic documents from the fourth century AD) were discovered in the mid-twentieth century. Interestingly, each of these libraries included one document that highlighted Melchizedek. These discoveries fueled a renewed scholarly interest in the potential non-canonical influences on the AH and his readers pertaining to Hebrews 7.[4] Scholars' views range from no influence[5] to significant.[6] Below is a brief summary of various references to Melchizedek in non-canonical literature. Then I will give

---

3. For comparison, Attridge subdivides into five sections: 7:1–3; 7:4–10; 7:11–19; 7:20–25; and 7:26–28 (*Hebrews*, 186); and Cockerill into three: 7:1–10; 7:11–25; and 7:26–28 (*Hebrews*, 293).

4. The scholarly literature here is significant. A classic and still valuable 'early' work is Fred L. Horton Jr, *The Melchizedek Tradition: A Critical Examination of the Sources to the Fifth Century A.D. and in the Epistle of Hebrews*, SNTSMS 30 (Cambridge: CUP, 1976).

5. So, e.g., Lane, *Hebrews 1–8*, 162–63; Cockerill, *Hebrews*, 298–99, n. 14; and Gard Granerod, 'Melchizedek in Hebrews 7,' *Bib* 90 (2009): 188–202.

6. So, e.g., to varying degrees, A. van der Woude, '11Q Melchizedek and the New Testament,' *NTS* 12 (1966): 301–26; Attridge, *Hebrews*, 194; and Andrei A. Orlov, 'The Heir of Righteousness and the King of Righteousness: The Priestly Noachic Polemics in 2 Enoch and the Epistle of Hebrews,' *JTS* ns 58 (2007): 45–66.

my view as to the possible effect this information has upon Hebrews 7.

Within the DSS is a fragmentary document termed Melchizedek (11QMelch, also referred to as 11Q13).[7] The person Melchizedek is presented as a heavenly judge who delivers God's people in an eschatological Day of Jubilee and brings judgment upon God's enemies. Portions of Psalms 82:1-2 and 7:7-8 are quoted to show that he is the head of God's divine council (11QMelch II, 10-13). Given this, most scholars connect Melchizedek to the archangel Michael.[8] Note, there is no connection to the priesthood of Melchizedek, although the Day of Atonement is mentioned (11QMelch II, 7-8).[9] Also, there is no explicit reference to Genesis 14:18-20 nor Psalm 110:4.

Second Enoch (Slavonic Apocalypse) is very difficult to date as it may have Christian interpolations. Scholars have proposed dates from first century BC to ninth century AD, with many concluding the first century AD.[10] The only extant versions exist in the Slavonic language. Melchizedek is discussed in 2 Enoch 71-72. He is the supposed son of the priest Nir (not mentioned in the Bible), who is the second son of Lamech, who is the father of Noah (Gen. 5:28-29; Luke 3:36). Nir was

---

7. Melchizedek is included in the Genesis Apocryphon (1QapGen), which is an apocryphal account of Noah and Abraham mostly covering Gen. 12-14. The account related to Abraham's meeting Melchizedek follows very closely to Gen. 14:18-20 (1QapGen XXII, 14-19). One detail added is that Salem is Jerusalem.

8. E.g., D. C. Allison Jr, 'Melchizedek,' *DLNT*, 729-30.

9. *Contra* Eric F. Mason who concludes that 'presumably' Melchizedek is a 'high priest conducting this eschatological Day of Atonement event' ('Hebrews 7:3 and the Relationship between Melchizedek and Jesus,' *BR* 50 [2005]: 41-62, esp. 57).

10. See discussion in F. I. Anderson, '2 (Slavonic Apocalypse of) Enoch,' *OTP*, 1:94-97. He 'is inclined to place [2 Enoch]—or at least its original nucleus—early rather than late; and in a Jewish rather than a Christian community.' Attridge concludes that 2 Enoch was written in the first century AD and that the Melchizedek discussion is 'certainly not a Christian interpolation and is probably an original component of the work' (*Hebrews*, 193).

not the actual father. Melchizedek's mother, Sothonim, the wife of Nir, conceived him miraculously in her womb. She died before giving birth and was wrapped in grave clothes by Noah and Nir. Subsequently, however, Melchizedek was miraculously 'birthed' from the dead Sothonim and came forth already clothed with priestly garments and was able to talk. Melchizedek is saved from the Noahic flood by an angel and is now being preserved miraculously in the heavenly "garden of Eden." He will eventually be head of a group of priests who will reign over God's people.[11] No reference is made to Genesis 14:18–20 nor Psalm 110:4.

Philo discusses Melchizedek in three passages, *Allegorical Interpretation* 3:79–83; *On the Life of Abraham* 235; and *On the Preliminary Studies* 99. He adds a few historical details to Genesis 14:18–20 (e.g., Melchizedek raised his hands to heaven). In two of the texts, Philo clearly moves from the historical details to allegory. In *Allegorical Interpretation*, Melchizedek, the king of peace, represents proper reason which brings peace.[12] Also, Melchizedek brought wine and not water. This wine represents the proper 'divine intoxication' of the soul. In *On the Life of Abraham*, the 'plain words' show that good fortune comes to those who please God. In addition, the allegory includes that the four kings represent four passions within us (pleasure, desire, fear, and grief) and the five kings, the five outward senses. In *On the Preliminary Studies*, Melchizedek is used to support tithing. All texts are connected to Genesis 14:18–20; there is no connection to Psalm 110:4.

Josephus has two brief mentions of Melchizedek, both related to Genesis 14:18–20. In a general discussion of Abraham, Josephus mentions the Melchizedek incident. He notes that Salem is later called Jerusalem and Abram gave a

---

11. Orlov sees 2 Enoch as a Jewish polemic in the first century AD against the Noachic priestly tradition that was trying to usurp the validity of the Aaronic priestly tradition ('The Heir of Righteousness and the King of Righteousness,' 50–55).

12. More than I do, Horton believes Philo connects Melchizedek's priesthood to the Logos (*The Melchizedek Tradition*, 59).

tenth of his booty (*Jewish Antiquities* 1.180–81). In a discussion concerning the checkered history of Jerusalem, Melchizedek is the first to build a temple in Salem/Jerusalem and is the first priest of God.

Concerning Rabbinic targums, for Genesis 14:18, in both Targum Jerusalem and Targum Pseudo-Jonathan, Melchizedek is explicitly stated to be Shem, who is the son of Noah. Also, both interpret Salem as Jerusalem. Targum Onkelos says nothing about Shem but does interpret Salem as Jerusalem. For Psalm 110:4, the Psalms Targum interprets 'priest' as 'leader' (Aramaic רב), and the 'order of Melchizedek' as 'merit of being a righteous king.' Clearly, the intent here is to remove any priestly connections from Psalm 110:4.

Melchizedek is negatively referenced in the Rabbinic b. Nedarim 32b.[13] According to R. Zechariah, God wanted to bring the priesthood through the bloodline of Shem and Melchizedek. However, since Melchizedek improperly blessed Abraham instead of blessing God in Genesis 14:19, God brought the priesthood through Abraham's line. Hence, Psalm 110:1 and 110:4 are properly referring to Abraham.

The Nag Hammadi codex NHC IX, 1 Melchizedek is extant in eleven pages of which approximately fifty percent per page is damaged and not readable. This fourth-century AD Coptic text may have existed as a Greek text extending back to the second century AD. In this 'Christian' gnostic text, Melchizedek is the 'true high priest of God most high' and revealer of the secrets of God that he received from heavenly luminaries. He is either connected to 'Jesus Christ, the Son of God' or is Christ himself. Christ/Melchizedek will be the eschatological savior of his people and a warrior who destroys enemies. The fragmentary nature of the text prohibits definite conclusions.[14] Excepting that Melchizedek is a high

---

13. Melchizedek is positively included in b. Baba Batra 14A within a list of those who authored part of the book of Psalms. No specific psalm is identified.

14. For good, brief discussion, see Birger A. Pearson, 'Melchizedek (NHC IX, 1),' *ABD* 4:688.

priest, there are no explicit connections to Genesis 14:18–20, Psalm 110:4, nor Hebrews 7.

To summarize the above, Melchizedek is presented as a heavenly figure in three sources, 11QMelch; 2 Enoch; and NCH IX, 1, Melchizedek. In 2 Enoch and NCH 1X, 1, Melchizedek, he is also clearly a priest. Interestingly, these three texts do not have explicit connections to Genesis 14:18–20 nor Psalm 110:4. Philo and Josephus clearly reference Melchizedek from Genesis 14:18–20 and take the biblical text at face value. Philo does see allegorical implications from the historical narrative. Neither discusses or alludes to Melchizedek from Psalm 110:4. The Rabbinic literature is mixed. Some texts take Genesis 14:18–20 in a straightforward way, although adding the detail that Melchizedek is actually Shem may be an implied polemic against those who read too much into the absence of Melchizedek's genealogy in Genesis. Other texts are clearly a polemic against a Melchizedekian priesthood (b. Nedarim 32b; Psalms Targum 110:4).

The question of dating offers a significant complication to all of the above when considering the possible impact upon Hebrews 7. Except for the DSS, Philo, and Josephus; the dating of 2 Enoch; NHC IX, 1 Melchizedek; and the Rabbinic literature is very tenuous. Related to this is the question of general awareness in the culture for *all* of the above sources. Would the AH and a portion of his congregation have known any of the above literature or at least known some of the ideas contained in this literature? My general view of Second Temple Judaism literature is that it is reasonably possible that some of the ideas were broadly 'in the air' during the first-century AD.[15] Hence, the AH and some of his readers were possibly aware of various interpretations of Melchizedek.

Given my conclusions that (1) some of the above

---

15. For a detailed discussion of the difficulties of dating the literature from Second Temple Judaism and my conclusions of the usefulness of various documents, see Cara, *Cracking the Foundation of the New Perspective on Paul*, 208–20.

interpretations of Melchizedek were 'in the air,' (2) the AH and his congregation were well acquainted with Judaism and its Levitical priesthood, and (3) some readers were being tempted to return to Judaism—*How do I see the above sources influencing Hebrews 7? In sum, virtually not at all.* The AH's conclusions concerning the typology of Melchizedek are based on the combination of Genesis 14:18–20; Psalm 110:4; and an argument from silence in Genesis. None of the above sources that contain a 'heavenly Melchizedek' remotely makes this unified argument. Further, solving how Christ could properly be a priest given his non-Levitical genealogy is a pertinent question for those well-acquainted with Judaism, whether or not other Melchizedek interpretations were known, either the 'heavenly Melchizedek' or Rabbinic varieties. Hence, I conclude that the AH did *not* use positively any of the above sources *nor* clearly make an argument against any of their specific points.[16] However, since Melchizedek ideas were 'in the air,' the AH and some of congregants would be aware of the broad contrast between Hebrews 7 and these ideas.

Melchizedek and Abraham (7:1–10)

The subunit Hebrews 7:1–10 of 7:1–28 has two paragraphs, 7:1–3 and 7:4–10. The first paragraph, which is really one sentence, concerns Melchizedek and Abraham's encounter mentioned in Genesis 14:17–20. It concludes with a typological statement comparing Christ's eternality with Melchizedek's lack of genealogy. The second paragraph expands upon the superiority of Melchizedek over Abraham/Levi. Tying this subunit together is the use of 'met' (συναντάω) in Hebrews 7:1 and 7:10.

7:1–2a *For this Melchizedek, king of Salem, priest of the highest God, the one meeting Abraham who was returning*[17] *from the slaughter of*

---

16. Of course, whether the AH did use any of these sources or not, Hebrews itself is Scripture, and the truths in it stand no matter the sources.

17. In the Greek, 'who was returning' (ὑποστρέφοντι, dative) clearly refers

the kings, the one who blessed him, to whom also Abraham divided a tenth of all;

Melchizedek is mentioned in the OT in Genesis 14:18–20 and Psalm 110:4. Hebrews 6:20 ends with a reference to Psalm 110:4. **For this Melchizedek** connects the Psalm 110:4 // Hebrews 6:20 reference to the following Genesis 14 discussion in Hebrews 7:1–10. More specifically, the AH gives reasons that Christ is a Melchizedek-type priest that is better than the Levi/Aaronic priesthood. This in turn implies that the congregation ought to continue in their reliance on Christ and not turn back to older truncated forms of Judaism.

Hebrews 7:1–2a uses much of the same LXX wording from Genesis 14:17–20.[18] Exact matches include 'Melchizedek, king of Salem,' 'priest of the highest God,' 'slaughter ... of the kings,' and 'tenth of all.' Similar wording but a cognate or different mood includes 'meeting,' 'returning,' and 'blessed.' Interestingly, both the HB and LXX use 'Abram' (אברם, Ἀβράμ) in Genesis 14 as God does not change his name to 'Abraham' until Genesis 17:5 (אברהם, Ἀβραάμ). But here and elsewhere in the book of Hebrews, the AH always uses 'Abraham' (Ἀβραάμ), as does the entire NT.

The AH notes that Melchizedek is both a **king** and **priest**. This has clear 'dual' typological connections to Christ.[19] Although the focus of Hebrews 7:1–10:18 will be on the priesthood of Christ and the connection to the priesthood of Melchizedek, the connection to Psalm 110 and the 'Son'/king emphasis of the book confirms the **king** portion of the typology. Further, in the immediate context, 'righteousness' and 'peace' in Hebrews 7:2b–c provide another messianic/

---

to Abraham. Ἀβραάμ, although indeclinable, is also in the dative case as the participle 'the one meeting' takes a dative as its object (BDAG, 965).

18. The LXX is a straightforward translation of the Hebrew. One exception is Gen. 14:19a. The Hebrew has 'he blessed him'; the LXX correctly clarifies, 'he blessed Abram.' The AH follows the Hebrew.

19. So also *Geneva Bible: 1602 Edition*, folio 111; Hughes, *Hebrews*, 247; and Schreiner, *Hebrews*, 208–09. Owen is less sure of the **king** typology than I am (*Hebrews*, 21:300–1).

king connection (cf. Zech. 6:12–13). Hence, as Melchizedek was both a **king** and **priest**, this was a foreshadowing of Christ who would be *the* **king** and *the* **priest**.

Melchizedek **blessed him** (Abraham). As recorded in Genesis 14:19–20, Melchizedek gives a priestly blessing/benediction.[20] His giving of a benediction parallels the requirements of Levitical priests to give benedictions (e.g., Num. 6:22–27; Deut. 21:5; cf. Heb. 11:20–21) and thus reinforces that Melchizedek is a proper priest.[21] The AH will expand upon the implications of this blessing in Hebrews 7:6–7.

The AH notes another priestly aspect of Melchizedek, **to whom** [Melchizedek] **also Abraham divided a tenth of all**.[22] The **all** in context of Genesis 14:20 means **all** of the booty that Abraham captured,[23] which matches to Hebrews 7:4. As Levitical priests received tithes, so did Melchizedek (e.g., Num. 18:21–32; Deut. 12:6–7, 19; 14:29; 18:1–8; 2 Chr. 31:2–12; Neh. 10:32–39; 12:44; cf. Gen. 18:18–22). Similar to the blessing, the AH will add to the implications of this tithe in Hebrews 7:4–10.

7:2b–c *first, [his name] is being translated, king of righteousness,*

---

20. I use the term 'benediction' for blessings offered by an authorized representative of God, such as an OT priest or NT ordained minister of the word. See further discussion at Heb. 13:20–21.

21. Gen. 14:18 notes that Melchizedek 'brought out bread and wine.' Many through church history connect this to the NT sacrament of the Lord's Supper (e.g., Clement of Alexandria, *Stromata* 4.25 [*ANF*, 2:439]; Cyprian, *Epistle* 62.4 [*ANF*, 5:359]). This would further reinforce connections to Christ.

22. Both the Hebrew and the LXX simply have 'he gave him a tenth of all' (Gen. 14:20). Who is the subject and who is object is not clear grammatically; although the context implies that Abraham gave a tenth to Melchizedek, which the AH makes explicit. Many critical scholars believe that Gen. 14:18–20 is an interpolation into proto-Gen. 14 in which the original Melchizedek saga had him giving gifts to Abraham but it got reversed (intentionally or unintentionally) when put into the context of Gen. 14 (so Joseph A. Fitzmyer, 'Melchizedek in the MT, LXX, and the NT,' *Bib* 81 [2000]: 63–69, esp. 66–67).

23. So also John D. Currid, *A Study Commentary on Genesis 1:1–25:18*, EP Study Commentary (Darlington, England: Evangelical Press, 2003), 287.

and then also [he is] king of Salem, that is, king of peace;

The AH returns to and expands upon the first two words/phrases from Hebrews 7:1, 'Melchizedek' and 'king of Salem.' As does the Second Temple Judaism tradition for both Hebrew (מלכיצדק) and Greek (Μελχισέδεκ) versions, the AH correctly **translate[s]** Melchizedek's name as **king of righteousness** (cf. Heb. 1:9).[24] Genesis 14:18 explicitly states that Melchizedek is the **king of Salem** (שָׁלֵם, *shalem*). The AH correctly notes that the city name of **Salem** is clearly related etymologically to **peace** in Hebrew (שָׁלוֹם, *shalom*).

Although the AH does not explicitly make the connection here, the fact that through translation Melchizedek is both **king of righteousness** and **peace** implies he is making messianic connections to Christ (cf. Ps. 72:7; Isa. 9:6–7; Zech. 6:12–13; 9:10). There is another messianic connection through **Salem**. The OT very often refers to Jerusalem as 'Zion' (e.g., 1 Kgs. 8:1; Ps. 147:12; Isa. 40:9; Zech. 9:9; cf. Heb. 12:22). Psalm 76:2 uses both 'Salem' and 'Zion' to refer to Jerusalem.[25] Psalm 110:2, the psalm that Hebrews 7 concentrates upon, connects the Messiah with 'Zion.' Hence, the AH sees the city of 'Salem' as another name for Jerusalem/Zion, the Messiah's city.

The historical Melchizedek was a king of a city named **Salem**, which apparently was located on the same site as Jerusalem. Melchizedek was probably known as both a righteous (i.e., just, cf. Heb. 11:33) and peaceful ruler. He was also a priest.

7:3 *without father, without mother, without genealogy, having*

---

24. The Hebrew מלכ is **king**, צדק is **righteousness**, and י is for pronunciation reasons, as opposed to the normal 'my.' (so also Owen, *Hebrews*, 21:328). *Contra* my view, some critical scholars argue that in the OT context the י does mean 'my' or part of a supposed king's name; thus, 'Melchizedek' should be properly translated as either 'my king is Zedek,' 'my king is righteous,' or 'Malki is righteous' (e.g., Fitzmyer, 'Melchizedek in the MT, LXX, and the NT,' 65; Gordon J. Wenham, *Genesis 1–15*, WBC 1 [Waco: Word, 1987], 316; and Attridge, *Hebrews*, 189).

25. Another aspect is the obvious etymological connection between Jeru*salem* and Salem (שלם/ירושלם).

neither beginning of days nor end of life, but having been made like the Son of God, he remains a priest[26] *continuously.*[27]

What is the basis by which the AH concludes that Melchizedek is **without father, without mother, without genealogy**? Given the prominence of Melchizedek in Genesis 14:18–20 and Psalm 110:4, the basis is the significant fact that Melchizedek is the only God-worshipping person in Genesis whose **genealogy** is *not* included.[28] Further, Melchizedek is the first priest mentioned in Genesis, and priests are expected to have a **genealogy**. That is, *this is an argument from a stunning silence.*[29] Similarly, the phrase **having neither beginning of days nor end of life** is based on neither Melchizedek's birth nor death being recorded in Genesis.

Does the AH believe that Melchizedek is literally **without father** and **without mother** and does not have **beginning of days nor end of life**? No, the AH is making a typological argument, as he does throughout the book.[30] The phrase **having been made like the Son of God** makes this clear. Melchizedek is certainly not the **Son of God** (cf. Heb. 1:5; 4:14) but is **like** Christ, that is, Melchizedek is typologically **like** Christ (cf. Heb. 7:15). In addition, I have mechanically translated the participle **having-been-made-like** with the

---

26. **Priest** is in the nominative case because the verb **remains** occasionally acts as a 'to be' verb and takes a predicate nominative (BDAG, 631, §1b).

27. The idiom εἰς τὸ διηνεκές is used in Heb. 7:3; 10:1, 12, 14 and nowhere else in the LXX and NT. It has slightly different nuances per context; here it clearly as a 'forever' aspect. See C. F. D. Moule, *An Idiom Book of New Testament Greek*, 2nd ed. (Cambridge: CUP, 1959), 164–65.

28. So also Chrysostom, 'Homily 12 on Hebrews,' *NPNF*[1], 14:423–24; Aquinas, *Hebrews*, 143–44; Hughes, *Hebrews*, 248–49; and Phillips, *Hebrews*, 225.

29. See Heb. 1:5 and 1:13 for other arguments from silence.

30. Ambrose well says, 'The Church doth certainly not hold [Melchizedek] to be an angel (as some Jewish triflers do), but a holy man and priest of God who prefigure[s] our Lord' (*On the Christian Faith* 3.88 [*NPNF*[2], 10:255]). Turretin gives a detailed defense of Melchizedek's humanity (*Institutes of Elenctic Theology*, 2:408–11).

full passive sense.³¹ Thus this is a 'divine passive' in that it was *God* who providentially created Melchizedek and had Moses not record Melchizedek's genealogy so the text would typologically point to Christ.³²

By using Melchizedek, what aspect(s) of Christ is the AH emphasizing here? There are two related aspects: (1) Christ has an eternal (divine) nature and (2) Levitical **genealogy** is not required for priesthood.³³ Note how Hebrews 7:16 combines these two.

The eternal and divine nature of Christ is shown from the typology that **he** [Melchizedek] **remains a priest continually**.³⁴ Grammatically, this clause is highlighted because (1) it is the only finite verb within Hebrews 7:1–3 and (2) it is the last clause. This then well matches to the final words of Hebrews 6:20 that are paraphrasing Psalm 110:4, 'Jesus, according to the order of Melchizedek has become a high *priest forever*.' That is, there is an emphasis on 'forever'/**continuously** in both Hebrews 6:20 and 7:1–3.³⁵ Melchizedek in a typological sense was **continuously** a priest as Genesis narrates neither the beginning nor the ending of his priesthood. The **Son of God** was truly in his divine nature a 'priest forever.' This

---

31. So also KJV and NASB. The ESV and NIV have 'resembling.' This has more of a Greek middle sense, which is grammatically legitimate as ἀφωμοιωμένος may be parsed as either a middle or a passive with no context.

32. Those agreeing to a divine passive include Lane, *Hebrews 1–8*; and Cockerill, *Hebrews*, 302 n. 23.

33. So also Aquinas, *Hebrews*, 143–44; Calvin, *Hebrews and 1 & 2 Peter*, 89–90; Hughes, *Hebrews*, 248–49; and Lane, *Hebrews 1–8*, 165–66. Several commentators put the sole emphasis here on the lack of **genealogy**, e.g., Owen, *Hebrews*, 21:332–37; and Brown, *Hebrews*, 327–28

34. As Charles Hodge points out, the proper subject/nominative of **remains** is all the way back to 'this Melchizedek' in Heb. 7:1. He surmises that some improperly interpret the subject of **remains** as **Son of God** as a misguided zeal to more explicitly declare the divinity of Christ (*Hebrews*, 56).

35. Possibly the AH used the expression **continuously** for Melchizedek and 'forever' for Christ to note that Melchizedek is only a type of Christ. This 'forever'/**continuously** concept is contrasted with Levitical priests who apparently finished working at age fifty (Num. 4:3; 8:25).

'forever' aspect of Christ from Psalm 110:4 is highlighted in Hebrews 7:16, 24–25, and 28. Further confirming the divine nature aspect is **having neither beginning of days nor end of life**. This evokes the grand statements about Christ's divine nature from Hebrews 1:12 ('you are the same, and your years will not fail') and 13:8 ('the same yesterday, today, and forever').[36] As discussed above in the Reflection section following Hebrews 5:1–10, Christ became our mediatorial priest at his conception and continues forever as our priest. But his eternal nature including eternity 'past' is a necessary part of the background to this mediatorial priesthood.

The **without father** and **without mother** language is intriguing relative to the Son's eternal nature. The AH realizes that the *divine* nature of the Son has a *divine* Father (e.g., Heb. 1:1–5) and the *human* nature of the Son has a *human* mother (e.g., Heb. 7:14), but here the AH emphasizes that the *divine* nature of the Son has no *human* parents, **without father** and **without mother**.[37] The wonderful language of **having neither beginning of days nor end of life** has been used often in church history to support the Son's divinity and eternality (e.g., included in text of Belgic Confession 10 and 19).

As noted above, in addition to emphasizing the eternal nature of the Son, the typology of Melchizedek also includes that a Levitical **genealogy** is *not* required for priesthood. This aspect corresponds to 'order of Melchizedek' from Hebrews 6:20 // Psalm 110:4. It will be explicitly discussed in Hebrews 7:5, 9–11, 14, and 16.

7:4–6 *Now[38] observe how great this [man was], to whom even Abraham, the patriarch, gave a tenth from the spoils. And on the one*

---

36. So also Bauckham, 'The Divinity of Jesus Christ in the Epistle to the Hebrews,' 27–32.

37. Gregory of Nazianzus comments, 'In his human nature he had no Father, but also in his divine nature no mother' (*Third Theological Oration* 19 [*NPNF*², 7:308]).

38. I here translate δέ as **now** as it is logically connecting Heb. 7:1–3 with 7:4–10. So also Owen, *Hebrews*, 21:344; KJV; NASB; and CSB17.

hand, those, from the sons of Levi, the ones receiving the priesthood, have a commandment according to the law to take tithes from the people; that is, their brothers, even though coming from the loins of Abraham, but on the other hand, the [man] not being descended from them received tithes from Abraham and blessed the one having the promises.

Hebrews 7:4–10 restates information and makes several implications from Hebrews 7:1–3 // Genesis 14:17–20. The overall point is to show that Melchizedek's priesthood is better than the Levitical priesthood.

The AH begins **observe how great this man** (Melchizedek) **was**. To show Melchizedek's greatness, he compares him to **Abraham, the patriarch**,[39] also **the one having the promises** (cf. Heb. 6:13). These two epithets enhance the prestige of Abraham, which in turn enhances the prestige of Melchizedek because (1) Abraham **gave a tenth from the spoils** to Melchizedek and (2) Melchizedek **blessed** Abraham. Surprisingly, given all the positive things said about Abraham throughout this book (Heb. 2:16; 6:12–15; 11:8–12, 17–19; 13:2), Abraham's association with Levi connects him to the Mosaic Covenant and its (God-ordained) deficiencies.[40]

Melchizedek's superiority over Abraham brings the AH to his real point. This superiority relates to the Levitical priesthood. The Levitical priesthood, **sons of Levi, the ones receiving the priesthood**, receives tithes from **the people**.[41] Both of these, the **people** and the **sons of Levi**, are **brothers** who are descended **from the loins of Abraham**. Melchizedek, **on the other hand**, is not related to Abraham nor his descendants (**them**), and despite this, Melchizedek still **received tithes from Abraham**. Hence, in

---

39. In Greek, **patriarch** is separated from **Abraham** and is at the end of Heb. 7:4 sentence. This gives more 'punch' to this epithet. So also Turner, *Style*, 107.

40. For more discussion, see Cara, 'Covenant in Hebrews,' 251–54.

41. More specifically, the whole tribe of Levi, including the priests, received a tithe from the people (Num. 18:21, 26, cf. Lev. 27:21).

Hebrews 7:4–6, Melchizedek's priesthood superiority to the Levitical priesthood is shown by Melchizedek's receiving tithes from one whom he is not related.

7:7 Now[42] *[it is] without any dispute [that] the lesser is blessed by the greater.*

Hebrews 7:7 is somewhat of a parenthesis within the tithes discussion, although it adds another angle to the superiority of Melchizedek over Abraham/Levi. The end of Hebrews 7:6 notes that Melchizedek 'blessed' Abraham. The AH adds a truism **that the lesser is blessed by the greater.**[43] Therefore by implication, Melchizedek is **greater** because he blessed Abraham, the **lesser**.

The truism **that the lesser is blessed by the greater** needs some qualifications. In the OT, there are many examples of 'lesser' humans blessing the 'greater' God, which are clearly understood as humans *praising* and/or *thanking* God (e.g., Deut. 8:10; 1 Kgs. 1:48; Ps. 103:1; 1 Chr. 29:20). Also in the OT, there are examples of 'lesser' humans blessing 'greater' humans, which do not match the AH's truism, such as subjects blessing their king (e.g., Gen. 47:7; 2 Sam. 14:22; 1 Kgs. 1:47; Ps. 72:15; cf. 2 Sam. 21:3).[44] On the other hand, matching to the above truism, there are the obvious examples of God the 'greater' blessing 'lesser' humans (e.g., Gen. 12:2; 22:17 // Heb. 6:14). In addition, there are examples of the 'greater' humans blessing the 'lesser' humans, such as parents blessing children (e.g., Gen. 27:27; 48:9) and priestly blessings

---

42. I here translate δέ as **now** as it is logically connecting to 'blessed' from Heb. 7:6.

43. **The lesser** (τὸ ἔλαττον) is clearly in the neuter gender, and **the greater** (τοῦ κρείττονος) is implied to be. This neuter gender, as opposed to the expected masculine, adds confirmation that this is a truism-type statement.

44. The verb 'to bless' (ברך) includes the broader nuance of 'to salute' and 'to greet' as part of a meeting (e.g., Gen. 47:7; 2 Kgs. 4:29) or departing (e.g., Gen. 24:60; 47:10) (see BDB, 139). For detailed discussions of various types of blessings in the Bible, see Owen, *Hebrews*, 21:316–21, 369–74 and Christopher Wright Mitchell, *The Meaning of* BRK *'To Bless' in the Old Testament*, SBLDS 95 (Atlanta: Scholars, 1987).

(e.g., Num. 6:22–27).[45] Here, the AH is using the truism relative to *priestly* blessings/benedictions.[46] In sum, in priestly situations, it is absolutely true **that the lesser is blessed by the greater**.

7:8–10 *And here, on the one hand, mortal men receive tithes, but there, on the other hand, it is witnessed that he lives. And so to speak,*[47] *even Levi, the one receiving tithes, has paid tithes through Abraham; for he was yet in the loins of the father when Melchizedek met him.*

Following the parenthesis related to blessing (Heb. 7:7), the AH returns again to the subject of tithes, but now with more specificity concerning the Levitical priesthood.

The Levitical priesthood are **mortal men**. But Melchizedek/Christ as a priest does not die, but **he lives**. Here the superiority is again based on the 'forever' aspect of the Melchizedek/Christ priesthood. Possibly **he lives** is intentionally connecting to the several 'living God' epithets in Hebrews (Heb. 3:12; 9:14; 10:31; 12:22; cf. 7:3). Concerning **there ... it is witnessed**, **there** and **it** refer to the Genesis account about Melchizedek.[48]

Although the AH has already shown the superiority of Melchizedek by his receiving tithes from Abraham, in Hebrews 7:9–10 this point is explicitly extended to the Levitical priesthood. It was not only Abraham that paid tithes, but also **Levi ... has paid tithes through Abraham** to Melchizedek. How is this possible since Levi was not alive

---

45. WLC 129 references Heb. 7:3 where superiors are to 'bless their inferiors.'

46. So also Calvin, *Hebrews and 1 & 2 Peter*, 92–93; Owen, *Hebrews*, 21:369; Brown, *Hebrews*, 332; and Cockerill, *Hebrews*, 310; *contra* Attridge, *Hebrews*, 196n134.

47. The idiom **so to speak** (ὡς ἔπος εἰπεῖν) only occurs here in the LXX and NT, and ἔπος alone only occurs once elsewhere in the LXX and NT (Sir. 44:5). This idiom occurs twenty-two times in Philo (e.g., *On Drunkenness* 51; *On Dreams* 1.96). When not in the idiom, ἔπος is translated in various Greek writings as 'word,' 'proverb,' and 'verse.'

48. So also Hughes, *Hebrews*, 253. CSB17 translates as 'Scripture testifies that he lives.'

during Abraham's time? **So to speak** he was because Levi **was yet in the loins of the father**, that is, Levi was present because he was an ancestor of Abraham.⁴⁹

Is it not an objection that Christ in his human nature, who was also **in the loins of the father** Abraham, paid tithes to Melchizedek? The answer is that here the AH is using the Melchizedek typology to refer to the divine nature of Christ as shown by the use of 'Son of God' (Heb. 7:3) and the **he lives** emphasis.⁵⁰

Reflections

God, the writer of Scripture, did not include the 'genealogy' of Melchizedek in Genesis. This *stunning silence* was intentionally orchestrated by God to teach us important aspects of Christ's person and his priesthood. Christ's divine nature has no human parents and has 'neither beginning of days nor end of life.' Christ's mediatorial priesthood will last from his conception until forever.

At least for me, this stunning silence further confirms my conviction that God wrote the Bible. 'What are the chances,' as the saying goes, that (1) no genealogy was provided for an enigmatic figure such as Melchizedek and (2) this happens to match aspects of Christ's divine nature?

May the Holy Spirit use all parts of the Bible, including Hebrews 7, to confirm in us the Bible's true nature.

Change in Priesthood (7:11–19)

Hebrews 7:11–19 is a coherent subunit as shown by 'perfection'/'perfected' and 'received-legislation'/'law' both being in 7:11 and 7:19. This forms an inclusio.⁵¹

---

49. Cockerill also connects **so to speak** to the **loins of the father** (*Hebrews*, 312).

50. So also Turretin, *Institutes of Elenctic Theology*, 2:410; and Hughes, *Hebrews*, 254.

51. As virtually all agree, e.g., Vanhoye, *Structure and Message of the Epistle of Hebrews*, 90.

The subunit begins with the imperfection of the Levitical priesthood (Heb. 7:11) and then asserts that with a change in priesthood, there must be a change in priestly requirements (Heb. 7:12). The AH confirms that Christ's priesthood is an obvious change in the priesthood (Heb. 7:13–14). As to the resulting changes in priestly requirements, they include an 'indestructible life' (Heb. 7:15–17) and a priesthood that provides a 'better hope' (Heb. 7:18–19). To summarize, the subunit Hebrews 7:11–19 includes three interrelated arguments as to the appropriateness of changing the Levitical priesthood to Christ's priesthood. (1) The mentioning of a Melchizedekian-like priesthood in Psalm 110:4 indicates a change was anticipated in the Aaronic priesthood. (2) The 'forever' comment in Psalm 110:4 is related to Christ's priesthood and his indestructible life. (3) The Aaronic priesthood did not attain eschatological perfection for God's people, which is the goal of a priesthood.

Interestingly, what on the surface could be seen as an objection to Christ's being a priest—he was not from the tribe of Levi—becomes part of the argument *for* his priesthood.[52] That is, Psalm 110:4 indicates that the priesthood will change; hence, the Levitical priesthood is deemed inferior as shown by its need to change. Therefore, it is positive that Christ is not from the tribe of Levi and its inferior priesthood.

7:11 *Therefore, if perfection were through the Levitical priesthood, for the people have received legislation concerning*[53] *it, what further need would [there be for] another priest to arise according to the order of Melchizedek and not be named according to the order of Aaron?*

---

52. Attridge alerted me to this point (*Hebrews*, 199).

53. The preposition ἐπί with the genitive has a wide range of meanings (BDAG, 363–67). I chose **concerning** as a more general use for this context (so also Hughes, *Hebrews*, 256; and Lane, *Hebrews 1–8*, 174) as opposed to more specific translations such as 'on the basis of' (e.g., CSB17) or 'under' (e.g., ESV).

Following the background discussion of Melchizedek in Hebrews 7:1–10, **therefore** is referring back to Hebrews 6:20 ('Jesus, according to the order of Melchizedek has become a high priest forever').[54] In Hebrews 7:11–19, the AH will make arguments from 'according to the order of Melchizedek' and 'forever.'

The AH's argument here in Hebrews 7:11, presented in a contrary-to-fact format, is that because the Levitical priesthood *did not* bring **perfection** to believers it makes sense that a subsequent priesthood is needed and that priesthood would not be of the imperfect Levitical lineage. This then dovetails with the Psalm 110:4 implication that **another priest** *not* from the **order of Aaron** would **arise** and he would be instead from the **order of Melchizedek**.

This is the first time in Hebrews that the term **perfection** and/or its cognates are related to believers. Previously, they have been related to Christ (see detailed discussion at Heb. 5:9). Here **perfection** is related to the design/end/purpose/fulfillment for which God's plan of salvation was ultimately intended, that is, the new covenant benefits for believers. Christ's 'perfection' as the high priest of the new covenant brings about believers' **perfection**. Although no specifics are given here in context, from the rest of Hebrews a believer's **perfection** includes sins truly being forgiven based on the reality of Christ's work (Heb. 9:26; 10:4), more access to God through Christ (Heb. 4:16; 7:19), personal sanctification (Heb. 10:14 [?]; 12:23), and the final enjoyment of the Triune God upon death (Heb. 12:23) and in the NHNE (Heb. 11:40).[55] Note that these new covenant realities also have benefits for OT believers (e.g., Heb. 9:15; 11:40; 12:23).

---

54. So also Lane, *Hebrews 1–8*, 180. Others see a looser connection (e.g., Brown, *Hebrews*, 336; and Attridge, *Hebrews*, 199); hence, many translations have 'now' (e.g., RSV, NASB, ESV).

55. Hodge defines **perfection** as 'the attainment of the end designed which was reconciliation with God' (*Hebrews*, 61). Silva emphasizes the eschatological aspect of **perfection** as opposed to *only* a moral aspect. For Silva, the AH's **perfection** is 'the enjoyment of the time of fulfillment, the new epoch introduced by the Messiah through his exaltation' ('Perfection and Eschatology in Hebrews,' 67).

In the parenthetical phrase **for the people have received legislation concerning it, it** grammatically refers to the **Levitical priesthood**. The verb **received-legislation** (νομοθετέω[56]) clearly alludes to the priestly and ceremonial aspects of the Mosaic law, as the reference to the **Levitical priesthood** makes clear.[57]

7:12 *For when the priesthood changes,[58] from necessity a change of law comes about also.*

Hebrews 7:12 expands (**for**) upon the implications of two interrelated points from 7:11, (1) there is a relationship between priesthood and legislation/law and (2) another priest will arise who is not from Aaron. Given these two points, the AH simply notes that **when the priesthood changes**, there must also be **a change of law**.

Most likely **comes about** (γίνομαι) refers to God making it happen, a so called 'divine passive.'[59] Hence, this verse is simply a truism about God's ordering of his world for his people. When God changes the priesthood, he will also (**from necessity**) inform his people through his written revelation.

Law here means priestly and cultic requirements, as can be seen from Hebrews 7:11 and 16. Pertaining to the Levitical priesthood, the **law** is part of the cultic legislation in the Mosaic law.[60] Pertaining to Christ's priesthood, most likely the **law** here is used in an expanded way. In the Hebrews 7 context, it includes Genesis 14:18–20 and Psalm 110:4. That

---

56. Etymologically, νομοθετέω comes from 'to place' and 'law.' This verb is only used in the NT here and in Heb. 8:6. In the LXX, νομοθετέω translates ירה, 'to teach/instruct,' which is related to the cognate noun תורה, which is often translated as 'law' (e.g., Exod. 24:12; Deut. 17:11; Ps. 24:8).

57. So also Mary Schmitt, 'Restructuring Views on Law in Hebrews 7:12,' *JBL* 128 (2009): 189–201, esp. 193–98.

58. **When the priesthood is changing** is a genitive absolute (so also Maximillian Zerwick and Mary Grosvenor, *A Grammatical Analysis of the Greek New Testament*, 2 vols. [Rome: Biblical Institute, 1974, 1979], 2:668).

59. So also Owen, *Hebrews*, 21:434.

60. Calvin restricts **law** to the cultic portions of the Mosaic law (*Hebrews and 1 & 2 Peter*, 96).

is, the AH is here using **law** to mean God's written revelation that pertains to priesthood, which is broader than simply the Mosaic cultic legislation, although it does include that.

Although not explicitly stated here, the AH assumes that God's law is related to God's covenants. Hence, for the priestly requirements of the Mosaic **law** to change, that requires a 'better covenant' (Heb. 7:22), which will be the emphasis in Hebrews 8:8–13.[61]

7:13–14 *For about whom these things are said has belonged to another tribe, from which no one has paid attention to the altar; for [it is] evident that our Lord has descended from Judah, to which tribe Moses said nothing concerning priests.*

In these two verses, the AH expands (first **for**) upon the point in Hebrews 7:11–12 that God intended a change in the Levitical priesthood and this change is related typologically to Melchizedek's priesthood. He makes this point very explicit that **about whom these things are said** refers to Jesus Christ, **our Lord**.

It is **evident** that Christ is not from the tribe of Levi, but he is from **another tribe**, that is, **Judah**. And since **Moses said nothing concerning** there being **priests** from that **tribe** (cf. 2 Chr. 26:16–21), there must be a change in the priestly requirements to reflect Christ's priesthood.[62]

By using **evident**, the AH implies that it was a well-known fact among the congregants that Christ's lineage was from the tribe of **Judah**. He may have in addition also been implying that it was **evident** from the OT that the OT Messiah/Son was from the tribe of **Judah** through the Davidic line (e.g., 2 Sam. 7:12–14; Ps. 78:70–72; Jer. 23:5; Rev. 5:5). Intriguingly, in an argument about Christ's priesthood, Christ's kingly line is referenced.

---

61. Chrysostom states, 'It is not possible that there should be a priest, without a covenant and laws and ordinances, nor that having received a different priesthood, he [God] should use the former covenant' ('Homily 13 on Hebrews' [*NPNF*[1], 14:428]).

62. Of course, Moses in the Pentateuch did discuss the tribe of Judah (e.g., Gen. 49:8–12) but not related to the priesthood.

Also intriguingly, in an argument that includes Christ's 'having neither beginning of days nor end of life' (Heb. 7:3), Christ's human nature is referenced.[63]

Concerning Christ's lineage being from **Judah**, based on Mary's cousin Elizabeth being from the tribe of Levi (Luke 1:5), a few in church history have argued that Christ descended from both Levi and Judah. This verse clearly argues against that conclusion. Owen offers that an 'antecedent intermarriage of those tribes' of Elizabeth took place and that 'Elizabeth's mother might be sister unto the father or grandfather of the holy Virgin.' He cites 2 Chr. 22:11 as an example of an antecedent priestly marriage that does not affect the kingly line. Therefore, Owen concludes that Christ is properly only from the tribe of Judah and not Levi (cf. Matt. 1:3, 6; Luke 3:31–33).[64]

7:15–17 *And yet it is even more evident since[65] another priest arises according to the likeness of Melchizedek, who has become [a priest] not according to a law of fleshly commandment but according to a power of an indestructible life. For it is witnessed[66] that 'You are a priest forever according to the order of Melchizedek.*

Hebrews 7:12 notes that a change in priesthood results in a change of priestly requirements. Hebrews 7:13–14 emphasizes that the priesthood did in fact change with Christ. Here in Hebrews 7:15–17, one of the resulting requirements that changed is emphasized—**an indestructible life**.

---

63. The Belgic Confession 17 and 18 reference Heb. 7:14 as proof of Christ's humanity and that he was in the line of David and Judah. The French Confession 14 references Heb. 7:14 to show that Christ was the 'true seed of Abraham and David.'

64. Owen, *Hebrews*, 21:440. Aquinas has a similar solution and cites Exod. 6:23 along with 2 Kgs. 11:2 // 2 Chr. 22.11 (*Hebrews*, 153–54).

65. **Since** is the 'causal' use εἰ; otherwise εἰ is normally translated as 'if' (BDAG 278). So also Owen, *Hebrews*, 447.

66. The majority text tradition has the verb 'to witness' in the active (μαρτθρεῖ) as opposed to the passive (μαρτυρεῖται); hence, the KJV translates as 'he testifieth.'

Coming from Psalm 110:4, the AH uses the expression 'according to the *order* of Melchizedek' (or 'Aaron') several times (Heb. 5:10; 6:20; 7:11). In Hebrews 7:15, he alters it to **according to the *likeness* of Melchizedek**. That is, the AH makes clear that he has always been using 'order' from Psalm 110:4 to more specifically mean **likeness**.[67] In confirmation of this, the verb cognate of **likeness** is used in Hebrews 7:3 ('having been made like') confirming the typological nature of Melchizedek to Christ (as opposed to Melchizedek being Christ).

The **law of fleshly** (σάρκινος) **commandment** relates to the priestly requirements of the Mosaic law. Why the adjective **fleshly** (cf. Heb. 9:10)? Chrysostom takes it as relating to outward aspects of the flesh such as washings and anointings.[68] Owen gives several options: (1) fleshly sacrifices for fleshly people, (2) a fleshly posterity of the priestly line, and/or (3) fleshly as opposed to the Holy Spirit and the Gospel.[69] I prefer Brown's definition of 'external and perishable things.'[70] I take **commandment** as a collective (see parallel to 'law' in Heb. 7:18–9), although the AH is probably highlighting here the priestly requirement concerning the Levitical (bodily) lineage.[71]

Again, the AH explicitly quotes Psalm 110:4, **'You are a priest forever according to the order of Melchizedek'** (cf. Heb. 5:6; 6:20; 7:21).[72] All agree that the **indestructible life**

---

67. Attridge states, 'The substitution of "likeness" for "order" clarifies the way the latter term has been understood throughout the exegesis of this key verse [Ps. 110:4]' (*Hebrews*, 202).

68. Chrysostom, 'Homily 13 on Hebrews,' (*NPNF*[1], 14:428).

69. Owen, *Hebrews*, 21:450.

70. Brown, *Hebrews*, 342.

71. So various English translations, e.g., RSV, NIV, ESV, CEB, and CSB17.

72. The Greek for the Ps. 110:4 quote in Heb. 7:17 (and 5:6) matches the LXX excepting the elimination of the implied 'to be' be verb εἶ. The Heb. 7:17 (and 5:6) quote is a word-for-word translation of the Hebrew (the Hebrew also has an implied 'to be' verb). For background on Ps. 110, see my discussion at Heb. 1:13.

of Christ is **witnessed** by **forever** in the Psalm 110:4 quote. That is, one of the new priestly requirements that God revealed through Psalm 110:4 by using the word **forever** is that the Melchizedekian priest will have an **indestructible life**. The disagreement comes as to when the **indestructible life** begins. Does it begin at Christ's resurrection and/or exaltation?[73] Or is the **power of an indestructible life** related more specifically to Christ's eternal divine nature?[74] I agree with the latter view. As previously argued at Hebrews 7:3, Christ's eternal divine nature is the necessary background to his mediatorial priesthood. Also, Christ's mediatorial priesthood begins in the state of humiliation (see discussion in Reflection section following Heb. 5:1–10). If this is so, Christ died as a priest, which is clearly not the intent of the expression and explains why many see this text as post-resurrection. But if the eternal nature of Christ is referred to, his divine nature was still active as a priest during his death and buried existence. Further, the use of the word **power** implies that it was something Christ already had that qualified him to become the mediatorial priest. Finally, **indestructible** best describes the **life** of a divine being, the eternal Son.

7:18–19 *For, on the one hand, the annulment*[75] *of the former commandment comes about on account of its weakness and uselessness*[76]*, for the law perfects nothing, but on the other hand, an introduction of a better hope comes about through which we draw near to God.*

---

73. So, e.g., Calvin, *Hebrews*, 98; Lane, *Hebrews 1–8*, 184; Johnson, *Hebrews*, 188; Lindars, *The Theology of the Letter to the Hebrews*, 78; and Schreiner, *Hebrews*, 223.

74. So, e.g., Owen, *Hebrews*, 21:451–53; Hodge, *Hebrews*, 63; Hughes, *Hebrews*, 264; and Cockerill, *Hebrews*, 323–25.

75. The noun ἀθέτησις only occurs in the LXX and NT in 1 Sam. 24:12; Heb. 7:18; and 9:26 and has the basic meaning of 'something set aside.' In non-canonical literature, it is often used in legal contexts (LSJ, 31) and is translated as 'annulment.' Given the legal context here, **annulment** is appropriate. The verb form is used in Heb. 10:28.

76. **Weakness** (ἀσθενής) and **uselessness** (ἀνωφελής) are adjectives used as abstract substantives.

With the priestly requirement of 'an indestructible life,' Hebrews 7:15–17 is partially answering the comment in Hebrews 7:12 that the priestly requirements changed. In 7:18–19, another changed requirement is noted (first **for**), the new priesthood should produce **a better hope**, which is contrasted with the inadequacies of the Levitical priesthood.

The various priestly and cultic requirements from the Mosaic law are here termed **the former commandment**. Note that **law** in the next clause is paralleled with **commandment**, with **law** certainly including all ceremonial laws, not only those of Levitical bodily lineage (e.g., Heb. 9:13–14).[77]

The **commandment** (**its**) is defined by **weakness and uselessness**.[78] These two are explained by (second **for**) the parenthetical clause **the law perfects nothing**. The AH is not saying that in an absolute sense that the Mosaic ceremonial law is useless, but that without Christ, the goal of the **commandment** is not reached.[79] This lack of 'perfection' refers back to Hebrews 7:11 (see extended discussion there and also at Heb. 8:7).

After stating the negative, the AH gives the positive that the new priesthood should accomplish **a better hope** (see discussion of 'hope' at Heb. 6:18–19) with all its new covenant benefits. Among other benefits, it is **through** this **hope** (**which**) that **we draw near** (ἐγγίζω) **to God**. This concept is similar to Heb. 4:16, 'let us approach (προσέρχομαι) with confidence the throne of grace' (see extended discussion there).

Reflections

In Hebrews 7:14, the AH remarks that 'our Lord has descended from Judah.' The only other places he uses 'our' to refer to any

---

77. Owen has the minority view that **law** includes all of the Mosaic commandments, including the moral law (*Hebrews*, 21:458, 464).

78. The Council of Trent quotes portions of Heb. 7:11 and 18 to confirm that due to the 'weakness of the Levitical priesthood' Christ's priesthood was needed (Doctrine of the Sacrifice of the Mass, ch. 1).

79. Calvin notes that **perfects nothing** implies that there is some good to be perfected (*Hebrews and 1–2 Peter*, 99).

of the persons of the Trinity is in the benediction, 'our Lord Jesus' (Heb. 13:20) and a quote of the Old Testament, 'our God is a consuming fire' (Heb. 12:29 // Deut. 4:24).

In Hebrews 7:14, I am struck by the use of 'our' in the midst of a technical argument concerning priesthood.[80] It is as if the AH's love for the person of Christ inserts itself into his argument. Christ is not only objectively of the Melchizedekian priesthood, he is '*our* Lord,' both the AH and the believing congregants.

Possibly the AH uses 'our' here because he comments on Christ's human nature ('descended from Judah'). The use of 'our' in the benediction is also in context of Christ's human nature, God the Father 'brought again from the dead, our Lord Jesus' (Heb. 13:20). Once given the divine majesty of the Son of God, his becoming a man for us is such a tremendous and heart-melting thought, that using 'our' in the midst of an argument is appropriate.

Yes, Christ is objectively 'the Lord of glory' (1 Cor. 2:8). But when two or three believers are gathered together, they may also say, 'He is *our* Lord of glory!'

Surety and Intercessor (7:20–25)

Hebrews 7:20–25 consists of two complicated sentences (Heb. 7:20–22 and 7:23–25). The first, using Psalm 110:4, notes that God the Father made an oath with Jesus and not with the Aaronic high priests. This leads to the conclusion that Jesus is the surety of a better covenant. The second, implicitly using Psalm 110:4, contrasts Jesus' permanent priesthood with the Aaronic priests who continually die. This leads to the conclusion that Jesus saves to the uttermost as our intercessor.

As a subunit within Hebrews 7:1–28, 7:20–25 is not clearly distinct. It continues the argument from 7:11–19 that Christ's priesthood is better than the Aaronic line. Also, it has an oath connection to the following subunit, Hebrews 7:26–28.

---

80. 'Lord' is probably due to the kingly aspect related to the tribe of Judah.

7:20–21 *And, inasmuch as [it was] not without an oath;*[81] *for, on the one hand, those have become*[82] *priests without oaths, and on the other, the one [has become a priest] by the one saying to him, 'The Lord swore and will not relent, "you are a priest forever"'*[83]*;*

The AH adds (**and**) another argument as to Christ's superior priesthood. Christ's priesthood came about **not without an oath**, which is to say, *with an oath*, but said with added rhetorical punch.[84] To confirm that an oath was sworn by the Father (**the one saying**) to the Son (**to him**), a portion of Psalm 110:4 is quoted, **'The Lord swore**[85] **and will not relent, "you are a priest forever."'**[86] Again the AH takes Psalm 110 as God the Father speaking to the Son. Portions of Psalm 110:4 have been previously quoted and alluded to (Heb. 5:6; 6:20; 7:17), but this is the first time that the portion containing **'The Lord swore and will not repent'** has been quoted.

In the OT, although there were ordination ceremonies for the high priests (e.g., Exod. 29; Lev. 8–9) and God did by divine command designate the Aaronic priesthood

---

81. The Greek word for **oath** (ὁρκωμοσία) in Heb. 7:20 (*bis*), 21, and 28 is a cognate of 'oath' (ὅρκος) in Heb. 6:16–17. There is no discernable difference in meanings between these two words in these two contexts.

82. The verb **have become** is a periphrastic perfect, also in Heb. 7:23. If the perfective aspect of the tense is pressed, one could conclude that the Aaronic high priests were still existing. Hence, a date prior to AD 70 would be necessitated for the writing of Hebrews. So Hughes, *Hebrews*, 267n31; and Ellingworth, *Hebrews*, 389–90. I agree to the dating of Hebrews, but I am reticent to put much weight on the perfective aspect for the argument.

83. Some ancient texts add 'according to the order of Melchizedek,' so the KJV. See Metzger, *TCGNT*², 597.

84. The phrase **not without an oath** includes a double negative and is an example of the rhetorical device of litotes—a strong positive affirmation using a negative.

85. The Greek verb 'to swear' (ὀμνύω) and the noun 'oath' (ὁρκωμοσία) are cognates.

86. The Hebrew and the LXX match very well. The LXX does have the explicit verb 'you are' (εἶ) where the Hebrew only has 'you' and the 'are' is implied. The only difference between the LXX and Heb. 7:21 is that the LXX has εἶ ('you are') and it is implied in Heb. 7:21. That is, Heb. 7:21 matches directly to the Hebrew.

(e.g., Exod. 28:1);[87] it is clear that the Aaronic high priests did *not* receive a direct oath from God himself. The **oath** implies among other things the permanent nature (**priest forever**). Apparently, the logic is that a divine command for the Aaronic priesthood applies for the appropriate redemptive-historical period, but an **oath** is by definition, **forever**.[88] The contrast between Christ's priesthood with an **oath** and the Aaronic **priests without oaths** is stark.[89]

God the Father's swearing an **oath** to the Son is quite an intra-Trinitarian statement (cf. Heb. 3:2). In addition, it is done here with obvious covenantal overtones. It recalls from elsewhere in Hebrews (1) the importance of God's swearing a covenantal oath to Abraham (Heb. 6:13–18); (2) the explicit Davidic covenantal connections and promises between the Father and Son in Psalm 2:7; 2 Samuel 7:14; Psalm 110:1, 4 as quoted in Hebrews 1:5, 13, and 5:5; (3) the bold statement by Christ related to Psalm 40:6–8 that he came to do the Father's will, which is quoted and expanded upon in Hebrews 10:5–10; (4) the immediate context of 'better covenant' (Heb. 7:22); (5) Hebrews 8:1–10:18 emphasizes the advantages of the new covenant related to Christ's priesthood; and (6) the benediction mentions 'the blood of the eternal covenant' (Heb. 13:20).[90] All this clearly indicates that some type of agreement exists between the Father and the Son (with the approbation of the Holy Spirit, cf. John 7:39; 14:26;

---

87. Note the 'covenant of peace' for the Aaronic priesthood related to Phinehas' actions (Num. 25:11–13; cf. Neh. 13:29). Owen argues that this does not contradict the AH as this covenant was 'not a complete, solemn covenant, confirmed either by oath or sacrifice, but only a naked promise or declaration of the will of God' (*Hebrews*, 21:487).

88. So also Schreiner, *Hebrews*, 229.

89. Cockerill well sees the difference between the two priesthoods as a difference 'in kind, not in degree' (*Hebrews*, 329). Heidelberg Catechism 31 references Ps. 110:4 and Heb. 7:21 regarding Christ's being 'our only High Priest.'

90. Swain also emphasizes the covenantal language in Hebrews related to the covenant of redemption ('Covenant of Redemption,' 120–21).

15:26; 16:7; Eph. 4:8–10[91]). Better yet, it appears to be a type of covenantal agreement.

When did this **oath** occur? Since (1) Christ knew of the agreement as he came into the world (Heb. 10:5–10); (2) the **oath** must be applicable in some sense when David penned Psalm 110; and (3) the contextual emphasis includes Christ's eternal person in Hebrews 7:3 and 7:16; therefore, this **oath** must have occurred in eternity 'past.'[92] Also dovetailing with this are (1) the statements that Christ's mediatorial work was known in the OT (e.g., Heb. 3:5; 4:2; 8:5; 9:9, 23; 10:1; cf. Acts 7:44); (2) Christ's new covenant atonement was effectual for the OT saints (Heb. 9:15); and (3) the benediction language of 'by the blood of the *eternal* covenant' (Heb. 13:20). That is, the eternal **oath** ties together the temporal old and new covenants. As Vos wonderfully puts it,

> The bond that links the Old and New Covenant together is not a purely evolutionary one, inasmuch as the one has grown out of the other; it is, if we may so call it, a transcendental bond; the New Covenant in its preëxistent, heavenly state reaches back and stretches its eternal wings over the Old.[93]

Of course, the **oath** when made in eternity 'past' concerned Christ's future temporal work as mediator.[94] Given this, many Reformed theologians distinguish between the agreement/**oath** made in eternity 'past' between the Father and the Son, termed either 'covenant of redemption' or '*pactum salutis*'; and the agreement between God and the elect in redemptive

---

91. List from Fesko, *The Trinity and the Covenant of Redemption*, 105.

92. So also Turretin, *Institutes of Elenctic Theology*, 2:243. Fesko adds that it must be a pre-temporal covenant because 'Scripture records no historical event when Yahweh uttered this covenantal oath to Jesus' (*The Trinity and the Covenant of Redemption*, 99).

93. Vos, 'Hebrews, The Epistle of the Diatheke,' 2:12.

94. As Owen notes, the Father's covenant with the Son is with 'the *person of the Son of God*, not absolutely considered, but with respect unto his *future incarnation* (*Hebrews*, 18:93, emphasis his).

history, termed 'covenant of grace.'[95] As Bavinck says, 'The covenant of grace in time does not hang in the air but rests on an eternal, unchanging foundation, [the covenant of redemption].'[96] Other Reformed theologians agree to some type of eternal agreement but would rather conflate this with the covenant of grace.[97]

7:22 *so much the more Jesus has become a surety of a better covenant.* Hebrews 7:22 completes the thought from the beginning of 7:20. Because of the 'oath,' **so much more** is the priesthood of **Jesus** superior to the Aaronic high priests. That is, there is a relationship of the importance of the 'oath' to non-oath

---

95. In favor of more clearly distinguishing the 'covenant of redemption' from the 'covenant of grace,' e.g., *Sum of Saving Knowledge*, 2.1–3; Owen, 'Federal Transactions between the Father and the Son,' in *Hebrews* 18:77–97; Owen, *Hebrews*, 489–90; Herman Witsius, *The Economy of the Covenants between God and Man: Comprehending a Complete Body of Divinity*, 2 vols. (Phillipsburg; Presbyterian and Reformed, 1990 [1693]), 1:177–81; Turretin, *Institutes of Elenctic Theology*, 2:177–78; Brakel, *The Christian's Reasonable Service*, 250–63; Hodge, *Systematic Theology*, 2:359–62; Dabney, *Systematic Theology*, 431–33; Bavinck, *Reformed Dogmatics*, 3:212–16; Vos, *Reformed Dogmatics*, 2:83–85; Berkoff, *Systematic Theology*, 265–71; Pink, *The Divine Covenants*, 20–25; van Genderen and Velema, *Concise Reformed Dogmatics*, 556–58; Kelly, *Systematic Theology*, 1:298–99; Swain, 'Covenant of Redemption,' 107–25; Fesko, *The Trinity and the Covenant of Redemption*; and Guy M. Richard, 'Covenant of Redemption,' in *An Introduction to Covenant Theology*, ed. Guy P. Waters, J. Nicholas Reid, and John R. Muether (Wheaton: Crossway, 2020), 43–62.

96. Bavinck, *Reformed Dogmatics*, 3:215. Similarly Vos, 'The counsel of peace [covenant of redemption] is the eternal pattern for the temporal covenant of grace' (*Reformed Dogmatics*, 2:92).

97. So, e.g., WSC 20 compared to WLC 31; James Fisher, *The Assembly's Shorter Catechism Explained by Way of Question and Answer* (Totton: Berith, 1998 [1765]), 107–8; John L. Girardeau, *The Federal Theology: Its Import and Its Regulative Influence* (Greenville: Reformed Academic, 1994 [1881], 16–18; and Letham, *Systematic Theology*, 431–39. The Associate Reformed Presbyterian denomination, founded in 1782, adjusted the *Sum of Saving Knowledge* to eliminate all references to the 'covenant of redemption' and replace them with 'covenant of grace.' They did this 'to void the improper distinction between the covenant of redemption, and the covenant of grace, which, in reality, are not two, but one and the same blessed covenant, viewed under different aspects' (*The Constitution and Standards of the Associate-Reformed Church in North-America* [New York: T. & J. Sword's: 1799], 588.).

proportional to the importance of the priesthood of **Jesus** relative to Aaron's. More specifically, **Jesus** is a better priest because he is a **surety of a better covenant**.

As the beginning of Hebrews 7:20 has rhetorical flair using the double negative 'not without an oath,' the ending of 7:22 also has rhetorical flair. In Greek, **Jesus** is the last word of the long sentence 7:20–22. Also adding to the punch of Hebrews 7:22 is the phrase **surety of a better covenant**. This phrase introduces more explicitly themes prevalent in the important Hebrews 8:1–10:18 section.

With **covenant** (διαθήκη) here, this is the first of twenty-five times that the word 'covenant' is used in Hebrews.[98] Twenty-one of the twenty-five are in Hebrews 8:1–10:18 (remaining four are Hebrews 7:22; 10:29; 12:24; 13:20). 'Covenant' in Hebrews refers to either the first/old (Mosaic) covenant or the second/new/better/eternal covenant. It is noted, however, that the AH has already clearly referenced the Abrahamic and Davidic covenants but without using the word 'covenant.'[99]

The **better covenant** has a better priesthood. Here **covenant** clearly refers to the 'new covenant' that is contrasted with the 'first'/'old'/Mosaic covenant (e.g., Heb. 8:13). As I will note often in this commentary, the context for designating the new covenant as **better** or 'new' relates to the *ceremonial* aspects of the Mosaic covenant's priesthood and sacrifices. For more discussion on 'covenant,' see Hebrews 8:6.

Relating this back to the eternal 'oath' and the covenant of redemption, the **better covenant** is the temporal outworking of the eternal 'oath' between the Father and the Son.

---

98. Actually, **covenant** is used explicitly seventeen times and idiomatically implied (e.g., the 'first' and the 'second' [Heb. 8:7] eight times. Explicit use of διαθήκη: Heb. 7:22; 8:6, 8, 9 (*bis*); 8:10; 9:4 (*bis*), 15 (*bis*), 16, 17, 20; 10:16, 29; 12:24; 13:10. Idiomatically implied: Heb. 8:7 (*bis*), 13 (*bis*); 9:1, 18; 10:9 (*bis*).

99. For a detailed overview of the Abrahamic, Mosaic, Davidic, and new covenants in Hebrews, see Cara, 'Covenant in Hebrews,' 247–66; and Lehne, *The New Covenant in Hebrews*.

Jesus is a **surety**[100] (ἔγγυος). This is the only use of ἔγγυος in the NT. Before making some conclusions, first, a brief word study on ἔγγυος and its close cognate, ἐγγύη, which is not included anywhere in the NT.[101] The general Greco-Roman background includes legal or financial proceedings where a surety 'ensures' or guarantees that his friend will comply with the legal/financial obligations owed to a third party.[102] That is, it something similar to a modern co-signer or one that puts up collateral for another.

In the LXX, ἔγγυος and its cognate ἐγγύη are only used as follows. In Maccabees 10:28, the Jewish army's virtue is the ἔγγυος for a victory; this is a figurative use. In Sirach 29:15–19, ἔγγυος and ἐγγύη are used to warn wise men that sinners take advantage of sureties. Similarly, ἐγγύη is used in Proverbs 17:18 and 22:26 to warn of the dangers of suretyship. The use in Sirach and Proverbs reasonably match the Greco-Roman use in that a pledge of some kind is made for a friend.[103] If the friend cannot meet the obligation, the surety must meet it to satisfy the third party to whom the obligation is owed. Although not using ἔγγυος, Genesis 43:8–9 and Philemon 18–19 are good illustrations of the concept.

Another angle here is that the language of **surety of a better covenant** is closely paralleled in Hebrews by 'mediator' (μεσίτης) as in 'the mediator of a better covenant' (Heb. 8:6) and 'mediator of a new covenant' (Heb. 9:15; 12:24). With no context, a 'mediator' is an 'umpire' or 'arbitrator' between two parties.[104] Given the priestly context in Hebrews, 'mediator' at

---

100. The Geneva Bible, KJV, and RSV translate as **surety**; the NIV and ESV as 'guarantor'; Latin Vulgate, *sponsor*.

101. Although ἔγγυος is an adjective that would normally be translated 'secured,' ἔγγυος in Heb. 7:22 is here used substantivally and translated **surety**. The normal noun form translated as 'surety' is ἐγγύη.

102. LSJ, 468.

103. The cognate verb ἐγγυάω is used eight times in the LXX and nowhere in the NT (Prov. 6:1, 3; 17:18; 28:17; Sir. 8:13 (*bis*); 29:14; Tob. 6:13). These uses match the use of ἔγγυος and ἐγγύη elsewhere in the LXX.

104. LSJ, 1106; cf. 1 Tim. 2:5.

least means that a high priest acts 'on behalf of men concerning the things toward God' (Heb. 5:1).

Now to the context of Hebrews 7:22 for **Jesus** as a priestly **surety** (ἔγγυος). It is presupposed that men are sinful and need atonement to have access to God as Hebrews 8:1– 10:18 will emphasize. The obligation of men to God in this context, once given they are sinful, is that they need atonement. This **surety** does more than simply promise to meet the obligation if need be. Given sinful man, the guarantee of this **surety** is that he and he alone will meet the obligation for the elect.[105] He will be both priest and sacrifice (Heb. 9:11–12), along with being an intercessor (Heb. 7:25). As a **surety**, **Jesus** is not here promising to fulfill God's part of the **better covenant** as if God could fail. God has given his 'oath'; there cannot be a higher guarantee.[106] **Jesus** is here, as part of the covenant of redemption, guaranteeing to fulfill man's obligations, which in turn makes the temporal new covenant **better**.[107] God's 'oath' to **Jesus** confirms that the new covenant will have an everlasting **surety**.

Concerning the relationship between 'mediator' and **surety**, obviously, the referent of both words is the same, it is the God-man, the Lord Jesus Christ. 'Mediator' *as a term* has the advantage of emphasizing that a priest is between God and man and his work is related to both.[108] This well captures the emphasis in Hebrews on both of Christ's natures; he is the God-man, the only perfect mediator.[109] **Surety** *as a term* is a

---

105. So also Owen, *Hebrews*, 21:500–9; Hodge, *Hebrews*, 66; Vos, *Reformed Dogmatics*, 2:94–95, 3:1–4; Hughes, *Hebrews*, 267; Pink, *Hebrews*, 407; and Bruce, *Hebrews*, 171, 175.

106. *Contra* those who see Jesus as primarily being a **surety** for God's promise, e.g., Attridge, *Hebrews*, 208–9; Koester, *Hebrews*, 370; and Schreiner, *Hebrews*, 230.

107. Brakel notes that by definition if a **surety** is involved, there must be *covenantal* obligations (*The Christian's Reasonable Service*, 1:255–56).

108. So also Turretin, *Institutes of Elenctic Theology*, 2:375.

109. Of course, Christ 'is not something *between* God and man, but *both* God and man' (Roderick Lawson, *The Shorter Catechism: With Explanatory

stronger word as to Christ's work, but weaker as to his being a full-fledged mediator. **Surety** relates more to the work of explicitly supporting the elect by fulfilling their obligation of a need of atonement, but it has less emphasis on Christ's roll to represent both God and man, as **surety** primarily relates to helping man.[110] The **surety** aspect will be more the emphasis of Hebrews 8:1–10:18. As can be seen by this discussion, both the terms 'mediator' and **surety** aid in having a full-orbed understanding of Christ.[111]

7:23–24 *And, on the one hand, those have become priests [are] many on account of being prevented by death to continue, but, on the other hand, the one on account of his remaining forever has a priesthood [that is] permanent[112]; ...*

And indicates another argument as to Christ's superior **priesthood**. **Death** prevented the Aaronic high priests from **continu[ing]**, but Christ's *person* **remains forever** and thus his **priesthood** is **permanent**. This argument recalls previous points made in Hebrews 7:3, 8, and 16–17, including using 'you are a priest forever' from Psalm 110:4. There Christ's eternal divine nature and his indestructible life are emphasized and the mortality of others is noted. Here the comparison is finally explicitly stated.

Forever is the same wording as just quoted in Psalm 110:4 // Hebrews 7:21 to which the AH is obviously referring. **Remaining** is the same verb from Hebrews 7:3, 'he remains a priest continuously.'

The Aaronic priests were **prevented by death to continue**.[113]

Notes and Review Questions [Ross-shire; Christian Heritage, 2017], 29, emphasis his).

110. 'God accepteth the satisfaction from a *surety*, which he might have demanded of them, and did provide this *surety*, his own only Son' (WLC 71, emphasis mine).

111. '[Christ] was thoroughly furnished to execute the office of a *Mediator* and *Surety*' (WCF 8.3, emphasis mine).

112. I take ἀπαράβατον (**permanent**) as a predicate adjective to **priesthood**. So also Allen, *Hebrews*, 428.

113. Cf. Num. 35:25, 28, 32. Josephus claims that there were eighty-three

But did not Christ die, at least as to his human nature (Heb. 9:16,27–28)? One answer is to say that Christ's **priesthood** did not start until his ascension.[114] I disagree. As discussed previously, I strongly believe that Christ's mediatorial priesthood began at his incarnation, not at his resurrection/ascension (see Reflection section following Hebrews 5:1–10). In context of all the statements in Hebrews 7 concerning Christ's eternal divine nature, certainly here the AH is referring to Christ's *person* as being forever,[115] including his body always being mysteriously connected to his person. Owen quips, Christ 'died *as a priest*; they [Aaronic priests] died *from being priests.*'[116] Christ's death was part of his wonderful priesthood, and amazingly, this did not prevent him from continuing to be a priest for us forever.

7:25 ... *wherefore he is even able to save to the uttermost those approaching to God through him, [because] he always lives*[117] *to intercede for them.*

One implication (**wherefore**) of Christ's 'priesthood that is permanent' is that **he is even able to save to the uttermost**. The verb **save** here is related to the noun 'salvation' elsewhere in Hebrews (1:14; 2:3, 10; 5:9; 6:9, 9:28), which includes a full-orbed salvation of justification, sanctification, and glorification.[118] The adjective **uttermost** (παντελής) has two general nuances: (1) unlimited as to time/duration, that is,

---

high priests from Aaron to Phanas. Phanas was the high priest at the time of the Jewish war with the Romans in AD 66–73. He mentions that the high priests at first held their office 'until the end of life, although afterward they had successors while they were alive' (*Jewish Antiquities* 20.224–29). I am not sure what to make of this comment.

114. So, e.g., Koester, *Hebrews*, 371.

115. So also Hughes, *Hebrews*, 269; and Cockerill, *Hebrews*, 333–34.

116. Owen, *Hebrews*, 21:517, emphasis his.

117. I translated the adverbial participle ζῶν as causal matching most major English translations.

118. In Hebrews, the verb **save** is only used here and Heb. 5:7. In Heb 5:7 it has a different sense because it relates to the Father saving the Son through his death.

forever or (2) unlimited as to quality, that is, completely.[119] Given **to save**, here **uttermost** clearly emphasizes completeness of salvation, although this completeness has a forever and eschatological aspect to it.[120]

Those approaching to God through him (Christ) obviously refers to believers. For a detailed discussion of the verb **approaching** and its priestly overtones, see discussion at Hebrews 4:16.

One reason for our assured salvation is **because he always lives to intercede**.[121] Here, Christ's eternal person (**he always lives**) is connected with his continual **intercession** to the Father for us. The priestly intercession of Aaronic high priests is interrupted by their deaths. To the contrary, Christ's priestly intercession never stops. This is quite an assurance of our perseverance in the faith.[122]

For which of our needs does Christ **intercede** in this context? Koester summarizes the options from the whole of Hebrews into two broad categories: (1) pleas for temporal assistance (Heb. 2:18; 4:16: 10:33–34; 13:3, 13) and (2) pleas

---

119. BDAG, 754.

120. This 'both' answer is agreed to by most, e.g., Owen, *Hebrews*, 21:528–29; Hughes, *Hebrews*, 269 n. 35; Koester, *Hebrews*, 365; Allen, *Hebrews*, 429; and Mitchell, *Hebrews*, 154. Others see it as only related to time/duration, e.g., Brown, *Hebrews*, 352; and Moffatt, *Hebrews*, 100.

121. The Greek verb ἐντυγχάνω in its infinitive form is translated **to intercede**. It has the general meaning of 'to meet with.' In the context of two humans, it could mean 'to petition' or 'to appeal' or 'to intercede; in the context of a deity, it could mean simply 'to pray,' or stronger, 'to intercede.' In several NT contexts, 'to intercede' is the proper translation (Rom. 8:27, 34, 11:2; Heb. 7:25; cf. Acts 25:24). The cognate noun ἔντευξις is only in 1 Tim. 2:1 ('intercession') and 1 Tim. 4:5 ('prayer'). See LSJ, 576, 578; BDAG, 341; and Silva, ed., "ἐντυγχάνω," *NIDNTTE*, 2:207–11.

122. One of Turretin's 'proof of perseverance' is 'the efficacy of [Christ's] intercession ... not on earth only (once and again) does he pray, but in heaven, seeing he ever lives to make intercession for us (Heb. 7:25)' (*Institutes of Elenctic Theology* 2:601–2). Similarly, WLC 79 gives 'his continual intercession' as one of the reasons a 'true believer ... can neither totally or finally fall away from the state of grace.'

for forgiveness/salvation (Heb. 2:17; 7:26–27; 8:12; 10:19).[123] Ultimately, Christ's intercession for us includes both, but the immediate context emphasizes his intercession for our personal full-orbed salvation.[124] Christ's making intercession is an aspect of his *applying* our salvation to us once given his *purchase* of it by his atonement.[125] For other key NT texts related to Christ's intercession, see Luke 22:32; 23:34; John 17; Romans 8:34; Hebrews 5:7; and 9:24 (cf. Isa. 53:12).[126]

Reflections

I have long loved noting that Jesus is my 'surety' (Heb. 7:22). In fact, I was just re-reading a commentary I had used in my twenties (Pink, *Hebrews*, 406). I noticed that I had hand written the following marginal note where Hebrews 7:22 was quoted, 'RJC loves this verse' (yes, I am RJC).

A small part of my love of the 'surety' concept is that my father co-signed for my loan when I bought a new car as I was graduating from college. This made a very positive impression on me. My father's love for me was shown by his agreeing to co-sign the loan. As it turned out, he did not need to ever meet my obligation.

Admittedly it is a weak analogy, but Jesus loved me by agreeing to be my 'surety' as my earthly father loved me. Jesus, however, was not simply a 'co-signer' but agreed to and did fulfill my obligation to the curse of the law. Further, he did not pay money; he gave his life. Glory be, Jesus ensures our salvation; Jesus is our 'surety.'

---

123. Koester, *Hebrews*, 366.

124. So also, Murray, 'The Heavenly, Priestly Activity of Christ,' 44–58, esp. 55–56; Bruce, *Hebrews*, 175; and Allen, *Hebrews*, 429.

125. For language of *purchased* and *apply*, see WCF 8.8. Similar language is used for the Holy Spirit's applying our salvation to us in WSC 30.

126. Also see WLC 55; Belgic Confession 26; and Calvin's Catechism 77.

Summary of Priesthoods: Law Versus Oath (7:26–28)

Hebrews 7:26–28 presents several contrasts between the Christ/Melchizedekian priesthood and the Aaronic. Christ is without sin, lives forever, sacrificed only once, his priesthood is appointed by God's oath, and is a Son. This is opposed to the Aaronic high priests who do sin, are mortal, sacrifice often, their priesthood is appointed by the Mosaic law, and are men.

These topics have been previously implicitly and explicitly covered in Hebrews 7:1–25, but also in 1:3, 5; 2:10, 17; 3:6; 4:14–15; 5:1–10; and 6:20. Two of these contrasting topics, one versus many sacrifices and the oath (new covenant) versus Mosaic law, will be especially emphasized in the immediately ensuing Hebrews 8:1–10:18 section. Hence, Hebrews 7:26–28 is somewhat of a summary of the argument so far as to the superiority of Christ's priesthood. This well prepares any reader before going into the amazing depths of Hebrews 8:1–10:18.

Hebrews 7:26–27 is one, fairly complicated sentence. Hebrews 7:28 covers most of the same points as 7:26–27 but with the punch of rhetorical parallelism.

7:26 *For it was indeed[127] fitting for us [that there is] such a high priest, pious,[128] innocent, undefiled, having been separated from sinners, and higher than the heavens;*

The AH begins his summary (**for**) by presupposing that a proper, and more specifically, a perfect **high priest** is required to truly save. Hence, **it was indeed fitting**, that is, Christ's priesthood, and none other, was exactly what was needed **for us**.

OT priests and especially high priests were expected to be morally upright (e.g., Lev. 21:6) and even without any

---

127. I take καί as in intensive (**indeed**) describing **fitting**.

128. Greek ὅσιος only occurs here in Hebrews. It has semantic overlap with the more common ἅγιος ('holy'), which with its cognates occurs 27 times in Hebrews. See BDAG, 728; and LSJ, 1260–61.

significant physical blemishes (e.g., Lev. 21:6, 18–20).[129] The high priest had a golden plate on his turban engraved with 'Holy (קדש, ἁγίασμα) to the Lord' (Exod. 28:36; 39:30). This moral aspect of the Levitical priesthood is typologically fulfilled by Christ.[130] Paralleling and exceeding this moral qualification for priests, Christ is **pious**, **innocent**, and **undefiled**.[131] In fact, he is 'without sin' (Heb. 4:15) and 'without blemish' (Heb. 9:14). This is referring to Christ's human-nature actions while on earth.[132]

In addition to being the only **high priest** truly morally qualified, Christ is **higher than the heavens**,[133] that is, Christ's *status* now as the ascended priest at God's right hand exceeds any status that the Aaronic high priests ever had (cf. Heb. 1:3; 2:8; 4:14; 8:1; 9:24; 10:12; 12:2; Luke 2:14). Both in moral qualifications and status, Christ is the only true **high priest**.

There is debate concerning the expression **having been separated from sinners**. Does this mean that because Christ is spatially now in heaven he is thus spatially **separated from sinners** on earth, which would match to the proceeding phrase?[134] Or does it mean that Christ's sinless moral character

---

129. Rabbinic literature has much to say about the disqualifying physical blemishes of priests and even their wives (cf. Lev. 21:13–15), see, e.g., m. Megillah 4:7; m. Ketubbot 7:7; m. Bekhorot 7:1–7; t. Bekhorot 5:1–9; b. Ketubbot 75a; b. Bekhorot 45b. These blemishes intentionally parallel to some degree the disqualifying blemishes of animals to be sacrificed (m. Bekhorot 7:1). Philo states, 'For the law designs that he [high priest] should be the partaker of a nature superior to that of man; inasmuch as he approaches more nearly to that of the Deity' (*On the Special Law* 1:116; cf. Philo, *On the Life of Moses* 2:131; and Josephus, *Jewish Antiquities* 3:192.).

130. Calvin remarks that Aaron had the same three qualities, 'but only in the smallest degree' (*Hebrews and 1 & 2 Peter*, 102).

131. These three adjectives of Christ are in several creeds, e.g., WCF 8.3; and Catechism of the Catholic Church §1544.

132. WLC 37 and WSC 22 reference Heb. 7:26 for Christ's sinlessness as a 'man.' Of course, Christ's human nature is always in union with his divine.

133. This exact expression only occurs here in the Bible.

134. So, e.g., Lane, *Hebrews 1–8*, 192; Attridge, *Hebrews*, 213; and Cockerill, *Hebrews*, 341.

and actions are *in kind* (qualitatively) **separated from** all humans, including the Levitical priesthood, who are also **sinners**, which would match to the previous three adjectives?[135] I opt for the latter based on the spatial wording of **separated from** being used logically, the mention of the Aaronic sins in the following verse, and the emphasis on Christ's being without sin (Heb. 4:15).

7:27 *who has no necessity daily, just as the high priests [do], to offer up sacrifices first for their own sins, then of the people; for he did this*[136] *once offering up himself.*

Although complicated grammatically, this verse conceptually has a wonderful balance to it. The Aaronic **high priests** have a **necessity** to **daily**/often **offer up sacrifices** for both **for their own sins** and for the sins **of the people**. In contrast, Christ (**who, he**) only **once offer[ed] up himself**, not for his own sins, but only for the sins **of the people**.

Hebrews 7:26 emphasized Christ's perfect character and exalted status that were implicitly superior to the Aaronic priesthood. Here, the implicit becomes explicit. The Aaronic **high priests** were not perfect and needed to sacrifice **first for their own sins** (Lev. 16:6, 17; cf. Lev. 4:3). Christ **ha[d] no necessity** for this 'own-sins' sacrifice.[137] Further, the Aaronic **high priests**, although positively sacrificing for the sins **of the people**, had to do this year after year on the annual Day

---

135. So most older exegetes, e.g., Chrysostom, 'Homily 13 on Hebrews,' *NPNF*[1], 14:430; Calvin, *Hebrews and 1 & 2 Peter*, 102; Owen, *Hebrews*, 21:558; also Hughes, *Hebrews*, 273–74.

136. The neuter τοῦτο (**this**) refers back to **offer up sacrifices** for the sins **of the people**, which in the Greek text is the immediately preceding phrase.

137. Referring to Heb. 7:26–27, Augustine asks rhetorically, 'Who then is so righteous and holy a priest as the only Son of God, who had no need to purge His own sins by sacrifice, neither original sins, nor those which are added by human life?' (*On the Trinity* 4.19 [*NPNF*[1], 3:79]). Heb. 7:26–27 goes a long way to destroy the modern argument that Christ assumed a *fallen* human nature (e.g., Karl Barth and T. F. Torrance). For a good discussion upholding the historic view, see Kelly, *Systematic Theology*, 310–15; and Letham, *Systematic Theology*, 526–33.

of Atonement (Lev. 16; 23:26–32; Num. 29:7–11). Since there is a need for multiple sacrifices, this implies that none of the sacrifices truly atoned for the people's sins. This foreshadows a better atonement. Christ again **ha[d] no necessity** of multiple sacrifices, he only had to **once** make an offering for **this**, that is, the sins **of the people**. This **once** indicates it was an effective atonement.

The expression **daily** (καθ' ἡμέραν) is a puzzle. On the Day of Atonement, which only occurs once per year (Lev. 16:34), the Mosaic legislation requires the high priest to offer sacrifices for both his own sins and the sins of the people (Lev. 16:6, 17; m. Yoma 4:2). Clearly, the AH is aware of this once-per-year requirement (Heb. 9:7, 25; 10:3; cf. Heb. 13:11). But why does he here use **daily**? Is this somehow related to the required twice-daily burnt offerings at the tabernacle/temple (Exod. 29:38–42; Num. 28:3–8; Ezek. 46:13–15)? Options to explain **daily** include: (1) By the time of the NT, the high priest did actually offer the required daily sacrifices.[138] (2) Even though the high priest did not actually offer the required daily sacrifices, he was considered in charge of them.[139] (3) The AH is purposely conflating the required daily sacrifices and the Day of Atonement.[140] (4) The expression **daily** refers to the Day of Atonement and the multiple once-per-year days that an individual high priest would sacrifice over his lifetime.[141] (5) Leviticus 4:3 requires priests (or high priests) to offer a sin offering if they sin grievously, this combined with multiple once-per-year days for the Day of

---

138. Sir. 45:14. Philo states, 'The high priest . . . offers up prayers and sacrifices every day (καθ' ἑκάστην ἡμέραν) on behalf of the whole nation' (*On the Special Laws* 3:131). This does not seem to be historically accurate if actually meaning every single daily sacrifice.

139. So Brown, *Hebrews*, 355–56; and Attridge, *Hebrews*, 213–14. M. Tamid 7:3 states that the high priest has the right to actually perform the daily sacrifices as he so chooses.

140. So Hughes, *Hebrews*, 277.

141. So Turner, *Style*, 111–12; Hodge, *Hebrews*, 68; and Cockerill, *Hebrews*, 343.

Atonement may be generalized as **daily**.[142] Options two, three and four are viable. If pressed, I prefer number four.

The adverb **once** and the phrase **offering up himself** are together a major theme to be expanded upon in Hebrews 8:1–10:18, especially see 9:28 and 10:10. **Once** (ἐφάπαξ) is grammatically the intensive of its cognate (ἅπαξ),[143] which is also translated as 'once' in Hebrews. The intensive has the added force of 'once for all' or 'once and never again' or 'once completely finished,'[144] although ἅπαξ does also have this force in some situations (e.g., Heb. 9:28). As noted above, **once** is compared to the many times that the Aaronic priesthood must sacrifice. It also indicates that Christ's atonement is effective; it was only done once, and does not need to be done again.

Offering up[145] **himself** is a grand phrase (cf. Heb. 9:14, 25; 10:10, 12, 14, 12:2, 24; 13:12, 20).[146] Both the Aaronic **high priests** and Christ **offer sacrifice(s)**; but glory be, Christ does not offer an animal (Heb. 10:4), he offers **himself**. Thus, the effectiveness of Christ's priestly work is not only that it is done **once**, but also that the sacrifice is Christ, **himself**. In fact, the starkness of **himself** takes the reader somewhat by surprise. A reader is expecting the discussion to emphasize Christ's priestly work of actively-offering-a-sacrifice paralleling the work of the Aaronic priests. This has been the emphasis since at least Hebrews 7:1. But instead, both the expected priestly work of actively-offering-a-sacrifice (**offering up**) and the *un*expected priestly work of passively-being-the-sacrifice

---

142. So Owen, *Hebrews*, 21:563–65.

143. In Hebrews, ἐφάπαξ in 7:27; 9:12; and 10:10; ἅπαξ in 6:4; 9:7, 26, 28; 10:2; 12:26; and 12:27.

144. The first two definitions are also found in BDAG, 417.

145. The verbs '**to offer-up**' (ἀναφέρω) and 'to offer' (προσφέρω) have significant overlap semantically in Hebrews. Compare Heb. 7:27; 13:15 (ἀναφέρω) and 9:7, 14, 25; 10:12 (προσφέρω). However, in Heb. 9:28, which includes both, ἀναφέρω is used in the sense of 'to bear.'

146. WSC 25 uses it. "Christ executeth the office of a priest, in his *once offering up of himself* a sacrifice to satisfy divine justice, and reconcile us to God, and in making continual intercession for us' (emphasis mine).

(**himself**) are heartwarmingly combined here in this phrase.[147] As Ambrose said about our Lord's priestly work, 'Priest and victim are one.'[148]

A few implications of Hebrews 7:27: (1) Although not explicit in Hebrews 7:26, the use of **himself** here indicates that the moral uprightness of Christ also applies to his being the sacrifice without blemish (Heb. 9:14), in addition to qualifying him for being *the* high priest. (2) Christ's **once offering up himself** clearly refers to his priestly work on earth. This is a strong argument against those who see Christ's priestly work as only ever occurring in heaven.[149]

7:28 *For the law appoints*[150] *men, high priests having weakness, but the word of the oath, the one after the law, [appoints] a Son, having been perfected forever.*

The rhetorical contrasting parallel between the Aaronic **high priests** and Christ is clear: the Mosaic **law // word of the oath**; **men // Son**; and **having weakness // having been perfected forever**.

---

147. Vos notes that the Aaronic 'high priest must with his own hand slay the sacrificial animal, Lev. 16:15.... In analogy with this the [AH] may have looked upon the self-surrender of Christ to death as an act of priestly nature' ('The Priesthood of Christ in the Epistle of Hebrews,' 2:603).

148. Ambrose, *Of the Christian Faith* 3.87 (*NPNF*², 10:255). Similarly Augustine, '[Christ] had the power to lay down his life, and the power to take it up again, for us was he unto you [God the Father] both victor and victim, and the victor as being the victim, for us was he unto you both priest and sacrifice, and priest as being the sacrifice' (*Confessions* 10.69 [*NPNF*¹, 1:162]). Aquinas answers affirmatively to his article question, 'Whether Christ was himself both priest and victim?' (*Summa Theologiae* 3a.22.2). Calvin, '[Christ is] the same one [who] was to be both priest and sacrifice' (*Institutes* 2.15.6); 'This high priest was Christ; he poured out his own blood; he himself was the sacrificial victim; he offered himself, obedient unto death, to the Father' (*Institutes* 4.14.21).

149. See my extended discussion in the Reflections section following Heb. 5:1–10. Brakel uses Heb. 7:26–27 as his first argument to prove that Christ was a priest in his humiliation state (*The Christian's Reasonable Service*, 1:541).

150. The verb **appoints** is present tense. Hughes sees this as confirming that the temple still stood (*Hebrews*, 279 n. 51). It may, but also it may simply indicate that the **law** as written *presently* speaks.

The **high priests** have **weakness**, which in context is their own sins and mortality (Heb. 7:23; 27; cf. Heb. 5:2–3). This dovetails with the previous statement that the 'first commandment' has 'weakness' (Heb. 7:18). (Christ is implied to have 'weaknesses' [Heb. 4:15], but this does not relate to moral deficiencies.) As usual, the aspects of the Mosaic **law** referred to are ceremonial.

Christ is a **Son** who **ha[s] been perfected forever**. The mention of Christ's being a **Son** recalls Hebrews 7:3 and his divine nature.[151] Hence, Hebrews 7:26–28, as several other places in Hebrews (e.g., Heb. 1:3), presents both Christ's human nature ('offered himself' to die) and his divine nature strikingly together. As discussed in detail at Hebrews 5:9, Christ's perfection is related to his being perfected for the task of priestly service. This includes aspects both in his state of humiliation and exaltation, not to mention his eternal divinity. Here the emphasis is on his heavenly priestly work. Cockerill well says summarizing a **Son having been perfected forever**, '[It] affirms his eternal sonship, incarnation, human obedience, self-offering, exaltation, and present session at God's right as the "[s]ource of eternal salvation" (5:9).'[152]

The eternal new covenant is termed **the word of the oath** and contrasted with the Mosaic **law**. Obviously, the **word of the oath** has reference to Psalm 110:4 and the discussion in Hebrews 7:20–22. As discussed at Hebrews 7:20–21, I understand the actual **oath** to have been made in eternity 'past' (covenant of redemption) about Christ's incarnational priesthood, although the actual prophetic inscripturation (**word**) of the **oath** did not occur until David wrote Psalm 110.[153] This inscripturation was related typologically to the prior Melchizedek events (Gen. 14:18–20).

With the comment that the **word of the oath, the one** *after*

---

151. So also Hodge, *Hebrews*, 69; and Vos, 'The Priesthood of Christ in the Epistle of Hebrews,' 2:590.

152. Cockerill, *Hebrews*, 345.

153. So also Owen, *Hebrews*, 21:577.

the law, the AH recalls the argument from Hebrews 7:11 and makes more explicit the redemptive-historical timeline argument as to the superiority of Christ's priesthood. Since Psalm 110:4 was written **after the** Mosaic **law**, although referencing typologically the Melchizedekian event before the Mosaic **law**, this **after** indicates that God intended another priesthood. The **weakness** of the Aaronic high priests and the **perfect[ion]** of the **Son** combine in context to confirm that the timeline argument is valid.[154] But could there not be another change in the future? No, the **Son** is **forever**.

Reflections

Christ as our high priest 'offer[ed] up himself' (Heb. 7:27). This reminds us that although it was other humans who nailed Christ to the cross (Luke 23:32; John 20:25–27), it is also true that Christ *himself* as priest offered up *himself* as an atoning sacrifice. (The Father and Holy Spirit were also involved as the works of any one person of the Trinity are inseparable from the other two, as there is ultimately only one divine being doing the work. For example, all three persons are involved in creation, see Gen. 1:1–2; John 1:3, 10; Heb. 1:2–3; 2:10; Rev. 4:11.)

We do not serve a weak Christ who could not stall the events of that Friday or only passively allowed them to happen. No. Our high priest marched himself up that hill. Our high priest in full awareness of all the typology of the slaughtered animals *offered himself*. Our high priest 'loved us and gave himself for us' (Eph. 5:2; cf. Gal. 2:20; Eph. 5:25; Heb. 12:2). Amen and Amen.

---

154. For other examples of redemptive-historical timeline awareness, see Heb. 1:1–2; 4:8; 7:11; 8:5–8, 13; 9:10, 28; 10:1, 9, 16; 11:39–40; 12:18–22, 27.

8.
New Covenant in My Blood
(8:1–10:18)

Hebrews 8:1–10:18 is one of five subsections of Hebrews 4:14–10:39.[1] Combined with Hebrews 7, 7:1–10:18 is the theological core of the AH's argument concerning the person and work of Christ as high priest. Speaking broadly, Hebrews 7 emphasizes more the *person* of Christ; the fact that he is a high priest, along with a justification of this. Hebrews 8:1–10:18 emphasizes more the *work* of Christ, including his work's connections to his priesthood, the OT tabernacle, and the new covenant, in addition to his work's significance for believers.[2] More specifically, Christ's work is a priestly new-covenant offering of himself, or as termed

---

1. The five subsections are Hebrews 4:14–5:10; 5:11–6:20; 7:1–28; 8:1–10:18; and 10:19–39.

2. Similarly, Frank J. Matera summarizes Hebrews 7 as explaining 'the superior nature of Jesus' priesthood to the Levitical priesthood' and summarizes Hebrews 8:1–10:18 as 'the meaning and significance of the Son's priestly sacrifice' ('The Theology of the Epistle to the Hebrews,' in *Reading the Epistle to the Hebrews: A Resource for Students*, ed. Eric F. Mason and Kevin B. McCruden, Resources for Biblical Study 66 [Atlanta: Society of Biblical Literature, 2011], 189–208, esp. 195). Grässer entitles Hebrews 7 as the 'dignity' (*Würde*) of the high priest and Hebrews 8:1–10:18 as the 'work' (*Dienst*) of the high priest (*Hebräer*, 2:ix). Kleinig intriguingly sees a movement from 'the appointment of Jesus as High Priest to the *location* of his liturgical ministry in the heavenly tent' (*Hebrews*, 387, emphasis mine).

269

elsewhere in the NT, the "new covenant in my blood" (Luke 22:20; 1 Cor. 11:25; cf. Heb. 12:24).

Most commentators see Hebrews 8:1–10:18 as a reasonably defined unit.[3] For purposes of this commentary, I will subdivide into eight sections: Hebrews 8:1–6; 8:7–11; 9:1–10; 9:11–14; 9:15–21; 9:23–28; 10:1–10; and 10:11–18.

Platonic Influence?

Within Hebrews 8:1–10:18, the AH makes a distinction between the heavenly tabernacle and the earthly tabernacle with the earthly/'shadow'/'copy' tabernacle being derivative of the 'true'/'better' heavenly tabernacle (Heb. 8:2, 5; 9:23–24). To many scholars, this derivative relationship is evidence of broad Platonic influence.[4] To solve the universal/particulars problem, Plato (427–347 BC) promoted the view that a true form/ideal existed immaterially in the realm of forms (above?) and all earthly examples of that form were defective to some degree. The perfect cat form exemplified 'catness' and existed in the realm of forms (universal); the imperfect copies are actual cats on earth (particulars). These earthly imperfect cats are only shadows of the real cat.[5] To understand the form (catness), we use our mind; to understand the particulars (our particular house cats, e.g., 'fluffy'), we use our senses.

Thompson is a well-known scholar who promotes that Platonism, or more accurately, 'middle Platonism,' had a significant influence on the AH. He nuances this to say that the AH is also influenced by Jewish eschatology (redemptive-

---

3. Vanhoye's minority view is that Hebrews 8:1–9:28 is the central section of the letter with Hebrews 7 and Hebrews 10 each subordinate (*Structure and Message of the Epistle to the Hebrews*, 40a–b, 89–97).

4. So, e.g., Johnson, *Hebrews*, 201–2; and Spicq, *Hébreux*, 1:39–91 (more specifically, Philo).

5. See Plato's famous cave analogy. He imagines severely chained prisoners in a dark area who are only able to see shadows of real people and not the real people themselves for all their lives. These prisoners would confuse the shadows (particulars on earth) for the reality (true form) (*Republic* book 7).

historical assumptions), but that he 'employed Platonic assumptions for his own purposes ... with his focus on what is eternal rather than transitory,... the stable, invisible, and untouchable reality.' Thompson concludes that of the two influences, Jewish eschatology and Middle Platonism, the AH put his 'emphasis' on Middle Platonism while still 'maintaining the traditional Jewish eschatological hope.'[6]

Other scholars dismiss the Platonic influence in favor of a solely Jewish Apocalyptic.[7] More specifically, it is the apocalyptic understanding of the heavenly sanctuary (e.g., 2 Bar. 4:6; 1 En. 14:15–20; cf. Wis. 9:8; Mekilta Shirata 10). They argue that since there are both vertical (heavenly) and eschatological aspects in these documents, the vertical influence need not come from Platonic influence.

My view is that the primary influences on the AH are the OT and the NT Christological events, with the ultimate influence being the Holy Spirit. An eternal God who is spirit and creator provides the understanding of universals and particulars.[8] The OT tabernacle/temple itself was clearly understood as *representing* aspects of God (e.g., 1 Kgs. 8:27;

---

6. James W. Thompson, 'What Has Middle Platonism to Do with Hebrews?,' in *Reading the Epistle to the Hebrews: A Resource for Students*, 31–52, esp. 51–52. Also see Thompson's influential *The Beginnings of Christian Philosophy: The Epistle to the Hebrews*, CBQMS 13 (Washington: Catholic Biblical Association), 1982; and his *Hebrews*, Paideia (Grand Rapids: Baker, 2008).

7. So, e.g., L. D. Hurst, *The Epistle to the Hebrews: Its Background of Thought*, SNTSMS 65 (Cambridge: CUP, 1990); and Barrett, 'The Eschatology of the Epistle to the Hebrews,' 389.

8. Cornelius Van Til emphasized this point in his writings. More specifically, the Triune God is both one substance and three persons; hence, 'unity and plurality are equally ultimate in the Godhead' (*An Introduction to Systematic Theology* [Phillipsburg: Presbyterian and Reformed, 1974], 220). This equal ultimacy shows that one does not have to choose between whether universal or particulars are ultimate (also called the 'one-and-many' problem). 'In God's being there are no particulars not related to the universal and there is nothing universal that is not fully expressed in the particulars' (*The Defense of the Faith*, 26).

Isa. 66:1).[9] Further, the AH explicitly says that Exodus 25:40 is proof that the tabernacle is a copy. Finally, the AH's multifaceted typological use of the Scriptures is based on an eternal Son along with a sovereign God who providentially controls all things. All of these adequately explains both the vertical (heavenly/earthly) and the redemptive-historical components in Hebrews.

OT Tabernacle Relates Both Forward and Upward

Allow me to continue some aspects of the above discussion. The OT tabernacle looks forward, and it also looks upward to the heavenly temple. That is, the OT tabernacle is not simply a shadow of the future reality of Christ (Heb. 3:5; 10:1), it is also a shadow of the heavenly reality about the preincarnate Christ, who existed when Moses wrote the Pentateuch (Heb. 8:5). To say it another way, in the new covenant, the old covenant and its association with the heavenly reality of the preincarnate Christ became the full substance of that reality in Christ's NT work. The OT tabernacle was a shadow of the new covenant both as it relates to (1) the heavenly, preincarnate Christ and (2) the future, full NT reality of Christ.[10] This heavenly reality that has always existed explains well (1) the use of 'eternal' (αἰώνιος) with (a) 'salvation' (5:9), (b) 'redemption' (9:12), (c) 'inheritance' (9:15), and (d) 'covenant' (13:20); and (2) the fact that Christ is 'the same yesterday and today and forever' (13:8). Hence, this heavenly and eternal reality

---

9. For further arguments that the OT itself is the foundation for understanding the earthly tabernacle as replica of the heavenly, see Cockerill, *Hebrews*, 352–53. Also see Goppelt's discussion denying a Philo-like connection because the AH bases his 'vertical typography' not on 'self-evident metaphysical fact, but bases it on Exod. 25:40' (*Typos*, 163–70, esp. 166–67). Beale notes the many inner OT connections between the OT tabernacle/temple, God's creation, and 'God's temple in heaven that eventually would encompass also the whole earth' (*A New Testament Biblical Theology*, 626–32, esp. 630).

10. Vos, 'Hebrews, the Epistle of the Diatheke,' 2:11–16; also see Geerhardus Vos' often-used triangle to represent this idea (*The Teaching of the Epistle to the Hebrews*, 57).

provides a fundamental grounding for the continuity between the old and new covenants and between the heavenly and earthly tabernacles.[11]

New Covenant: Earthly Priests Versus the Heavenly Priest (8:1–6)

Hebrews 8:1–6 begins with a grand statement that Christ is our high priest who is now in heaven and ministers at the true tabernacle (8:1–2). The heavenly aspect of this statement is then supported by Hebrews 8:3–6, which contrasts earthly priests and the heavenly priest. Earthly priests offer earthly sacrifices (Heb. 8:3–4). These earthly aspects are a shadow of the heavenly aspects, as Exodus 25:40 proves (Heb. 8:5). But Christ's heavenly ministry is superior, which relates to a better covenant and better promises (Heb. 8:6; cf. Heb. 7:22).

The contrast of the true/heavenly tabernacle versus the shadow/earthly tabernacle has been alluded to previously (Heb. 4:14; 6:20). But it is introduced fully here in Hebrews 8:1–6 and is an integral part of the argument within Hebrews 8:1–10:18.

The conclusion to Hebrews 8:1–6 that Christ's heavenly priesthood is connected to a better covenant (Heb. 8:6) sets up Hebrews 8:7–13,[12] where the new (better) covenant is confirmed by a long quote from Jeremiah 31:31–34.

8:1–2 *Now*[13] *[the] main point of the things which are being said:*[14]

---

11. This paragraph is copied from Cara, 'Covenant in Hebrews,' 251.

12. A minority view is to include Hebrews 8:6 with 8:7–13 as opposed to with 8:1–5, e.g., Owen, *Hebrews*, 22:3; and Spicq, *Hébreux*, 2:232. The usual rebuttal is that the use of 'minister' and 'ministry' in 8:2 and 8:6, respectively, ties this pericope together.

13. As to **now**, I am taking δέ as a 'marker linking narrative segments, *now, then, and*' (BDAG, 213, emphasis theirs). So also many English translations, e.g., Geneva Bible, KJV, NIV, ESV, and CEB.

14. The phrase **now the main point of the things which are being said** is a nominative absolute (**main point** [κεφάλαιον] is in the nominative). Nominative absolutes often act as headings. See discussion of nominative

We have such a high priest,[15] *who sat at the right hand of the throne of the Majesty in the heavens; a minister of the sanctuary*[16] *and the true tabernacle,*[17] *which the Lord pitched, not man.*

It is not completely clear as to whether the **main point** is summarizing the previous discussion from the whole letter or giving the thesis statement for Hebrews 8:1–10:18 or some combination of both. In any event, Hebrews 8:1b–2 is an important statement.

The AH is appealing to and comforting his readers. **We have such a high priest**, as opposed to the human OT priests and the pagan temple priests, **who sat** (and continues to sit) **at the right hand of the throne of the Majesty in the heavens** (cf. Heb. 1:3; 10:11). Here is the combination of Christ as a priest and a king. This combination parallels the emphasis in Hebrews 7:28, but differs from the remainder of Hebrews 8:1–10:18, which concentrates on Christ's priesthood. Christ as priest and king matches well to the use of Psalm 110:1 and 110:4 in Hebrews, along with Hebrews 1:3; 5:5–6; 10:12–13; and 13:20 (cf. Zech. 6:12–13; Jer. 33:14–18).

Christ's priestly office is further defined as being an authorized **minister** (λειτουργός) **of the sanctuary and the true tabernacle**. I take **sanctuary** (emphasizing the two holy rooms) and **tabernacle** (entire structure) as virtual synonyms.[18]

---

absolutes in Wallace, *Greek Grammar Beyond the Basics*, 49–51.

15. **Such a high priest** is the same wording as Heb. 7:26.

16. The Greek is τῶν ἁγίων. In various tabernacle contexts, it has different nuances. These include **the sanctuary** (the two rooms and utensils), 'the holy things' (utensils in the sanctuary), the 'holy place' (outer room) or 'the holy of holies' (the special one inner room).

17. Greek is σκηνή, which is simply 'tent' with no context. The LXX uses σκηνή for tents in general, but especially for the special tent (מִשְׁכָּן, 'dwelling-place') that Moses had constructed. The Latin Vulgate translates as *tabernaculum* for the special tent, which obviously relates to the English **tabernacle**. Wycliffe's NT (1380) translates as 'tabernacle' as does Tyndale, Geneva Bible, KJV, NASB, NIV, and CSB17. The RSV, ESV, and CEB translate as 'tent.'

18. So also Chrysostom, 'Homily 14 on Hebrews' (*NPNF*[1], 14:433); Hughes, *Hebrews*, 290; Ellingworth, *Hebrews*, 400; Koester, *Hebrews*, 376; and Schreiner, *Hebrews*, 242. Hence, I take the **and** (καί) as epexegetical. Many do

The key point is the word **true** (cf. Zech. 8:3); hence, the **true tabernacle** is not the OT structure, but the **tabernacle** that is **in the heavens**. This heavenly **tabernacle** is a metaphor for heaven itself.

To reinforce the understanding of **true** and **in the heavens**, the AH adds **which**[19] **the Lord pitched, not man**. Yes, the Lord was providentially involved in pitching the OT tabernacle, but the stark expression **the Lord pitched not man** means the Lord made heaven by himself.

This distinction between the **true tabernacle** and the one made by man is important. It shows broadly that there is *continuity* as both the heavenly and earthly have a **tabernacle**, a high priest, and a sacrifice(s). While **true** indicates potential *contrasts*, either antithetical contrasts (e.g., stand versus sit, Heb. 10:11–12) or graded (better, superior, escalating) contrasts (e.g., better sacrifices, Heb. 9:23).[20]

8:3–4 *For every high priest is appointed to offer gifts and sacrifices; wherefore, [it is] necessary [that] this [one] also have something that he offered. Now,*[21] *if he were on earth, he would not be a priest*[22] *[because] there are [priests]*[23] *who offer gifts according to the law;*[24]

---

not see these two as synonyms. E.g., Grässer takes 'sanctuary' as the 'holy of holies' that would be in the **tabernacle** (*Hebräer*, 2:82–83). Some older exegetes take **tabernacle** to be the church (e.g., Aquinas, *Hebrews*, 164) or Christ's body (e.g., *Geneva Bible: 1602 Edition*, folio 112; and Owen, *Hebrews*, 22:17–18). See Hughes' extended discussion of the older exegetes (*Hebrews*, 283–90).

19. **Which** (ἥν) grammatically connects to **tabernacle**.

20. For more discussion of my 'contrasts within continuity' view within Hebrews, see Cara, 'Covenant in Hebrews,' 249–51.

21. I interpret οὖν as resumptive, hence **now** (BDAG, 736). So also Attridge, *Hebrews*, 219.

22. **If he were on earth, he would not be a priest** is in the traditional Greek format for a contrary-to-fact sentence (second-class conditional sentence). So also Hebrews 8:7. For a convenient chart of various types of conditional sentences, see Wallace, *Greek Grammar Beyond the Basics*, 689.

23. The majority-text manuscripts do include **priests**. It is clearly implied in the other manuscripts.

24. **Because there are priests who offer gifts according to the law** is a causal, genitive-absolute participial phrase.

Hebrews 8:3–5 proves the thesis from 8:1–2 (**for**) that Christ is a heavenly priest who serves at the heavenly tabernacle, which necessarily also includes the contradistinctive point that Christ does not serve at the earthly tabernacle.

The AH begins by asserting the general truth that **every high priest is appointed to offer gifts and** (τε καί[25]) **sacrifices** (similar in language to Heb. 5:1). This includes Christ also. **Wherefore, it is necessary that this one** (Christ) **also have something that he offered.** The AH is using understatement here. Amazingly, Christ did offer **something**, himself!

With **now**, the AH is jumping back to Hebrews 8:2 and supporting the point that Christ is a *heavenly* high priest.[26] At first glance, the logic of **if he were on earth, he would not be a priest** is confusing. The AH has readily admitted often that part of Christ's priestly work was **on earth**, preeminently, the sacrifice of himself. So, in what sense is Christ's work *not* **on earth**?[27] There is an interrelated two-part answer. The first relates to **because there are priests who offer gifts according to the law**. **Law** is the ceremonial aspects of the Mosaic law. It obviously requires that the Levitical priesthood **offer gifts** here **on earth**. Since Christ is not part of this priesthood, he cannot be an earthly priest. Further, using an argument to the contrary, he must be a heavenly priest.[28]

The second part of the answer relates to seeing Christ's priestly ministry as a whole, including both work on earth and in heaven. As Vos puts it, 'if Christ's priesthood *now* and *as a whole* were exercised on earth, He could not legitimately be a

---

25. By the use of τε καί as opposed to simply καί, the AH considers **gifts and sacrifices** to be one unit. For a grammatical discussion of τε καί, see Hebrews 2:4.

26. So also Hodge, *Hebrews*, 72.

27. Moffitt argues that Christ's priestly work was *not* in any sense on earth (*Atonement and the Logic of Resurrection in the Epistle to the Hebrews*, 198). For my response to this, see the Reflections section following Heb. 5:1–10.

28. So also Owen, *Hebrews*, 22:32; Hughes, *Hebrews*, 291; and Kleinig, *Hebrews*, 391.

priest.'[29] Calvin adds the nuance that the power and efficacy of the earthly death for spiritual fruit in believers comes from heaven.[30] In sum, Christ is not an 'earth-only' priest like the Levitical priests.

Concerning the dating of Hebrews: Was it before or after the AD 70 destruction of the temple? The use of the present tense for both **every high priest** *is appointed* **to offer** and **who** *offer* as compared to the past (aorist) for **he** (Christ) **offered** is strong evidence for a pre-AD 70 date.[31]

8:5 ... *those [priests] serve a copy and shadow of the heavenly [things], just as Moses had been instructed when he was about to erect the tabernacle, 'see,' he says, 'you will make all [things] according to the archetype that is being shown to you on the mountain.'*

The argument for Christ's being a heavenly priest who ministers at a heavenly tabernacle continues. In brief, the **tabernacle** that the Levitical priests **serve** is **a copy and shadow** of Christ's **heavenly** one. Exodus 25:40 shows that there is both an **archetype** and a **copy**, which then confirms that there is a **heavenly** and an earthly **tabernacle**.

Within this pericope, the AH has referred to the OT tabernacle as being 'on earth' and 'according to the law' (8:4). It is not 'true' nor 'in the heavens' (8:1–2). Here he expands his vocabulary and labels the OT tabernacle as a **copy** (also Heb. 9:23, cf. 4:11) **and shadow** (also Heb. 10:1) **of the heavenly things**. This is not all bad! The earthly **tabernacle** does have a positive relationship with the heavenly one—as

---

29. Vos, 'The Priesthood of Christ in the Epistle to the Hebrews,' 2:602–3.

30. Calvin, *Hebrews and 1 & 2 Peter*, 106; similarly, Owen, *Hebrews*, 22:32. Hughes adds that Christ's 'abiding sphere of his priesthood is heavenly and eternal, not earthly and temporal' (*Hebrews*, 291). Brakel (and others) adds an interesting complementary argument. He notes that the Aaronic high priest had to sacrifice the animal outside of the tabernacle and then go into the holy of holies. Christ sacrificed himself on earth (outside the tabernacle) and then went into heaven (the heavenly holy of holies) (*The Christian's Reasonable Service*, 1:542–43). I am not convinced that the AH intended this.

31. So also Owen, *Hebrews*, 22:32; and Hughes, *Hebrews*, 292.

a **copy and shadow**[32] it matches in a divinely intended way (continuity).[33] On the other hand, it is not 'true'—it is only a **copy and shadow** (contrast).

As a proof that there is a heavenly and earthly distinction, Exodus 25:40 is quoted. The introductory comment for the quote is **just as Moses had been instructed when he was about to erect the tabernacle.** Some brief background is useful. Following Moses' giving of the ten commandments with associated laws (Exod. 20:1–23:32) and the confirmation of the covenant (24:1–8), God again calls Moses to ascend Mount Sinai, and he stays forty days (Exod. 24:9–18). Moses receives detailed instructions that relate to the tabernacle and the outer court, along with all the commensurate utensils, priestly clothing, furniture, and altars (Exod. 25–31).

While Moses is on the mountain, the golden calf incident occurs and Moses descends (Exod. 32). Eventually, the tabernacle and appurtenances are constructed with the craftsmen, Bezalel and Oholiab, leading the way (Exod. 35:30–40:33).

The Exodus 25:40 quote is **'see,' he [God] says [to Moses], 'you will make all things according to the archetype that is being shown to you on the mountain.'**[34] In addition to this verse, three additional times in fairly similar language

---

32. I take these as virtually synonymous terms. So also Hodge, *Hebrews*, 72.

33. Origen notes the positives. He quotes Hebrews 8:5 and concludes that Mosaic 'forms of worship' were 'a sort of schoolmaster to those who by it were to be conducted to Christ' (*On the Principles* 3.6.8 [*ANF*, 4:348]).

34. The LXX is fairly close to the Hebrew. The Hebrew text includes 'make a pattern of *them*'; the LXX does not include 'them.' A minor grammatical change is that the Hebrew has the imperative 'make' and the LXX has the future 'you will make,' which is not a conceptual difference. Hebrews 8:5 follows the LXX fairly closely. Hebrews 8:5 inserts the explanatory **he says** and **all things**. The **all things** conceptually relates to the Hebrew 'them' or it may have come from the 'all things' in Exod. 25:39. Philo's quote of Exod. 25:40 includes 'all things,' although it differs on other particulars (*Allegorical Interpretation* 3:102). A very minor difference is the aorist participle **being shown**, with the LXX being a perfect participle and Hebrews 8:5 a present participle.

Moses is told to make these items according to what God shows him (Exod. 25:9; 26:30; 27:8; cf. Exod. 31:18; Num. 8:4; 1 Chr. 28:11; Acts 7:44). Specifically related to Exodus 25:40, this verse concludes the instructions concerning the lampstand (Exod. 25:31–39). Possibly, Exodus 25:40 refers all the way back to 25:10 to include the ark of the covenant and the shewbread table, along with the lampstand;[35] or possibly this verse and the other three similar ones are all general comments (or 'mantras') that are not necessarily related to the specific items in the immediate context, but they are periodic reminders within Exodus 25–31 of Moses' task.

What rationale does the AH use to conclude that what Moses saw was reflective of a heavenly tabernacle from Exodus 25:40? Could not one argue that the pattern that Moses saw looked exactly like a miniature earthly tabernacle, that is, it was an earthly-tabernacle pattern and not reflective of the heavenly tabernacle? Similarly but conversely, could not one argue that the earthly tabernacle is the true/real tabernacle and what God showed Moses is just a pattern? Is not the physical more real than a pattern? Many critical scholars believe that the AH's exegesis cannot be justified as a proper interpretation of Exodus 25:40.

Before answering, a linguistic discussion is useful. The Greek word that I translate as **archetype** is τύπος (type).[36] This matches the LXX and is a translation of the Hebrew תבנית, which has a broad semantic range of 'pattern' or 'plan' or 'image' or 'copy' (e.g., Exod. 25:9; Deut. 4:16; 1 Chr. 28:11–12; Ps. 106:20).[37] In Hebrews 9:24, ἀντίτυπος (antitype), the opposite of τύπος (type), clearly means a derivative model/copy as it clearly refers to the earthly tabernacle.[38] In Hebrews 8:5 and

---

35. Based on 'them' from the Hebrew of Exod. 25:40.

36. BDAG gives one definition as 'an archetype serving as a model, *type, pattern, model.*' Another is 'embodiment of characteristics or function of a model, *copy, image*' (p. 1020, emphasis theirs).

37. *HALOT*, 1686–87.

38. Note, the AH uses τύπος (**archetype**) and ἀντίτυπος (derivative model,

9:23, ὑπόδειγμα (**copy**) also refers to the earthly tabernacle. In Hebrews 8:5 and 10:1, σκιά (**shadow**) also clearly refers to the earthly tabernacle. Hence, in Hebrews, three terms, ἀντίτυπος, ὑπόδειγμα, σκιά (derivative-'model,' **copy, shadow**, respectively), clearly have the referent of the earthly tabernacle. One term, τύπος (**archetype**), must be different from these three because (1) it is the opposite of ἀντίτυπος, and (2) it is contrasted with the earthly **copy and shadow** in Hebrews 8:5. Hence, to conclude this linguistic discussion, in Hebrews, τύπος (**archetype**) is *not* the earthly tabernacle *nor* a copy of the earthly tabernacle, but it is closely tied to the heavenly things.[39]

Now to justify the AH, or more accurately, to humbly understand his exegesis: He argues that **archetype** in Exodus 25:40 implies that there is also a **copy** (earthly tabernacle), because otherwise it would not be an **archetype** if there was nothing made from it. This is fairly straightforward. But why does the AH assume that the **archetype** is 'true' and that the earthly tabernacle is a derivative, 'non-true,' **copy and shadow**? I answer that this is based not on the specific Hebrew or Greek words used (תבנית, τύπος), but based on (1) the theo-Christological worldview that assumes heavenly and eschatological realities are ultimate, and (2) other places in the OT that indicate the earthly tabernacle/temple is only representative of the true presence of God (e.g., 1 Kgs. 8:27; Isa. 66:1; cf. Gen. 1:1).[40] But how can the **archetype** in and

---

Heb. 9:24) in a reverse way as opposed to the normal Greco-Roman usage and the usage in Christian history. In Christian history, as in 1 Pet. 3:21, ἀντίτυπος (antitype) is the reality and τύπος (type) is the typological model pointing to the reality.

39. So also Owen, *Hebrews*, 45; Hughes, *Hebrews*, 293–95; and Kleinig, *Hebrews*, 392. In Wis. 9:8, the temple was 'a copy (μίμημα) of the holy tabernacle that you [God] prepared from the beginning.' The 'holy tabernacle' in this quote may refer to a preexisting heavenly tabernacle, and thus be similar to the AH. If the 'holy tabernacle,' however, simply refers to the earthly tabernacle being a pattern for the later temple, there is no overlap with the AH.

40. *Contra* Aquinas who answers this with one of his typical emphases;

of itself, that is, what Moses saw, be so closely connected to the heavenly tabernacle and at the same time provide the architectural plan of the earthly tabernacle? The general answer must be that it was *God* who **show[ed]** this and spoke to Moses. God could make this happen.[41] After that, we are in the realm of mystery.[42]

8:6 *But now he has obtained a superior ministry,[43] by as much as even he is a mediator of a better covenant, which has been enacted upon better promises.*

Hebrews 8:6 is a transitional verse that connects the heavenly/earthly contrast to the Mosaic-covenant/new-covenant contrast. Beginning with this verse through 10:18, the word **covenant** will be used often.

As opposed (**but**) to the priests who minister at the earthly tabernacle, the priestly **ministry** of Christ (**he**) is **superior**. How **superior** is it? Its superiority is commensurate (**by as much as**) with how much **better** the new **covenant** and its related **promises** are to the Mosaic covenant and its promises.

The **better covenant** is here contrasted with the ceremonial aspects of the Mosaic covenant and its associated priestly ministry. Note that it is simply assumed that issues related to priesthood are necessarily connected to covenants. Concerning terminology within Hebrews, the new covenant is referred to using five Greek adjectives, two of which are

---

he notes that 'the Lord wills that we be led by the hand from sensible things [earthly tabernacle] unto intelligible and spiritual things [heavenly realities]' (*Hebrews*, 166). Also *contra* others who simply argue Platonic influence, e.g., Johnson, *Hebrews*, 201; see above 'Platonic Influence?' section.

41. One rabbinic answer, which includes a quote of Exod. 25:40, is that 'an ark made of fire, a table made of fire, and a candlestick made of fire came down from heaven; Moses saw them and copied the pattern' (b. Menahot 29a).

42. With what I assume is understatement, Owen remarks concerning the specifics of exactly what and how God showed the heavenly tabernacle to Moses, '[it] is hard to determine' (*Hebrews*, 22:45).

43. **Ministry** (λειτουργία) is the intentional cognate of 'minister' (λειτουργός) in Hebrews 8:2.

synonymous: **better** (7:22; 8:6), 'second' (8:7; 10:9), 'eternal' (13:20), 'new'/καινός (8:8, 13; 9:15), and 'new'/νέος (12:24).[44] This **better covenant** has the advantage of **better promises**. These **better promises** are as opposed to the promises associated with the ceremonial aspects of the Mosaic covenant (e.g., forgiveness of sins by death of animals); however, the **better promises** are not here defined. One would assume that these **better promises** would include the advantages within the following quote from Jeremiah 31 and all other promises in Hebrews (especially Abrahamic[45]).

Christ is a 'surety' (Heb. 7:22) and **mediator**.[46] In Hebrews, **mediator** (μεσίτης) is a key term related to covenant and is only used explicitly of Christ and the new covenant (Heb. 8:6; 9:15; 12:24; cf. 1 Tim. 2:5; Job 9:33). Conceptually, it is contrasted to the OT Levitical high priest (Heb. 5:1; 8:6) and implicitly to Moses himself (Heb. 3:2–5; 9:19–20; cf. Gal. 3:19).[47] Lincoln argues that **mediator** is 'the key [Christological] concept' in Hebrews because it (1) bridges the immense gap between a holy God and sinful man and (2) explains the dual emphasis in Hebrews of Christ's being both God and sinless man.[48]

I note that this verse confirms that the term **covenant** used in a biblical context may include **promises**, priestly **ministry**, and a **mediator**; and it certainly does include all of these for the new **covenant**.

---

44. With the notable exceptions of Spicq (*Hébreux*, 2:409) and Westcott (*Hebrews*, 329), virtually all commentators agree that the two Greek words for 'new' are synonymous.

45. For a discussion of the relationship between Abrahamic promises and the new covenant, see Cara 'Covenant in Hebrews,' 252–54.

46. For a discussion as to the overlap and differences between these two terms, see commentary at Heb. 7:22.

47. Both Moses (e.g., Exod. 18:19; 20:19–21; 24:6–8) and the high priests (Exod. 19:24; Lev. 16) function as mediators in the OT. Philo explicitly calls both Moses (*On the Life of Moses* 2:166) and the high priest (*On the Special Laws* 1:116) a 'mediator' (μεσίτης). Moses is explicitly called a 'mediator of his [Lord's] covenant' in the *Testament of Moses* 1:14.

48. Lincoln, *Hebrews*, 85–89, esp. 85. Some of the wording in this paragraph is directly from Cara, 'Covenant in Hebrews,' 261.

Reflections

'We have such a high priest' (Heb. 8:1). Yes, for believers, there *is* a high priest. Others claim to know the 'road to heaven,' or they even believe that 'all roads lead to heaven,' or there is no 'road' to heaven because there is no heaven. But the one in union with Christ knows he *has* a high priest, who is the only high priest.

Hebrews 8:1 also notes that our high priest is currently 'in the heavens,' and not with us in the flesh. In fact, if Christ 'were still on earth, he would not be a priest' (Heb. 8:4). The 1614 Confession of the Evangelical Church in Germany (Reformed as opposed to Lutheran) instructs believers that it is wrong to assume that 'Christ is not able to help us unless He is with us in the flesh.' It then quotes John 16:6–7; Hebrews 8:4; and 1 John 3:24.[49] Understanding that (1) Christ's human body is now in heaven and (2) part of Christ's priestly work involves his being in heaven should reduce the anxiety of not seeing his body here and now. Scoffers say that a living Christ is a myth because they cannot see him (cf. John 20:24–29). The Christian responds, 'Glory be that we do not see him now. He is my high priest in heaven now and needs to be for my complete salvation. One future day I will see him face-to-face and be with him forever.'

New Covenant: Jeremiah 31:31–34 (8:7–13)

With Hebrews 8:7–13, the AH is expanding upon and justifying the 'better covenant' and 'better promises' comments from 8:6 within an overarching argument that Christ's priesthood is 'superior' to the Aaronic (Heb. 7:1–10:18). To do this, Jeremiah 33:31–33 is quoted (Heb. 8:8b–12) and bookended with an introductory comment (Heb. 8:7–8a) and a concluding comment (Heb. 8:13). The key term from the quote is *new* from 'new covenant' (Heb. 8:8; cf. 8:13). The bookended comments

---

49. Confession of the Evangelical Church in Germany 23 (*Reformed Confessions of the 16th and 17th Centuries*, 4:62–63).

emphasize the deficiencies of the Mosaic/'old' covenant.

At the end of Hebrews 7:1–10:18, the Jeremiah quote is again used, although in a truncated form. There, the AH emphasizes the existential benefits of the new covenant ('laws on hearts,' Heb. 10:16 // Jer. 31:33) and the forensic benefits ('remember their sins ... no more,' Heb. 10:17 // Jer. 31:34). The concluding comment will further emphasize the forensic benefits (Heb. 10:18) and connect this to Christ's sacrifice.

Given the Jeremiah quote, some background as to covenantal language in Jeremiah is helpful.[50] Within Jeremiah as a whole, explicit covenantal statements abound. Judah and Israel are condemned for not following the Mosaic covenant (Jer. 7:21–26; 11:1–8; 22:8–9; 31:32; cf. 16:14–15; 23:7–8). Positively, the Mosaic covenant includes the promise 'I will be your God, and you shall be my people' (Jer. 7:23; cf. 30:22) and an unbreakable 'covenant with the Levitical priests' (Jer. 33:21). The Davidic covenant is very prominent and includes 'righteous Branch' language (Jer. 23:5–6; 30:9; 33:15–17, 21–22; cf. 30:22). The new covenant will include a renewed 'heart' (Jer. 24:7; 31:33; 32:39–40), the promise 'you shall be my people, and I will be your God' (Jer. 30:22; cf. 24:7; 31:33), the assurance of being brought back to the land (Jer. 16:14–15; 23:7–8; 25:11–12; 29:10),[51] and it is called an 'everlasting covenant' (Jer. 32:40; 50:5). Finally, the permanence of the day-and-night aspect of the Noahic covenant is used to confirm the permanence of God's covenantal promises (Jer. 33:20–21; cf. Gen. 8:22; Jer. 31:35). As is mentioned in virtually every scholarly discussion of Jeremiah's new covenant compared to previous covenants, there are both discontinuities and continuities.[52]

---

50. The remainder of this paragraph is taken from Cara, 'Covenant in Hebrews,' 262.

51. These land promises implicitly refer also to the Abrahamic covenant (cf. Jer. 33:26).

52. For a standard discussion, see Willem A. VanGemeren, *Interpreting the Prophetic Word: An Introduction to the Prophetic Literature of the Old Testament* (Grand Rapids: Academic, 1990), 313–17.

8:7–8a *For if that first were blameless, no place would be sought for a second.*[53] *For finding fault with them,*[54] *he says,*

With the 'better covenant' reference in Hebrews 8:6, **first** relates to the Mosaic covenant, and **second**, the new covenant.[55] Hence, the initial **for** relates directly back to 8:6 to argue that the new/**second** covenant is 'better' than the Mosaic/**first** covenant; but more broadly, it is connecting Hebrews 8:7–13 with 8:1–6. The broad argument will include (1) the simple implications of having a **first** and **second** covenant (Heb. 8:7, 13), (2) the negative comments about the Mosaic covenant (Heb. 8:9), and (3) the positive comments ('better promises') about the new covenant (Heb. 8:8, 10–12).

Hebrews 8:7 begins the argument by simply noting that the existence of a **second** covenant strongly implies a replacement or adjustment or expansion of the **first**. It further implies some defect in the **first**, or why else would a **second** be needed? Of course, a first-to-second sequence does not always imply this (cf. Gal. 3:15, Acts 12:10). But given the previous multiple arguments for a change in priesthood and the disappointing portions of Israel's history confirmed by Jeremiah's direct statement (Jer. 31:32 // Heb. 8:9; cf. Heb. 3:16–4:2), the AH well concludes that the **first** was not **blameless**. The sequential logic of this argument parallels his previous argument from Psalm 100:4 concerning a future Melchizedekian priest (Heb. 7:11) and the 'rest' discussion (Heb. 4:8).

---

53. Heb. 8:7 is a contrary-to-fact sentence in form and concept. See footnote at Heb. 8:4.

54. Manuscripts differ as to αὐτούς or αὐτοῖς. If taken to be the direct object of the **finding fault**, there is no difference in meaning. This is my view (so also *TCGNT*², 597; Attridge, *Hebrews*, 225; Mitchell, *Hebrews*, 167, 170; Kleinig, *Hebrews*, 384; and most major English translations). If αὐτοῖς is original and taken as the indirect object of **he says** plus an implied 'it' (i.e., the first covenant), then the reading 'finding fault with it, he says to them.' This eliminates the supposed incongruity between blaming the Mosaic covenant per se and the people under the Mosaic covenant (so Lane, *Hebrews 1–8*, 202; Hughes, *Hebrews*, 298; and ESV footnote).

55. The Mosaic covenant is referred to as **first** in Hebrews 8:7, 13; 9:1, 15, 18; 10:9. Only in Hebrews 9:15 is the full expression 'first covenant.' The new covenant is referred to as **second** in Hebrews 8:7; 10:9.

The clause **for finding fault with them, he says** prefaces the Jeremiah quote. The implied grammatical subject is clearly God. **Them** is focused on the wilderness generation (Heb. 8:9) but would include the whole visible covenant community from the Mosaic covenant unto the new. Here, the AH moves from a sequence-logic argument to the relatively ineffectualness of the Mosaic covenant.

In what sense was the Mosaic covenant to blame? The positive comments about Moses personally (Heb. 3:1–6; 8:5; 11:23–28), that *God* initiated the Mosaic covenant (Heb. 3:4–5), and that believers living under the Mosaic covenant were commended and used as positive examples (e.g., Heb. 3:2; 11:23–12:1; 12:5; 13:5–6) mitigates against understanding the blame in a radically negative way. Further, the noted lack of attainable 'perfection' (Heb. 7:11, see extended discussion there) confirms a less than radical understanding. The Mosaic covenant per se was not to blame in a redemptive-historical sense, that is, the blame was not a moral fault.[56] God's plan was to clearly reveal the substance of Christ's priesthood and sacrifice/intercession using the Mosaic covenant as a pointer (Heb. 3:5). Also, the new covenant would bring *proportionally* greater spiritual benefits (see my exegesis of Heb. 8:10–12). Notwithstanding the redemptive-historical explanation, those under the Mosaic covenant did incur moral blame for significant sin (**finding fault with them**), as opposed to the Mosaic covenant per se, which has no moral fault.[57]

---

56. Owen, 'The first covenant ... could not accomplish the *perfect administration* of the grace of God unto the church, nor was ever designed unto that end' (*Hebrews*, 22:103, italics his). Lane, '[God] fully intended the first covenant to be provisional' (*Hebrews 1–8*, 209).

57. Herman Witsius presents seven 'defects' of the old covenant (*The Economy of the Covenants between God and Man*, 2:362–78). (1) Cause of salvation was not present, (2) Obscurity, (3) Rigour and unrelenting threatenings, (4) Bondage to the elements of the world, (5) Servile economy (Rom. 8:15), (6) Grace was less in respect of extent and degree, and (7) Hunger for a better condition (this is presented as a quasi-positive).

8:8b–12 *'Behold, days are coming, says the Lord, when*[58] *I will establish a new covenant with the house of Israel and with the house of Judah, not according to the covenant that I made with their fathers on the day of my taking their hand to lead them out from the land of Egypt, because they were not remaining in my covenant, and I neglected them, says the Lord. Because this is the covenant that I will covenant with the house of Israel after those days, says the Lord: [I will] put my laws in their mind, and I will write them on their hearts, and I will be to them God, and they shall be to me a people; and they shall not teach, each his citizen*[59] *and each his brother, saying, "Know the Lord," because all shall know me from the least to the greatest of them. Because I will be merciful to their unrighteous [acts] and I will remember their sins*[60] *no more.*

Hebrews 8:8b–12 is a quote of Jeremiah 31:31–34.[61] It is the longest OT quote in the NT. There are no major differences between the Hebrew, LXX, and Hebrews. There are several minor differences of which two have been of interest to some interpreters. First, **laws** and the related pronoun **them** are plural in Hebrews 8:10 and the LXX but singular in the Hebrew. Second, the Hebrew uses the idiomatic verb כרת ('to cut') for 'to cut (establish) a covenant' three times in Jeremiah 31:31–33. The LXX consistently translates this verb with διατίθημι. In Hebrews 8:8–10, however, three different verbs are used as shown above in the translation, to **establish** (συντελέω), to **make** (ποιέω), and to **covenant** (διατίθημι).

---

58. Καί includes 'when' within its semantic range. See Zerwick, *Biblical Greek* §455δ; and BDF §442.4.

59. The Hebrew has the traditional word for 'neighbor' (רע). Most LXX manuscripts have 'citizen' (πολίτης), although a few have 'neighbor' (πλησίον). Most NT manuscripts have **citizen** including those in the majority text tradition; however, the Textus Receptus has 'neighbor,' as can be seen in the KJV. See *TCGNT*², 597. There is no substantial difference in context between the two.

60. The majority text tradition has 'sins and lawless [acts]' matching to Hebrews 10:17, as can be seen in the KJV.

61. MT Jer. 31:31–34 matches to LXX Jer. 38:31–34. The LXX of Jeremiah has several chapters in different locations compared to the MT.

How is the AH using the quote? As discussed above, it is easy to see how the comment 'finding fault with them' (Heb. 8:8a) matches to Israel's sin (**they were not remaining in my covenant**, Heb. 8:9). But it is not immediately clear how this quote relates to the Hebrews 8:1–7 argument about the changes in the ceremonial law. In fact, some commentators believe the AH misunderstands Jeremiah. They assume that for Jeremiah the **new covenant** and its **laws** do *not at all* relate to any ceremonial aspects and that AH *did* see a relationship.[62] Below I present several arguments to justify the AH's use of the Jeremiah quote that includes both the ineffectiveness of the Mosaic covenant to change hearts and the anticipated change in ceremonial laws:[63]

(1) A weakness of the Mosaic covenant itself is that its laws were not adequately written on hearts (Heb. 8:10).[64]

(2) The fact that the expression '*new* covenant' is used by Jeremiah implies that aspects of the old covenant were not adequate. This matches the AH's concluding comments (Heb. 8:13) following the Jeremiah quote (Heb. 8:8–12).[65] (Also see discussion at Heb. 8:7).

(3) 'Law' as used by Jeremiah, although not exclusively referring to the ceremonial laws, certainly includes them (Heb. 8:10).

(4) The book of Jeremiah condemns many ceremonial sins in addition to civil and moral (e.g., Jer. 7:8–10; 8:19; 17:21–23);

---

62. So Lehne, '[The AH] infuses the new covenant metaphor, which bears no relationship whatsoever to the cult in Jeremiah's prophecy on the new covenant, with cultic content that is rooted elsewhere in the OT' (*New Covenant in Hebrews*, 120). Johnson sees the AH as 'reinterpreting the purpose of the covenant' (*Hebrews*, 211). Mitchell considers the original point to be that 'the Law did not change in Jeremiah's view, but the people had to' (*Hebrews*, 170).

63. These arguments and other aspects of the new covenant discussion are from Cara, 'Covenant in Hebrews,' 261–65.

64. So also Calvin, *Hebrews and 1–2 Peter*, 109.

65. So Chrysostom. He notes that after showing priestly reasons, the AH 'shows more clearly by express words' that the Mosaic covenant has ended ('Homily 14 on Hebrews' [*NPNF*[1], 14:433–38, esp. 434]).

hence, it is proper in prophetic language to indicate that ceremonial laws, among others, would be written on hearts.

(5) The AH, although not agreeing that the ceremonial laws continue in a straight one-to-one manner, does apply ceremonial-law language to his congregation (e.g., Heb. 10:22; 13:10–16). Hence, at some level, ceremonial laws are written on NT believers' hearts.

(6) **I will remember their sins no more** (Heb. 8:12) is taken absolutely by the AH based on the work of Christ (cf. Heb. 10:18). Therefore, this shows the inadequacies of the ceremonial laws to forgive sins.[66]

***

The AH focusses upon the term **new covenant**. In the OT, this exact term is only used once, which is this quote.[67] Within Hebrews, 'new' is used explicitly in reference to covenant in 8:8, 13; 9:15 (καινός) and 12:24 (νέος). The AH understands **behold, days are coming** and **after those days** as referring to the **new covenant** inaugurated by Christ (Heb. 8:8b, 10).[68] He

---

66. David Peterson emphasizes that the AH sees Jeremiah's quote 'in priestly and sacrificial terms' because he sees the whole OT as pointing toward Christ's sacrifice with its 'definitive cleansing of the conscience or forgiveness which is the basis of Jeremiah's prophecy' ('The Prophecy of the New Covenant in the Argument of Hebrews,' *RTR* 38 [1979]: 74–81, esp. 77, 81).

67. Cf. the use of 'new' in Ezek. 11:19–20 and 36:26–28. In the DSS, CD makes mention of 'the new covenant in the land of Damascus,' which apparently is a veiled reference to the community itself (VI, 19; VIII, 1). Given the law emphasis in this document, it appears to have no relationship to Jer. 31:31. Str-B note that Jer. 31:31–34 is rarely mentioned in Rabbinic literature (p. 3:704). In 2 Maccabees 2:1–8, Jeremiah hides the ark in a cave and tells the deportees that 'the law should not depart from their hearts' (2 Macc. 2:3, cf. 2 Macc. 1:4). Based on early church familiarity, Kistemaker surmises that Jer. 31:31–34 had significant 'liturgical usage' (*Psalm Citations in the Epistle to the Hebrews*, 41).

68. From the book of Jeremiah, one might get the impression that the new covenant begins at the end of the exile and their return to Canaan. But this is not the AH's view. Therefore, the return from exile must be another aspect of typology pointing toward Christ's inauguration of the new covenant at his first coming.

uses the expressions **house of Israel, house of Judah**, and **my people** to refer especially to NT believers (Heb. 8:8b, 10).

Not according to the covenant that I made with their fathers (Heb. 8:9) clearly refers to the Mosaic covenant. It is focused on the wilderness generation (cf. Heb. 3:16–4:2) but includes the whole visible covenant community from the Mosaic covenant unto the new.[69] Several commentators note the AH's use of **made** for the Mosaic covenant (Heb. 8:9) as opposed to **establish** for the new (Heb. 8:8b). They see these as intentional changes from the Hebrew/LXX to show that the new covenant, unlike the Mosaic covenant, will never change.[70] I see these changes as only stylistic.[71]

God will **write them** (laws) **on their hearts** emphasizes the grace and divine initiative of the new covenant (Heb. 8:10). This grace is strengthened further when one considers Christ's priesthood. Within Hebrews, the congregation is exhorted not to have an 'unbelieving heart' (Heb. 3:12, cf. 3:8) and to draw near to God with a 'true heart' (Heb. 10:22). Also, the AH refers to 'heart' in a similar way for OT believers (Heb. 3:8, 14; cf. Jer. 24:7). Hence, the heart aspect of the new covenant cannot imply that no one in the OT had the law in their hearts. Upon putting together the grace and divine initiative emphasis of the new covenant as to 'heart' with the fact that at some level the OT people of God had a 'heart' for God, the result is a proportional understanding of the heart. The new covenant emphasis on heart is not *absolutely* different than the OT—God's initiative versus no initiative. It is, rather, *proportionally* different—more emphasis on God's initiative in the new covenant as compared with the old.[72] As

---

69. *Contra* Owen who restricts this to only the wilderness generation (*Hebrews*, 22:126–27).

70. So, e.g., Cockerill, *Hebrews*, 368–69.

71. So also Lane, *Hebrews*, 209.

72. WLC 35 references Hebrews 8:8, 10–11 regarding the NT 'in which grace and salvation are held forth in more fulness, evidence, and efficacy, to all nations' relative to the OT. Similarly, see WCF 7.6 and 20.1 where new covenant realities offer 'more' efficacy relative to the OT.

to whether there are any specific exegetical implications to the AH's plural **laws** (so also the LXX) as opposed to the Hebrew singular 'law,' I see none.

The Jeremiah quote includes the grand covenantal language of **I will be to them God, and they shall be to me a people**. This language is part of the new covenant (Heb. 8:10; Rev. 21:3) and has connections to all redemptive covenants (e.g., Gen. 17:7; Exod. 6:7; 29:45; 2 Kgs. 11:17; Jer. 7:23; 24:7; 30:22).[73] Within Hebrews, similar language is used in a Davidic covenant context, 'I will be to him a father, and he shall be to me a son' (Heb. 1:5) and in an Abrahamic context, 'God is not ashamed to be called their God' (Heb. 11:16). This all points to significant continuity across the covenants. In addition, this covenantal language dovetails well with the emphases in Hebrews to 'draw near to God' (Heb. 4:16; 7:25; 10:22; 11:6) and 'not neglecting to meet together' (Heb. 10:25).[74]

The Jeremiah quote includes that in the new covenant there will be no need for teaching each other (Heb. 8:11). Why is no teaching required? **All shall know me**. I take the emphasis of this verse as parallel to the previous **mind/heart** language. God will sovereignly put his laws in our **minds**, and equally so, he will make all true believers to **know** him (cf. John 6:45). As Owen rightly states, 'In the new covenant, there being an express promise of an *internal, effectual, teaching by the Spirit of God.*'[75] Again, similar to the heart language, I take this new covenant reality as proportional to the old covenant—God

---

73. See the classic discussion in Robertson, *The Christ of the Covenants*, 45–52.

74. Overstating it in my view, but Michael D. Morrison sees the covenant motif as primarily used in Hebrews for exhortations related to community (*Who Needs a New Covenant?: Rhetorical Function of the Covenant Motif in the Argument of Hebrews*, PTMS 85 [Eugene, OR: Pickwick, 2008], 158–60).

75. Owen, *Hebrews*, 17:160, emphasis his. Schreiner goes a significant step beyond me and further infers that the old covenant was a "mixed community" (regenerate and unregenerate) and the new covenant community is not mixed (*Hebrews*, 252–53, 476). As a response to Schreiner's 'new covenant' view, see Scott R. Swain, 'New Covenant Theologies,' in *Covenant Theology: Biblical, Historical, and Theological Perspectives*, 551–69.

did make believers know him in the OT (e.g., Exod. 6:7; 31:13; Deut. 29:6; Ps. 100:3; Isa. 45:3; Jer. 9:24), but relative to that, he will do so with greater emphasis in the NT.[76] Also, this internal knowledge does not negate the NT teaching ministry as the whole book of Hebrews is itself a teaching ministry (Heb. 13:22), the AH refers to teachers (Heb. 5:11–12; 13:7), and all are exhorted to stir up each other to good works (Heb. 10:24–25).

Others emphasize the eschatological nature of **all shall know me** as its primary intention. That is, in the NHNE this statement will be absolutely true and not simply proportionally and/or partially true.[77] In addition, however, this view does see partial fulfillment now (a now/not-yet relationship). My view has significant overlap with this 'eschatological' view as there is only an emphasis disagreement concerning the purpose of the quote. I see the primary aim as making a *proportional* argument, and secondarily, yes, it foreshadows the NHNE. The eschatological view is basically the converse.

Hebrews 8:10–11 emphasizes a significant existential benefit to the new-covenant believer (change of **heart/mind, know the Lord**). Hebrews 8:12 emphasizes the forensic benefit (**I will remember their sins no**[78] **more**). These two benefits are again emphasized in the truncated Jeremiah quote in Hebrews 10:16–17. These reflect the two broad benefits believers receive related to their union with Christ, both existential (i.e., sanctification and glorification) and forensic

---

76. So also Calvin, *Hebrews*, 113; Hodge, *Systematic Theology*, 2:376; and Brown, *Hebrews*, 373.

77. So, e.g., Hughes, *Hebrews*, 301–2; Richard L. Pratt Jr., 'Infant Baptism in the New Covenant,' in *The Case for Covenantal Infant Baptism*, ed. Gregg Strawbridge (Phillipsburg: P&R, 2003), 156–74; and Swain, 'New Covenant Theologies,' 559–62.

78. The negative is emphatic (οὐ μή plus the aorist subjunctive). Also the same emphatic grammatical construction is in **they shall not teach**. This construction is common in the NT in the midst of LXX quotations. See Turner, *Syntax*, 95–96; and BDF §365.

(i.e., justification).[79] Calvin famously termed these two graces as *duplex gratia*.[80] Note that here, and in Hebrews 10:18, the existential benefits are predicated upon (**because**, Heb. 10:12) the forensic benefit.[81] Hence, I would argue that there is a *logical* priority to the forensic, although not a temporal priority as one's justification and beginning-sanctification are temporally the same.[82] Further, the strong emphasis of Christ's sacrifice *for sins* within Hebrews confirms the logical priority of justification.[83]

8:13 *By speaking of the new, he has made obsolete the first; and what is becoming obsolete and growing old is near disappearance.*

The AH adds a concluding comment to the Jeremiah quote. It parallels Hebrews 8:7, which has 'first'/'second' language and here it is **first/new**. The point is the same. **By speaking of the new**, God shows that the Mosaic covenant has (God-intended) deficiencies (cf. Heb. 10:9). With the inauguration of the **new**, God **has made obsolete the first** (Mosaic covenant). This refers to the ceremonial aspects of the Mosaic covenant and the relative lack of power they have to change God's covenant people.

The statement **and what is becoming obsolete and growing**

---

79. One might say this summarizes justification and sanctification/glorification. Calvin's Catechism 17 (AD 1537) makes this exact point and references Jer. 31:33; Hebrews 8:10 and 10:16.

80. Calvin, *Institutes*, 3.11.1. In addition to the *duplex gratia* language, Calvin also famously says here that justification is 'the main hinge on which religion turns.'

81. So also Owen, who terms Hebrews 8:12 as the 'foundation' and 'the grounds' for the benefits in Hebrews 8:10–11 (*Hebrews*, 22:168).

82. As to logical priority of justification relative to sanctification, see Turretin, *Institutes of Elenctic Theology*, 2:691; Bavinck, *Reformed Dogmatics*, 4:182, 190; Vos, *Reformed Dogmatics*, 4:6; *The Pauline Eschatology* (Phillipsburg: P&R, 1986 [1930]), 149; and Berkhof, *Systematic Theology*, 536.

83. So also R. Michael Allen as to this emphasis in Hebrews (*Justification and the Gospel: Understanding the Contexts and Controversies* [Grand Rapids: Baker, 2013], 63–67. He makes the additional helpful distinction that justification is the *ground* of the Gospel and sanctification/glorification is the *goal* of the Gospel (pp. 37–53).

old is near disappearance is a truism or proverbial.[84] This is confirmed by the neuter **what** as opposed to the feminine **new** and **first** referencing the feminine 'covenant.' Hence, the present tense aspect of this verse does *not* mean that the Mosaic covenant is in the process of **becoming obsolete** when the AH was writing. The present tense is simply part of the proverbial statement. The first half of the statement is confirmed—God **has made obsolete the first** covenant at the first coming of Christ.[85]

Reflections

In God's covenant of grace, he will be our God, and we will be his people. One of the benefits of that is a changed heart. A heart changed ultimately by God. 'I will write them [my laws] on their hearts' (Heb. 8:10).

Christians should love God's law. Understanding God's law should give us joy. Doing God's law should bring us joy. Hopefully, we can agree with the psalmist, 'Oh how I love your law' (Ps. 119:97).

It is not that we love 'law' in the abstract, that is, law abstracted from or separated from everything. It is *'my* law.' It is *God's* law. It is a law that is *personal*—it comes from a 'tri-personal' God.[86] It is also a 'law' that fits God's *creation*. It is made for us as we live in God's creation.

---

84. So also Owen, *Hebrews*, 22:176; and Attridge, *Hebrews*, 228.

85. *Contra* Kenneth A. Vandergriff who takes an 'apocalyptic' interpretation of the quote. According to Vandergriff, the AH uses 'after those days' to refer to only to the NHNE. Hence, the Mosaic covenant will not fully pass away until the second coming of Christ ('Διαθήκη καινή: New Covenant as Jewish Apocalypticism in Hebrews 8,' *CBQ* 79 [2017]: 97–110).

86. Certainly, the Triune God is not impersonal. But in what sense, if any, are we to think of the one God as 'personal' as opposed to impersonal? I prefer to say that the one God is 'tri-personal.' This is a subject that quickly becomes mysterious. For discussions promoting the tri-personal nature of God, see Bavinck, *Reformed Dogmatics*, 301–4; Van Til, *An Introduction to Systematic Theology*, 218–19, 229–32; and Frame, *The Doctrine of God*, 25–26, 703–4. Bavinck comments, 'It belongs to God's very essence to be triune. In that regard personhood is identical with God's being itself" (pp. 303–4). For a sympathetic interaction with Bavinck and Van Til, see Lane G. Tipton, *The Trinitarian Theology of Cornelius Van Til* (Libertyville, IL: Reformed Forum, 2022), 74–86.

'I will write my laws on their hearts.' This shows both God's grace and our desire to do his will. 'I will write' shows that any true love we have for God's personal law is because God gave us this love. 'My laws on their hearts' shows that we are a changed people. We desire in our hearts to do God's will/laws. Of course, due to sin ...

Pray that God will more and more write his laws on our hearts.

First Covenant Tabernacle (9:1–10)

Hebrews 8:13 uses the Jeremiah passage's mention of a 'new covenant' to conclude that the 'first' covenant is 'obsolete.' Hebrews 9:1–10 concerns the deficiencies of the 'first' covenant and the associated tabernacle. This will then be contrasted in Hebrews 9:11–10:18 with the 'second'/'new' covenant and the heavenly tabernacle.

Within Hebrews 9:1–10, the tabernacle's furniture and appurtenances along with some priestly worship duties are briefly summarized. The focus is on the tabernacle's separation between the Holy Place and the Holy of Holies, which results in restricted access to the Holy of Holies. This restricted access is especially highlighted on the Day of Atonement. This separation and resulting restricted access has typological significance. It shows that full access to God and a perfected conscience would have to wait until the 'time of reformation,' that is, the new-covenant inauguration by Christ. This fuller connection to God matches the internal heart emphasis and full forgiveness of sins noted in Hebrews 8:10–12 // Jeremiah 31:33–34.

The AH uses the terms 'first' and 'second' several times to refer to the two sections of the tabernacle, the Holy Place and the Holy of Holies, respectively. These designations are unique. Why does he use these unique terms for the earthly tabernacle? Is he making typological connections between the 'first' and 'second' sections of the tabernacle to the 'first' and 'second' covenants? I answer, 'yes.' For the AH, the earthly tabernacle has both a vertical/eternal relationship and a forward-looking relationship to the heavenly tabernacle.[87] This is similar to the ceremonial aspects of the Mosaic covenant that reflect both an eternal covenant and the later new covenant. That is, there is both an eternal and redemptive-historical relationship for both the earthly/heavenly tabernacles and the Mosaic/new covenants. In Hebrews 9:1–10, the AH is using the spatial distinctions within the earthly tabernacle as a reflection of the temporal redemptive-historical relationships (not the eternal ones) of the tabernacles and covenants. The 'first' section of the earthly tabernacle represents (a) itself (more accurately, the whole earthly tabernacle) and (b) the 'first' covenant. The 'second' section of the tabernacle is a type of (a) Christ's heavenly-tabernacle work in his death/resurrection/ascension and (b) the later 'second'/'new' covenant. To conclude, the AH uses the unique terms for the tabernacle of 'first' and 'second' to better show the connection to the 'first' and 'second' covenants. Further justification of this view is presented below in the exegesis section.

The flow of Hebrews 9:1–10 is as follows: An overarching observation is given that the first covenant had worship regulations and an earthly tabernacle (9:1). Concerning earthly tabernacle and appurtenances, a brief description is given of the Holy Place and then the Holy of Holies (9:2–5). Concerning the worship regulations, priestly duties are explained for the Holy Place and then the Holy of Holies (9:6–7). Finally, typological implications are made based on the distinction between the Holy Place and the Holy of Holies (9:8–10).[88]

---

87. See previous section at the beginning of this book chapter entitled, 'OT Tabernacle Relates Both Forward and Upward.'

88. Felix H. Cortez argues instead that Hebrews 9:6–10 is a unit ('period') that sets up Hebrews 9:11–10:18. He notes that the three themes of multiple vs. single priests, continuous vs. one entrance, and unrestricted access vs. restricted with blood access are all in both Hebrews 9:6–10 and 9:11–10:18 ('From the Most Holy Place: The Period of Heb 9:6–10 and Day of Atonement as a Metaphor of Transition,' *JBL* 125 [2006]: 527–47).

9:1 Now[89] *the first [covenant]*[90] *also had regulations of worship and the sanctuary [that was] worldly.*[91]

Although the **first covenant** was deficient, it **also** included **worship** similar to the second (Heb. 8:7). Further, there are typological connections based on the **regulations for worship and the sanctuary** between the two covenants.

Here the entire wilderness tabernacle is termed **the sanctuary** (τό ἅγιον, מקדש, קדש). 'Sanctuary' (holy place) in biblical language often refers to the two-room arrangement, whether as related to the tabernacle (e.g., Exod. 26:8), Solomon's temple (e.g., 1 Chr. 22:19), or the second/Herod's temple (e.g., Mal. 2:11).

The **sanctuary** is described as **worldly** (κοσμικός). Given the cognate connection between **worldly** (κοσμικός) and the universe (κόσμος), is the AH implying that the tabernacle/temple/**sanctuary** is intentionally imitating the created universe? Unrelated to this verse, many ancient Jewish and Christians interpreters thought so. Josephus argues that tabernacle fabric, the clothes of the priests, the furniture 'were every one made in way of imitation and representation of the universe.' For example, the twelve loaves of bread reflect the twelve months. The candelabra with its seven lights matches the seven planets. The high priest's clothing has blue for the sky and bells for thunder.[92] Several ancient Christian interpreters also see similar connections. Gregory of Nanzianzus sees the tabernacle as a figure of 'the whole creation ... entire system of things visible and invisible.'[93]

---

89. Taking οὖν as a 'marker of continuation of a narrative' (BDAG, 736).

90. The word **covenant** is not in the Greek, but as all agree, the word **first** refers to **covenant** based on Hebrews 8:13. So also Chrysostom, 'Homily 15 on Hebrews' (*NPNF*[1], 14:438); Calvin, *Hebrews and 1 & 2 Peter*, 115; Moffatt, *Hebrews*, 112; Johnson, *Hebrews*, 216; Geneva Bible, KJV, ESV, and CEB. A few Greek manuscripts have 'tabernacle,' and this is reflected in the Tyndale translation.

91. My stilted translation 'a sanctuary that was worldly' reflects that κοσμικός is here technically a predicate adjective.

92. Josephus, *Jewish Antiquities* 3.179–87; also 3.123. Similarly, Philo, *On the Life of Moses* 2.80; 102–5; *Who is the Heir?* 225–28.

93. Gregory of Nanzianzus, *Second Theological Oration* 31.

Although, other Christian interpreters do not agree to these connections.[94] My view is that here, as opposed to **worldly** being used as morally evil (e.g., Titus 2:12), it simply means 'earthly' tabernacle as opposed to the heavenly tabernacle. This is confirmed by 'on earth' in Hebrews 8:4 and 'not of this creation' in 9:11.[95] That is, there is no special emphasis on imitating the created universe.

9:2 *For the tabernacle was built, [it included] the first [section], in which were the lampstand and the table and the presence of the breads, which is called the Holy Place;*[96]

To expand upon the details related to the 'sanctuary' mentioned in the previous verse (**for**), the AH specifically recalls the wilderness-generation **tabernacle**, of which Moses received the divine 'archetype' (Heb. 8:5). As presented in Exodus, the **tabernacle** is a movable tent that has layers of cloth, goat hair, and animal skin pulled over a wooden frame that was overlaid with gold (Exod. 26:1–14; 36:8–38; 40:18–19). The plan dimensions are 30 by 10 cubits, and the height is 10 cubits (Exod. 26:2, 15–25, 36:14–30).[97] The **tabernacle** had two rooms. The room upon entering was 20 by 10 by 10 cubits and

---

94. So, e.g., Fairbairn, *Typology of Scripture*, 2:219–21.

95. So also virtually all modern interpreters, e.g., Calvin, *Hebrews and 1 & 2 Peter*, 116; Hughes, *Hebrews*, 305; and Lane, *Hebrews 9–13*, 214. Aquinas adds the nuance that **worldly** implies this tabernacle was 'temporal and not perpetual' (*Hebrews*, 177). Owen adds that the 'efficacy extended only unto worldly things ... in opposition unto that which is heavenly' (*Hebrews*, 22:189).

96. The Greek is ἅγια. It is neuter plural and mechanically would be translated as 'holies' or 'holy places.' However, as most do here, I translate ἅγια as **Holy Place** in contrast to ἅγια ἁγίων as **Holy of Holies** in Hebrews 9:3. Elsewhere in Hebrews, ἅγια refers to the Holy of Holies (9:8, 12, 24, 25; 13:11).

97. One cubit equals approximately 1.5 feet or 0.46 meters. To determine the plan dimensions from the Exodus description is not clear-cut. For a detailed explanation how the 'frames' (panels) may fit together to produce the 30 by 10 plan, see Richard Elliott Friedman, 'Tabernacle,' *ABD*, 6:292–300. The plan dimensions of Solomon's temple are 60 by 20 cubits and 30 cubits high (1 Kgs. 6:2).

is commonly called the **Holy Place**. The second room was a 10-cubit cube and is commonly called the 'Holy of Holies.' There is a veil at the entrance and a veil separating the two rooms (Exod. 26:33).

The AH uses the term **first** to refer to the **Holy Place**. This was the first room one entered, and it also fits the typology related to the 'first' covenant (Heb. 9:8–9). He notes that the **Holy Place** contains the **lampstand**[98] (Exod. 25:31–40; 37:17–24) and the **table**[99] that has the twelve **breads**[100] upon it (Exod. 25:23–30; 37:10–16; Lev. 24:5–9). The word **presence** (πρόθεσις) is an approximation of the Hebrew idiom 'the bread of faces' that implies before God's face (e.g., Exod. 25:30; cf. Mark 2:26). Hence, **presence** implies God's presence. More fully, the expression **presence of breads** means the bread that is presented to God in and for his presence.

On the surface, there are a few oddities. The altar of incense is also in the **Holy Place** (Exod. 30:6; 40:26; Luke 1:11); however, it is not mentioned here. More on this below at Hebrews 9:4. The **lampstand** is pure gold (Exod. 25:31), and the **table** is overlaid with gold (Exod. 25:24). This creates another oddity because gold is mentioned in connection with the articles in the Holy of Holies and not here (Heb. 9:4). I have no answer to this except to say that more detail is given for articles in the Holy of Holies.

9:3–5a *and behind the second veil was a tabernacle called the Holy of Holies, having a golden censer and the ark of the covenant covered entirely with gold, in which was a golden jar having the manna, and Aaron's rod, the one that budded, and the tablets of the covenant, and above it were the cherubim of glory overshadowing the mercy seat;*

---

98. The **lampstand** (λυχνία) has seven lights on it and was placed on the southside. It is *menorah* (מנרה) in Hebrew and *candelabrum* in Latin (Exod. 25:31; 37:18). In Solomon's temple there were ten lampstands, five on the northside, and five, southside (1 Kgs. 7:49).

99. The **table** was two cubits long by one cubit wide by 1.5 cubits high. It was placed on the northside.

100. The KJV translates as 'shewbread.'

***

Excursus:
Translation of Θυμιατήριον as 'Censer' in Hebrews 9:4

My translation of **censer** (instrument to carry coals and incense that produces sweet smelling smoke[101]) as opposed to the 'altar of incense' is currently the minority view. Primarily, the earlier English Bible translations and many earlier commentators opt for 'censer';[102] however, modern translations and commentators favor 'altar of incense.'[103]

Before getting into the technicalities of whether **censer** or 'altar of incense' is the correct translation, I present a brief description of both. The altar for incense is one cubit squared by two cubits high and overlaid with gold. It has 'horns' on it resembling the horns on the large bronze altar where animals are sacrificed. Upon it incense is burned (Exod. 30:1–10; 37:25–29). The overwhelming-majority view, to which I also agree, is that this altar is in the Holy Place (more on this below). The details of the **censer** are less clear. It appears that a **censer** is a 'firepan', or a special type of firepan or bucket, in which incense is placed over coals. For the bronze altar, bronze firepans were made for the coals (Exod. 27:3; 38:3). Nothing is explicitly said in the Bible as to the making of censers related to the altar of incense. Twice daily, the priest would take hot coals from the bronze altar and combine them with incense in the **censer.** He then would place the **censer** upon the altar of

---

101. The English word 'censer' is a cognate of 'incense,' coming into English through French.

102. So, e.g., Wycliffe, Tyndale, Geneva Bible, KJV, Douay-Rheims, ERV, and NKJ. The Latin Vulgate has censer (*turibulum*), which explains the Wycliffe and Douay-Rheims translations. Commentators opting for censer include Aquinas, *Hebrews*, 179 (although again he was following the Vulgate); Owen, *Hebrews*, 22:198, 201; Brown, *Hebrews*, 380; and Hodge, *Hebrews*, 78.

103. So, e.g., ASV, RSV, NASB, NIV, ESV, CEB; Calvin, *Hebrews and 1 & 2 Peter*, 116; Moffatt, *Hebrews*, 113–14; Bruce, *Hebrews*, 200; Hughes, *Hebrews*, 310–12; Attridge, *Hebrews*, 234; Allen, *Hebrews*, 460; and Cockerill, *Hebrews*, 376.

incense (Exod. 30:8, 34–38; 40:27; m. Tamid 6:2). On the Day of Atonement, a special amount of incense was used in the **censer** and it was taken into the Holy of Holies to create a significant incense-cloud (Lev. 16:12–13; m. Yoma 5:1).

Why the importance of this translation issue? If one translates as 'altar of incense' and assumes the traditional view that this altar should be in the Holy Place, then the AH placed the altar of incense in the wrong room. There are multiple explanations for this surface-level discrepancy, some consistent with a high view of the accuracy of the Bible and some clearly not.[104] On the other hand, if one translates as **censer**, there are no factual discrepancies, but one presumably must explain why the altar of incense is not mentioned at all. This translation issue deserves an extended discussion since, at least partially, it touches upon the inspiration and inerrancy of the Bible.[105] Although, in the context of Hebrews 9, this translation issue does not have special importance as the placement of the **censer** or altar of incense does not affect the primary point—there were two rooms in the tabernacle.

First, a linguistic discussion: The Greek term in question is θυμιατήριον (*thymiatērion*) This is a clear cognate of the noun 'incense' (θυμίαμα) and the verb 'to offer incense' (θυμιάω). The suffix -τηριον normally refers to either the location where the implied action took place or the instrument for that action.[106] In this case, location and instrument nuances merge together so that the general meaning is incense-burner. Surveying Greco-Roman uses, LSJ gives 'censer,' 'vessel for fumigation,' and 'incense-burner' for *thymiatērion*.[107] As will be discussed

---

104. E.g., Lindars flatly calls the placement of the altar of incense a 'mistake' (*The Theology of the Letter of Hebrews*, 86).

105. Ellingworth, who does not hold to a traditional inerrancy view, rightly states, 'Ways of explaining the discrepancy tend to reflect theological views concerning how far the inspiration of scripture extends to inerrancy about such factual details' (*Hebrews*, 426).

106. Moulton and Howard, *Accidence and Word-Formation*, 340–44; and Robertson, *A Grammar of the Greek New Testament*, 154.

107. LSJ, 809; LSJ/Supplement, 153.

below, in the context of the Jewish tabernacle or temple, it clearly could refer to the altar of incense (e.g., Philo, *Who is the Heir?* 226), although, with no context, 'censer' would be the default translation.[108]

Within the Bible, the incense-burning altar is referred to as the 'altar of incense'[109] or the 'golden altar'[110] (golden is used to distinguish it from the bronze altar). Nowhere in the Bible is it referred to by *thymiatērion*; however, the altar of incense is referred to by *thymiatērion* in Philo and Josephus. Philo uses *thymiatērion* six times to refer to the altar of incense, [111] and one use is questionable.[112] Josephus uses *thymiatērion* to refer to the altar of incense five times[113] and censer(s) five times.[114]

Within the LXX, θυμιατήριον is only used three times and clearly refers to a censer, although not the censer used with the altar of incense.[115] In the NT, *thymiatērion* is only used here in Hebrews 9:4. In the LXX, 'censer' is more commonly translated by πυρεῖον ('firepan'), although implying in context a firepan with coals and incense. A golden censer connected to an altar is referenced in Revelation 8:3 and 8:5, which is related to the seventh seal. The Greek here for 'censer' is λιβανωτός, which can also be translated simply as 'frankincense' (e.g., 1 Chr. 9:29) and is a cognate of the more common word for frankincense,

---

108. BDAG indicates 'censer' is the 'usual' translation, although 'altar of incense' is attested, 'esp. of the incense altar in the Jewish temple,' (p. 461).

109. Exod. 30:27; 31:8; 35:15; 1 Chr. 6:49; 28:18; 2 Chr. 26:16, 19; Luke 1:11; cf. Rev. 8:3. The translation from the original languages is straight-forward, מזבח הקטרת, τὸ θυσιαστήριον τοῦ θυμιάματος.

110. Exod. 39:38; 40:5, 26; Num. 11:2; 1 Kgs. 7:48; 2 Chr. 4:19; cf. Rev 8:3, 5. The translation from the original languages is straight-forward, מזבח הזהב, τὸ θυσιαστήριον τὸ χρυσοῦν.

111. Philo, *Who is the Heir?* 226, 227; *On the Life of Moses* 2.94, 101, 105, 146.

112. Philo, *On the Special Laws* 1.231: τὰ τοῦ θυμιατηρίου ('things of the altar of incense' or 'things related the censer'). Either way, the plural 'things' creates uncertainty for the translation.

113. Josephus, *Jewish Antiquities* 3.147, 193, 198; *Jewish War* 5.216, 218.

114. Josephus, *Jewish Antiquities* 4.32, 54, 57; 8.92; *Jewish War* 1.152. Several of these clearly refer to the censers related to the altar of incense.

115. 2 Chr. 26:19; Ezek. 8:11; 4 Macc. 7:11.

λίβανος (e.g., Exod. 30:34; Matt. 2:11; Rev. 18:13).[116]

In sum of the linguistic discussion: *Thymiatērion* etymologically refers to a place or instrument by which one burns incense, that is, an incense-burner. In Greco-Roman usage, it refers to a censer. In the LXX, it never refers to the altar of incense and occasionally refers to a censer, but never the ones used with the altar of incense.[117] In both Philo and Josephus, *thymiatērion* does refer to the altar of incense; and in Josephus, it also refers to censers, including ones used with the altar of incense. Hebrews 9:4 is the only use of *thymiatērion* in the NT.[118] Conclusion is that on the surface both translations are defensible. Although, because the AH often uses LXX technical terms, the default position with no other considerations would be to translate as **censer**.

Now to justify *thymiatērion* meaning **censer** beyond the linguistic argument: The primary argument is, given the emphasis on the Day of Atonement (Heb. 9:7, 12), that it is factually true that on the Day of Atonement a **censer** is taken into the Holy of Holies (Lev. 16:12–13; m. Yoma 4:4; 5:1; t. Kippurim/Yoma 2:14; b. Yoma 52b–53b). Conversely, it is not factually true (to most) that the altar of incense is in the Holy of Holies.

One counter argument is that the biblical texts are clear that the altar of incense is overlaid with gold, but nothing is said of a *golden* **censer**.[119] In response, first I note that this argument may prove too much. Hebrews 9:4 clearly notes that **ark is covered entirely with gold** (i.e., it is wood overlaid with gold), but it says that the *thymiatērion* is **golden**, which

---

116. LSJ, 1047.

117. Some manuscripts indicate that the later Theodotion and Symmachus Greek translations have θυμιατήριον in Exod. 30:1 for 'an altar to burn incense.' See Göttingen LXX edition, p. 338. Thanks to my colleague William A. Ross for double checking me on this.

118. A few NT manuscript witnesses move θυμιατήριον to Heb. 9:2 to put it in the Holy Place. Apparently θυμιατήριον is interpreted as 'altar of incense' as this would eliminate the altar being in the wrong room (Metzger, *TCGNT*², 598).

119. So, e.g., Hughes, *Hebrews*, 311; and Lane, *Hebrews 9–13*, 215.

strongly implies it is solid gold, which the altar of incense is not (Exod. 30:1–3).[120] Further, since the other smaller utensils in the tabernacle are all solid gold (e.g., Exod. 25:29, 36) and the firepans for the bronze altar are solid bronze (Exod. 27:3), one would expect the **censer** for the altar of incense, at least the one used on the Day of Atonement, to be solid gold. Josephus references golden censers in connection with both Moses' tabernacle and Herod's temple.[121] Finally, the symbolism in Revelation includes a 'golden censer' (8:3; cf. 8:5; 9:13) and a 'golden bowls of incense' (5:8).

The second counter argument is that *thymiatērion* must refer to the altar of incense because otherwise the AH forgot to mention a major piece of furniture in the Holy Place and instead mentioned a censer that is not explicitly included in Exodus.[122] In response, first note that Hebrews 9:5b is a strong hint that not all items in the tabernacle are discussed, e.g., no discussion of utensils on the table except to mention the bread (Exod. 25:29).[123] Possibly, the altar of incense is not mentioned by the AH because of its intimate connection with the **censer** on the Day of Atonement. The altar of incense is taking on a secondary role as the means of incense on this one day, or better, the **censer** is taking the place of the altar because the altar cannot be moved into the Holy of Holies (Lev. 16:12–13).[124] Finally, again, this argument may

---

120. Although, as mentioned above, the altar of incense is sometimes termed the 'golden altar'; however, in this context, one would expect a parallel explanation with the **ark** of overlaid gold if the AH were referring to the altar of incense.

121. Josephus, *Jewish Antiquities* 8.92; *Jewish War* 1.152.

122. So, e.g., Hughes, *Hebrews*, 312; Bruce, *Hebrews*, 200; Mitchell, *Hebrews*, 174; and Cockerill, *Hebrews*, 376. Of course, censers are mentioned in Leviticus (e.g., Lev. 16:12) and Numbers (e.g., Num. 16:17).

123. Josephus also gives a summary that does not include all items. 'Now Moses commanded them to make use of all the utensils which were necessary to the structure of the tabernacle, for covering the tabernacle itself, the candlestick, and the altar of incense, and the other vessels, that they might not be at all hurt when they journeyed' (*Jewish Antiquities* 3.193). Note that the table is not mentioned.

124. Although, blood is sprinkled on the altar of incense on the Day of

prove too much. If the altar of incense is so obvious that it must be included, this heightens the discrepancy of its being in the wrong room.

For those who favor the 'altar of incense' translation, what rationales are offered to explain its being included within the Holy of Holies? There are two related explanations, of which I consider the first one plausible and the second one not. Both explanations begin well by noting that the altar of incense and the ark of the covenant have a close association. In the tabernacle, there is a close association spatially as the altar of incense is put 'before' the ark, although the curtain separates them (Exod. 30:6; 40:5, 26; cf. 1 Kgs. 6:20, 22). On the Day of Atonement, there is another connection in that blood is sprinkled on both the altar of incense and the ark (Exod. 30:6; Lev. 16:17).

First explanation favoring 'altar of incense':[125] This view begins by assuming that the AH clearly understood that the altar of incense and the ark were in different sections of the tabernacle, that is, the altar and the ark were close to each other but separated by the veil. This is confirmed by the priests offering twice daily incense upon the altar (Exod. 30:7–8; Luke 1:8–10), which must be in the Holy Place because only the high priest may enter the Holy of Holies once a year. Given the close association both spatially and due to the blood, the AH 'does not "relocate" this altar within the inner sanctuary but closely associates it with the Most Holy Place in accord with it function.'[126] Again, I see this explanation as plausible; although of course, I prefer to simply translate as **censer**.

Atonement (Exod. 30:10).

125. For extended discussions agreeing with this view, see Bruce, *Hebrews*, 200–2; Hughes, *Hebrews*, 310–13; and Cockerill, *Hebrews*, 375–77.

126. Cockerill, *Hebrews*, 377. Cockerill also appeals to **having** (Heb. 9:4) as implying that location is not implied (p. 377). Hughes, who agrees with Cockerill's overall view, dismisses this as part of the solution (*Hebrews*, 313n53).

Second explanation favoring 'altar of incense':[127] This view first assumes that historically the altar of incense and the ark were separated by the veil. However, despite this, it asserts that the AH confused the close association of the altar of incense and the ark in the biblical material to mean that they were both in the Holy of Holies and/or he wrongly followed actual Jewish traditions that had both in the Holy of Holies.[128] Johnson has a typical view, 'The language of the LXX is sufficiently vague to allow a reader—such as the AH—to suppose that it [altar of incense] was placed near the ark of the covenant within the second tent [Holy of Holies].'[129] Given the reality of divine inspiration and the very low probability that someone in the first century AD wrongly thought the altar of incense was/is in the Holy of Holies, this view is not plausible.

***

Following his description of the Holy Place (**and**), the AH now describes the **Holy of Holies**. The **second veil** refers to the curtain/veil that separates the Holy Place from the **Holy of Holies** (cf. Matt. 27:51). It is the **second** in the sense that the first veil is the curtain at the entrance to the Holy Place (Exod. 26:33). The **second** terminology recalls 'first' in reference to the first section of the tabernacle. Here **tabernacle** is used in the sense of the *second section* of the **tabernacle**.

The participle **having** refers to two items in the **Holy of Holies**: (1) **the golden censer** and (2) **the ark of the covenant**. The remainder of the description refers to the **ark of the covenant** and associated items with the **ark**.

---

127. For extended discussions agreeing with this view, see Moffatt, *Hebrews*, 113–15; Lane, *Hebrews 9–13*, 215, 220; Ellingworth, *Hebrews*, 425–28; and Attridge, *Hebrews*, 234–38.

128. The best evidence for the altar and ark both being in the Holy of Holies is quite tenuous. It hangs upon 2 Baruch 6:7, which itself is a translation problem between 'censer' and 'altar of incense.' The Rabbinic tradition clearly has the altar and ark separated into the two rooms (e.g., m. Menahot 11:7; m. Tamid 1:4, 3:1, 6, 9; 6:1–3), as does Josephus (e.g., *Jewish Antiquities* 3.147) and Philo (e.g., *Life of Moses* 2.101).

129. Johnson, *Hebrews*, 220.

For the **golden censer**, see the above excursus. The **ark**[130] **of the covenant** is a rectangular box that is two and one half by one and one half cubits in plan and one and one half cubits high and made of acacia wood **covered entirely with gold** (Exod. 25:10–11; 37:1–2; Deut. 10:3).[131] The **ark** has a lid made of pure gold that matches the plan dimensions and is called the **mercy seat**[132] (Exod. 25:17; 37:6). As part of the lid and fashioned as one piece with it are two pure gold **cherubim of glory** set at each end of the lid facing each other with their wings spread out toward each other **overshadowing the mercy-seat** (Exod. 25:18–20; 37:7–9). The **ark** is a symbol of God's special presence (e.g., Exod. 25:22; 30:6, Judg. 20:27; 1 Sam. 4:4; Pss. 80:1; 99:1; 132:8; Isa. 37:16; cf. Jer. 3:16–17; Rev. 11:19). The **cherubim** are winged angelic beings that are connected with God's **glory** due to their association with the **ark** (e.g., 1 Sam. 4:4, 21; Ezek. 10:19; 11:22; cf. Gen. 3:24; Ezek. 28:14).[133] Although the AH is in the midst of making an argument as to the inferiority of the Mosaic covenant, note the implied high view he has of the **ark** and its associated items.

Associated with the **ark** are **a golden**[134] **jar having the manna** (Exod. 16:33–34; cf. Rev. 2:17)**, and Aaron's rod, the**

---

130. In Latin Vulgate, *arca*.

131. In the OT, the **ark of the covenant** is referred to with a variety of names. The most common are 'ark of the covenant of the Lord' (e.g., Num. 10:33), 'ark of the covenant' (e.g., Josh. 3:8), 'ark of the testimony' (e.g., Exod. 25:22), and 'ark of God' (e.g., 1 Sam. 3:3).

132. In Hebrew, it is termed כפרת. This is a clear cognate of the Hebrew verb כפר, which has the meanings of 'to cover' (qal) and 'to atone' (piel) (*HALOT*, 493–95). The LXX and Hebrews 9:5 use ἱλαστήριον, which has a variety of cognates related to 'propitiation'/'expiation'/'atonement'/'mercy' (see Silva, ed., *NIDNTTE*, 2:531–41).

133. In Solomon's temple within the Holy of Holies were two large cherubim statues overlooking the **ark**. Each was ten cubits high with a wing span of ten cubits and made with olive wood overlaid with gold (1 Kgs. 6:23–28).

134. The OT does not explicitly say that the **jar** was **golden** (pure gold), but given that all the instruments in the tabernacle are either pure gold or overlaid with gold, this is a reasonable assumption. Philo also has a 'golden jar' (*On the Preliminary Studies* 100). The Rabbinic Mekilta Vayassa 6 explicitly refers to an earthen jar related to Exod. 16:33 and predicts that at the restoration of Israel, Elijah will bring with him that jar of manna.

one that budded (Num. 17:8–10; cf. 20:8–11), **and the tablets**[135] **of the covenant** (Exod. 25:16, 21; 40:20; Deut. 10:5; 1 Kgs. 8:9; 2 Chr. 5:10).[136] On the surface, it appears that the AH places the three items inside the **ark**, although the preposition **in** (ἐν) has a broad enough semantic range to include both inside and adjacent to the **ark**[137] It is clear in the Mosaic biblical material that the **jar** and the **rod** are in the Holy of Holies with the **ark**, but it is not clear whether they are inside or adjacent to the **ark**. Later in redemptive history at the dedication of Solomon's temple, it is clear that only the **tablets** are in the **ark** (1 Kgs. 8:9 // 2 Chr. 5:10). (The **jar** and the **rod** are not mentioned beyond the Mosaic biblical material.) There are two plausible options to explain this.[138] (1) The **jar** and the **rod** were initially inside the **ark**, but then taken out and lost either when the Philistines captured it (1 Sam. 4:11–6:21), or less likely, while at Abinadab's house (1 Sam. 7:1–3).[139] (2) The **jar** and the **rod** were initially adjacent to the **ark**, but the broad semantic range of ἐν accommodates this.[140] I prefer option one.

---

135. These two **tablets** are the ones made by Moses with the ten commandments written upon them by God. Moses had broken the previous tablets because of the golden calf incident (Exod. 34:1–7, 28; Deut. 10:1–4). The previous tablets had been both made by God and written upon by God (Exod. 24:12; 31:18; 32:15–16; Deut. 4:13).

136. Also associated with the **ark** but not mentioned here is Moses' 'book of the law' (Deut. 31:26).

137. BDAG lists as one option 'within the range of, at, near' (p. 326 [1.c]).

138. Bruce says both are legitimate. It is only speculative to assume that the **jar** and **rod** were either inside or adjacent to the **ark** (*Hebrews*, 203–4). Allen agrees here with Bruce (*Hebrews*, 461–2). Of course, some commentators simply believe the OT never portrayed the **jar** and the **rod** as being inside the **ark**, but the AH did, i.e., the AH is wrong on this detail (e.g., Moffatt, *Hebrews*, 115).

139. So Hughes, *Hebrews*, 315. Pseudo-Philo recounts the apocryphal story of Kenaz putting the twelve tribal stones in the ark with the tablets (LAB 26:9–12). Another OT pseudepigraphic author recounts that Jeremiah hid the 'ark of the law and the things in it' before the temple was captured (*Lives of the Prophets* 2:11).

140. So Calvin, *Hebrews and 1 & 2 Peter*, 116; and Owen, *Hebrews*, 22:206.

9:5b *concerning which it is not now [time] to speak in detail.*[141]

Similar to Hebrews 11:32 (cf. Heb. 6:3), the AH notes time and/or length constraints in the writing of his letter, or maybe, the constraint is due to the disruption in the flow of his argument.

Which refers back to all the items in both rooms in the tabernacle. **In detail** certainly refers to not mentioning all of the specifics of the tabernacle furniture and appurtenances (e.g., various utensils on the table, the cherubim likenesses woven into the second veil, etc.). In addition, **in detail** most likely refers to the typological implications of various items in the tabernacle. That is, the upcoming arguments in Hebrews 9–10 will make typological implications from the tabernacle and the activity of the priests, but there are many additional ones that could have been made.

9:6–7 *And thus these things having been prepared,*[142] *on the one hand,*[143] *priests go into the first [section of the] tabernacle continually performing the worship [duties]; but on the other, only the high priest [goes] into the second [section] once per year,*[144] *not without blood*[145] *that he offers for himself and the ignorance of the people;*

The AH now moves from the tabernacle and appurtenances (**and thus these things being prepared**) to the 'regulations of worship' (Heb. 9:1) performed by the **priests** and the **high priest**. He is driving home the difference between the Holy Place (**first**) and the Holy of Holies (**second**).

Multiple **priests** go into the Holy Place (**first section of the tabernacle**). Furthermore, they do this **continually**.

---

141. The Greek for **in detail** is κατὰ μέρος, mechanically 'according part.' It is being used distributively, 'according to *each* part', so also Zerwick and Grosvenor, *A Grammatical Analysis of the Greek New Testament*, 2:672.

142. The opening participial phrase is a genitive absolute construction.

143. Reflecting the μέν ... δέ of Hebrews 9:6–7.

144. The Greek is ἅπαξ τοῦ ἐνιαυτοῦ ('once of year'); ἐνιαυτοῦ is a genitive of time used distributively. See Turner, *Syntax*, 235.

145. **Not without blood** is a double-negative understatement for rhetorical effect (literary term, 'litotes').

The **continually** functions of **priests** *in the Holy Place* are primarily to (1) twice-daily burn incense on the altar of incense (Exod. 30:7–8); (2) twice-daily tend to the lampstand (Exod. 27:20–21; Lev. 24:1–4); and (3) every Sabbath change the twelve breads on the table (Exod. 25:30; Lev. 24:5–9). (In addition, just outside of the Holy Place, the **priests** offer two lambs daily for the burnt offering [Exod. 29:38–42].)

Contrasted with the activity in the Holy Place, **only the high priest goes into the second section once per year**.[146] On the Day of Atonement (Lev. 16), the **high priest** brings the censer of incense into the Holy of Holies and sprinkles blood on the mercy seat of the ark. He does this twice, first for **himself** and his family (Lev. 16:6, 11) and then for **the people** (Lev. 16:15). The 'scapegoat' (Azazel) is also part of the ceremony, but the AH does not mention it here (Lev. 16:20–22).

As will be seen in the next verses, the main point is the restricted access to the Holy of Holies (cf. parallels of Heb. 9:7 to 9:11–12 and 9:25). **Priests** are in the Holy Place **continually**, but **only the high priest** is in the Holy of Holies **once per year**. The Holy of Holies is restricted both as to who may enter and the number of times per year. There is an additional restriction, **not without blood**. Although not needed for his argument, this additional restriction anticipates typological connections with Christ (Heb. 9:12, 22, 25: 10:4; 13:20).

Interestingly, the AH does *not* say that the **high priest** *sprinkled* the **blood**, which would be expected, but that it was *offer[ed]* (προσφέρω). Normally, animals that are killed are *offered*, and blood is *sprinkled*. Apparently, the AH uses **offers** to connect it to Christ's death on the cross (Heb. 9:25, 28; 10:12; cf. 12:24). Although the Levitical **high priest** literally sprinkled the blood on the mercy seat, that was typological of Christ's offering himself to die on the cross.[147]

---

146. **Once per year** means one *day* per year as the **high priest** enters the Holy of Holies twice on the same day as part of the Day of Atonement ceremony (Lev. 16:11–15).

147. See excellent discussion in Norman. H. Young, 'The Gospel According to Hebrews 9,' *NTS* 27 (1981): 198–210, esp. 207–9. Young is especially zealous to counteract the view that Christ's atoning sacrifice was

The AH terms the sins of **the people** as **ignorances**[148] (ἀγνόημα; cf. cognate ἀγνοέω in Heb. 5:2). As part of the Levitical sin offering (Lev. 4:2, 13) and guilt offering (Lev. 5:14, 17–18), there is a category of sins that are committed unintentionally (שגגה, LXX mostly ἀκούσιος).[149] However, for the Day of Atonement, all categories and types of sins are forgiven (Lev. 16:21). Clearly, here **ignorances** is used in a broader sense in that all sins, unintentional and intentional, include some level of morally culpable ignorance.[150] The use of ἀγνόημα and its cognate verb (ἀγνοέω) in the LXX often confirms this broad morally-culpable nuance related to ignorance (e.g., Num. 12:11; 1 Sam. 14:24; 2 Chr. 16:9; Hos. 4:15; Tob. 3:3; Sir. 23:2; 51:19; 1 Macc. 13:39; cf. 1 Tim. 1:13; Heb. 5:2).

9:8–10 *[by] this the Holy Spirit signifies*[151] *[that] the way into*[152] *the Holy of Holies [was] not yet manifested while the first [section of the] tabernacle had standing,*[153] *which [is] a parable for the time having*

---

not on the cross but occurred only in heaven. Although Young was writing before Moffitt, Moffitt is currently the most influential proponent of the general view that Young is countering (Moffitt, *Atonement and the Logic of Resurrection in the Epistle to the Hebrews* [2011]).

148. The KJV translates as 'errors'; ESV as 'unintentional sins;' CEB as 'sins ... committed in ignorance.' All are adequate translations.

149. Gordon J. Wenham notes that sin and guilt offerings each distinguish two categories of sin. His terms for them are as follows: for the sin offering between 'inadvertent sin' (Lev. 4:1–35) and 'sins of omission' (Lev. 5:1–13); and for the guilt offering, between 'inadvertent sin' (Lev. 5:14–19) and 'deliberate sin' (Lev. 6:1–7) (*The Book of Leviticus,* NICOT [Grand Rapids: Eerdmans, 1979], 87). Num. 15:27–30 distinguishes between unintentional sins and the extremely heinous sins of the 'high hand.' Concerning a broader discussion of the sin of ignorance, see G. C. Berkouwer, *Sin,* Studies in Dogmatics (Grand Rapids: Eerdmans, 1971), 290–94.

150. So also Calvin, *Hebrews and 1 & 2 Peter,* 117; Owen, *Hebrews,* 22:233; Brown, *Hebrews,* 384; Moffatt, *Hebrews,* 117; and Cockerill, *Hebrews,* 380 n. 43. Ellingworth disagrees. He sees **ignorances** being used in a limited sense; hence, there is a 'discrepancy' relative to the Day of Atonement (*Hebrews,* 435–36).

151. The participial phrase **by this the Holy Spirit signifying** is a genitive absolute construction.

152. In the expression **way into the Holy of Holies**, **Holy of Holies** is taken as an objective genitive or 'genitive of direction,' which is common with the head noun **way** (BDF §166).

153. The participial phrase **while the first section of the tabernacle had**

been present, according which gifts and sacrifices were being offered [that] were not able to perfect the worshiper according to conscience, [but to perfect] only with foods and drinks and differing baptisms regulations of flesh being imposed until the time of reformation.

The Greek syntax of Hebrews 9:8–10 is notoriously difficult as can be seen by the variations in the standard translations. The main translation issue is whether τῶν ἁγίων ('of the holies') should be **Holy of Holies** (my view) or the less specific 'holy places' implying either the entire earthly tabernacle or the heavenly tabernacle. This then relates to the understanding of **first**. Is **first** being used spatially to refer to the **first section of the** (earthly) **tabernacle** (my view[154]), or is **first** being used temporally to refer to the *entire* earthly tabernacle?[155]

In either case, the ultimate interpretation is not that much different. Both translations see (1) either the earthly Holy Place (**first section**, my view) or the entire earthly tabernacle (**first**) as representative of the first covenant and (2a) either the earthly **Holy of Holies** (my view) or the entire earthly tabernacle ('holy places') as typological of the heavenly tabernacle and the second covenant or (2b) 'holy places' is a direct reference to the heavenly tabernacle and the second covenant. That is, all options agree that there is an earthly/heavenly tabernacle distinction that matches with the first/second covenant distinction. Also see discussion above at the beginning of this section (First Covenant Tabernacle).

For the AH, the very limited access to the *earthly* **Holy of Holies** is an indication that God had not yet **manifested**/revealed and Christ had not yet accomplished the true nature of the atoning work to gain access to the *heavenly* **Holy of Holies**. Here, the earthly **Holy of Holies** is typological (**parable**[156]) of the heavenly tabernacle. The revelation would

---

standing is a genitive absolute construction.

154. So also Aquinas, *Hebrews*, 182–83; Brown, *Hebrews*, 385–86; Lane, *Hebrews 9–14*, 216, 223; Attridge, *Hebrews*, 240; Cockerill, *Hebrews*, 381; and Young, 'The Gospel According to Hebrews 9,' 198.

155. So Owen, *Hebrews*, 22:245; Spicq, *Hébreux*, 2:253–54; Bruce, *Hebrews*, 208–9; and Johnson, *Hebrews*, 225.

156. I translated παραβολή with the English cognate. Obviously, the AH

not be clear as long as the earthly **first section of the tabernacle had standing**. I take **had standing**, not as physical existence, but as a quasi-legal term to mean as long as God intended the tabernacle/temple worship regulations to be in force.[157] The first **which** refers back to the **first section of the tabernacle** (Holy Place).[158] I take **the time having been present** to mean while the Holy Place **had standing**, which is paralleled by **being imposed until the time of reformation**.

The various ceremonies connected to the tabernacle (and temple) that included **gifts, sacrifices, foods, drinks,** and **baptisms** could not **perfect** the **conscience**, but rather, they were only related to the **flesh**. I take the distinction between **conscience** and **flesh** to be true inward realities effected from a real atonement compared to outward-only ceremonies (cf. Heb. 9:13–14). The outward-only ceremonies may or may not be indicative of an inward reality.[159] Brown well captures the difference, '[The ceremonies] cleansed body from ceremonial defilement but not the soul from moral guilt.'[160]

Baptisms (βαπτισμός) or 'washings' within the Mosaic ceremonies include the full range of submerging, dipping, and sprinkling (e.g., Exod. 29:4; Lev. 15:8, 16; Num. 8:7; cf. Heb. 6:2).[161]

By this in the phrase **by this the Holy Spirit signifies** refers to the arrangement of the Mosaic tabernacle and the priestly functions. Given that the AH explicitly connects the OT text

---

is using **parable** more broadly than the modern usage. See similar use of παραβολή in Heb. 11:19.

157. So also Owen, *Hebrews* 22:242; Lane, *Hebrews 9–13*, 216; and Attridge, *Hebrews*, 240. For semantic range of **standing** (στάσις), see BDAG, 940.

158. See Lane for a refutation of the view that **which** looks forward to **parable** (*Hebrews 9 -13*, 223–24).

159. I do not take **flesh** to be negative per se, as is often in Paul, but to simply refer to the outward aspect of the body or material things.

160. Brown, *Hebrews*, 389.

161. Seeing a broad semantic range of **baptisms** as to mode of the washings, the Westminster divines referenced Hebrews 9:10 regarding Christian baptism, along with Hebrews 9:19–22. 'Dipping the persons into the water is not necessary; but baptism is rightly administered by pouring or sprinkling water upon the person' (WCF 28.3).

to the Holy Spirit's speaking in Hebrews 3:7 and 10:15–17, it is safe to assume that the expression **the Holy Spirit signifies** refers to an OT text also.[162] In Hebrews 9:1–7, the AH is clearly referring to Leviticus 16 and the Day of Atonement ceremony. These ceremonial specifics in Leviticus are presented as a direct quote of what the 'Lord (Yahweh) said to Moses' (Lev. 16:2). Many Reformers used these two texts (Lev. 16:2 and Heb. 9:8) with their relationship of the 'Lord' and the **Holy Spirit** to show the divinity of the **Holy Spirit**.[163]

Reflections

Christians through the centuries have been fascinated by the physical tabernacle structure, its furniture and appurtenances, the associated ceremonies, and the clothes worn by the priests and high priest. Why? First of all, these are very interesting in their own right. The dimensions, the materials, the colors, the locations of the furniture, the imagined smells, and the clothes connected to this ancient worship site make an aesthetic impact and spark our intellectual curiosity.

But more than this, Christians know that God so designed the tabernacle to teach both OT and NT saints about himself and our salvation, with a special focus on the person and work of Christ. As the AH says in reference to the tabernacle, 'the Holy Spirit signifies' (Heb. 9:8). Finally, seeing Christ in the tabernacle is a confirmation and deepening of our faith in Christ. The tabernacle is only a shadow, but it is a shadow that deepens our trust in the reality.

For a Christian, the typological significance of Christ related to the tabernacle is a joy to contemplate. The Bible invites us to do this. As we think through the typological

---

162. Although primarily referring to the accomplished inspiration when first written, **signifies** also shows that the **Holy Spirit** is active in anyone's true understanding of the original text.

163. So, e.g., Mastricht, *Theoretical-Practical Theology*, 2:573. For a discussion of these two texts and a variety of similar other combination texts as used by the Reformers to prove the divinity of the Holy Spirit, see Muller, *Post-Reformation Reformed Dogmatics*, 4:357–59.

significances, we try to take the whole Bible into account, but we also realize that there are levels of exegetical certainty for our interpretation of various aspects of the tabernacle and that some aspects may have no typological significance.

In Thomas Aquinas' commentary, he notes that the AH did not have time to make all the typological connections (Heb. 9:5). Thus Aquinas, who apparently had plenty of time (!), took the opportunity to make several connections for his reader, of which most of his connections are to Christ.[164] The lampstand and its light is Christ, as he is the 'light of the world' (John 8:12). That Christ is present in both the OT and NT is shown by the three branches on each side of the lampstand. The table is related to refreshment; hence, the twelve breads are the refreshing doctrine of Christ brought by the twelve apostles. The tablets of the ten commandments are Christ's wisdom. The rod is his eternal priesthood or power. The manna is the sweetness of grace given by Christ. The mercy seat is Christ's propitiation (1 John 2:2).

No, I do not agree with all of these connections.[165] However, I do agree with Aquinas' effort to see Christ because it is a worthwhile task. May the reader and I be encouraged and have joy in seeing Christ in the tabernacle, even if we are not sure of every connection.

The Blood of Christ (9:11–14)

Hebrews 9:11–14 breaks up nicely into two sentences, 11–12 and 13–14. Hebrews 9:12 and 9:14 are somewhat parallel verses that proclaim Christ's priestly offering of his own atoning blood/death and the resulting benefits he/it has for us. 'The blood of Christ,' which in fact was 'his own blood,' procured 'eternal redemption' and 'purifi[ed] our conscience

---

164. Aquinas, *Hebrews*, 178–80.

165. For a Reformed and more biblically justified treatment of the typology of the tabernacle, see Owen, *Hebrews*, 213–22; Fairbairn, *The Typology of Scripture*, 2:178–344; and Vern S. Poythress, *The Shadow of Christ in the Law of Moses* (Phillipsburg: P&R, 1991), 9–40.

from dead works to serve the living God.' These two verses have been quoted and alluded to by Christians down through the centuries. They are especially prominent in various creeds of the church.[166] As WLC 57 succinctly puts it, '*Christ*, by his mediation, *hath procured redemption*, with all other benefits of the covenant of grace' (with references to Heb. 9:12 and 2 Cor. 1:20, emphasis mine).

Up to this point in Hebrews, not much has been said explicitly about Christ's sacrifice (although Heb. 1:3; 7:27). The previous section, Hebrews 9:1–10, emphasizes the earthly tabernacle and associated priestly functions, with 9:7 anticipating Christ's sacrifice in its description of the Day of Atonement. Starting with Hebrews 9:11,[167] however, and continuing through 10:18, the related themes of blood, sacrifice, offering, and covenant are emphasized.

Allow me a few comments on a minority view concerning Christ's atoning sacrifice that is disturbingly gaining influence. As has been discussed several times in this commentary, some scholars see Christ's priesthood as beginning only upon his resurrection/ascension.[168] A related corollary is that Christ's death on earth was not Christ's offering, but Christ offered himself only in heaven. That is, the death of Christ on the cross is *not* an atoning sacrifice or offering. This view is now strongly associated with David M. Moffitt.[169] There are also 'tweener' views—Christ's death on earth was part of the

---

166. E.g., Heidelberg Catechism 46, 80; Belgic Confession 21, 34; WCF 8.7, 19.3; WSC 25; WLC 34, 38, 44, 55, 57; First Confession of Basel 4 (*Reformed Confession of the 16th and 17th Centuries*, 1:289); Bohemian Confession 17 (*Reformed Confession of the 16th and 17th Centuries*, 3:380); French Confession 23; *Thirty-nine Articles* 31; Council of Trent, Doctrine of the Sacrifice of the Mass 1; Catechism of the Catholic Church §§1085, 2100.

167. Vanhoye sees Hebrews 9:11 as the dead center of the entire outline structure of Hebrews (*Structure and Message of the Epistle of Hebrews*, 40a-b). This is going too far for me.

168. See my rebuttal of this view in the Reflections section following Hebrews 5:1–10.

169. Moffitt, *Atonement and the Logic of Resurrection in the Epistle to the Hebrews*, 42–43, 216–18, 220–30.

offering, but it was not finalized until also offered in heaven.[170]

My view is the traditional one—Christ's death on the cross was the sacrifice/offering resulting in the finalization of his priestly atoning/redemptive work. Following that, Christ's priestly work continues in heaven, but in heaven, it is his work of intercession that applies his completed atoning work. This is the standard distinction concerning Christ's redemption between 'accomplished and applied' or 'purchased and applied.'[171]

In addition to my exegetical arguments below and throughout this commentary, my broad-based arguments against the above views include: (1) The whole sweep of biblical revelation outside of Hebrews views Christ's death as the pinnacle and ending of Christ's atoning work (e.g., Isa. 53; John 19:30; Rom. 3:25; 1 Pet. 1:19; 1 John 3:16). With God as the author of Scripture, one would expect Hebrews to be compatible. (2) Related to the first and no matter one's assumed date of Hebrews, the AH and his first-century readers would have been surely aware of the existing Christian tradition concerning the sacrificial death of Christ. (3) The NT writers, including the AH, saw Christ as the typological fulfillment of a variety of the OT sacrificial ceremonies (e.g., Day of Atonement, Passover, Water of Impurity [Num. 19]). Add to this the complication that Christ is both priest and victim and has both a divine and a human nature. And finally, the earthly tabernacle is typological of both redemptive-historical and eternal/vertical/heavenly realities. Hence, not every detail of

---

170. For a useful summary of many options upon a wide continuum since 1950, see Jamieson, 'When and Where Did Jesus Offer Himself? A Taxonomy of Recent Scholarship on Hebrews,' esp. the chart on 343. Jamieson concludes that the traditional view is still the 'most popular contemporary position' (p. 345).

171. See the very influential book by John Murray, *Redemption Accomplished and Applied* (Grand Rapids: Eerdmans, 1955). The Westminster Standards use 'purchased' and 'applied' (WCF 8.5, 8.8, 20.1, 20.4, WSC 29, WLC 59).

every ceremony could woodenly connect to Christ or connect in the exact same way. Therefore, it is flawed to use the Day of Atonement ceremony in a wooden way.[172] (4) To argue in verse after verse in Hebrews that Christ's *blood* does not mean his *sacrificial* death (or only part of his sacrifice) is exegetically odd and goes against, again, first-century Christian traditions that connect Christ's blood to his sacrificial atoning death (Acts 20:28; Rom. 3:25; 5:9; Col. 1:20; 1 John 1:7; Rev. 1:5).[173]

9:11–12 *But Christ, [after] having come about [as] high priest of the good [things] having come,*[174] *by virtue of a greater and more perfect tabernacle, not hand-made, that is, not of this creation, not by virtue of [the] blood of goats and calves but by virtue of his own blood, entered once*[175] *into the Holy of Holies [after] having obtained eternal redemption.*

Grammatically, the main structure of this complicated sentence is **Christ ... entered once into the Holy of Holies after having obtained eternal redemption**. As in Hebrews 9:7, here **Holy of Holies** is referring to the heavenly reality with the emphasis on God's presence.[176] Thus, **Christ entered** the heavenly reality at his ascension. This ascension occurred

---

172. Bruce well remarks, 'There have been expositors who, pressing the analogy of the Day of Atonement beyond the limits observed by [the AH], have argued that the expiatory work of Christ was not completed on the cross ... but while it was necessary under the old covenant for the sacrificial blood first to be shed in the court and then to be brought into the holy of holies, no such division of our Lord's sacrifice into two phases is envisaged under the new covenant' (*Hebrews*, 213–14).

173. Moffitt argues that 'blood' denotes, not death, but 'Jesus' life/living presence appearing in the presence of God' (*Atonement and the Logic of Resurrection in the Epistle to the Hebrews*, 273).

174. Many manuscripts have **good things *to come*** (μελλόντων), probably implying in the NHNE. Metzger assumes this reading is secondary because of the confusion with similar wording in Hebrews 10:1 (*TCGNT*², 598).

175. Greek is ἐφάπαξ. See discussion at Hebrews 7:27.

176. There is no implied split in the heavenly tabernacle between two rooms.

after having obtained[177] **eternal redemption**, that is, after his atoning death on the cross.

The word for **redemption** (λύτρωσις) and its cognate ἀπολύτρωσις (Heb. 9:15) have at their core the idea of a *ransom* paid to deliver from a state of bondage or captivity, that is, ransom from the guilt of sin and its effects.[178] This word and its cognates are used in several important NT verses (Matt. 20:28; Mark 10:45; 1 Tim. 2:6; 1 Pet. 1:18). The background metaphor of price paid is certainly in this context due to **blood of goats and calves**.[179]

Once and **eternal** make sense together. If an atonement

---

177. **After having obtained** (εὑράμενος) is an aorist participle. Although the essence of an aorist is not necessarily past-temporal and is highly aspectual, in the vast majority of NT cases, adverbial aorist participles *are* logically or temporally prior to the main verb (see insightful aorist-participle discussion by Moule, *An Idiom Book of New Testament Greek*, 99–100). Given the statistical prevalence and the assumption that Christ's death on the cross is sacrificial, surely this participle 'obtaining' should be seen as occurring temporally before the main verb **he entered**, hence my translation of *after having obtained*. So also Owen, *Hebrews*, 22:281; Brown, *Hebrews*, 393; Spicq, *Hébreux*, 257–58; Bruce, *Hebrews*, 213; Hughes, *Hebrews*, 328 n. 84; Barry C. Joslin, 'Christ Bore the Sins of Many: Substitution and the Atonement in Hebrews,' *SBTJ* 11 (2007): 74–103, esp. 82; Kenneth Schenck, 'Hebrews as the Re-presentation of a Story: A Narrative Approach to Hebrews,' in *Reading the Epistle of Hebrews: A Resource for Students*, 171–88, esp. 186; Cockerill, *Hebrews*, 395 n. 37; Geneva Bible, KJV, NASB, and CSB17. *Contra* Attridge, *Hebrews*, 248–49; Lane, *Hebrews 9–13*, 230; Ellingworth, *Hebrews*, 453; Johnson, *Hebrews*, 237; R. B. Jamieson, *Jesus' Death and Heavenly Offering in Hebrews*, SNTSMS 172 (Cambridge: CUP, 2019), 57–63, 70; RSV, NIV, ESV, and CEB.

178. Benjamin Breckinridge Warfield complains that 'ransom' should be used more often than 'redeem' in our theological vocabulary ('Redeemer and Redemption,' and 'The New Testament Terminology of Redemption,' in *The Person and Work of Christ*, ed. Samuel G. Craig [Philadelphia: P&R, 1970], 325–50, 429–78, respectively). '"Redeem" implies to buy *back* and ["ransom"] means rather to buy *out*' (p. 330, emphasis his). 'The NT does not set forth the saving work of Christ as a redemption, but as a ransoming; and does not present him to us therefore so much as our Redeemer as our Ransomer' (pp. 334–35). Warfield also points out that redemption/ransom in the NT including Hebrews has both present and future salvific effects (pp. 465–66; 474–75). I note that the OT verb (גאל) and concept of a kinsman redeemer do have a significant 'redeem' (buy back) aspect and are related to λύτρωσις and its cognates.

179. So also Warfield, 'The New Testament Terminology of Redemption,' 464.

has **eternal** effects, it is done only **once**; thus subsequently, Christ only **once** needs to ascend after his atonement. The **once** emphasis, of course, comes typologically from the Levitical high priests only entering the **Holy of Holies** one day per year. Calvin nicely quips that this 'solemn' Levitical requirement was 'a vague pre-figuring of the unique sacrifice of Christ.'[180] Intriguingly, since the Levitical high priests enter once *per year*, the AH will later compare the 'per year' aspect to Christ's **once** absolutely to show that Christ's sacrifice is better (Heb. 9:25–26; 10:1–3). Hence, the *once*-per-year aspect is used *typologically* to refer to Christ by emphasizing the 'once'; and the 'per year' aspect is considered *literally* to show the superiority of Christ's sacrifice.

In the phrase **not by virtue of the blood of goats and calves but by virtue of his own blood**, the translation **by virtue of** takes the preposition διά instrumentally.[181] This is as opposed to simply meaning 'with,' as in the priest carried blood 'with' him. Part of the qualification (**by virtue of**) for the Levitical high priest on the Day of Atonement to enter the **Holy of Holies** was to have the **blood of goats and calves** (Lev. 16:3–5); so also the qualification (**by virtue of**) of Christ to **enter** the heavenly **Holy of Holies** was to have **his own blood** shed on the cross. The rhetorical effect of this double-blood phrase is powerful and will be amplified in Hebrews 9:13–14 (cf. Heb. 13:11–12).

Christ is described as **having come**[182] about as **high priest**, which I take as occurring upon his arrival on earth (cf. Heb. 9:26).[183] The **good things having come** refers to all of Christ's new-covenant benefits, now and in the NHNE.

---

180. Calvin, *Hebrews and 1–2 Peter*, 119.

181. Most scholars take διά (plus the genitive) instrumentally here. I have added the instrumental nuance of **by *virtue* of**; so also Owen, *Hebrews*, 22:280; Brown, *Hebrews*, 396; Bruce, *Hebrews*, 213; Hughes, *Hebrews*, 328; and Kistemaker, *Hebrews*, 249.

182. **After having come** is an aorist participle that I take as occurring before the main verb **he entered**.

183. So also, e.g., Grässer, *Hebräer*, 2:143; *contra* Koester who takes it as Christ's arrival in heaven (*Hebrews*, 407).

As all agree, **by virtue of a greater and more perfect tabernacle** is a notoriously difficult phrase. The first issue is whether the phrase modifies Christ's **having come** or that Christ **entered into the Holy of Holies**. The second is whether the preposition διά should be translated instrumentally (**by virtue of**) or spatially ('through'[184]). The third is whether **tabernacle** refers to Christ's body (either while on earth or in heaven), the heavenly reality, just the outer part of the heavenly reality matching to the Holy Place, or the heavenly/new-covenant age. I will simply give my view. I take the phrase as modifying **having come**, the preposition διά instrumentally, and **tabernacle** to be the heavenly/new-covenant period. Therefore, the AH is making the point that Christ's arrival is **by virtue of** the new covenant age. The new-covenant **tabernacle** is **not hand-made** and **not of this creation**.

9:13–14 *For if the blood of goats and bulls and the ash of a heifer sprinkling those having been defiled sanctify for the purification of the flesh, how much more shall the blood of Christ, who through the eternal spirit offered himself without blemish to God, purify our*[185] *conscience from dead works to serve the living God.*

In Hebrews 9:13–14, the AH supports (**for**) his statement that Christ's 'own blood ... obtained eternal redemption' (Heb. 9:12). He does this with a lesser-to-greater argument (cf. Heb. 2:2–3).[186] Yes, the **blood** and **ash** of animals related to

---

184. Similar to διά plus the genitive, in English, 'through' has both an instrumental sense (e.g., I learned Greek *through* hard study) and a spatial sense (e.g., I ran *through* the field). The spatial sense can expand into a temporal sense (e.g., Christ has been preached down *through* the centuries). In Hebrews, the instrumental sense is dominant, although the spatial sense (e.g., 11:29) and temporal sense do exist (e.g., 13:15).

185. Many manuscripts have 'your.'

186. This if/then sentence is a first-class conditional sentence. The 'if' clause of first-class conditionals indicates 'the assumption of truth for the sake of the argument' (Wallace, *Greek Grammar Beyond the Basics*, 690, emphasis removed) or 'emphasis on the reality of the assumption' (BDF §371). Note that BDF more emphasizes the assumed truth of the 'if' clause where Wallace is looser and more context dependent. However, in this context of OT law, the AH would agree to the truthfulness of the 'if' clause

various Levitical ceremonies *did* **sanctify for the purification of the flesh**; if that is true, **how much more shall the** *blood of Christ* **... purify your conscience from dead works to serve the living God**. Although Hebrews 9:11–12 is explicitly related to the Day of Atonement, here, with the wording of **goats and bulls** referring to all types of Levitical sacrifices[187] and especially with the **ash of a heifer** (Numbers 19), the general nature of various Levitical **purification** ceremonies is contrasted with the glorious atoning death of Christ.[188]

Why include the 'waters for impurity'[189] ceremony from Numbers 19 (cf. Num. 31:23)? First, an explanation of the ceremony: God tells Moses and Aaron to get a red **heifer** without blemish and give it to Aaron's son Eleazar. Someone slaughters the animal in the presence of Eleazar. The blood is used to sprinkle toward the tabernacle. Then the animal, blood, cedarwood, hyssop, and scarlet yarn (cf. Heb. 9:19) are burned, resulting in an **ash**. This **ash** is safely kept and then mixed with water to cleanse, usually by **sprinkling**, **those having been** ceremonially **defiled** (e.g., touching a dead body). Somewhat confusingly, it is also described as a sin offering (Num. 19:9), although clearly the primary use is to **sanctify** those ceremonially unclean and enable them to return to normal community activities.

Do we learn anything from Jewish tradition? Josephus describes the ceremony closely matching to Numbers 19 except

---

as opposed to just assuming for argument's sake.

187. Note the change from 'goats and *calves*' in Hebrews 9:12 to **goats and bulls** to indicate all ceremonies. So also Owen, *Hebrews*, 22:286.

188. This argues against Moffitt's view that Christ only presents his sacrifice in heaven based on the analogy of the Day of Atonement's blood upon the ark. Note here that multiple Levitical ceremonies are contrasted with the **blood of Christ** and his atoning work. Hence, a view solely driven by one aspect of one ceremony is misguided.

189. In Hebrew, always מי נדה, 'waters of impurity' (e.g., Num. 19:9). The noun נדה also translates as 'menstruation' in other contexts (e.g., Lev. 12:2). In the LXX, ὕδωρ ῥαντισμου, 'water of sprinkling' (e.g., Num. 19:9) except once ὕδωρ τοῦ ἁγνισμοῦ, 'water of cleansing' (Num. 31:23).

he explicitly says that the high priest kills the heifer (*Jewish Antiquities* 4.78–81).[190] In the important Qumran document, The Community Rule, this Numbers 19 ceremony is mentioned twice as it is apparently used in a community-joining ceremony (1QS III, 1–12). The Rabbinic Mishnah has a whole tractate on Numbers 19, m. Parah.[191] Much of it concerns what to do if the ash or water are spilled and if an insect gets into the mix (m. Parah 6:1–11:9). It is not clear if the one killing the heifer needs to be the high priest or not; and in this discussion, the Day of Atonement is mentioned (m. Parah 3:1). The Epistle of Barnabas discusses the typology of Numbers 19. It notes, for example, that the ceremony has three boys pick up the ash and do the sprinkling (Barnabas 8:4). Although a second-century Christian document, it may have information that reflects former Jewish practices. In sum, the above shows that the waters-of-impurity ceremony was somewhat known during first-century AD.

So why is the waters-of-impurity ceremony mentioned in Hebrews? Possible answers are the connection with the high priest, or an implicit rebuttal to the Dead Sea Scrolls community or similar group,[192] or another sin offering,[193] or related to the 'baptisms' of Hebrews 9:10[194] or connected to the Day of Atonement,[195] or sprinkling **blood** toward the tabernacle (Num. 19:4), or the *dead* bodies (Num. 19:11) connected with *dead* **works**,[196] or the **heifer** and Christ are both **without blemish** (Num. 19:2), or burned outside the camp (Num. 19:3; Heb. 13:11). My view begins with acknowledging that the AH understands

---

190. I assume the high priest connection is due to Eleazar, who later in Numbers becomes the high priest (Num. 20:22–29).

191. So named because 'parah' (פרה) is Hebrew for heifer.

192. So surmises Hughes, *Hebrews*, 363–64.

193. Attridge sees both the high priest and sin offering connections (*Hebrews*, 249–50).

194. So Cockerill, *Hebrews*, 396–97.

195. So m. Parah 3:1.

196. So Ellingworth, *Hebrews*, 458.

the Numbers 19 ceremony as typological of Christ.[197] Given this, the **without blemish** connection in context is the most compelling, along with sprinkling **blood** toward the tabernacle. Another angle here could be that modern believers are not that familiar with the waters-of-impurity ceremony relative to how well known it may have been in first-century Jewish circles. Hence, modern believers unconsciously assume more of a rationale is needed to include this ceremony as opposed to a rationale to include the more well-known sacrificial ceremonies.

For us, our Lord **offered himself without blemish to God**. This is another inspiring statement in Hebrews. Christ is both the priest (**offered**) and the victim (**himself without blemish**). **Without blemish** clearly connects to the many Levitical animal sacrifices that have the same requirement (e.g., Exod. 12:5; 29:1; Lev. 1:3; Num. 19:2). For Christ, the antitype, this refers to his moral character, 'without sin' (Heb. 4:15), as opposed to physical characteristics. Interestingly, 'offered himself' in context of Hebrews 7:26–27 has more of an emphasis on the priestly qualifications of Christ, and here, **offered himself** *without blemish* emphasizes the sacrificial/victim qualifications.

Christ **offered himself** with the instrumental aid (**through**) of the **eternal spirit**.[198] The meaning of **spirit** is not clear. Does **spirit** indicate the Holy **Spirit**,[199] which is **eternal**; or does

---

197. Owen gives seven typological connections to Christ from Num. 19 (*Hebrews*, 22:289).

198. Some Greek manuscripts and the Latin Vulgate have 'holy' in place of **eternal**. Metzger gives **eternal** an 'A' level of certainty (highest) based on a scribe's being more likely to 'correct' **eternal** to 'Holy' as opposed to the reverse (*TCGNT*², 598–99). All major English translations have **eternal**, except Douay-Rheims, which is based on the Latin.

199. So Calvin, *Hebrews and 1 & 2 Peter*, 121; Pink, *Hebrews*, 492–93; Bruce, *Hebrews*, 217; Kistemaker, *Hebrews*, 251–52; Lane, *Hebrews*, 230, 240; Ellingworth, *Hebrews*, 457; Martin Emmrich, '"Amtscharisma": Through the Eternal Spirit (Hebrews 9:14),' *BBR* 12 (2002): 17–32; George Smeaton, *The Doctrine of the Holy Spirit* (Carlisle: Banner of Truth, 2016 [1889]), 128–30; and Schreiner, *Hebrews*, 270–71.

spirit indicate Christ's **eternal** divine nature,[200] which is **spirit**? In favor of Holy Spirit would be that on the cross Christ's human nature was aided by the Holy Spirit while undergoing the wrath of God (cf. Isa. 42:1; Matt. 3:16; Luke 1:35; John 3:34; Rom. 8:11). Also, the Holy Spirit is clearly mentioned several times in Hebrews.[201] Since I do believe that the Holy Spirit did aid Christ's human nature at all times, but certainly during his time on the cross, this view is very plausible. Here, however, I am persuaded that the AH is referring to Christ's divine/eternal nature, the eternal Son. Arguments in favor of this include: (1) Hebrews 7:16 ('indestructible life') refers to Christ's divine nature in a priestly context.[202] (2) There is an emphasis in Hebrews on the eternal Son (e.g., Heb. 1:3, 8, 10–12; 7:3, 16; 13:8, 20). (3) In context of Hebrews 9:13–14, the emphasis is on *Christ's* dignity and worth, it was not just one human's **blood** that was sacrificed, but it was the **blood** of the human nature of Christ that was/is united to his divine nature; that is, it was the person of the God-man who **offered himself**.[203] (4) The parallel to Hebrews 9:12 with *Christ's*

---

200. So Ames, *The Marrow of Theology*, 133; Owen, *Hebrews*, 22:306; Brown, *Hebrews*, 402; Vos, 'The Priesthood of Christ in the Epistle to the Hebrews,' 590–92; Spicq, *Hébreux*, 2:258; Hughes, *Hebrews*, 358–59 (?); and John J. McGrath, *Through the Eternal Spirit: An Historical Study of the Exegesis of Hebrews 9:13–14* (Rome: Pontificio Universitas Gregoriana, 1961), 90–103. Several commentators downplay any two-nature assumptions and see **spirit** as simply Christ's own, e.g., Moffatt, *Hebrews*, 123; and Attridge, *Hebrews*, 251.

201. Explicit references to the Holy Spirit, Heb. 2:4; 3:7; 6:4; 9:8; 10:15; virtually explicit, Heb. 10:29. References clearly not to the Holy Spirit, Heb. 1:7, 14; 12:9, 23.

202. Often, if one sees the 'indestructible life' from Heb. 7:16 as beginning at Christ's ascension as opposed to his eternal divine nature, then one opts for the Holy Spirit view here, e.g., Emmrich, 'Amtscharisma,' 20–22. The reverse is not necessarily true. For example, Cockerill favors eternal divine nature in Heb. 7:16 but opts ('probably') for the Holy Spirit view here (*Hebrews*, 323, 398).

203. *Contra* James W. Thompson who sees that 'the blood of Jesus was actually offered in the heavenly tabernacle. It is this fact which gives Jesus' sacrifice metaphysical superiority to the blood of bulls and goats' ('Hebrews 9 and Sacrifice,' *JBL* 98 [1979]: 567–78, esp. 571–72).

'having obtained *eternal* redemption' works better if **through the *eternal* spirit** refers to *Christ's* **spirit**.

Both options, the Holy Spirit or Christ's eternal/divine nature, make the same point that the Almighty Godhead was involved intimately in the crucifixion.[204] Glory be.

Of course, Christ's redemption accomplishes many things. Here it will **purify your conscience from dead works to serve the living God**. The verb **purify** (καθαρίζω) is intentionally playing off its cognate **purification** (καθαρότης). As the Levitical ceremonies accomplish **purification of the flesh** (cf. Heb. 9:22), in a much greater way, Christ's redemption changes us. Before Christ in one's life, one's **conscience** (inner man) was interested in **dead works** (cf. Heb. 6:1). But with Christ, one is changed (**purify**) and now gloriously **serve(s) the living God**. Note the rhetorical contrast between **dead** and **living**.[205] As is seen in Hebrews 9:22, our purification (change of inner man) presupposes the forgiveness of sins.

Reflections

Christians have been appropriately interested in the biblical expressions that refer to our Lord's blood. The exact expression 'the blood of Christ' (Heb. 9:14) is found also in 1 Corinthians 10:16, Ephesians 2:13, and 1 Peter 1:19. There are many similar well-known verses that include 'blood' (e.g., Matt. 26:28; John 19:34; Acts 20:28; Rom. 3:25; Eph. 1:7; Col. 1:20; Heb. 13:20; 1 John 1:7; Rev. 5:9; also see discussion below at Heb. 9:22b). Often Christians hear the words of institution at communion, 'This cup is the new covenant in my blood' (1 Cor. 11:25).

---

204. In the Holy Spirit view, Hebrews 9:14 includes all three members of the Trinity. In the divine-nature-of-Christ view, Hebrews 9:14 includes both natures of Christ. The Westminster Standards are not clear on their interpretation. In WCF 8.5, the wording 'through the eternal Spirit' appears by the capitalization to imply the Holy Spirit (although WLC 7 also has capitalized 'Spirit,' and it is clearly not referring to the Holy Spirit). WCF 8.7 and WLC 38, on the other hand, imply the divine nature of Christ.

205. Possibly there is also an allusion to the 'waters of impurity' ceremony that cleanses one who touched a *dead* body (Num. 19:11).

Christians understand the seriousness of sin and the need for atonement. In one sense, the idea of our Lord being physically killed, and furthermore, this death being compared to a sacrificed/slaughtered animal, is extremely off-putting. But on the other hand, the expression 'the blood of Christ' brings a solemn joy to Christians as it highlights the depths of love that Christ had/has for them.

This solemn joy is reflected in many Christian songs that include references to Christ's blood. I have sung many such songs at churches that I have attended. Interestingly, many of these songs include the blood reference in the first line. 'Just as I am without one plea but *thy blood* was shed for me'; 'What can wash away my sin? nothing but the *blood of Jesus*'; 'And can it be that I should gain an int'rest in the *Savior's blood?*'; 'There is a fountain filled with *blood* drawn from *Immanuel's* veins'; and 'Alas! and did my *Savior bleed*, and did my Sovereign die.'[206]

Inauguration of Covenants by Death and Blood (9:15–22)

As Hebrews 9:11–14 emphasizes the 'blood of Christ' in relationship (a graded contrast) to the Mosaic covenant's 'blood of goats and bulls,' so also Hebrews 9:15–22 connects the death/blood of the Mosaic covenant to the new covenant. The connection (continuity) in these verses primarily emphasizes that both covenants were *inaugurated* by death/blood. A secondary emphasis is the connection (graded contrast[?]) in both covenants between death/blood and the forgiveness of sins.

As to the flow of Hebrews 9:15–22, 9:15 is the thesis statement that Christ is the mediator of a new covenant connecting his death to the new-covenant benefits. Anticipating the question of when the new covenant was inaugurated, Hebrews 9:16–17 picks up on the death comment in 9:15 to show that deaths and

---

206. Titles in order, 'Just as I Am without One Plea'; 'Nothing but the Blood'; 'And Can It Be That I Should Gain'; 'There is a Fountain'; and 'Alas! and Did my Savior Bleed.'

the establishing of covenants are related. Hebrews 9:18–22a further confirms this by showing the extensive nature of death, and more specifically blood to show death, in the inauguration of the Mosaic covenant. This blood emphasis then echoes back to the 'blood of Christ' from Hebrews 9:11–14 to confirm that the new covenant has been inaugurated by Christ's death/blood. Hebrews 9:22b is a truism connecting blood to the forgiveness of sins, which anticipates the further discussion of 9:23–10:18 concerning Christ's death and the forgiveness of sins.

9:15 *And on account of this, he is the mediator of a new covenant, so that, a death having occurred for redemption of the transgressions during*[207] *the first covenant,*[208] *those having been called may receive the promise of the eternal inheritance.*

And on account of this refers back to Hebrews 9:11–14 and Christ's being a high priest who offered his own blood.[209] This priestly activity, especially that it is related to blood/death, supports that Christ is **the mediator**[210] **of a** *new covenant*. (At this point, the AH has not completely explained the blood/

---

207. Taking ἐπί temporally (BAGD, 367, §10.b) as opposed to 'basis for a state of being' (BAGD, 364, §6a).

208. **A death having occurred for redemption of the transgressions during the first covenant** is a genitive-absolute participial phrase.

209. **On account of this** with no context grammatically may refer backwards or forwards. I have taken it to refer backwards as do most commentators, so, e.g., Hodge, *Hebrews*, 85; Hughes, *Hebrews*, 364; and Attridge, *Hebrews*, 254. Others see it as referring forward to Heb. 9:15b to support the thesis statement that Christ is the mediator, so, e.g., Chrysostom, 'Homily 14 on Hebrews,' (*NPNF*[1], 14:443); and Moffatt, *Hebrews*, 126. There is not a significant difference between the two views, although the 'backwards' view emphasizes the death/blood connection more.

210. Concerning Christ's being a **mediator**, see discussions at Heb. 8:6 and 12:24, along with the connection to 'surety' at 7:22. Cyprian states, 'This is our God, this is Christ, who, as the mediator of the two, puts on man that he may lead them to the Father. What man is, Christ was willing to be, that man also may be what Christ is' (*The Treatises of Cyprian* 6.11 [*ANF*, 5:468]). Irenaeus states, 'For it was incumbent upon the Mediator between God and men, by His relationship to both, to bring both to friendship and concord, and present man to God, while He revealed God to man' (*Against Heresies* 3.18.7 [*ANF*, 1:448]).

death connection to the new covenant, but he will go a long way toward that explanation in Hebrews 9:16–22.) The AH then connects the blood/death (**death having occurred**) to the new covenant benefits that the mediator-priest brings (**the promise of the eternal inheritance**).

In the participial phrase, **a death having occurred for redemption of the transgressions during the first covenant**, there are several connections back to Hebrews 9:11–14. **Death** connects to 'his own blood' (9:12) and 'blood of Christ' (9:14); **redemption** (ἀπολύτρωσις) to 'eternal redemption (λύτρωσις)' (9:12); **transgressions** to 'dead works' (9:14); and **first covenant** to 'blood of goats and calves/bulls' (9:12–13). Here **death** clearly refers to Christ's death, and significantly, Christ's **death** provides real **redemption**/atonement for even those who are morally liable for **transgressions** *during the first covenant*. That is, Christ's death does not simply atone for those in the new covenant era; it atones for all believers in all eras, including those who sinned **during the first covenant** (from Moses up to the NT era) (cf. Heb. 9:26; 11:40; 12:23; 13:8; Rom. 3:25; Acts 17:30).[211] Christ's death has 'eternal' implications, both retrospectively and prospectively (Heb. 5:9; 6:2; 9:17, 25–26; 10:2–3, 11; 13:20, for retrospectively, see further discussion at Heb. 9:25–26; 10:2–3; and 10:11). The Westminster divines said it well, 'Although the work of redemption was not actually wrought by Christ, till after his incarnation, yet the virtue, efficacy, and benefits thereof, were communicated unto the elect in all ages ... being yesterday and today the same and for ever' (WCF 8.6).[212] In context, possibly some Christian-Jewish believers were wondering about a true atonement for their OT heroes since Christ's atonement surpassed that of the tabernacle/temple sacrifices. The comforting answer is that Christ's atonement is for all believers, past, present, and future.

---

211. So also *Geneva Bible: 1602 Edition*, folio 112; Owen, *Hebrews*, 22:228–29; Hodge, *Hebrews*, 85; Brown, *Hebrews*, 414; Moffatt, *Hebrews*, 127; Hughes, *Hebrews*, 367; Leon Morris, *The Cross in the New Testament*, Biblical and Theological Classics Library (Carlisle, UK; Paternoster, 1995), 292; Attridge, *Hebrews*, 255; and Catechism of the Catholic Church §592.

212. Also see WCF 7.4, 8.5, and WLC 152.

Although the emphasis in Hebrews 9:15–22 is on the new covenant's connection to death/blood, the AH does summarize the big-picture benefits of Christ's mediatorial role with the clause, **those having been called may receive the promise of the eternal inheritance**. The benefits do include forgiveness of sins, but so much more, **the eternal inheritance**. This **inheritance** includes aspects of our salvation now but ultimately is fulfilled in the NHNE. This **eternal inheritance** (κληρονομία) is related to the Abrahamic-covenant **promise** (Heb. 6:13; 11:8, 16; cf. Heb. 8:6; Rom. 4:16) and to the Davidic-covenant **promise** to Christ as he is 'heir (κληρονόμος) of all things' (Heb. 1:2; cf. Heb. 1:5, 14; 5:5–6). Again in Hebrews we see the various OT covenants being fulfilled in Christ and the new covenant. Also, this text combines aspects of Christ's priestly and kingly offices. Finally, the idea of **inheritance** has as its background our being adopted sons into the family of God and being fellow-heirs with Christ our brother (cf. Rom. 4:13; 8:17; Gal. 4:7; Heb. 2:12; 12:7).

9:16–17 *For where a covenant [is], death of the one covenanting must be brought forth. For a covenant [is] valid upon dead ones, otherwise it is not in force when the one covenanting lives.*

Hebrews 9:16–17 is well known in scholarship for an interpretation issue that then results in a translation difference. Virtually all agree that διαθήκη in the LXX and the vast majority of NT should be translated as 'covenant' due to its connection to ברית ('covenant') in the OT, including all instances of διαθήκη in Hebrews excepting Hebrews 9:16–17. Also, all agree that διαθήκη should be translated as 'testament' (in the sense of 'last will and testament') in the vast majority of instances within secular Greco-Roman literature in the first century AD.[213] The debate concerns which context controls the

---

213. For διαθήκη as 'testament,' see LSJ, 394–95. Similarly, the cognate verb διατίθημι is predominantly used as 'to make a will,' see LSJ, 415. As LSJ's multiple references show, although the predominant secular use is for 'testament' and 'to make a will,' these two Greek words are used for 'covenant' and 'to make a covenant,' respectively, in a few non-biblical

understanding/translation of διαθήκη in Hebrews 9:16–17.[214] Should διαθήκη be understood/translated as 'testament' (or 'will') (e.g., KJV, ESV, NIV) assuming the AH is intentionally using a secular parallel?[215] Or should it be understood/ translated as 'covenant' (e.g., NASB) assuming consistency with the rest of Hebrews?[216] This debate exists among all types of scholars, no matter their theological presuppositions. It has even existed in the (conservative) Reformed tradition within the last 150 years,[217] although before that the tradition mostly opted for 'testament'.[218]

---

contexts. In secular contexts for 'covenant/agreement' and 'to make a covenant/agreement,' more commonly used are συνθήκη and συντίθημι, respectively; see LSJ 1717, 1727. Both of these are used sparingly in the LXX, primarily referring to general agreements. Συνθήκη is not in the NT. Συντίθημι is used as 'to make a general agreement' in Luke 22:5; John 9:22; and Acts 23:20.

214. A few interpret διαθήκη as 'testament' consistently throughout Heb. 9:15–22 (e.g., KJV; James Swetnam, 'A Suggested Interpretation of Hebrews 9:15–18,' *CBQ* 27 [1965]: 373–90); however, the references to the 'first διαθήκη' must surely mean the first/Mosaic covenant.

215. So, e.g., Moffat, *Hebrews*, 127–28; Spicq, *Hébreux*, 2:260–63; Attridge, *Hebrews*, 253–56; Ellingworth, *Hebrews*, 462–64; Koester, *Hebrews*, 417–18; Johnson, *Hebrews*, 240–41; Scott R. Murray, 'The Concept of διαθήκη in the Letter to the Hebrews,' *CTQ* 66 (2002): 41–60; and Schreiner, *Hebrews*, 275–76.

216. So, e.g., Frederic Gardiner, 'On διαθήκη in Heb. ix. 16, 17,' *JBL* 5 (1885): 8–19; J. J. Hughes, 'Hebrews IX 15ff and Galatians III 15ff: A Study in Covenant Practice and Procedure,' *NovT* 21 (1979): 27–96; Lane, *Hebrews 9–13*, 230–32, 242–43; Scott W. Hahn, 'A Broken Covenant and the Curse of Death: A Study of Hebrews 9:15–22,' *CBQ* 66 (2004): 416–36; Guthrie, 'Hebrews,' 973; Morrison, *Who Needs a New Covenant?*, 144–46; Cockerill, *Hebrews*, 404–6; and Compton, *Psalm 110 and the Logic of Hebrews*, 128–32.

217. So, e.g., pro-'testament': Vos, 'Hebrews, The Epistle of the Diatheke,' 614–18; John Murray, *The Covenant of Grace: A Biblico-Theological Study* (Phillipsburg: Presbyterian and Reformed, 1988), 29–30; and Phillips, *Hebrews*, 314–15. So, e.g., pro-'covenant': Brown, *Hebrews*, 407–8; and Robertson, *God's People in the Wilderness: The Church in Hebrews*, 39–43.

218. So, e.g., Calvin, *Hebrews and 1 & 2 Peter*, 123–24; Geneva Bible; Owen, *Hebrews*, 22:319–21, 335–42; Turretin, *Institutes of Elenctic Theology*, 2:170–71; Gouge, *Hebrews*, 2:639–42; and WCF 7.4. It should be noted that these understand 'testament' within the framework of biblical covenants (e.g., WCF 7) as opposed to others who understand 'testament' in Hebrews 9:16–17 as simply an analogy

As the reader can see from my above translation, I interpret διαθήκη as **covenant** as opposed to 'testament' or 'will'; and likewise, the substantival-participle of διατίθημι as **the one covenanting** as opposed to 'testator'. My broad justification for this is: (1) In biblical literature, and in Hebrews specifically, the default understanding of διαθήκη should be 'covenant' unless the context cannot reasonably support it. (2) The death of animals as part of self-maledictory oaths/promises associated with covenant ceremonies well supports the 'covenant' view that death is associated with the inauguration of covenants. (3) Although 'inheritance' (Heb. 9:15) does match well to the 'testament' view, it also matches well to the 'covenant' view through inheriting the covenantal promises (Heb. 6:12; 11:8). (4) The 'wherefore' in Hebrews 9:18 connecting 9:18–22a to 9:16–17 indicates that 9:16–17 is foundational truth that then applies to the Mosaic covenant and by implication to the new covenant. This is not cogent if 9:16–17 is simply an analogy from the common Greco-Roman form of a last will and testament.

The **for** in Hebrews 9:16 is supporting the aspect of 9:15 that 'a *death* having occurred for redemption' is appropriate to Christ's being the 'mediator of new *covenant*.' This then begins the discussion through 9:22 connecting death/blood to the establishing of covenants. Of course, since deaths are connected to covenants, then it makes sense that Christ's death would be connected to the new covenant. Hence, the AH begins with a general truism about biblical covenants, **for where a covenant is, death of the one covenanting must be brought forth**.

In several biblical covenants, death is part of the ceremony

---

from the secular Greco-Roman context. For modern views with a close connection between 'testament' and biblical covenants, see Bruce, *Hebrews*, 221–24; Meredith G. Kline, *Treaty of the Great King: The Covenant Structure of Deuteronomy: Studies and Commentary* (Grand Rapids: Eerdmans, 1963), 41; and Hughes, *Hebrews*, 356–70. Bruce in fact translates as a 'testamentary covenant' (p. 224). Although I do not agree with this view, I find it significantly more helpful than the bare Greco-Roman analogy view.

to confirm and inaugurate the covenant between the two parties (e.g., Gen. 15:7–17; Exod. 24:3–8; Ps. 50:5; Jer. 34:17–20).[219] It is not, however, the death of either of the parties, but it is the death of animals to represent the implied punishment if one of the parties does not fulfill the terms of the covenant. The covenant ceremony includes oaths with promises and punishments. Hence, as represented by the death of the animals, a self-maledictory oath is involved; one pledges punishments similar to the death of the animals upon oneself if one does not keep the covenantal promises.[220]

Given this self-maledictory aspect of covenants, **the one covenanting** (διατίθημι) refers to the *symbolic* **death** of the person making the oath as shown by the death of the animals.[221] And until the covenant ceremony that involves death is performed, the **covenant** is not **valid** nor is it **in force**. This view of the *symbolic* death best explains why the plural **dead ones**, that is, dead animals, is connected to the singular **the one covenanting**.[222]

Of course, some understand where the AH is going even though he has not explicitly said it yet. Christ is the high priest and mediator of the new covenant. But Christ did *not* die a *symbolic* death to confirm and inaugurate the covenant,

---

219. Some arguing against the 'covenant' view note that not all biblical covenants are explicitly tied to death. Fair enough, although, a similar argument could be leveled at the 'testament' view because not all wills are inaugurated at the death of the testator; for ancient examples of this, see Hughes, 'Hebrews IX 15ff. and Galatians III 15ff.,' 61–63; also Luke 15:12.

220. For a discussion of self-maledictory oaths in the Bible, see Meredith G. Kline, *By Oath Consigned: A Reinterpretation of the Covenant Signs of Circumcision and Baptism*, 13–22, 39–49; and Robertson, *The Christ of the Covenants*, 128–37. For self-maledictory oaths in the ANE, see McCarthy, *Treaty and Covenant*, 27–152.

221. So also Robertson, 'The reference ... is to the symbolic representation of the death of the covenant-maker as a necessary step in the establishment of a covenant relationship, as is seen by the connection to the phrase with the 'making firm' of a covenant' (*God's People in the Wilderness*, 41).

222. Because 'dead' in English can be a collective, the English translations do not clearly bring out the Greek plural νεκροῖς (**dead ones**) in Hebrews 9:17.

but a *real* death as **the one covenanting**. Further, he did not personally break the covenant (i.e., sin), but he did agree to stand in the place of others (surety, Heb. 7:22). Possibly, the AH only mentions the singular **the one covenanting**, as opposed to two people taking oaths and covenanting, because he is alluding to the one mediator/surety. In addition, the covenant of redemption may come into play here. Christ agreed in eternity 'past' to represent his people and undertake their punishment which came to fruition with Christ's death on the cross. This goes a long way toward explaining the use of 'eternal' in 'the blood of the eternal covenant' (Heb. 13:20) and Christ's death applying to all believers in all ages. In one sense, the covenant is eternal; and in another, it is new.

9:18 *Wherefore not even the first was inaugurated without blood.*

Hebrews 9:16–17 states the general principle that biblical covenants are confirmed/validated/inaugurated upon a death. Given this (**wherefore**), the Mosaic (**first**) covenant was certainly also **inaugurated** with **blood**. Note the double negative (**not, without**) for rhetorical punch (also Heb. 9:22b).

The AH moves from 'death' in Hebrews 9:15–16 to **blood**, which harkens back slightly further to 9:11–14 where both the 'blood' of animals and the 'blood of Christ' are discussed. Also, the self-maledictory ceremonies referred to in Hebrews 9:16–17 evoke images of a bloody death.

9:19–20 *For, after every commandment according to the law being spoken by Moses to all the people,* [223] *[and] after taking the blood of the calves and the goats with water, and scarlet wool, and hyssop, he sprinkled both the book itself and all the people, saying, 'this is the blood of the covenant that God commanded concerning*[224] *you.'*

Hebrews 9:19–22a is giving evidence (**for**) that the Mosaic covenant was confirmed with blood (Heb. 9:18). To prove

---

223. **After every commandment according to the law being spoken by Moses to all the people** is a genitive-absolute participial phrase.

224. Πρός here in the sense of 'with reference/regard to,' see BDAG, 875 (§3e). It matches the LXX.

his point, as one would expect, the AH refers to the formal inauguration of the Mosaic covenant in Exodus 24:3–8.

In the Hebrews account, there are a few extra details that are not explicit in Exodus 24:3–8. But first, what is in the Exodus 24:3–8 account? Moses conveys the words of God to the people, and they respond positively (24:3). Then Moses writes the words down and makes an altar (24:4). He has others offer burnt offerings and oxen/calves for peace offerings (24:5). From the blood related to the animal offerings, Moses throws half the blood on the altar (24:6). After Moses' reading from the 'book of the covenant,' the people again respond positively (24:7). Finally, Moses throws the remaining blood on the people and makes a statement about the 'blood of the covenant' (24:8).

The AH adds the detail that **goats** were involved.[225] This is a proper implication of the burnt offerings (e.g., Lev. 1:10; 4:24). **Water, and scarlet wool, and hyssop** are not mentioned in Exodus 24, although they are elsewhere (Exod. 12:22; Lev. 14:4–7; Num. 19:6, 51; cf. Ps. 51:7; John 19:29). The **water** was used to dilute the blood and allow it to be used for a significant number of sprinklings. The **hyssop**[226] was used to sprinkle the blood. The **wool** was wrapped around the **hyssop** to partially soak up the blood to aid in sprinkling. Again, this is a proper implication of Moses' **sprinkl[ing]** of **all the people** as opposed to using his finger. Finally, the AH notes that Moses also sprinkled the **book itself**. The 'book of the covenant' is mentioned in Exodus 24:7 (cf. 24:4), although its being sprinkled is not. This again, however, is a reasonable implication.[227]

---

225. Some Greek manuscripts do not include **goats**. Some scholars believe it was omitted intentionally assuming that Exod. 24:5 was understood as not including them. See *TCGNT*², 599.

226. **Hyssop** is a plant/shrub that 'was tied into bunches and was used as a brush to sprinkle blood .... Its hairy leaves can absorb liquids' (Irene Jacob and Walter Jacob, 'Flora,' *ABD* 2:803–17, esp. 812).

227. For a similar defense of the AH's interpretation of Exod. 24:3–8, see Owen, *Hebrews*, 22:344–47. *Contra* Johnson who sees it as 'extremely loose'

The AH quotes Exodus 24:8, which itself is a direct quote of Moses. **'This is the blood of the covenant that God commanded concerning you.'**[228] This quote clearly confirms that **God** intended that sacrificial blood/death is to be connected to the inauguration of the Mosaic covenant. So much so, that it is termed **the blood of the covenant** (cf. Heb. 10:29; 13:20). This expression is wonderfully very reminiscent of Christ's words of institution at the Lord's Supper, 'This cup is the new covenant in my blood' (1 Cor. 11:25; cf. Matt. 26:28; Mark 14:24; Luke 22:20). Again, although not explicitly stated yet, the AH is preparing to connect the death/blood of the Mosaic covenant to Christ's death/blood of the new covenant.

9:21–22a *And likewise he sprinkled with blood the tabernacle and also all the vessels of ministry. And almost all things are purified with blood according to the law,*

The **tabernacle** was not yet built at the time of the initial inauguration of the covenant. The AH points out that later Moses also **sprinkled with blood the tabernacle** and **all the vessels** associated with its ceremonial **ministry**. The AH is making reasonable implications from a variety of texts to make this claim (e.g., Exod. 40:9 [oil]; Lev. 8:15, 19; 30;[229] 16:14–20; 17:11; Num. 7:1 [oil]; 19:4–6).

Given the amount of ceremonies **according to the law** that include sacrificial blood, **almost all things are purified with blood** is a summarizing statement further emphasizing that **blood** is connected to covenants. Note the **almost**. An exception, for example, would be a poor person who could not afford an animal offering but uses flour instead (Lev. 5:11).

---

and 'inaccurate' (*Hebrews*, 241–42).

228. The LXX follows the OT Hebrew text very closely. Hebrews 9:20 changes 'behold' to **this**; 'has made' (כרת, διατίθημι) to **commanded**; and 'Lord' to **God**.

229. Josephus, similar to the AH, concludes that Moses sprinkled the **tabernacle** and **vessels** with oil and **blood** (*Jewish Antiquities* 205–6). Philo includes a discussion of the mixing of oil and blood for the initial ordination of the priests (*On the Life of Moses* 2.146–52).

9:22b *and without the shedding of blood there is no forgiveness.*

The AH concludes this pericope with a general principle, **without the shedding of blood there is no forgiveness**. Note the double negative (**without, no**) for rhetorical punch (also Heb. 9:18).

Here, **forgiveness** of sin is made explicit as an aspect of being 'purified' (Heb. 9:22a). 'Forgiveness' and 'sin' are used in Hebrews 10:18, which is the final verse of this long section (8:1–10:18). As noted above at Hebrews 9:14, Christ's blood 'purifies' us (change of inner man), and this presupposes our **forgiveness** of sins.

Tantalizingly, this expression has clear connections to the Mosaic covenant (Lev. 4:18–20; 5:13; 17:11,[230] 14; 19:22; Num. 15:25–28; cf. Gen. 9:4–5), but it is stated in a such a way to entice the congregant to understand that true **forgiveness** only comes through Christ's sacrifice, as Hebrews 10:4 will make crystal clear and 9:15 has already stated.[231]

The noun *shedding*-**of-blood**[232] further stresses that a bloody death is required for **forgiveness**. This implicitly harkens back to the 'blood of Christ' in Hebrews 9:14. The 'shedding' aspect reminds us of Christ's flogging (Matt. 20:19 // Mark 10:34; John 19:1), his crown of thorns (Matt. 27:29 // Mark 15:17; John 19:2–5), the nails in his hands (John 20:25), and the blood from his pierced side (John 19:34, 37; 20:25; cf. Zech. 12:10).

Reflections

'This cup is the new covenant in my blood. Do this, as often

---

230. Lev. 17:11 is discussed several times in the Talmud. The question concerns why the laying of hands is required in certain ceremonies (e.g., Lev. 1:4) if it is only the blood, as stated in Lev. 17:11, is necessary for forgiveness. See b. Yoma 5a; b. Zevahim 6a; and b. Menahot 93b.

231. Referencing Heb. 9:22 and 1 Pet. 1:18–19, WLC 152 states, 'Every sin ... cannot be expiated but by the blood of Christ.'

232. The Greek is αἱματεκχυσία. It only occurs here in the NT and does not occur in the LXX. It is a combination of 'blood' (αἷμα) and 'to pour out' (ἐκχέω).

as you drink it, in remembrance of me' (1 Cor. 11:25). The sacrament of the Lord's Supper incorporates many biblical truths. How does it relate to Hebrews 9:15–22?

Christ is the mediator of a *new covenant* (Heb. 9:15). A major aspect of the inauguration of covenants is that *death* is involved (Heb. 9:15–17). More specifically, a death that involves the shedding of *blood* (Heb. 9:18–22). The Mosaic covenant and its *blood of the covenant* is typological of the new covenant (Heb. 9:20). This shedding of Christ's blood in the new covenant effects in believers *purification* and assures *forgiveness* of sins and an *eternal inheritance* (Heb. 9:15, 22).

Two points of interest connecting the Lord's Supper to Hebrews 9:15–22: First, there is the reminder that although the Lord's Supper is obviously typological of the Passover (Exod. 12:1–28, 43–51; Luke 22:7–8), this text highlights another typological connection, that is, the inauguration of the Mosaic covenant in Exodus 24:3–8. The Mosaic covenant was inaugurated with Moses' speaking and writing down God's words and performing a ceremony that included sprinkling both the book and the people with blood. That covenant ceremonies include God's words matches the Lord's Supper. Both the preaching of the Word and the 'words of institution' go together with the bread and wine. Commenting on Hebrews 9:20, Calvin says, 'What kind of sacrament would it be unless the Word preceded it?'[233]

Second, Hebrews 9:15–22 highlights that the Lord's Supper is a *covenantal* ceremony, both as to its inauguration on that Thursday night and our continuing observance of the sacrament. And as a covenantal ceremony, blood/wine is involved representing the sacrificial death.[234] Given this, the WLC 174 encourages Christians during the Lord's Supper to 'affectionately meditate on his [Christ's] death and suffering ... in the renewing of their covenant with God.'

---

233. Calvin, *Hebrews and 1 & 2 Peter*, 126.

234. The bread and wine are also normal aspects of a meal and thus represent our spiritual sustenance.

Once to Die, Then Judgment (9:23–28)

Hebrew 9:23–28 continues the discussion of Christ as the true 'high priest' (Heb. 9:11) and the 'mediator of the new covenant' (Heb. 9:15) relative to the ceremonies of the Mosaic covenant. More specifically, the AH begins by making an implication from the Mosaic blood-purification ceremonies discussed in Hebrews 9:16–22—Christ's sacrifice is needed for purification, and it is better (Heb. 9:23). How is it better? Christ's sacrifice relates to eternal/heavenly/new-covenant realities, not just earthly realities (Heb. 9:24). Also, Christ's sacrifice of himself only occurred once, not every year, showing it truly dealt with sin and will bring eschatological salvation (Heb. 9:25–28).

9:23 *Therefore, [it was] necessary that the copies of the things in the heavens be purified by these, and that the heavenly things [be purified] by better sacrifices than these.*

Looking back to Hebrews 9:16–22a, the AH notes that the Mosaic-covenant inauguration, the tabernacle, and vessels are **copies of the things in the heavens**. That is, they are typological of the true heavenly and eternal realities. He also has in mind the truism that 'without the shedding of blood there is no forgiveness' (Heb. 9:22b). **Therefore**, the AH concludes that two things are **necessary** from God's perspective. (1) It is **necessary** that the things associated with the Mosaic covenant **be purified by** various blood-purification ceremonies/sacrifices (first and second **these**[235]). (2) It is **necessary** that **the heavenly things be purified by better sacrifices**.

Obviously, **better sacrifices** refers to Christ's one sacrifice, which the AH will be emphatic about this 'once' aspect in the immediately context (Heb. 9:25–28). The plural **sacrifices** is used because its typological Mosaic equivalent is plural.[236]

---

235. The first **these** (τούτοις) is neuter plural and refers back to the Mosaic purification ceremonies. The second **these** (ταύτας) is feminine plural and refers more explicitly to **sacrifices**, that is, the sacrifices of the Mosaic purification ceremonies.

236. So virtually all commentators, e.g., Aquinas, 'Although one

Why is it **necessary** that **the heavenly things be purified**? This issue has puzzled commentators of all stripes.[237] Obviously, it cannot be that God himself is sinful and needs to be cleansed. The various proposed solutions depend on differing definitions of **heavenly things**, and for some, defining **purified** as only referring to inauguration (cf. Heb. 9:18) as opposed to cleansing from sin (cf. 9:22). Also coming into play is whether one sees Christ's blood being brought into the heavenly tabernacle, a view with which I strongly disagree. I will simply give my view with a truncated argument. The **heavenly things**, as opposed to 'heaven itself' (Heb. 9:24), are the heavenly/new-covenant realities (matching my view of 'a greater and more perfect tabernacle,' Heb. 9:11) for God's people, now and into the eschatological future. This includes their personal salvation but also the ordinances of Christ's church. Since those who become God's people are sinful and to be in his kingdom one must be cleansed, **purified** primarily refers to God's people being cleansed.[238] The inauguration view has some attraction because it equates the consecration/dedication of the Mosaic tabernacle (cf. Exod. 40:9; Heb. 9:18) to the purification of heavenly tabernacle and side steps the assumption of a tainted tabernacle.[239] The primary problem with this view is that the main emphasis of the purification in

---

[Christ's sacrifice], yet it was prefigured by a plurality of sacrifices in the Old Testament' (*Hebrews*, 196).

237. R. B. Jamieson states that 'in the eyes of modern commentators ... [this] is one of the strangest, most intractable statements in this elusive epistle' ('Hebrews 9:23: Cult Inauguration, Yom Kippur and the Cleansing of the Heavenly Tabernacle,' *NTS* 62 [2016]: 569–87). For good summaries of options, see Hughes, *Hebrews*, 379–82; and David J. MacLeod, 'The Cleaning of the True Tabernacle,' *BSac* 152 (1995): 60–71.

238. In general, so also Chrysostom, 'Homily 16 on Hebrews' (*NPNF*[1], 14:444–45); Aquinas, *Hebrews*, 195–96; Calvin, *Hebrews and 1 & 2 Peter*, 128; Owen, *Hebrews*, 22:374; Bruce, *Hebrews*, 226; and Attridge, *Hebrews*, 262 (with a Platonic twist).

239. In general, so Spicq, *Hébreux*, 2:266–67; Ellingworth, *Hebrews*, 475–78; Moffitt, *Atonement and the Logic of Resurrection in the Epistle to the Hebrews*, 225 n. 20; and Koester, *Hebrews*, 421.

the Hebrews 9 context is to deal with the forgiveness of sin.[240] Secondarily, it is not clear that Moses' tabernacle inaugural 'purification' was not also against the background of sin.

9:24 *For Christ did not enter into the Holy of Holies[241] made with hands, [which is] a type of the true, but [he entered] into heaven itself, now to appear before the face of God for us.*

Hebrews 9:24–28 is an expansion (**for**) on Christ's work being a 'better sacrifice.' It begins with the heavenly-intercessory aspect of Christ's work that resulted from the 'better sacrifice.'

On the Day of Atonement, the high priest enters the **Holy of Holies** (Lev. 16:1–14). As opposed to the high priest, **Christ entered heaven itself** and is **before the face of God**. As the Geneva Bible comments, 'The Leuvitical hie Priest ... appeared before the Arke, but Christ before God himselfe.'[242]

This verse includes the comforting words **for us**. This re-reminds any Christian of Christ's intercessory work before the Father (Heb. 2:18; 4:15; 7:25).[243] Of course, this intercessory work presupposes the atonement, which is the emphasis of this section of Hebrews.

Note the 'contrast within continuity' aspect of this verse. The priest's entering the **Holy of holies** is a **type** (ἀντίτυπος[244]) **of the true** spiritual realities. This typology shows a level of continuity. An escalating contrast (**but**, ἀλλά) is shown by the difference between the ark and God's presence and

---

240. So also Schreiner, *Hebrews*, 283.

241. The Greek ἅγια, which is plural, with no context could be 'holy places' or an idiom for **Holy of Holies**. Similar to Hebrews 9:12, I prefer **Holy of Holies**, so also Owen, *Hebrews*, 22:339; Attridge, *Hebrews*, 262; and Schreiner, *Hebrews*, 284.

242. *Geneva Bible: 1602 Edition*, folio 113.

243. Creedal references using Hebrews 9:24 for Christ's intercessory work include WCF 8.4, WLC 55, and Heidelberg Catechism 49.

244. AH uses τύπος ('archetype,' Heb. 8:5) and ἀντίτυπος (**type**) in a reverse way as opposed to the normal Greco-Roman usage and the usage in Christian history.

an antithetical contrast by the tabernacle being **made with hands** versus God and his heaven that is/was not made with human hands.

9:25–26 *Nor [did he enter] in order to offer himself often, just like the high priest enters into the Holy of Holies every year with the blood of another; otherwise it would have necessitated him to suffer often from the foundation of the world, but now*[245] *he has appeared once at the end of the ages for removal of sin through his sacrifice.*

To show that Christ's work was 'better' (Heb. 9:23), Hebrews 9:24 stresses that Christ 'did not enter' the manmade tabernacle, but entered into the Father's presence. Now in Hebrews 9:25–26, AH adds that Christ did not **offer himself** *often* but only **once**, and that Christ **offered** *himself*, not **the blood of another**.

Interestingly, the AH uses a *reductio ad absurdum* argument to show that Christ's sacrificial death only occurred **once**. High priests were only able to offer sacrifices **every year** because they offered **the blood of another** (i.e., animal blood). If Christ was similar to the high priests in how often he performed his sacrificial duties, he would have had to **suffer often** as a **sacrifice**, that is, die **every year**. How many times would Christ have had to die? As many years as there are **from the foundation of the world**, or more pedantically, since Adam's first sin (cf. Luke 11:50). Given Christ's human nature, this is absurd because men cannot die numerous times. (This point will be expanded upon in Hebrews 9:27–28.) Since Christ's sacrifice only happened **once**, this is further evidence that it is 'better.' How? It confirms that it was truly effective for **the removal of sin**; it did not have to be repeated (cf. Heb. 10:1–2, 10–11).[246]

---

245. Here, **now** (νυνί) is mostly logical as opposed to temporal. BDAG notes νυνί may be used to 'introduc[e] the real situation after an unreal conditional clause or sentence' (p. 682), which is this scenario.

246. Morris, 'The very fact that there is a continuing need for these sacrifices seems to him [AH] to show conclusively that they have no real effectiveness. A sacrifice that really takes away sin would not have to be repeated indefinitely' (*The Cross in the New Testament*, 290).

With the use of **from the foundation of the world**, the AH presupposes the preexistence of Christ (divine nature). Further he presupposes that Christ's one death covers the sins of the elect going all the way back to Adam (see further discussion at Heb. 9:15, 10:2–3, and 10:11).[247] Christ's died **once**; this death has eternal significance!

Christ' incarnation is referred to as **he has appeared once at the end of the ages**. The expression **end of the ages** matches to 'in these last days' (Heb. 1:2) and refers to the decisive Christ event that was long predicted (cf. Gal. 4:4). Since Hebrews 9:28 refers to Christ's second appearing on earth, clearly **he has appeared** refers to Christ's first appearing on earth. This first appearing is also connected to his **sacrifice**. Therefore, *contra* some scholars, Christ's sacrificial atonement occurred on earth, not in heaven.[248]

9:27–28 *In as much as it is appointed for men to die once, and after this, judgment; thus also Christ, having been offered once to bear the sins of many, will be seen a second time, not [to deal] with sin, [but] for salvation for those eagerly awaiting him.*

The AH now states a general biblical truism and then relates it to Christ (**in as much as … thus also**) to further confirm that Christ's sacrifice and its results are 'better'.

The biblical truism is: **It is appointed for men to die once, and after this, judgment**. This truism that men die began upon the Adamic fall and will continue up to the NHNE (cf. Gen. 2:17; Rom. 5:12–14; 1 Cor. 15:22).[249] Death

---

247. So also Calvin, *Hebrews and 1 & 2 Peter*, 129; *Geneva Bible: 1602 Edition*, folio 113; Owen, *Hebrews*, 22:398; Moffatt, *Hebrews*, 133; and Koester, *Hebrews*, 422.

248. So also Hughes, *Hebrews*, 384; and Allen, *Hebrews*, 487; *contra* Socinians and Moffitt, *Atonement and the Logic of Resurrection in the Epistle to the Hebrews*, 280–81.

249. But what about Enoch (Heb. 11:5), Elijah (2 Kgs. 2:11), and those present at Christ's second coming? They did not nor will not die. The usual response is that in that moving from this world to the next is a type of death (cf. 1 Cor 15:51) (e.g., Calvin, *Institutes* 2.17.17).

is a consequence of sin.²⁵⁰ In addition to the Bible, general revelation foretells of a judgment (Rom. 1:18–20; 2:14–16). The word **judgment** (κρίσις) with no context is neutral and is so here. Depending on the person being judged, there could be a positive or negative result.²⁵¹

The AH connects this truism to Christ's redemptive-historical acts. Men dying **once** matches to Christ who also died **once**. Men experiencing a future **judgment** matches, not to Christ's being judged, but to his bringing the judgment **salvation** to the elect at his **second** coming.

The fact that Christ's human nature²⁵² can only die **once** *as per the truism* adds additional support to the previous *reductio ad absurdum* argument of Hebrews 9:25–26 that Christ will not die multiple times. Yes, Christ will again come to earth. That coming, however, will not involve dying as did his first coming. At Christ's **second** coming, as opposed to the first, he will come **not to deal with sin**, otherwise he would have to die again. To the contrary, there will be **salvation for those eagerly awaiting him** (cf. 1 Thess. 1:10).²⁵³ There will also be negative judgment for those outside of Christ, but that is not the point here.

Having been offered once to bear the sins of many is another wonderful statement. The phrase **to bear the sins of**

---

250. 'Shall all men die? Death, being threatened as the wages of sin, it is appointed unto all men once to die, for that all have sinned' (WLC 84). References are Rom. 6:23; Hebrews 9:27; and Rom. 5:12.

251. Κρίσις in Hebrews 10:27 is clearly negative. 'Eternal judgment' in Hebrews 6:2, using the cognate κρίμα, is a neutral context.

252. Ambrose, 'The death is not the death of [Christ's] eternal Godhead but of his weak human frame' (*Of the Christian Faith* 3.19 [*NPNF*², 10:254]). See further discussion 7:23–24 as to Christ's person always living.

253. Some see Christ's appearing as analogous to the high priest's appearing after coming out from the Holy of Holies on the Day of Atonement based on Sir 50:5 ('How glorious he was when the people gathered round him as he came out of the inner sanctuary' [RSV]), e.g., Hughes, *Hebrews*, 388–89; and Lane, *Hebrews 9–13*, 250. I disagree as Lev. 16:17–18 gives no hint of this and the immediate analogy is not to the Day of Atonement but to the die-and-then-judgment truism.

many is linguistically very close to Isaiah 53:12.[254] Christ as both priest and victim matches to this section of Hebrews and to the wonderful Isaiah 52:13–53:12 passage; hence, I assume **to bear the sins of many** is an intentional reference to Isaiah 53:12. **Having been offered** is in the passive. The Greek verb προσφέρω behind **having been offered** is used often in Hebrews, but in reference to Christ, it is otherwise in the active, 'he offered himself' (Heb. 9:14, 25; 10:12). Here we see the planning work of the Father to have the Son offer himself (cf. Heb. 10:5–9).

Reflections

As the KJV translates, 'It is appointed unto men once to die, but after this the judgment' (Heb. 9:27). Clearly, not all cultures accept that death is followed by judgment. Many tombstones in the Greco-Roman world indicated there was nothing after death.[255] Reincarnation is still popular in parts of the modern world.[256]

In the modern West, it is generally a mixed bag. Among many there is agnosticism as to what happens upon death, which then leads to squelching any serious discussion of the issue. Others see a type of heaven where one's departed relative is looking down upon us smiling. There is no mention of a judgment. It is simply assumed that one's departed was good enough to get to heaven, and so also will they be. This is typical in many televised funerals of the famous, actors for instance.

---

254. The LXX is very close to the Hebrew excepting 'sin' is singular in the Hebrew (חטא) and plural in the LXX (ἁμαρτίας). The LXX and Hebrews 9:28 are very close given the mood difference of the verb 'to bear.' LXX: αὐτὸς ἁμαρτίας πολλῶν ἀνήνεγκεν ('he bore the sins of many'). Heb. 9:28: εἰς τὸ πολλῶν ἀνενεγκεῖν ἁμαρτίας ('to bear the sins of many'). Also cf. 1 Peter 2:24: τὰς ἁμαρτίας ἡμῶν αὐτὸς ἀνήνεγκεν ('he bore our sins').

255. Tombstones had the Latin acronym *NFFNSNC*, which stands for *non fui, fui, non sum, non curo* ('I was not, I was, I am not, I care not').

256. After quoting Heb. 9:27, the Catechism of the Catholic Church flatly states, 'There is no "reincarnation" after death' (§1013).

Others, whether they know Hebrews 9:27 or not, at times feel in their bones that there will be a judgment following this life. Unfortunately, they do not trust in the Savior, but seek to merit heaven by their works. This produces a level of anxiety that is often suppressed, but comes more to the surface when they attend a funeral or pass one of life's milestones or as they themselves can more clearly see death approaching.

The Bible continues to toll the bell, 'It is appointed unto men once to die, but after this the judgment.' For some, this is nonsense; for others, it produces anxiety. For the Christian, it is a hard truth that we will die, but it is a glorious truth that our 'judgment' will result in being face to face with our Savior based on his 'offering himself' as atoning 'sacrifice'. In addition to thanking our Savior, let us pray for and interact with those who need the Gospel.

Not Blood of Bulls and Goats (10:1–10)

Hebrews 9:25–26 contrasts the Levitical repeated once-per-year sacrifices with Christ's one sacrifice. In Hebrews 10:1–10, the AH expands upon this. Hebrews 10:1–4 shows the inadequacies of the Levitical repeated sacrifices and further adds the inadequacies of animal sacrifices. By using Psalm 40:6–8, in Hebrews 10:5–10 the AH confirms the Levitical inadequacies by showing that Christ's one sacrifice with his body was God's plan all along.

10:1 *For the law, having a shadow of the good things to come, not the image itself of the things, is never able to perfect those approaching every year by the same sacrifices which they offer*[257] *continually.*

---

257. The verb is προσφέρουσιν is active (**they offer**). **They** being the high priests that offer sacrifices on the Day of Atonement for the general worshipers. So also Owen, *Hebrews*, 22:427; Koester, *Hebrews*, 429; and Johnson, *Hebrews*, 246. Some see προσφέρουσιν as functionally a passive which makes **sacrifices** as the subject and eliminates priests (**they**) from the sentence. So Moffatt, *Hebrews*, 136; James Hope Moulton, *Prolegomena*, 3rd ed., vol. 1 of *A Grammar of New Testament Greek* (Edinburgh: T & T Clark,

In Hebrews 10:2–4, the AH will give the specific rationales as to why the Levitical sacrifices are deficient. Here he simply states it. The grammatical center of this verse is **the law ... is never able to perfect those approaching**. **Law** is, as usual, the ceremonial law, with special reference here to the Day of Atonement (**every year, continually**). **Those approaching** refers to general 'worshipers' (Heb. 10:2). **To perfect** is full-orbed and true salvation, which the **law** cannot do (cf. Heb. 7:19).[258]

The **law** is not completely deficient; it is a **shadow of the good things to come**.[259] This parallels Hebrews 8:5 where the earthly tabernacle is a 'copy and *shadow* of the heavenly things.' The phrase **good things to come** is from the perspective of the **law** (cf. Heb. 3:5; 9:11), that is, it refers to the new covenant's current and future benefits that the readers enjoy and will enjoy.

Negatively, the **law is not the image itself of the** new covenant **things**. The Greek behind **image** is εἰκών. In context, it clearly means reality and is being contrasted with **shadow** as all commentators through the ages agree. Hence, many modern translators understandably do not use the potentially confusing term **image** but 'true' and/or 'reality' (e.g., RSV, NIV, ESV, CEB). This is the only time that the AH uses εἰκών. It is used elsewhere in the Bible to mean reality or exact replica (e.g., 2 Cor. 4:4; Col 1:15; Rom 8:29; cf. Gen. 1:26; Col 3:10); however, it is also used to mean not the reality, but simply an image of a reality (e.g., Isa. 40:19; Ezek. 23:14; Dan. 3:1; Matt. 22:20; Rom. 1:23).

Following Greek philosophy, Philo uses **shadow** (σκία) and **image** (εἰκών) interchangeably (e.g., *Allegorical Interpretation*

1908), 58–59; Zerwick and Grosvenor, *Grammatical Analysis*, 2:675; Lane, *Hebrews 9–13*, 255; and ESV. Grammatically this does not work because ἅς (or αἷς) (**which**) clearly refers to **sacrifices** and is not a nominative.

258. For discussion of 'perfection' of believers, see Hebrews 7:11. For discussion of 'perfection' of Christ, see Heb. 5:9.

259. This positive use of the ceremonial law is referenced in the Catechism of the Catholic Church §128, WCF 19.3, and WLC 34.

3.96; *On the Migration of Abraham* 12). The fact the AH does not follow this word usage is another evidence that he is not under the sway of Platonic influence (see discussion at the beginning of the Heb. 8:1–10:18 section).[260] Another ancient Greek usage of the two words relates to a painting. The painter first drew an outline, called the σκία. The painter then filled the outline in with colors for the final version of the painting, called the εἰκών. Chrysostom assumed that this is how the AH uses the words. The OT law/tabernacle is the outline (σκία), and the new-covenant/heavenly-tabernacle is the completed painting (εἰκών).[261] Although this painting analogy is interesting, the AH is influenced by the biblical usage of εἰκών as it relates to a reality.[262]

10:2–3 *Otherwise would they*[263] *not have ceased to be offered on account of the worshipers having been once purified would no longer still have consciousness of sins? But in these [there is] a reminder of sins every year.*

The AH gives another angle to the rationale as to why the law is deficient. His key assumption is that if a sacrifice is a true sacrifice, it would only need to be offered **once** because it would truly take care of sins, including past, present, and future (see discussion at Heb. 9:15, 25–26, 10:11). This assumption is possible because of the divine-human nature of Christ and the eternal heavenly tabernacle.[264] Thus, if **worshipers** were truly

---

260. Cockerill well says, '[This word usage] betrays the distance between his [AH's] worldview and Platonic dualism espoused by Philo' (*Hebrews*, 428).

261. Chrysostom, 'Homily 17 on Hebrews,' (*NPNF*[1], 14:448). So also Calvin, *Hebrews and 1 & 2 Peter*, 132; and Brown, *Hebrews*, 433.

262. Owen is against the painting view because the book was written primarily to Jewish people, 'who of all people were the least acquainted with the art of painting' (*Hebrews*, 22:421).

263. **They**, that is, the sacrifices.

264. Aquinas argues that since sin is spiritual, it needs a 'heavenly' purification. Further, since Christ has perpetual/eternal power (Heb. 9:12, 23), thus this 'perpetual power suffices for those sins to be committed and those already committed' (*Hebrews*, 203).

purified and this would only need to occur **once**, then they **would no longer still have consciousness of sins**. But in fact, the ceremonies of the law continue to be **a reminder of sins**, especially with the sacrifices (**these**) in the Day of Atonement ceremony (**every year**).[265]

The AH is using **consciousness of sins** to mean being still under the judgment of sin, that is, for those who have not been justified by faith (cf. Heb. 9:22).[266] This remembrance/ **consciousness of sins** wonderfully contrasts with God's *non*-remembrance of believers' sins from the Jeremiah quote (Heb. 8:12; 10:17). By the repeated sacrifices, the **worshipers** were being taught (1) that these sacrifices did *not* truly justify and (2) sins were serious and needed to be atoned for. Given this, the **worshipers** were to conclude that these repeated sacrifices pointed to a true, one sacrifice.

But are not believers, those who have been justified, supposed to be conscious of their sins (e.g., Matt. 6:12)? Also, does not the AH admit that even for believers there is 'sin which clings closely' (Heb. 12:1)? Owen well answers, 'Our remembrance of sin and confession of it respect only the *application* of the virtue and efficacy of the atonement once made, without the least desire or expectation of a new propitiation.'[267]

As to the date of Hebrews, Bruce notes that it appears that the sacrifices are still being made at the Jerusalem temple; otherwise, the AH would have had to explain why they had ceased. Hence, Hebrews 10:2–3 is an 'incidental pointer to the dating of the epistle before AD 70.'[268]

---

265. For Philo, sacrifices offered by impious men are not sacrifices at all and only remind the impious of their sin (*On Planting* 108; *On the Life of Moses* 2.107). Jub. 5:19 and 34:19 have an emphasis on righteous actions and mourning producing forgiveness on one day per year.

266. So also Owen, *Hebrews*, 22:434; and Brown, *Hebrews*, 436. Cockerill includes both justification and aspects of sanctification (*Hebrews*, 431).

267. Owen, *Hebrews*, 22:438, emphasis mine.

268. Bruce, *Hebrews*, 236. Ellingworth rebuts this by taking the various present tenses in Hebrews 10:1–4 as 'gnomic or timeless,' not an indication that the offerings were continuing (*Hebrews*, 490).

10:4 *For [it is] impossible [for the] blood of bulls and goats to take away sins.*

Hebrews 10:4 supplements (**for**) the argument from 10:2–3 to show the ineffectiveness of the Levitical sacrifices. Yes, the sacrifices were ineffective due to the logic of being repeated, but in addition, these sacrifices were just *animals*. Since Hebrews 9:22 has shown that the 'shedding of blood' is needed for forgiveness, the emphasis here is not on **blood**, but on the ineffectiveness of **bulls and goats** (cf. 9:12). This then sets up Hebrews 10:5–10 with its emphasis on the body of Christ.

In essence, the AH has made this point previously in Hebrews 9:11–14 comparing animal blood to Christ's using a lesser-to-greater argument. Here in Hebrews 10:4, however, the point is made starkly and with rhetorical flourish. **For it is impossible for the blood of bulls and goats to take away sins.**[269] Probably, the AH is using **bulls and goats** to refer to all Levitical sacrifices.

Although the AH does not expand explicitly upon the reasons that animals were not good enough, several reasons are clear from the book of Hebrews. (1) God simply did not intend animals to be the true sacrifice (e.g., Heb. 10:5–9). (2) The priest/sacrifice needed an indestructible life (Heb. 7:16–17). (3) The priest/sacrifice needed to be a brother to represent his people (Heb. 2:11–17; 4:15). (4) The animal does not willingly give itself to die, but the true sacrifice had to willingly offer himself (Heb. 10:9; 12:2). (5) There is a moral/spiritual aspect to sin that cannot be eliminated simply by material (animal) means (Heb. 8:9; 9:11, 23, 27; 13:20). (6) The pinnacle of God's creation is man, and an animal substitute does not match man's inherent glory (Heb. 2:6–9; 4:14–16; 11:6; 12:22–24).

10:5–7 *So then, when coming into the world, he said, 'you did not*

---

269. Ellingworth comments that Hebrews 10:4 'contains perhaps the author's strongest negative statement about the levitical sacrifices' (*Hebrews*, 497).

desire sacrifice and offering, but you prepared a body for me; you took no pleasure in burnt offerings and sin offerings. Then I said, behold I have come (in the scroll of the book it is written concerning me) to do, O God, your will.'

Given that repeated animal sacrifices were insufficient (**so then**), the AH quotes Psalm 40:6–8 to emphasize that Christ's **body**, not an animal's, was/is the true sacrifice. The further implications of the quote concerning the law-versus-new-covenant and the repeated-versus-once aspects will be noted in Hebrews 10:8–9 and 10, respectively.

As to the linguistic technicalities of the quote between the Hebrew, the LXX, and the book of Hebrews, there is only one point of substance.[270] It concerns the phrase 'you have dug (כרה) ears for me' (Ps. 40:6), which in the book of Hebrews is **you prepared a body for me** (Heb. 10:5). The LXX is a mixed bag with some manuscripts matching exactly the NT, and others having 'you prepared *ears* for me.'[271] The Hebrew phrase 'you have dug ears for me' is somewhat opaque but

---

270. Excepting the one issue, the very minor linguistic differences between the Hebrew and the LXX include: (1) The Hebrew 'scroll' (מגלה) is translated as 'little head' (κεφαλίς). This makes sense as the wooden stick that is within the rolled scroll sticks out with a 'little head.' (2) The Hebrew has the passive participle 'written' and the LXX has a perfect passive indicative 'it has been written.' The minor and inconsequential differences between the LXX and the NT book of Hebrews include: (1) The LXX has singular 'burnt offering,' and the NT has the plural **burnt offerings**. (2) The LXX has 'you did not ask/require' (αἰτέω), the NT has **you took no pleasure** (εὐδοκέω). (3) The LXX has the vocative 'O my God' following 'your will,' and the NT drops 'my,' and moves the vocative **O God** to follow **to do**.

271. The Rahlfs and the Rahlfs/Hanhart editions surprisingly choose 'ears' as the original despite the major manuscripts B, S, and A all having 'body.' The Vulgate has 'ears.' Some scholars believe that the AH had 'ears' in his LXX copy and intentionally changed it to **body**. This initial change is then picked-up in later LXX manuscripts. So Owen, *Hebrews*, 22:457–58; Karen H. Jobes, 'Rhetorical Achievement in the Hebrews 10 "Misquote" of Psalm 40,' *Bib* 72 (1991): 387–96; and Guthrie, 'Hebrews,' 977. However, most scholars believe that 'body' was in the AH's copy of the LXX. So Moffatt, *Hebrews*, 138; Bruce, *Hebrews*, 240; Koester, *Hebrews*, 433; and Jared Compton, 'The origin of ΣΩΜΑ in Heb 10:5: Another Look at a Recent Proposal,' *TJ* 32ns (2011): 19–29 (this article is a rebuttal of Jobes).

refers to God's making the author capable of obeying. 'Dug' refers to God's fashioning the author's body, and 'ears' is representative for hearing/obeying.[272] Whether the LXX had 'body' or 'ears', the translation of the Hebrew 'you have dug ears for me' as **you prepared a body for me** is reasonable. First, it uses a synecdoche: the part ('ears') is appropriately replaced by the whole (**body**). Second, it replaces the opaque 'dug' by the straightforward **prepared**. Third, "ears" are related to obeying, which the AH understands as Christ's **body** as obeying.

Before elaborating on how the AH uses this text, some background on Psalm 40 is helpful. Psalm 40 is ascribed to David. It has two major sections: 1–10 is a thanksgiving for God's past deliverance of the author, and 11–17[273] is a lament/request to be currently delivered from both the author's 'iniquities' and more so from enemies.[274] Although this psalm emphasizes the individual, it does include several comments that this individual will proclaim God's mercies to the congregation (Ps. 40:5, 9–10; cf. Heb. 2:12) and gives proverbial advice that applies to any individual (Ps. 40:4, 16). Intriguingly, the author of the psalm states that he is written about elsewhere in the 'scroll of the book' (Ps. 40:7), that is, elsewhere in Scripture. Given the David reference in the superscription, these 'one and many' nuances, and the 'scroll of the book' comment, Psalm 40 appears to be written by David[275] and shows how any Israelite king represents, [276] or should represent, his people and also

---

272. Isa. 50:4–5 is a reasonably close parallel. As with almost all other commentators, I do not see Exod. 21:6 as a parallel.

273. Ps. 40:13–17 parallels closely to Ps. 70:1–5.

274. The sequence of thanksgiving and then lament is unusual in the Psalms, although Pss 9–10; 27; 44; and 89 have this sequence. The unusual sequence does make sense; one looks for future deliverance from a current problem based on past deliverances. So also Belcher, *The Messiah in the Psalms*, 173.

275. Many critical scholars see this psalm as post-exilic, e.g., Terrien, *Psalms*, 341.

276. Based on the one and many, Craigie comments, 'Thus, implicit

looks forward to *the* king.

Psalm 40:6–8, which is quoted in Hebrews 10:5–7, is within the thanksgiving section of Psalm 40. On the surface, David is saying that various offerings are not desired by God, but David was at some point enabled to understand that ('dug my ears,' Ps. 40:6). Following this ('then,' Ps. 40:7), David did God's will and had internalized God's law. Since God's will and law did include giving sacrifices during David's lifetime, it is assumed that David is using hyperbole to make the point that sacrifices offered without the correct heart motive are useless.[277] This point is made often in the OT (e.g., 1 Sam. 15:22; Pss. 50:8–15; 51:16–17; Isa. 1:10–13; Jer. 7:21–26; Hos. 6:6; Amos 5:21–23).[278]

Now back to the AH. As all agree, the AH understands that the quote is spoken by Christ to God the Father. In the introductory phrase to the quote, **when coming into the world, he said**, this clearly refers to Christ at his incarnation (Heb. 10:5). Also, within the quote itself, the phrases **you prepared body for me** and **I have come ... to do, O God, your will** confirm that the **I/me** is Christ and **you/O God** is God the Father.

What potentially prompted the AH to see Psalm 40 as ultimately being spoken by Christ?[279] First, note that the AH sees this speech being spoken by Christ prior to but referring to his incarnation (**when coming into the world, I have come**). The prior-to aspect is more clearly seen with **in the scroll of the book it is written concerning me**. As Richard notes, 'These works had already been written down in Scripture

---

in the psalm is a principle of representation within the kingdom of God' (*Psalms 1–50*, 317).

277. Possibly, the emphasis on improper sacrifices is prompted by Saul's sin, as Saul was the king prior to David (1 Sam. 15:1–23, esp. 15:22).

278. Kistemaker comments, 'There are clear indications in several OT passages which show that offering to God is not to be found in the thing (sacrifice), but in the person (the heart)' (*The Psalm Citations in the Epistle to the Hebrews*, 126).

279. See the excellent article by Brandon D. Crowe, 'Reading Psalm 40 Messianically,' *RF&P* 2:2 (2017): 31–44.

(Heb. 10:7) long before the Son ever took on flesh and dwelt among us, which means that they must have been determined in the counsels of God [covenant of redemption] even before that.'[280] These words are spoken as Christ is considered in his mediatorial role (cf. Heb. 2:12–13). Thus, this matches the AH's high view of Christ and his pre-incarnational existence.

Primarily, however, the AH sees kingly psalms as typological and/or directly predictive of Christ the Son, who is also the high priest (e.g., Heb. 1:5, 8–13; 2:6–8; 5:5–6; 7:21).[281] Most likely here the AH saw Psalm 40 about David and understood it in a prophetically escalating way that Christ is the more perfect David.[282] As noted above, many aspects of the psalm show a representative and obedient king (cf. the obedience of Christ, Heb. 2:10; 3:2; 4:15; 5:7; 12:2–3; 13:13). Certainly, the parenthetical comment **in the scroll of the book it is written concerning me** would lead one to see more than a psalm simply about David.[283]

Hebrews 10:5–7 is another amazing example of intra-Trinitarian speech. The AH assumes that the persons of the Trinity do communicate and that some of these communications are recorded in Scripture! See Hebrews 1:5, 2:12, and 7:20–22 (cf. John 17).

---

280. Richard, 'The Covenant of Redemption,' 49. For more discussion on the covenant of redemption, see Hebrews 7:20–21.

281. I have argued elsewhere that 'every psalm in *some sense* refers to *both* Christ and Christians … some psalms [are] primarily about Christ and secondarily about believers; and other psalms, conversely, [are] primarily about believers and secondarily about Christ' (Cara, 'Psalms Applied to Both Christ and Christians: Psalms 8, 22, 34, 118 and Romans 15:3 // Psalm 69:9,' 97–111, esp. 98, emphasis original).

282. The psalm author commenting upon his 'iniquities' (Ps. 40:12) often has caused some concern as applying this psalm to Christ. The best answer is to see that Christ took on himself the 'iniquities' of his people (cf. Isa. 53:5, 8, 10). So also Calvin, *Hebrews and 1 & 2 Peter*, 134; Brown, *Hebrews*, 440; and Belcher, *The Messiah and the Psalms*, 175. Schreiner argues differently. NT believers understood that 'Jesus was greater than David, that David's faults were not replicated in the life of Jesus' (*Hebrews*, 297).

283. Possibly, David was originally referring to Deut. 17:14–20; but as the psalm ultimately refers to Christ, it would include all of Scripture (e.g., Luke 24:25–27). B. Yevamot 77a sees David as the speaker in Ps. 40:7 and was referring to Gen. 19:15 and Ps. 89:21. B. Gittin 60a–60b uses Ps. 40:7 in arguments as to whether the whole Torah is one scroll or multiple scrolls.

10:8–9 *Above when saying 'you did not desire nor took pleasure in sacrifices and offerings and burnt offerings and sin offerings' (which are offered according to the law), then he has said, 'Behold, I have come to do your will.' He takes away the first in order to establish the second.*

He, God the Father, **takes away the first in order to establish the second**. In addition to just arguing that the Psalm 40:6–8 quote required a human 'body', in Hebrews 10:8–9 the AH makes the related point that the quote anticipated the redemptive-historical movement from the **first** (Mosaic covenant and the associated Levitical sacrifices) to the **second** (new covenant and the associated sacrifice of Christ).[284]

In requoting (**above when** [Christ was] **saying**), the AH appropriately shortens the quote of Psalm 40:6–8 to **you** (God the Father) **did not desire nor took pleasure in sacrifices and offerings and burnt offerings and sin offerings, then he** (Christ) **has said, 'Behold, I** (Christ) **have come to do**[285] **your will**. How does this show a movement from **first** to **second**? The first key is to see that the AH interprets **then** from **then he has said** and **I have come** as occurring (or planning to be) temporally later then the OT sacrifices. The second key is to see that the OT statements that God does not desire animal sacrifices is not just a hyperbolic complaint about sacrificing without the proper heart motive but is foreshadowing that ultimately God's forgiveness will not be based on animal sacrifices, no matter the heart motive. Of course, a congregant

---

284. Confirming that first/second language refers to covenants, see Heb. 8:7, 13; 9:1, 15, 18; cf. 1 Cor. 15:47; Rev. 20:6. Also, Heb. 10:16 quote of Jer. 31:33 in context points to covenant. Somewhat confusingly, both **first** and **second** are in the neuter ('covenant' and 'sacrifice' are both feminine). I have no explanation for this. *Contra* Schreiner who relates the first/second language 'to the passing away of OT sacrifices, which are no longer required now that the sacrifice of Christ has been offered'(*Hebrews*, 300 n. 483). Ultimately, there is little difference between our views.

285. The majority-text manuscripts include 'O God' matching to Heb. 10:7; hence, it is included in the Geneva Bible and the KJV. Metzger argues it is 'clearly a secondary assimilation to v. 7 and/or to the Septuagint text of Ps. 39:9 [ET 40:9]' (*TCGNT*², 600).

is also predisposed to see this redemptive-historical movement based on the Jeremiah 31 discussion in Hebrews 8:8–13.

The AH inserts into the quote about the Levitical sacrifices the parenthetical statement **which are offered according to the law**. Again, he associates the ceremonial aspects of the Mosaic covenant (**first**) with the term **law**. Also note that multiple OT sacrifices and offerings, not just those associated with the Day of Atonement, are considered typological of Christ.

10:10 *By which will we have been sanctified through the offering of the body of Jesus Christ once.*

Although grammatically expanding upon 'second' from the previous sentence, the AH here concludes Hebrews 10:1–9 as he brings in aspects of the quote (**will, offering, body**) and drives home the repeated-versus-once aspect from Hebrews 10:1–3 (**once**).

Will refers to 'your will' (Heb. 10:7, 9). This is God the Father's **will** as fulfilled and carried out by Christ (cf. John 10:17–18). More specifically, it is that Christ's atonement would sanctify the church. Although implied multiple times, Christ's atonement is here for the first time termed an **offering**.[286] This is stated again in Hebrews 10:14 and strongly implied in 10:18. Christ's **body** relates back to the quote (Heb. 10:5) and is as opposed to animals (Heb. 10:4). The adverb **once** (ἐφάπαξ[287]) emphasizes[288] that there was only one **offering**, and there will never be any more.[289]

---

286. Although Moffitt agrees that 'coming into the world' does refer to the incarnation, he still insists that **offering** and **body** (and 'blood') are referring to 'Jesus's body being offered in heaven' and not on the cross (*Atonement and the Logic of Resurrection in the Epistle to the Hebrews*, 229–56, esp. 232).

287. Heb. 10:2 has 'once' (ἅπαξ). For discussion of synonyms ἅπαξ and ἐφάπαξ, see Heb. 7:27.

288. Ellingworth sees its position at the end of the sentence as grammatically emphatic (*Hebrews*, 505).

289. So also Zerwick and Grosvenor, *Grammatical Analysis of the New Testament*, 2:676; Lane, *Hebrews 9–14*, 256; Ellingworth, *Hebrews*, 505; Koester, *Hebrews*, 434; and Schreiner, *Hebrews*, 301; *contra* Cockerill who

The exact expression **Jesus Christ** is only used in Hebrews three times, 10:10, 13:8, and 13:21. Hebrews 13:8 and 13:21 are certainly grand and creedal-type statements about him.[290] Hence, this adds rhetorical weight here because Hebrews 10:10 is one of the intentionally overarching creedal-type statements.[291] Yes, it is gloriously true that **we have been sanctified through the** one and only **offering of the body of Jesus Christ!**[292]

The nuance of the phrase **we have been sanctified** (ἁγιάζω) is not clear. Linguistically, 'to be sanctified' ('to be made holy') does have a general 'set apart' sense and, if related to humans, a more specific existential moral holiness sense.[293] Further, in the NT the moral holiness sense has two related theological/conceptual meanings. (1) 'Definitive sanctification' is the radical break from a pagan mindset and life to turn to God and live for him that occurs at conversion and this state continues throughout our life (cf. Rom. 6:1–14; 8:9). [294] (2) Progressive sanctification' is the continuing advancement in holiness throughout the life of the believer (cf. 1 Thess. 4:3). Now, more specifically in the book of Hebrews, the verb ἁγιάζω refers in 2:11 to Christ and believers (both present participles); 9:13 to OT believers being ceremonial clean (present indicative);10:10 to believers (periphrastic perfect indicative); 10:14 to believers (present participle); 10:29 to believers[295] (aorist participle); and 13:12 to believers (aorist subjunctive).

---

attaches it to **we have been sanctified** (*Hebrews*, 445 n. 53). Grammatically, Greek adverbs do not normally modify nouns/substantives; but here by sense (and context of Heb. 10:1–3) **once** modifies **offering** with **offering** apparently being taken verbally as 'Jesus Christ was offered.' Smyth does admit that 'rarely' adverbs may modify 'substantives' (*Greek Grammar*, 283).

290. 'Christ Jesus' does not occur in Hebrews. 'Christ' by itself occurs 9 times. 'Jesus' by itself occurs 11 times.

291. Attridge refers to it as a 'solemn combination' (*Hebrews*, 277 n. 118).

292. As expected, Hebrews 10:10 is referenced in many creeds, e.g., Augsburg Confession 24; Heidelberg Catechism 80; French Confession 23; WCF 8.4, 11.3; WLC 71; and Catechism of the Catholic Church §614.

293. BDAG, 9–10.

294. See John Murray, 'Definitive Sanctification,' *Collected Writings of John Murray*, 2:277–84.

295. Not all agree that the reference is to believers here. Some see it as referring to an apostate, others to Christ.

Here in Hebrews 10:10 with the use of the perfect, **we have been sanctified**, the options for me are either (1) a general having been 'set apart' for God's purposes focused on the believer's broad salvation (including justification, sanctification, and glorification), or (2) more specifically, definitive sanctification. Supporting option one is the meaning of 'to perfect' in Hebrews 10:1; the summary big-picture creedal-type statement of 10:10; and the end of the following pericope includes both sanctification and justification, with the emphasis being on justification (Heb. 10:15–18). Supporting option two is the appropriate concern in Hebrews for personal sanctification (e.g., 12:14), and given the definitive/progressive relationship, it may explain the present tense usage (progressive sanctification) elsewhere of ἁγιάζω.[296] I prefer option one here.[297] Also, I think this option plausibly works for the other ἁγιάζω passages. To be sure, since option two is a subset of option one, the differences between these two options does not affect the overall theology of Hebrews.

Reflections

Hebrews 10:1–10 contains two memorable verses: 'It is impossible for the blood of bulls and goats to take away sins' (Heb. 10:4), and 'we have been sanctified through the offering of the body of Jesus Christ once' (Heb. 10:10).

The juxtaposition of the offering of animal bodies with the offering of the body of Jesus Christ is striking. A casual observer of the Jewish sacrifices in the first century AD (pre-AD 70) and a casual reader of the OT would assume that the multiple animal sacrifices do in fact take away sins. But no, declares the AH, anyone who saw Christ on the cross and risen (1 Cor. 15:1–8)

---

296. The use of the cognate noun 'saints' (ἅγιος) in Hebrews 6:10 and 13:24 (cf. Heb. 3:1) could argue for both options as saints are set apart to be holy; although, it probably favors option two.

297. So also Owen, *Hebrews*, 22:478; and Brown, *Hebrews*, 443. Favoring definitive sanctification, Bruce, *Hebrews*, 243; Kleinig, *Hebrews*, 483; Allen, *Hebrews*, 500 ('objective sanctification,') and Schreiner, *Hebrews*, 301 ('Sanctification here is positional, something true of believers upon conversion'). Kistemaker favors progressive sanctification based on present tense use in Heb. 2:11 and 14 (*Hebrews*, 282).

and/or is a deep reader of the OT knows that Jesus Christ and his one sacrifice/offering alone is the reality that brings God's benefits to his people.

This juxtaposition is enhanced when one considers that Jesus Christ as the eternal divine Son is the one who agreed to take on a body. It is not simply a comparison between animal bodies and a human body, but it is between animal bodies and the person of the Son, who is the *divine*-human mediator.

Another juxtaposition is the power of the two types of offerings. The animal offerings were continuous, but this ultimately simply showed their ineffectiveness. The offering of the body of Jesus Christ only occurred once and needed to be only once. This one offering was so powerful that it was effectual for both OT and NT saints and ensured their getting to the new heavens and the new earth.

After noting Hebrews 10:10, the Waldensian Confession 15 (AD 1662) exhorts us: 'Let us therefore cling to this one and true sacrifice of Christ.'[298]

Jeremiah 31 Again (10:11–18)

Hebrews 10:11–18 ends the great theological section of 8:1–10:18, which along with Hebrews 7, emphasize the person and work of Christ as the high priest. Following 10:18, the AH begins another exhortation section.

Hebrews 10:11–18 clearly breaks down between 10:11–14 and 10:15–18. The first section describes Christ's priestly work as including both his sacrifice on earth and his current sitting on the throne in heaven. His sacrificial work is compared to the Levitical priests' work in somewhat of a summary of Hebrews 10:1–4, if not back to 9:11.[299] Hebrews 10:11–14 does add one component, which is a comparison of Christ's sitting

---

298. *Reformed Confessions of the 16th and 17th Centuries*, 4:505.

299. Calvin emphasizes the summary/conclusion aspect, 'This is the conclusion of the whole argument, namely that the practice of daily sacrifice is wholly inconsistent with and foreign to the priesthood of Christ' (*Hebrews and 1–2 Peter*, 137). Hodge connects Hebrews 10:11–12 directly to the 'once' of Hebrews 10:10 (*Hebrews*, 99).

versus the standing of the other priests. This comparison is another proof that Christ's one sacrifice does take away sins and the multiple sacrifices of the other priests do not. The ascension language, which includes Christ's sitting, is based off of Psalm 110:1, which then evokes the similar language from Hebrews 8:1 (also Heb. 1:3, 13; 12:2).[300]

The second section, Hebrews 10:15–18, reuses a portion of the Jeremiah 31:31–34 quote already used in Hebrews 8:8–12. This truncated quote is used to authoritatively confirm the statements in Hebrews 10:11–14, with the emphasis on the forgiveness of sins that then further demonstrates that Christ's one sacrifice is sufficient.

10:11 *And, on the one hand,[301] every priest has stood daily ministering and offering repeatedly the same sacrifices, which are never able to take away sins;*

Hebrews 10:11–14 is introduced with a non-specific **and** (καί). See immediately above for the connections backwards.

Here the argument of Hebrews 10:1–4 is condensed to one verse but with the additional argument based on the standing-versus-sitting comparison. There is also the slight change from the once-a-year Day of Atonement sacrifice by the high priest to **every priest** and all the various **daily** offerings.

In order for any priest to do the work of **ministering and offering**, he needs to stand.[302] In fact, there has always been a Levitical **priest** who **has stood daily**[303] since the erection of the tabernacle and continues with the temple. The implication of

---

300. Ellingworth objects to Hebrews 10:11–18 being viewed as a summary. It is a 'step forward' due to the stand-versus-sit argument and the 'gradual change in temporal perspective' based on re-emphasizing Christ's sitting (*Hebrews*, 507).

301. **On the one hand** and the 'but on the other' in Hebrews 10:12 is my wooden translation of the Greek μέν ... δέ expression.

302. In fact, the OT emphasizes that a priest stands before the Lord to do his work (e.g., Deut. 10:8; 17:12; 18:7; 2 Chr. 29:11; cf. 1 Kgs. 8:11; 13:1).

303. **Daily** and **same sacrifices** invokes the daily morning and evening lamb sacrifices (Exod. 29:38; Num. 28:4), but it probably also includes all types of other occasional offerings and sacrifices.

this standing is that the work is not completed, and further, uncompleted work shows that these **sacrifices ... are never able to take away sins**.³⁰⁴ The use of **daily, repeatedly,** and **same** drives this point home. Again note the assumption that if a sacrifice **takes away sins**, this would include past, present, and future sins, and thus there is no need for another sacrifice (see discussion at Heb. 9:15, 25–26, 10:2–3, and 10:11.)

10:12–13 *but on the other hand, this [one after] offering*³⁰⁵ *one sacrifice for all time*³⁰⁶ *sat at the right hand of God, from that time on*³⁰⁷ *waiting until his enemies be made a footstool for his feet.*

As compared to the Levitical priests (**but on the other hand**), Christ (**this one**), **after offering one sacrifice,** *sat.* This sitting of Christ is another argument that his **sacrifice** (of himself!) will not be offered again because one needs to stand to do the work of sacrificing.

The wording **sat at the right hand of God ... until his enemies be made a footstool for his feet** is a quote of Psalm 110:1 with slight modification. The OT Hebrew and LXX, along with Hebrews 1:13, have the imperative 'sit'. But wonderfully so, here the imperative is changed into the past (aorist) indicative **sat**. In Psalm 110:1, the Father told the Son to

---

304. As usual in these types of verses, Hughes argues that the tenses show that priests are still standing (perfect **has stood** implies they were and still are standing) with the implication that the temple is still standing (*Hebrews*, 400 n. 63). Also as usual, Ellingworth notes that the tenses show only a 'general principle' and there is no implication about the temple (*Hebrews*, 508).

305. For a defense of the translation *after* **offering**, which is an aorist participle, see discussion of similar grammar related to *'after* having obtained' in Hebrews 9:11–12.

306. Grammatically, the prepositional phrase being used adverbially, **for all time** (εἰς τό διηνεκές), may modify **offering** (e.g., KJV, RSV, NIV, ESV) or **sat** (e.g., Tyndale, Geneva Bible, NAB, NJB). In context, both options make sense. My justification for εἰς τό διηνεκές modifying the participle **offering** is that elsewhere in Hebrews (7:3; 10:1; 12:14) εἰς τό διηνεκές always follows the verb it is modifying. As to the translation of εἰς τό διηνεκές, see Hebrews 7:3.

307. **From that time on** is my translation of τό λοιπόν, which generally has the meaning of 'remaining,' but when used temporally, as here, the English must be idiomatic (cf. Gal. 6:17).

sit, at that point, a future event. But as the AH writes, the Son has ascended and is seated on the throne; hence, he uses **sat**.[308] Given that Psalm 110:4 connects the kingship and priesthood of Christ, the AH interprets Christ's sitting as implying, among other things, that it was purposely as opposed to the priests' standing.[309]

10:14 *For the one offering has perfected for all time those being sanctified.*

Hebrews 10:14 gives the grounds (**for**) for Hebrews 10:11–13, but especially 10:12a, probably emphasizing the **for all time** aspect.[310] It does so in a summary-type manner.[311]

As elsewhere in Hebrews, the AH uses **perfected** related to believers to indicate the design/end/purpose/fulfillment for which God's plan of salvation was ultimately intended, that is, the new covenant benefits for believers.[312] The earthly-work

---

308. The only other changes are the grammatically required changes due to the quote not being the first-person speech of God the Father. Hence, 'my' is **God**; the two uses of 'your' referring to Christ are **his**; and the active 'I make' is the passive **be made**. The AH did insert the words **from that time on waiting**, although he made no explicit use of them. Chrysostom and Aquinas see the reason for the **waiting** as God's desire to show mercy on those who have not yet believed before Christ comes back in judgment (cf. Isa. 30:18; Heb. 9:28; 2 Pet. 3:9) ('Homily 18 on Hebrews,' [*NPNF*[1], 14:452]; *Hebrews*, 208, respectively).

309. For the many other connections the AH makes to Ps. 110:1, see discussion at Heb. 1:13.

310. So also Hodge, *Hebrews*, 100.

311. This summary-type manner explains why Heb. 10:14 is referenced in many creeds, e.g., Thirty-Three Articles (Anabaptist) 19, Augsburg Confession 24, Heidelberg Catechism 21, Belgic Confession 21, WCF 8.5, 11.5, First Confession of Basil 4 (*Reformed Confessions of the 16th and 17th Centuries*, 1:289), Bohemian Confession 6 (*Reformed Confessions of the 16th and 17th Centuries*, 1:308), First London Confession 18 (*Reformed Confessions of the 16th and 17th Centuries*, 4:281), Waldensian Confession 15 (*Reformed Confessions of the 16th and 17th Centuries*, 4:505), and Catechism of the Catholic Church §1544.

312. For a discussion of 'perfection' of believers, see Hebrews 7:11. For discussion of 'perfection' of Christ, see Hebrews 5:9.

portion of this plan is accomplished by Christ's **one offering for all time**. It is effective for both OT and NT saints (**those being sanctified**).³¹³

As discussed in more depth at Hebrews 10:10, there is disagreement over the nuance of the verb 'to sanctify' in Hebrews. Here it is substantival present participle, **those being sanctified**. Many see the meaning here as progressive sanctification, especially given the present tense.³¹⁴ I prefer to see 'to sanctify' with the broad nuance of 'set apart,' meaning set apart for full-orbed salvation, which would of course include progressive sanctification.³¹⁵ For me, the present tense here is 'gnomic' (truism) and/or 'iterative' in the sense that throughout redemptive-history believers have been, are, and will be 'set apart' by the application of Christ's work.³¹⁶ Contextually, this matches the parallel Hebrews 10:10 use of 'to sanctify'; the meaning of **perfected**; and the emphasis of Hebrews 10:18 on the forgiveness of sins, which is the logical ground for all new covenant benefits.

10:15 *And the Holy Spirit also witnesses to us, for after he has said;*

In addition to the argument in Hebrews 10:11–14 based on the stand-versus-sit comparison to prove that Christ's one sacrifice 'has perfected for all time' believers (Heb. 10:14), **the Holy Spirit also witnesses** to this same conceptual point by the partial quote of Jeremiah 31:33–34.³¹⁷

---

313. That is, this verse supports the Reformed doctrine of limited atonement.

314. So, e.g., Allen, *Hebrews*, 502–3; and Cockerill, *Hebrews*, 452.

315. So also Owen, *Hebrews*, 22:493 ('dedicated to God'). Bruce and Schreiner are also against the 'progressive' view. Bruce interprets 'to sanctify' here as 'eternally constituted God's holy people' (*Hebrews*, 247). Schreiner has what I term the 'definitive sanctification' view (*Hebrews*, 306).

316. Bruce opts for a 'timeless' (i.e., gnomic) present (*Hebrews*, 247). For definitions of gnomic and iterative presents, see Wallace, *Greek Grammar Beyond the Basics*, 520–25.

317. In Hebrews 8:8b–12, the full Jer. 31:31–34 quote is the (God-designed) deficiencies of the first covenant.

The **Holy Spirit** in the past inspired Jeremiah 31 (**has said**), but also, the **Holy Spirit** currently **witnesses**[318] **to us**.[319] This past and current aspect matches Hebrews 3:7 where through Psalm 95 the Holy Spirit is speaking 'today'. Since it is the **Holy Spirit** who **witnesses**, this current witness is an *authoritative* witness. Note that the Scripture and the **Holy Spirit** together are the witness/authority, not to mention God is also speaking the words of Jeremiah 31:31–34 as stated in the introduction to the quote in Hebrews. 8:8.[320]

A few have connected 'declares the Lord (Yahweh)' (Jer. 31:33 // Heb. 10:16) to the **Holy Spirit**, that is, the **Holy Spirit** is directly equated to Yahweh. Hughes argues, 'That the Holy Spirit and Yahweh are one is plainly implied by the equation of what the Holy Spirit says with the Lord (in the Hebrew, Yahweh) says.'[321] Although plausible, I prefer, however, to see the speaking of the **Holy Spirit** here, as in Hebrews 3:7, only in the sense of the divine person who (primarily) inspired the words of Scripture and the current implications that flow from that.

With the use of **after** in the phrase **after he has said**, the AH apparently is referring to Hebrews 10:16, that is, **after he has said** 10:16. This then has the implication that what

---

318. The verb **witnesses** (μαρτυρέω) is also used in Hebrews 7:17 explicitly related to Scripture, and implicitly in 7:8 (cf. John 5:39). Philo often uses 'to witness' (μαρτυρέω) as in God witnesses through the Scripture (e.g., *Allegorical Interpretation* 3.2, 37, 129, 196, 217; *Sacrifices* 67). He also uses 'to witness' unrelated to Scripture (e.g., Aristotle witnesses to Plato [*Eternity* 16]; Philo himself witnesses to the grace of certain government officials [*Against Flaccus*]).

319. So also to this past and current aspect, Owen, *Hebrews*, 22:495; Lane, *Hebrews 9–14*, 268; Kleinig, *Hebrews*, 486; and Cockerill, *Hebrews*, 454–55.

320. WCF 1.4–5 well says, 'The authority of Holy Scripture ... dependeth ... wholly upon God (who is truth itself), the author thereof.... Our full persuasion and assurance of the infallible truth, and divine authority thereof, is from the inward work of the Holy Spirit, bearing witness by and with the word [Holy Scripture] in our hearts.'

321. Hughes, *Hebrews*, 403. So also Mastricht, *Theoretical-Practical Theology*, 2:573. Emmrich has another nuance. He sees this as direct speech by the **Holy Spirit** ('*PNEUMA* in Hebrews: Prophet and Interpreter,' 60–63).

follows is the primary point, which would be 10:17. Hence, many translations because of **after he said** add something like 'then he adds' at the beginning of 10:17 (e.g., RSV, NIV, NKJ, ESV).[322] I agree with this view as Hebrews 10:18 confirms that 10:17 is primary.

10:16–17 *'This is the covenant that I will covenant with them after those days, says the Lord, [I will] put my laws on their hearts and I will write them in their mind,' and [then he adds],*[323] *'I will remember their sins and their lawless [acts] no more.'*

This is the second time Jeremiah 31 is quoted. Hebrews 8:8b–12 quotes Jeremiah 31:31–34 in full.[324] Here, the AH/'Holy Spirit' has truncated the quote to first include Jeremiah 31:33a-b (Heb. 8:10a-b) **and then he adds** Jeremiah 31:34c (Heb. 8:12). Even where the two Hebrews quotes overlap (Heb. 8:10a-b // Heb. 10:16 and Heb. 8:12 // Heb. 10:17), there are a few minor changes, although these appear to be simply stylistic.[325]

As noted above, the quote is designed to prove that Christ's one offering 'perfected for all time' believers (Heb. 10:14). **Covenant** is clearly the new covenant (Jer. 31:31 // Heb. 8:8) and is connected to Christ's work. Hence, we see the Holy Spirit's witnessing that God the Father's covenantal promise and benefits have been accomplished by Christ's work (yes, note the Trinity). The truncated quote includes from Christ's

---

322. So also Owen, *Hebrews*, 22:495; Brown, *Hebrews*, 447; and Lane, *Hebrews 9–14*, 256. The contrary view is to see **after he has said** to only refer to Hebrews 10:16a, and 'declares the Lord' as the beginning of what follows, that is, Hebrews 10:16b–17 is the primary point. So Attridge, *Hebrews*, 281; Johnson, *Hebrews*, 254; and Cockerill, *Hebrews*, 455.

323. See discussion at Hebrews 10:15 to justify **and then he adds**.

324. As discussed at Hebrews 8:8b–12, the quote has only minor differences between the Hebrew, LXX, and Hebrews.

325. Hebrew 10:16 changes 'with the house of Israel' (Heb. 8:10a // Jer. 31:33a) to **with them**, and reverses the 'mind ... hearts' parallel (Heb. 8:10b // Jer. 31:33b) to **hearts ... mind**. Hebrews 10:17 eliminates 'because I will be merciful,' and substitutes **lawless acts** for 'unrighteous acts' (Heb. 8:12 // Jer. 31:34c), A very minor change, which makes no translation difference, is that **remember** is future indicative in Heb. 10:17 and aorist subjunctive in 8:12.

work both sanctification (**I will put my laws on their hearts and I will write them in their mind**) and justification (**I will remember their sins and their lawless acts no more**). These two clearly show that believers are 'perfected', but the 'one offering for all time' aspect is still by implication. The AH will make that implication explicit in the next verse.

10:18 *Where[326] [there is] forgiveness of these, [there is] no longer an offering for sins.*

Hebrews 10:18, by using the Jeremiah quote, is the conclusion that shows 10:14 is true. This involves two points: believers are 'perfected' and there was only 'one offering for all time.'

From the Jeremiah quote that included both sanctification and justification, the AH here emphasizes justification (**forgiveness**).[327] **These** refers to 'sins' and 'lawless acts' from the previous verse. Why the emphasis on justification to show believers are 'perfected'? As I argued previously, the importance of justification is due to its *logical* priority.[328] Once given this, all the other salvific benefits follow.

The AH must also show that only 'one offering for all time' is required. First, again, note the AH assumes that **forgiveness** of sins includes past, present, and future sins and has objectively been accomplished. Given this proper understanding of **forgiveness** and the reality that only Christ's death (as opposed to animals) can produce true **forgiveness**, then **there is no longer an offering for sins**. That is, the Jeremiah quote shows there will be only 'one offering for all time' and no others, and Christ was that 'one offering.'

---

326. As in English (cf. 'whereas'), **where** in Greek (ὅπου) can have a logical sense of these existing circumstances are the premise for my conclusion. See BDAG, 717; and BDF §456.3.

327. This emphasis is also shown by 'and then he added' in Heb. 10:17. As to Heb. 10:17 being the emphasis, so also Owen, *Hebrews* 22:496; Hodge, *Hebrews*, 102; Brown, *Hebrews*, 447; Moffatt, *Hebrews*, 141; Ellingworth, *Hebrews*, 512; Johnson, *Hebrews*, 254; and Schreiner, *Hebrews*, 310. *Contra* Cockerill, *Hebrews*, 455.

328. See discussion at the end of Hebrews 8:8b–12.

Reflections

As we come to the end of Hebrews 7:1–10:18, the reader and I have now looked closely at one of the most thrilling, and sometimes mysterious, sections of Scripture. Both the person and work of the high priest, Jesus Christ, has been presented with glorious nuances—as if he and his benefits to us are a brilliantly-shining multifaceted diamond. Also, we have been exposed to God's wisdom and providence in his institution of the old covenant. The numerous ways, both positively and negatively, God has foreshadowed Christ as mediator of the new covenant is also glorious. These amazing realities about Christ and the God-designed relationship between the old and new covenants have driven Christians throughout the ages to their knees in wonder concerning and thankfulness to the Triune God.

Maybe I should not have been, but I was surprised at a two-paragraph section in Owen's magnificent seven-volume commentary on Hebrews.[329] It comes right after he ends his exposition of Hebrews 10:18. He notes that this is the end of the dogmatic portion of Hebrews that is filled with 'heavenly and glorious mysteries.' Then, maybe somewhat uncharacteristic for his commentary, he says,

> I do therefore here, with all humility, and sense of my own weakness and utter disability for so great a work, thankfully own the guidance and assistance which have been given to me in the interpretation of it, so far as it is or may be of use unto the church, as a mere effect of sovereign and underserved grace.[330]

Needless to say, I can relate to Owen's statement, especially the 'humility' comment. Who is sufficient to delve into the interpretation of 'so great a work' such as Hebrews 7:1–10:18

---

329. Brown in his commentary also notes this section from Owen (*Hebrews*, 448).

330. Owen, *Hebrews*, 22:497.

so that the church may use it for her edification (cf. 2 Cor 2:16)? As Owen is, I am 'thankful for the guidance and assistance.' In context, Owen mentions the assistance of the 'worthy labour of others' and preeminently the Holy Spirit. As can be seen by my many footnotes, I am also thankful for the assistance of others and, I trust, the special assistance of the Holy Spirit (cf. 2 Cor. 3:5–6). Any truth I glean is the 'mere effect of sovereign and undeserved grace.'

Similar to Owen and me, I assume that many of my readers are also studying Hebrews with the goal of preaching/teaching its riches to the church. May all of us present these glorious realities and truths with power from the Scripture, but may we also realize that the means of our understanding of 'so great a work' drives us to personal humility.

9.
Exhortations Based on the Great Priest (10:19–39)

Hebrews 10:19–39 is the fifth of five subsections of Hebrews 4:14–10:39.[1] More specifically, it is the hortatory section immediately following the conclusion of the core theological statements concerning the priesthood of Christ (7:1–10:18).[2] As expected, the exhortations in this section are primarily grounded upon those priesthood realities. Also, there are clear verbal and conceptual parallels back to the priestly comments in Hebrews 4:14–16.[3] But in addition to these backward looking aspects, Hebrews 10:19–39 also anticipates later discussions in Hebrews. One obvious example is the discussion of 'faith' (Heb. 10:22, 38–39) that relates to Hebrews 11.[4]

Hebrews 10:19–39 itself breaks down into three pericopes.[5]

---

1. The five subsections are Hebrews 4:14–5:10; 5:11–6:20; 7:1–28; 8:1–10:18; and 10:19–39.

2. As I construe it, there are six hortatory sections in Hebrews: 2:1–4; 3:7–4:13; 4:14–16; 5:11–6:12; 10:19–39; and 12:1–13:17.

3. See discussion at opening section of Hebrews 4:14–5:10.

4. Given this forward looking aspect, some see 10:19–12:29 as one, large hortatory unit, so Hughes, *Hebrews*, 404; and Cockerill, *Hebrews*, 460.

5. So also many commentators, e.g., Ellingworth, *Hebrews*, 515–16.

The first has three positive exhortations, although one includes a negative sub-point (10:19–25). The second is a severe warning (10:26–31). The third is a renewed call for perseverance (10:32–39).[6]

Three Exhortations (10:19–25)

Hebrews 10:19–25 is one complex sentence. It includes three exhortations that are grounded upon two realities. The three exhortations are 'let us approach' (10:22), 'let us hold fast the confession' (10:23), and 'let us consider each other' (10:24).[7] The first and third exhortations each have two related participial phrases: 'having been sprinkled' and 'having been washed' connect to 'let us approach' (10:22); and 'not forsaking' and 'exhorting' connect to 'let us consider each other' (10:24–25). Interestingly, the well-known triad of faith, hope, and love is included as each exhortation mentions one of the three.

The two realities that ground or provide the basis for the three exhortations are 'having confidence ... by the blood of Christ' (10:19–20) and 'having a great priest' (10:21). These two realities are a summary of Hebrews 7:1–10:18. Possibly, this two-fold summary revolves around Christ as Victim (10:19–20) and Christ as Priest (10:21), that is, he 'offered himself' (9:14).[8]

10:19–20 *Therefore, brothers, having confidence for the entrance*[9]

---

6. Vanhoye splits my third section into two, Hebrews 10:32–35 and 10:36–39 (*Structure and Message of the Epistle of Hebrews*, 99). Schreiner agrees with my first two sections, but extends the third section from 10:32–12:3 (*Hebrews*, 311–12).

7. In Greek, all three are present hortatory subjunctives.

8. Not all will agree here. The more one sees the emphasis in Hebrews 10:19–20 as Christ as 'forerunner' (Heb. 6:20), then the less Christ as Victim applies.

9. To obtain a smooth reading, most English Bibles translate this prepositional phrase **for the entrance** as the infinitive 'to enter.'

into[10] *the Holy of Holies by the blood of Jesus, which he inaugurated a fresh*[11] *and living way for us, by the veil, that is, by his flesh;*

The **therefore** connects the previously just discussed priesthood and work of Christ to the three exhortations in Hebrews 10:23–25. This is the reality that drives the exhortations. But before getting directly to the three exhortations, the AH summarizes Hebrews 7:1–10:18 with two points. The first is Hebrews 10:19–20. The primary emphasis is that one's **confidence**[12] **for the entrance into the Holy of Holies**, that is, to be connected to Christ who is in the heavenly tabernacle, is based on and merited **by the blood of Jesus** (i.e., by Christ's priestly sacrifice). The mention of **blood** especially reminds the reader of Hebrews 9:11–10:18 and anticipates 10:29. Further, the **blood** emphasis is implied in the clause **which (entrance) he (Jesus) inaugurated a fresh/'new' and living way** through the word **inaugurated**. How so? This clause relates to the new covenant and its benefits. This new covenant **inaugurat[ion]** parallels 'not even the first covenant was *inaugurated* without *blood*' (Heb. 9:18).

Much scholarly ink has been spilt over **by (διά) the veil, that is, by his flesh.**[13] Virtually all agree that the background

---

10. **Into** is included because the genitive τῶν ἁγίων is a genitive of direction. For discussion of this type of genitive, see Wallace, *Greek Grammar Beyond the Basics*, 100–1. Surprisingly, BDF puts the use here as an objective genitive that is 'loosely used' as opposed to a genitive of direction (§§163, 166).

11. The Greek is πρόσφατος, and this is its only use in the NT. In secular usage it has the nuances of 'new', 'fresh, not decomposed,' and 'recent' (LSJ, 1529). I opted for **fresh** due to the contextual association with **living**.

12. **Confidence** is also used in Hebrews 3:6; 4:16; and 10:35.

13. E.g., Joachim Jeremias, 'Hebräer 10:20: τοῦτ' ἔστιν τῆς σαρκός αὐτοῦ,' *ZNW* 62 (1971): 131; Norman H. Young, 'ΤΟΥΤ' ΕΣΤΙΝ ΤΗΣ ΣΑΡΚΟΣ ΑΥΤΟΥ (Heb. 10:20): Apposition, Dependent or Explicative?,' *NTS* 20 (1973): 100–4; Daniel M. Gurtner, 'LXX Syntax and the Identity of the NT Veil,' *NovT* 47 (2005): 344–53; Mark A. Jennings, 'The Veil and the High Priestly Robes of the Incarnation: Understanding the Context of Heb 10:20,' *PRSt* 37 (2010): 85–97; Westcott, *The Epistle to the Hebrews*, 319–21; Hughes, *Hebrews*, 407–10; Ellingworth, *Hebrews*, 518–21; and Moffitt, *Atonement and the Logic of Resurrection in the Epistle to the Hebrews*, 281–83.

reference of **veil** is to the tabernacle veil that hangs between the Holy Place and the Holy of Holies, and the background reference to **entrance** is to the OT high priest's entrance to the Holy of Holies on the Day of Atonement. But how does this relate to Christ's **flesh**? In broad strokes, the interrelated 'questions' are: (1) Is the metaphorical veil an obstacle, an entrance point, or some combination for Christians getting to the heavenly tabernacle? (2) Does Christ's **flesh** relate to **veil** or go further back to **way** or refer to the whole preceding grammatical unit (Heb. 10:19–20a)? (3) Should the preposition διά be translated as 'through' (spatial/local) or as **by** (instrumental) before **veil** and **flesh**, and should that choice be consistently applied to both?

Without going through all the options and sub-options, although several are mentioned in the footnotes, I will primarily only present and justify my view. I take **flesh** as metaphorically referring to **veil** based on the consistent use of **that is** in the five other places it occurs in Hebrews.[14] I take the **veil** as the obstacle that must be overcome in order to allow entrance.[15] That is, Christ's **flesh**, the metaphorical **veil**, refers to Christ's sacrificial death (**by the blood of Jesus**).[16] As the OT priest had to push aside the material veil to enter the **Holy of Holies**, so similarly, Christ's sacrificial death had

---

14. **That is** (τοῦτ' ἔστιν) is used in Hebrews 2:14; 7:5; 9:11; 11:16; and 13:15. In every instance, the case of the word following **that is** matches the case of the initial word. Hence, **flesh** is in the genitive because **veil** is in the genitive, i.e., it is an appositive. So also, e.g., Young, 'ΤΟΥΤ' ΕΣΤΙΝ ΤΗΣ ΣΑΡΚΟΣ ΑΥΤΟΥ (Heb. 10:20): Apposition, Dependent or Explicative?,' 104; Attridge, *Hebrews*, 286; and many commentators. Westcott, to the contrary, connects **flesh** to **way** ('a way consisting in His flesh') to relieve the difficulty of seeing Christ's flesh as an 'obstacle' to getting to God and insisting on a 'complete parallelism between the description of the approach of Christ to God and the approach of a believer to God' (*Hebrews*, 320).

15. A common option in church history is to take **veil/flesh** as the means to hide Christ's divine nature, e.g., Aquinas, *Hebrews*, 211; Calvin, *Hebrews*, 141; and the *Geneva Bible: 1602 Edition* folio 113. Brown takes **veil** as the visible heavens that Christ passed spatially through (*Hebrews*, 456–57).

16. So also Athanasius, *Incarnation of the Word* 25.5 (*NPNF*[2], 4:50); Owen, *Hebrews*, 22:505; Moffatt, *Hebrews*, 143; Bruce, *Hebrews*, 253; Hughes, *Hebrews*, 408–10; and Schreiner, *Hebrews*, 315.

to push away the barrier of sin to allow Christians to enter the heavenly tabernacle. Supporting this is that the synoptic authors tell us that at Christ's death 'the veil of the temple was rent in twain from the top to the bottom' (Mark 15:38 KJV; cf. Matt. 27:51; Luke 23:45).

What about the preposition διά?[17] Many admit they understand it as 'through spatially' the **veil** but then 'by the instrumental means of' **his flesh**. For some, this incongruity (i.e., spatial versus instrumental) drives them away from seeing **flesh** connected to **veil**;[18] for others, it is simply an inconsistency they can accept.[19] I propose that the inconsistency is solved by understanding that the spatial and instrumental nuances conflate with a stress on the instrumental use when a door or veil/curtain are in view. Consider the expression, 'I went in through the front door' as opposed to the expression 'I went through the forest.' In the latter expression, 'through' is purely spatial. Concerning the door, however, one does not mean that he walked through the door per se, that is, that he cut a hole in the door in fireman-like fashion, and then walked through without ever actually opening the door. No, he means that he opened the door (instrumental) to provide the access inside, and then stepped through the doorway (spatial). Similarly, when we say that the OT priest went 'through' the veil, we do not mean that he cut a hole in it and went through the hole. To the contrary, we mean that he pushed the veil aside to provide access to the Holy of Holies. One spatially enters a house or the Holy of Holies by the instrument of manipulating the door or veil, respectively. Hence, it is proper to see διά as primarily the instrumental use (**by**) in pushing

---

17. I am assuming, as most do, that the διά before **veil** is implied as also before **flesh**.

18. So, e.g., Jeremias, 'Hebräer 10:20: τοῦτ' ἔστιν τῆς σαρκός αὐτοῦ,' 131; Westcott, *Hebrews*, 320; and Spicq, *Hébreux*, 2:316.

19. So, e.g., Young, 'ΤΟΥΤ' ΕΣΤΙΝ ΤΗΣ ΣΑΡΚΟΣ ΑΥΤΟΥ (Heb. 10:20): Apposition, Dependent or Explicative?,' 104; Ellingworth, *Hebrews*, 521; Lane, *Hebrews 9–13*, 275–76; Mitchell, *Hebrews*, 211; and Cockerill, *Hebrews*, 471.

aside the veil to obtain access and διά as the instrumental use (**by**) of Christ's sacrifice to push aside the barrier/penalty of sin to obtain access to God. There is no inconsistency; both expressions primarily have the instrumental use of διά, which secondarily provide spatial access.

Given my above view, I do not see this text making a parallel between Christians' **entrance** and Christ's entrance into the heavenly tabernacle. Yes, in Hebrews 6:19 there is a parallel that both Christ and Christians have entered behind the veil. There Christ is our 'forerunner'. But here the issue is the method by which Christians gain access. How was the veil pushed aside? It was **by the blood of Jesus, by his flesh.**

10:21 *and [having]a great priest over the house of God;*

The second ground of a Christian's 'confidence' is that Christ is a **great**[20] **priest**. This priesthood connects back to the previous ground ('the blood of Jesus,' Heb. 10:19) as Christ as **priest** presented himself as the sacrifice.

Christ's priesthood relates to his people. Here the redeemed are again referred to as **the house of God** (Father) matching Hebrews 3:6 (cf. Num. 12:7; Zech. 3:6–7).[21] This would include all OT and NT believers.

Interestingly, in Hebrews 3:1–6 Christ is 'faithful as a *son* over his (Father's) house' and here he is the **great priest**. Again in Hebrews, Christ as Son (King) and Christ as Priest are intimately related.

10:22 *let us approach with a true heart in full assurance of faith, having been sprinkled [with respect to* [22] *our] hearts from an evil*

---

20. For **great** (μέγας), see linguist footnote at Hebrews 4:14.

21. So also most commentators. Some, however, see **house** as referring more specifically to the heavenly temple, e.g., Hodge, *Hebrews*, 104; Brown, *Hebrews*, 458; and BDAG, 699.

22. **Hearts** is not technically the subject of the participle **having been sprinkled**, and similarly, **body** is not the subject of **having been washed**. They are 'accusatives of respect.' So also Zerwick and Grosvenor, *Grammatical Analysis of the New Testament*, 2:67. For a general discussion

conscience and[23] *having been washed [with respect to our] body with pure water;*

The first of the three exhortations is **let us approach**. It parallels 'let us approach with confidence the throne of grace' (Heb. 4:16; cf. Heb. 7:25; 11:6), which emphasized prayer. Primarily then, the purpose of our intimate connection here is for prayer and the blessings that come from that.[24] For a discussion of the priestly and theologically charged connotation of the verb 'to approach' and a variety of aspects of prayer, see discussion at Hebrews 4:16.

In what manner should we come to God?—**with a true heart in full assurance of faith** and not with an **evil conscience** (cf. Heb. 6:11, 'full assurance of hope'). The AH's use of **heart** recalls the use in Hebrews 8:10 and 10:16 as part of the Jeremiah quote. His use of **faith** looks forward to the use in Hebrews 10:38–39 and significantly in chapter 11.

The two participles are **having been sprinkled** and **having been washed**. They both are passives implying that God changed and is changing the congregants. They are motivations for coming to God in addition to the two in Hebrews 10:19–21. The OT metaphorical background is probably the Numbers 19 heifer ceremony previously discussed in Hebrews 9:13. This ceremony includes both sprinkling and washing (Num. 19:12, 19), although Hebrews 9:13 only refers to sprinkling.[25] Further,

---

of 'accusatives of respect,' see Wallace, *Greek Grammar Beyond the Basics*, 203–4. Hence, my overly mechanical translation is **with respect to.** The two participles are nominative plurals connecting to the **us** in the exhortation. This justifies the addition of **our**.

23. A minority of commentators take the participial phrase **and having been washed … water** to be connected with Heb. 10:23, so, e.g., Hodge, *Hebrews*, 104, and ASV.

24. So also Lane, *Hebrews 9–13*, 286. Referencing this text for prayer is the Belgic Confession 26 and the Confession of La Rochelle 19 (*Reformed Confessions of the 16th and 17th Centuries*, 3:314).

25. Other plausible options are that the **sprinkling** and **washing** relate to the ordination of priests (Exod. 29:4, 21; Lev. 8:6, 30). On the Day of Atonement, the **washing** of the high priest is explicit (Lev. 16:4), the **sprinkling** is less clear. Peter J. Leithart connects to the ordination of priests

Ezekiel 36:25–27 has definite connections as that passage has 'sprinkling clean water,' 'heart,' '(Holy) Spirit,' all within the context of the implied new covenant.[26] Some see **hearts** and **body** as representing the inner change (**hearts**) that results with outward actions done by the **body**.[27] Following the majority, I prefer to see these as parallel statements, primarily referring to the inner change that initially occurred at regeneration and continues.[28] Most likely the AH is here alluding to Christian baptism (cf. Heb. 6:2; 1 Pet. 3:21).[29] There is an inward change of **heart** caused by the Holy Spirit that is represented by an outward **washing** of the **body**.

10:23 *let us hold fast the unbending[30] confession of hope, for the one who promised is faithful;*

The second exhortation is **let us hold fast the unbending confession of hope.** Not only should true Christians 'approach' God now, they should have also realized the truth

---

and then argues that 'Heb. 10:19–22 states precisely that baptism confers priestly privileges' ('Womb of the World: Baptism and the Priesthood of the New Covenant in Hebrews 10.19–22,' *JSNT* 78 [2000]: 49–65, esp. 51).

26. Jason P. Kees argues that Ezek. 36:25–26 is the 'proper referent' for Hebrews 10:22 and is a 'bridge' connecting Levitical priesthood purification rites to the new covenant ('Having our Hearts Sprinkled Clean: The Influence of Ezek. 36:25–26 on Hebrews 10:22,' *WTJ* 83 [2021]: 237–50, esp. 249–50).

27. So Owen, *Hebrews*, 22:513–14; Gouge, *Hebrews*, 712; and Cockerill, *Hebrews*, 474.

28. This best fits with both participles being perfects.

29. So also Brown, *Hebrews*, 463; N. A. Dahl, 'A New and Living Way: The Approach to God According to Hebrews 10:19–25,' *Int* 5 (1951): 401–12, esp. 407–11; Bruce, *Hebrews*, 255; Hughes, *Hebrews*, 412; Attridge, *Hebrews*, 289; and Schreiner, *Hebrews*, 319. Typically, commentators who see **hearts** and **body** referring to inner change and outward actions, respectively, do not see a connection to baptism.

30. **Unbending** (ἀκλινής) is an adjective describing **confession**, so also Bruce, *Hebrews*, 256; and Attridge, *Hebrews*, 289. Most major English Bibles translate with an adverbial sense ('without wavering') modifying **let us hold fast**, also Lane, *Hebrews 9–13*, 288–89; and Koester, *Hebrews*, 445. Although adjectives sometimes also act as adverbs, I could find no clear example of this for ἀκλινής (LSJ, 51).

that Christ's priesthood guarantees the future. Therefore, they should now have and continue to have a **confession of hope**. This **hope** is one of the factors that aids their perseverance. For a discussion of **hope**, including its relationship to faith, see Hebrews 6:11–12 and Hebrews 11:1.

As the above exhortation parallels Hebrews 4:16, this one parallels Hebrews 4:14, 'let us hold firm the confession.' Also, Christ is called 'the apostle and high priest of our confession' (Heb. 3:1). For a discussion of the usefulness of confessions, see the Reflections section following Hebrews 3:1–6.

Besides the two grounds in Hebrews 10:19–21, the AH adds another one (**for**) that dovetails well with the content of **hope—the one who promised is faithful**. Promise and **hope** are both future-oriented concepts. The **unbending[ness]** of one's **confession of hope** is commensurate, or at least should be, with the trustworthiness of the **one who promised**. It was none other than God the Father who is **the one who promised**. Therefore, since he is **faithful** to his promises/covenants and does not lie (Heb. 6:17–18; cf. Heb. 3:6; 1 Thess. 5:24; Titus 1:2; Rev. 1:5), be exhorted to **hold fast** to your **confession of hope**.

10:24–25 *And let us consider one another toward a stirring up of love and good works, not forsaking the assembling together of ourselves,*[31] *as [is] a habit of some, but exhorting, even so much more as you see the Day drawing near.*

The third exhortation is **let us consider one another toward a stirring up of love and good works**. As the 'house of God,' Christ's work has clear corporate implications that drive believers to **consider one another**.[32] The purpose, at least here, is **toward a stirring up of love and good works**. The noun **stirring up** (παροξυσμός) and the cognate verb

---

31. The third person reflexive pronoun ἑαυτοῦ is used for first and second person especially in the plural; so also in Hebrews 10:34. See Zerwick, *Biblical Greek* §209.

32. The corporate aspect is summarized in the Abrahamic covenant, 'I will bless you and multiply you' (Heb. 6:14; cf. Heb. 11:12), and the new covenant, 'I will be their God, and they shall be my people' (Heb. 8:10).

παροξύνω are normally in very negative contexts and are translated 'sharp disagreement' and 'to provoke (to anger),' respectively. (e.g., Num. 14:11; Deut 29:27; Acts 15:39; 17:16; 1 Cor 13:5).[33] Several examples, however, do exist where the verb παροξύνω connotes 'to provoke (toward good works)' (Prov. 27:17; Josephus *Jewish Antiquities* 16.125).[34] Here the use is positive for the noun παροξυσμός.[35] But it does indicate that the interaction is to be done with some vigor as the translation **stirring up** indicates.

Interestingly, the noun **love** (ἀγάπη) only occurs elsewhere in the letter at Hebrews 6:10, where it is also combined with 'work'.[36] Confirmed by the parallel with Hebrews 6:10, the **love and good works** are those directed toward other believers. It is noted that Hebrews 10:22–24 includes the famous faith-hope-love triad (as does Heb. 6:10–12); the first exhortation includes 'faith,' the second, 'hope,' and the third **love**.[37] See discussion below in the Reflections section on the triad.

The two participles, **not forsaking** and **exhorting**,[38] give the location and means to carry out the third exhortation.[39]

---

33. Both of these are related to the noun 'sharp' (ὀξύς).

34. Although in the LXX and NT, there is mostly a negative connotation, LSJ gives several positive examples of 'spur on, stimulate' in non-biblically related Greek literature (pp. 1342–43).

35. So also virtually all other commentators. This is despite the fact that excepting Hebrews 10:24, I could not find one clearly positive use of the noun παροξυσμός; however, the semantic range of the cognate verb and the context confirm the positive use. Moffatt says that the AH's use of the noun 'seems to be an original touch' (*Hebrews*, 146). For the minority view that παροξυσμός in Hebrews 10:24 is negative, see Otto Glombitza, 'Erwägungen zum kunstvollen Ansatz der Paraenese im Brief an die Hebräer 10:19–25,' *NovT* 9 (1967): 132–50.

36. The verb ἀγαπάω only occurs in Hebrews 1:9 and 12:6, which are both OT quotes with Son/Lord doing the loving. The noun 'brotherly love' (φιλαδελφία) is a different cognate (Heb. 13:1).

37. The triad is also in Hebrews 6:10–12 but has a different order, 'love,' 'hope,' and 'faith.' Also, Hebrews 6:10–12 has a more broad use of the triad compared to Hebrews 10:22–24.

38. For the broad semantic range of **exhorting** (παρακαλέω), see footnote on 'encouragement' at Hebrews 6:18.

39. This contrasts with the first two exhortations. In both of the first two

The noun **assembling together** (ἐπισυναγωγή[40]) refers to the ongoing formal gatherings that would include worship.[41] The seriousness of the next pericope confirms this (Heb. 10:26–31). That is, not attending general and/or informal gatherings was not the primary concern.[42] Is the **forsaking ... as is a habit of some** referring to the complete abandonment of Christianity or the lessening of the commitment to attend the gatherings?[43] I prefer to see this as including both. Certainly the serious warning in the next pericope implies that complete abandonment was a possibility for some in this visible church. But the comments in Hebrews 10:32–35 concerning public suffering by being associated with the congregation may argue that others had less heinous motivations not to attend the services. Of course, either way, **forsaking the assembling together** is unhealthy for the individual and the congregation as the individual is not part of the **exhorting** that enhances

---

the additional information increases one's confidence in the exhortation, 'having been sprinkled' and 'having been washed,' along with 'the one who promised is faithful.' Here the additional participles are expanding upon how to perform the exhortation.

40. **Assembling together** (ἐπισυναγωγή) only occurs once in the LXX (2 Macc. 2:7) and twice in the NT (Heb. 10:25; 2 Thess. 2:1). It is a cognate of συναγωγή, which is used very often in the LXX for the assembled covenant people of God (e.g., Exod. 12:7, 34:31; Lev. 16:5; Deut. 5:22; Ps. 111:1). In the NT, συναγωγή is almost always used for a Jewish synagogue (e.g., Matt. 4:23), with the exception of a Christian assembly in James 2:2.

41. So also Calvin, *Hebrews and 1 & 2 Peter*, 144–45; Owen, *Hebrews*, 22:522; Bruce, *Hebrews*, 228; and Attridge, *Hebrews*, 290–91. As expected, creeds use this text to encourage attending worship services, e.g., WCF 21.5, 26.2; Cambridge Platform 13.1 (*Reformed Confessions of the 16th and 17th Centuries*, 4:401); Waldensian Confession 27 (*Reformed Confessions of the 16th and 17th Centuries*, 4:510); and Catechism of the Catholic Church §2178.

42. Of course, informal gatherings are good also (e.g., Heb. 13:1–2).

43. Morrison considers the **forsaking of assembling** as the 'most explicit danger' to which the warnings in Hebrews are directed. Because 'covenant' emphasizes 'allegiance to the community,' he sees it as 'the term that links doctrine and exhortation in the argument of Hebrews' (*Who Needs a Covenant?*, 160). Attridge sees the 'stern warnings' in Hebrews as 'largely hypothetical' with only Hebrews 10:25 being a 'specific reference to some who have abandoned Christian fellowship' (*Hebrews*, 66; 66 n. 40).

love and good works.[44] Wonderfully, God has promised that he will not 'forsake' true believers (Heb. 13:5).

The clause, **even so much more as you see the Day drawing near**, adds another motivation for the exhortation. As most commentators do, I take **Day** as referring to the final Day of the Lord (e.g., Joel 1:15; 1 Thess. 5:2) that involves both joy for believers and negative judgment for the unrepentant (cf. Heb. 4:9, 13; 9:27–28; 11:16; 12:14).[45] Since for all there will be the **Day**, and in God's timing we do not know when it will come (2 Pet. 3:8–10), but we are assured it is **drawing near**; therefore, Christians out of concern for **one another** should be motivated to encourage perseverance. Also, even when perseverance is not the prime issue, Christians should always be meeting to promote **love and good works** in light of *the Day* so as to glorify God now and in the future to have our good works on earth be publicly acknowledged by God as a testament to his grace in our lives.

Reflections

The triad of faith, hope, and love occurs several times in Scripture.[46] In Paul for the triad, he generally implies 'faith' in Christ, 'love' of other Christians, and 'hope' in eschatological salvation associated with the Second Coming (e.g., Col. 1:4–5). There is obvious overlap between the three. Depending on the

---

44. Later Rabbinic material also encouraged gathering together, 'Whoever has a synagogue in his town and does not go in there to pray is called a bad neighbor' (b. Berakhot 8a). Also see b. Berakhot 6a for stress on synagogue attendance.

45. For the minority view that this refers to the coming AD 70 destruction of Jerusalem, see Owen, *Hebrews*, 22:526; and Randall C. Gleason, 'The Eschatology of the Warning in Hebrews 10:26–31,' *TynBul* 53 (2002): 97–120.

46. I separate the references into more clearly triadic structure and more broad use of the triad plus other terms. The former includes 1 Cor. 13:13; Gal. 5:5–6; 1 Thess. 1:3; 5:8; Col. 1:4–5; and Heb. 10:22–24; and the latter includes Rom. 5:1–5; Eph. 4:2–5; Heb. 6:10–12; and 1 Peter 1:20–23. The similar triad of faith, love, and steadfastness (ὑπομονή) occurs in 2 Thess. 1:3–4; 1 Tim. 6:11; 2 Tim. 3:10; and Titus 2:2.

Pauline context, one of the three is usually emphasized.[47]

In Hebrews, the triad broadly exists in 6:10–12, but it is more clearly used in 10:22–24 as shown:

10:22: 'Let us approach with a true heart in full assurance of *faith*.'
10:23: 'Let us hold fast the unbending confession of *hope*.'
10:24: 'Let us consider one another toward a stirring up of *love* and good works.'

The intentionality of using the triad in Hebrews 10:22–24 is confirmed by (1) its use in 6:10–12, (2) 'full assurance of hope' (Heb. 6:11) is intentionally altered to 'full assurance of faith' (Heb. 10:22), (3) the noun 'love' (ἀγάπη) only occurs in the two triad locations (Heb. 6:10; 10:24), (4) the three exhortations each have one of the triad, and (5) the general Christian usage outside of Hebrews.

As noted above in Paul it is also true in Hebrews that there is an overlap of the meanings and implications of the three terms, 'faith,' 'hope,' and 'love.' In fact, the AH will closely relate 'hope' to 'faith' in his definition of 'faith' (Heb. 11:1) and will relate conceptually future hope to 'faith' for most of the chapter-eleven heroes.

In the context of Hebrews 10:22–24, 'faith' is faith in the Triune God based on the reality of the priestly aspects of the person and work of Christ. 'Hope' is conviction that God has graciously promised that a true Christian will persevere to enjoy the future eschatological benefits. 'Love' is a Christian's love for other Christians that motivates good works. Of course these are interrelated, for example, 'hope' and 'love' are partially driven by one's 'faith' in the reality of Christ's atonement. These definitions and interrelatedness in Hebrews 10:22–24 broadly match to Paul's. Again note that biblical authors, even the same author, do not always use the exact same nuance for each of three terms.[48]

---

47. See Cara, *1 and 2 Thessalonians*, 36–37, 144.

48. For example, 'love' is usually love for other Christians, but possibly includes in some contexts a Christian's love for both other Christians and non-Christians (1 Thess. 1:3?; Gal. 5:6 with 6:10?). 'Love' is clearly God's

There are many good summaries of the Christian life. And faith-hope-love is a good one. It does not say everything, but it does deserve appropriate emphasis. And in fact, the Christian church has historically used this triad, although in different ways.[49] In the Protestant churches that I have attended in my lifetime, the triad as a triad per se has not been particularly emphasized. Of the three, certainly faith and love have been emphasized, with hope maybe being under emphasized, although it is included conceptually in a strong redemptive-historical reading of Scripture. One advantage of using the triad is that 'hope' gets appropriately included, which also fills a cultural need. As Western culture generally frowns on discussions of death, judgment, and the final blessings (and curses), having 'hope' included in a summary of the Christian life is especially advantageous.

Warning: No More Sacrifice for Sins (10:26–31)

Hebrews 10:26–31 is a stern warning for those who abandon the Christian faith. The consequences are catastrophic.

It is assumed by virtually all commentators that this stern warning is against the same sin as the one described in Hebrews 6:4–6, that is, apostasy. Although, not all agree to the specific definition of apostasy and whether true believers can commit this sin. See the extended discussion about the apostasy options at the beginning of Hebrews 6:4–8 section.[50] To reiterate my view, which will be assumed below: Apostasy means irrevocable apostasy, and the people referred to in Hebrews 6:4–6 and 10:26–31 are not true believers but are non-believers associated with the visible church.

---

love for us in Rom. 5:5.

49. See Augustine, *The Enchiridion* (*NPNF*[1], 3:237–76); Aquinas, *Summa Theologiae* 1a2ae.62, 2a2ae.1–46 (Aquinas considers faith, hope, and love/charity as the three theological virtues, which are distinct from the four cardinal virtues of prudence, justice, temperance, and fortitude. For me, this is an unbiblical nature/grace dichotomy); Calvin, *Institutes* 3.2.41–43; and the Russian Orthodox document, The Longer Catechism of the Eastern Church 62–608 (Schaff, *Creeds of Christendom*, 2:455–541).

50. The discussions at Heb. 3:6b and 3:14 are also relevant.

The flow of Hebrews 10:26–31 begins with the thesis that abandoning Christ includes abandoning the only method to forgive sins, which is Christ's 'sacrifice' and consequently also the 'fearful expectation' of a negative judgment (10:26–27). The AH then highlights both the severity and certainty of this judgment (1) by using a lesser-to-greater rhetorical argument comparing OT sins and their judgment to the greater sin of disparaging Christ and the greater expected judgment for this (10:28–29), and (2) by quoting Deuteronomy 32:35–36 to show that in fact God will judge (10:30). The pericope ends with somewhat of a curt and dramatic summary—'It is a fearful thing to fall into the hands of the living God' (10:31).

10:26–27 *For [if] we willfully sin*[51] *after receiving the knowledge of the truth, [there] no longer remains a sacrifice concerning sins, but [there remains] a certain*[52] *fearful expectation of judgment and a zeal of fire [that] will consume the adversaries.*

By asserting the negative consequences of abandoning Christ, Hebrews 10:26–27 is providing a rationale (**for**) to why the congregants need to be serious about the just-mentioned three exhortations (Heb. 10:22–25), including appropriately 'not forsaking the assembling together.' Of course, this rationale is also simply an aspect of the broader rationale to persevere in Christ. Also, this negative assertion recalls the parallel positive one in Hebrews 10:18.

The words **willfully sin** in and of themselves do not necessarily refer to apostasy,[53] but the following three-fold description of one abandoning Christ (Heb. 10:29) and the parallel with Hebrews 6:4–8 confirm that **willfully sin** in this

---

51. **If we willfully sin** is a conditional (hence **if**), genitive-absolute, participial clause.

52. I take τὶς as an intensifier and thus the translation of **certain**. So also BDAG, 1008; and BDF §301.1.

53. In Greek, **willfully** (ἑκουσίως) is in the emphatic position and **sin** is a present participle. These two grammatical points are consistent with a persistent and explicitly conscious permanent rejection of Christ.

context certainly does refer to apostasy.[54] As noted above, not all define apostasy in the same way, but I take it as irrevocably apostasy that is committed by those who are/were part of the visible church but were never true believers. The phrase **after receiving the knowledge of the truth** further confirms that this sin is attributed to one who was at one point part of the visible church. I take the conditional **we** to be anyone in the visible church.

The obvious consequence of permanently abandoning Christ is that **there no longer remains a sacrifice concerning sins**. Based on the AH's discussion in Hebrews 7:1–10:18, this presupposes that Christ's **sacrifice** is the only instrument that God has designed to forgive **sins**. Given that the congregation includes a significant portion of those who had previously attended Jewish services, the wording **no longer remains a sacrifice** would be especially poignant to those considering going back to trusting in the temple sacrifices.[55]

If there is no remedy for the punishment due for **sins**, then **there** only **remains a certain fearful expectation of** negative **judgment** by God. **And**[56] this judgment is defined as **a zeal of fire that will consume the adversaries**.[57] Although not an exact quote, the AH is alluding to Isaiah 26:11 for the wording of **zeal of fire that will consume the adversaries**.[58] 'Zeal,' 'fire,' 'consume' (different mood), and 'adversaries' are included in the LXX of Isaiah 26:11 with the LXX closely matching to the

---

54. So virtually all commentators, e.g., Calvin, *Hebrews and 1 & 2 Peter*, 146; Moffatt, *Hebrews*, 149; Attridge, *Hebrews*, 292; and Johnson, *Hebrews*, 262. Lane has an extended discussion comparing Heb. 6:4–8 and 10:26–31 and concluding they each have the 'same process': (1) experience the Christian life, (2) apostasy, (3) renewal impossible, and (4) covenant curses (*Hebrews 9–13*, 291, cf. 296–97).

55. So also Owen, *Hebrews*, 22:531; and Hughes, *Hebrews*, 421.

56. That is, **and** is epexegetical. So also Ellingworth, *Hebrews*, 535.

57. As is clear in Greek, **that will consume the adversaries** describes **fire**, not **zeal**. Both **fire** and the participle μέλλοντος, translated as **will**, are in the genitive, whereas **zeal** is in the nominative.

58. The partial quote of Isa. 26:20 in Heb. 10:37 confirms that this is an allusion. For background on Isa. 26, see discussion at Heb. 10:37–38.

Hebrew.⁵⁹ In Isaiah 26:11 as well as here, God's punishment of the unrepentant is affirmed, and it is affirmed with strong evocative language, **fire that will consume**.

10:28–29 *Anyone annulling⁶⁰ the law of Moses dies without compassion [based] upon two or three witnesses; how much worse, do you think, will he deserve punishment, the one who has trampled under foot the Son of God, and considered profane⁶¹ the blood of the covenant, by which one was sanctified, and insulted the Spirit of grace?*

Although there is no explicit conjunction to Hebrews 10:26–27, the AH in 10:28–29 is clearly proving the truth of the severity and the certainty of God's punishment of apostates. He does this by a lesser-to-greater rhetorical argument.⁶² In brief, OT law requires the physical death penalty for specific heinous crimes. As serious as this is, it is considered by the AH a lesser sin and a lesser punishment. An apostate disparaging Christ is a greater sin and deserves a greater punishment, which is implied to be eternal.⁶³ Now to the details of this argument.

The AH is quoting from Deuteronomy 17:6 for **dies ... based upon two or three witnesses**.⁶⁴ The context of

---

59. 'Fire,' 'zeal,' and a synonym for **consume** are included in Zeph. 1:18 and 3:8. Other verses that refer to God and consuming fire include Deut. 4:24; Isa. 33:14; Ezek. 36:5; and Heb. 12:29; cf. 2 Baruch 48:39.

60. Generically, ἀθετέω would be translated 'setting aside,' but in context of law, I prefer **annulling**. See discussion of the cognate noun ἀθέτησις at Heb. 7:18.

61. Κοινός may be translated as 'common' or 'unclean' or **profane** depending on the context. Cf. the verb cognate κοινόω in Heb. 9:13.

62. The AH makes similar lesser-to-greater arguments in Heb. 2:2–3 and 12:25 related to punishments. Also see Heb. 9:13–14 for a lesser-to-greater argument related to salvation.

63. Philo uses a similar argument. After he notes the serious OT punishments for crimes against one's parents and lying under oath, he argues that the punishments for blaspheming God as creator Father and showing contempt for God's name by perjury will be much worse. See *On Flight and Finding* 83–85; and *On the Special Laws* 2.252–55.

64. There are very slight differences between the OT Hebrew, the LXX, and Hebrews. Wooden translations are as follows. The OT Hebrew has

Deuteronomy 17:2–7 is a law related to 'transgressing the covenant' if one 'has served other gods and worshipped them' (17:2–3). In this case, assuming there are at least **two or three witnesses**,[65] the death penalty is required. Given this, **annulling the law**[66] **of Moses** is not simply a violation of the law for which there is a sacrifice; no, this language implies the very serious sin of completely abandoning God and his law as the context of Deuteronomy 17:2–7 and Hebrews 10:26–31 both confirm.[67] For more on **two or three witnesses**, see the Reflection section below.

Without compassion shows that this sin and other heinous sins that required capital punishment (e.g., Exod. 21:14; Num. 35:30) were normally unpardonable (see Deut. 13:8; 19:13).[68] The point is that since punishment for OT heinous crimes is *certain* (i.e., no pardon), the punishment for abandoning Christ will also be certain, and will be even more certain because God will be the judge.

With jarring language that is commensurate with the heinousness, the AH describes the apostate with three parallel, substantival, aorist participles.[69] An apostate is one who has:

'upon the mouth (פי) of two witnesses or three witnesses the one dying will be put to death.' The LXX has 'upon two witnesses or upon three witnesses the one dying will die.' Heb. 10:28 has 'upon two or three witnesses he dies.' The AH appropriately rewords 'the one dying' as **anyone annulling the law of Moses.**

65. For other biblical references to **two or three witnesses**, see Deut. 19:15; Num. 35:30; 1 Kgs. 21:10–13; Matt. 18:16; 26:60; John 8:17; 2 Cor. 13:1; 1 Tim. 5:19; and Rev. 11:3.

66. This is the only use of **law** in Hebrews that refers to the 'civil' use. All other eleven uses of the singular 'law' refer to ceremonial aspects. The plural of 'law' is used twice in the Jeremiah quotes. See Cara, 'Covenant in Hebrews,' 259.

67. So also Attridge and Schreiner. Attridge comments that the verb 'suggests ... the rejection of the Law as a whole' (*Hebrews*, 294). Schreiner understands it as 'blatant and outright rebellion' (*Hebrews*, 325). Cf. Isa. 24:16 (LXX only) and Ezek. 22:26.

68. 'Unpardonable,' so also Aquinas, *Hebrews*, 217.

69. There is only one definite article controlling the three participles confirming that all three refer to one generic apostate.

(1) **trampled under foot the Son of God** (cf. Heb. 4:14; 6:6), (2) **considered profane the blood of the** new **covenant**, and (3) **insulted the** Holy **Spirit of grace**[70] (cf. Matt. 12:31–32).

The **blood of the covenant** refers to the new covenant and Christ's own blood (Heb. 9:12), which was foreshadowed by the blood of the Mosaic covenant (Heb. 9:18–22). Virtually all Jews in the first century who knew something about Jesus would have agreed that he was crucified. If one was not a believer and saw that Jesus himself or his followers considered Jesus' death/blood as related to a new covenant, this would have been revolting. This unbeliever, even one unrelated to the church, would have considered Jesus' blood as **profane**. How much worse would be the sin of an apostate who had received 'the knowledge of the truth' and most certainly would have partaken of the Lord's supper. At that supper, the apostate would have often heard the words of institution, 'This cup is the new covenant in my blood' (1 Cor. 11:25) and partook of the wine.[71] Despite all this, he now considered that blood **profane**.

There is debate concerning the expression ἐν ᾧ ἡγιάσθη, which I have translated as **by which one was sanctified**. All agree that **by which** grammatically refers to **blood**, and thus the **blood of the covenant**. The verb, however, does not have an explicit subject and one needs to be supplied. I supplied the generic **one**, meaning this **blood** that results in the full

---

70. In consideration of 'aggravations that make some sins more heinous than others,' the WLC 151 references Heb. 10:29 and Matt. 12:31–32 as proof that offending the Holy Spirit is a significant aggravation. The Formula of Concord concludes that those who 'willfully turn themselves away again ... and embitter the Holy Spirit [results in] their last state [being] worse than their first' (Solid Declaration 9). The Council of Trent takes this aggravation and wrongly uses it as an argument as to why post-baptism sins need 'satisfaction' through penance (On the Most Holy Sacraments of Penance and Extreme Unction, ch. 8 [Schaff, *Creeds of Christendom*, 2:156; Denzinger[43] §1690]).

71. Chrysostom emphasizes the Lord's supper connection ('Homily 20 on Hebrews,' [*NPNF*[1], 14:458]).

salvation of a true believer (**sanctified**);[72] that is, **one** does not refer to an apostate.[73] Others translate as 'he' meaning the apostate, and that the apostate was truly converted (**sanctified**) but no longer is.[74] Still others also translate as 'he' but meaning Christ. Christ was set apart (**sanctified**) for his work by his death (**blood**).[75] Finally, one could translate as 'it' referring to the new **covenant** with the understanding that the new **covenant** was set-apart/made-special by Christ's **blood**.[76] As to be expected, given that the subject of ἡγιάσθη is not explicit, the arguments for and against each view are primarily driven by the commentator's broader understanding of Hebrews.

10:30 *For we know the one who said, 'Vengeance is mine, I will repay,' and again,*[77] *'The Lord will judge his people.'*

In addition to the lesser-to-greater argument to confirm the severity and certainty of God's judgment on apostates, the AH quotes from portions of Deuteronomy 32:35 and 32:36 to reinforce (**for**) this same severity and certainty.

Deuteronomy 32:1–43 is the Song of Moses, from which the AH has already quoted in Hebrews 1:6 (Deut. 32:43). This song is spoken by Moses before Israel enters the promised land and is somewhat of a warning for Israel to persevere in allegiance to the Lord (Deut. 31:27–29). The song includes a list of gross sins by the Israelites and God's punishments of them (32:5–25). God will, however, graciously save them eventually, which saving will partially include punishments of those against his people (32:26–43). One scholarly debate concerns

---

72. See my discussion of 'sanctified' at Heb. 10:10.

73. So also Brown, *Hebrews*, 474; Bruce, *Hebrews*, 262; Hughes, *Hebrews*, 423; and Ellingworth, *Hebrews*, 541.

74. So, e.g., DeSilva, *Hebrews*, 349; and Cockerill, *Hebrews*, 489.

75. So, e.g., Owen, *Hebrews*, 22:545.

76. Several commentators mention this possibility, but I found none that concluded this was the correct view.

77. The majority text tradition has 'the Lord says' after **again** as can be seen in the KJV translation.

the identity of 'nation' (גוי/ἔθνος) in Deuteronomy 32:28, which then controls through 32:38 who it is that will be punished. Does this refer to non-Israelite nations or it is an ironic label for unrepentant Jews within Israel or both?[78]

Vengeance is mine, I will repay is from Deuteronomy 32:35.[79] The AH clearly applies this to the apostates. As mentioned above, it is not clear as to the identity of the enemies in the original context of the Song of Moses. No matter exactly who the original enemies were, by implication, the **vengeance** of Deuteronomy 32:35 properly applies to all unrepentant enemies of God.[80]

The Lord will judge his people is from Deuteronomy 32:36.[81] The verb **judge** in both Greek and Hebrew (κρινω, דין) has a wide semantic range that includes governing, vindicating, and punishing.[82] In Deuteronomy 32:36, the immediate context of this specific verse argues for 'to vindicate'/protect **his people** as the next line is 'and have compassion on his servants.' The AH, however, takes **judge** in the sense of 'to punish' and **his people** in the sense of those in the covenant community who have apostatized.[83] Clearly the wider context of the

---

78. For a discussion of options, see Currid, *Study Commentary on Deuteronomy*, 506–07. Currid opts for unrepentant Jews. See A. D. H. Mayes for 'nation' being non-Israelite nations (*Deuteronomy*, NCB [Grand Rapids: Eerdmans, 1979], 389–90). The Damascus Document from the Dead Sea Scrolls quotes Deut. 32:28 and applies it to evil ones within Israel (CD V, 17).

79. The OT Hebrew, LXX, and Heb. 10:30a do differ at the word level. Wooden translations are as follows. The Hebrew has 'to me is vengeance and recompence.' The LXX (and Ode 2) has 'in [the] day of vengeance I will repay.' Heb. 10:30a has 'to me is vengeance, I will repay.' The targums also differ slightly among themselves with none being an exact match to the Hebrew nor the LXX. Interestingly, Rom. 12:19 is an exact match to Heb. 10:30a. See Kistemaker, *Psalm Citations in the Epistle of Hebrews*, 45–46.

80. In Rom. 12:19, Paul accurately infers from this same verse that it is *God* and not Christians who are the ultimate avenger.

81. The OT Hebrew, LXX, and Heb. 10:30b match exactly as does Ps. 135:14.

82. See LSJ, 996; LEH, 267–68; and Robert D. Culver, 'דין,' *TWOT*, 188.

83. *Contra* those who take **judge** and 'fall into the hands' as both positives anticipating Heb. 10:32–39. So James Swetnam, 'Hebrews 10:30–

Song of Moses includes God's punishing the unrepentant in his covenant community. But even for this verse itself, to 'vindicate' believers, God has to punish any enemies including those within his covenant community—that is, vindication and punishment are corollaries. Hence, the AH is justified in using this verse because 'by good and necessary consequences' (WCF 1.6) it does relate to punishment of apostates.[84]

10:31 *[It is] a fearful [thing] to fall into the hands of the living God.*
As mentioned above, this verse is a curt and dramatic summary of Hebrews 10:26–30. Johnson comments that it is 'chilling in its simplicity.'[85] This description of the future reality of negative eternal judgment for an apostate serves as a warning to those in the covenant community. This warning provides at least one of many motivations for non-believers still in the visible church to repent and truly believer.[86] Also, this warning is used by God to aid true Christians in their perseverance.

The adjective **fearful** recalls 'a *fearful* expectation of judgment' (Heb. 10:27, cf. 12:21) and could easily be translated as 'terrifying'. The expression **to fall into the hands of the living God** is stressing *God* (!). Specifically, it is stressing his power and ability to mete out eternal damnation to those who abandon and rebel against his Son.[87] Yes, some in this life may escape the hands of *men*, but no one can escape

---

31: A Suggestion,' *Bib* 75 (1994): 388–94; and John Proctor, 'Judgement or Vindication? Deuteronomy 32 in Hebrews 10:30,' *TynBul* 55 (2004): 65–80.

84. So also J. A. Thompson, *Deuteronomy: An Introduction and Commentary*, TOTC (London: Inter-Varsity, 1974), 302–03; Brown, *Hebrews*, 477; Bruce, *Hebrews*, 264–65; and Hughes, *Hebrews*, 425. Calvin prefers the sense of 'to govern' and comments 'God cannot govern his church without purifying it' (*Hebrews and 1 & 2 Peter*, 150).

85. Johnson, *Hebrews*, 266.

86. Although specifically referencing Heb. 10:27, the WLC 83 and Belgic Confession 37 both note that the wicked do have some sense of a dreadful judgment for the ultimately unrepentant.

87. Occasionally, this expression has a positive context. See 2 Sam. 24:14 // 1 Chr. 21:13 and Sirach 2:18.

from the future and eternal judgment of Almighty God (cf. 2 Macc. 6:26; 7:31; 2 En. 39:8).

Reflections

The original AD 1611 KJV included an eleven-page preface termed 'The Translators to the Reader.'[88] The penultimate sentence of this preface quotes Hebrews 10:31.[89] But first some background before getting to the quote.

The document begins with a several paragraph expectation that any 'zeal to promote the common good,' especially for 'he that meddleth with men's religion,' is often met with complaints and suspicion instead of thanks. Hence, the translators provide a defense of their work and 'seek to approve ourselves to every one's conscience.'

Next, the Scriptures are praised. 'But now what piety without truth? What truth (saving truth) without the word of God? What word of God (whereof we may be sure) without the Scripture?' A variety of biblical verses and church fathers are quoted to show the importance of reading the Scriptures and hearing them preached. The Scriptures have 'the author being God, not man; the inditer, the Holy Spirit, not the wit of the Apostles or Prophets.' The Scriptures have saving effects.

Arguing explicitly against the 'Church of Rome,' which was hindering people from reading the Scriptures in their native language, the document declares that translations are necessary. 'How shall they understand that which is kept close in an unknown tongue?' The document then moves to argue against some Protestants who asked, 'Was their translation good before? Why do they now mend it?' Yes, the previous English translations were good, but we 'do endeavor

---

88. See the wonderful source by Enroll F. Rhodes and Liana Lupas, eds., *The Translators to the Reader: The Original Preface of the King James Version of 1611 Revisited* (New York: American Bible Society, 1997). This includes a 'facsimile' of the original, an easily readable 'transcription' of the facsimile with updated spelling and explanatory footnotes, and a 'modern form' translation. Miles Smith, an OT scholar and one of the translators, is the primary author, although the document as it appears in the KJV is anonymous.

89. I was alerted to this quote by Bruce, *Hebrews*, 266.

to make that better which they left so good.' And 'we never thought from the beginning that we should need to make a new translation, nor yet to make a bad one a good one …, but to make a good one better, or out of many good ones one principal good one.'

The document then explains and justifies several of the translators' translation methodologies. For example, the use of occasional alternate translations in the margins and the situations where different English words are required for the same Hebrew or Greek word.

In the final paragraph, the emphasis is on God and his grace for those who read the Scriptures. The readers are to love the Scriptures 'above gold and silver.' On the other hand, the readers are not to despise the Scriptures and the Savior as this will ultimately lead to God's vengeance. Then comes the grand ending that asks the reader to consider his options, to be cursed or to be blessed.

> *It is a fearful thing to fall into the hands of the living God*; but a blessed thing it is, and will bring us to everlasting blessedness in the end, when God speaketh his word before us, to read it; when he stretcheth out his hand and calleth, to answer, 'Here am I, here we are to do thy will, O God.' [May] the Lord work a care and conscience in us to know him and serve him, that we may be acknowledged of him at the appearing of our Lord Jesus Christ, to whom with the Holy Ghost, be all praise and thanksgiving. Amen.

Do Not Throw Away Your Confidence (10:32–39)

Hebrews 10:32–39 is the third pericope of exhortations within 10:19–39. It is another exhortation to persevere in the Christian life, with the key verse being 'do not throw away your confidence' (Heb. 10:35). Although an exhortation, it is one that is presented in an encouraging way. The AH commends the congregation's former good works, their exhibited confidence in their future heavenly home, and their current faith to encourage them to persevere. The AH makes clear to the congregation that he considers the vast majority of them as true believers, and as true believers, they will certainly persevere.

This encouraging exhortation follows the stern warning of Hebrews 10:26–31. Both Chrysostom and Aquinas use the analogy of a physician who puts a soothing balm on a patient after cutting them. The cutting is the stern warning of Hebrews 10:26–31, and the balm is 10:32–39.[90] This pattern of a stern warning followed by a balm matches Hebrews 6:4–8 followed by 6:9–12.[91]

The pericope begins with the AH asking the congregants to remember their good works in difficult times and their understanding of their future home that sustained them during those times (Heb. 10:32–34). Given this, they should persevere to the end (Heb. 10:35–36). To drive home his points, he alludes-to/quotes Isaiah 26:20 and Habakkuk 2:3–4, which includes a reference to persevering 'faith' (Heb. 10:37–38). The AH ends the long exhortation section (Heb. 10:19–39) and this pericope specifically by noting that 'we,' himself and the vast majority of the readers, will have 'faith' that perseveres until the end (Heb. 10:39). This 'faith' then anticipates the heroes of faith in Hebrews 11.

10:32 *But remember the former days, in which after being enlightened, you endured a hard struggle of sufferings,*

Before getting to the primary exhortation to persevere in Hebrews 10:35, the AH lays the groundwork in 10:32–34 so that the exhortation will have an encouraging aspect. He tells the congregation to **remember the former days in which** (days) they **endured a hard struggle of sufferings**. Since these **sufferings** occurred **after** becoming members of the visible

---

90. Chrysostom, 'Homily 21 on Hebrews,' (*NPNF*[1], 14:461); and Aquinas, *Hebrews*, 221.

91. Although not necessarily using the physician metaphor, virtually every commentator notes the parallel patterns between Heb. 6:4–12 and 10:26–39.

church (**being enlightened**[92]), they are related to hardships due to being a Christian. Therefore, since **you** have already **endured** difficulties in your Christian life for Christ, this in-and-of itself shows you can persevere, which is an encouragement to continue to persevere. Or to say it somewhat negatively, Calvin quips, 'It is a shameful thing when you have started well to grow tired half way, and even more shameful to go back when you have made considerable progress.'[93]

Although not clear, **former days**, past (aorist) tense of **endured**, and **hard struggle** indicate that these **sufferings** were more severe previously than they are as the AH writes the letter. Aspects of these **sufferings** are fleshed out more in Hebrews 10:33–34.

The Greek word behind **struggle** is ἄθλησις (etymologically related to 'athletic') and is most likely an allusion to the famous Greek athletic games (cf. Heb. 12:1).[94] This athletic angle adds that the readers were *actively* resisting, at least internally, these negative situations; they were not simply *passive*.[95] Further, as athletic contests have endings, this metaphor probably also adds that the **hard struggle** eventually did end, at least the **hard** aspect of it.

10:33–34 *sometimes, on the one hand,*[96] *being publicly exposed to reproaches and*[97] *afflictions, and sometimes, on the other hand, being*

---

92. **Enlightened** is the same participle as used in Heb. 6:4. See discussion there.

93. Calvin, *Hebrews and 1 & 2 Peter*, 151.

94. So also Attridge, *Hebrews*, 298; Lane, *Hebrews*, 298; Johnson, *Hebrews*, 268; and Cockerill, *Hebrews*, 497. For an extended discussion of athletic imagery and moral exhortation, see DeSilva, *Hebrews*, 361–64.

95. Koester, 'A criminal was expected to bear up passively under blows inflicted for punishment, but an athlete remained active and resistant when receiving blows in a boxing match' (*Hebrews*, 464).

96. The Greek behind **sometimes on the one hand ... and sometimes on the other** is τοῦτο μὲν ... τοῦτο δὲ, which occurs nowhere else in the LXX and NT. It is common in Herodotus. See LSJ, 1276 (C.8.3); and BDF §290.5.

97. **Reproaches** is linked to **afflictions** by τε καὶ, which shows very

partners with those being thus treated. For even you sympathized with prisoners[98] *and you accepted the plunder of your possessions with joy, [because]*[99] *knowing you yourselves*[100] *had a better and enduring possession.*

The 'sufferings' and the positive responses are presented in a chiastic structure: (a) **publicly exposed to reproaches and afflictions**, (b) **being partners with those being thus treated**, (b') **sympathized with prisoners**, and (a') **accepted the plunder of your possessions**.

Some in the congregation were **publicly exposed to reproaches and afflictions**.[101] Most likely this included some level of well-known public verbal scorn and humiliation and/or false charges (**reproaches**) along with possibly public beatings (**afflictions**). The beatings did not, however, result in death as Hebrews 12:4 makes clear. In addition, some lost their **possessions**. Whether this **plunder** was approved by magistrates or actions of a mob is not stated. The readers are not explicitly said to have been **prisoners**, but I assume some were, based on Hebrews 13:3 (cf. Heb 11:36). The implicit wording is probably due to the chiastic structure in order to be parallel with **being partners**. They may have been put in prison on trumped up charges or financial debts due to losing property. In any event, the magistrates were involved at some level. For how these 'sufferings' impact the dating of Hebrews, see the Introductory Matters section.

'closely related' concepts (BDAG, 993).

98. Some manuscripts have 'bonds' (δεσμοῖς, cf. Heb. 11:36) as opposed to **prisoners** (δεσμίοις), which is the difference of one letter. Some add 'my' to 'bonds.' See Metzger, *TCGNT*², 600–1. Based on 'my bonds,' Owen sees confirmation of Pauline authorship (*Hebrews*, 22:568).

99. I take **knowing** as a causal participle; hence, the addition of **because**. So also Hodge, *Hebrews*, 109; and Cockerill, *Hebrews*, 502.

100. The third person reflexive pronoun ἑαυτοῦ is used for first and second person especially in the plural; so also in Heb. 10:25. See Zerwick, *Biblical Greek* §209.

101. Grässer argues that these persecutions would have been typical of any NT congregation (*Hebräer*, 3:65).

Heartwarmingly, the concern for others within the church is shown by the 'b' and 'b'' phrases, **being partners with those being thus treated** and **sympathized with prisoners**, respectively. **Being partners** with those receiving **reproaches and afflictions** in apparently some tangible way exposed the members to these same dangers. For example, tangible and public ways may have included helping with the public defense or administering medical aid upon initial beatings.

The AH commends the readers because they **sympathized with prisoners**, especially (exclusively?) Christian ones (cf. Heb. 13:3). This would have included visiting and taking items to the **prisoners**.[102] In the Greco-Roman world, the conditions in prison generally necessitated prisoners' families to supply the prisoner with most or all of his food and clothing.[103] As numerous examples in the early church show, Christians considered the Christian **prisoners** as family and took care of them. See Reflections below for more discussion.

The AH further commends the congregation for their rationale as to why they **accepted the plunder of** their **possessions with joy—knowing** they **themselves had a better and enduring possession**. That is, the congregants knew that their eternal (**enduring**) and future **possession**, their home in the NHNE (cf. Heb. 11:16), was so much **better** than their current **possessions** that suffering for Christ's sake could be done **with** an appropriate **joy**. Yes, the forced loss of **possessions** was disappointing, which is assumed in the AH's argument, but those affected are commended for seeing the 'long run' advantages of Christ that enables an overarching attitude of **joy** in the midst of true disappointment (cf. Heb. 12:2; 13:6; Matt. 6:19; 2 Cor. 6:10; Jas. 1:2).

---

102. The Greek behind **sympathize** is συμπαθέω, from whence English gets the word. Semantically, it primarily involves 'fellow-feeling' (LSJ, 1680; cf. Heb. 4:15). But the immediate context and the well-known Christian actions with prisoners in the early church argues for both feelings and concrete actions. So also Attridge, *Hebrews*, 299.

103. See Brian Rapske, *The Book of Acts and Paul in Roman Prison*, vol 3 of *The Book of Acts in Its First Century Setting* (Grand Rapids: Eerdmans, 1994), esp. 9–35; 209–19.

10:35–36 *Therefore, do not throw away your confidence, which has a great reward. For you have need of endurance in order that, after doing the will of God, you may receive the promise.*

Do not throw away your confidence is grammatically the main exhortation in 10:32–39. The previous verses set the groundwork for that **confidence**, that is, boldness in belief and actions relative to Christ.[104] The obvious implication (**therefore**) is that they continue in this **confidence**. Although it is put negatively (**do *not* throw away**), the fact that the AH refers to their existing **confidence** puts this exhortation in quite a positive light.

The AH gives one reason why they should keep their **confidence**. Because[105] it will result in **a great** future **reward**. The **reward** generally matches to the just mentioned 'better and enduring possession' and the **promise** in the next verse (cf. Heb. 11:6, 26). These refer to the wonders of the eternal NHNE. Here, and in many places in the Bible, **reward** may be defined as 'God fulfills what he promises.'[106] It is grace based, as the broader context of Christ's priestly work makes plain. Of course, sometimes the word 'reward' does refer to human merit by works (e.g., Rom. 4:4), but that use is not in view here. The expectation of a God-given gracious **reward**, which includes being with God!, is one of many motivations that the Bible uses for sanctification.

---

104. **Confidence** (παρρησία) is also in Heb. 3:6; 4:16; and 10:19.

105. The indefinite relative pronoun ἥτις here has a causal use. So also Robertson, *A Grammar of the Greek New Testament*, 728. The gender of ἥτις clearly connects it to **confidence**.

106. This quote is from Van Genderen and Velema, *Concise Reformed Dogmatics*, 667 (emphasis removed). Robert Bruce similarly comments, 'There are two kinds of reward or recompense: there is a reward that is earned, and there is a promised reward that is undeserved' (*Preaching Without Fear or Favour: Previously Unpublished Sermons on Hebrews 11*, trans. and ed. David Searle [Ross-shire: Christian Heritage, 2019], 396). The Reformed tradition normally speaks of 'gracious rewards' (Belgic Confession 37). See Heidelberg Catechism 63; Second Helvetic Confession 16; WCF 16.6; 19.6; WLC 45; Calvin, *Institutes* 3.18.1–5; Bavinck, *Reformed Dogmatics*, 4:236; and Cara, *Cracking the Foundation of the New Perspective on Paul*, 53–56.

Hebrews 10:36 is an explanation (**for**) of 10:35, although it is somewhat conceptually repetitive. To persevere, yes, **you will need endurance** (cf. Heb. 12:1–2). This **endurance** will result in **receiv[ing] the** substance of the **promise**, which here is the glories associated with the future NHNE.[107]

Endurance involves **doing the will of God**. This **will of God** is presented generally and certainly involves a Christian's obeying the 'revealed' commands **of God** (cf. Heb. 13:21). Possibly, in a secondary sense, it presupposes the 'secret' **will of God** as in God has providentially placed some believers in difficult situations.[108] These two may be combined to say that God's commands include instruction for a believer to act appropriately when providentially placed in difficult situations. This would be similar to Christ's first coming as he also did God's 'will' (Heb. 10:5–10).

10:37–38 *For 'Yet [in] a very little while, the one coming shall come and not delay; and the righteous one*[109] *shall live by faith, and if one shrinks back, my soul has no pleasure in him.'*

The AH presses home and confirms the veracity of several of his previous points (**for**) by quoting a very small portion of Isaiah 26:20 and quoting/alluding-to/applying Habakkuk 2:3–4. He also adds an encouragement by noting the 'endurance' will not last forever and Christ is truly coming.

The AH's use of these two OT texts is instructive as he shows awareness of the larger OT contexts combined with redemptive-historical realities.[110] Another point of interest is that there are

---

107. 'Promises in Hebrews have been partially realized in the Old Testament (Heb. 6:15; 11:9, 33) and have significant continuity with (and escalation into) the current New Testament age and the coming new heavens and new earth (e.g., 4:1; 10:18, 36; 11:39)' (Cara, 'Covenant in Hebrews,' 253).

108. For a standard Reformed explanation of 'revealed' and 'secret' wills, see Berkhof, *Systematic Theology*, 77. Owen also sees aspects of both wills in Heb. 10:36 (*Hebrews*, 22:579–80).

109. Some manuscripts include 'my' resulting in 'my (God's) righteous one.' Metzger considers it original, although with a 'B' rating (*TCGNT*², 601).

110. Kistemaker, 'The [AH] has given the combined quotation a

moderate word-level differences for Habakkuk 2:3–4 between the original Hebrew, the LXX, and Hebrews 10:37–38. Allow me to first exegete Hebrews 10:37–38 without significant reference to the OT. Then I will consider the AH's use of the OT. (I will not be considering the Commentary on Habakkuk from the Dead Sea Scrolls.[111])

The AH understands the **one coming** as Christ, and given the redemptive-historical situation, this would now refer to his second coming (cf. Heb. 9:28; Matt. 11:3; 21:5, 9; 23:39; John 12:13; 2 Thess. 1:10; Rev. 1:8; 22:20).[112] For the believer, Christ's appearance will be **in a very little while**, he will **not delay**. Taking the whole Bible into account, this will be true at either the believer's death or the actual second coming (cf. 2 Cor. 5:8; Phil. 1:21; 2 Pet. 3:8–10).[113] This **little while** point is meant to be encouraging to the readers. Also, the fact that the OT properly understood confirms that Christ is truly the **one coming** is also encouraging.

Two types of people in the covenant community are referred to during the time of 'endurance' (Heb. 10:36). The first is a **righteous one**. Grammatically, **by faith** can be connected directly to **the righteous one** or to **shall live**. By 'theological logic,' however, if **by faith** applies to one of these two, it must also apply to the other (cf. Heb. 6:1; 11:7). Due to the nature of faith, both of these options have the person looking outside of himself to God.[114] That is, if a person is

---

decidedly messianic interpretation considered from an apocalyptic point of view' (*The Psalm Citations in the Epistle to the Hebrews*, 48).

111. Points of interest: The 'vision' of Hab. 2:3 relates to the 'final generation,' and God told the 'Teacher of Righteousness,' not Habakkuk, when this would happen (1QpHab VII, 1–5). The 'vision' will be accomplished by 'men of truth who keep the Law' (1QpHab VII, 11). The 'righteous' ones are those 'who observe the Law,... [are] suffering and ... [have] faith in the Teacher of Righteousness' (1QpHab VIII, 1–3). (Translation from Geza Vermes, *The Complete Dead Sea Scrolls in English*, rev. ed. [New York: Penguin, 2004], 512–13.)

112. So also Hodge, *Hebrews*, 110; Hughes, *Hebrews*, 435; Cockerill, *Hebrews*, 508; and Schreiner, *Hebrews*, 334.

113. So also Aquinas, *Hebrews*, 224.

114. While discussing Hab. 2:4b, O. P. Robertson affirms that 'by faith' is grammatically connected with 'shall live' rather than the one declared

initially declared righteous by the instrument of faith, then that one would also live by a persevering faith. Conversely, if a person lives by a persevering faith, then that one would also have been previously declared righteous by faith. Matching both to the context of Habakkuk and Hebrews, the emphasis here is on **shall live by** a persevering **faith**.[115] In Romans 1:17 and Galatians 3:11, Paul also quotes Habakkuk 2:4b with his emphasis in context concerning 'by faith' being that 'faith' is the instrument for being declared righteous. However, Paul also clearly affirms that one who is declared righteous by faith also lives by faith (e.g., Rom. 6–8; Gal. 5).

The second type of person that might be in the covenant community is **one** who **shrinks back**. I translated using the generic **one**, as opposed to 'he,' to make clearer that this person was *not* formerly a **righteous one** (true Christian) and then shrank back.[116] This translation best matches with the bifurcation in the next verse and the original Hebrew of Habakkuk 2:4. As is confirmed by the next verse (Heb. 10:39), the **one** who **shrinks back** is an apostate whose end is 'destruction'.[117] In somewhat of an understatement, God (**my soul**[118]) **has no pleasure in** the apostate (**him**) (cf. Heb. 10:6).

---

righteous. This 'may appear to leave open the question of *how* a person becomes righteous. But the resulting emphasis only reinforces the fact that the source of true righteousness always remains outside the person. If continuing life is a gift received by faith, then the righteousness that is the basis of life must have the same source' (*The Books of Nahum, Habakkuk, and Zephaniah*, NICOT [Grand Rapids: Eerdmans, 1990], 178, emphasis his).

115. So also Owen, *Hebrews*, 22:588; Bruce, *Hebrews*, 275; and Schreiner, *Hebrews*, 335.

116. So also Owen, *Hebrews*, 22:587, 589. *Contra* Brown, *Hebrews*, 487; Moffatt, *Hebrews*, 158; Attridge, *Hebrews*, 302; and Cockerill, *Hebrews*, 510.

117. So most commentators. *Contra* T. W. Lewis. He connects the hiding in Isa. 26:20 to **shrink back**, which is not apostasy but a misplaced 'mode of endurance' that the AH wants the readers to discontinue ('"... And If He Shrinks Back" [Heb. X. 38b],' *NTS* 22 [1975]: 88–94, esp. 94).

118. Koester comments that **soul** (נפשׁ) is sometimes used in the OT when God's emotion is highlighted, e.g., Isa. 1:14; 42:1; Jer. 6:8; 15:1 (*Hebrews*, 463). Bruce K. Waltke notes the infrequent use of נפשׁ relative to God but when used it 'express[es] forcefully his passionate disinclination or inclination toward someone' ('נפשׁ,' *TWOT*, 587–91, esp. 591.) This usage of **soul** for

Now I consider the OT connection to Isaiah 26:20 and Habakkuk 2:3–4 in more detail. The first thing to note is that the AH does not have the usual clear indication that he is quoting Scripture (Heb. 13:6 appears to be another exception). He simply says **for**, and then goes into the quotes. Although, the very idiomatic expression ὅσον ὅσον from Isaiah 26:20 (see below) and the well-known clause **the righteous one shall live by faith** argue that the AH assumes many in the congregation would/should know that these at least are biblical quotations.[119] Possibly, this lack of specific reference to Scripture explains the looser-quotation-and-more-application character of Hebrews 10:37–38.[120]

Yet in a very little while (ἔτι ... μικρὸν ὅσον ὅσον) is from Isaiah 26:20. The idiomatic use of ὅσον ὅσον confirms this.[121] Isaiah 26:11 has just been alluded to in Hebrews 10:27, which further confirms the connection to Isaiah 26:20. Isaiah 26 is a 'song' (26:1) that includes significant eschatological statements (26:1–6, 19–21), including glorious statements concerning the resurrection from the dead (26:19).[122] Punishment of the wicked is mentioned, and at least some of this is eschatological (26:5–6, 11, 21). As to the Isaiah 26:20 quote per se, God is coming in negative judgment and gives protective instructions (metaphorical?) to his redeemed people. 'Come, my people,

---

'passionate disinclination' matches the Heb. 10:38 context.

119. So also Spicq, *Hébreux*, 2:331. Lane assumes that Isa. 26:20 is very well known in synagogues as Isa. 26:9–20 is in the LXX as Ode 5. Because it is well known, the congregants would have immediately understood that Scripture was being quoted (*Hebrews*, 304).

120. Understating the case from my perspective, Brown calls it 'a mere allusion' to Habakkuk (*Hebrews*, 484).

121. The phrase ὅσον ὅσον is only used in Greek biblical literature at LXX Isa. 26:20 (Ode 5:20) and Heb. 10:37 (also in 1 Clem. 50:4, which is a quote Isa. 26:20). The double ὅσον ὅσον adds an intensive sense (**very**). The Hebrew phrase is mechanically translated as 'as/yet a little while' (כמעט־רגע).

122. For an overview of Isa. 26, see J. Ridderbos, *Isaiah*, 209–14; Young, *The Book of Isaiah*, 2:203–31; and Brevard S. Childs, *Isaiah*, OTL (Louisville: Westminster, 2001), 186–92.

enter your chambers, and shut your doors behind you;[123] hide yourselves *for a little while* until the fury passes by. For behold, the LORD [Yahweh] is coming out of his place to punish the inhabitants of the earth for their iniquity' (26:20–21a ESV).

The context of Isaiah 26 generally and the specific context of 26:20–21 have clear conceptual connections to Hebrews 10:32–39. These connections include an eschatological context of both salvation and negative judgment, God's providing encouragement/instructions as the final Day approaches, and God himself will be coming.[124] The AH's understanding of **yet in a little while** as an encouragement to Christians matches to God's encouragement/ instructions for believers to hide 'for a little while' during a period of negative judgment. Also, Yahweh's 'coming' well matches to Christ as **the one coming**.[125]

Before getting to the Habakkuk 2:3–4 quote, a brief summary of the book of Habakkuk (Hebrew, not LXX) in its original context is useful.[126] The prophet complains that justice is perverted in Judah because evil exists and prospers in the covenant community (Hab. 1:2–4). God responds that, yes, there is evil in Judah, and surprisingly, the Chaldeans (Babylonians) will be his instrument of destructive judgment upon Judah (Hab. 1:5–11). This prompts a second complaint

---

123. 'Shut your doors behind you' is similar to Noah and the ark language (Gen. 7:16).

124. Going beyond me, Ellingworth believes that for the AH the context of Isa. 26 dominates his thought more than Hab. 2 (*Hebrews*, 555).

125. The verb for God's *coming* in Isa. 26:21 (יצא, ἐπάγω) is not the same as Heb. 10:38 (ἔρχομαι), although conceptually it is close. Based 'on the principle of verbal analogy,' Guthrie sees 'coming' as the key for the AH's connecting Isa. 26:20–21 with Hab. 2:3–4 ('Hebrews,' 982). I would rather say it is ultimately a *conceptual* analogy.

126. For useful overviews of Habakkuk, see Robertson, *Nahum, Habakkuk, and Zephaniah*; 135–248; F. F. Bruce, 'Habakkuk,' in *The Minor Prophets: An Exegetical and Expository Commentary*, ed. Thomas Edward McComiskey, 3 vols. (Grand Rapids: Baker, 1992–1998), 2:831–96, esp. 2:831–40; and Raymond B. Dillard and Tremper Longman III, *An Introduction to the Old Testament* (Grand Rapids: Zondervan, 1994), 409–13.

from the prophet. It is not morally just for God to use the very evil Chaldeans to punish the less evil in Judah. Further, again, it looks like the evil, now the Chaldeans, are prospering (Hab. 1:12–17). God responds by giving a 'vision' that will be accomplished at the 'end'. The 'vision' may seem like it never comes, but it will. The vision declares that there are two types of people; (1) those 'puffed up' who are 'not upright' and (2) the 'righteous' who 'shall live by faith' (Hab. 2:2–4). In context, the 'puffed up' are the Chaldeans and also, if only implicitly, the proud evil ones in Judah. The 'righteous' are the true believers living in Judah during these difficult times. The 'vision' goes on to affirm that the Chaldeans will be eventually punished (Hab. 2:6–20). The broad two points of Habakkuk 2:2–4 are that (1) it will not be until the 'end' that it will be clearly seen that evil ones do *not* prosper and (2) until that time the righteous are to have faith in God and his providential ways. This persevering faith in God and his ways, especially during difficult circumstances, is reiterated in Habakkuk's long prayer (Hab. 3:1–19), especially the wonderful words of 3:17–18. Clearly, there are several themes in Habakkuk that match Hebrews 10:32–39. They include, for example, eschatological salvation and judgment; a covenant community experiencing persecution; a covenant community that includes within it those against God; and a call for true believers to persevere.

The LXX has two modifications of the original Hebrew of Habakkuk 2:3–4 that are of note. The first is that the Hebrew has 'for it shall surely come,' with the subject 'it' being the 'vision' (Hab. 2:3d). The LXX alters this to 'for (a?) coming one shall come,' with the subject being an undefined masculine, which eliminates 'vision' (feminine) as an option.[127] Most likely the LXX implies it is God who is the one coming because he is the real subject to accomplish the vision.[128] The AH has

---

127. Possibly, the infinitive absolute בא was mistakenly taken as a participle.

128. That God is the one coming is explicit in Hab. 3:3, 8.

the one coming and understands the 'vision' (final judgment) to be accomplished by Christ.[129] When the 'vision' will be accomplished in Habakkuk is not completely clear,[130] but whether it is directly speaking of the final judgment or not, it is at least typological of the final judgment. Once given a Trinitarian understanding of God, the AH correctly identifies Christ as **the one coming** to accomplish the 'vision' at the final judgment.

Concerning the second modification, the Hebrew has 'behold his soul swelled; it [soul] is not upright in him' (Hab. 2:4a). The LXX alters this to 'if one shrinks back, my soul has no pleasure in him.' This matches exactly to wording of the AH, although the AH has reversed the order of the two clauses in Habakkuk 2:4.[131] The AH functionally connects **if one shrinks back** to 'his soul swelled.' The AH apparently understands that a significantly proud person ('his soul swelled') is one who **shrinks back** from God and his commands.[132] At some level, all have a form of knowledge of God, and the 'proud' have moved away from him (cf. Rom. 1:18–32). This would be especially true for those evil ones in Judah. They were in the covenantal community and **shr[a]nk back**, which directly matches the concern of the AH. The AH also functionally connects **my soul has no pleasure in him** to 'it [soul] is not upright in him.' These two clauses are logically related. God's **soul** obviously **has no pleasure in him** who is 'not upright' in the sight of God.

10:39 *But we are not [of those] of shrinking back to destruction but [of those] of faith to preservation of soul.*

---

129. The AH added **the**. This eliminates any ambiguity as to this 'coming' being one of many comings.

130. It could include the destruction of Judah by the Chaldeans, and/or the destruction of the Chaldeans by the Persians, and/or the final judgment.

131. This LXX clause may be describing that the one/thing 'coming' may shrink back. This would only be true if God is not the assumed one that is coming. However, since the AH reversed the order of the clauses, he clearly does not connect the **shrinks back** to **the one coming**.

132. So also Calvin, *Hebrews and 1 & 2 Peter*, 155.

The AH ends this pericope and this whole exhortation section on a very positive and encouraging note. In Greek, **we** is especially emphasized.[133] It includes the AH and the vast majority of congregants in that visible church. The **we** are **those of faith** who will persevere to the end (**preservation of soul**).[134] This is conceptually very similar to Hebrews 6:9.

The AH uses the language of the two groups from the just quoted Habakkuk 2:4—those defined as **of shrinking back**[135] and those defined as **of faith**, although in inverse order. The quote implied the eschatological results of these two groups. But here the results are made explicit, either **destruction** or **preservation** to the end.[136] Again, although two groups are mentioned, by the use of **we**, the AH sees the vast majority as having **faith**. This **faith** emphasis here and in the quote sets up chapter 11.

Reflections

The AH commends the readers for their concern for prisoners, 'you sympathized with prisoners' (Heb. 10:34). Later he encourages them to continue this, 'remember the prisoners' (Heb. 13:3).

As noted above, prisoners usually needed help from those on the outside for food and clothing. Predominantly, this help came from family members. The early church was well known for taking care of and having concern for Christian prisoners as those in the church considered each other as family.

---

133. 'Double emphatic, by position and by being expressed at all,' Zerwick and Grosvenor, *Grammatical Analysis of the Greek New Testament*, 2:678–79.

134. Heb. 10:39 is referenced to prove that true **faith** results in eschatological salvation in Heidelberg Catechism 20, WCF 14.1, WLC 72, and WSC 86.

135. The noun **shrinking back** (ὑποστολή) is the obvious cognate to the verb 'shrinks back' (ὑποστέλλω) from the quote.

136. Owen, 'Scripture everywhere testifieth, that in the visible church there is a certain number of false hypocrites, whose end and lot it is to be destroyed' (*Hebrews*, 22:592–93). Lane perceptively comments that this has covenantal overtones of blessings and curses (*Hebrews 9–13*, 307).

In approximately AD 96, Clement includes in a prayer, 'ransom our prisoners' (1 Clement 59:4). In the *Apology of Aristides*, written somewhere between AD 125–161, the Christian Aristides notes the good deeds Christians have done for the disadvantaged. They include 'if they hear that one of their number is imprisoned or afflicted on account of the name of their Messiah, all of them anxiously minister to his necessity, and if it is possible to redeem him they set him free' (§15 [*ANF* 10:277]).

Tertullian (AD 160–225), in *To the Martyrs*, begins by noting the 'provision [from] our lady mother the Church … and [from] each brother out of his private means [helps with] your bodily wants in prison.' He then immediately comments that by this treatise he is going to provide 'spiritual sustenance' (§1 [*ANF* 3:693]). In his *Apology*, Tertullian lists the perceived 'peculiarities of the Christian society.' These include helping those Christians 'in the mines, or banished to the islands, or shut up in the prisons for nothing but their fidelity to the cause of God's church.' He then famously comments, 'But it is mainly the deeds of a love so noble that lead many to put a brand on us. "See," they say, "how they love one another."' This comment was used pejoratively by the non-Christians. Another complaint by the non-Christians is that the Christians 'call each other brethren' (§39 [*ANF* 3:46]).

One of the more interesting discussions relating the early church's helping of prisoners comes from a pagan satirist, Lucian of Samosata (AD 125–180).[137] In *The Passing* [death] *of Peregrinus*, Lucian pokes fun at Peregrinus Proteus who as a pagan Cynic commits suicide in front of a crowd by burning himself. Lucian argues this was simply done for 'love of notoriety.' Although Peregrinus later rejects Christianity, at one point he does join the church. This joining, according to Lucian, was for nefarious reasons. While connected to the church, Peregrinus is put in prison. 'The Christians …

---

137. For a brief summary of Lucian, see Everett Ferguson, *Backgrounds of Early Christianity*, 3rd. ed. (Grand Rapids: Eerdmans, 2003), 352–53.

left nothing undone in the effort to rescue him.... Elaborate meals were brought in, and sacred books of theirs were read aloud.' Part of the logic for this kindness was that 'their first lawgiver [Christ] persuaded them that they are all brothers of one another' (§§1, 11–13 [Harmon, LCL]). Even though Lucian was unimpressed by Peregrinus, he unwittingly provides confirmation that Christians performed deeds of mercy because of their love of Christ and their doctrine of adoption ('brothers').

As shown from Hebrews and other evidence in the first and second centuries AD, Christians helped those wrongly imprisoned because of their Christian faith. This encouraging historical fact should be more well-known among modern Christians. May the watching world see modern Christians' love for each other, and exclaim, whether mockingly or not, 'See how they love one another.'

10.
Heroes of Faith
(11:1–40)

Hebrews 11 is a wonderful and well-known chapter. Most pastors at one time or another have preached through this chapter; and more than many other chapters in the Bible, sermons on this chapter have often been published.[1] There are many things in Hebrews 11 to attract one's attention. It has an emphasis on faith, an interesting presentation of the joys and difficulties of OT men and women, an orientation to a future and everlasting city, a creation statement understood as affirming *creatio ex nihilo*, and obvious practical implications for living one's life now in light of the future. And all of this is presented with significant rhetorical flair.

Hebrews 11 is a separate unit based on the genre, content, and the ending inclusio (Heb. 11:39 with 11:1–2). The primary theme, although not the only theme, of Hebrews 11 is the persevering faith of the OT saints; a faith based on divine promises (or more specific commands), and a faith that results

---

1. I have especially enjoyed reading two that were preached about the same time, the Scot, Robert Bruce, *Preaching Without Fear or Favour: Previously Unpublished Sermons on Hebrews 11* (preached AD 1590–1592 at St. Giles in Edinburgh); and the Englishman, William Perkins, *Commentary on Hebrews 11*, vol. 3 of *The Works of William Perkins*, ed. Randall J. Pederson and Ryan M. Hurd (Grand Rapids: Reformation Heritage, 2017 [1607]) (preached at Great St. Andrews in Cambridge, although the exact date is unknown, maybe AD 1590–1600).

409

in commendable actions. The obvious implicit purpose of this theme is to exhort the readers to strengthen their faith now so as to also persevere to the end of their lives, and thereby receive the full, promised eschatological benefits. Thus, chapter 11 is not an exhortation per se, but its purpose is clearly exhortative.

The pericopes before and after Hebrews 11, 10:35–39 and 12:1–3, are explicit exhortations that make the same point as Hebrews 11. They include both verbal and conceptual similarities to each other and to Hebrews 11, e.g., 'faith' (Heb. 10:38, 39, 11:1; 12:2), and 'endurance' (10:36; 11:13 [concept]; 12:1). Several commentators see Hebrews 11 as an explicit expansion on the 'righteous one shall live by faith' (Heb. 10:38 // Hab. 2:4).[2] In addition to the connections to the prior and subsequent pericopes, both the theme and the purpose of Hebrews 11 recall the previous comment, 'be imitators of those who through faith and patience inherit the promises' (Heb. 6:12).[3]

The genre of Hebrews 11 may be loosely defined as using a list of biblical characters and/or events presented fairly compactly for a clear exhortative purpose. There are other biblical examples of a somewhat similar listing of redemptive-historical persons and events (Josh. 24:1-13; Neh. 9:6–31; Pss. 78; 105; 106; 135; 136; Ezek. 20:5–29; Acts 7, Jude 5–16), and non-biblical examples (Sir. 44–50; 1 Macc. 2:1–60; 4 Macc. 16:16–23; 4 Ezra 7:106–111; 1 Clement 17; *Apostolic Constitutions* 7.37, 8.12 [*ANF* 7:474–75, 487–89, respectively]). As in the above examples, the AH uses the list to make his point.[4] He properly asserts, whether the OT texts explicitly

---

2. So, e.g., Calvin, *Hebrews and 1 & 2 Peter*, 157; Koester, *Hebrews*, 481; and Johnson, *Hebrews*, 279. This is going a little too far for me unless one also includes 'promise' and future blessings into 'the righteous one shall live by faith.'

3. Several commentators put an emphasis on 'patience' as part of the theme/purpose for Heb. 11, so Calvin, *Hebrews and 1 & 2 Peter*, 157; and Moffatt, *Hebrews*, 158.

4. N. T. Wright notes that Sirach 44–50's list of heroes has its climax with the high priest Simon (high priest from 219–196 BC). This is contrasted with Hebrews that ends with the high priest Christ (Heb. 12:1-3). Wright sees the AH providing a 'clear subversion of the story in Ben-Sirach 44–50' (*The New*

mention it or not, that the positive character and/or actions of these 'heroes' is the result of their faith, and this faith is to be imitated (Heb. 13:7).[5] These positive examples of faith (πίστις) are contrasted with the negative example of those in the wilderness generation who had no faith (ἀπιστία, Heb. 3:19).

As to an outline of Hebrews 11, it depends on how granular one wants to get. I prefer to split it into four sections: (1) Definition, creation, and Abel through Noah (11:1–7); (2) Abraham through Joseph with an interlude (11:8–22); (3) Moses through Rahab (11:23–31); and (4) a rapid summary of persons and actions with a conclusion (11:32–40).[6]

Faith: Definition through Noah (11:1–7)

Hebrews 11:1–7 has three well-known verses, 11:1, 3, and 6. Two of them note important aspects of faith (11:1, 6), and the third confirms an important insight to creation (11:3).

The flow of Hebrews 11:1–7 begins with a truncated definition of faith (11:1). Then there is the comment that God approved the faith of the OT saints (11:2), which sets up the list of heroes in 11:4–40. This flow is straightforward, except for the creation statement in 11:3. It begins with 'faith', but it does not invoke one of the heroes; in fact it invokes 'we' and the congregation's faith. As will be discussed below, apparently Hebrews 11:3 is giving more insight to the second half of the definition (11:1b) before embarking on the faith of the heroes.

The heroes list begins in earnest at Hebrews 11:4. First is the faith of Abel (11:4) and then Enoch (11:5). Hebrews 11:6 is a parenthetical expansion upon Enoch's pleasing of God that importantly expands the definition of faith. Finally, Noah finishes out the first section (11:7).

Testament and the People of God [Minneapolis: Fortress, 1992], 410).

5. Speaking of departed believers, the Second Helvetic Confession 5 notes, 'we do *imitate* the saints, for we desire, with the most earnest affections and prayers, to be followers of their *faith* and virtues' (emphasis mine).

6. So also Vanhoye, *Structure and Message of the Epistle to the Hebrews*, 100–4; and Lane, *Hebrews 9–13*, 321.

11:1–2 *Now faith is an assurance of [things] hoped for and a conviction of things not*[7] *seen. For by this, the elders were commended.*

The first point to make about this Hebrews 11:1 definition of **faith** is that it is only partial. As Calvin quips about this definition, 'he selects that part which best fits his purpose'; Lane, 'rhetorical and aphoristic in character.'[8]

The definition includes two parallel statements, **assurance of things hoped for** and **conviction of things not seen**.[9] The **things hoped for** are blessings that are chronologically in the future. The **things not seen** clearly includes these future blessings. This includes blessings that will be visible when one receives them, although they are currently **things not** literally **seen** (e.g., being saved from flood, Heb. 11:7; heavenly country, Heb. 11:13–16). In addition to blessings that are able to be seen in the future, in the context of Hebrews 11, **things not seen** also includes (1) the invisible God, which is metaphorically 'seen' by us now (Heb. 11:27), and (2) 'invisible' causes that create visible effects, of which the prime example is the power of God that created the visible world (Heb. 11:3).

This definition of **faith**, especially **things hoped for**, is fitted to the congregation's context as it primarily refers to the future blessings in the NHNE that Christ's work has

---

7. Why the negative οὐ as opposed to the expected μή before the participle **things seen**? BDF sees οὐ as similar to an alpha privative (§426, cf. §430). That is, the substantival participle is considered a noun with a 'not' before it.

8. Calvin, *Hebrews and 1 & 2 Peter*, 157; Lane, *Hebrews 9–13*, 328. Virtually all agree to a partial definition, so, e.g., Vos, *Reformed Dogmatics*, 4:77; Robert Bruce, *Preaching Without Fear or Favour*, 5–6; Hodge, *Hebrews*, 113; Hughes, *Hebrews*, 438; Attridge, *Hebrews*, 307; and S. M. Baugh, 'The Cloud of Witnesses in Hebrews 11,' *WTJ* 68 (2006): 113–22, esp. 119. Famously, Aquinas does not agree. 'The Apostle completely defines faith, albeit obscurely' (*Hebrews*, 231). This is partially explained by Aquinas' (and Aristotle's) interest in having the 'end' or 'purpose' of a substance included as an important part of its definition, which **things hoped for** provides for him. Also it matches his emphasis on the beatific vision. Further, Aquinas asserts, somewhat confusingly, that any object of faith cannot be seen (see *Summa Theologiae* 2a2ae.1.4–6, 4.1).

9. Rom. 8:24–25 also connects 'hope' to what is not seen.

provided for. It carries the exemplary implication that their **faith**, matching to the OT saints, is to be forward looking and thus enabling perseverance and endurance, especially during difficult times. The forward-looking aspect is also a secondary proof of the AH's larger redemptive-historical point that Christ's first and second comings are anticipated in the OT.[10] This forward-looking aspect also dovetails with the AH's emphases on 'promise' (e.g., Heb. 10:36; 11:9) and 'heir'/'inheritance' (e.g., Heb. 6:17; 9:15; 11:7, 8).

My translations of ὑπόστασις as **assurance** and ἔλεγχος as **conviction** are common but debated. The concept of faith or belief itself has both a subjective aspect and an objective aspect. The subjective aspect refers to the internal act of believing, as in 'he believes.' The objective aspect refers to what or whom one believes or trusts in, as in 'he trusts *his sister.*' As it turns out, the semantic ranges of both ὑπόστασις and ἔλεγχος also have subjective and objective aspects. Hence, ὑπόστασις may be translated as either 'assurance'/'confidence' (subjective) or 'reality'/ 'substance' (objective).[11] Similarly, ἔλεγχος may be translated as either 'conviction' (subjective) or 'evidence' (objective).

Given the parallel nature of the faith definition in Hebrews 11:1, the two terms should be understood as either both subjectively or both objectively. As can be seen by my translations of **assurance** and **conviction**, I have chosen the subjective aspect.[12] For those who choose the objective

---

10. Baugh well notes this redemptive-historical point, but he sees it as primary in Heb. 11 with the exemplary point being secondary ('The Cloud of Witnesses in Hebrews 11,' 113–14, 120). I see the reverse.

11. See LSJ, 1895. Examples of the subjective aspect include Heb. 3:14; Ruth 1:12; Ps. 39:7; 2 Cor. 9:4; and 11:7, although in Greco-Roman literature the objective aspect is more prevalent. The objective aspect is used in Heb. 1:3. The statement in BDAG that examples 'cannot be found' of 'confidence' and 'assurance' is simply in error (p. 1041).

12. So also Brown, *Hebrews*, 488–89; Moffatt, *Hebrews*, 159; Hodge, *Hebrews*, 113; Bruce, *Hebrews*, 277; Schreiner, *Hebrews*, 339; ASV, RSV, NASB, NIV, and ESV. *Contra* Owen, *Hebrews*, 8–10; Gouge, *Hebrews*, 758; Attridge, *Hebrews*, 308–10; Lane, *Hebrews 9–13*, 325–26; Geneva, KJV, NAB, and CSB17.

aspect, many times this is qualified. The AH did not mean that the **things hoped for** exist in one's **faith** or that having **faith** somehow makes these **things** real. But metaphorically speaking (or as a metonymy), one's **faith** is so strong and the reality of **things hoped for** becomes so 'real' that it is *as if* **faith** makes the **things hoped for** to exist. Given this qualification by those who advocate for the objective option, there is, therefore, not much difference between my subjective view and the qualified objective view.

More specifically in this Hebrews 11 context, What object is the object of **faith** that one puts trust in? On the surface it is **things hoped for**. But this is a subset of God's promises (Heb. 6:12; 10:38: 11:9), that is, his word making those promises (Heb. 11:3, 18). This promise/word is in turn a subset of trusting in God himself (Heb. 6:1; 11:6).[13] The AH will then go on to show in Hebrews 11:4–38 that this **faith** will produce effects in a believer's life.

For by this ('faith'), **the elders were commended** by God. The **elders** are the OT heroes, paralleling the use of 'fathers' in Hebrews 1:1. The AH is proving (**for**) his point that the definition of 'faith' is correct because God **commended** those who had this type of faith. Therefore, the AH is also correct in that there is still a future aspect to the blessings that both the **elders** and the congregation look forward to. Thus, the strong implication being that the congregants also ought to have this type of faith and will have future benefits with it.

11:3 *By faith, we understand the ages were prepared by the word*[14] *of God, so that the thing seen has not*[15] *come about from things visible.*

---

13. WCF 14.2 defines faith as believing 'to be true whatsoever is revealed in the *word*, for the authority of *God himself* speaking therein.' This includes 'embracing the *promises* of God for this life and the life to come.' But more specifically, the 'principal acts of saving faith, are accepting, receiving and resting upon Christ alone for justification, sanctification, and eternal life, by virtue of the covenant of grace' (emphasis mine).

14. The Greek behind **word** here is ῥῆμα and also in Heb. 1:3, which is a similar creation context. In the expression 'word of God' in Heb. 4:12 and 13:7, the Greek is λόγος.

15. As most translations do, I take the **not** (μή) as negating **has come**

This is the first of the many times that **by faith** is used to introduce a new subsection (anaphora).[16] Further, each of them does not have a conjunction (asyndeton). The combination of the same word and no conjunctions creates a noticeable rhetorical effect.

Hebrews 1:2 includes faith ('it') and the 'elders.' One would expect that the next verse would include faith and the first hero. Although the AH does include **faith**, he begins with **we** and creation, not the first hero. Apparently, he is expanding upon the definition of faith from the second part of Hebrews 1:1, 'conviction of things not seen.' By the use of **we**, he is encouraging the congregants by reminding them that they do agree with his definition of faith.

The ages (entire universe, 'worlds') **were prepared** (created, cf. Heb. 10:5) **by the word of God**. The **word of God** relates to Genesis 1:1, where God speaks/creates the universe, and also to Psalm 33:6, 'By the word of the Lord, the heavens were made; and by the breath of his mouth, all their hosts' (cf. 2 Pet. 3:5). Clearly in Hebrews 11:3, the spoken **word of God** is referred to, but also the written **word** because **we** learn about this spoken word from the written word. This interplay between spoken and written matches to God's promises in the history of redemption; the promises are orally given and then inscripturated. The AH has previously mentioned creation in Hebrews 1:2–3, 10 and 2:10.

How does **the thing seen has not come about from**

---

about. Others take it as negating the participle **things visible** (e.g., Attridge, *Hebrews*, 315). This results in the alternate translation 'so what is seen was made from the things *not* visible (NRSV, similarly CEB). Grammatically, the problem with the NRSV translation is that it would normally require ἐκ μή φαινομένων, that is, the μή captured within the prepositional phrase for this to be the correct translation. However, the text has μή outside of the prepositional phrase, and it is part of the prepositional articular infinitive phrase εἰς τὸ μὴ ... τὸ βλεπόμενον γεγονέναι. The possible theological problem with this alternate translation is that opens the door to God's making visible creation out of existing invisible matter.

16. Spicq comments, 'Chapter 11 furnishes the best example of anaphora in the whole Bible and possibly in all of secular literature' (*Hébreux*, 1:362, my translation).

things visible prove 'conviction of what is not seen' from the definition of faith? The AH is presupposing that it is normal to see a visible thing made from another visible thing. For example, one watches someone cut down a tree branch and whittle it into a figurine. It would be abnormal if one made a figurine out of something invisible. For the AH, **the thing seen** is the visible world, and **things visible** is any existing matter.[17] Therefore, based on the Scripture, the believer **understands** that the visible world **has *not* come about** by using any existing matter. Instead, there was an invisible cause, the **word of God**, God's breath/wind/Spirit (cf. John 3:8, Rom. 1:20, Ps. 33:6). God needed no existing material to create the world. Thus, relative to creation, faith is the 'conviction of what is not seen' for two reasons. (1) There was an invisible cause (**word of God**). (2) No human was there at the beginning of creation to see it. The AH is probably emphasizing the first reason.

See the following Reflection section for a discussion of *creatio ex nihilo*.

11:4 *By faith, Abel offered a better sacrifice to God, through which he was commended to be righteous, God testifying to his gifts,[18] and through it, [although] being dead, yet he speaks.*

As also with Enoch in the next verse, it is not clear in what way Abel's **faith** demonstrates an 'assurance of things hoped for" (Heb. 11:1). Apparently, the AH understands that Abel and Enoch did good works that were driven by their faith. Further, if they had true faith, at least a part of this included believing God's promises of future blessings.

The story of Cain and Abel is in Genesis 4:1–10.[19] The Lord approved of both Abel himself and his 'gift'/offering of the 'firstborn of his flock and their fat portions' (Gen. 4:4). The

---

17. Yes, the AH believes that reality also includes non-visible things, e.g., love, faith, God. This, however, is not his point here.

18. **God testifying to his gifts** is a genitive absolute, participial phrase.

19. NT references to Abel are Matt. 23:35; Luke 11:51; Heb. 12:24; and 1 John 3:12; Cain is only in Jude 11.

Lord did not approve of Cain's 'gift'/offering of the 'fruit of the ground' (Gen. 4:3). Thus, **by faith, Abel offered a better sacrifice to God** than Cain. The Genesis text does not explicitly say why Abel's offering was **better**. It does state that Abel himself was approved as well as his offering. As mentioned often in the Bible, an offering without the correct heart motivation is not approved by God (e.g., Isa. 1:11). Hence, it is the faith of Abel as opposed to the lack of faith of Cain (cf. Gen. 4:7) that explains God's acceptance.[20] True, but is there more?

The LXX translators add to the Hebrew text that Cain did 'not divide correctly' his offering (Gen. 4:7 LXX); that is, there was nothing wrong with his offering per se, but he did not present/divide it correctly when offering it to God.[21] I do not accept this interpretation. The Genesis text does seem to emphasize Abel's offering more; his is the 'firstborn of the flock and of their fat portions' (Gen. 4:4).[22] Interestingly, the AH terms Abel's 'gift' a **sacrifice**. That is implied in the OT text, but the actual word 'gift' (מנחה, δῶρον) is used for both Abel and Cain (Gen. 4:3–4). Obviously, later in redemptive history sacrificed animals become the norm. Also, the AH emphasizes 'sacrifices' throughout Hebrews. These include the sacrificial animals from the Mosaic legislation (e.g., 8:3), the

---

20. Many commentators see this as the total answer. Abel had faith, and Cain did not. The type of offering is irrelevant. So, e.g., Calvin, *Hebrews and 1 & 2 Peter*, 160; Bruce, *Hebrews*, 281; Koester, *Hebrews*, 475; and Bruce K. Waltke, 'Cain and His Offering,' *WTJ* 48 (1986): 363–72. The Pseudo Jonathan targum seems to agree as it expands upon Gen. 4:8 with Cain complaining to Abel about God's fairness and dismissing that 'there will be a good reward to the righteous.'

21. Josephus argues that Abel's offering was better per se because an animal grows 'naturally' (κατὰ φύσιν) as opposed to planting crops that consists in manipulating the ground (*Jewish Antiquities* 1.54). Philo also argues that Abel's sacrifice was better per se but based on the animal being older and living than Cain's crops (*On the Sacrifices of Cain and Abel* 88). He qualifies this elsewhere to note that Abel's better character also contributed (*Questions and Answers on Genesis* 1:61).

22. Possibly, Cain's grain offering was not a *first* fruits of the ground (cf. Exod. 23:19).

sacrifice of Christ (e.g., 10:12), and the metaphorical sacrifice of praise (13:15–16). Given these factors, I conclude that the AH believes that Abel's *animal* **sacrifice** is more appropriate per se than Cain's grain offering.[23] Of course, this **sacrifice** was presented as a result of Abel's **faith**, and both are needed for an appropriate offering.

Paralleling the comment in Genesis 4:4b that God approved Abel's offering, the AH comments that **through which** (faith[24]) **he** (Abel) **was commended to be righteous, God testifying to his gifts. Righteous** refers back to the Habakkuk quote in Hebrews 10:38. It designates Abel as a true believer (**through** faith). More specifically, a true believer who demonstrates his faith by his offering (cf. Jas. 2:24;[25] 1 John 3:12). Interestingly, since his offering is a **sacrifice**, this demonstration of a good work includes an admittance of sin and a need for an atonement (cf. Heb. 10:18).[26]

The AH connects the Abel discussion directly to any believer, **through it** (faith), **although being dead, yet he** (Abel) **speaks**. The pronoun **he** is not explicit in the Greek and grammatically could be 'it.' Many opt for 'it' referring to Abel's blood that 'cried out' (Gen. 4:10).[27] This view is supported by Hebrews 12:24 that clearly does refer to Abel's

---

23. Although not always having my logic, those who also conclude that an animal sacrifice was better per se than a grain offering include Aquinas, *Hebrews*, 234; Perkins, *Hebrews*, 32, 37; Owen, *Hebrews*, 23:23; and Brown, *Hebrews*, 494.

24. **Which** is feminine and could refer to either of the two feminine nouns, **faith** or **sacrifice**. Given the emphasis on **faith** in context, it refers to **faith**. Although, this is a **faith** that results in a **sacrifice** showing there is not much difference between the two grammatical options.

25. So also connecting this to Jas. 2:24, Owen, *Hebrews*, 23:26; and James Buchanan, *The Doctrine of Justification: An Outline of its History in the Church and of its Exposition from Scripture* (Carlisle: Banner of Truth, 1961 [1867]), 357.

26. The ultimate ground of Abel's righteousness is the imputed righteousness of Christ. The emphasis in Hebrews on forgiveness of sins through Christ's offering himself confirms this.

27. So, e.g., Aquinas, *Hebrews*, 235; Owen, *Hebrews*, 23:28; Bruce, *Hebrews*, 283–84; and Koester, *Hebrews*, 481.

blood metaphorically speaking. However, this view does not explain well the comment, **through** faith. Abel's death was not something he did **through** faith. Hence, Abel **yet speaks** in the sense that his faith and faith-driven-actions are recorded in Scripture.[28] Of course, this point is then to be applied to all of the following heroes.

11:5–6 *By faith, Enoch was changed so that he did not see death, and he was not being found because God changed him. For, before the change, he was commended [as] to having pleased God. Now, without faith, [it is] impossible to please [him]; for the one approaching God must believe that he exists and he is a rewarder of those seeking him.*

Enoch[29] is mentioned in Genesis 5:18-24, with the key verse being 'Enoch walked with God, and he was not because God took him' (Gen. 5:24). There are several clear implications from this text that the AH makes and/or he is simply agreeing with the LXX's expansive translation.[30] Enoch was **not being found** on earth as God took him to heaven. This meant that **God changed him** so as to be fit for heaven. Enoch's walking with God and being taken to heaven implies (**for**) that **before the change**, Enoch **pleased God**. AH also makes another implication, as he does for all the heroes; **faith** is the key to understanding Enoch's life.

Interestingly, the first hero dies a violent death, and the second one does not die in the traditional sense but goes to

---

28. So also Moffatt, *Hebrews*, 164; Lane, *Hebrews*, 335; Cockerill, *Hebrews*, 528; and Schreiner, *Hebrews*, 344–45.

29. There is another Enoch in the Genesis account (4:17–18). Because of two Enochs, Jude distinguishes them by designating the famous Enoch as the seventh from Adam (Jude 14). Also, Jude quotes Enoch as to God's future judgment (Jude 14–15; cf. 1 En. 1:9). Jubilees 4:17 has Enoch writing a 'book of signs of the heaven according to the order of their months' (*OTP*, 2:62). According to Wisdom 4:10, Enoch 'pleased God and was loved by him' (RSV); similarly, according to Sirach 44:16, 'Enoch pleased the Lord and was taken up; he was an example of repentance to all generations' (RSV). A variety of books are attributed to Enoch and are designated by scholars as 1 Enoch (Ethiopic), 2 Enoch (Slavonic), and 3 Enoch (Hebrew).

30. The AH does not quote Gen. 5:24 explicitly, but he is obviously referring to the verse. The LXX of Gen. 5:24 is slightly expansive, and in fact, the AH uses several key words as shown: 'Enoch *pleased* God and *was not being found* because God *changed* him' (LXX Gen. 5:24).

heaven. Cockerill sees this as related to Christ's humiliation and exaltation. Further, based on the verb 'lives' from Hebrews 10:38, Cockerill sees Abel as the 'paradigmatic example' of how to conduct an 'earthly life,' and Enoch as one who 'obtains eternal life.'[31] I am not convinced of these views, but they are worth considering.

With Hebrews 11:6, the AH inserts a parenthetical comment that somewhat elaborates on his faith definition from 11:1. The direct connections to Hebrews 11:5 are that Enoch had **faith** and it **pleased God**.

The AH's first point is that **faith** is not simply an important thing, but **without faith, it is impossible to please** God (cf. Rom. 14:23; Heb. 13:16, 21). That is, it is a necessary condition (*sine qua non*) in order to **please** God.[32] Since the AH is connecting this to Enoch's pleasing of God, it is clear that this is not referring to a general faith in any type of deity, but a true faith in the God of the Bible. Possibly, the point is also that **faith** is needed because sinners need to trust Christ's redemptive work.[33]

The AH adds that a true believer, **one approaching God** and one **seeking him, must believe** (at least) two things: (1) God **exists**, and (2) God **is a rewarder**. In a sense, that God **exists** is an obvious requirement (cf. Exod. 3:14; Rom. 1:20; 1 Tim. 1:17; 4 Macc. 5:24).[34] Maybe the AH pastorally adds this because he understands that at least some congregants are being tempted (a) to believe in a general deity as opposed to the God of the Bible or (b) to doubt any God exists. Or maybe this is a part of some type of creedal formulation (Exod. 3:14).[35]

---

31. Cockerill, *Hebrews*, 526, 529–30.

32. Works done by unregenerate men are not properly speaking 'good works,' see Belgic Confession 24 and WCF 16.7.

33. So also Gouge, *Hebrews*, 768.

34. Donald E. Hartley disagrees with the traditional translation 'he exists' and prefers that the adjective 'faithful' be supplied resulting in 'he is faithful.' According to Hartley, this then eliminates the awkwardness of the AH making the obvious point about believing God exists ('Heb 11:6—A Reassessment of the Translation "God Exists,"' *TJ* ns 27 (2006): 289–307).

35. So Lane, *Hebrews 9–13*, 328.

Of the many attributes of God, the AH chose to mention that he is a **rewarder**, that is, faithful to his promises.³⁶ This emphasis reflects the context of Hebrews 10:34–12:2. The AH has previously stated that God will provide a 'great *reward*' (Heb. 10:35; cf. 11:26). Also, the emphasis on ensuring one gets to the future NHNE fits nicely with God's attribute of being a **rewarder**. Finally, the two-part statement seems to match in reverse order Hebrews 11:1—'assurance of things hoped for' = God is a **rewarder**; and 'conviction of things not seen' = God **exists**.³⁷

11:7 *By faith, Noah, after being warned concerning the things not yet seen, being reverent,³⁸ built an ark for the salvation of his house, through which he condemned the world and became an heir of righteousness according to faith.*

Genesis 6:8–9:28 is the well-known OT narrative concerning Noah (cf. Ezek. 14:14; Matt. 24:37–38; Luke 17:26–27; 1 Pet. 3:20–21; 2 Pet. 2:5; Sir. 44:17–18; Wis. 10:4). The AH is especially interested in God's commanding Noah to **build an ark** because of a future destroying flood for the purpose of delivering his family (Gen. 6:13–18; 7:4). The AH deftly terms this as **being warned concerning the things not yet seen**. The **things not yet seen** are the future rain, flood, and destruction. Obeying this warning will result in the physical **salvation of his** (Noah's) **house**.³⁹ This is tied to the 'things not seen' definition of faith in Hebrews 1:1 and the larger point of Hebrews 11. As Noah had **faith** in God's word about future physical unseen events that resulted in physical **salvation**, so also the readers are to have faith in

---

36. For a discussion of rewards, see Heb. 10:35–36.

37. So also Attridge, *Hebrews*, 318; and Cockerill, *Hebrews*, 531.

38. **Being reverent** (εὐλαβέομαι) is a cognate of 'reverence' (εὐλαβείας) in Heb. 5:7 and 12:28. See discussion at Heb. 5:7–8.

39. **House** (בית, οἶκος), meaning family members of the household, is from Gen. 7:1.

God's promises concerning the unseen future NHNE that will result in spiritual and physical salvation.

Noah's faith (**through which**) contributed to two parallel results: (1) Noah **condemned the world**, and (2) Noah **became an heir of righteousness according to faith**. As Chrysostom notes, including the negative condemnation also shows the readers the result of *un*belief in addition to belief.[40] It is not clear in what way(s) Noah's faith brought condemnation. Peter calls Noah a 'preacher of righteousness' (2 Pet. 2:5).[41] Apparently, driven by his faith, Noah's example of righteous living (Gen. 6:8–9) and also his explicit testimony/preaching about why he was building the ark contributed to the ultimate condemnation of that evil generation.

Heir of righteousness according to faith is a heart-warming phrase. With **heir**, the AH brings back to the fore the significant realities of grace and adoption along with the Abrahamic promises (cf. Heb. 1:2; 6:12, 17). The merit of this inheritance is based on Christ's work. **Righteousness** refers to character traits and actions that match God's law. With no context in the Bible, designating a believer as 'righteous' may be a broad statement about a believer's general character and actions, while acknowledging they do commit sins (e.g., Luke 1:5–6), or it may also be used in a narrow and specific sense to denote perfect righteousness (e.g., Rom. 3:21; 4:6). In the Genesis text, Noah is considered 'righteous' in the broad sense (Gen. 6:8–9; 7:1; cf. Ezek. 14:14). Note, he is also shown to sin (Gen. 9:20) and offers sacrifices presumably for sins (Gen. 8:20). But here, I see **righteousness** being used in the narrow sense. Based on **heir** (grace) and on the logic of **faith** (not works per se), **righteousness** here must mean a perfect righteousness. One that is imputed to a believer

---

40. Chrysostom, 'Homily 23 on Hebrews' (*NPNF*[1], 14:469).

41. Somewhat similarly, 'To [Noah], God himself spoke as follows from heaven: "Noah, embolden yourself, and proclaim repentance to all the peoples, so that all may be saved"' (Sib. Or. 1:125 [*OTP*, 1:338]).

based on the perfect righteousness of Christ.[42] Of course, this language of **righteousness according to faith** is very similar to Paul's (cf. Rom. 4:13). This should not be unexpected as both Paul and the AH knew Timothy (Heb. 13:23).

Reflections

The Christian church has long taught that God the creator made the universe out of nothing, that is, he did not make the world out of preexisting matter. By his initial creation, God 'brought the entire world out of nonbeing into a being that is distinct from his own being.'[43] This doctrine has long been known as *creatio ex nihilo* ('creation out of nothing'). These exact words are not in the Bible, but the concept certainly is. Hebrews 11:3 is often and correctly cited as confirmation of this doctrine.[44]

References to the *creatio ex nihilo* concept are in the OT Apocrypha/Pseudepigrapha and are numerous in the early church. 'God did not make them [heaven and earth] out of things that existed' (2 Macc. 7:28 RSV).[45] 'Before anything that existed at all, from the very beginning, whatever is I created from non-being into being, and from the invisible things into visible' (2 En. 24:2, cf. 25:1 [*OTP*, 1:25]). 'God who dwells in heaven and created that which is out of that which is not' (Shepherd of Hermas, Vision 1.1.6 [Lake LCL]). Irenaeus states, '[God] himself called into being the substance of his creation, when previously it had no existence.'[46] Similarly

---

42. So also Perkins, *Hebrews*, 113; Robert Bruce, *Preaching Without Fear or Favour*, 112–13; Owen, *Hebrews*, 23:55; Gouge, *Hebrews*, 774; Hughes, *Hebrews*, 464; Phillips, *Hebrews*, 432; Turretin, *Institutes of Elenctic Theology*, 2:645; Belgic Confession 23; and Michael Allen, *Sanctification*, New Studies in Dogmatics (Grand Rapids: Zondervan, 2017), 192.

43. Bavinck, *Reformed Dogmatics*, 2:416.

44. E.g., Turretin, *Institutes of Elenctic Theology*, 1:432; and Craig's Catechism (*Reformed Confessions of the 16th and 17th Centuries*, 3:553).

45. Also 2 Baruch 14:17; 21; Jubilees 12:4. Although, Wisdom 11:17 could be taken as denying *creatio ex nihilo*.

46. Irenaeus, *Against Heresies* 2.10.4 (*ANF*, 1:370).

Augustine, 'Lord God Almighty, in thy wisdom,... [did] create something, and that out of nothing. For thou did create heaven and earth, not out of thyself, for then they would be equal to thee.'[47]

The medieval church strongly affirmed *creatio ex nihilo*. The AD 1215 Fourth Lateran Council, chapter 1, is the first creed to explicitly affirm this doctrine, '[God] the creator of all things, visible and invisible, spiritual and corporal, who by his almighty power from the beginning of time made at once out of nothing (*de nihilo*) both orders of creatures, the spiritual and the corporeal.'[48] Aquinas affirms that 'to create (*creare*) is to make something from nothing (*ex nihilo*).'[49]

The Reformation churches also strongly affirmed *creatio ex nihilo*. 'It pleased God the Father, Son, and Holy Ghost ... in the beginning, to create, or make *of nothing*, the world, and all things therein, whether visible or invisible' (WCF 4.1, emphasis mine; cf. WSC 9, WLC 15; Heidelberg Catechism 26).[50]

In addition to the obvious emphasis in the Bible concerning God's initial creation of the universe out of nothing (e.g., Gen. 1:1; Heb. 11:3), part of the reason for the phrase *creatio ex nihilo* was to counteract the ancient philosophical phrase *ex nihilo nihil fit* ('from nothing comes nothing'). Hence, according to this view, matter is eternal and there is no creation in a biblical sense. Maybe without all the philosophical trappings, this ancient view is unfortunately still the view of many in the modern world. By grace through faith, may 'we understand that the worlds were prepared/created by the word of God' (Heb. 11:3).

---

47. Augustine, *Confessions* 12.7 (*NPNF*[1], 1:77).

48. Denzinger[43] §800. The Roman Catholic Church further affirms *creatio ex nihilo* in the AD 1870 First Vatican Council, session 3, canon 1 (Denzinger[43] §3025); and the Catechism of the Catholic Church §§296–98.

49. Aquinas, *Summa Theologiae* 1a.45.1.

50. See typical discussions in Ussher, *A Body of Divinity*, 83–86; Turretin, *Institutes of Elenctic Theology*, 1:431–33; Van Mastricht, *Theoretical-Practical Theology*, 3:108–18; and Bavinck, *Reformed Dogmatics*, 2:416–20.

Faith: Abraham through Joseph (11:8–22)

Hebrews 11:8–22 is primarily about Abraham, but does include Sarah his wife, and Isaac, Jacob, and Joseph, Abraham's son, grandson, and great-grandson, respectively. The AH refers to Abraham explicitly in four contexts (Heb. 2:16; 6:13–15; 7:1–10; 11:8–19) and implicitly in one context (Heb. 13:2).[51] The extended discussion here of Abraham is no surprise given his prominence in the OT and the explicit OT statement about his faith (Gen. 15:6),[52] along with his prominence in Second Temple Judaism literature for being faithful in trial(s).[53]

Previously, the AH has included all believers in the 'seed of Abraham' (Heb. 2:16) that Christ helps. The Jewish-Christian congregants would be especially attracted to the example of Abraham. By highlighting Abraham's faith, the AH is implicitly making the point that it is not his ethnicity that is ultimately what one ought to be proud of. Hence, all the congregants, no matter their ethnicity, should positively embrace Abraham's faith as an example.

All aspects of Abraham's life, of course, are not covered in Hebrews 11:8–19. The AH does comment on Abraham's calling (11:8), sojourning (11:9), fathering of Isaac by Sarah (11:12–13), and offering of Isaac (11:17–19).[54] Given Hebrews 10:38a and 11:1–2, it is Abraham's faith related to these events that interests the AH. And in turn, the AH intends that the congregation make connections to their situation.

As to the flow of Hebrews 11:8–22; the obvious markers are 'by faith' (πίστει) at 11:8 (Abraham), 11:9 (Abraham),

---

51. For a summary of Abraham in the OT, see introductory section to Heb. 6:13–20. For a summary of Abraham in Hebrews, see Cara, 'Covenant in Hebrews,' 251–54.

52. Interestingly, Gen. 15:6 is not quoted in Hebrews. Although, the ending of Heb. 11:7 is very close, 'heir of righteousness according to faith.'

53. E.g., 1 Macc. 3:52; Sir. 44:19; m. Abot 5:3; cf. 1 Clem. 10:1; 31:2.

54. Although a significant amount of Abraham's life in Gen. 12–22 is covered, there are few direct quotes in the Hebrews narrative, excepting Heb. 11:18 // Gen. 21:12 and Heb. 11:21 // Gen. 47:31.

11 (Sarah), 17 (Abraham), 20 (Isaac), 21 (Jacob), and 22 (Joseph). Using a slightly different marker, 'according to faith' (κατὰ πίστιν), the AH introduces an 'interlude' that comments on Abraham, Sarah, Isaac, and Jacob's understanding of the promises (11:13–16).

11:8 *By faith, when being called, Abraham obeyed to go out[55] to a place that he was about to receive for an inheritance, and he went out not knowing where he was going.*

The AH appropriately interprets Genesis 12:1, the call of God upon Abraham. The call includes the command for him to go 'to a land (**place**) that I will show him (**not knowing where he was going**).' It is not explicit that this land will be an **inheritance** for his offspring as part of the call, but later it becomes obvious (e.g., Gen. 12:7; 13:14–15; cf. Acts 7:5; Ps. 105:9–11).

Genesis 12:4 has Abraham's response, 'Abraham went out just as God said to him.' The AH notes that the response was immediate, **when** (or 'as soon as') **being called, Abraham obeyed to go out**.[56] Given Abraham had to both leave his homeland and go to an unknown **place**, the AH concludes that it was only **by faith** that Abraham would do this. Abraham's **faith** is highlighted by his trusting in God and his word (**being called** by God).[57] Also, the forward-looking aspect of his **faith** includes his believing God's promise about a land whose location was unknown to him (**not knowing where he was going**). Further forward-looking aspects from

---

55. The infinitive **to go out** grammatically goes better with 'obeyed' (e.g., NASB) than 'being called' (e.g., ESV) due to proximity. So also Lane, *Hebrews 9–11*, 333–34; and Johnson, *Hebrews*, 287. Although the difference is negligible because for either option **to go out** is explicit with the one verb and implied with the other.

56. The present participle **when being called** confirms the immediacy of Abraham's response. So also, e.g., Hughes, *Hebrews*, 466; and Cockerill, *Hebrews*, 538. Philo comments, 'As soon as he [Abraham] was commanded, he migrated with his soul even before his body' (*On the Life of Abraham* 66).

57. Perkins terms the call of God as the 'cause or ground' of Abraham's faithful obedience (*Hebrews 11*, 123).

the Genesis context include Abraham's believing he is to be blessed and be the father of a great nation (Gen. 12:2–3).

11:9–10 *By faith, he sojourned to the land of promise, as a foreign [land], dwelling in tents*[58] *with Isaac and Jacob, fellow heirs of the same promise. For he was waiting for the city having the foundations, whose*[59] *craftsman and maker [is] God.*

In Genesis, Abraham (**he**) is shown and described as one who **sojourn(s)** in Canaan (e.g., Gen. 12:5; 17:8, 23:4),[60] as are also **Isaac and Jacob** (Gen. 26:3; 47:9).[61] To enforce the point about being sojourners, the AH notes that all three were **dwelling in tents**, as opposed to permanent homes in a city.[62]

Canaan is termed the **land of promise**, or the 'promised land.'[63] There is some irony in this comment. Given Israelite history, one might initially understand that the physical land of Canaan is Abraham's 'inheritance' (Heb. 11:8) and his **land of promise**, which inheritance/land his descendants will eventually obtain. And so it is at one level (Josh. 1:6; Judg. 11:24; Neh. 9:7–8). But on the other hand, Hebrews 3:7–4:13 and 11:39–40 confirm that the land and 'rest' were not ultimately the physical land of Canaan, but there will be a future and better rest. Yes, the AH is saying, Abraham was a sojourner relative to the physical land of Canaan, but since he was a believer in the God of great promises (e.g., Heb. 8:6; 9:15; cf. Luke 20:38), he knew that there is more to God's promises than earthly-physical land and

---

58. The Greek for **tents** (σκηνή) I have elsewhere translated as 'tabernacles' (e.g., Heb. 8:2, 5). See discussion at Heb. 8:1–2.

59. **Whose** (God's) refers back to **city** as both are grammatically feminine.

60. Abraham is also shown to sojourn in Egypt (Gen. 12:10; 15:13; Acts 7:6).

61. The verb for **sojourned** (παροικέω) is the same one used in LXX of Gen. 17:8; 26:3; and 47:9. The substantival adjective 'sojourner' (πάροικος) is in Gen. 23:4.

62. The AH is not saying that all three lived in the same tent at the same time. So also Calvin, *Hebrews and 1–2 Peter*, 168; and Owen, *Hebrews*, 23:66.

63. This is the only place in the Bible where the term 'promised land' occurs. See introductory section of Heb. 6:13–20 for discussion of the term 'promise.'

earthly cities.⁶⁴ The congregant is to understand that he is in the same situation as Abraham. The AH expands upon this topic in Hebrews 11:13–16.

For he was waiting for the city having the foundations, whose craftsman and maker is God. This verse clears up the possible misunderstanding of the irony.⁶⁵ Obviously, this is the heavenly city, and I take it as a description of the NHNE.⁶⁶ Note the emphasis of the articles, it is *the* **city** that has *the* **foundations**.⁶⁷ In one sense, God's providential control builds all cities, but *the* **city** has only one **craftsman and maker**, that is almighty **God**.

11:11–12 *By faith, even Sarah herself*⁶⁸ *received power to [be] the foundation of [the] seed, even beyond*⁶⁹ *[the] season of age, since she considered faithful the one who had promised. So then, even from one [man],*⁷⁰ *although*⁷¹ *having been dead, they were birthed just as [many as] the stars of heaven in number and as [many as] the innumerable sand of the seashore.*

---

64. Similarly, 2 Baruch 4:1–6 has God saying he is not speaking of physical-earthly cities, but that he showed Abraham and Moses that there would be a future 'Paradise' city.

65. Cockerill terms it a 'touch of irony' (*Hebrews*, 540).

66. So also Cockerill (*Hebrews*, 541); and Beale, *A New Testament Biblical Theology*, 758. See further discussion at Heb. 12:22.

67. I assume that many translations drop **the** before **foundations** because it is implied with **the** before **city** (e.g., RSV, NIV, ESV). Others have 'a' before both **city** and **foundations** assuming there would only be one city built by God. Lane notes that **the** before **foundations** is 'emphatic' to emphasize their 'eternal' nature (*Hebrews*, 344).

68. Some Greek manuscripts include 'barren' (στεῖρα). Metzger opts for including it, although he gives a low level ('C') of certainty. He admits that part of the reason is seeing Abraham as the grammatical subject (*TCGNT*², 602). I do not include it (so also *THGNT*). My primary reason is that the manuscript evidence is very weak.

69. The semantic range of παρά includes **beyond**; see BDAG, 757–58 (C.3).

70. **One** is masculine, hence the insertion of **man**.

71. Καὶ ταῦτα before a participle is often a concessive, hence the insertion of **although**. See Herbert Weir Smyth, *Greek Grammar*, rev. Gordon M. Messing, rev. ed. (Cambridge, Harvard University Press, 1956 [1920]) §§ 947, 2083.

The land aspect of the Abrahamic covenant is highlighted in Hebrews 11:8–10; in 11:11–12, it is the people, the 'great nation' (Gen. 12:2). In Genesis, this promised covenantal people are further clarified as being tied to the son of Abraham and Sarah. However, when this is revealed by God, Abraham is one hundred years old, and Sarah, ninety (Gen. 17:15–21). At that point, they had not had any children together, that is, Sarah was 'barren' (Gen. 11:30). Neither Abraham nor Sarah can initially believe this promise as they both cynically laugh at it (Gen. 17:17; 18:12). In Sarah's case, upon her laughter, she then overhears God ask Abraham, 'Is anything too hard for the Lord?' (Gen. 18:14). And apparently this restores her faith in God's promise of a child. And in fact, later Abraham and Sarah do produce a child, whom they name Isaac[72] (Gen. 21:1–3).

Before getting to the exegesis, commentators disagree over the interpretation/translation of Hebrews 11:11 concerning whether Sarah or Abraham is the grammatical subject of the sentence.[73] The Greek explicitly has **Sarah**. But some see Abraham as the implied subject of the verbs **received** and **considered**, thus making Sarah only a parenthetical comment in the verse. For example, Mitchell translates, 'By faith, he received power of procreation, even beyond the normal age—with Sarah, who was barren—since he considered him faithful who had promised.'[74] Older commentators overwhelmingly preferred Sarah as the grammatical subject; but in the last hundred years, it is roughly an even split. The major English

---

72. The name Isaac (יצחק) is a cognate to the verb 'to laugh' (צחק).

73. Pro-Sarah: so Chrysostom, 'Homily 23 on Hebrews' [*NPNF*[1], 14:471]; Gouge, *Hebrews*, 2:783–84; Owen, *Hebrews*, 23:73–76; Hodge, *Hebrews*, 116; Brown, *Hebrews*, 514; Moffatt, *Hebrews*, 171; Spicq, *Hébreux*, 2:349; Hughes, *Hebrews*, 473; Johnson, *Hebrews*, 288, 292; Allen, *Hebrews*, 549–52; Cockerill, *Hebrews*, 542–44; and Schreiner, *Hebrews*, 351–53. The Latin Vulgate has Sarah as the grammatical subject; hence, those using it naturally interpret Sarah as the subject (e.g., Aquinas, *Hebrews*, 242). Pro-Abraham: so Bruce, *Hebrews*, 294–96; Attridge, *Hebrews*, 325–26; Kistemaker, *Hebrews*, 323–24; Lane, *Hebrews 9–13*; 345; Ellingworth, *Hebrews*, 586–88; Grässer, *Hebräer*, 3:121, 130–31; DeSilva, *Hebrews*, 397–98; and Koester, *Hebrews*, 487–88.

74. Mitchell, *Hebrews*, 235.

translations, however, have primarily sided with Sarah, with only two opting for Abraham (NIV84; NRSV).[75] As can be seen from my translation above, I see **Sarah** as the grammatical subject.

The crux of the debate for those favoring Abraham is the prepositional phrase εἰς καταβολὴν σπέρματος, which is understood by them as an idiom ('toward throwdown of seed') that only applies to a male in the procreation process. This is then combined with the immediate context that includes Abraham in the previous verses (Heb. 11:8–10) and the following verse (Heb. 11:12).

The primary argument for Sarah as subject is simply that all Greek manuscripts have her in the nominative case.[76] This makes her the obvious subject of **received** and **considered**. The context of Hebrews 11:11–12 secondarily confirms this. One would expect both Sarah (11:11) and Abraham (11:12) to be included given the events surrounding the miraculous nature of Isaac's conception as portrayed in Genesis. Hence, to use the unclear phrase εἰς καταβολὴν σπέρματος to overturn the clear grammar is not warranted.

Now to the linguistic aspects of εἰς καταβολὴν σπέρματος: The noun σπέρμα is fairly straightforward in both the general Greco-Roman and LXX/NT contexts.[77] Its base meaning is 'seed', and similar to English, it can be used as a collective. It can mean 'seed' in an agricultural context (e.g., Gen. 1:11; Matt. 13:32) and 'semen' in a male procreation context (e.g., Lev. 15:16). It can also mean 'offspring' or 'descendants' in a family generations context, either the offspring reference from a male (e.g., Gen. 9:9; Luke 1:55) or from a female

---

75. 'By faith he received power of procreation, even though he was too old—and Sarah herself was barren—because he considered him faithful who had promised' (NRSV).

76. Admittedly, uncial manuscripts do not normally include iota subscripts. Thus some pro-Abraham scholars have argued that both **Sarah** and **herself** were originally in the dative ('with Sarah herself') (e.g., Attridge, *Hebrews*, 321). This is pure conjecture.

77. LSJ, 1626; BDAG, 937; LEH, 434.

(e.g., Gen. 3:15; Rev. 12:17). In Hebrews, it is clearly used in both 2:16 and 11:18 in the sense of 'offspring'.

The noun καταβολή and the cognate verb καταβάλλω etymologically come from 'throw' and 'down'. In the Greco-Roman world, the verb has the basic meaning of 'throw down' or 'strike down.' In addition, the verb and noun often are using for 'sowing' in an agricultural context and 'laying a foundation' in a building context.[78] In the NT, bracketing out Hebrews 11:11, the noun καταβολή occurs ten times and is only used as 'foundation', including in Hebrews 4:3 and 9:26 (both 'foundation of the world'). The noun is only used once in the entire LXX, also with the meaning 'foundation' or 'building' (2 Macc. 2:29). In the NT, the verb καταβάλλω is only used twice, once for 'strike down' (2 Cor. 4:9) and once 'laying' in reference to a metaphorical foundation, which is in Hebrews 6:1. The verb is used forty-seven times in the LXX with the meanings 'throw down' and 'strike down.'[79] Bracketing out Hebrews 11:11, in sum, neither the noun nor the verb in the LXX and NT are ever used for 'sowing', either in reference to a farmer or male procreation.[80] This is not true in Greco-Roman literature.

The argument from the pro-Abraham scholars is as follows: In Greco-Roman literature, including Jewish Second Temple literature, the combination of either καταβολή or καταβάλλω with σπέρμα is so standardized as a male-procreation idiom that it must mean the male 'sowing of a seed' related to procreation in Hebrews 11:11, despite no example with this meaning in the LXX or NT. Yes, I respond, there are a number of examples of καταβολή/καταβάλλω with σπέρμα meaning male procreation.[81] However, there are examples where

---

78. LSJ, 884–85.

79. LEH, 231.

80. Σπείρω is the primary verb used in the LXX and NT relative to agricultural sowing and related metaphors (LEH, 433; BDAG, 936).

81. E.g., Epictetus, *Discourses* 1.13.3; Gk. Apoc. Ezra 5:12; Philo, *On the Creation of the World* 67, 132; *On the Special Laws* 3.361 ; *On Drunkenness* 211; and *On the Eternity of the World* 98. See more examples in LSJ, 884–85

this expression is used in which it does not refer to the act of procreation, but instead uses καταβάλλω in the negative sense of throwdown to destroy and σπέρμα as 'offspring'. In Psalm 106:27 (LXX 105:27), καταβάλλω with σπέρμα occurs and is translated as 'throwdown the offspring'; also in Psalms of Solomon 17:7, 'God will throwdown (καταβάλλω) them and remove their offspring (σπέρμα).'

There are several plausible interpretations of εἰς καταβολὴν σπέρματος that all support **Sarah** as being the grammatical subject of Hebrews 11:11. (1) 'Foundation of semen'—Sarah's body is the receptacle of Abraham's semen.[82] (2) 'Foundation of offspring'—Sarah is the foundation and establishment of the Jewish nation and spiritual descendants, not speaking of the procreation act per se.[83] (3) 'sowing of semen'—this is Abraham's act, but Sarah is given power in reference to it.[84] I prefer the second option because: (a) Psalm 106:27 and Psalms of Solomon 17:7 evidence that σπέρμα in this expression may be taken as 'offspring'. (b) Elsewhere in Hebrews, καταβολή is 'foundation' and σπέρμα is 'offspring'. (c) Hebrews 11:12 and 11:18 emphasizes the corporate nature of the seed.

Back to exegesis: The AH includes **Sarah** in his list of heroes. She and Rahab (Heb. 11:31) are the two females that are explicitly named but Moses' mother ('parents,' Heb. 11:23) and other women are included (Heb. 11:35). Given that Sarah was beyond the age of menstruation (**beyond the season of age**), God miraculously gave her the **power to be the foundation of the seed**. As noted above, I understand **foundation of the**

(καταβάλλω, II.6; καταβολή, 1.a).

82. This is probably the view of those who conclude that the expression must somehow relate to Sarah's ability to conceive, e.g., Chrysostom, 'Homily 23 on Hebrews' [*NPNF*[1], 14:471] and most English translations. So Moffatt, who comments, 'Probably it was what the writer meant, though the expression is rather awkward' (*Hebrews*, 171).

83. So also Spicq, *Hébreux*, 2:349; and Hughes, *Hebrews*, 473. Swetnam argues for only the 'spiritual' **seed**/descendants (*Jesus and Isaac*, 100–118).

84. So, e.g., Johnson, *Hebrews*, 288, 292; and Cockerill, *Hebrews*, 542–44. Yes, this is the same view of this expression as the pro-Abraham scholars, but it is not used to overturn Sarah as the grammatical subject.

seed to be the establishment of the offspring/descendants. She is the physical mother of the ethnic Jewish nation and the spiritual mother of all true believers (cf. Isa. 51:2; Gal. 4:21–31; 1 Pet. 3:6). Of course, to be the mother of physical descendants, one needs to begin with the first child, which is Isaac.

Specifically, what aspect of **faith** is here related to **Sarah**? **She considered** God to be **faithful** to what he **had promised** regarding that she and Abraham would miraculously have a son, and that son's descendants would be a great nation. This well matches the forward-looking emphasis of the faith definition in Hebrews 11:11. Also note the symmetry between her **faith** (πίστις) and God's being **faithful** (πιστός).

Given the miraculous conception and eventual birth of Isaac, it is true (**so then**) that **from one man** (Abraham) many **were birthed** to become a great nation. And this is true despite Abraham's **having been** metaphorically **dead**[85] relative to having a child with Sarah.[86]

The greatness of this nation is shown by its large population. Metaphorically, the population is **as many as the stars of heaven in number** and the **innumerable sand of the seashore**. These two metaphors are a conflation of Genesis 15:5; 22:17; 26:4; and 32:12, with 22:17 being the closest.[87] All of these verses include 'seed' (זֶרַע, σπέρμα) in the sense of 'offspring,'

---

85. Cf. similar metaphorical language in Rom. 4:19.

86. Later Abraham has children through his new wife, Keturah (Gen. 25:1–2). Hence, **dead** may refer to (1) his inability to produce a child due solely to the older Sarah, and not himself or (2) his inability to produce a child due to his age irrespective of Sarah, which would then include the conclusion that his children by Keturah were also miraculous. Augustine's solution matches option one but includes the nuance that old men can have children with young women (e.g., Gen. 16:16), but they cannot have children if both the man and the woman are old; hence, Abraham's children with Keturah were natural as Keturah was young (*City of God* 29.28 [*NPNF*², 2:327]).

87. The Hebrew and Greek of Gen. 22:17 linguistically matches exactly to **stars of heaven** and **sand of the seashore**. However, **in number** and **innumerable** conceptually match, but not at the linguistic level. Interestingly, the first part of Gen. 22:17 is quoted in Heb. 6:14 and the second half more-or-less quoted in Heb. 11:12.

matching, at least in my exegesis, to **seed** in Hebrews 11:11.

The AH is implicitly including the believers in the congregation as part of the **stars**, the **sand**, and the **seed**. Similarly, Paul connects NT believers to Abraham's 'seed', which is ultimately related to *the* seed, Christ (Gal. 3:7–9, 16, 29).[88]

Possibly, the AH is purposely alluding to a motif of life coming from one who was **dead**. This would metaphorically relate both to Isaac's conception/birth and his being 'sacrificed' (Heb. 11:19). Naturally, this would then relate to the Christian life that comes from the death of Christ.[89]

11:13–14 *According to faith, all these died, not receiving the promises, but having seen and greeted them from afar, and confessing that they are strangers and exiles in the land. For saying such things makes clear that they seek a home-country.*[90]

Hebrews 11:13–16 is an 'interlude' within the catena of the heroes of faith. The congregation is immediately alerted to this because of the different introductory maker, **according to faith** (κατὰ πίσιν) as opposed to **by faith** (πίστει). The content differs in two ways: (1) it includes comments about multiple people, and (2) it uses **faith** slightly differently as people died with their forward-looking faith intact, as opposed to their faith driving their belief or actions.

It expands upon the land discussion of Hebrews 11:8–9, which concerns Abraham but also mentions Isaac and Jacob. Sarah is mentioned in 11:11 in relation to the promised son, but she obviously was also with Abraham in his sojourning in the land. Hence, **all these** refers directly to Abraham, Sarah,

---

88. With the language of **one man**, **dead**, and many descendants, Attridge believes that the AH is purposely alluding to Christ (so Attridge, *Hebrews*, 326–27) or to resurrection in general.

89. So also Attridge, *Hebrews*, 326–27, although he has more certainty than I do.

90. The Greek behind **home-country** is πατρίς, which is etymologically related to 'father'. As expected, therefore, German Bibles translate as 'fatherland' (*Vaterland*).

Isaac, and Jacob, but by implication, it refers to all believers.[91]

As to the grammatical flow of Hebrews 11:13–14, the main subject/verb clause is **all these died**. This clause is followed by four subordinate participles describing or summarizing their lives. The first is negative, **not having received the promises**; **but** despite this, three positive participles, **seeing, greeting,** and **confessing**. The obvious (**makes clear**) conclusion (**for**) to make from these four participles is that these people's lives were characterized by the fact that they truly did **seek a heavenly home-country**.

The expression **not receiving the promises** means not receiving *what* was *ultimately* promised, as clearly promises were made to the patriarchs and portions of them were fulfilled. As noted above (see Heb. 11:8–9), there is a sense that **all these** did receive temporally/earthly aspects of **the promises** in that the 'seed' promised was born (Heb. 6:14–15). Also, their descendants will actually own the temporal/earthly promised land of Canaan, although the patriarchs did not. True, these four were sojourners in the physical land of Canaan as they did not own that land (Gen. 23:4; 26:2–3; 47:9). But they were aware, as should be all believers, that the ultimate promised land is the NHNE, thus making believers sojourners here on earth (e.g., 1 Chr. 29:15; Ps. 39:12; Phil. 3:20; 1 Pet. 2:11). Hence, the AH says about the four that they lived **confessing that they are strangers and exiles in the land**. Why did they consider themselves **exiles**? While living, they **ha[d] seen and greeted** the true promises of the NHNE **from afar**. This **see[ing]** and **greet[ing]** was, while at their best, their life-long habit.[92]

The participle **confessing** (ὁμολογέω, cf. Heb. 13:15) recalls the important cognate noun 'confession' (ὁμολογία) from

---

91. So also Perkins, *Hebrews 11*, 190; Owen, *Hebrews*, 23:84; Brown, *Hebrews*, 516; and Cockerill, *Hebrews*, 547. Some include only Abraham, Isaac, and Jacob (e.g., Attridge, *Hebrews*, 329). Chrysostom includes back to Abel, excepting Enoch ('Homily 23 on Hebrews' [*NPNF*[1], 14:470]).

92. Referencing Heb. 11:13 and 1 Tim. 4:8, WCF 14.2 notes that a Christian with true saving faith 'embrac[es] the promises of God for this life and that which is to come.'

Hebrews 3:1; 4:14; and 10:23. Thus, the content of this confession, **they are strangers and exiles in the land**, has rhetorical punch. New covenant believers also should confess, at a church service or to their neighbor, 'we are strangers and exiles in this world' (see below Reflection section).

11:15–16 *And if they were making mention of that [land][93] from which they went out, they would have had cause to return; but now, they desire a better [home-country], that is a heavenly [home-country]. So then, God is not ashamed of them [so as][94] to be called their God, for he prepared for them a city.*

In Hebrews 11:15–16a, the AH is further proving the point of 11:14 that Abraham, Sarah, Isaac, and Jacob were looking for a **better home-country, a heavenly** one. How? By disproving a possible objection that they called themselves sojourners in Canaan because they wanted to get back to **that land from which they went out**, that is, Ur. He uses a contrary-to-fact argument[95]—it is *not* true that they had **cause** or reason to return to Ur, because if they wanted to, they would have. Since they did not, this confirms that they considered themselves sojourners because they were looking forward to the **heavenly home-land**, not to Ur.

Note that translations differ as to the tense of the verb 'to desire' (or 'to look'). In Greek form (ὀρέγονται), the verb is present tense; although in some contexts, a Greek present would be used for a past event to add vividness or dramatic

---

93. Primarily based on context, but also because **that** and **which** are feminine, they clearly refer back to the feminine 'land' in 11:14. 'Home-country' is also feminine, but context eliminates it as the antecedent.

94. Most English translations understandably drop **of them** (αὐτούς) and the implied **so as** for smoothness, e.g., KJV, RSV, NIV, ESV, and CEB. The Tyndale and Geneva Bible retain **of them**. 'Wherefore God is not ashamed of them even to be called their God' (Tyndale).

95. This is grammatically a second-class conditional (contrary-to-fact) sentence. The protasis ('if' clause) has εἰ plus an indicative (imperfect); the apodosis ('then' clause) has ἄν plus an indicative (imperfect). For conditional sentences with an explanatory chart, see Wallace, *Greek Grammar Beyond the Basics*, 689.

effect.⁹⁶ If one considers this verb a historical present, it would be translated as 'they were desiring/longing/looking' (e.g., NJB, NLT, NIV) and thus would refer to while they were on earth. If one translates as **they desire**, as I do (also KJV, NASB, ESV, CSB17, CEB), the implication is that during the AH's time frame, Abraham, Sarah, Isaac, and Jacob are currently in heaven still looking forward to the **city**, that is, the NHNE.⁹⁷ Partially confirming this view is the comment that God **prepared** (ἑτοιμάζω) **for them a city**. The verb 'to prepare' is used in other similar NT eschatological contexts (e.g., Matt. 25:34, 41; John 14:3; 1 Cor. 2:9; Rev. 21:2).

As to the comment, **God is not ashamed of them so as to be called their God**, why bring this up in this context? First, I note that the OT covenantal promises often include God's stating that he is the God of the covenantal people, and more specifically, he is the God of Abraham, Isaac, and Jacob (e.g., Exod. 3:6, 15). This, however, does not explain this comment's inclusion here. What might prompt one to assume that God might be ashamed so that the AH has to specifically say **God is not ashamed**? Possibly, it is that they were 'strangers and exiles' who oriented their lives around the promising God. Often, others are ashamed of those who are strangers and exiles. Further, this may relate to the congregation (cf. Heb. 2:11). Are they also ones of whom others (non-Christians) are ashamed?

11:17–19 *By faith, when being tested, Abraham had offered Isaac, indeed, the one having received the promises was offering [his] only begotten [son], of whom it was said, 'Through Isaac your seed shall be called'; considering that God is able to raise even from [the] dead, wherefore he received him back, and in parable.*

---

96. If that is the case, it is called a 'historical present.' 'For the sake of vividness or dramatic effect a writer sometimes imagines that he and/or his readers are present and are witnessing a past event' (James A. Brooks and Carlton L. Winbery, *Syntax of New Testament Greek* [Lanham, MD: University Press of America, 1970], 87).

97. So also Hughes, *Hebrews*, 480.

Genesis 22:1–19, the *Aqedah*,[98] narrates Abraham's taking of Isaac to Moriah to sacrifice him and the stunning provision by God of a ram to be offered in place of Isaac. This is the obvious background to Hebrews 11:17–19. Previously, the AH has quoted from this pericope, clearly so in Hebrews 6:14 (Gen. 22:17a) and opaquely in Hebrews 11:12 (Gen. 22:17b).[99] The sacrificial act recalls Hebrews 11:4 and anticipates 12:2.[100]

The primary point in Hebrews 11:17–19 is that Abraham's great **faith** in God was evidenced by his willingness to offer Isaac, despite that Isaac was his son and that Isaac was the heir through which the promised nation would come.[101] The forward-looking aspect of this **faith** is shown in that Abraham, **the one having received the promises**, trusted God's promise about a nation coming from Isaac and that a future resurrection would somehow resolve the obvious dilemma he was in.

Matching to Genesis 22:1, the AH includes that Abraham was **being tested** by God.[102] In a rhetorically interesting manner, the AH states that **Abraham** *had offered* (Greek perfect tense) **Isaac** and then immediately also states that he *was offering* (Greek imperfect tense) Isaac. This well matches Genesis 22. As to Abraham's intent, he **had offered** Isaac. But

---

98. The events of Gen. 22:1–19 are often referred to as the *Aqedah*, which is Hebrew for the 'binding' (implied of Isaac), coming from the verb 'to bind' (עָקַד) in Gen. 22:9.

99. Other *Aqedah* references in the NT are James 2:21 and most likely Rom. 8:32 // Gen. 22:16. For second temple and rabbinic literature, see 1 Macc. 2:52; 4 Macc. 16:20; 18:11; Sir. 44:20; LAB 18:5; 32:2–4; 40:2; Jub. 17:15–18:19; Philo, *On Abraham* 171–205; Josephus, *Ant.* 1.222–36; Mekilta Pisha 7, 11; t. Berakhot 1:15; b. Sanhedrin 89b; and b. Rosh Hashanah 16a–b.

100. So also Attridge, *Hebrews*, 333.

101. Van Mastricht cites Heb. 11:17 to show that 'faith supplies to the believer an unconquerable strength by which we may conquer ... ourselves and our own passions' (*Theoretical-Practical Theology*, 2:33).

102. The same verb (πειράζω) is in the LXX Gen. 22:1 and Heb. 11:17. Rabbinic literature emphasizes various tests for Abraham. M. Abot 5:3 mentions that Abraham had ten tests. According to Jubilees 17:15–16, similar to the book of Job, it is 'prince Mastema' who suggests to God that he ought to test Abraham with Isaac; in b. Sanhedrin 89b, it is Satan.

as to the actual events, he **was** in the process of **offering** him when God provided the ram.[103]

In what sense was Isaac the **only begotten son**?[104] Abraham already had one son, Ishmael, by Hagar (Gen. 16:15). Thus, Isaac is the **only begotten son** as to being the proper heir according to the promise. This previous promise about Isaac (**of whom it was said**) is referenced by quoting from Genesis 21:12, '**through Isaac your seed shall be called.**'[105]

The AH gives a rationale to explain Abraham's **faith**-driven obedience. The AH assumes Abraham's prior knowledge of the promise and then concludes that Abraham must have **consider[ed] that God is able to raise even from the dead**. In addition to the obvious promise implications, What factors in Genesis may have contributed to the AH's conclusion? In Genesis 22:5, Abraham tells others that he and Isaac ('we') will return from the sacrifice.[106] Also, in reference to Sarah conceiving, the Lord said to Abraham, 'Is anything too hard for me?' (Gen. 18:14; cf. Mark 10:27).[107] If conception is not hard, neither is resurrection. Of course, the resurrection comment has connections to Christ (Heb. 13:20) and the congregation (Heb. 6:3).

Commentators disagree as to the understanding of ἐν παραβολῇ, which I translate mechanically as **and in parable**. The two options are: (1) translate as 'figuratively speaking' — meaning that Abraham's **receiv[ing] back** of Isaac is *as if*

---

103. Here, the imperfect **was offering** is considered as having a 'conative' use. Conative is defined as a 'action attempted, but not completed' (Burton, *Syntax of the Moods and Tenses in New Testament Greek* §27). Also see Turner, *Syntax*, 65; and Wallace, *Greek Grammar Beyond the Basics*, 550–51.

104. The Greek for **only begotten** is μονογενής, which conceptually connects to the Hebrew יחיד ('only') in Gen. 22:2, 13, 15. The LXX does not follow the Hebrew text but has instead ἀγαπητός ('beloved'). Is the use of μονογενής by the AH an echo of John's use referring to Christ (John 1:14, 18; 3:16, 18; 1 John 4:9)?

105. The Hebrew, LXX, and Heb. 11:18 all match exactly, cf. Rom. 9:7. Note the Gen. 22 context includes Ishmael.

106. So also Bruce, *Hebrews*, 304; and Schreiner, *Hebrews*, 357.

107. So also Koester, *Hebrews*, 499.

Isaac was resurrected from the dead,[108] or (2) translate as 'typologically'—meaning that Abraham's **receiv[ing] back** of Isaac is typological of new-covenant resurrection realities.[109] My view is option two primarily based on the only other use of παραβολή in Hebrews, which is 9:9, where it clearly refers to new-covenant typology. What **parable**/typology is the AH referring to in Hebrews 11:19? In context, he is referring to resurrection, and from my perspective, this would involve the interrelated resurrections of Christ and believers.[110]

11:20–22 *By faith, Isaac blessed even*[111] *concerning future things Jacob and Esau. By faith, Jacob, when dying, blessed each of the sons of Joseph and bowed upon the top of his staff. By faith, Joseph, coming to an end, mentioned the exodus of the sons of Israel and instructed concerning his bones.*

In rapid succession, Isaac, Jacob, and Joseph are commended. For all three, it is what they said, not their actions, that is the focus.[112]

Genesis 27 narrates Jacob's deceiving of his father, Isaac, to obtain the blessing due to his elder brother, Esau. Isaac's blessings of Jacob are recorded in Genesis 27:27–29 and

---

108. So Calvin, *Hebrews and 1 & 2 Peter*, 172; Perkins, *Hebrews 11*, 240–43; Owen, *Hebrews*, 23:118; Moffatt, *Hebrews*, 177; RSV, NIV, ESV, and CEB.

109. So Chrysostom, 'Homily 25 on Hebrews' [*NPNF*[1], 14:478]; Augustine, *City of God* 16.32 [*NPNF*[1], 2:329]; Aquinas, *Hebrews*, 248; Robert Bruce, *Preaching Without Fear or Favour*, 260–61; Bruce, *Hebrews*, 304; Hughes, *Hebrews*, 484 n. 54; Attridge, *Hebrews*, 335; Cockerill, *Hebrews*, 558; Swetnam, *Jesus and Isaac*, 119–23; NASB, and NAB.

110. Several commentators restrict this typology to the future resurrection of believers (e.g., Lane, *Hebrews 9–13*, 347, 363; and Cockerill, *Hebrews*, 558). Others focus on Christ (e.g., Chrysostom, 'Homily 25 on Hebrews' [*NPNF*[1], 478]; and Schreiner, *Hebrews*, 358). As to typology in Gen. 22, Augustine connects Isaac's carrying of the wood to Christ's carrying the cross; ram as an offering to Christ as an offering; ram's horns being caught in a thicket to Christ's crown of thorns; and Abraham spared not his son to God the Father not sparing his Son [*City of God* 16.32 [*NPNF*[1], 2:329]. Similar to Augustine is Clement of Alexandria (*The Instructor* 1.5 [*ANF* 2:214–15]).

111. I take καί as emphatic related to the future blessings; so also Lane, *Hebrews 9–13*, 347.

112. Schreiner alerted me to this point (*Hebrews*, 359).

28:3–4; and of Esau, in Genesis 27:39–40. These blessings are somewhat of a combination of a last-will-and-testament and a blessing.[113] The AH emphasizes that **Isaac blessed** *even concerning future things* for both **Jacob and Esau**. How is this related to Isaac's forward-looking **faith**? Since, normally a blessing of a child by a parent would relate to the future, the AH is intending something more here. This blessing is related to God's covenantal promises that Isaac believed. This is further confirmed by the expression **future things** (μέλλω), which is used in Hebrews with an eschatological nuance.[114] Of course, the blessing related to **Esau** includes what he will *not* receive relative to **Jacob** (cf. Heb. 12:16–17).

Genesis 47:29–48:22 relates to Hebrews 11:21. It begins with the comment that Jacob (also called 'Israel') is near death (**when dying**) and asks that Joseph come to him. Jacob asks Joseph to ensure that he will be carried from Egypt and buried in Canaan (cf. 49:29–50:14). Upon Joseph agreeing, Jacob **bowed**, apparently in worshipful thankfulness to the Lord. Later Joseph brings his two sons, Manasseh and Ephraim, to Jacob, and he blesses Joseph, and **the sons of Joseph**. Interestingly, similar to **Jacob and Esau**, Joseph's sons are not blessed in the 'correct' order of older then younger. What aspect of Jacob's forward-looking **faith** is being emphasized by the AH? It is not clear, but it certainly includes that the posterity of Joseph's two sons will in fact get to Canaan, which would be a continuation of God's covenantal promises (cf. Gen. 48:3–4). Also, it may be that Jacob received and believed a revelation from God that Ephraim's posterity will be greater than Manasseh's. The readers know that this eventually did happen (cf. Josh. 16–17; Hos. 6:4).

---

113. Mitchell terms these and others by the patriarchs as 'testamental blessings' (*The Meaning of BRK 'To Bless' in the Old Testament*, 79–90). Owen terms these patriarchal blessings as 'paternal benedictions ... accompanied with a spirit of prophecy' (*Hebrews*, 21:318).

114. See Heb. 1:14; 2:5; 6:5; 10:1; 10:27; 11:8; 13:14, with 8:5 as the only exception. So also Attridge, *Hebrews*, 336; and Koester, *Hebrews*, 497.

The use of **staff** in the expression **bowed upon the top of his staff** is worthy of comment. The expression comes from Genesis 47:31. The original (consonantal and unpointed) Hebrew text would have had מטה, which, depending on the pronunciation (vowel pointing), could be understood as 'bed' (מִטָּה) or as 'staff' (מַטֶּה). The Masoretes chose 'bed'; the LXX and the AH chose 'staff.' From my perspective, 'staff' is the best understanding of the original Hebrew text.[115] Another plausible understanding is that the AH understood that Jacob was sitting on the side of his bed while leaning on his staff to keep him in the seated position.[116]

Following Genesis 50:24–25, the AH comments on two statements Joseph made at the end of his life (**coming to an end**, τελευτάω[117]).[118] Joseph **mentioned the exodus of the sons of Israel** and **instructed** others **concerning his bones** that he would be embalmed and eventually buried in Canaan. Of course, both the **exodus** of Israel from Egypt (Exod. 14:30) and the embalming and burying of Joseph in Canaan did occur (Gen. 50:26; Exod. 13:19; Josh. 24:32; Acts 7:15–16; cf. Sir. 49:15; Philo, *On the Migration of Abraham* 17). Joseph's forward-looking **faith** showed itself as he believed the covenantal promises concerning inheriting the land of Canaan, which in order to accomplish, given his situation, an **exodus** of Israel from Egypt was required. Also, in addition to his confidence in a future **exodus**, Joseph had **faith** that his **bones** would also get to Canaan (cf. Gen. 48:21).[119]

---

115. So also Hughes, *Hebrews*, 489. I assume the Masoretes chose 'bed' due to Gen. 48:2. Although understandable, this is confusing the two contexts of Gen. 47:29–31 with 48:1–7. Also, to lean/bow on the 'top of a staff' makes more sense than to lean/bow on 'top/head of a bed.'

116. So Owen, *Hebrews*, 23:129; and Bruce, *Hebrews*, 306.

117. Referring to Joseph's death, τελευτάω is used in Gen. 50:26; to Jacob's, Acts 7:15.

118. Besides the bones, various other aspects of Joseph's life are commented upon in Ps. 105:17–19; Acts 7:9–15; Wis. 10:13–14; 1 Macc. 2:53; and 4 Macc. 18:11.

119. Bruce comments that Joseph's temporary residence is also emphasized (*Hebrews*, 307).

Reflections

'Confessing that they are strangers and exiles in the land' (Heb. 11:13) is a quote and concept that has captured Christians' imaginations down through the centuries—with the prime example being Bunyan's *Pilgrim's Progress*. Although this world is made and ruled by God, sin does exist. This world has importance, but the 'land' that is ultimate for Christians is the NHNE. Hence, Christians are 'strangers and exiles' in this world.

The anonymous Epistle to Diognetus was written approximately AD 200.[120] Chapters 5–6 are an apology and explanation to a non-Christian to explain the relationship of Christians to the world. 'They [Christians] dwell in their own fatherlands, but as if sojourners in them; they share all things as citizens, and suffer all things as strangers. Every foreign country is their fatherland, and every fatherland is a foreign country' (Diogn. 5:5 [Lake, LCL]). 'They pass their time upon the earth, but they have their citizenship in heaven' (Diogn. 5:9 [Lake, LCL]).

The *Valley of Vision* contains Puritan prayers. One includes, 'I am a stranger, with a stranger's indifference; My hands hold a pilgrim's staff, My march is Zionward, My eyes are toward the coming of the Lord, My heart is in thy hands without reserve.'[121]

Although there are many God-given temporal blessings and responsibilities in this life, may the Christian reader and I remember that we 'are strangers and exiles in the land.' So much so, that we even are 'confessing' it to others.

Faith: Moses through Rahab (11:23–31)

Following the previous discussion of Abraham and the patriarchs (Genesis 12–50), Hebrews 11:23–31 covers aspects

---

120. So Robert M. Grant, 'Diognetus, Epistle to,' *ABD*, 2:201.

121. Arthur Bennett, ed., *The Valley of Vision: A Collection of Puritan Prayers & Devotions* (Carlisle: Banner of Truth, 1975), 198.

of Moses' life through the crossing of the Red Sea and then moves to the destruction of Jericho (Exod. 2–14; Josh. 2, 6). It is natural that the AH would move from Joseph to Moses and his exodus generation. This matches the movement from the end of Genesis to the beginning of Exodus, and it matches to Joseph's 'mention[ing] the *exodus* of the sons of Israel' (Heb. 11:22).

More specifically, the AH commends the faith of Moses' parents (11:23), the faith of Moses in three situations (11:24–28), the faith of the Israelites at the Red Sea and at Jericho (11:29–30), and the faith of Rahab related to the Jericho conquest (11:31). As opposed to the difficulties that the patriarchs faced related to the land and to the seed, the various examples of 'faith' in Hebrews 11:23–31 are exhibited in the midst of significant temporal danger, and this will continue through 11:38. This danger aspect, although not as extreme (cf. Heb. 10:33–34; 12:4), relates to the congregation's situation.

11:23 *By faith, Moses, after being born, was hidden three months[122] by his parents[123] because they saw [that] the child was special and they did not fear the edict of the king.*

Exodus 1:8–22 narrates Pharaoh's attempts to reduce the Israelite population in Egypt. He first makes their jobs more difficult. Then he orders the Hebrew midwives to kill all male children at birth. Finally, he orders that all of his subjects are responsible to kill all Hebrew male children at birth by throwing them into the Nile. It is in the context of this final broad order that Moses is born. The well-known story of Moses' deliverance from this broad order is in Exodus 2:1–10

---

122. Τρίμηνον (**three months**) is an accusative of duration; so also Zerwick and Grosvenor, *A Grammatical Analysis of the Greek New Testament*, 682. For different nuances per case related to 'time' words, see Wallace, *Greek Grammar Beyond the Basics*, 202–3.

123. The Greek behind **parents** is the plural of πατήρ, which with no context would normally be translated as 'fathers'. Given the context and other examples in secular Greek (see LSJ, 1348 [VII.2]), virtually all agree **parents** is correct here.

(cf. Acts 7:19–22). Moses' mother, after hiding him for **three months**, puts him in a basket to float on the Nile while Moses' sister keeps watch. Pharaoh's daughter finds the basket and eventually Moses lives with her as her son.

What does the AH note about this story? Although **Moses** is the grammatical subject of Hebrews 11:23, that is, the subject of the passive verb **was hidden**, the **faith** being described is of Moses' **parents**, Amram and Jochebed (Exod. 6:20; Num. 26:59).[124] Two reasons are given for their actions. (1) **They saw that the child was special**. The exact meaning of **special** (ἀστεῖος) is not clear; hence, my more generic translation. The Hebrew text of Exodus 2:2 has טוב, which is a very common word with a broad semantic range that is often translated 'good'. The LXX has ἀστεῖος, as does the AH. Although not as broad as טוב, the semantic range of ἀστεῖος in secular sources is broad. When referring to humans, it ranges from 'polite' to 'refined' to 'charming' to 'handsome'.[125] In the NT, ἀστεῖος is only elsewhere used in Acts 7:20, where again referring to Moses, it is said that he is 'ἀστεῖος to God.'[126] Does ἀστεῖος in Hebrews 11:23 relate to outward appearance? It probably does include this, but the more central point is that the **parents** knew somehow that Moses was **special** to God's people and needed to be rescued, as the parallel 'ἀστεῖος to God' of Acts 7:20 implies.[127]

---

124. Although Exod. 2:1–3 only mentions Moses' mother, obviously both **parents** would be involved in seeing Moses and hiding him for **three months**. The LXX makes this assumption as it has plural verbs for 'saw' and 'hid' in Exod. 2:2. Philo also has 'parents' (*On the Life of Moses* 1.9). In Josephus, Amram, Moses' father, is told in a dream by God prior to his birth that Moses would be special (*Jewish Antiquities* 2.210–18). In LAB, before his wife has conceived, Amram makes a heroic speech to the Jewish elders to defy the king's degree so that God's covenant people may continue (9:3–8).

125. LSJ, 260–61.

126. In the LXX, ἀστεῖος occurs seven times, including Exod. 2:2. It exhibits a variety of meanings reasonably matching to the secular use. See LEH, 67.

127. More or less, so also Calvin, *Hebrews and 1 & 2 Peter*, 176; Owen, *Hebrews*, 138–39; Bruce, *Hebrews*, 309; and Lane, *Hebrews 9–13*, 370. Koester asserts that God would not use physical looks to indicate importance (*Hebrews*, 501).

(2) **They did not fear the edict of the king.** Exodus does not explicitly say that Moses' mother did not fear Pharaoh, although this is obviously implied.[128] A little later it will be said that Moses 'was not *fearing* the wrath of the king' (Heb. 11:27; cf. Heb. 13:6). Part of true **faith** is doing the right thing no matter the future consequences, even when the consequences are dire (cf. Dan. 3:16–18; Acts 4:18–19; 5:27–29). **Faith** drives out fear. One knows **by faith** that the possible negative consequences are temporary compared to eternity with God.[129]

11:24–26 *By faith, Moses, being full grown, refused to be called the son[130] of Pharaoh's daughter, choosing rather to be mistreated with the people of God than to have fleeting pleasure of sin, considering the reproach of Christ greater wealth [than] the treasures of Egypt, for he was looking toward the reward.*

Here begins three 'by faith' comments about Moses (Heb. 11:24, 27, 28). Moses has previously been highlighted in Hebrews 3:1–6, where he is said to be 'faithful (πιστός)' similar to Jesus' being faithful.[131] Moses is obviously also included in Hebrews as the human writer of the first/old covenant.

I understand Hebrews 11:24–26 to be an accurate summary of a portion of Moses' life rather than specifically referring to his killing of the Egyptian and its immediate aftermath

---

128. Concerning the midwives it is explicit that they 'feared God' as opposed to Pharaoh (Exod. 1:21).

129. *Contra* Pamela Michelle Eisenbaum, who states, 'The πίστις [faith] that each exemplar exemplifies is not necessarily demonstrated by something they do, or think, as vv. 23 and 30 show, but by something God does for/with/to them' (*The Jewish Heroes of Christian History: Hebrews 11 in Literary Context*, SBLDS 156 [Atlanta: Scholars, 1997], 167).

130. **Son** is in the nominative case, where one might expect an accusative as **son** is the object of the infinitive 'to be called.' However, the nominative case may be used in infinitive situations where the 'object' is 'identical with the subject of the verb on which it depends,' i.e., **Moses** equals **son**. See Zerwick, *Biblical Greek* §393.

131. For a discussion of Moses in Hebrews, see Cara, 'Covenant in Hebrews,' 257–61; and D'Angelo, *Moses in the Letter of Hebrews*.

(Exod. 2:11–15).¹³² **Being full grown**¹³³ is in contrast to being a child in the previous verse. As Moses came of age, at some point he internally **refused to be called the son of Pharaoh's daughter** (cf. Exod. 2:10; Acts 7:21).¹³⁴ Why? Being **called the son of Pharaoh's daughter** in Moses' specific context was apparently wrapped up with denying **the people of God**.¹³⁵ This internal refusal set in motion various outward actions by Moses and resulting consequences.

This internal decision (**by faith, considering, looking**) has temporal negative consequences. Moses **cho[se] rather to be mistreated with the people of God**. It was not simply being identified with God's people that would bring on the negative consequences from Exodus 1. In Moses' case, since he was the adopted **son of Pharaoh's daughter**, he would be giving up the advantages of his very high position. These advantages include the 'lesser' **wealth** of **the treasures of Egypt** and the supposed advantages of the **fleeting pleasure of sin**.¹³⁶ The **pleasure of sin** partially includes various gross sins that those in power typically have ample opportunity to indulge in.¹³⁷

What does the expression **the reproach** (ὀνειδισμός) **of Christ** refer to?¹³⁸ In the immediate context, **reproach** is Moses' being **mistreated with the people of God**. Elsewhere in Hebrews, **reproach** is used (1) to refer to the difficulties of the congregants (10:33), and (2) to make the connection between

---

132. So also Owen, *Hebrews*, 23:146; and Allen, *Hebrews*, 559.

133. The Greek matches exactly LXX Exod. 2:11.

134. The name of Pharaoh's daughter is not given in Scripture. She is given different names in Second Temple Judaism: 'Thermuthis' (Josephus, *Jewish Antiquities* 2.224); 'Tharmuth' (Jub. 47:5); and 'Merris' (Artap. 27:3).

135. For a discussion of the term **people of God**, see Heb. 4:9.

136. Chrysostom quips, 'For when Heaven was set before him, it was superfluous to admire an Egyptian Palace' ('Homily 24 on Hebrews' [*NPNF*¹, 483]).

137. So also Brown, *Hebrews*, 544.

138. For a good, brief summary of various early church, Reformation, and modern views of this expression see Nathan MacDonald, 'By Faith Moses,' in *The Epistle to the Hebrews and Christian Theology*, 374–82.

the congregants' difficulties and Christ's **reproach** (13:13). What does **of Christ** add? Even though Moses lived during the OT, **Christ** must refer at least to his partial knowledge of the Lord Jesus Christ (cf. Heb. 3:5; 8:5). Further, it shows that the **reproach** endured by both OT and NT believers for the sake of God are in the same category; thus, this is another confirmation of the unity of the **people of God** (body of **Christ**) across the OT and NT.[139] In addition, as Hebrews 13:13 makes explicit, the **reproach** that **Christ** suffered is a general pattern for believers' suffering.[140] Finally, 'the **reproach** Moses suffered for *God's* sake is attributed to Jesus **Christ**';[141] hence, this is a confirmation of a Trinitarian understanding of God.

For he was looking toward the reward gives an additional rationale as to why **wealth** and **fleeting pleasure of sin** were renounced by Moses. Note the contrast of time. The eternal heavenly **reward**[142] is contrasted with **fleeting** (cf. Ps. 84:10; Prov. 16:8). This brings to the fore again Hebrews 11:1, 'assurance of things hoped for.'

11:27 *By faith, he left Egypt, not fearing the anger of the king; for he persevered as seeing the invisible [one].*

Moses **left Egypt**. Commentators disagree as to which event in Moses' life the AH is referring to. There are two basic options, of which the second has two sub-options. I prefer option two-b. (1) Moses **left Egypt** to go to Midian after killing the Egyptian (Exod. 2:11–15), where he stayed for forty years

---

139. Emphasized by Calvin, *Hebrews and 1 & 2 Peter*, 177.

140. Further solidifying this is the connection between **reproach**, Christ, and believers in Ps.s 69:9 and 89:50–51. Ps. 69:9 uses the cognate verb ὀνειδίζω and Rom. 15:3 explicitly connects this to Christ, which in turn is used as a pattern for Christians. See Robert J. Cara, 'Psalms Applied to Both Christ and Christians,' 108–10. Psalm 89:50–51 uses both the noun (ὀνειδισμός) and verb (ὀνειδίζω) to connect the **reproach** of believers to the **reproach** of the anointed king (מָשִׁיחַ, χριστός). Cf. Matt. 5:11–12; Gal. 6:17; Phil. 1:29; 1 Pet. 4:14.

141. Schreiner, *Hebrews*, 363, emphasis mine.

142. For an extended discussion on **reward**, see Heb. 10:35.

(Acts 7:30)?¹⁴³ The disadvantage with this view is that after killing the Egyptian and this action became known, Moses 'was afraid' and 'fled from Pharaoh' who 'sought to kill him' (Exod. 2:14–15).¹⁴⁴ Those who favor this view respond that Moses' 'fear' was a rational fear realizing that the time was not right for a revolt.¹⁴⁵ (2) Moses **left Egypt** (a) following the Passover (Exod. 13:18),¹⁴⁶ or (b) considered an extended event from the ten interviews with Pharaoh culminating with leaving following the Passover (Exod. 7:1–13:18).¹⁴⁷ The disadvantage with this view is that the next verse (Heb. 11:28) refers to the Passover which reverses the historical order of the leaving and Passover. This disadvantage is overcome by option two-b.

For he persevered as seeing the invisible one gives an aspect of Moses' **faith** that aided him in standing up to the **anger of the king**. This harkens back to Hebrews 11:1, 'conviction of things not seen' (cf. Heb. 11:3, 6). Although Moses did see visible manifestations of God (e.g., Exod. 3:2–3; 33:21–23), the Godhead is **the invisible one**. The point being that Moses' life of **faith** was so strong that it is *as if* Moses was

---

143. So, e.g., Moffatt, *Hebrews*, 181–82; Bruce, *Hebrews*, 313; Hughes, *Hebrews*, 499; Ellingworth, *Hebrews*, 615; and Schreiner, *Hebrews*, 364.

144. Stories abound in Second Temple Judaism literature about Moses. In one legend, Moses is exonerated because he killed the Egyptian, Chenephres, in self-defense, spoiling a plot to kill him after his mother had died (Artap. 27:15–18). Chenephres was jealous of Moses, for among other things, Moses had led a rag-tag Egyptian army successfully against Ethiopians (Artap. 27:7–10). Josephus also records this war with Ethiopia and Moses' amazing strategies as a general (*Jewish Antiquities* 2.238–53). Another author notes that while in Midian, Moses says, 'I wander in a foreign land,' connecting his plight to the patriarchs (Ezek. Trag. 58 [*OTP* 2:810]).

145. So well argued by Bruce, *Hebrews*, 313; and Hughes, *Hebrews*, 498–9.

146. So, e.g., Calvin, *Hebrews and 1 & 2 Peter*, 178; Owen, *Hebrews*, 23:161; and Westcott, *Hebrews*, 373.

147. So, e.g., Spicq, *Hébreux*, 2:359; Kistemaker, *Hebrews*, 339; Koester, *Hebrews*, 504; Cockerill, *Hebrews*, 574–75; and Kleinig, *Hebrews*, 567. This view entails seeing the verb **left** as a 'culminative aorist,' which is defined as 'emphasis is placed on the conclusion or the results of the completed action' (Brooks and Winbery, *Syntax of New Testament Greek*, 100).

always **seeing** God (cf. John 1:18; Rom. 1:20; Col. 1:15; 1 Tim. 1:17; 6:16; Heb. 12:2, 14; 1 John 4:20).

11:28 *By faith, he kept*[148] *the Passover and the sprinkling of blood in order that the one destroying the firstborn would not touch them.*[149]

God instructed Moses and Aaron about the Passover ceremony (Exod. 12:1, 28). As the representative of the people and the one who delivered God's instructions to the Israelites (Exod. 12:21), Moses **kept the Passover** (Exod. 12:1–28) **and the sprinkling of blood** (Exod. 12:7, 22). This prevented **the one destroying**[150] **the firstborn**[151] Egyptian humans and animals from **touch[ing]** any of the Israelite (**them**) humans and animals (Exod. 11:4–7; 12:23).

What **faith** did Moses exhibit? He trusted and obeyed God's word (Exod. 12:1, 21, 28; 13:1–3).[152] This recalls Hebrews 11:3, 'understand ... by the word of God.' Interestingly, three aspects of the faith definition ('assurance of things hoped for,' 'conviction of things not seen,' 'understand ... by the word of God') in Hebrews 11:1, 3 are exhibited by Moses in 11:24–28. Also, with Moses' **faith** being highlighted, Perkins states the obvious, but it is worth repeating, 'If any man could be justified by the works of the law, it must be Moses, who gave the law,...

---

148. The combination of ποιέω and πάσχα is an idiom meaning 'to keep the Passover' (e.g., Exod. 12:48; Num. 9:2; Deut. 16:1; Matt. 26:18). This idiom mechanically follows the Hebrew עשׂה פסח. Ποιέω is in the perfect tense probably because this emphasizes both the inauguration and continuation of the Passover ceremony; so also BDF §342.4.

149. The direct object **them** is in the genitive because the verb **touch** usually takes a genitive. So also at Heb. 12:20. See LSJ 801.

150. The **one destroying** (ὀλοθρευω) is also used in LXX Exod. 12:23. The cognate noun 'destroyer' (ὀλοθρευτής) is used in 1 Cor. 10:10 with the same referent. Is the **one destroying** a good angel (e.g., 1 Chr. 21:15), evil angel (e.g., Ps. 78:49?), or an impersonable force? I prefer a good angel (so also John D. Currid, *Exodus*, 2 vols. EP Study Commentary [Darlington: Evangelical Press, 2000–2001], 1:251; and Owen, *Hebrews*, 23:168). But in any event, God was providentially in control.

151. **Firstborn** is neuter confirming the reference to both men and animals.

152. So also Calvin, *Hebrews and 1 & 2 Peter*, 180; and Brown, *Hebrews*, 559.

[but] the thing that commends Moses and makes him stand before God is not his works but his faith.'[153]

The AH does not explicitly connect **the Passover** ceremony **and the sprinkling of blood** upon the lintel and doorposts typologically to Christ (cf. 1 Cor. 5:7). Given the context of the book, however, the AH certainly intends for the congregation to see the connection.[154] The **Passover** is another emphasis on sacrifice within Hebrews 11 along with Abel (11:4) and Abraham/Isaac (11:17), not to mention the Tabernacle animal sacrifices and *the* sacrifice of Christ (8:1–10:18) elsewhere in Hebrews. Similarly, the **blood** emphasis of Christ is prominent in Hebrews (e.g., 9:12, 18–22; 10:4; 13:20).

11:29 *By faith, they crossed the Red Sea as through dry land, which*[155] *the Egyptians while making an attempt drowned.*[156]

The grand story of God's salvation of Israel at the **Red Sea**[157] is narrated in Exodus 14 and referred to in Scripture many times thereafter (e.g., Exod. 15:1–12; Neh. 9:11; Pss. 78:13; 106:9–12; 136:13–15; Isa. 50:2; 51:10; 63:12; Acts 7:26; cf. Wis. 10:18–19).

Here the AH does not explicitly refer to Moses' **faith** but to the Israelites' (**they**). What aspect of **faith** is emphasized? As Exodus 14:1–3 makes clear, the Israelites were boxed in with the **Red Sea** at their backs.[158] Upon seeing the coming Egyptian

---

153. Perkins, *Hebrews 11*, 295.

154. So also Chrysostom, 'Homily 26 on Hebrews' (*NPNF*[1], 14:487); Attridge, *Hebrews*, 343; and Cockerill, *Hebrews*, 580. *Contra* Calvin, *Hebrews and 1 & 2 Peter*, 179; and Koester, *Hebrews*, 504.

155. **Which** (ἧς) is grammatical feminine and could refer back to either the feminine **Sea** or feminine **land**. Either way, the point is the same.

156. The Greek verb translated as **drowned** (καταπίνω) is more literally 'gulp, swallow up' (LSJ, 905). So in Exod. 15:12.

157. For a defense that the **Red Sea** (ים סוּף, ἐρυθρά θάλασσα) in the OT refers to the northern portion of the modern Gulf of Suez of the Red Sea, see Currid, *Exodus*, 1:280–81. The common critical view is that it refers to marshes in the delta of the Nile. For a summary of views, see John R. Huddlestun, 'Red Sea,' *ABD*, 5:633–42.

158. See Josephus' dramatic description of this dilemma (*Jewish Antiquities* 2.321–25).

army, 'they feared greatly' (Exod. 14:10) and bitterly complain to Moses. Moses then tells the Israelites that God will save them from this danger, and in fact, they do escape **through dry land**. Although initially wavering, the Israelites had **faith** to trust God's word ('go forward,' Exod. 14:15) and go **through dry land** trusting it would not disappear partly through as it did for the **Egyptians**. That is, they trusted God's word about the unique provision in the face of danger. The Exodus episode ends with a comment about their **faith**, 'they [Israelites] *believed* in the LORD and in his servant Moses' (Exod. 14:31). Given the AH's earlier negative comments concerning the faith of this generation that left Egypt (Heb. 3:16–19; cf. 1 Cor. 10:5), not all who went through the **Rea Sea** had true **faith**. One can imagine that, given the dire circumstances, many had no choice but to opt to go ahead through the opening in the water without necessarily having a true saving **faith** in God.[159]

Obviously, **the Egyptians** do not believe in God and are judged by **drown[ing]**. This anticipates the ultimate judgment. Many ancient commentators notice the irony of Pharaoh's drowning of the male children in the water of the Nile (Exod. 1:22) and Pharaoh's male army **drown[ing]**.[160] In the Rabbinic Mekilta, it is likened to a wheel that indicates the rotation of God-directed fortune.[161] This wheel matches to the modern saying, 'what goes around, comes around.'

11:30 *By faith, the walls of Jericho fell, after being encircled for*[162] *seven days.*

Given the disappointment of the wilderness generation, the AH skips ahead to the next generation (Josh. 5:1–9). He

---

159. Calvin comments, 'It is certain that many in that multitude were unbelievers, but God granted it to the faith of the few that the whole multitude should cross the sea dry-shod' (*Hebrews and 1 & 2 Peter*, 180).

160. E.g., Jub. 48:14; Wis. 18:5.

161. Mekilta, Beshallah 7.

162. The preposition ἐπί with an accusative can indicate duration (see Zerwick, *Biblical Greek* §125).

focuses on the events connected to **Jericho**.¹⁶³ It is the first major city that the Israelites defeat upon crossing the Jordan River. Joshua 2 concerns Rahab's initial interaction with the two spies; and Joshua 6, the defeat of the city, along with the rescue of Rahab.

The AH very briefly summarizes the events, **the walls of Jericho fell, after being encircled for seven days**. Similar to the previous verse, it is the **faith** of the Israelites that is being highlighted. Although here, they are not the grammatical subject, but the obvious implied subject as they were the ones marching in a circle around the city.

How does the Israelite **faith** contribute to the destruction of the **walls**?¹⁶⁴ Clearly, it is God who miraculously destroys the **walls**, but God chooses to use the very unusual secondary means of marching around the city. The **faith** that is commended is that the Israelites listened to God's word in the form of Joshua's 'military' instructions (Josh. 6:2, 7).¹⁶⁵ Also, they would have to trust that God's power would accomplish his purposes. And these purposes in Canaan are related to God's divine promises related to the land (Josh. 23:10–11).

11:31 *By faith, Rahab the prostitute did not perish with the disobedient having received the spies with peace.*

Continuing the events related to Jericho, the AH mentions **Rahab**.¹⁶⁶ At the destruction of Jericho, she **did not perish**

---

163. Multiple civilizations have lived at the Jericho site (Tell es-Sultan). Significant evidence of several destructions has been found, although to date any of these to Joshua's time is beyond the specificity of the current evidence. For an up-to-date summary of various archaeological digs and conclusions at the Jericho site, see John D. Currid, *The Case for Biblical Archaeology: Uncovering the Historical Record of God's Old Testament People* (Phillipsburg: P&R, 2020), 122–24.

164. Given that Rahab's house was part of the wall, the location of the scarlet cord, and the eventual rescue of Rahab from her house (Josh. 2:15, 18; 6:22), it is a reasonable assumption that not every single part of the wall fell. So also Owen, *Hebrews*, 23:175.

165. So also Lane, *Hebrews 9–13*, 378; and Johnson, *Hebrews*, 304.

166. Although spelled the same in English Bibles, **Rahab** (רחב) the woman

(Josh. 6:22–25) **with the disobedient** residents (Josh. 6:20–21). Why not? The AH summarizes her **faith**-based actions as **having received**[167] the two **spies with peace**, which refers to her hiding and stealthily sending away the **spies** (Josh. 2:8–21, cf. Heb. 13:2).[168]

But what of her **faith** per se? Before meeting with the **spies**, **Rahab** somehow hears about God's drying up of the Red Sea and the military victories and thus believes in him. She rehearses this with the **spies** and concludes with, 'the LORD, your God, he is God in the heavens above and the earth below' (Josh. 2:11; cf. Ruth 1:16–17). **Rahab** believes God will destroy Jericho, but she also believes that her **faith** in him will save her (Josh. 2:12–13). Somewhat similar to Moses, she throws her lot in with God's people. In the end, Joshua and the **spies** did rescue her and her family—'and she dwelled in the midst of Israel until this day' (Josh. 6:25).

The same term **disobedient** (ἀπειθέω) is also used in Hebrews 3:18 to refer to many in the wilderness generation. Thus, as with the Egyptians (Heb. 11:29) and the wilderness generation, the fate of the people of Jericho is another implicit warning to the congregation that there will be a future judgment (cf. Heb. 9:27), and potentially for some, it will be disastrous.

These comments about **Rahab** mark an end to the AH's 'by faith' format.[169] But what an ending it is. There is quite the rhetorical punch by ending upon, of all possibilities, **Rahab the prostitute**.[170] First of all, she is not ethnically Jewish

---

and 'Rahab' (רהב) the one who rages, representing Egypt and a sea creature (e.g., Isa. 30:7; 51:9, respectively), are two different Hebrew spellings.

167. **Having received** is a causal participle. Many English translations make this explicit by including 'because' (e.g., RSV, NIV, ESV, CEB).

168. 'For her faith and hospitality Rahab the harlot was saved' (1 Clem. 12:1 [Lake, LCL]).

169. Cockerill especially emphasizes Rahab as 'a most appropriate conclusion ... to the discourse in vv. 1–31' (*Hebrews*, 584).

170. 'Many of the heroes, like Noah, Abraham, and Moses are natural choices; they are the pride of the tradition. On the other hand, some of the

(i.e., in the line of Abraham). Second, she has the epithet, **prostitute**.[171] Given she had faith before the **spies** visited her home, possibly it is assumed that she just recently ceased practicing her profession (cf. Heb. 12:16; 13:4), although many in Jericho may not have known this.[172] For sure, the Joshua text and AH understand that when she joined Israel after the destruction, she was no longer a **prostitute** (Josh. 6:25). Thus, the epithet identifies her by denoting her *former* profession, paralleling 'Matthew the tax collector' (Matt. 10:3) and 'Simon the zealot' (Mark 3:18).[173] Despite this qualification, it is still quite a shock to hold up a former **prostitute** as a heroine of the faith. But this simply matches the Bible's inclusion of her, and the general portrayal of the amazing grace of God. **Rahab** plays an important part in Joshua 2 and 6. She is used as an example in James 2:25. She, being a Gentile and a **prostitute**, marries Salmon and is in the blood line of Jesus Christ (!) (Matt. 1:5; cf. Ruth 4:29; Heb. 7:14; Josh. 11:1).

But what about the lie of **Rahab** to protect the **spies**? Is God commending this? See Reflections section below.

Reflections

In Christian ethics, there is debate as to whether lying is morally acceptable in extreme circumstances. The short-hand way to refer to this is 'Nazis at the door.'[174] Rahab is faced with a similar dilemma (Josh. 2:1–7). She had hidden the two spies in her house. The agents of the king of Jericho, unaware that

---

author's selections are surprising, most notably Rahab' (Eisenbaum, *The Jewish Heroes of Christian History*, 82).

171. Aspects of Jewish tradition downplayed the **prostitute** epithet by referring to her as an innkeeper, e.g., Targum Josh. 2:1 (פונדקית); and Josephus, *Jewish Antiquities* 5.8, 30. Elsewhere, however, she is clearly identified as a prostitute; e.g., Mekilta, Amalek 3; and b. Megillah 14b.

172. Aquinas comments about the **spies** coming to her home, 'She was a harlot to whom they went not to sin but to hide' (*Hebrews*, 256).

173. So also Gouge, *Hebrews*, 855; and Hughes, *Hebrews*, 503.

174. E.g., Christopher O. Tollefsen, *Lying and Christian Ethics*, New Studies in Christian Ethics (Cambridge: CUP, 2014), 175.

she has hidden them, request that Rahab hand over the spies. She lies. 'Oh, Mr. police officer, those two guys were spies! I did not know that. Yes, they were here, but they have already left my home, and in fact, I think they just left the city. You should be able to catch them if you hurry.' Maybe the ethical debate should be termed, 'Jericho police at the door' (Josh. 2:3).

To the debate per se, the absolutist position is that in no situation should a Christian lie (intentional deceive with words, writing, or gestures).[175] That is, if asked, a Christian should *not* tell the Nazis at the door that there are no Jews hiding in the house.[176] To be sure, the absolutist position understands lies to help others as significantly less heinous than traditional lies, but nevertheless one is still morally culpable for these. This position is strongly against lying because of its connection to the character of God as one who tells the truth. Those favoring the absolutist position in the Christian tradition is impressive, with the fountainhead being Augustine.[177]

The allowable-in-extreme-circumstances position understands God's law as having levels of priorities to be applied in extreme circumstances. Protecting the life of the Jew supersedes not deceiving the Nazi, that is, the sixth commandment outranks the ninth commandment. This deception would not be a sin.

---

175. The classic definition by Augustine is 'a man lies who has one thing in his mind and utters another in words, or by signs of whatever kind' (*On Lying* 3 [*NPNF*[1], 3:458]).

176. The absolutist would prefer that one simply not respond to the Nazis (so, e.g., James Henley Thornwell, 'Sincerity,' in *The Collected Writings of James Henley Thornwell*, 4 vols. [Carlisle: Banner of Truth, 1974], 2:519–42, esp. 541). Tollefsen, an absolutist, recommends not answering as to whether Jews are in the house, but in addition, he suggests telling the Nazi that 'he is engaged in a wicked activity and to encourage his repentance' (*Lying and Christian Ethics*, 177).

177. So, e.g., Augustine, *On Lying* 42 (*NPNF*[1], 3:476–77); *To Consentius: Against Lying* 41 (*NPNF*[1], 3:500); Aquinas, *Summa Theologiae* 2a2ae.100; Turretin, *Institutes of Elenctic Theology*, 2:129–34; and Murray, *Principles of Conduct: Aspects of Biblical Ethics*, 135–43. In their sermons on Heb. 11:31, both Robert Bruce (*Preaching Without Fear or Favour*, 481) and Perkins (*Hebrews 11*, 341) felt the need to comment that Rahab sinned when she lied.

Hodge uses the example of a murderer attempting to kill a child. The mother has the 'perfect right to mislead him by any means in her power because the general obligation to speak the truth is merged or lost, for the time being, in the higher obligation.'[178] Obviously, this principle can be easily abused. The burden of proof is on one who claims a circumstance requires deception. This position is based on the good and necessary consequences from biblical examples where it appears deception is appropriate (e.g., Exod. 1:15–21; Josh. 8:3–8; 1 Sam. 16:1–5).

Both views appeal to the Bible, although I side with the allowable-in-extreme-circumstances position.[179] What does Hebrews 11:31 add to the discussion? The text explicitly commends Rahab for 'having received the spies with peace.' Does this commendation include her deception? Obviously, not everything a biblical character does is to be imitated — as the 'judges' listed in Hebrews 11:32 makes clear! So it is certainly possible that in principle the deception is not part of the commendation; however, here I believe that the deception is included with the commendation. Rahab knew the two men were spying, which involves at least their deceptive actions.[180] These spies were sent by Joshua (Josh. 2:1), who was himself one of the twelve spies that God told Moses to send (Num. 13:1, 16). Hence, spying in this case is appropriate. In Hebrews 11:31, to distinguish between deceptive actions of God-approved spies and deceptive words by Rahab to protect

---

178. Charles Hodge, *Systematic Theology* 3:442. For an excellent discussion defending the allowable-in-extreme-circumstances position, see Frame, *The Doctrine of the Christian Life*, 224–28; 834–39.

179. Although maybe at some level a contradiction by me, but I do think one should tell the truth no matter the circumstance, including the threat of death, when asked to personally deny Christ. That is, although being threatened with death is an extreme circumstance, it is *not* allowable to deny Christ. Cf. Dan. 3:14–18; Matt. 10:33; Heb. 11:35. Within the levels-of-priorities understanding, the first and second commandments outrank the sixth.

180. Intriguingly, soon after Rahab's deception, she and the spies make an oath based on the assumption that neither is being deceptive (Josh. 2:12–14; 6:22).

the spies seems more than the text can bear.[181] Of course, to settle the question between the absolutist and the allowable-in-extreme-circumstances positions requires the whole Bible to be taken into account.

Faith: Rapid Summary (11:32–40)

In Hebrews 11 so far, the AH has used the rhetorical feature of 'by faith.' Now in 11:32–38 he uses a different rhetorical feature—a rapid summary of OT names and actions/consequences, which is introduced by a rhetorical question. Also, within the list of actions/consequences there is a rhetorically effective split between the positive faith-based actions (Heb. 11:33–35a) and the negative consequences (in this world) that came upon some of those who had faith (Heb. 11:35b–38). In addition, another rhetorical feature is that none of the actions is explicitly tied to any person. This encourages any reader to connect some of them from his OT knowledge, although the rapid nature of the listing allows only a few names at most to come to mind upon first reading. A final rhetorical feature is the parenthetical statement within the listing of the negative-consequences section that 'of whom the world was not worthy' (Heb. 11:38). It breaks the flow, but given the horrible things the 'world' did to God's people of faith, it is a satisfying comment.

The flow of this section is as follows: A rhetorical question

---

181. Calvin disagrees with me as he has an absolutist position, but he also has a nuanced view as to Rahab's deception. In his work on Joshua he comments, 'Although our purpose be to assist our brethren, to consult for their safety and relieve them, it never can be lawful to lie, because that cannot be right which is contrary to the nature of God. And God is truth. And still the act of Rahab is not devoid of the praise of virtue, although it was not spotlessly pure. For it often happens that while the saints study to hold the right path, they deviate into circuitous courses' (*Commentaries on the Book of Joshua*, trans. Henry Beveridge, Calvin's Commentaries 4 [Grand Rapids: Baker, 1996], 4:1:47). Augustine comments, 'God did good to the Hebrew midwives, and to Rahab the harlot of Jericho, this was not because they lied, but because they were merciful to God's people' (*To Consentius: Against Lying* 32 [*NPNF*[1], 3:495]).

and its implied answer (Heb. 11:32a); seven named men and the generic 'the prophets' (Heb. 11:32b); the positive faith-based actions of those just named (Heb. 11:33–35a); non-named others and the negative consequences resulting from their faith (Heb. 11:35b–38); and the conclusion of the whole chapter (11:39–40), with 11:39 recalling 11:1–2 and 11:40 explicitly connecting to the readers.

11:32 *And what more shall I say? For the time will fail me*[182] *[if]*[183] *recounting*[184] *concerning Gideon, Barak, Samson, Jephthah, David and Samuel, and the prophets,*

As noted above, the AH takes a surprising rhetorical turn. He ceases using the 'by faith' format. Instead, he asks rhetorically, **And what more shall I say?** There is an implied two-fold answer. (1) Enough has been said to prove the point about faith as defined in Hebrews 11:1–2 by using Abel through Rahab, ending with a significant event of the conquest of Canaan. (2) There are so many examples from the conquest forward that there is not enough **time** to mention a representative sample of them along with a specific **recounting** like previously done in Hebrews 11:4–31; hence, even though it is not needed, a rapid summary of OT names and actions/consequences is nevertheless provided.

For the names, the AH begins with four judges. It appears that he is continuing with the next phase in Israelite history

---

182. Similar expressions to **for the time will fail me** are used in other written documents that are clearly not originally intended to be oral presentations, e.g., Philo, *On the Sacrifices of Cain and Abel* 27; *On the embassy to Gaius* 323; and Josephus, *Jewish Antiquities* 257; for more ancient examples, see Spicq, *Hébreux*, 2:362. This fact gives significant caution for using this expression to argue for Hebrews' being originally an oral sermon.

183. I take the participle **recounting** as a conditional participle. So also Zerwick and Grosvenor, *A Grammatical Analysis of the Greek New Testament*, 683; and Turner, *Syntax*, 157. Most translations functionally assume this by translating the participle as an infinitive (e.g., ESV, 'to tell'); others use a finite verb and add 'if' (e.g., NASB, 'if I tell').

184. The participle **recounting** is masculine singular, and the grammatical antecedent is **me**. Hence, as to authorship, the writer is a male.

after the initial conquest by Joshua. Curiously, the names are not given in historical/canonical order. The AH uses the order of **Gideon, Barak, Samson**, and **Jephthah**.[185] The historical order is Barak (Judg. 4:1–5:31), Gideon (Judg. 6:11–8:32), Jephthah (Judg. 10:6–12:7), and Samson (Judg. 13:1–16:31). This apparently random order adds to the sense of a rapid summary.[186] These four judges are presented with significant flaws in Judges. Yes, all believers sin, but some of these flaws are significant. Thus, many ask, Why these judges? All of these were warriors who fought against significant odds and won. Their enemies, for the most part, were those opposing the divine promises of Israel taking Canaan. These warriors had faith in God. For more discussion on Jephthah specifically, see Reflections section below.

David and Samuel are also reversed as to their historical order. Most likely this is done so that **and the prophets** may be added following **Samuel**. Although **Samuel** was both a judge (1 Sam. 7:15) and a prophet (1 Sam. 3:20), here the prophetic office is stressed.

11:33–35a *who through faith conquered kingdoms, administered justice,*[187] *obtained promises, blocked mouths of lions, quenched power of fire, escaped edges*[188] *of sword, were empowered from weakness, became strong in war, routed foreign armies. Women received their dead [ones] by resurrection;*

The relative pronoun **who** refers back to the those mentioned in the previous verse and is the grammatical

---

185. In 1 Sam. 12:11, the order of Jerubbaal (Gideon), Bedan (Barak?), Jephthah, and Samuel. In the *Apostolic Constitutions*, the order is Gideon, Samson, Jephthah, Barak, Samuel, and David (§7.37 [*ANF*, 7:474–75]).

186. So also Hughes, *Hebrews*, 506; Lane, *Hebrews 9–13*, 383; and Cockerill, *Hebrews*, 588.

187. Mechanically, **administered justice** could be translated 'worked righteousness' (εἰγάσαντο δικαιοσύνην). The context of mostly leaders justifies the translation of **administered justice** in a governmental context (cf. Ps. 15:2 [LXX Ps. 14:2]).

188. Plural **edges** implies a two-edged **sword**, cf. Heb. 4:12.

subject of the following nine third-person-plural verbs.[189] That is, one or more of those named plus the many possible 'prophets' are potential subjects for each verb, especially given that 'prophets' may be used loosely. As noted above, upon first reading (or hearing) at a normal pace, one's mind cannot possibly think of all those that are potential references to each verb. Of course, Scripture is also meant to be read over-and-over and studied; hence, taking time to consider as many references as possible is appropriate.

Some see an orderly pattern of three sets of three each for the nine verbs. For example, Johnson sees the first three as 'positive accomplishments,' the second as 'astonishing escapes,' and the third as 'power to overcome.'[190] I disagree. For me, the nine are relatively random similar to the names.

Three of the nine clearly refer to military victories, **conquered kingdoms**, **became strong in war**, and **routed foreign armies**. This would apply at least to the four judges and David. **Escaped the edges of sword** could also refer to military battles in the sense of not being killed during a battle, but it may refer to Elijah (1 Kgs. 19:2–18), Elisha (2 Kgs. 6:31–7:2), and Jeremiah (Jer. 36:26) as these prophets escaped being killed by indignant rulers. **Administered justice** is a quasi-governmental function that would apply to the four judges, David, and Samuel (acting as a judge).

Blocked mouths of lions and **quenched power of fire**, which are listed together, apply in the first place to Daniel (Dan. 6:22) and his three friends (Dan. 3:23–27), respectively (cf. 1 Macc. 2:59–60). In addition, **blocked mouths of lions**

---

189. So also Owen (*Hebrews*, 23:187) and Brown (*Hebrews*, 583). The only possible exception to this would be Daniel's three friends in the fiery furnace; however, they are included either because they are closely connected to the prophet Daniel or they themselves are considered prophets loosely defined. *Contra* Ellingworth who takes **who** (οἵ) as an indefinite pronoun. Thus he interprets οἵ as 'such people' because 'there is no close correlation between the individual names in v. 32 and the achievements listed in the following verses' (*Hebrews*, 624).

190. Johnson, *Hebrews*, 306. Attridge sees the first three as 'military and political accomplishments,' the second as 'acts of deliverance,' and the third as 'military valor' (*Hebrews*, 348).

would also apply to Samson (Judg. 14:5–6) and David (1 Sam. 17:34–36).[191]

Concerning the phrase, **were empowered** by God **from weakness, weakness** (ἀσθέναια) is used elsewhere in Hebrews in significant texts concerning physical limitations (Heb. 4:15; 5:2; 7:28). Possibly this phrase includes Samson's regaining his strength (Judg. 16:23–31); David's defeating his superior opponent, Goliath (1 Sam. 17:41–49); and Hannah's overcoming barrenness with Samuel (1 Sam. 1:12–20; 2:4).[192]

Obtained the results of the **promises** refers to various *temporal* plural promises as opposed to the ultimate promise of being with God. This is confirmed by the later use of the singular 'promise' noting that the OT saints 'did not receive the promise' (Heb. 11:39). Examples of temporal promises received include Gideon's victories (Judg. 6:15–18), David's offspring (2 Sam. 7:12), and Israel's conquests (Neh. 9:22–25).

Women received their dead ones by resurrection is a slight change in format. The previous nine verbs had **who** as their subject. Here, **women** is the grammatical subject, which explains the slight change in format. Yet, despite **women** being the subject, the probable reason for including this comment is the role played by two prophets, Elijah and Elisha. Elijah was involved in the raising of the son of the widow of Zarephath (1 Kgs. 17:8–24), and Elisha was involved in the raising of the son of the Shunammite woman (2 Kgs. 4:8–37). The **women** had faith that God would work through the prophets. Clearly, here **resurrection** only means a temporal returning to life and these two sons will eventually die, which is different than its use in Hebrews 11:35b.[193]

---

191. Cf. 2 Sam. 23:20; 2 Tim. 4:17.

192. Cf. Isa. 38:1–5. Although he convinced only a few, Chrysostom interpreted this phrase as the Jews in their exilic weakness being returned to Israel ('Homily 27 on Hebrews,' [*NPNF*[1], 14:488]). Clement applies this to women, including Judith and Esther (1 Clem. 55:3–6). Hughes notes that this phrase could relate to all mentioned in Heb. 11:32–38 (*Hebrews* 510). Aquinas (*Hebrews*, 261), Calvin (*Hebrews and 1 & 2 Peter*, 182), and Owen (*Hebrews*, 23:192–93) cite Hezekiah (Isa. 38:1–5) as the intended reference.

193. So all commentators, e.g., Chrysostom, 'Homily 27 on Hebrews,' (*NPNF*[1], 14:488).

11:35b *but others were tortured,*[194] *not*[195] *accepting the release in order that they would obtain a better resurrection;*

Hebrews 11:35a and 11:35b are connected grammatically by **but others**. So why then separate them as I have done? It is because the content significantly changes. In addition to exclusively going to unnamed saints, the AH switches from positive actions by the OT saints to very negative this-world consequences that may occur to those who put their faith in God. This negative chord continues down through Hebrews 11:38. If one were reading this text out loud, the reader would emphasize **but others** and insert a long pause following it before continuing with **were tortured ...**

Although the verb **tortured** per se does not indicate tortured to death, the context of this verse and the next does. The victims were **tortured**/killed because of their faith (cf. Matt. 5:11–12).[196] In the biblical record, it is often stated that 'prophets' were killed, implying (1) they were killed for their faithful words and (2) at least some of them were killed by torture (e.g., 1 Kgs. 18:13; Neh. 9:26; Matt. 23:34; Luke 11:47; Acts 7:52; Rom. 11:3). Although I am not convinced that the AH was referring to the Maccabees, there are gruesome stories of torture in 2 Maccabees 6–7 and 4 Maccabees 6–7 (cf. Wis. 3:1–4).[197]

---

194. The verb translated **were tortured** (τυμπανίζω) is also used in the sense 'to beat' a drum. Τύμπανον, the cognate noun, refers to a normal 'drum' or a torture instrument (e.g., 2 Macc. 6:19, 28, see LSJ, 1834). Although not clear, some by combining the verb and the cognate noun surmise that the verb τυμπανίζω refers to stretching one's body over a rack matching to stretching skin over a drum, and then beating the body to death with blunt instruments matching to beating a drum with drumsticks. E.g., Tyndale and the Geneva Bible translate τυμπανίζω as 'racked.' Chrysostom understood τυμπανίζω here to refer to beheading ('Homily 27 on Hebrews,' [*NPNF*[1], 14:488]).

195. Since **accepting** is a participle, one would expect the negative μή instead of the negative οὐ. This change of expectations normally means an emphasis on the **not**, which perfectly matches the context. So also BDAG, 733.

196. In a pseudepigraphal account, using the same verb, Amos is said to have been **tortured** (τυμπανίζω) by Amaziah and eventually is clubbed to death (Liv. Pro. 7:1).

197. Many others are convinced, so, e.g., Owen, *Hebrews*, 23:200; Hughes, *Hebrews*, 512; Attridge, *Hebrews*, 349–50; and Johnson, *Hebrews*, 308.

In some situations, victims were given a chance to disavow their faith in God; however, they refused, or as the AH says it, **not accepting the release**. Why did they refuse? — **in order that they would obtain a better resurrection**. 'Resurrection' in Hebrews 11:35a refers to the temporal benefits of being raised from the dead. Here, **resurrection** is contrasted with a similar temporal 'resurrection' of being released from torture to live by denying God. But these victims did not want that if it meant giving up the **better resurrection**, which is the final bodily **resurrection** at the last day (cf. Heb. 6:2; 13:20).[198] The God-given faith of these **others** enabled them to suffer well as they looked forward (cf. Matt. 10:28; 2 Cor. 4:17–18; Phil. 1:21).

11:36 *but others*[199] *received an experience of mockeries and scourges, and moreover*[200] *chains and imprisonment.*

As opposed to those who were tortured and killed in Hebrews 11:35b, apparently here **others** were abused but *not* killed.[201] They **received an experience of mockeries and scourges** (floggings). After this, they (some?) were put in **chains and imprisonment** for a time. Jeremiah would be the prime exhibit of an OT saint being mocked, beaten, and put in prison (Jer. 20:7–10; 37:15; 38:6).[202]

As opposed to the list of positive actions in Hebrews 11:33–35a, this verse relates more directly to the congregants. As Hebrews 10:32–34 and 13:3 clearly indicate, some of them were mocked, suffered, and put in prison, although they had not yet been killed

---

198. So also Perkins, *Hebrews 11*, 376; Owen, *Hebrews*, 14:200; Bruce, *Hebrews*, 327; and Allen, *Hebrews*, 565; *contra* Koester who sees this as raised to eternal life, not specifically eschatological resurrection (*Hebrews*, 514).

199. I have translated both ἄλλοι (Heb. 11:35b) and ἕτεροι (Heb. 11:36) as **others**. In classical Greek, 'ἄλλος strictly means *other* (of several), ἕτερος *other* (of two)' (Smyth, *Greek Grammar* §1271). In the NT, this distinction does not hold in general and certainly not here (so also Robertson, *A Grammar of the Greek New Testament*, 748–49).

200. The Greek behind **moreover** is ἔτι used in the sense of 'that which is added to what is already at hand' (BDAG, 400 [2b]).

201. So also Owen, *Hebrews*, 23:201; and Bruce, *Hebrews*, 327.

202. Also imprisoned were the prophets Micaiah (1 Kgs. 22:24–28) and Hanani (2 Chr. 16:7–10).

(Heb. 12:4). Of course, this verse would also remind them and us that Christ suffered these things also. The cognate verbs for the nouns **mockeries** and **scourges** are used often in the Gospels.[203] They are used together in reference to Christ in Matthew 20:19 (and the synoptic parallels, Mark 10:34; Luke 18:32–33; cf. Heb. 12:2–3).

11:37–38 *They were stoned, they were sawn apart, they died by murder of the sword, they went around in sheepskins, in skins of goats, being destitute, being afflicted, being mistreated—of whom the world was not worthy—wandering upon deserts and in mountains and in caves and in holes in the ground.*

Hebrews 11:37–38 is a summary of negative consequences that have happened to various unnamed OT saints. It probably includes those in 11:35b–36. As 11:35b–36 began with death and then suffering short of death, so also 11:37–38 begins with death and then sufferings short of death. This summary in 11:37–38 is rhetorically powerful with its short staccato-like opening three finite verbs followed by a longer finite clause. This longer finite clause includes three short staccato-like participles followed by a longer participial phrase. In addition to all of this is the powerful parenthesis.

The first three statements all relate to death, **they were stoned, they were sawn apart, they died by murder of the sword**. Naboth (1 Kgs. 21:13) and Zechariah the son of Jehoiada (2 Chr. 24:20–21) **were stoned** (cf. Matt. 23:37; Luke 11:51; Acts 7:59). Jewish pseudepigraphical tradition and patristic sources report that Jeremiah was **stoned** in Egypt.[204] Concerning **they were sawn apart**, this cruel death possibly had been inflicted on many as various kings killed various prophets, although no specific mention is given in Scripture of this type of death.[205] There are, however, several Jewish sources (pseudepigraphic and rabbinic) and patristic sources that report

---

203. 'To mock' (ἐμπαίζω), 'mockery' (ἐμπαιγμός), 'to scourge'/'to flog' (μαστιγόω), 'scourge'/'flogging' (μάστιξ).

204. E.g., Liv. Pro. 2:1; Tertullian, *Scorpiace* 8 [*ANF*, 3:640]; 4 Bar. 9:27–32.

205. The LXX of Amos 1:3 records one of the transgressions of Damascus to be sawing apart pregnant women.

that Isaiah was **sawn apart**.[206] One gruesome account has Isaiah being mocked by Manasseh's men as they are sawing him. They want Isaiah to recant by him saying, 'I lied in everything I have spoken; the ways of Manasseh are good and right.' But Isaiah refused. 'While Isaiah was being sawed in half, he did not cry out, or weep, but his mouth spoke with the Holy Spirit until he was sawed in two' (Mart. Ascen. Isa. 5:1–6 [*OTP*, 2:163–64]).

Following the opening three finite clauses, the remainder of the sentence is controlled by the finite verb **they went around**. The nameless OT saints **went around in sheepskins, in skins of goats, being destitute, being afflicted, being mistreated—of whom the world was not worthy—wandering upon deserts and in mountains and in caves and in holes in the ground**. OT and Jewish pseudepigraphic/apocryphal connections abound.[207]

The parenthesis **of whom the world was not worthy** following the three staccato-like participles **being destitute, being afflicted, being mistreated** is rhetorically powerful and emotionally satisfying. The piling up of the list of evils that the **world** (non-believers, whether in the OT covenant community or outside of it) did to the OT saints, and considering that some of these evils have been perpetrated upon the congregation's own covenant community, brings very negative emotions. This parenthesis then is somewhat of an emotional safety valve—yes, it is truly said, **the world was not worthy** of even having these OT saints in their midst. Brown says this parenthesis 'is peculiarly beautiful.'[208]

11:39–40 *And all these, [although][209] having been commended*

---

206. E.g., Mart. Ascen. Isa. 1:9; 5:1–16; Liv. Pro. 1:1; b. Yevamot 49b; Justin Martyr, *Dialogue with Trypho* 120 [*ANF*, 1:259]; Tertullian, *Scorpiace* 8 [*ANF*, 3:640]; Origen, *To Africanus* 9 [*ANF*, 4:388]; cf. b. Sanhedrin 103b.

207. E.g., Judg. 6:2; 1 Sam. 22:1; 1 Kgs. 18:4; 19:4; Neh. 9:26–27, 30; Ps. 107:4; Amos 7:10–12; 1 Macc. 2:28, 31; 2 Macc. 5:27; 6:11; 10:6; Pss. Sol. 17:17; Mart. Ascen. Isa. 5:10–11; cf. Matt. 8:20; 1 Clem. 17:1.

208. Brown, *Hebrews*, 591.

209. The participle **having been commended** is clearly being used concessively; hence, I added **although** to the translation. So also Zerwick and Grosvenor, *A Grammatical Analysis of the Greek New Testament*, 683.

through [their]²¹⁰ faith, did not receive the promise [since]²¹¹ God has provided something better concerning us in order that they would not be made perfect without us.

With Hebrews 11:39–40, the AH concludes chapter 11. He notes that **all these**, that is, the above OT saints, were positively **commended** by God **through their faith** (cf. Heb. 11:2). Despite this positive point, however, they **did *not* receive the promise**. Note that **promise** here is singular as opposed to the plural in Hebrews 11:17 and 11:33 that refer to temporal (this world) promises. On the other hand, in Hebrews 11:13 'promises' is plural and refers to ultimate promises. Hence, here **the promise** is most likely a collective term indicating all of the grand ultimate promises associated with Christ and his eternal benefits, but, as I will argue below, the emphasis seems to be on the aspect of **the promise** related to the bodily resurrection of believers on the last day.

Hebrews 11:40 gives the rationale as to why the OT saints did not receive **the promise—since God has provided something better concerning us in order that they would not be made perfect without us**. Scholars disagree as to whether this verse refers to the benefits specifically with Christ's first coming,²¹² his second coming,²¹³ or is non-specific.²¹⁴ I see this as related to Christ's second coming and the associated

---

Most major English translations in one way or another include a concessive nuance, cf. RSV, NIV, ESV, and CEB.

210. I interpret the definite article before **faith** as indicating the particular faith of each of the OT saints; hence, I translate as **their**, as also do many other major English translations, e.g., RSV, NASB, NIV, NJB, ESV, and CEB. Note, there is no definite article before 'faith' in Heb. 11:33.

211. **God has provided** is a genitive-absolute participial construction. It is also clearly causal; hence, I added **since**. Other major English translations agree and typically add 'since' also, e.g., NIV, ESV, and NRSV.

212. So, e.g., Owen, *Hebrews*, 23:214; Turretin, *Institutes of Elenctic Theology*, 2:261; Kistemaker, *Hebrews*, 358; Johnson, *Hebrews*, 309; and Cockerill, *Hebrews*, 598.

213. So, e.g., Robert Bruce, *Preaching Without Fear or Favour*, 557; Brown, *Hebrews*, 597–98; R. C. H. Lenski, *The Interpretation of the Epistle to the Hebrews and the Epistle to James* (Minneapolis: Augsburg, 1966), 420–21; Koester, *Hebrews*, 520–21; and DeSilva, *Hebrews*, 424.

214. So, e.g., Lane, *Hebrews 9–13*, 392–94; and Ellingworth, *Hebrews*, 636.

benefit of bodily resurrection as believers move into the NHNE. Since the souls of OT saints are in heaven with Christ as the AH writes, I consider the **something better concerning us** that is also something that the OT saints would not obtain **without us** must be referring to the future resurrection and the promised NHNE. This view dovetails well with (1) the overall point of chapter 11 that land foreshadows the NHNE, (2) that 'resurrection' in Hebrews 11:35b refers to bodily resurrection; and (3) my view of 'rest' and 'Sabbath rest' in Hebrews 3:7–4:11 that it is solely future and eschatological.[215]

Reflections

For some, including Jephthah in the heroes of faith is somewhat disturbing (Heb. 11:32; Judg. 10:6–12:7). Did he not make a rash vow and kill his daughter (Judg. 11:29–40)?[216] As noted above, the primary reason for including him, and others from Judges, is that he was a warrior who fought God's opponents in the face of significant odds. His faith in God aided him. But should not the heinousness of this rash vow disqualify him?

From my perspective, yes, Jephthah did make a rash vow. But it is not clear that his honoring of that vow was to kill his daughter; in fact, I believe it was instead to dedicate her to the Lord, that is, to commit her to perpetual virginity. This virginity view, although not held by the majority, has a venerable tradition.[217]

The vow itself is given in Judges 11:30–31. The Hebrew grammar is masculine singular as to who/what comes from the house (יֵצֵא, הַיּוֹצֵא) and to who/what is offered up (וְהַעֲלִיתִהוּ). In Hebrew, masculine singular could be a male person;

---

215. The verb **to be made perfect** does not decide this disagreement as it and its cognate noun 'perfection' refers in Hebrews to multiple benefits of being connected to Christ. See discussion at Heb. 7:11.

216. LAB 40 has an extended discussion. Jephthah's daughter's name is Seila. She forgives her father and gives a long lament before being killed.

217. So, e.g., Aquinas, *Hebrews*, 258; Perkins, *Hebrews 11*, 349; and Gouge, *Hebrews*, 872–73. For listing of exegetes pro and con, see the excellent article by Henry M. Knapp, 'Jephthah's Daughter in English Post-Reformation Exegesis,' *WTJ* 80 (2018): 279–97; esp. 286–89.

a generic person, whether male or female; or a non-person, for example, a lamb. Possibly, Jephthah expected to sacrifice an animal. He certainly did not expect his daughter to be the first out of the house to greet him. In Judges 11:37 the daughter weeps for her virginity as opposed to weeping for her death. This implies that the offering-up of the daughter was to dedicate her to perpetual virginity.[218] Even doing this is not proper, but it is less heinous than killing her. Jephthah made a rash vow and furthered his sin by honoring it.[219] Admittedly, the Judges passage is not clear, but when adding in the commendation of Jephthah in Hebrews, the perpetual virginity view is the best understanding.

---

218. See Gouge's twelve arguments favoring the virginity view (*Hebrews*, 872–3).

219. WCF 22.4 and 22.7 indicate that rash oaths and vows that require sinful actions to fulfill them should not be fulfilled.

11.
Endurance
(12:1–29)

Although not much rides on the differences, commentators disagree moderately on the outline of Hebrews 12. As mentioned in the introduction to Hebrews 11, some connect Hebrews 12:1–3 to chapter 11 and thus see 12:4–29 as a unit.[1] Another area of difference is 12:12–13, should it be connected to the subunits of 12:4–11 or 12:14–17?[2]

I see Hebrews 12:1–29 tied together in one way or another by the theme of endurance. For convenience, I have separated chapter 12 into five sections: 1–3; 4–11; 12–17; 18–24; and 25–29.

Endurance: Jesus and a Cloud of Witnesses (12:1–3)

As discussed in the introduction section to Hebrews 11, Hebrews 12:1–3 is very closely tied to Hebrews 11 in that they both include exhortations to endure. The exhortations in Hebrews 11 are *implicit* using the examples of OT saints. The exhortations in Hebrews 12:1–3 are *explicitly* referring back to the OT saints as a group but also adding Jesus to the discussion. My rationale for separating Hebrews 12:1–3 from chapter 11 is simply the difference in genre.

---

1. So, e.g., Cockerill, *Hebrews*, 514–15, 613–14.

2. E.g., connected to 12:4–11 is Schreiner (*Hebrews*, 381–82); connected to 12:12–17 is Bruce (*Hebrews*, 347).

As to the flow of Hebrews 12:1–3, verses 1–2 are one sentence exhorting the congregants to 'lay aside the weight' and 'run the race' including the 'cloud of witnesses' and 'Jesus' as motivations.[3] Verse 3 is somewhat of a restatement of verses 1–2. The congregants are exhorted to 'not be weary nor faint,' but here only Jesus is mentioned as a motivation.

12:1 *Consequently, [since] we indeed[4] are surrounded by so great a cloud of witnesses, let us lay aside[5] every weight and the sin that easily encompasses, [and] let us run[6] with endurance the race that is set before us,*

By using **consequently**, **witnesses**, and **endurance** (cf. Heb. 10:32, 36), the AH is clearly referring back to chapter 11. But he also intermixes this with a Greek-games athletic metaphor (cf. Heb. 10:32).[7] The metaphor refers to a long race in an arena with spectators.

The **cloud of witnesses** is primarily the just mentioned OT saints plus all other believers who are in heaven (cf. Heb. 13:7), although not the NHNE. Why a **cloud**? This is often used in

---

3. A few see a chiastic structure in Heb. 12:1–2 with the center being 'gazing upon the leader and perfector of faith, Jesus.' See, e.g., David Allen Black, 'A Note on the Structure of Hebrews 12:1–2,' *Bib* 68 (1987): 543–1. A questionable angle for this chiastic structure is to equate the implied sitting of the witnesses as spectators with the sitting of Jesus on the throne.

4. Καὶ ἡμεῖς is emphatic; hence, my translation of **we** *indeed*. As to its emphatic character, so also Owen, *Hebrews*, 23:221; and Ellingworth, *Hebrews*, 637.

5. As most translations do, I take the participle ἀποθέμενοι as attendant circumstance with **let us run**. Hence, the participle is translated as a first-person imperative, **let us lay aside**. For a discussion of attendant circumstance participles including this one, see Wallace, *Greek Grammar Beyond the Basics*, 640–45, esp. 644.

6. **Let us run** is a hortatory subjunctive.

7. As a definite minority view, Zoe Hollinger argues against the athletic imagery and prefers the translation of 'let us undergo ... the struggle' for **let us run ... the race** ('Rethinking the Translation of τρέχωμεν τὸν .. . ἀγῶνα in Hebrews 12:1 in Light of Ancient Graeco-Roman Literature,' *BT* 70 [2019]: 94–111, esp. 94). For athletic imagery in Paul, see 1 Cor. 9:24–25; Phil. 3:12–14; 1 Tim. 6:12; and 2 Tim. 4:7–8. Also see 4 Macc. 14:5 and 17:11–16.

Greco-Roman literature as a 'compact, numberless throng.'[8] In the metaphor, the **witnesses** are the spectators, but given the context, these would be spectators who have previously completed the race acting both as vocal encouragers and as examples to the runners to complete the long race. In reality, believers know of their lives and are encouraged by their examples.[9] Why the word **witnesses**? The cognate ('commended') is used in Hebrews 11:2, 4, 5, and 39, and the departed saints are conceived of as witnessing by their lives on earth to the positive benefits of faith.

The **race that is set before us** is the Christian life from now and until death. The congregants are encouraged to complete the race. But how? They are to **lay aside every weight** and **run with endurance**. At the race metaphor level, the **weight** might be body fat and/or extra clothing, and **endurance** is required as opposed to a sprinter's speed. At the reality level, the **weight** is defined as **the sin that easily encompasses**.[10] I take **the sin** broadly as including the believer's sin and also the difficulties of living in a sin-cursed world.[11] Interestingly, the metaphor and reality levels merge in **easily encompasses**. Clothing is removed by runners as it slows them down by

---

8. BDAG, 670. Cf. Isa. 60:8 and Ezek. 38:9, 16.

9. Referencing this text and the **cloud of witnesses**, the Catechism of the Catholic Church recommends that 'we can and should ask them to intercede for us and for the whole world' (§2683). I disagree.

10. **Easily encompasses** (εὐπερίστατος) may be a word that the AH invented. It combines 'well'/'good' (εὖ) + 'around' (περί) + 'to stand' (ἵστημι).

11. Commentators have varying views on **the sin**. Calvin takes it not 'as actual sins, but the fount of sin itself, that is the lust which so possesses all of us that we feel that we are held by its snares on every side' (*Hebrews and 1 & 2 Peter*, 188). Brown connects to **weight** as primarily being the undue attachment to things that are not in and of themselves sinful (*Hebrews*, 607–8). Moffatt sees **the sin** as any sin that leads to apostasy (*Hebrews*, 194). Hughes takes it as 'precisely sin, of whatever kind, that impedes or slows down the Christian in the spiritual race, and conversely, anything, however innocent in itself, which impedes' (*Hebrews*, 520). Lane takes it as 'sin itself,' not specific sins (Lane, *Hebrews 9–13*, 409). WLC 78 references Heb. 12:1 as to the remaining internal sin of believers that 'hinders in all their spiritual services.'

easily entangling/encompassing their legs and arms; and similarly, sin in its many aspects easily entangles/encompasses a believer thereby increasing his difficulties while living the Christian life. **Endurance** at the reality level is a reminder that the Christian life is an extended affair and often has significant difficulties (cf. Rev. 2:2–3, 19; 3:10; 13:10; 14:12).

12:2 *gazing upon the leader and perfecter of faith, Jesus, who for*[12] *the joy that was set before him endured a cross, despising shame,*[13] *[and] has been seated at the right hand of the throne of God.*

In what manner or what is an aid to 'lay aside every weight' and 'run with endurance'? In addition to considering OT saints, one should be **gazing upon ... Jesus**.[14] The present tense of this participle strongly suggests that this should be continuously practiced throughout the Christian life.[15]

Is Jesus simply another, but better, example similar to the 'cloud of witnesses'? No, Jesus is more than an example as his redemptive actions are included here; but yes, he does have exemplary characteristics that surpass those in the 'cloud'.[16]

Two summaries of Jesus are presented: (1) **the leader and perfecter of faith**,[17] others translate as 'author and finisher of our faith' (KJV) and (2) **who for the joy that was**

---

12. As most do, I take ἀντί to mean **for** as opposed to 'in place of joy.' A similar usage of ἀντί exists in Heb. 12:16. BDAG (p. 88) is ambiguous on usage of ἀντί in Heb. 12:1 (p. 88), as is Mitchell (*Hebrews*, 266).

13. **Shame** is in the genitive (αἰσχύνης) as the verb 'to despise' takes the genitive for direct objects (BDAG, 529).

14. First Clement 7:4 uses a similar phrase, 'let us gaze upon the blood of Christ,' although he uses a different verb for 'gaze' (ἀτενίζω as opposed to AH's ἀφοράω).

15. So also Owen, *Hebrews*, 23:237; and Lane, *Hebrews 9–13*, 399.

16. Contra those who *only* see exemplary aspects of Jesus, e.g., Moffatt, *Hebrews*, 196; and Johnson, *Hebrews*, 317–18. For discussions of Jesus' being both our redeemer and example, see, e.g., Owen, *Hebrews*, 23:236–37; and Hughes, *Hebrews*, 522–23. Lenski sees no aspect of Jesus' being an example, only that Jesus gives believers faith (*Hebrews and James*, 426–27).

17. The grammar confirms that **leader and perfecter** are one unit because only one article governs both of them.

set before him endured a cross, despising shame, and has been seated at the right hand of the throne of God. The first summary is not completely clear. **Leader** (ἀρχηγός) is also used in Hebrews 2:10 (see extended discussion there, cf. also 'forerunner' in Heb. 6:20). There Jesus leads the sons to salvation and sanctifies them in a context where he shows trust. As to **perfecter** (τελειωτής), its cognate 'to perfect' (τελειόω) is also in Hebrews 2:10. In context of Hebrews 2:10, Jesus is perfected in the sense of being fit for service as a leader and the one who sanctifies. In Hebrews 2:10 specifically, Jesus is a **perfecter** of his people, that is, he is their redeemer. In Hebrews 12:2, the prepositional phrase translated **of faith** does have an article in the Greek. I take this use of the article as referring to faith broadly and abstractly, that is, in this context, primarily the faith of believers (see reflection section below for whether this also includes Jesus' faith).[18] Hence, **Jesus** is the **leader and perfector** of the faithful saints in that he is both their redeemer, including ultimately giving them faith and seeing it through to the end,[19] and their supreme example of **endur[ance]**.

Possibly, in addition to the reference back to Hebrews 2:10, the expression **the leader** (ἀρχηγός) **and perfecter** (τελειωτής) may have been used because of the cognate connection to Christ as 'the Alpha and Omega, the beginning (ἀρχή) and end (τέλος)' (Rev. 22:13, cf. Heb. 13:8), with ἀρχὴ and τέλος also

---

18. Τῆς πίστεως. I understand the articular usage as referring to an abstract noun—in English abstract nouns normally do not have the article. For a discussion of the abstract articular usage in Greek, see Wallace, *Greek Grammar Beyond the Basics*, 226–27.

19. Concerning this text including at least partially Christ's giving and completing faith in believers, so also Chrysostom, 'Homily 28 on Hebrews' (*NPNF*¹, 14:493); Augustine, *On the Predestination of the Saints*, 31 (*NPNF*¹, 5:513); Owen, *Hebrews*, 23:238; Hughes, *Hebrews*, 522; Koester, *Hebrews*, 523; and Schreiner, *Hebrews*, 378. Also see the Westminster Standards, which reference Heb. 12:2 for both 'Christ ... effectually persuading them by his Spirit to believe and obey' (WCF 14.3) and 'Christ, who is the author and finisher of our faith' (WCF 14:3).

used in relation to his eternality in Hebrews 7:3 (cf. 3:14). [20] If so, this would be highlighting Christ's divinity, which in turn adds support to his initiating and completing faith in believers (divine actions) and also adds rhetorical punch to his suffering on the **cross** for us.

Jesus is summarized as the one who went to the **cross** and now sits at the **right hand of the throne of God** (cf. Heb. 1:13 // Ps. 110:1; Heb. 8:1). This humiliation/exaltation pattern of Christ is common in Hebrews and the NT (see references at Heb. 1:3). In context, this pattern shows Christ's redemptive work, but it is also somewhat exemplary for believers who will have difficulties in this life (**endured**) and then be with God in a fuller sense.

Christians have long marveled at the clause **for the joy that was set before him endured a cross**. Of course, Christ's being on the **cross** per se was not a **joy**. Instead, it was doing the will of the Father (Heb. 10:9), his love for the brethren (Heb. 2:12), and their resulting redemption (Heb. 10:10; 13:12) that explains the **joy** as he 'offered himself' (Heb. 9:14). Given the physical pain/torture of a **cross**, the separation from the Father, being a curse (cf. Deut. 21:22–23; Gal. 3:13), 'hostility' (Heb. 12:3), and the **shame**; this **joy** is another wonder as to Christ's love for the church.[21]

12:3 *For consider the one who has endured such hostility against himself*[22] *from the sinners in order that you may not be weary nor faint*[23] *in your souls.*

Hebrews 12:3 is somewhat of a restatement of 12:1–2. The **for** is not giving a reason per se, but re-summarizing in a slightly different way. This is a self-evident conclusion.[24]

---

20. So also Attridge, *Hebrews*, 356 n. 49; and Cockerill, *Hebrews*, 607.

21. Leaders of the church are also to have **joy** as they lead (Heb. 13:17).

22. Some other Greek manuscripts have 'him,' and some have 'them.' See Metzger, *TCGNT*², 604–05.

23. I take the participle ἐκλυόμενοι as 'attendant circumstance' with the finite verb **weary**. Hence, I translate as the finite verb **faint**.

24. Brown translates **for** as 'moreover' (*Hebrews*, 615). BDAG calls this

The AH also reverts back to the athletic metaphor in 12:3b with **weary** and **faint**. Finally, the AH moves from 'we' in Hebrews 12:1-2 to 'you' in 12:3 and following.

The emphasis here is more on Christ (**the one**) as an example of **endur[ance]** as opposed to being the redeemer. **The sinners** in context are those (some Jewish and Roman leaders and possibly some in the crowd) who are responsible (from a human perspective) for Christ's being on the cross (cf. Matt. 26:45; Luke 23:18-25; Acts 2:23; 1 Cor. 2:8). Their actions are termed **such hostility**.

Believers are to **consider** the greatness of this **hostility** and the commensurate greatness of Christ's **endur[ance]**. This is an example to believers who are currently undergoing some level of **hostility** (cf. 1 Pet. 2:21-22). To describe the **endur[ance]** that results upon **consider[ing]** Christ, the AH reverts back to the long-distance race metaphor of Hebrews 12:1. The result is that **you may not be weary nor faint** (cf. Gal. 6:9; 2 Thess. 3:13; Heb. 12:5; Rev. 2:3) as one continues (runs) toward the completion (finish line) of the Christian life in this world.

Reflections

Does the expression 'leader and perfecter of faith' in Hebrews 12:2 include that Jesus had personal 'faith'? As noted above, the words τῆς πίστεως ('faith'; or 'the faith'; or 'our faith') in Hebrews 12:2 are somewhat ambiguous. Related to this question is whether Christ's 'trust' (πείθω) in God the Father (Heb. 2:13; cf. Acts 2:26) or his 'faithful' (πιστός) work as the Son (Heb. 3:2, 6) are equivalent concepts to 'faith'. Further related to this is whether the exegete understands the expression 'leader and perfecter' to refer to Christ as redeemer only, an example only, or a combination of redeemer and example.

Given the above, there is disagreement as to whether Hebrews 12:2 refers at all to Christ's personal 'faith'. Some

---

use of **for** here as a 'marker of inference' making a 'self-evident conclusion' (p. 190).

have emphatically answered 'no'. Aquinas says 'no' based on his understanding of faith, as defined by Hebrews 11:1, that it must include knowing 'a Divine thing not seen.' Aquinas continues, '[Even since] conception Christ always saw God's Essence fully,' thus he never had faith.[25] Lenski also says 'no' based on the exegetical consideration that the Greek article related to 'faith' refers back to the 'faith' of believers in Hebrews 11:1, not Jesus' faith, and that, according to him, 'Scripture nowhere speaks of Christ as a believer.'[26] In addition, Spicq and Cockerill also say 'no' in the sense that Jesus did not live 'by faith' as Hebrews 11 uses that term because to live 'by faith' is to be dependent on Christ.[27] Finally, if an exegete has the view that the 'leader and perfecter of faith' only relates to Jesus' initiating and completing faith in believers, then this view would not agree that this text refers to Jesus' personal faith.[28]

Others answer an unqualified 'yes.' Usually, this is also tied to only seeing Christ as an example in this passage. Moffatt sees Christ as the 'perfect exemplar of πίστις ['faith'] in his earthly life.... He has realized faith to the full, from start to finish.'[29] Pink states, 'Yes, the life which Jesus lived here upon earth was a life of faith.'[30] Hughes, who does believe that Christ is here both redeemer and example, states that Christ's faith here is 'without qualification. His whole earthly life is the very embodiment of trust in God.'[31]

Still others like Turretin and Allen agree to a *qualified* 'yes.' Turretin notes that Christ's faith does *not* relate to an

---

25. Aquinas, *Summa Theologiae*, 3a.7.3 (trans. Laurence Shapcote, *Summa Theologiae* [Lander, WY; Aquinas Institute, 2012], 19:87). In the same location, Aquinas also notes that often that 'faith ... implies a certain defect with regard to [a] matter, and this defect was not in Christ.'

26. Lenski, *Hebrews and James*, 426–28, esp. 426.

27. Spicq, *Hébreux*, 2:385; and Cockerill, *Hebrews*, 608.

28. So, e.g., Owen, *Hebrews*, 23:238–39.

29. Moffatt, *Hebrews*, 196.

30. Pink, *Hebrews*, 905.

31. Hughes, *Hebrews*, 522.

'apprehension of the mercy of God' related to forgiveness of sins, but it *does* relate to the 'assent' of 'the doctrine revealed of God' and 'rests in the goodness of God providing all things necessary for us.'[32] Allen is more specific in the context of Hebrews 11. He suggests that Christ had faith in 'the divine promises made within the intra-Trinitarian fellowship and applicable to Jesus' own life, suffering, and resurrection' (i.e., the Covenant of Redemption). Allen also notes that this would then dovetail with the reward promised in Hebrews 11:6.[33]

My view is *weak* 'no.' As noted above in the exegesis, although I do view Christ as the 'leader and perfecter of faith' both as Redeemer and as an example of endurance; for me, however, the use of 'faith' in Hebrews 12:2 relative to the context of Hebrews 10:36–12:3 is significant. Previously I argued that Noah's faith through which he 'became an heir of righteousness according to faith' (Heb. 11:7) did refer to saving faith as opposed to works and included forgiveness of sins. Also consider Hebrews 10:37–38 (// Hab. 2:3–4), which includes 'the one coming' and 'the righteous one shall live by faith.' The AH considers Christ as 'the one coming' at his second coming; hence, Christ is not considered in this text as one living by faith. Further, from my perspective, no other Scripture refers at the word level to Christ's 'faith.'[34] Hence, given (1) the ambiguity of 'faith' in Hebrews 12:2, (2) my exegesis of Hebrews 10:37–38 and 11:7—both of which are in the context of Hebrews 10:36–12:3, and (3) no other Scripture

---

32. Turretin, *Institutes of Elenctic Dogmatics*, 2:348.

33. R. Michael Allen, *The Christ's Faith: A Dogmatic Account*, T & T Clark Studies in Systematic Theology (Edinburgh: T & T Clark, 2012), 101. I do disagree with Allen that the Pauline expression 'faith of Christ' (πιστίς Χριστοῦ) refers to Christ's own faith/faithfulness (pp. 8–15, 214). For his intriguing discussion of the faith of Jesus in the NT, also see Michael Allen, '"From the time he took on the form of a servant": The Christ's Pilgrimage of Faith,' *International Journal of Systematic Theology* 16 (2014): 4–24. Pages 7–19 deal with Hebrews.

34. I view the Pauline expression 'faith of Christ' (πιστίς Χριστοῦ) and its equivalents as referring to our faith in Christ, not as Christ's personal faith/faithfulness (e.g., Rom. 3:22; Gal. 2:16).

text explicitly refers to Christ's personal faith; I conclude that Hebrews 12:2 is not referring to Christ's 'faith'. I would rather simply say that his *trust* (Heb. 2:13) and being *faithful* (Heb. 3:2, 6) related to endurance are included in Hebrews 12:2. But the loaded term of 'faith' is not. Although, in the end, the 'qualified yes' view and my 'weak no' view are probably not that far apart.[35]

Endurance: Discipline (12:4–11)

Hebrews 12:4–11 continues the theme of endurance from 12:1–3 with the emphasis on discipline from God. This discipline is intertwined with endurance (Heb. 12:7). Further, being disciplined is to be expected and is, in fact, a sign of being one of God's sons.

The flow of this pericope revolves around Proverbs 3:11–12. After a mild rebuke (Heb. 12:4–5a), the AH quotes Proverbs 3:11–12 (Heb. 12:5b–6). Then there is an exposition/ application of this OT quote (Heb. 12:7–11), emphasizing 'discipline' and 'son' from the quote.

Greco-Roman Background for Concept of *Paideia* in Hebrews?[36]

The quote of Proverbs 3:11–12 in Hebrews 12:5–6 includes the common LXX word παιδεία (*paideia*), which is then used in Hebrews 12:7, 8, 11. It is usually translated 'discipline' in a biblical context, but with no context, it could be 'training' or 'education', in addition to 'discipline'. It is a scholarly trend among some to argue that the concept of *paideia* in Hebrews 12:4–11 is not really coming from the Proverbs quote (or a general OT conceptual background) but is significantly dependent on Greco-Roman and/or Stoic concepts of *paideia*. The following is a typical view: Concerning the upbringing

---

35. I could not find any Reformation creeds that address this specific question.

36. For a somewhat similar question as to possible Platonic influence in Hebrews, see the discussion at the beginning of the Heb. 8:1–10:18 section.

of (free) children through the teen-age years, Greco-Roman *paideia* is primarily characterized as education focused (educative) but does include difficult *training*. This is typically termed 'non-punitive discipline.' This is contrasted with an emphasis on correction and/or *punishment* for wrongdoing (including corporal punishment), albeit for a positive purpose, which is termed 'punitive discipline.' Second Temple Jewish and OT *paideia* for children and adults have a much heavier concentration on punishment for wrongdoing (i.e., punitive discipline). Given this, those with the view that Greco-Roman *paideia* dominates Hebrews 12 see the AH using *paideia* as non-punitive and educative, using the training metaphor. They argue that the punishment-for-wrong-doing aspect of the Proverbs quote is not used by the AH.[37]

From my perspective, for purposes of exegesis, it is too reductionistic to see Greco-Roman *paideia* as primarily educative and training oriented, and OT and Jewish Second Temple Jewish *paideia* as oriented toward positive correction/ punishment of wrongdoing.[38] Although, broadly, this probably has some truth to it,[39] it is not specific enough to make a determination in an individual case, whether in the Bible or another Greco-Roman document. Admittedly, there are significant parallels between OT and Second Temple

---

37. For the influential monograph supporting this view, see N. Clayton Croy, *Endurance in Suffering: Hebrews 12.1–13 in Its Rhetorical, Religious, and Philosophical Context*, SNTSMS 98 (Cambridge: CUP, 1998).

38. Philip A. Davis, Jr. agrees with Croy as to *paideia* being non-punitive in Hebrews, but he notes that both Greco-Roman and Jewish *paideia* included corporate punishment. He sees Hebrews as using the image of corporal punishment, although not for the punishment or correction for wrongdoings (*The Place of Paideia in Hebrews' Moral Thought*, WUNT 2/475 [Tübingen: Mohr Siebeck, 2018], 239–41).

39. This would make sense because the God of the OT is significantly concerned with holiness and sin as part of his covenantal relationship with his people. But on the other hand, God also educates his people as to his character, works, and laws. Hence, the broad truth is that *comparatively*, Greco-Roman *paideia* is more educative because of its low view of sin and holiness.

Jewish *paideia* and Greco-Roman *paideia* as to the eventual benefits from difficult training. Also, the AH's use of athletic metaphors in Hebrews 12:1–13 parallels the athletic training aspect of Greco-Roman *paideia*.[40] Further, another possible point of connection between Hebrews and Greco-Roman *paideia* is gymnasia (cf. γυμνάζω in Heb. 12:11), which are places that often included both moral/educative and physical/athletic training.[41]

As all would agree, for a Christian author aware of the LXX, the word *paideia* in the first-century AD certainly had a semantic range that included (1) from general training to corporal punishment and (2) from education/instruction to positive punishment for wrongdoing.[42] My view is that despite the parallels to Greco-Roman *paideia*, the primary conceptual background of *paideia* in Hebrews is from Proverbs, and more generally, the OT (cf. Deut. 8:5; 11:2; Ps. 103:8–13). Hence, as I will show with more exegesis below, I do see the AH including, although not emphasizing, punishment for wrongdoing. The primary argument for the OT conceptual background is simply that the AH does quote

---

40. E.g., two quotes from the stoic Seneca (the Younger) have a lot of connections to Heb. 12. 'Cruel fortune bears hardest upon the inexperienced; to the tender neck the yoke is heavy. The raw recruit turns pale at the thought of a wound, but the veteran looks undaunted upon his own gore, knowing that blood has often been the price of his victory. In like manner God hardens, reviews, and disciplines those whom he approves, whom he loves' (*On Providence* 4.7 [Basore, LCL]). 'No prizefighter can go with high spirits into strife if he has never been beaten black and blue; the only contestant who can confidently enter the lists is the man who has seen his own blood, who has felt his teeth rattle beneath his opponent's fist ... For manliness gains much strength by being challenged' (*Epistle 13* [Gummere, LCL]).

41. Johnson emphasizes the gymnasia connection (*Hebrews*, 319–21). For a discussion of gymnasia, related to Greco-Roman and *Jewish* cultures, see B. W. R. Pearson, 'Gymnasia and Baths,' *DNTB*, 435–36.

42. See LSJ, 1286; also the cognate verb παιδεύω, LSJ, 1287. 'In the LXX, the vb. παιδεύω seems to remain nearer in meaning to the OT notion of "chastening," while the noun παιδεία tends more in the direction of the [Greco-Roman] idea of culture, "instruction"' ('παιδεύω,' Silva, ed., *NIDNTTE*, 3:584 – 90, esp. 586–87).

Proverbs (!), and the quote itself includes punishment, not to mention the many other OT quotes in Hebrews that would lead one to presuppose an OT conceptual background.[43] On the other hand, secondarily, I do agree that the athletic metaphors are from the Greco-Roman world, although not necessarily connected to Greco-Roman *paideia* as general athletic metaphors were ubiquitous in Greco-Roman culture (cf. 1 Cor. 9:24–26).

12:4 *You have not yet resisted until [the shedding] of blood [while] struggling[44] with sin.*

I take **sin** to be both the broad physical difficulties that *all* the readers are experiencing from those outside the church, that is, persecution (e.g., Heb. 10:32–34) and also the resultant internal sin for *some* as they question their commitment to Christ and whether the endurance needed for the Christian life is worth it (cf. Heb. 5:11–14). I justify this view as both types of sins are in the context of Hebrews 12.[45] Physical difficulties from outsiders would include 'sinners' who put Christ to death (Heb. 12:3) and many of the heroes of faith in Hebrews 11. Internal sins for some include the lack of a robust desire to endure (Heb. 12:3, 12–13) and apparent squabbles within the church (Heb. 12:14–15; cf. 13:4–5). 'Chastises' from the Proverbs quote confirms that some were sinning.

The AH notes that, yes, some of you are being persecuted, but your persecutions are not as severe as they could be—**you have not yet resisted until the shedding of blood**. You have not been crucified as Christ was (Heb. 12:2) nor martyred as

---

43. For a view similar to mine that is primarily interacting with Croy, see Ched Spellman, 'The Drama of Discipline: Toward an Intertextual Profile of PAIDEIA in Hebrews 12,' *JETS* 59 (2016): 487–506.

44. **Struggling** is a temporal present participle; hence, the addition of **while**.

45. Some commentators agree with me that **sin** includes external persecution and internal sins (e.g., Owen, *Hebrews*, 23:250–51; and Schreiner, *Hebrews*, 382). Others see **sin** as only persecution (e.g., Lane, *Hebrews 9–13*), and others as only internal sins (e.g., Koester, *Hebrews*, 525–26).

some of the heroes (Heb. 11:4, 35–37). Thus, the AH begins this section with an acknowledgement of their external difficulties but also includes a mild rebuke for some who are growing 'weary and faint.' But quickly, in the next verse, the AH will offer consolation and encouragement related to their being 'sons'.

Given the more clear athletic metaphor in Hebrews 12:1, and most likely also 12:12–13, the participle **struggling** and the verb **resisted** are also to be seen as athletic metaphors. Because of **blood**, the metaphor is probably some form of boxing.

12:5–6 *And you have forgotten the exhortation*[46] *that addresses you as sons,*[47] *'My son, do not take lightly the discipline of the Lord, nor faint [when] being reproved*[48] *by him; for whom the Lord loves, he disciplines, and he chastises every son whom he receives.'*

Continuing the mild rebuke for those who were wearying, **you have forgotten the exhortation** from Proverbs **that addresses you as sons**. But within this rebuke is consolation — you are **sons**. This consolation not only applies to the weary congregants but would also apply to all of the congregation. They all lived in a culture that included persecution of Christians, whether they personally experienced it or not.[49] As the AH will make clearer in a few verses, the providential hand of God that brings external difficulties is not necessarily a sign of being rejected.

Another aspect of the consolation is the connection to Christ's sonship. Christ is God's unique 'son' (Heb. 1:5), and the readers are also **sons** (Heb. 2:10), and thereby, 'brothers'

---

46. See semantic discussion at Heb. 6:18.

47. This clause could just as easily be translated as a question, so, e.g., RSV, ESV, and Lane, *Hebrews 9–13*, 420.

48. I take **being reproved** as a temporal present participle; hence, the addition of **when**.

49. Robertson connects the 'wilderness' typology (Heb. 3:7–4:13) to the discipline described here, which includes all believers (*God's People in the Wilderness*, 134–35).

of Christ (Heb. 2:12). In addition, Christ also underwent external difficulties, although not for his personal sin, and 'learned obedience' (Heb. 5:8). Further, many of the external difficulties that the congregants are undergoing are due to their being followers of Christ. Hence, there is a Christological connection to being a son and undergoing discipline in Hebrews that does not match Greco-Roman *paideia*.[50]

The **exhortation** is a quote of Proverbs 3:11–12.[51] In Proverbs, these two verses conclude the pericope that begins at 3:1. This pericope has a human father addressing 'my son' and giving a series of admonitions and resulting blessings.[52] For example, in 3:1–2, the son is admonished not to forget the father's 'teaching' and 'commandments' for this will increase the son's 'length of days.' It also includes the well-known 'trust in the LORD ... and he will make straight your paths' (Prov. 3:4–5). Proverbs 3:11–12 functions in this pericope as more of a conclusion.[53] It presupposes that the son has received instruction and experienced difficulties, some self-inflicted (e.g., Prov. 13:24). Therefore, the son should **not take**

---

50. So also Cockerill, *Hebrews*, 618, 618n16.

51. The Hebrew, LXX, and NT match well with only a few minor differences. Two differences are worth mentioning. In Prov. 3:11 // Heb. 12:5, the Hebrew has 'my son,' the LXX 'son,' and the NT is back to 'my son,' also the initial position of 'my son' in the NT matches the LXX and not the Hebrew. In Prov. 3:12 // Heb. 12:6, the Hebrew has 'as a father' with the implied 'reproves', the LXX 'he chastises' with the implied 'father,' and the NT follows the LXX. Apparently the Hebrew כאב, כ 'as' with אב 'father,' was understood by the LXX as the (hiphil?) verb כאב 'to cause pain' (*HALOT*, 454).

52. Tremper Longman III comments, 'This wisdom poem contains a series of admonitions marked by imperatives as the father addresses the son (Prov. 3:1, 3, 5–6a, 7, 11). The father also offers motivation for following the imperatives by naming the positive consequences that will flow from obedience (Prov. 3:2, 6b, 8, 12)' (*Proverbs*, Baker Commentary on the Old Testament Wisdom and Psalms [Grand Rapids: Baker, 2006], 130). Also see Bruce K. Waltke, *The Book of Proverbs: Chapters 1–15*, NICOT (Grand Rapids: Eerdmans, 2004), 236–39.

53. So also Waltke, *Proverbs 1–15*, 239, 248–50. Guthrie calls it a 'crowning exhortation' ('Hebrews,' 986).

lightly the discipline of the Lord as ultimately this discipline shows that the Lord loves him (**for whom the Lord loves, he disciplines**, cf. Rev. 3:19). In the long run, because the Lord loves him, the son will receive the various blessings. The Hebrew for the noun 'discipline' is מוסר (LXX παιδεία) which includes a broad semantic range from training (e.g., Prov. 1:2, 7; 8:10) to correction and/or punishment for wrongdoing (e.g., Prov. 6:23; 13:24; 23:13).[54]

Note that **addresses** is in the present tense. This is quite a high view of Scripture! An OT text of Scripture, which in the Proverbs' context is Solomon exhorting a generic son, is considered to be also **address[ing]** Christians in the first-century AD. Obviously, the AH considers the ultimate author of Scripture to be God (e.g., Heb. 10:17), but he probably did not explicitly say 'God addresses' because the quote itself includes **the Lord** in third person (cf. Gal. 3:8). In any event, the AH has equated God's speaking with the Scripture's **addressing**, and this is true for the first readers of Proverbs as well as all subsequent believing readers.

Intriguingly, the AH also refers to his letter as an **exhortation** (Heb. 13:22). Is this a possible hint that the AH was aware of the canonical authority of his letter? Also, note that an **exhortation** can come from a written source. That is, 'exhortation' in Hebrews 13:22 is not necessarily an oral allusion.

12:7–8 *You are enduring*[55] *[trials]*[56] *for discipline as God is treating you as sons. For what son is [there] whom the father does not discipline? And if you are without discipline, which all have become partakers, then you are illegitimate and not sons.*

The AH expands on the meaning of the Proverbs 3:11–12. Being **sons** is good because the believing congregants are

---

54. See *HALOT*, 557; and E. Merrill, 'יסר,' *NITDOTTE*, 2:479–82, esp. 480–1.

55. **You are enduring** in form could also be an imperative.

56. As to assuming **trials**, so also Lane, *Hebrews 9–13*, 401; and Ellingworth, *Hebrews*, 650; *contra* Koester, *Hebrews*, 528.

receiving **discipline**, and this in turn aids in **enduring** through **trials**. That is, trials produce **discipline**, and the positive results of that **discipline** aid in **enduring** the next trial. All this is part of the means of God's preservation of his children. (Although the emphasis here in Hebrews is related to discipline in the midst of difficulties, the broader context of both Proverbs and Hebrews also includes discipline in the sense of straightforward instruction unrelated to external difficulties.)

The congregation is reminded that difficulties are a sign that **God is treating you as sons**. In fact, **if you are without discipline, which all** believers **have become partakers** of discipline, **then you are illegitimate and not sons**.[57] That is, for a believer, one should *not* necessarily take providential difficulties as a sign of God's indifference, that is, as an **illegitimate** son who typically would receive no **discipline**. Rather, the difficulties are an evidence that **God** is your loving **father**. Of course, having difficulties is not certain proof that one is a Christian, but the complete absence of them is a proof of not being a Christian (cf. 2 Tim. 3:12; Jas. 1:2–4).

12:9–10 *Furthermore, on the one hand, we[58] have had our fathers of flesh, discipliners, and we respected [them]. But, on the other hand, should it not be[59] that much more that we are subject to the Father of spirits, and we will live? For they disciplined for a short time[60] according to what seems [best] to them, but he [disciplines] for what profits in order to share his holiness.*

---

57. Philo notes the advantages for those with discipline as compared to those who are abandoned to no discipline in *That the Worse Attacks the Better* 144–46 and *Preliminary Studies* 175–77. In *Preliminary Studies* he quotes Prov. 3:11–12 (§177). Other Second Temple Judaism and Rabbinic texts that relate include Jdt. 8:27; Sir. 18:14; 30:8; Wis. 3:11; 2 Macc. 6:12–17; 7:33; 10:4; Pss. Sol. 3:4; b. Berakhot 5a (includes quote of Prov. 3:12); and b. Sanhedrin 101a ('suffering is precious'). The Formula of Concord, Solid Declaration 6 quotes Heb. 12:8 to show that Christians need the 'law's daily instruction and admonition.'

58. Note the change from second person in Heb. 12:7–8 to first person in 12:9. The AH includes himself in one who needs discipline to endure.

59. Since the question begins with οὐ, an affirmative response is expected.

60. Literally, 'for a few days.'

The AH adds another point (**furthermore**) using an explicit lesser-to-greater argument (**should it not be that much more**). It begins with the general observation about a father's typical actions in raising his children. Human fathers (**fathers of flesh**), who are **discipliners**, do a reasonably, although not perfectly, good job of discipline (**according to what seems best to them**).[61] Also, as a general rule, typical earthly fathers are **respected**.[62] Given this, there is a greater and better discipline from the divine-creator **Father** that is exactly what one needs (**what profits in order to share his holiness**) to live spiritually now and into the NHNE (**we will live**). Also, a believer's respect and love (**subject to**) of the divine **Father** should far exceed that of an earthly father. Finally, a human father's discipline lasts only **for a short time**; God's discipline, it is implied, is throughout one's lifetime as a believer.

The expression **share his holiness**[63] refers to a believer's personal sanctification/holiness that is patterned after God's perfect **holiness** (i.e., **holiness** is a communicable attribute; cf. 1 Pet. 1:15–16). Although some take this to occur only when a believer enters heaven,[64] I view it as related to both now in this life and in heaven.[65] For me, Hebrews 12:14 confirms the 'now' aspect (cf. Heb. 2:11; 10:14).

The exact wording **Father of spirits** is unique in the Bible. It is close to 'God of the spirits of all flesh' in both

---

61. WLC 127 references Heb. 12:9 related to the fifth commandment in that 'inferiors' should have 'due submission to their corrections.' On the other hand, WLC 130 references Heb. 12:10 in that 'superiors' should not be 'correcting them [inferiors] unduly.'

62. See Luther's somewhat comical discussion within the fourth commandment (for Reformed, the fifth) section of his Large Catechism complaining that human parents do not get enough respect.

63. The Greek behind **holiness** (ἁγιότης) is unusual. This exact form is used only in the LXX in 2 Maccabees 15:2 (referring to a holy day) and nowhere in the NT. However, this odd form does not seem to have any special meaning beyond the typical 'holy' cognates. So also Kleinig, *Hebrews*, 608.

64. So Brown, *Hebrews*, 128–29; Bruce, *Hebrews*, 344; and Lane, *Hebrews 9–13*, 421.

65. So also Calvin, *Hebrews and 1 & 2 Peter*, 193; Owen, *Hebrews*, 23:270; Hughes, *Hebrews*, 231; and Attridge, *Hebrews*, 363.

Numbers 16:22 and 27:16, where the subject ('flesh') is humans.[66] In Hebrews 12:9, **Father of spirits** is clearly parallel to **fathers of flesh**. There is the obvious contrast of divine and human. But there is also the similarity that both are creators, although at different levels. Specifically, to what does **spirits** (πνεῦμα) refer? Upon bracketing out the Holy Spirit, the AH uses 'spirit' to refer to angels (1:7, 14), humans (4:12; 12:23), and Christ's divine nature (9:14). Given the AH does include humans in his semantic range of 'spirit', I conclude that here he is referring to humans.[67] More specifically, does **spirits** refer to the immaterial souls or to humans in general? Based on 'spirit' in Hebrews 4:12 and 12:23, and the **flesh/spirits** contrast here, I view **spirits** as human souls.[68] Although God ultimately makes all bodies and souls, this contrast stresses God's more mysterious sense of providential involvement in and perfect knowledge of the creation of all humans as animate beings with souls made in the image of God. Hence, the expression **Father of spirits** emphasizes God's transcendence.[69]

How does my exegesis relate to the historic creationism-versus-traducianism debate concerning the origin of the soul in every human? The creationism view is that God immediately

---

66. This is the translation of the Hebrew (אלהי הרוחת לכל־בשר). The LXX has 'God of the spirits *and* all flesh.' Targum Pseudo-Jonathan for Num. 16:22 has 'God, who has put the spirit of life in the bodies of the sons of men.' Cf. 2 Maccabees 3:24, 'the Sovereign of the spirits and all authority.' Here 'spirits' probably does not refer to humans. First Enoch uses 'Lord of the spirits' numerous times referring to angels (e.g., 1 En. 37:2, 4; 38:4; 39:12).

67. Some understand **spirits** as angels and humans, e.g., Shedd, *Dogmatic Theology*, 441; Lenski, *Hebrews and James*, 437; Allen, *Hebrews*, 582; and Kleinig, *Hebrews*, 608. Others take **spirits** as in 'spiritual Father' of humans e.g., Bruce, *Hebrews*, 344; and Hughes, *Hebrews*, 530–31.

68. So also Calvin, *Hebrews and 1 & 2 Peter*, 192; and Owen, *Hebrews*, 269. Of course, to have my view, one must presuppose the traditional (substance) dichotomous view of man consisting of both body and soul/spirit.

69. Although not agreeing with my 'soul' view, others agree with the transcendence emphasis (e.g., Lane, *Hebrews 9–13*, 424; and Cockerill, *Hebrews*, 625).

(i.e., without means) creates souls.[70] The traducianism view maintains that both body and soul are derived mediately from the parents.[71] Hebrews 12:9 is a key verse in the debate (along with Gen. 2:7; Num. 16:22; 27:16; Eccl. 12:7; Zech. 12:1). My exegesis has some affinity with the creation view in that God's providential activity concerning souls is emphasized, but it disagrees with creationism, at least here, if this verse is used to conclusively show that God immediately creates souls.

12:11 *And, on the one hand, all discipline for the present does not seem to be [for] joy but [for] pain, but, on the other hand, later it yields peaceful fruit of righteousness to those having been trained by it.*[72]

Hebrews 12:11 is somewhat of a restatement of verse 10, or maybe better, a proverbial restatement. Yes, while undergoing **discipline** from the Father, it **does not** always **seem to be for joy**, but in fact, it may include **pain**, whether physical or emotional. However, this is not the whole story.[73] In the longer run (**later**), this **discipline (it) yields** positive results.

---

70. Those *strongly* favoring creationism include Aquinas, *Summa Theologiae* 1a.118.2; Turretin, *Institutes of Elenctic Theology*, 1:477–82; and Van Mastricht, *Theoretical-Practical Theology*, 3:455–56, 474–75. Those *weakly* favoring it include Hodge, *Systematic Theology*, 2:65–76; and Bavinck, *Reformed Dogmatics*, 2:580–88. The Roman Catholic Church is by creed committed to creationism; see Fifth Lateran Council (AD 1517) (Denzinger[43] §1440); *Humani Generis* (AD 1950) (Denzinger[43] §3896); and Catechism of the Catholic Church §366. Augustine famously commented several times that he could not decide between the two views (e.g., *Letter 166* [*NPNF*[1], 1:525–26]; *On the Soul and Its Origin* 16 [*NPNF*[1], 5:322]). Berkouwer sees the question as moot because he does not believe in a dichotomous view of man (*Man: The Image of God*, 279–309).

71. Favoring traducianism are, e.g., Tertullian, *A Treatise on the Soul* 27 (*ANF*, 3:207–8); Shedd, *Dogmatic Theology*, 430–82; and Letham, *Systematic Theology*, 343–47. During the Reformation, most Lutherans favored traducianism. The term derives from the Latin *tradux*, a 'branch' or 'sprout.'

72. **It** refers to **discipline** as both are feminine.

73. Heidelberg Catechism 28 puts it beautifully concerning our responses to God's fatherly providence, 'That we may be *patient* in adversity, *thankful* in prosperity, and for what is future have good *confidence* in our faithful God' (emphasis mine). For similar language, see Calvin, *Institutes* 1.17.7.

The positive results are termed the **peaceful fruit of righteousness**. This term is quite broad.[74] It includes both external and internal benefits that a believer has 'now' and into the NHNE.

The Greek behind **those having been trained** is the participial form of the verb γυμνάζω, which is a cognate of the well-known gymnasia (see further linguistic discussion at Heb. 5:14). Due to the athletic metaphors already in this context, γυμνάζω is here to be taken as an athletic metaphor.

Reflections
Being labeled a 'son' by Almighty God is a humbling thought. This adoption into God's family is one of the many benefits of Christ's work for us (cf. Rom. 8:5, 14; Gal. 3:26; 4:5; Eph. 1:5), and for many Christians, it is especially heart-warming. As the WLC 74 puts it, Christians are 'under his [God's] *fatherly care* and dispensations, admitted to all the liberties and privileges of the sons of God' (emphasis mine). Calvin, in his introduction to his section on justification, notes that one result of faith is that we 'have in heaven instead of a Judge, a *gracious Father*.'[75]

Hebrews 12:4–11 confirms that Christians have a fatherly relationship with God. The specific emphasis is that this relationship includes discipline that is sometimes difficult. Christians, however, are still comforted because they know discipline is from a caring and gracious father, not a judge.[76] Psalm 103:13 wonderfully notes in a context that includes the discipline of believers, that 'like as a father pitieth his children, so the LORD pitieth them that fear him' (KJV). Yes, we may be sometimes under 'God's fatherly displeasure' (WCF 11.5) or

---

74. Possible connections in Hebrews include 7:2; 11:7; 11:31, 33; 12:14, and 13:20. Also cf. Prov. 3:9; 11:30; Isa. 57:19; Amos 6:12; Zech. 6:13; 8:12; 2 Cor. 9:10; Gal. 5:22; and Phil. 1:11.

75. Calvin, *Institutes* 3.11.1, emphasis mine.

76. See insightful discussion concerning the "Righteousness of God's Punishments" by Vern S. Poythress, *The Shadow of Christ in the Law of Moses*, 120–24.

have been 'chastened by him as by a father' (WCF 12), but the end game is the 'peaceful fruit of righteousness.'

Endurance: Make Straight Paths (12:12–17)

Hebrews 12:12–17 continues the broad exhortation for endurance in the Christian life. It begins with an athletic metaphor to persevere despite being exhausted (Heb. 12:12–13). This looks back to the previous pericope concerning the advantages of fatherly discipline (Heb. 12:4–11).[77] This discipline will aid one in continuing and completing the athletic event.

The athletic metaphor also looks forward to the subunit of 12:14–17. This subunit begins with the imperative to 'pursue peace ... and holiness' (12:14), where the athletic metaphor becomes ethically concrete. To continue in the Christian life is positively defined as to pursue peace and holiness. This initial imperative is followed by a subordinate imperative, 'see' or 'be concerned' (12:15). This subordinate imperative is cautionary in that it relates three grammatically parallel dangers (12:15–16a). The third danger, the combination of 'sexual impurity' and 'profane', is elaborated upon by the example of Esau (12:16b–17).

Hebrews 12:12–17 includes several OT allusions. They include, at a minimum, Isaiah 35:3 (Heb. 12:12); Proverbs 4:26 (Heb. 12:13); Psalm 34:14 (Heb. 12:14); Deuteronomy 29:18 (Heb. 12:15); Genesis 25:31–34 (Heb. 12:16); and Genesis 27:30–40 (Heb. 12:17).

12:12–13 *So then, straighten the drooping hands and the weakened knees, and make straight paths for[78] your feet in order that what [is] lame may not be dislocated[79] but rather be healed.*

---

77. As noted at the beginning of my discussion of Heb. 12, some see Heb. 12:12–13 as part of the previous pericope.

78. I take **make** in the athletic metaphor as determine *in your mind* to take the best route (**straight path**) for the race. Others take **feet** as an instrumental dative, 'with your feet.' That is, have your feet determine the best route (so, e.g., Cockerill, *Hebrews*, 630).

79. The verb ἐκτρέπω generally means 'to veer off,' but it also has a technical medical use meaning a bone or joint 'to be dislocated' (BDAG, 311).

Picking up on the previous athletic metaphors in Hebrews 12:1, 4, 11, the AH encourages the congregants to **straighten** your **drooping hands and** your **weakened knees** (probably a boxing metaphor) and **make straight paths for your feet** (race metaphor).[80] **So then** relates back to the discipline of Hebrews 12:4–11. Putting these together, the discipline should encourage the athlete to continue in the difficult athletic event even if tired because he has been trained/disciplined to complete it. Similarly, the Christian should be encouraged because the loving Father has disciplined him so that he may complete the journey despite his current lackluster spiritual state.

Somewhat surprisingly, the athletic metaphors here are stated using wording/allusions from the OT. **Straighten the drooping hands and weakened knees** reasonably parallels Isaiah 35:3,[81] both in wording and context.[82] Isaiah encourages those to strengthen themselves in the current difficult 'desert' time as God will eventually make it 'blossom' (Isa. 35:1–10). **Make straight paths for your feet** is quite close in wording and content to Proverbs 4:26a.[83] In the Proverbs 4:20–27

---

80. Chrysostom comments, '[The AH] speaks to runners, and boxers, and warriors' ('Homily 30 on Hebrews' [*NPNF*[1], 14:503]). Philo allegorizes the wilderness events related to the temptations of the soul, and includes an athletic metaphor. 'Weakening the hands, like exhausted athletes (ἀθληταί), they determined to return to Egypt to the indulgence of their passions' (*On Preliminary Studies* 1.164). Most modern commentaries confirm an athletic metaphor (e.g., Lane, *Hebrews 9 – 13*, 426–27), although many older ones, excepting Chrysostom, do not mention it (e.g., Aquinas, *Hebrews*, 278; Calvin, *Hebrews and 1-2 Peter*, 193–95; Owen, *Hebrews*, 23:279–83).

81. The Hebrew and LXX of Isa. 35:3 match except that the Hebrew has two synonymous verbs and the LXX only has one verb to cover both 'hands' and 'knees'. The wording of Heb. 12:12 that matches exactly to the LXX are '**hands**,' and '**weakened knees**.' There is a close cognate for **drooping**.

82. Apparently, the combination of both 'hands' and 'knees' having difficulties is a stock expression (e.g., Job 4:4–5; Ezek. 7:17; 21:7; Zeph. 3:16; Sir. 25:23).

83. The Hebrew and LXX slightly differ. The Hebrew has a singular 'foot' as opposed to the LXX's 'feet'. Also, the Hebrew has a 'you' (singular), and the LXX has dropped it. LXX has added 'straight'. Heb. 12:13 follows the

context, the son is to metaphorically make his path straight by following godly wisdom and not swerving into sin.

I take **what is lame** to refer in the athletic metaphor to the **hands, knees,** and/or **feet**, that is, whatever is out of joint. But **straighten[ing]** these and **mak[ing] straight paths** will reduce the further harm done by getting them totally **dislocated**. **Rather** in fact, these strategies will have them **be healed**. At the reality level, Christians who are experiencing difficulties (**what is lame**) can still get back to a robust spiritual state (**be healed**).

12:14 *Pursue peace with all and holiness, without*[84] *which no one will see the Lord,*

Hebrews 12:14–16 is one sentence. Although there is no conjunction connecting this sentence to 12:12–13, I take it as the concrete version of metaphorically straightening the hands and knees and making straight paths for your feet.

The main grammatical verb of the sentence is the imperative **pursue** with two direct objects, **peace** and **holiness**.

To **pursue** or seek **peace** is a wonderful biblical expression (e.g., Ps. 34:14 // 1 Pet. 3:11; Rom. 12:18; 14:19; 2 Tim. 2:22; cf. Matt. 5:9; cf. m. Abot 1:12). It is not clear if **with all** refers specifically to only other Christians or include humans without exception, although I take it as other Christians as the entire sentence deals with covenantal community matters.[85] Since **peace** in Hebrews is not especially emphasized or a particularly theologically charged word, I take **peace** here as referring to the general welfare of others, which does include both internal and external components.[86] Of course, this

---

LXX except for having a plural imperative **make** and adding a **you** (plural).

84. In Greek, this is a rare instance of the preposition **without** (χωρίς) following its object (**which** [οὗ]), although I translated in the normal English order (BDF §216(2).

85. So also Attridge, who cites Heb. 13:1-3, 7, 16–17 as support (*Hebrews*, 367). Many commentators do take as **all** without exception.

86. **Peace** only occurs elsewhere in Hebrews in 7:2 (Salem equals peace), 11:31 (idiom for welcome), and 13:20 ('God of peace' in the benediction).

general welfare is from a Christian perspective and would include appropriate caveats.

The readers are also to **pursue ... holiness**. Just previously, they have been told that God's discipline will aid them to be able 'to share his holiness' (Heb. 12:10). The **holiness** here refers to a believer's personal sanctification (cf. Heb. 10:36; 2 Cor. 7:1; 1 Thess. 4:3),[87] which ultimately comes from the work of God in Christ (cf. Heb. 13:12). Elsewhere in Hebrews, Christians are termed 'holy brothers' (Heb. 3:1) and 'saints' (6:10; 13:24, 'saints' is a cognate of 'holy'). A true believer will have some level of sanctification/**holiness** and is encouraged to continually increase/**pursue** it.[88] This holiness is one significant evidence of being a Christian because **without which** (i.e., **holiness**) **no one will see the Lord**.

The expression **see the Lord** refers broadly to entering heaven. Does **Lord** refer to God the Father, God the Son incarnate, or simply the Godhead? It is not clear. In Hebrews, 'Lord' is often used for Yahweh in OT quotes (Heb. 1:10; 7:21; 8:8–11; 10:16, 30; 12:5–6; 13:6). Of these, one is clearly the preincarnate Son (Heb. 1:10), and two are clearly God the Father (Heb. 7:21; 12:5–6). The others in the quotes are either the Godhead or God the Father. 'Lord' is also used clearly sometimes for the incarnate Christ (Heb. 2:3; 7:14; 13:20). For cases in Hebrews where 'Lord' is used referring to God's actions in the OT and is not part of an OT quote (e.g. Heb. 8:2), these references could be either to the Godhead or God the Father. Now back to **Lord** in Hebrews 12:14. The closest

---

87. WCF 13.1 includes both 'definitive' sanctification ('the dominion of the whole body of sin is destroyed') and 'progressive sanctification' ('the several lusts thereof are more and more weakened and mortified, and they are more and more quickened and strengthened in all saving graces, to the practice of true holiness, without which no man shall see the Lord'). The Heb. 12:14 quote is in reference to progressive sanctification.

88. So also Bavinck, *Reformed Dogmatics*, 4:235, 4:253. For a recent discussion of multiple facets of sanctification from a Reformed perspective, including a discussion of the relationship of the concepts of justification and sanctification in Hebrews, see Allen, *Sanctification*, esp. 190–97.

context is Hebrews 12:5–6 where 'Lord' is God the Father. However, given the use of **see**[89] and the predominate use of 'Lord' elsewhere in Hebrews for the Son when not in a quote, I weakly conclude that **Lord** refers to the incarnate Christ.[90] In any event, to **see the** Lord, whether it is aspects of the Godhead's glory or the resurrected body of Christ, is a grand future benefit for believers (John 17:24, Acts 7:55). Upon death, we will 'behold the face of God in light and glory' (WCF 32.1).

12:15–16 *oversee lest someone [be] falling short of the grace of God; lest some root of bitterness growing up troubles, and by it*[91] *many are defiled; lest someone [be] a fornicator or profane as Esau, who gave over his own birthright*[92]*in exchange for one meal.*

Continuing from the main imperative 'pursue' (Heb. 12:14) is a subordinate imperative **oversee**.[93] **Oversee** (ἐπισκοπέω) is the same verb used for elders' responsibilities in 1 Peter 5:2. It is also the cognate of an 'overseer' (ἐπίσκοπος), that is, an elder (Acts 20:28; Phil. 1:1; 1 Tim. 3:2; Titus 1:7; 1 Pet. 2:25). Here, however, **oversee** is an imperative that all in the covenant community should be concerned for all other members, although it would especially apply to the leaders (Heb. 13:17).

The imperative **oversee** is followed by three grammatically parallel clauses that each contain a potential danger.[94] These three dangers or warnings conceptually overlap.[95] Believers

---

89. I do not want to place all of my exegetical weight on **see** as several biblical passages seem to use sight metaphorically when referring to the Godhead (e.g., Pss. 11:7; 17:15; 63:2; Heb. 11:27) or metaphorically referring to Jesus (Heb. 12:2). Also, Heb. 12:23 could imply seeing God.

90. So also Hodge, *Hebrews*, 132; and Brown, *Hebrews*, 637; *contra* Koester, *Hebrews*, 531.

91. **It** is feminine singular referring to **root** that is feminine singular.

92. The 'dictionary form' of **birthright** is neuter plural. Possibly this implies that a **birthright** comes with multiple rights.

93. Technically, **oversee** is an attendant circumstantial participle that takes on the imperatival aspects of 'pursue'. As such it is subordinate.

94. All three clauses begin with μή τις, translated as 'lest some(one).'

95. For a discussion of warnings in the subjunctive mood, see Moulton, *Prolegomena*, 177-79.

are to be concerned about others in their covenant community to eliminate potential negative effects. The first reason or warning to be concerned is **lest someone be falling short of the grace of God**.[96] That is, some might not have even attained the initial **grace of God,** and without it they will not get to heaven.

The second reason is **lest some root of bitterness growing up troubles** (others), **and by it many are defiled**. The wording **lest... troubles** is a short quote taken from Deuteronomy 29:18.[97] Deuteronomy 29 matches very well to the Hebrews situation. This chapter is Moses' speech related to the covenant renewal at Moab, and it includes warnings against abandoning the covenant by following idols. These warnings include noting how individual covenant breakers may negatively influence the broader community (Deut. 29:16–28). In addition to the evil of blatant idol worship, it also warns of one who in his heart commits idolatry but outwardly acts as a covenant keeper (Deut. 29:19). The **root of bitterness** metaphor is a bitter **root** that produces bitter fruit. By this metaphor, both Moses and the AH are warning that an individual who does not really believe (**root of bitterness**) may negatively affect others in the covenant community (the resulting bitter fruit)[98]—**by it** (the root) **many are defiled**.[99] Thus, this second reason notes the

---

96. The same verb **falling short** (ὑστερέω) is used in Heb. 4:1, which has a similar context.

97. The Hebrew reads 'lest there is among you a root bearing poison and wormwood.' The LXX comes in two versions, 'lest there is some root among you growing up with gall and bitterness' or 'lest there is some root among you troubles with bitterness.' Apparently, 'with gall' (ἐν χολῇ) has been confused with 'troubles' (ἐνχολῇ). The AH drops 'among you,' opts for 'troubles', and connects by a genitive 'bitterness' to 'root'.

98. Commenting on Deut. 29:18, Peter C. Craigie states, 'The [root] metaphor indicates the permeation of evil throughout Israel because of the action of an individual, family, or tribe. To express it in another way, "no man is an island"' (*Deuteronomy*, NICOT [Grand Rapids: Eerdmans, 1976], 368). Similarly, 1QH XII, 14–15 has the 'teachers of lies' as 'a root bearing poisoned and bitter fruit is in their designs' (trans. Vermes, *The Complete Dead Sea Scrolls in English*).

99. To **defile** (μιαίνω) is a strong word used very often in the LXX

danger of not the individual covenant breaker per se, but the additional negative consequences this brings to others (cf. leaven in 1 Cor. 5:6 and Gal. 5:9).

The third reason is **lest someone be a fornicator or profane**. Not spiritual caring about others in the covenant community might lead some to the gross sin of being a **fornicator** (πόρνος)[100] or the more general sin of being **profane** (βέβηλος). **Profane** might be described as *ir*religious, *ir*reverent, opposite of holy, or only caring about worldly things and not God.[101] In context, **profane** would be simply not caring about the things of God in any serious way.

Possibly also referring to **fornicator**,[102] but clearly relating to **profane**, the AH uses **Esau** as an example (Gen. 25:29–34; 27:36; cf. Heb. 11:20). The firstborn had the **birthright**.[103]

(e.g., Lev. 5:3; Num 5:3; Deut. 24:4; Hos. 5:3; cf. Titus 1:5). The adjective cognate '*un*defiled' (ἀμίαντος) is used in Heb. 7:26 (Christ) and 13:4 (marriage bed).

100. Some take πόρνος to mean **fornicator** in a metaphorical sense (spiritual fornication), that is, one seeks the love of other gods as opposed to the true God to which one is 'married'. This use per se is not in the LXX or NT but cognates of πόρνος do occur with this meaning in Judg. 2:17; Exod. 34:15; and Ezek. 23:5, 8, 44. Also, πόρνος is used with this meaning in Philo, *Allegorical Interpretation* 3.8. In addition, the feminine πόρνη ('harlot,' 'prostitute') is used several times in conjunction with **profane** by Philo (*On Flight and Finding* 114; *On the Special Laws* 1.102). Finally, the metaphorical use is usually driven by the view that the OT does not present Esau as a fornicator. In favor of this view include Lenski, *Hebrews and James*, 447; Attridge, *Hebrews*, 369; and Lane, *Hebrews 9–13*, 439. The clear use of πόρνος in Heb. 13:4 as literal sexual sin is conclusive against the metaphorical view.

101. Only occurrences in the NT are 1 Tim. 1:9; 4:7; 6:20; 2 Tim. 2:16; and Heb. 12:16. Aquinas takes it to mean a prohibition against gluttony due to the Esau context (*Hebrews*, 281).

102. Does the OT portray Esau as a **fornicator**? Esau's marriage to two Hittite women causes his parents bitterness (Gen. 26:34–35; 27:46). Possibly this makes Esau a **fornicator** if these marriages are illegitimate. In Obadiah, Edom is condemned and referred to as Esau, although no allusions to sexual sins are made. Outside of the OT, Esau is portrayed as a **fornicator** (e.g., Philo, *On the Virtues* 208). In b. Baba Batra 16b, Esau is said to have immoral sexual relations with a betrothed women (not one of the Hittite women) based on the connection of 'field' in Gen. 25:29 and Deut. 22:25.

103. In both Hebrew and Greek, **birthright** (בכרה, πρωτοτόκια) and

This **birthright** consisted in a double portion of the father's inheritance and priority related to order of succession (Deut. 21:15–17; 1 Chr. 5:1–2; 2 Chr. 21:3). The **birthright** of **Esau** as the firstborn had importance in-and-of itself, but because his **birthright** was (seemingly) also tied to Isaac who had a covenant from God, this **birthright** was very important. Given this importance, however, **Esau** shows his lack of concern for the things of God (**profane**) as he **gave over his own birthright in exchange for one meal**. Similarly, anyone who has no concern for Christ is also acting in a **profane** manner.

12:17 *For you know that even afterwards, desiring to inherit the blessing, he was rejected, for he found no place of repentance even though having sought it with tears.*

The AH now moves to an incident later (**afterwards**) in the Jacob and Esau story (Genesis 27). Jacob, with Rebekah's help, has tricked Isaac into giving him the special patriarchal blessing. This blessing includes material benefits, and that others, including his extended family, will serve him (Gen. 27:26–29). This blessing ultimately relates to the Abrahamic covenant (cf. Gen. 28:3–4). Esau, realizing that Jacob has secured this blessing instead of him, cries out bitterly to his father. Isaac confirms that he cannot revoke the special blessing that has just made Jacob 'lord' of Esau (Gen. 27:30–37). The incident concludes with Esau receiving a secondary (negative) blessing. He then in anger commits to kill Jacob (Gen. 27:39–41), although he personally does not follow through on this (Genesis 33). Another aspect to this incident and previous giving away of the birthright is that God reveals to Rebekah that he has predestined Jacob to be the leader (Gen. 27:22–23).

Now to Hebrews 12:17. What exact point is the AH making by saying that **afterwards** (i.e., after the birthright incident)

'firstborn' (בכר, πρωτότοκος) are clear cognates. Note 'firstborn' in Heb. 1:6; 11:28; and 12:23.

Esau **was rejected** by Isaac (and God!), **although** Esau was **desiring to inherit the** patriarchal **blessing**? On the surface, the first **for** is supporting Esau's giving up of his birthright, which is supporting the previous point that Esau is 'profane', which is in turn part of a general discussion of endurance and the possible consequences of not doing so. I take **for** as adding the aspect of *permanence* to Esau's birthright decision. Some decisions are set in stone. Related to the AH's readers, the implication by analogy is that a decision now not to endure in Christ's community may have serious and permanent effects. That is, there is such a thing as irrevocable apostasy (see extended discussion related to Heb. 6:4–8).

The second **for** enforces the permanence. **Even though having sought it (the blessing**[104]**) with tears,**[105] Esau could not reverse his rejection of the birthright and its accompanying **blessing**.

Commentators disagree concerning the clause **he** (Esau) **found no place** (opportunity[106]) **of repentance**. Whose lack of **repentance** is referred to—Isaac's[107] or Esau's[108]? Those favoring Esau note the connection to 'repentance' in Hebrews 6:6 combined with asserting that Esau had a false repentance (Gen. 27:41). Hence, they understand the clause

---

104. It is feminine and refers back to the feminine **blessing**. Although **repentance** is also feminine, it is not the head noun of the phrase **place of repentance**, where **place** is masculine. Grammatically, the pronoun **it** needs to refer to a head noun. So also the Geneva Bible, Owen, *Hebrews*, 23:303; Bruce, *Hebrews*, 351; Lane, *Hebrews 9–13*, 440; Koester, *Hebrews*, 533; Cockerill, *Hebrews*, 641; and Schreiner, *Hebrews*, 393.

105. Although the Genesis text does not explicitly use **tears**, this is the implication of Gen. 27:34. So also Jubilees 26:32; and Josephus, *Jewish Antiquities*, 1.275.

106. Wisdom 12:10 also has 'place of repentance,' where this phrase clearly refers to an opportunity or chance to repent.

107. So many older commentators, e.g., Owen, *Hebrews*, 23:303; and Brown, *Hebrews*, 642n1.

108. So some older and most modern commentators, e.g., Chrysostom, 'Homily 31 on Hebrews' (*NPNF*[1], 14:507); Aquinas, *Hebrews*, 282; Bruce, *Hebrews*, 351; Hughes, *Hebrews*, 541n147; and Attridge, *Hebrews*, 370.

as Esau **found no place** in his own heart **of** true **repentance** for his sin of rejecting the birthright despite his sincerity for material **blessing** (cf. 2 Cor. 7:10). I argue, however, that **repentance** refers to Isaac's refusal to change his mind. This (1) more clearly matches the Genesis incident, and (2) eliminates the awkwardness of interpreting (a) **he *found no place*** as referring to Esau's inner confusion and (b) Esau's **repentance** as false, which seems to be the opposite of what **having sought [the blessing] with tears** seems on the surface to imply.

Reflections
'Sports teaches you about life.' I often heard coaches quote this proverb to me, and then many years later other coaches quoted it to my son. The implications were that the player learned more than just the mechanics of the game and that the experience will teach one *positive* lessons. For some reason, this proverb did not sit well with me. I always wanted to nuance it. Well, yes, playing sports does give opportunities to learn teamwork, how to be a good loser and a humble winner, to follow rules, that hard work pays off, etc. But I noticed that sports often also encouraged, whether intentionally or not, unhealthy pride, misplaced priorities, a dislike for others, winning is everything, abusing one's body, etc. Of course, I was/am being pedantic, it is just a proverb, which by definition does not include all the nuances.

As noted above, Hebrews 12:12–13 includes athletic metaphors, probably referring to boxing and running a long race. In these metaphors, it is assumed that the athlete is having difficulties. He is tired and his body is failing. He needs to 'straighten' his hands and knees and run in a 'straight' path. The athlete is encouraged to keep going, do not quit, and exhibit endurance. This needed endurance is a metaphor for the Christian life, especially for those currently spiritually struggling. The broader context of the book of Hebrews confirms that the ability for this endurance is from God himself in the work of Christ and applied by the Holy Spirit.

Back to my complaint about the sports proverb. First, if the Bible also uses an athletic metaphor to teach us about life, I probably should quit whining so much! Second, the endurance aspect to sports is well understood by coaches and athletes. Yes, it is well applied to enduring through the difficulties of, for example, employment. But more important is enduring through difficulties related to one's commitment to Christ.

If you will permit a slight nuance, I would rather say, 'Sports *often* teaches you about *Christian* life.'

Endurance: Mount Zion and the Mediator (12:18–24)

Hebrews 12:18–24 is clearly a coherent unit with two sections contrasting the (unnamed) Mount Sinai (12:18–21) with the (named) heavenly Mount Zion (12:22–24). Each section has contrasting parallel beginnings: 'you have not approached' versus 'but you have approached.' Each section has a list of substantives in the dative, each separated by an 'and' (καί) that describe aspects of each mountain. There are seven for Sinai: 'what is felt,' 'blazing fire,' 'darkness,' 'gloom,' 'tempest,' 'blast of trumpet,' and 'voice of words.' There are eight for Zion: 'Mount Zion,' 'city of the living God,' 'myriad of angels,' 'church of the firstborn,' 'God, the judge of all,' 'spirits of the righteous,' 'mediator of the new covenant,' and 'blood of sprinkling.'[109]

The exact nature of Mount Sinai is debated, which then entails the point(s) of the contrast between the two mountains. Some see a straightforward contrast between the old and new

---

109. Some argue that the καί preceding 'city of the living God,' should be understood as '*even* city of the living God' and not '*and* city of the living God.' This would then make seven substantives in the list for Mount Zion matching to the seven for Mount Sinai. So Hughes, *Hebrews*, 545; Lane, *Hebrews 9–13*, 441; and Kleinig, *Hebrews*, 642. I disagree because in *form* there are still seven versus eight καίs.

covenants,[110] or similarly, law and gospel.[111] Others see the contrast in more platonic terms between the physical and the spiritual.[112] I see the contrast as between *truncated* aspects of the Sinai events and the new covenant. The AH is emphasizing those who did not believe at Sinai and in the wilderness and their subsequent punishment (cf. Heb. 2:2; 3:16–4:2).[113] They did not see the gracious aspects of the Mosaic covenant that looked forward to the new. Several arguments in context favor a truncated understanding. (1) Hebrews 11 has Moses and several other heroes after Moses who are believers. (2) 'Spirits of the righteous' (Heb. 12:23) in the Mount Zion section refers to both OT and NT saints who have died. (3) Christ's blood is explicitly compared with Abel's and not the Mosaic legislation (Heb. 12:24). (4) Neither Mount Sinai nor the Mosaic Covenant are explicitly mentioned. (5) The somewhat poetical and contrasting parallel nature of this text probably implies it is more summative. And (6) the negative judgment motif is further expanded in Hebrews 12:25–28 with the understanding that those who refuse the new covenant will have great judgment showing that judgment is not restricted to the Mosaic economy.

Although all agree that Hebrews 12:18–24 is a coherent unity, how it fits into the flow of Hebrews 12 is somewhat debated. That is, exactly what is the implication of the conjunction 'for' (γάρ) in 12:18? Some relate it directly back to 12:14–17, giving a rationale as to why one should live in

---

110. So Chrysostom, 'Homily 32 on Hebrews' (*NPNF*[1], 14:510); and Hughes, *Hebrews*, 542.

111. So Aquinas, *Hebrews*, 284; Calvin, *Hebrews and 1 & 2 Peter*, 199; Beza's Confession 23 (*Reformed Confessions of the 16th and 17th Centuries*, 2:274), and Bruce, *Hebrews*, 354. Cf. Gal. 4:24–25.

112. So Moffatt, *Hebrews*, 214; James Thompson, *Hebrews*, Paideia (Grand Rapids: Baker Academic, 2008), 261–62; and Johnson, *Hebrews*, 329. For a useful critique of platonic views, see Gareth Lee Cockerill, 'Hebrews 12:18–24: Apocalyptic Typology or Platonic Dualism,' *TynBul* 69 (2018): 225–39.

113. Cockerill agrees, '[The AH] is not concerned with old and new, before and after, but with belief and unbelief, with apostasy and faithfulness' (*Hebrews*, 643). Also see similar discussion in Lenski, *Hebrews and James*, 450–51.

peace (Heb. 12:22–24) and not be susceptible to a punishment like Esau's (Heb. 12:15–17),[114] or more emphasizing the punishment aspect.[115] Others see 'for' as supporting the general thrust of Hebrews 11–12 as a further encouragement for endurance,[116] and/or supporting the general thrust of the whole epistle.[117] I see Hebrews 12:18–24, and then also including 12:25–29, as more of a broader encouragement toward endurance somewhat summarizing Hebrews 11–12. Of course, this broader encouragement would also include relating to Hebrews 12:14–17.

12:18–19 *For you have not approached*[118] *to what can be felt and blazing fire and darkness and gloom and tempest and blast of a trumpet and voice of words,*[119] *which*[120] *those having heard entreated [that] the word not continue to them.*

See above for the clear contrasting parallelism between Hebrews 12:18–21 and 12:22–24, what Mount Sinai represents, and the implications of **for**.

Although not named, here the AH refers to Mount Sinai and the events associated with it (cf. 'mountain'[121] in Heb. 12:20). These events are initially narrated in Exodus 19:16–20:21, where Israel is at the foot of Mount Sinai while God descends to the top of the mountain in the midst of natural phenomena that frighten the people. Moses goes up the mountain and is told the ten commandments. Following this, the people ask

---

114. So, e.g., Lane, *Hebrews 9–13*, 440.

115. So, e.g., Kleinig, *Hebrews*, 641.

116. So, e.g., Brown, *Hebrews*, 644; and Cockerill, *Hebrews*, 649 n. 34.

117. So, e.g., Owen, *Hebrews*, 23:306; and Schreiner, *Hebrews*, 395.

118. The verb προσέρχομαι ('to approach') when followed by a substantive is normally in the dative case (see BDAG, 878). Thus, **what can be felt**, **fire**, **darkness**, **gloom**, **tempest**, **blast**, and **voice** are all in the dative. For a discussion of the use of προσέρχομαι in Hebrews, see Heb. 4:16.

119. Greek has two common words for 'word.' Here **words** is plural of ῥῆμα and **word** is singular of λόγος.

120. **Voice** is clearly the antecedent of **which** as both are feminine singular.

121. Many Greek manuscripts also include 'mountain' following **what can be felt**. See Metzger, *TCGNT*², 605.

Moses not to allow God to speak directly to them. Moses then again recounts these events in Deuteronomy 4:9–14 and 5:22–27. At least in my view, Moses also includes one aspect (Moses' fear) from the subsequent golden calf episode that occurred at Mount Sinai. This episode is initially narrated in Exodus 32 and recounted again in Deuteronomy 9:13–21, with the key verse being Deuteronomy 9:19 (see discussion below at Heb. 12:21).

The AH characterizes the true Christians congregants as *not* **hav[ing] approached** or come to Mount Sinai with the emphasis on negative judgment and separation from God. Further confirming that Mount Sinai is intended is that several of the terms in Heb. 12:18–19 match the LXX.[122] The description **what can be felt** refers to the earthly reality of Mount Sinai and the command for the people not to touch it (Exod. 19:12–13, cf. Heb. 12:20). That is, the people had the ability to touch it, but they did not have permission. The AH is probably also indicating that Mount Sinai is *only* earthly, contrasting this with Christ's work that has both earthly and heavenly components (see discussion at Heb. 8:3–4).

The implied threat of negative judgment (**voice of words**) was so terrifying that in the historical event many of the Israelites **having heard** these words **entreated** God **that** his message/**word not continue** to be spoken **to them**. Here the AH paraphrases Exodus 20:19; Deuteronomy 4:12; and 5:23–27.

12:20–21 *For they did not bear the order, 'If a beast touches the mountain, it shall be stoned.' And the sight was so*[123] *terrifying, Moses said, 'I am terrified and trembling.'*

For gives the rationale for why the Israelites were afraid of God's message (**they did not bear the order**), it involved severe judgment at disobedience. With **'If a beast touches**

---

122. **Approach** (Deut. 4:11), **blazing fire** (Exod. 19:18; 20:18), **darkness** (Exod. 20:21; Deut. 4:11; cf. Exod. 10:22), **tempest** (Deut. 4:11; 5:22; cf. Exod. 10:22), **trumpet** (Exod. 19:13, 16, 19), and **voice of words** (Deut. 4:12).

123. Here οὕτως has the meaning of 'marker of a relatively high degree, *so*' as opposed to the more common 'thus' (BDAG, 741–42 [3]).

the mountain, it shall be stoned,' the AH paraphrases and truncates Exodus 19:12–13. He eliminates that if humans touch the mountain they also will be stoned or killed with a javelin/dart. Apparently, the AH is using a lesser-to-greater argument concerning the seriousness of the command and resulting judgment. If even a beast that wanders onto the mountain is to be killed, how much more is the seriousness if a human knowingly does it.[124]

Neither the Exodus 19:16–20:21 nor Deuteronomy 4:9–14 and 5:22–27 indicate explicitly that Moses was afraid. However, Deuteronomy 9:19 does state this explicitly, whose LXX wording matches Hebrews 19:21.[125] Hence, as noted above, I take the AH's comment concerning Moses' fear to be referring to the subsequent golden calf incident (Exod. 32; Deut. 9:13–21) that also occurred at Mount Sinai.[126] In sum, the **sight** of the natural phenomena at the mountain, whenever it occurred, was very **terrif[ying]** and emphasized God's judgment.

12:22–24 *But you have approached Mount Zion, and to the city of the living God, the heavenly Jerusalem, and myriads of angels in festive gathering, and the church of the firstborn having been enrolled in heaven, and God, the judge of all,*[127] *and the spirits of*

---

124. The Rabbinic document Mekilta (Bahodesh 3) debates whether only domestic animals or also wild animals were to be killed if they touched the mountain; similarly, whether men only or also women. It concludes that both domestic and wild animals are to be killed but only men are to be killed. Pope Innocent III in AD 1199 used this verse to preclude 'unlearned' people [beasts] from 'touching the sublimity of Sacred Scripture [mountain] or preach it to others' (*Cum ex Iniuncto* [Denzinger[43] §771]).

125. LXX Deut. 9:19, ἔκφοβός εἰμι διὰ τὴν ὀργὴν ('I am terrified on account of the anger'). Heb. 12:21, ἔκφοβός εἰμι καὶ ἔντρομος (**I am terrified and trembling**).

126. So also Cockerill, *Hebrews*, 650; and Schreiner, *Hebrews*, 398. *Contra* many that connect Moses' fear to Exod. 19:16–20:21. In these views, the AH makes assumptions from Exod. 19:16, or from the general assumption that one is afraid when meeting God, or from implications based on Exod. 3:6 and Acts 7:32; or from the Rabbinic tradition (based off of one cited reference, b. Shabbat 88b).

127. **God, the judge of all** could be translated as 'the judge, God of all'

the righteous having been perfected, and the mediator of the new[128] *covenant, Jesus, and the blood sprinkled, which speaks better than [the blood of] Abel.*

As opposed to negative judgment and separation from God associated with Mount Sinai, Hebrews 12:22-24 includes various glorious descriptions of the heavenly realities. **Mount Zion** is a joyous place that includes the Triune God, angels, and believers.

Most of these glorious descriptions are prominent in the Bible, and several have a particular emphasis in Hebrews: **Mount Zion** (see Reflections section below); **city of the living God** (Heb. 3:12; 9:14; 10:31; 11:10, 16; 14:14; Phil. 3:20; Rev. 3:12); **heavenly Jerusalem** (Heb. 3:1; 6:4; 8:5; 9:23; 11:16; Ps. 122:2; Gal. 4:26; Rev. 3:12; 21:2; 21:10); **myriad of angels in festive gathering** (Heb. 1:6, 14; Ezek. 46:11); **church of the firstborn** (Heb. 1:6; 2:12; 11:4, 28; Gen. 4:4; Exod. 4:22; Deut. 4:10; Jer. 31:9; cf. Heb. 12:16); **enrolled in heaven** (Exod. 32:32; Ps. 69:28; Isa. 4:3; Luke 10:20; Acts 13:48; Phil. 4:3; Rev. 21:27; cf. Heb. 10:7); **God the judge of all** (Heb. 9:27; Gen. 18:25; Ps. 68:5); **spirits of the righteous having been perfected**[129] (Heb. 10:38; 11:4; 12:9; 2 Cor. 5:8; Phil. 1:21; Rev. 14:13); **mediator of the new covenant, Jesus** (Heb. 8:6, 8, 13; 9:15, 17; Jer. 31:31; Luke 22:20; 1 Cor. 11:25; 2 Cor. 3:6; 1 Tim. 2:5); **blood sprinkled** (Heb. 9:12, 13, 19, 20; 10:22, 29; Exod. 24:8; Rom. 3:25; Col. 1:20; 1 Pet. 1:19; Rev. 1:5); and **the blood of Abel** (Heb. 11:4; Gen. 4:4, 10).

True believers **have approached Mount Zion**, that is, they have arrived. Although still on earth, they are still in some sense now part of the heavenly city. **Mount Zion** includes

---

as the Greek is somewhat ambiguous.

128. In Hebrews, the expression **new covenant** is used four times. Three use καινός for 'new' (8:8, 13; 9:15), and here it is νέος. Virtually all commentators see καινός and νέος as synonymous. Spicq (*Hébreux*, 2:409) and Westcott (*Hebrews*, 329) are exceptions who see the choice of νέος as intentional to stress the recent establishment as opposed to its character.

129. For a discussion of 'perfected' and cognates, see Heb. 5:9 for perfection of Christ and 7:11 for perfection of believers.

the **church** or assembly **of the firstborn**. The **firstborn** (plural in Greek) refers to all elect believers, both OT and NT, both the Church militant and triumphant (cf. Exod. 4:22).[130] This election is confirmed by their **having been enrolled in heaven**. Intriguingly, Christ *the* 'firstborn' (Heb. 1:6, singular in Greek) is head of the **firstborn**. The description of **God** as **the judge of all** at first glance seems out of place if this solely refers to negative judgment. Here, however, **judge** emphasizes the positive and vindicating judgments God makes relative to believers due to context. The **spirits** (souls) **of the righteous having been perfected** refers to all OT believers and those NT believers who have died (i.e., the intermediate state, the Church triumphant).[131] They are **perfected** in the sense that at this point in redemptive history they are at the pinnacle; however, they are awaiting a further perfection of glorified bodies in the NHNE (cf. Heb. 13:14).

The last two items in the list are **mediator** and **blood**. Believers have come to **Jesus**, who is the **mediator of the new covenant**. The AH has already discussed several aspects of Christ's mediatorial role, but here he re-emphasizes Christ's **blood** that was typologically **sprinkled** (cf. Heb. 9:15–22). Christ's redemptive activity gives the ground as to why believers, both OT and NT, **have**/will-have **approached Mount Zion**. Thus, possibly for emphasis, **Jesus** is mentioned last in this glorious list.

Upon the mention of Christ's **blood**, the AH comments **which** (Christ's blood) **speaks better than the blood of Abel**. Note, the AH does not compare it to the blood in the Mosaic

---

130. So also the vast majority of commentators, e.g., Owen, *Hebrews*, 23:338; Attridge, *Hebrews*, 375; Lane, *Hebrews 9–13*, 469; and Johnson, *Hebrews*, 332. *Contra* Aquinas who understood **firstborn** as the Apostles (*Hebrews*, 288); Calvin as prominent OT believers (*Hebrews and 1 & 2 Peter*, 201); and Moffatt as only the Church militant (*Hebrews*, 217).

131. So also the vast majority of commentators, e.g., Calvin, *Hebrews and 1 & 2 Peter*, 201; Hodge, *Hebrews*, 135; Lenski, *Hebrews and James*, 458; Moffitt, *Atonement and the Logic of Resurrection*, 210–11; Cockerill, *Hebrews*, 656–57, and the Westminster Standards (WCF 32.1; WLC 86; WSC 37).

Covenant, further confirming that the two mountains do not represent per se the old and new covenants. Curiously, he does compare it to **the blood of Abel**. **Abel** has been previously mentioned in Hebrews 11:4 with the comment that he 'yet speaks' in the sense that his faith and faith-driven-actions (not his death) are recorded in Scripture. Here, the AH picks up on God's statement to Cain, 'the voice of the blood of your brother [Abel] is crying out to me [God]' (Gen. 4:10). Yes, **the blood of Abel** had/has some level of effectiveness in its 'crying out,' but Christ's **blood** that metaphorically **speaks** is qualitatively **better** because it has ultimate effectiveness.[132] I assume one reason to bring up **Abel** here is to connect back to the beginning of the heroes-of-faith chapter showing all true believers, OT and NT, are included in **Mount Zion**.

Hebrews 12:22–24 is useful for partially seeing the AH's sweep of redemptive history and his understanding of the heavenly city. **Mount Zion** in some sense existed in the OT and exists now (and will into the future NHNE). Further, the 'now' component has both earthly and heavenly aspects, especially with the phrase **you have approached** in the sense of have arrived at **Mount Zion**, while still living on earth.[133] It is also clearly shown that Christ's work effects both OT and NT believers.

Reflections

Within the Scriptures, 'Mount Zion' is an evocative term. It is associated with Jerusalem, the temple, the people of God, the Davidic kingdom, joy (usually[134]), the presence of God,

---

132. Commentators differ significantly on the implications from **blood of Abel**. Although I disagree with his conclusions, see Kyu Seop Kim for a good summary of options ('Better than the Blood of Abel? Some Remakes on Abel in Hebrews 12:24,' *TynBul* 67 [2016]: 127–36).

133. As to the now/not-yet aspect, see also G. K. Beale, *A New Testament Biblical Theology*, 320–21; and Grässer, *Hebräer*, 3:310–11. For a discussion of the redemptive-historical time-line in Hebrews, see my 'Covenant in Hebrews,' 249–51.

134. There are a number of verses especially in Lamentations and

and eschatological realities (e.g., 1 Kgs. 8:1; Pss. 2:6; 110:2;[135] 48:2; 87:2; 133:3; Isa. 8:18; 62:11; Joel 3:16–17; Zeph. 3:16; Zech. 9:9; Rom. 11:26; 1 Pet. 2:6; Rev. 14:1).[136] 'Zion' is like a loving nickname one spouse gives to another. For example, 'my sweetheart,' which is intended not only to refer to one's spouse but to evoke positive emotional connotations about the spouse. Fittingly, the AH uses 'Mount Zion' as the starting point for his joyous description of the heavenly realities—'you have approached Mount Zion.'

'Zion' was originally the name of the stronghold of the Jebusites that David conquered and renamed Jerusalem (2 Sam. 5:7). As the city expanded, the ark was placed and then the temple was built upon a higher elevation to which the name Zion or Mount Zion was also given (e.g., 1 Kgs. 8:1; 2 Kgs. 19:31; Pss. 48:2; 132:13). Hence, both Jerusalem broadly and the temple mount specifically were termed 'Zion' or 'Mount Zion.'[137] In addition, given the location, the term 'Zion' also was semantically extended to denote the people of God (e.g., Pss. 87:2; 125:1; 133:3; Isa. 34:8). Given the temple location, 'Zion' also became the metaphorical location of God's presence and redemptive activity (e.g., Isa. 28:16; 33:5; 52:8–9; Jer. 31:6–7; Mic. 4:2–3).

Jeremiah that use Zion to evoke negative emotions in lament and/or pending judgment contexts. These verses presuppose a positive view of Zion that then makes the negative comments so devastating (e.g., Jer. 9:19; 26:18; Lam. 1:4; 2:1; 5:18).

135. Pss. 2 and 110 are quoted elsewhere in Hebrews although not these specific verses.

136. Although overlapping with my summary to some degree, John T. Strong summarizes OT Zion under three interrelated headings: 'The Lord is the Great King,' 'The Great King-Protector,' and 'The Great King-Provider' ('Zion: Theology of,' *NIDOTTE*, 4:1314–21); and Jon D. Levenson summarizes the theology of OT Zion under three different headings, 'Enthronement after Victory,' 'The Election of Zion and David,' and 'Visions of Peace,' ('Zion Traditions,' *ABD*, 6:1098–102).

137. The city of Jerusalem itself is in essence a small mountain ranging in elevation from 2,100 to 2,500 feet. The temple mount has an elevation of 2,400 feet.

Two of my favorite hymns include 'Zion'. The first, words by John Newton sung to Hayden's 'Austrian Hymn,' begins 'Glorious Things of Thee are Spoken, Zion, City of our God.' Here, 'Thee,' 'Zion,' and 'City' all refer to the church. These opening words are a reworking of Psalm 87:1–3.

The second is more specific to my denomination, the Associate Reformed Presbyterian Church. The denomination was founded in 1782 and its founding documents require that 'all Judicatories, Sessions excepted, are to close their meetings, after prayer, with singing the 133d or some other Psalm, and pronouncing the Apostolic Benediction.'[138] Every 'stated' presbytery meeting and every annual denominational meeting (Synod) that I have attended since 1984 has ended with singing the same version of Psalm 133, which is entitled 'Christian Unity.'[139] It emphasizes the joy of Christian unity and the joy of Christians simply physically being together. As does the Psalm, it mentions 'Zion's hills,' which represents simultaneously the city of Jerusalem and the people of God. And it is there in Zion that 'the blessing God commands, Life that shall never end.'

Endurance: With Reverence and Awe (12:25–29)

Hebrews 12:25–29 completes the unit of 12:1–29. It is normally designated as the final "warning" passage (i.e., warning of apostasy), with the others being 2:1–4; 3:12–19; 6:4–6; and 10:26–31.[140]

Concerning the flow of the Hebrews 12:25–29, it is split into two sections, 12:25–27 and 12:28–29. The first section

---

138. *Constitution and Standards of the Associate-Reformed Church in North America*, 583.

139. #280 in *Bible Songs* (Due West: ARP Board of Publication, 1931) and #197 in *The ARP Psalter with Bible Songs* (Pittsburgh, Crown & Covenant, 2011). Tune is 'Ortonville' by Thomas Hastings.

140. See extended discussion at Heb. 6:4–8 concerning apostasy.

is the warning per se; the second section based on an implication from the first is an exhortation to be grateful by worshiping God properly. More specifically, the first section begins with an explicit warning ('see that you do not refuse the one speaking') and includes a lesser-to-greater argument comparing the Sinai/wilderness warnings to the current warning. This is partially explained by using a quote from Haggai 2:6 that relates the warning to 'shaking', which also includes that eternal things will not be destroyed by the shaking. The second section makes an implication from the eternally remaining kingdom of Christ. The true Christian is exhorted to gratefully worship God in 'reverence and awe.'

12:25 *See[141] [that] you do not refuse the one speaking; for if those who refused the one who warned upon earth did not escape, [how] much more will we, those turning away from him [who warns] from heaven, [not escape],*

Picking up on the metaphorical language that Christ's blood 'speaks' from the previous verse, here the AH refers to **the one speaking**, that is, God.[142] God spoke through Moses at Mount Sinai and in the wilderness (**upon earth**), and he now speaks through his Son (**from heaven**). This well matches Hebrews 1:1–2 (cf. Heb. 2:1–4; 4:12–13). The emphasis here as to what God spoke/speaks is the warnings about apostasy (**the one who warned**).

---

141. **See** in the sense of 'watch out.' Cf. Heb. 3:12 for the same verb (βλέπω) and very similar usage and context.

142. The majority of interpreters see God as being **the one who speaks** (e.g., Calvin, *Hebrews and 1 & 2 Peter*, 202; Brown, *Hebrews*, 656–9; Hughes, *Hebrews*, 555; Lane, *Hebrews 9–13*, 476; Johnson, *Hebrews*, 334; Allen, *Hebrews*, 595; and Gene R. Smillie, '"The One Who Is Speaking" In Hebrews 12:25,' *TynBul* 55 [2004]: 275–94). Chrysostom ('Homily 32 on Hebrews' [*NPNF*[1], 14:512]) and Moffatt (*Hebrews*, 220) opt for Moses being the **upon earth** speaker. A portion of the Reformed tradition sees Christ as the ultimate speaker both at Sinai and now (Owen, *Hebrews*, 23:353–56; Gouge, *Hebrews*, 1008; WSC 23; WLC 151 [?]). For a modern argument that Christ is the speaker, see Daniel J. Treier, "Speech Acts, Hearing Hearts, and Other Senses," in *The Epistle to the Hebrews and Christian Theology*, 337–50, esp. 346–49.

The AH uses a lesser-to-greater argument to add to the seriousness of the warning. **For if those who refused the one who warned upon earth did not escape, how much more will we, those turning away from him who warns from heaven, not escape**. Although in principle this warning would include all warnings throughout the OT, here the AH primarily refers to Sinai and the wilderness events, as the next verse will make clear (cf. Heb. 3:16–4:2). The verb **escape** (ἐκφεύγω) is the same one used in Hebrews 2:3, which also has a very similar context. The point is that if apostasy in the wilderness was punished, **how much more** will apostasy from the even clearer new covenant revelation be punished.

12:26–27 *whose voice shook the earth then but now has promised saying, 'Yet once more I will cause to quake not only the earth but also the heaven.' And this*[143] *'yet once more' signifies the removal of things shaken, as [things] having been made, in order that the things not shaken remain.*

To reinforce both that the warnings have consequences (**signifies the removal of things shaken**) and the lesser-to-greater aspect (**then but now, yet once more**), the AH uses the concept of shaking. Shaking in general implies that non-fixed or non-permanent items will fall and be destroyed.

Whose (God's) **voice shook** (σαλεύω) **the earth** is in reference to God's descending upon Mount Sinai. Among other things, 'the whole mountain shook violently' (Exod. 19:18, cf. Ps. 68:8).[144] The AH continues the shaking theme by quoting Haggai 2:6 (cf. Hag. 2:21), **'Yet once more I** (Lord of hosts) **will**

---

143. The quote is introduced by the neuter article, which I translated as **this**. For more on this usage, see Turner, *Syntax*, 182.

144. This clause in Exod. 19:18 is in the Hebrew Bible but not in the LXX. One implication of this is to further confirm that the AH did not use the LXX slavishly, or at least the version we understand to be the LXX. Relevant usage of the Greek 'to shake' (σαλεύω) in the LXX includes Judg. 5:5; Pss. 18:7; 77:18; and 114:7; for 'to cause to quake' (σείω), Judg. 5:4; Ps. 68:8; Isa. 33:20; Ezek. 38:20; Dan. 2:20; and Hag. 2:6, 21. The Rabbinic Mekilta connects the shaking mountain of Exod. 19:18 to Judg. 5:5 and Ps. 68:17 (Bahodesh 4).

cause to quake (σείω) not only the earth but also the heaven.'[145] In the context of Haggai 2:1–9, this shaking/quaking is aimed at the nations so that the 'treasures of the nations' (Hag. 2:7) will aid in making the glory of the second temple greater than the first and confirm that God is with Israel. Later in the book, using similar language, the shaking will 'overthrow the throne of kingdoms' and make Zerubbabel 'like a signet ring' (Hag. 2:20–23). These prophecies (**has promised**) had partial fulfillment in the rebuilding of the temple and Zerubbabel's leadership, but they have ultimate fulfillment in the kingdom of Christ (Heb. 12:28) and the defeat of his enemies. The AH understands the final shaking (**yet once more**) to be the final judgment.[146]

Exactly what does the AH mean by **heaven** in **I will cause to quake not only the earth but also the heaven**? In Haggai, it clearly means the created heavens as in Genesis 1:1. I also take it to mean that here.[147] The point being that not only will God shake certain places on earth (e.g., Mount Sinai, nations), but he will shake the whole created universe. How do I explain that this seems to be a different use than 'from heaven' in the previous verse? (1) The AH is using **heaven** from a quote which modifies the context, (2) the shaking for possible negative

---

145. The LXX follows fairly closely the Hebrew. Minor changes are that the LXX dropped 'little while,' changed the verb to finite as opposed to a participle, and has 'heaven' as singular as opposed to plural. The AH follows the LXX by dropping 'little while,' but deletes 'and the sea and dry ground' which is in both the Hebrew and LXX, and reverses and expands the Hebrew/LXX's 'the heaven and the earth' to 'not only the earth but also the heaven.' In the similar Hag. 2:21, note that the Hebrew has the shortened 'the heavens and the earth' while the LXX has 'the heaven, and the earth, and the sea, and the dry ground.'

146. So most commentators. A few take it as Christ's first coming as this dovetails with their view that Christ is the one speaking (e.g., Owen, *Hebrews*, 23:364; and Gouge, *Hebrews*, 1008). The concept of shaking is often associated with eschatological judgment in OT pseudepigraphic literature, e.g., Sib. Or. 3:675; 4 Ezra 6:14–16; 10:26; 2 Bar. 32:3–3; 59:3.

147. So also Bruce, *Hebrews*, 364–65; Hughes, *Hebrews*, 558; Grässer, *Die Hebräer*, 3:331–32; Cockerill, *Hebrews*, 666; and Schreiner, *Hebrews*, 406. *Contra* Lane, *Hebrews 9–13*, 479–80; and Koester, *Hebrews*, 547.

judgment of the new covenant heavens does not make clear sense, and (3) matches 'heavens' in Hebrews 1:10–12.

This future shaking (**and this 'yet once more'**), that is, eschatological judgment, will result in both (1) **the removal of things shaken** (negative judgment) and (2) the **remain[ing]** of **things not** able to be **shaken** (the current and future new covenant realities).

As many acknowledge, **as things having been made** is a difficult phrase. I take it as created things qualified by **the removal of things shaken**; thus meaning created things that do *not* have permanence (cf. Heb. 9:11). Or to say it another way, I do see most, but not all, of the current creation completely destroyed in all senses. However, there are some permanent things that will remain, although even they will be significantly transformed as part of the NHNE (e.g., believers' bodies).[148]

12:28–29 *So then since we are receiving an unshakable kingdom, let us be grateful by which let us acceptably offer worship*[149] *to God with reverence and awe, for indeed*[150] *our God is a consuming fire.*

The new covenant realities are the **unshakable kingdom**[151] of Christ. These realities in some sense existed in the OT, exist now, and will exist into the NHNE. Given this (**so then**), the AH urges true believers **let us be grateful**.[152] This **kingdom**

---

148. Within evangelical and Reformed theology, there is disagreement as to what portion of the current world will be part of the NHNE. I tend to be on the more minimalistic side.

149. The verb in Greek (λατρεύω) may mean generically 'serve,' or more specifically **offer worship** and 'worshiper' (substantival participle). Given its usage elsewhere in Hebrews referring to literal service by a priest or a worshiper in a tabernacle or typological tabernacle context (Heb. 8:5; 9:9, 14; 10:2; 13:10), I translate here as **offer worship** (and as a hortatory subjunctive). This is confirmed by the cognate noun λατρεία ('worship') in Heb. 9:1 and 9:6.

150. I am taking καί as an intensive; so the translation **indeed**.

151. For **kingdom** connections in Hebrews, see 1:8 and 11:33; cf. Hag. 2:22. This then naturally connects to many of the 'Son' and royal texts in Hebrews (e.g., Heb. 1:5, 13; 2:8; 5:5).

152. The Greek is ἔχωμεν χάριν. This is a hortatory subjunctive with χάριν

and Christ's work for us should produce a **grateful** attitude. In turn, this **grateful** attitude (**by which**[153]) should drive us toward, among many other spiritual activities, **acceptably offer[ing] worship to God**.[154] **Worship** here includes corporate worship (cf. Heb. 10:25; 12:22–25; 13:7) and most likely also private worship (cf. Rom. 12:1). What a fitting dual exhortation with which to end chapter 12. **Let us be grateful**, and as a result **let us acceptably offer worship to God**.

By the prepositional phrase **with reverence and awe**, the AH gives at least a partial explanation of **acceptably**. **Reverence** (εὐλάβεια)[155] here clearly means the appropriate attitude of a believer due a magnificent God who has made Mount Sinai quake, prepared the heavenly Mount Zion, is able to shake the universe, and is in fact a **consuming fire**. **Awe** (δέος) in most Greco-Roman contexts has the meaning of 'alarm,' 'fear,' or '[having] reason for fear.'[156] It is a rare word in biblical literature, and due to the context here, moves from being afraid of negative consequences to **awe**.[157] There

---

being idiomatic for **grateful** as opposed to the full import of 'grace'. So most modern commentators and modern English Bible translations. For idiomatic use, see Luke 17:9; 1 Tim. 1:12; and 2 Tim. 1:3. For 'let us have grace,' see Acts 2:47; 2 Cor. 1:15; so Spicq, *Hébreux*, 2:412–13; and KJV. Although in the end in this context, the difference between the two is slight.

153. In Greek, **which** is feminine referring back to **grateful** which is feminine.

154. DeSilva sees significant connections between a believer's **gratitude** to God and the Greco-Roman patron-client social custom (*Hebrews*, 473–77). For Pauline interpretation and here, I think these connections are overdone in NT scholarship.

155. As most agree, the translation **reverence** is appropriate as it combines the connotations of respect, amazement, and appropriate 'fear' (in the OT sense of a believer 'fearing God'). The noun and cognate adjective are not that common in biblical literature. The noun εὐλάβεια only occurs in the LXX/NT in Josh. 22:24; Prov. 28:14; Wis. 17:8; Heb. 5:7 (see discussion there); and 12:28. The adjective εὐλαβής only occurs in the LXX/NT in Lev. 15:31; Mic. 7:2; Luke 2:25; Acts 2:5; 8:2; and 22:12. The cognate verb εὐλαβέομαι does occur 38 times in the LXX, although many of them are unrelated to God; and only once in the NT in Heb. 11:7.

156. LSJ, 379.

157. The only occurrence of δέος in the NT is here. The only occurrences in the LXX are in 2 Macc. 3:17, 20, 12:22; 13:16; 15:23). It occurs 139 times in

is an intriguing overlap of **reverence and awe** with Paul's use of 'fear and trembling' in Philippians 2:12 (cf. 1 Cor. 2:3; 2 Cor. 7:15; Eph. 6:5). As many have pointed out, **reverence and awe** are ultimately internal motivations; hence, proper worship of God must include correct motives.[158]

The clause **for indeed our God is a consuming fire**, which is quoted/alluded to from Deuteronomy 4:24, has generated a modicum of debate. Grammatically, this is at least one motivational ground (**for**) to encourage the covenant community toward grateful and acceptable worship. The debate concerns the logical connection between **God is a consuming fire**, which most take as God's negative judgment upon unbelievers, and the motivation for believers to worship God.

Before going further, I will consider the context of the OT quote(s)/allusions and the broader use of judgment fire in Hebrews. In Deuteronomy 4:15–24, Moses exhorts the Israelites before entering Canaan not to forget the covenant they made with the Lord, and more specifically, not to make idols. Moses ends this discussion with 'For the Lord your God is a consuming fire, he is a jealous God' (Deut. 4:24).[159] God's being 'jealous' shows that he desires worship solely of himself as confirmed by its reference in the second commandment (Exod. 20:4–6; Deut. 5:8–10; cf. Exod. 34:14).[160] In the Deuteronomy 4 context, God's being a 'consuming fire'

Josephus, and 41 times in Philo. All of these occurrences are probably best translated as 'fear' or 'alarm' (cf. LEH, 99).

158. So, e.g., Aquinas, *Hebrews*, 293; and Calvin, *Hebrews and 1 & 2 Peter*, 203. WCF 21.3 and 21.5 reference Heb. 12:28 regarding internal motivations in worship.

159. The LXX matches very well to the Hebrew. The AH adds the intensive **indeed**, changes 'your' to **our,** and does not include 'the Lord' nor 'he is a jealous God.'

160. Craigie, commenting on this verse, notes the connections between God's covenant and his love. Thus he concludes, 'Jealousy . . . is, as it were, the reverse of love' (Craigie, *Deuteronomy*, 138). See Rabbinic discussion concerning Deut. 4:24 as to whether God is more jealous against a human who worships an idol or the idol itself (b. Avodah Zarah 54b–55a).

is at some level a statement of the reality of punishment for abandoning the covenant by improper worship but also an affirmation of God's desire for his people to properly worship. The expression 'consuming fire' is also in Deuteronomy 9:3. Moses encourages the Israelites to cross the Jordan because God as a consuming fire goes before them and will destroy their enemies. The same 'consuming fire' is also mentioned in Exodus 24:17 where God's glory on Mount Sinai is compared to it.[161] Isaiah 33:14 uses this expression in the context of God's negative judgment.[162] In Psalm 50:3, 'God comes ... a fire before him consuming,' the context here is judgment, both positive and negative.[163] In sum of OT usage of 'consuming fire,' it shows God's glory, his power, and his zeal for proper worship. This power may be used as negative judgment against those within the covenant community (improper worship) and those outside of it (improperly fighting against God's people) and in one text as both positive and negative judgment (Psalm 50).

Within Hebrews (and the entire NT), the exact expression **consuming fire** (πῦρ καταναλίσκω) only occurs here. There are, however, two other conceptually similar statements in Hebrews: 'thorns and thistles ... which the end is to be burned (καῦσις)' (Heb. 6:8); and 'there remains a certain fearful expectation of judgment and a zeal of fire (πῦρ) that will consume (ἐσθίω) the adversaries' (Heb. 10:27). Both of these clearly deal with negative judgment upon unbelievers, which in the context of Hebrews includes those not worshiping God through his Son. There are two other uses of 'fire' in Hebrews: Mount Sinai is described as a 'blazing fire' (καίω

---

161. Linguistically, the Hebrew of Exod. 24:17 has the same 'consuming fire' (אש אכלת/ה) as Deut. 4:24 and 9:3, although in Exod. 24:17 the LXX has 'flaming' (φλέγω) as opposed to καταωαλίσκω in Deut. 4:24; 9:3; and Heb. 12:29. Of course, one cannot help to think of the burning bush that was not consumed (Exod. 3:1–6).

162. Similar to Exod. 24:17, Isa. 33:14 linguistically has the same 'consuming fire' (אש אכלה), but the LXX has 'burning' (καίω).

163. The Hebrew matches to Deut. 4:24 (אש־לפניו תאכל), although the LXX has 'burning' (καίω).

πῦρ); and angels are described as God's 'ministers a flame a fire' (πῦρ φλόξ). These are not as clearly related to judgment but do dovetail with it.

Given both the OT and Hebrews contexts, it is fairly clear that **consuming fire** in Hebrews 12:29 refers at some level to an acknowledgement of judgment upon unbelievers. Many see this as the primary or sole point.[164] That is, believers' **reverence and awe** are increased when one realizes what the consequences are for turning away from God. This also matches the context of the warning of apostasy. Further, the Bible often puts together that God is both (1) merciful and (2) holy in his negative judgment. Calvin ends his discussion of this verse with a quasi-quote of Exodus 34:6–7 showing well both God's mercy and his judgment.[165] I have a slightly different view in *this* context. I acknowledge that the expression **consuming fire** presupposes God's judgment on unbelievers, but I view this as a secondary background point here, which would apply to those in the covenant community who are not true believers. The primary point, however, is to consider God's mercy through the 'mediator of the new covenant,' given God's holiness and punishment of those who reject him.[166] That is, knowledge of our sins and the punishment due them (**God is a consuming fire**) further drives us **to be grateful** that our undeserved redemption was mercifully provided for by the sacrificial blood of Christ (cf. Rom. 11:22). Yes, our motivation to worship the Triune God is increased when we consider what we truly deserved (**God is a consuming fire**) and simultaneously understand what he did to provide our salvation. This better explains the conjunction **for** with its grammatical connection to **let us be grateful**, along with *our* **God** and the intensive **indeed**. Our

---

164. So, e.g., Owen, *Hebrews*, 377; Moffatt, *Hebrews*, 223; Attridge, *Hebrews*, 383; and Koester, *Hebrews*, 562.

165. Calvin, *Hebrews and 1 & 2 Peter*, 203.

166. So also Bruce, *Hebrews*, 366; Cockerill, *Hebrews*, 673; Lindars, *Theology of the Letter to the Hebrews*, 117; and Schreiner, *Hebrews*, 407.

glorious God who is all powerful and zealous for worship has been and is merciful to us in an amazing manner through the priestly work of Christ. Yes, we should **offer worship to God with reverence and awe**!

Reflections

The AH encourages his readers, 'let us be grateful' and thus by this gratitude 'let us acceptably offer worship to God with reverence and awe' (Heb. 12:28). The word 'grateful' could easily be translated as 'thankful'.

Although not referencing Hebrews 12:28, the Heidelberg Catechism (AD 1563) uses 'thankfulness' as its primary motivation for good works. In doing so, this matches well to this biblical text. (Of course, in the Bible there are many motivations to do good works, and thankfulness is an important one.)

There are two important questions/answers in the Heidelberg Catechism that relate to this thankfulness (also see Q/A 28 and 116). Q/A 2 sets up the whole Catechism into three major sections. It reads, 'How many things are necessary for you to know, that in this comfort you may live and die happily? Three things: First, the greatness of my sin and misery [Q/A 3–11]. Second, how I am redeemed from all my sins and misery [Q/A 12–85]. Third, how I am to be *thankful* to God for such redemption [Q/A 86–129]' (emphasis mine).

Q/A 86 is the beginning of the *thankfulness* section. It reads,

> Since, then, we are redeemed from our misery by grace through Christ, without any merit of ours, why must we do good works? Because Christ, having redeemed us by his blood, renews us also by his Holy Spirit after his own image, that with our whole life we show ourselves *thankful* to God for his blessing, and that he be glorified through us, then also, that we may be assured of our faith by the fruits thereof; and by our godly walk also win others to Christ.[167]

---

167. Translations from *Reformed Confessions of the 16th and 17th Centuries*, 2:771, 789. Emphasis mine.

The thankfulness section then primarily covers the ten commandments and the Lord's Prayer.

For the readers and me, may *thankfulness* of God's great mercy be a wonderful motivation for us to live for God.

12.
Ending Exhortations and Closing (13:1–25)

Chapter 13 of Hebrews contains a variety of exhortations followed by a typical letter closing. A common breakdown of the chapter is to see the staccato list of exhortations in 13:1–6 as a unit. This is followed by a looser list of exhortations in 13:7–17 that begin and end referring to 'leaders' and also includes comments about Christ and attending exhortations. Finally, the AH ends with a closing in 13:18–25 that is fairly typical of letters. This closing does include some exhortations, although ones that are personally related to the AH, an expanded benediction, greetings, and ends with a brief grace benediction.[168]

It is noted by all that Hebrews 13 represents a change in the flow of the letter. Many term this chapter as a 'postscript.'[169] Previous to chapter 13, the letter contains many exhortations, but they are primarily related to encouraging (and warning) the readers to continue their faith in the great Christ and his work. This main thrust of the letter may be reasonably said to end

---

168. As to the outline of Heb. 13:1–6, 7–17, 18–25, so also, Cockerill, *Hebrews*, 676. Vanhoye has 13:1–6, 7–19, 20–25 (*Structure and Message of the Epistle to the Hebrews*, 40b, 107–9).

169. So, e.g., Moffatt, *Hebrews*, 224; Spicq, *Hébreux*, 2:415; and Hughes, *Hebrews*, 561. Schreiner terms it an 'epilogue' (*Hebrews*, 409).

with Hebrews 12:18–29. The exhortations in chapter 13 include more explicitly 'practical' exhortations (e.g., hospitality [13:2], obey leaders [13:17]). Although on the other hand, there are exhortations that well match those of the previous chapters (e.g., do not follow strange teachings [13:9], let us go to Christ who is outside the camp [13:13]; no lasting city [13:14]). Also, some of the 'practical' exhortations relate back to previous topics (e.g., visit prisoners [13:3 with 10:34]; avoid sexual sins [13:4 with 12:16]). In addition to these exhortations that relate back to chapters 1–12, chapter 13 contains examples of similar OT usage (e.g., exemplary use of Abraham [13:2] similar to Hebrews 11),[170] Day of Atonement implications [13:11–12]), and explicit OT quotes [13:5–6]). Hence, from my perspective, it is an overstatement to call this a postscript. I see chapter 13 as typical of many NT letters where following the main doctrinal section(s) that include explicit or implied exhortations, a list of more explicit exhortations are included that include both generic exhortations relevant to any church in the Greco-Roman world and also more specific exhortations appropriate to the church addressed (e.g., 1 Thess. 4–5; Eph. 4–6; 2 Pet. 3:14–18).[171] In sum, the fairly integrated nature of chapter 13 with chapters 1–12 and the matching of other typical letters argues against a 'postscript.'

Of course, if an interpreter believes that the same author wrote all of Hebrews as I do, then the differences between my view and labeling chapter 13 a 'postscript' are significantly reduced. Although most critical scholars do conclude that the

---

170. David L. Allen sees the exemplary use of OT characters in Heb. 13:1–8 with its connection to Heb. 11 as proof that the same author wrote all of Hebrews ('Constructing "Janus-Faced" Exhortations: The Use of the Old Testament Narratives in Heb 13:1–8,' *Bib* 89 [2008]: 401–09). I agree with his conclusion, but I think he overstates the case.

171. So also Owen, *Hebrews*, 23:379; and Bruce, *Hebrews*, 367. Koester (*Hebrews*, 554–56) and Cockerill (*Hebrews*, 674–76) also argue that chapter 13 is intimately connected and not a postscript, but they do so based on chapter 13 being a 'peroration' (an ending from rhetorical speech categories) and the logical implications of God's holiness from Heb. 12:28–29.

author of chapters 1–12 also wrote chapter 13,[172] a persistent minority continues to question the authorship of chapter 13.[173] At a minimum, the integration of themes from chapters 1–12 within chapter 13 and the practice for normal letters to exhibit concluding exhortations confirm the same author wrote all thirteen chapters.

Ending Exhortations: First Group (13:1–6)

Hebrews 13:1–6 contains a staccato list of eight imperatives/exhortations (13:1–5b) followed by two OT quotes (Josh. 1:5 and Ps. 118:6 // 13:5c–6). The two OT quotes relate to the seventh and eighth imperatives. The second OT quote is an additional exhortation, although implied. The eight explicit imperatives/exhortations and one implicit are:

(1) Let brotherly love continue.
(2) Do not neglect hospitality.
(3) Remember the prisoners.
(4) [Remember] those being mistreated.
(5) Let marriage be considered honorable.
(6) Let the [marriage] bed be undefiled.
(7) Let [your] manner be not loving money.
(8) Be content with present things.
(9) Say 'The Lord is my helper....' (implicit)

For most of the above, there are no conjunctions connecting them (asyndeton). This adds to the staccato sense. Although three of these nine are *grammatically* linked together in some way. Three and four are linked because the imperative 'remember' in three is not repeated for four but is grammatically

---

172. So, e.g., Clarence Russel Williams, 'A Word-Study of Hebrews 13,' *JBL* 30 (1911): 129–36; Attridge, *Hebrews*, 384; and F. V. Filson, *'Yesterday': a Study of Hebrews in Light of Chapter 13* (London: SCM, 1967).

173. So, e.g., A. J. M. Wedderburn, 'The "Letter" to the Hebrews and Its Thirteenth Chapter,' *NTS* 50 (2004): 390–405; and Gert J. Steyn, 'The Ending of Hebrews Reconsidered,' *ZNW* 103 (2012): 235–53 (this article mostly deals with Heb. 13:22–25).

required. Five and six are linked by the conjunction 'and'. Nine is grammatically linked to seven and eight by 'for'.

In addition to the three explicit grammatical connections, several of the nine are linked *conceptually* with no grammatical markers. Seven and eight are obviously a unit related to material possessions. Two, three, and four are reasonably connected as they relate to helping those in need. The order of five / six (marriage) is related to seven / eight (material possessions) as they follow the order of the seventh (adultery) and eighth commandments (stealing).

Are these exhortations specific to the congregation's situation or more general related to any church in the Greco-Roman world or some combination? As noted in the section above concerning chapter 13, there are several clear connections back to chapters 1–12 (e.g., prisoners). On the other hand, several of these exhortations would easily apply anywhere in the Greco-Roman world (e.g., hospitality, marriage). Thus for me, it seems that these exhortations in Hebrews 13:1–6 are some combination. No matter where one comes out on this question, the exegesis per se is not affected that much. Where it could matter more is if one assumes these exhortations are very specific, then one's conclusions about the original audience would be reasonably affected.

13:1 *Let brotherly love continue.*

The AH begins his moral exhortations with **brotherly love** (φιλαδελφία[174]), which is a common exhortation in the NT (Rom. 12:10; 1 Thess. 4:9; 1 Pet. 1:22; 2 Pet. 1:7; cf. Ps. 133:1; Rom. 9:1–5; 1 Pet. 2:17; 1 John 4:20).[175] This is a broad command and is fitting for an opening exhortation. By using **continue**, the AH acknowledges that the congregants are reasonably exhibiting this love.

---

174. This is a combination of 'love' (φιλέω) and 'brother' (ἀδελφός). The city name 'Philadelphia' (Rev. 1:11; 3:7) is obviously related, although with a slightly different spelling in Greek (Φιλαδέλφεια).

175. Whether intentionally or not by the AH, this command is rooted in the OT's 'love your neighbor as yourself' (Lev. 19:18) and Jesus' related comments (Matt. 22:37–40).

Brotherly here and elsewhere in the NT refers to other believers, not biological siblings. Specific to Hebrews, 'brother(s)' is used ten times. Notable is Christ's statement that he is not ashamed to call believers 'brothers' and had to be made like them (2:11–12, 17). Also, the AH terms the congregation 'holy brothers' (3:1) and refers to 'our brother Timothy' (13:23). Of course, 'brothers' implies as appropriate brothers and sisters (cf. αδελφή, Rom. 16:1; 1 Cor. 7:15; Jas. 2:15).

The rhetorical punch of using the term 'brothers' for non-biological siblings is heightened when compared to the use of 'brotherly love' in non-Christian circles in the Jewish and Greco-Roman world. Intriguingly, 'brotherly love' (φιλαδελφία) was often commented upon in these contexts, but it (virtually?) always referred to biological siblings.[176] Plutarch's *On Brotherly Love* (Περὶ Φιλαδελφηίας) is well known and a prime example.[177] He lived from AD 46–119, during which time Hebrews was written. The use of **brotherly love** by Christians to refer to other believers made an impact. For example, Clement comments that the Corinthian church was well known for its 'brotherly love' (φιλαδελφία) (1 Clem. 47:5).[178]

13:2–3 *Do not neglect*[179] *hospitality for by this some being hospitable to angels were unaware. Remember the prisoners as being bound together, [remember] those being mistreated as also you yourselves being in body.*

---

176. In Jewish contexts, e.g., Josephus, *Jewish Antiquities* 2:161; 4:26; 12:189; Philo, *On the Embassy to Gaius* 13:1; and 4 Macc. 13:23, 26; 14:1. For Greco-Roman references, see LSJ, 1931.

177. Some interesting comments by Plutarch (*On Brotherly Love*) include: Brotherly love accords with nature (φύσις) (478D); it shows proof of one's honor for parents (480A–F), especially when splitting the inheritance after the parents' death (482D); friendships with non-siblings is a faint imitation of sibling friendship (479D); and siblings should be kind to their siblings' spouses and children (491D).

178. See similar comments by Tertullian quoted in the Reflections section following Heb. 10:32–39.

179. The verbs **neglect** and **remember** take the genitive as their 'direct' object; hence, **hospitality, prisoners** and **those being mistreated** are in the genitive (BDAG, 375, 652, although Phil. 3:13).

Hebrews 13:2–3 are concrete examples of 'brotherly love' and are probably grouped together because they refer to helping those in need.

Hospitality was praised as a virtue in many ancient cultures.[180] As expected, there is a significant emphasis on it in the OT and NT.[181] The AH has previously alluded to **hospitality** with his praise of Rahab (Heb. 11:31) and has more remotely alluded to it with his praise of Sarah (Heb. 11:11–12; Gen. 18:1–15). Here an additional incentive is given (**for**) to encourage it—**by this (hospitality) some being hospitable to angels were unaware**. I assume that the AH is again alluding to Genesis 18 with Abraham and Sarah, although he might be also including Lot (Gen. 19:1–3; cf. Manoah, Judg. 13:3–15).[182] The point is that God is pleased by **hospitality**, and even more so when the guest is previously unknown to the host. Given the relative ease of traveling in the Greco-Roman empire, the somewhat dubious reputation of inns,[183] and the positive connections between churches, it would have been natural for Christians to open their homes to traveling Christians whom they previously would not have known.[184]

---

180. See S. C. Barton, 'Hospitality,' *DLNT*, 501–7; John Koenig, 'Hospitality,' *ABD*, 3:299–301; and Str-B 4:565–72.

181. Examples and commands include Gen. 18:1–8; 19:1–3; Deut. 10:19; Judg. 13:3–15; Isa. 58:7; Matt. 25:35; Luke 4:13; Rom. 12:13; 16:1–2; Phlm. 22; Jas. 1:27; 1 Pet. 4:9; and 3 John 5–8. In Rabbinic literature, see, e.g., m. Shabbat 18:1; and b. Berakhot 63a. Rabbi Isaac concludes based on Abraham's offering a 'fine meal' in Gen. 18:6 that 'a woman is more grudging than a man is when it comes to guests' (b. Bava Metzi'a 87a). Rabbi Yohanan remarked that there were six things that have benefits in this world, '*hospitality to guests,* visiting the sick, introspection in prayer, early rising to the schoolhouse, raising one's children for study of the Torah, and giving one's fellow the benefit of the doubt' (b. Shabbat 127a, emphasis mine).

182. Clement comments on the 'hospitality' of Abraham (1 Clem. 10:7) and Rahab (1 Clem. 12:1). The Rabbinic document Mekilta concludes that Abraham thought the angels were pagan worshipers of idols. Thus Rabbi Gamaliel concludes that hospitality should extend even to wicked people (Amalek 3).

183. Theophrastus, speaking of 'shameless person,' states, 'He is apt to keep an inn or run a brothel or be a tax collector, and he rejects no disgraceful occupation' (*Characters* 6:5 [Rusten, LCL]).

184. See comments about hosting traveling Christians in the *Didache* 11:4–6;

This **unaware** aspect may also be part of a Greek pun. The noun **hospitality** (φιλοξενία) is a combination of 'love' (φιλέω) and 'stranger' (ξένος), and the participle **being hospitable** (ξενίζω) is related to 'stranger.'[185] Further, the two verbs **neglect** (ἐπιλανθάνομαι) and **unaware** (λανθάνω) are cognates.

In addition to being kind to traveling Christian strangers, the readers are to **remember the prisoners** and **remember those being mistreated**. The AH is referring to Christians, whom it is assumed were unjustly put in prison.[186] Most likely, **those being mistreated** are a subset of those in prison, that is, some **prisoners** were also being physically **mistreated/** tortured beyond the normal difficulties of an average prisoner. Of course, to **remember** implies also to physically help. Previously, the AH has commended the congregation concerning its sympathy and help for Christians who were in prison (Heb. 10:34). (See my expanded discussion at Heb. 10:34 and the Reflection section following Heb. 10:32–39.)

Here the AH adds two rationales (**as**) for why the readers should help the **prisoners**. They are **bound together** metaphorically by their commitment to Christ and their being brothers and sisters. Also for **those being mistreated** physically, **you yourselves being in body**. This phrase **being in body** is understood by Calvin as metaphorically Christ's body.[187] However, most other commentators, including me, take it as referring to having physical bodies; therefore, they are able to relate to their fellow Christians in prison who are **being** physically **mistreated**.[188]

12:1–5. In addition to positive comments are warnings not to let the guests stay too long, at maximum three days.

185. Josephus comments that when Abraham saw the angels, he thought they were strangers (ξένος) (*Jewish Antiquities* 1:196).

186. So also, e.g., Aquinas, *Hebrews*, 296; Owen, *Hebrews*, 23:293–94; Brown, *Hebrews*, 674; Attridge, *Hebrews*, 387; Cockerill, *Hebrews*, 681; and Schreiner, *Hebrews*, 412.

187. Calvin, *Hebrews and 1 & 2 Peter*, 205.

188. So also, e.g., *Geneva Bible: 1602 Edition*, folio 114; Owen, *Hebrews*, 23:398; Moffatt, *Hebrews*, 226; Hughes, *Hebrews*, 564–65; Lane, *Hebrews 9–13*, 510; and Cockerill, *Hebrews*, 682.

13:4 Let[189] marriage[190] be [considered] honorable by all[191] and let the [marriage] bed be undefiled for God will judge fornicators and adulterers.

Marriage is to **be considered honorable**. This should be true for all people in all societies (**by all**). This ought to be especially true for those influenced by the ten commandments because the seventh commandment is against adultery (Exod. 20:14; Deut. 5:18; cf. Gen. 2:24). Further, the NT has much to say about **marriage** (e.g., Matt. 5:31–32; 19:1–12; 1 Cor. 7:1–16; Eph. 5:22–33; 1 Thess. 4:3; 1 Tim. 4:3; 1 Pet. 3:1–7). As one would assume, Hebrews 13:4 is quoted and referenced in many Reformed creeds in discussions related to marriage.[192] (For comments about **honorable**, see Reflections section below.)

Using the euphemism **bed** for sexual activity (Num. 31:17

---

189. As most do, in the absence of an explicit verb, I have assumed a third-person imperative 'to be' verb. This applies to **let marriage be considered honorable, let the marriage bed be undefiled**, and 'let your manner be not loving money' (Heb. 13:5). These imperatives are justified due to the explicit imperatives in Heb. 13:1–3.

190. Both **marriage** and **bed** have 'generic articles'; so also Zerwick and Grosvenor, *A Grammatical Analysis of the Greek New Testament*, 687. Generic articles emphasize the noun as an entire class. See Wallace, *Greek Grammar Beyond the Basics*, 227–31.

191. In Greek, ἐν πᾶσιν in form could be taken as **by all** or 'among all.' I am taking πᾶσιν as a masculine and relating it to people. If πᾶσιν is taken as a neuter, it would be translated as 'in all points' or 'in every respect'; thus relating it to circumstances. Virtually all translations and commentators take it as a masculine; Tyndale and CEB, however, take it as a neuter.

192. E.g., Second Helvetic Confession 29; Heidelberg Catechism 108; Thirty-Three Articles 25 (Anabaptist); Calvin's Catechism 8; Bohemian Confession 21 (*Reformed Confessions of the 16th and 17th Centuries*, 3:425); WCF 24.3; WLC 139. The Roman Catholic Church has a high view of marriage, and in fact, it is considered one of the seven sacraments (sacrament of matrimony). Although there are significant discussions concerning marriage in her official creedal documents, I was not able to find a reference to Heb. 13:4. See Council of Trent, Doctrine on the Sacrament of Matrimony (Schaff, *Creeds of Christendom*, 2:193–98; Denzinger[43] §§1797–816); Vatican Council II, *Gaudium et spes* 47–52 (Austin Flannery, ed., *Vatican Council II: The Conciliar and Post Conciliar Documents*, rev. ed., Vatican Collection 1 [Northport, NY: Costello, 1992], 949–57); and Catechism of the Catholic Church §§1601–66.

[LXX]; Wis. 3:13, 16; T. Reu. 1:6), the AH notes that the **bed** should be **undefiled**. That is, married persons should have no sexual activity outside of their **marriage** bond. Possibly, the term **undefiled** is used hinting at OT sacrificial and purity laws and is used for Christ as the high priest (Heb. 7:26).

In addition to the obvious and unnamed benefits of **marriage**, which is an 'honorable estate' that *God* instituted, the AH adds further incentive (**for**) to honor it by giving a warning—**God will** negatively **judge** (cf. Heb. 10:30) **fornicators and adulterers**.[193] **Fornicators** (cf. Heb. 12:16) are those who are not married and have sexual activity with those who are married and those not. **Adulterers** are those who are married and have sexual activity outside of their marriage. Judgment of **fornicators and adulterers** is often mentioned in the OT (e.g., Lev. 20:10; Deut. 22:20–25; Job 24:15–25; Prov. 5:15–23; cf. Sir. 15:17–20; 23:18–23; Wis. 14:24; 1 Cor. 6:9–20). Of course, there is forgiveness for those who repent and believe on Christ.

13:5–6 *Let [your] manner be not loving money. Be content[194] with present things. For he has said, 'I will not leave you and I will not forsake you' so that we may confidently say, 'The Lord is a helper to me, and I will not fear. What can man do to me?'*

The two imperatives in Hebrews 13:5 relate to greed in reference to material possessions. I have translated **let your manner be not loving money** and **be content with present things** very mechanically. **Not loving money** is a one-word adjective in Greek.[195] **Present things** refers to possessions that one has.

---

193. In Greek, **God** is at the end of the sentence adding an emphatic punch to whom it is that will do the judging.

194. **Be content** is in Greek form a participle; however, I take it as an attendant circumstance participle that takes on imperatival force due to context. For a general discussion of attendant circumstance participles, see Wallace, *Greek Grammar Beyond the Basics*, 640–45.

195. **Not-loving-money** is ἀ-φιλ-άργυρος (also used in 1 Tim. 3:3). Note, this is the third time φιλέω is used within a larger word in Heb. 13:1–5 as it is also included in 'brotherly love' (13:1) and 'hospitality' (13:2).

As the previous verse relates to the seventh commandment, this verse relates to the eighth commandment, which is against stealing (Exod. 20:15; Deut. 5:19). In addition to the seventh and eighth commandments, the condemnation of sexual sin and material greed in the same context occurs often in the Bible (e.g., Luke 16:9–18; Rom. 13:9; 1 Cor. 5:1–6:11; Eph. 5:3–5; Col. 3:5; 1 Thess. 4:3–7; 1 Tim. 1:10; cf. T. Jud. 18:2). Yes, these generic exhortations against greed relative to material possessions would apply anywhere in the Jewish and Greco-Roman world,[196] but most likely these exhortations have a more specific relevance as at least to the congregants who had their property taken from them (Heb. 10:34) and/or were in prison. Were those affected believers grieving too much over their material losses? Did this provide temptations for non-affected believers to keep inordinately their possessions, thus not giving appropriately to other believers in need? Ecclesiastes adds with some rhetorical flair to this discussion, 'He who loves money will not be satisfied with money' (Eccl. 5:10a).

Previously, the AH has argued that the reality of the future with God puts the difficulties of this life into perspective (e.g., 10:34; Heb. 11:24, 39–40). Here, with two OT quotes, the AH adds more incentives (**for**) to aid in adhering to the two imperatives—God's present and covenantal presence with the resulting providential help. These incentives dovetail well with his previous points. Further, the second OT quote acts as an implied imperative.

The first OT quote is **'I will not leave you and I will not**

---

196. In fact, the exact Greek expression **be content with present things** occurs numerous times in non-Christian Greco-Roman literature. See references in BDAG, 132. For similar NT references, see Phil. 4:11–12; 1 Tim. 6:6, 8; cf. 2 Cor. 12:9. The WSC 80 and WLC 147 reference Heb. 13:5 in regard to 'full contentment with our own condition' in their discussions of the tenth commandment. Craig's Catechism (AD 1581), while discussing the daily bread petition in the Lord's Prayer and referencing Heb. 13:5, states, 'Why do we ask for this day only? To teach us to be content with his [God's] present provision' (*Reformed Confessions of the 16th and 17th Centuries*, 3:584).

forsake you.' This quote is introduced simply by **he has said**, with the **he** referring to God, which then matches the **I** in the quote. There are four relatively close versions of this in the OT relating that God will not **leave** nor **forsake** either Joshua or David (Josh. 1:5, Joshua; Deut. 31:6, 8, Joshua; 1 Chr. 28:20, David; cf. Gen. 28:15, Jacob). Since Joshua 1:5 is the only one of the four that explicitly has God speaking in first person, it is the text the AH is referring to.[197] In the OT context, God's promise that **'I will not leave you and I will not forsake you'** is directly related to Joshua as he assumes leadership. Note that the AH expands its application to all believers. God's covenantal presence is emphasized for all those who trust in Christ, the mediator of the covenant.

Given that the Joshua 1:5 quote is promised to all believers, **we may confidently say, 'The Lord is a helper to me, and I will not fear. What can man do to me?'** Here, the AH quotes Psalm 118:6 as the logical implication (**so that**) of the Joshua 1:5 promise of God's covenantal presence.[198] That is, Joshua 1:5 is God's promise, and Psalm 118:6 is the believer's **confiden[ce]** in that promise. The context of Psalm 118 is an individual speaker who leads the congregation in thanksgiving for God's deliverance of him from enemies. I take the speaker to

---

197. So also, e.g., Owen, *Hebrews*, 23:414; Brown, *Hebrews*, 681–82; and Hughes, *Hebrews*, 568. Koester opts for Deut. 31:6, 8 (*Hebrews*, 559). Interestingly, both the Heb. 13:5 Greek text and the LXX match well to the Hebrew of Josh. 1:5, but they do not match each other at the word level. Excepting the third person, the LXX of Deut. 31:6 matches well to the Greek of Heb. 13:5. Another twist to this is that the Greek of Heb. 13:5 does match exactly to Philo, *On the Confusion of Tongues* 166. Guthrie concludes that 'it seems likely that Hebrews and Philo both depend on a common text form that in some way conflates the texts from Genesis and Deuteronomy' ('Hebrews,' 992). I prefer, however, that the AH translated directly from the Hebrew text of Josh. 1:5 or used another Greek translation that did.

198. As opposed to the Josh. 1:5 quote, here the Greek of Heb. 13:6 matches virtually exactly to the LXX. (The exception is the 'added' **and** in Heb. 13:6, although one major LXX manuscript does also include it. There is no **and** in the Hebrew.) The LXX/NT differs from the Hebrew in that the LXX/NT explicitly adds **helper**, which is a correct implication of the Hebrew.

be a king who has won a military victory against his foreign enemies and also had to deal with internal strife. Similar to what he did with Joshua 1:5, the AH applies the words of the kingly psalmist (**me, I**) to all believers (**we**). Thus, the AH is engendering contentment in the congregants that God will aid them spiritually and bring them through physical difficulties resulting in their finally arriving at the NHNE. He is implicitly exhorting them to **say**/apply-to-themselves the words of Psalm 118:6.

Two points concerning hermeneutics gleaned from these quotes: (1) Passages in Scripture that are person specific, here Joshua (Josh. 1:5) and the psalmist (Ps. 118:6), may at least sometimes be applied to all believers. (2) In the NT, Psalm 118 is quoted by NT authors and *applied to both believers* (Ps. 118:6 // Heb. 13:6) *and to Christ* (Ps. 118:22 // Luke 20:17; Acts 4:11; 1 Pet. 2:7; Ps. 118:22–23 // Matt. 21:42; Mark 12:10–11; Ps. 118:25–26 // Matt. 21:9; Mark 11:9–10; John 12:13; Ps. 118:26 // Matt. 23:39; Luke 13:35; 19:38). This application to both believers and Christ also explicitly occurs in Psalms 8, 22, and 34, and maybe in Psalm 2 (cf. Ps. 69:9 with Rom. 15:3). This shows that God intended to have each psalm apply in some sense to both believers and Christ.[199]

Reflections

'Let marriage be considered honorable[200] by all' (Heb. 13:4). Phrases connecting 'honorable' or 'honor' to marriage have long existed in the English speaking world. For example, marriage is often referred to as an *'honorable* estate.'

Where did these phrases connecting 'honorable' to marriage

---

199. See my essay for a much more detailed argument, 'Psalms Applied to Both Christ and Christians: Psalms 8, 22, 34, 118 and Romans 13:3 // Psalm 69:9,' 97–111.

200. The Greek adjective τίμιος, that I translate as 'honorable,' is only used here in Hebrews. Its cognate noun τιμή, 'honor,' occurs in Heb. 2:7, 9; 3:3; and 5:4. All of these are in combination with 'glory'/'glorify,' and they all refer directly or indirectly to Christ. This confirms that 'honorable' in Heb. 13:4 has weighty significance.

come from? Ultimately, they come from Hebrews 13:4 (cf. 1 Thess. 4:4), but I assume that the continuing prevalence of them is from the liturgical language at traditional Protestant wedding ceremonies.[201] Most Protestant ceremonies in the English-speaking world harken back to the first Anglican prayer book, by Cranmer, published in 1549. The ceremony begins:

> Dearly beloved friends, we are gathered together here in the sight of God, and in the face of his congregation, to join together this man and this woman in holy matrimony, which is an *honourable estate* instituted of God in paradise, in the time of man's innocence, signifying unto us the mystical union that is betwixt Christ and his church; which holy estate Christ adorned and beautified with his presence and first miracle that he wrought in Cana of Galilee, and is commended of Saint Paul *to be honourable among all men*.[202]

The marriage ceremony begins in a similar way in the Presbyterian tradition. Although there are variations, here is one example:

> Dearly beloved, we are assembled here in the presence of God, to join this Man and this Woman in holy marriage; which is instituted of God, regulated by His commandments, blessed by our Lord Jesus Christ, and *to be held in honor among all men*.[203]

---

201. The expression 'honorable estate' does not begin with Cranmer. In 1529, *Farrel's Summary* 38 uses the language 'holy and honorable estate' and references Heb. 13:4 (*Reformed Confessions of the 16th and 17th Centuries*, 1:101).

202. Robert Van de Weyer, ed. and compiler, *The First English Prayer Book* (Harrisburg: Morehouse, 1999), 59 (emphasis mine). Note the assumption that Paul wrote Hebrews.

203. *The Book of Common Worship: Approved by the General Assembly of the Presbyterian Church in the United States of America* [Northern Presbyterian Church] (Philadelphia: General Assembly Board of Publication, 1946), 183. On a personal note, this version was part of the liturgy at my wedding in

Given the difficulties traditional marriage is currently having in the Western world (e.g., high divorce rate), terming marriage as 'honorable' is commendable. May the reader, if married, consider his or her marriage as worthy of honor. Also, may the historic expressions 'honorable estate' and 'be held in honor by all' continue to be used by Christians. If done in an everyday conversation, it would probably make an impact.

Today's world needs many things. 'Let marriage be considered honorable by all' (Heb. 13:4) would help a lot!

Ending Exhortations: Second Group (13:7–17)

Hebrews 13:7–17 is a looser list of exhortations compared with Hebrews 13:1–6. It begins and ends with exhortations related to 'leaders' (Heb. 13:7, 17) and includes a wonderful creedal-type statement about Christ (Heb. 13:8). Hebrews 13:9–16 is a somewhat complicated discussion that begins with a negative exhortation against bad teaching that includes a wrong view of foods. This then is related to correct Christian teaching based on using typology from the Day of Atonement to affirm that Christians do offer sacrifices, properly understood.

By my count there are eight explicit imperatives/exhortations and one implicit. Although, the first two listed below are closely related as are items eight and nine. The list is as follows:

(1) Remember your leaders.
(2) Imitate their faith.
(3) [Believe] creedal statement about Jesus Christ (implicit).
(4) Do not be carried away by bad teachings.
(5) Let us go to [Christ] outside the camp bearing his reproach.
(6) Offer up sacrifice of praise with lips.
(7) Do not neglect doing good and sharing.

1979. The Directory for the Publick Worship of God by the Westminster Assembly has the phrase 'honourable estate of marriage, the covenant of their God' (The Solemnization of Marriage section).

(8) Be persuaded by your leaders.
(9) Yield to your leaders.

13:7 *Remember your leaders, those who spoke to you the word of God, whose conduct considering*[204] *the outcome.*[205] *Imitate [their] faith.*

Echoing 'remember the prisoners' (Heb. 13:3), the readers are exhorted to **remember your leaders**.[206] As opposed to the 'leaders' in Hebrews 13:17 and 13:24, these **leaders** have died. This is shown by (1) **spoke** being in the past tense, and more importantly (2) **outcome**, which assumes an end of life.[207] I take **outcome** to mean their dying with their Christian faith intact, which then encourages one to look at the **conduct** of their whole Christian life. This **conduct** includes their moral actions and practices along with their teachings (**spoke to you the word of God**[208]).[209]

Imitate their faith functionally restates the same point.

---

204. Several translations take **considering** as an imperative based on attendant circumstances with **remember** or **imitate** (e.g., RSV, NIV, ESV); others see this clause as a subset of the imperative **remember** or **imitate** (e.g., KJV, NJB, CSB17, CEB). As can be seen by my awkward translation, I do not see it as an imperative because the clause begins with ὧν (**whose**), which would be an odd way to begin an attendant-circumstance imperatival clause. I instead see it as a subset of **remember**.

205. Concerning **outcome** (ἔκβασις), the etymological meaning is 'the way out.' This then has a variety of meanings (e.g., 'way out of a sea,' cf. 1 Cor. 10:13), but when used of a person's life, it refers to the 'end,' 'termination,' or 'completion' (e.g., Wis. 2:17), or more broadly 'accomplishment' or 'result' based on the life. See LSJ, 501–2.

206. Two different Greek words are used for 'remember,' μιμνήσκω in Heb. 13:3 and μνημονεύω in Heb. 13:7. The remember aspects are similar in that neither the prisoners or the dead leaders are physically present when this letter is read to the congregation. But of course, they differ in that the prisoners are living on earth and the dead leaders are now with the Lord. I take the difference in verbs as simply rhetorical.

207. All commentators agree that the **leaders** have died, e.g., Aquinas, *Hebrews*, 298; Calvin, *Hebrews and 1 & 2 Peter*, 207; and Lane, *Hebrews 9–13*, 527. This does not, however, refer to martyrdom as Heb. 12:4 implicitly confirms.

208. Concerning **word of God**, cf. Heb. 1:1–2; 4:12; 5:12–13; 6:5; 12:24; and 13:22.

209. One implication for modern Christians is to read Christian biographies.

The reason to **remember your leaders** was to appropriately **imitate** them (cf. Heb. 6:12; Philo, *On the Life of Moses* 1.158).[210] By using **faith**, the AH recalls the positive examples within Hebrews 11 and the negative example of Hebrews 3:7–4:13 (cf. Heb. 3:19). The meaning of **faith** here is probably quite broad as the connection to **leaders** would imply. It would include the subjective internal trust-in-Christ of the **leaders**, their persevering and faithful commitment to the end, and the content of their doctrines that they affirmed and taught.

Clearly Hebrews 13:7 encourages the Church to properly honor/**remember** some dead believers. In the Reformation period, the Protestant churches thought the Roman Catholic church had gone too far in this regard. Referencing Hebrews 13:7, the Waldensian Confession (AD 1662) provides balance: "That those who have eternal life by faith and by their good works must be considered holy and honored for their virtues, *imitated* in the noble actions of their life, but not worshiped or called upon, for we must pray but to one God through Jesus Christ" (Article 23, emphasis mine).[211]

13:8 *Jesus Christ [is] the same yesterday, today, and forever.*[212]

This is a glorious creedal-type statement.[213] The creed-like features are shown by the comprehensive temporal language of **yesterday, today, and forever** similar to 'I am the first and

---

210. WLC 127, referring to honor that inferiors owe to superiors, includes 'imitation of their virtues and graces.' Cf. Did. 4:1–2.

211. *Reformed Confessions of the 16th and 17th Centuries*, 4:507. Similarly, see the Bohemian Confession 17 (AD 1535) (*Reformed Confessions of the 16th and 17th Centuries*, 1:332). Cf. Catechism of the Catholic Church §§971, 2683.

212. The Greek inserts **the same** (ὁ αὐτός) after **today** and before **forever**. This order is used in the Tyndale and Geneva Bibles, along with the partial quote in WCF 8.6. Thus, for example, the Geneva Bible reads, 'Iesus Christ yesterday, and to day, the same also is for euer' (original spelling). The placement of **the same** in the Greek does not affect the meaning but does add rhetorical flair.

213. Attridge calls it a 'solemn affirmation' (*Hebrews*, 392). Several commentators assume it has liturgical aspects (so, e.g., Lane, *Hebrews 9–13*, 704–05).

I am the last' (Isa. 44:6; cf. Rev. 22:13) and 'who is and who was and who is to come' (Rev. 1:4). In addition, this creedal aspect is confirmed by the use of the full name **Jesus Christ**, which only occurs in Hebrews here, 10:10; and 13:21.[214] Further, the lack of a conjunction before and after this verse adds to the rhetorical punch commensurate with this great creedal statement. Finally, this statement is not simply about a miscellaneous topic barely related to the book of Hebrews, but it is highlighting important aspects of the center of the book, **Jesus Christ**.

The phrase **yesterday, today, and forever** emphasizes the *eternality* of Christ's person, highlighting his divine nature; the use of **same** emphasizes his *immutability* (cf. Heb. 6:17). Of course, for the Triune God, eternality and immutability are interrelated. In addition to the creedal nature of the statement, What further confirms that **yesterday** does not simply refer to while the 'leaders' were alive or only extends back to Christ's incarnation or ascension?[215] (1) A significant argument is the use of **same** also in Hebrews 1:12, 'You are the *same*, and your years will not fail.' Hebrews 1:10–12 refers to Christ's divinity related to his being creator, which in context is supporting the creator comments in Hebrews 1:3. (2) Hebrews often discusses aspects of the divinity of Christ (e.g., Heb. 1:8; 3:5; 7:3, 15–16, 24, 28; 13:20). (3) The exhortation concerning 'faith' in the previous verse (Heb. 13:7) recalls the OT heroes of

---

214. So also Koester, *Hebrews*, 567.

215. Confirming that **yesterday** refers to the eternal aspects of Christ, so, e.g., Chrysostom, 'Homily 33 on Hebrews,' 515; Aquinas, *Hebrews*, 299; Owen, *Hebrews*, 23:427; Gouge, *Hebrews*, 1078; Geerhardus Vos, 'The Eternal Christ,' in *Grace and Glory: Sermons Preached in the Chapel of Princeton Theological Seminary* (Carlisle: Banner of Truth, 1994 [1922]), 197–208; Attridge, *Hebrews*, 393; Bauckham, 'The Divinity of Christ in the Epistle of Hebrews, 34–36; Koester, *Hebrews*, 560; Johnson, *Hebrews*, 346; Cockerill, *Hebrews*, 691; and Schreiner, *Hebrews*, 418. Others, while not necessarily denying the eternal aspects of Christ, see **yesterday** in a limited way, e.g., Moffatt, *Hebrews*, 223; and Hughes, *Hebrews*, 570. The Socinians, who do deny the divinity of Christ, only see **yesterday** as referring back at most to the incarnation. See Owen's interaction with this view in *Hebrews*, 23:426.

Hebrews 11 who, even in the OT, had faith in Christ, properly understood.[216] (4) This dovetails well with the tabernacle being heavenly during the OT.[217]

Yes, this verse confirms the ontological divinity of the Son, but the creedal statement is not simply making that point, as important as it is. It is also emphasizing that Christ's mediatorial attributes and benefits are always the same, including, in the context of Hebrews, his kingly care ('Son') and salvific work ('priest') for his people, whether in the OT or NT.[218] Of course, it is true that the eternal Son took on a human nature, and in that sense there is change (e.g., Heb. 5:8), but the AH still declares that the *person* is the **same yesterday, today, and forever** (cf. WCF 8.7). Hallelujah!

One advantage of a broad creed-like statement such as this one is that it has numerous implications depending on the context. Here, Hebrews 13:8 applies to both what goes before and after.[219] Related backwards to the dead leaders (Heb. 13:7), of whom the congregants are to imitate their life and faith, the AH is confirming and encouraging them

---

216. So also Turretin, 'It is supposed that "yesterday" denotes the day of his flesh.... This is repugnant to the aim of Paul, which is to exhort to constancy of faith' (*Institutes of Elenctic Theology*, 2:195).

217. See 'OT Tabernacle Relates Both Forward and Upward' section in the introduction to Heb. 8:1–10:18.

218. Calvin, 'The apostle is not discussing the eternal being of Christ but the knowledge of Him which flourished among believers in every age and which was the lasting foundation of the Church' (*Hebrews and 1 & 2 Peter*, 208; also see *Institutes* 2.10.4). Although I would want to nuance Calvin's 'eternal being' comment, his point is well taken. Owen, 'It is from his divine person, that, in the discharge of his [mediatorial] office, he was ὁ αὐτός, "the same"' (*Hebrews*, 23:427). Turretin, 'Christ as Mediator can be safely said *in a certain sense* to have sat down at the right hand of God as without flesh even before the incarnation; thus from the beginning of the world because he always was the head and King of the church who governed and defended it (Ps. 2:6; *Heb. 13:8*)' (*Institutes of Elenctic Theology*, 2:371, my emphasis). Note that also in the context of Ps. 102 God's/Christ's eternality and immutability are related to his concern of his people.

219. So also many commentators, e.g., Owen, *Hebrews*, 23:427–28; Moffatt, *Hebrews*, 232; Bruce, *Hebrews*, 571; and Hughes, *Hebrews*, 571.

ENDING EXHORTATIONS AND CLOSING (13:1–25)   541

by noting that the leaders followed and had faith in the same Christ that they do. This **same** Christ who sovereignly accomplished the final perseverance of the leaders is also their Son and Priest. (Also related would be the confirmation that Joshua's statement in Heb. 13:5 and the psalmist's in 13:6 may be applied to the congregants,[220] not to mention the lessons of Hebrews 11.) Related forwards, the AH warns against following false teachings (Heb. 13:9). Hence, Hebrews 13:8 confirms that truths about Christ do not change because the person of Christ does not change.

See Reflection section below for more on Hebrews 13:8.

13:9–10 *Do not be carried away by various and strange teachings, for [it is] good [that] by grace the heart be confirmed, not by foods by which those so being occupied*[221] *were not benefited. We have an altar from which those serving the tabernacle have no authority to eat.*

As opposed to the one, uniform teaching about Christ that properly understood relates to believers in both the OT and NT (Heb. 13:8), the congregation is exhorted, **do not be carried away by various and strange teachings** (cf. Heb. 5:11–6:3). These bad **teachings** are understood to be the opposite of **grace** that grounds, **confirm[s]**, and strengthens one's **heart**. In context, **grace** is related to 'faith' (Heb. 13:7) and 'Jesus Christ' (Heb. 13:8). That is, Christ's work merits our salvation (**grace**), and the instrument is faith.

Most acknowledge that aspects of Hebrews 13:9b–16 are difficult.[222] One of the problems revolves around defining **foods**. As many others do, I take **foods** here to be some type of

---

220. Aquinas sees the Joshua connection as possibly intentional (*Hebrews*, 299).

221. **Those so being occupied** is my translation of οἱ περιπατοῦντες, which etymologically translates as 'those walking around' but often means to 'walk,' 'live' or 'conduct oneself' (cf. Eph. 4:17; 1 Thess 2:11; 2 John 6). In Hebrews, this verb only occurs here.

222. Owen calls it 'abstruse' and the 'reasonings ... not easy to comprehend' (*Hebrews*, 23:429). Lane claims that Heberews 13:9–14 is 'one of the most controversial passages in Hebrews' (*Hebrews 9–13*, 530).

sacred meals with a Jewish flavor that are unrelated to meals associated with the Jerusalem temple or Passover per se.[223] These meals apparently arose as some sort of expanded version of the OT offerings that included eating portions of the sacrificed animal (e.g., guilt offering [Lev. 7:6]; peace offering [Lev. 7:11–18]). There are several extant references to various types of Jewish sacred meals being celebrated by Jews at this time.[224] They were partially designed to bring one closer to God in a special way. Confirming that **foods** does not here refer specifically to OT sacrificial meals (as it does in Hebrews 9:10) is that it would be odd for the AH to refer to the Mosaic legislation as **various and strange teachings**.[225] The congregants are aware of these Jewish-inspired sacred meals, of which there may also be Jewish-Christian versions. Either of which some congregants may have previously participated, are currently participating, or are tempted to participate.

As opposed to the **grace** related to Christ, **those so being occupied** with these meals **were not** and continue not to be spiritually **benefited**. It was not simply that some were participating in religious meals, it is that they also infused significant importance to them (**those so being occupied**) to the extent that it denied Christ. In addition, it probably also continued to foster an improper attachment to OT ceremonial laws so that the typological connections to Christ were not being seen.

Although there is no conjunction, the AH is clearly countering the wrong use of **foods** by proclaiming **we have an altar**. The wrong view was eating **foods** from a supposed altar. Christians, on the other hand, also **have an altar**, which clearly refers to Christ and his earthly sacrifice on the cross

---

223. So, e.g., also Spicq, *Hébreux*, 2:423–24; Bruce, *Hebrews*, 377; Hughes, *Hebrews*, 572; Attridge, *Hebrews*, 394–96; Koester, *Hebrews*, 569; Johnson, *Hebrews*, 347; and Cockerill, *Hebrews*, 692.

224. See 1QSa II, 17–22; Josephus, *Jewish Antiquities* §§213, 258; Philo, *On the Contemplative Life* §§64–85; and m. Berakhot 6:1–8.

225. So also Moffatt, *Hebrews*, 233; Kistemaker, *Hebrews*, 416–17; and Koester, *Hebrews*, 569.

('through his blood,' Heb. 13:12).[226] The true **altar** is obviously based on typology related to sacrifices upon the OT altar.[227] In this pericope, the AH will typologically use aspects of the Day of Atonement offering (Heb. 13:10b–14) and the peace offering (Heb. 13:15–16).

How does **foods** relate to the clause **from which** (the true altar) **those serving the tabernacle have no authority to eat**? In the Mosaic legislation, the priests (**those serving the tabernacle**) were allowed to eat portions of some sacrifices (e.g., guilt offering [Lev. 7:1–6]; cf. Num. 18:8–10) but not from the sin offering (Lev. 4:11; 6:30) nor the Day of Atonement offering(s) (Lev. 16:27–28). Based on the AH's references elsewhere (e.g., Heb. 7:27; 9:7) and 'high priest' (Heb. 13:11), he is referring to the Day of Atonement legislation. Given this, the AH contrasts the eating at the improper current sacred-meal ceremonies with the OT command that priests **have no authority to eat** portions of the Day of Atonement sacrifices. Typologically considered, those participating in these improper ceremonies are as wrong as a priest eating from the Day of Atonement sacrifices.[228] Why? The true

---

226. Referencing Heb. 13:10, the Catechism of the Catholic Church states, 'The altar of the New Covenant is the Lord's Cross, from which the sacraments of the Paschal mystery flow' (§1182). Leo the Great connects **altar** and 'outside the camp' (Heb. 13:11), '[Christ] offering himself to the Father a new and true sacrifice of reconciliation, was crucified not in the temple, whose worship is now at an end, and not within the confines of the city which for its sin was doomed to be destroyed, but outside, "without the camp," that, on the cessation of the old symbolic victims, a new Victim might be placed on a new altar, and the cross of Christ might be the altar not of the temple but of the world' ('Sermon 59,' §5; *NPNF*², 12:172).

227. If only referring to Christ as a sacrifice, this typology is using a metonymy, i.e., **altar** is used to denote the sacrifice upon the **altar**. If including the *cross* along with Christ as the sacrifice upon it, then this is a synecdoche, i.e., **altar** is used to refer to the cross and those things upon it.

228. Note the present tense of **have** in **those serving the tabernacle** *have* **no authority to eat** and 'is brought' and 'are burned' in Heb. 13:11. Although in one sense referring to past priests in the **tabernacle**, these present tenses are explained by its typological use to refer to the current situation. Thus, I do not see it as an explicit argument for Hebrews being written prior to AD 70; however, it does not argue against it either and, in fact, dovetails

altar and the true Day of Atonement are related to Christ. Therefore, among other things, the physical eating of portions of actual sacrificed animals upon the altar in Jerusalem has 'theologically' ceased.[229]

13:11–12 *For animals—whose blood concerning sin is brought in the Holy of Holies*[230] *by the high priest—bodies of these are burned outside the camp. So then also Jesus suffered outside the gate in order to sanctify through his own blood the people.*

Hebrews 13:11 proves the point (**for**) of 13:10b that for the sacrifices related to the Day of Atonement (**animals—whose blood concerning sin is brought in the Holy of Holies by the high priest**) priests were not allowed nor able to eat from these offerings because the **bodies of these** animals **are burned outside the camp**. That is, yes, portions were consumed on the altar, but their remains were later completely destroyed (**burned outside the camp**). Once making this point, the AH subtly makes two more typological points related to the Day of Atonement, now more focusing upon the requirement that the animals be **burned** *outside the camp*. The **outside the camp** aspect foreshadows (1) Christ's death **outside the gate** of Jerusalem (Heb. 13:12) and (2) the negative 'reproach' that Christians will experience in this world paralleling the

---

well with the 'camp'/'gate' relationship possibly alluding to current Jerusalem sacrifices being 'outside the gate' of Jerusalem (Heb. 13:11–12). Although I do not agree with all of his arguments, Peter Walker views the 'reproach' (Heb. 13:13) that the Jewish Christians would have received from non-Christian Jews making more sense prior to the temple's destruction ('Jerusalem in Hebrews 13:9–14 and the Dating of the Epistle,' *TynBul* 45 [1994]: 39–71).

229. As a Christian church, surely the congregants were participating in the Lord's Supper. Why is it not mentioned here? I assume that the Lord's Supper (1) explicitly relates to Christ as opposed to a denial or significantly downplaying Christ and (2) involves eating/drinking bread and wine with a spiritual emphasis as opposed to killing and eating sacrificed animals from a supposed altar without a proper spiritual emphasis.

230. Similar to Heb. 9:12, I take τὰ ἅγια ('the holies') as specifically the **Holy of Holies**. So also Hughes, *Hebrews*, 575; Attridge, *Hebrews*, 397; and Lane, *Hebrews 9–13*, 541.

stigma of Christ's death in the cursed area **outside the camp** (Heb. 13:13–14).

Given that the animals from the Day of Atonement were **burned outside the** wilderness **camp**, this typologically parallels (**so then also**) that **Jesus suffered outside the** Jerusalem city **gate**. Being **outside** both the **camp** and **gate** indicates a cursed location for death (cf. Lev. 24:10–16; Num. 19:3; Acts 7:58; Luke 20:15; Gal. 3:13). Here, **suffered** (πάσχω) includes death as **through his own blood** makes clear (cf. Heb. 2:9).[231] Note that the AH assumes that the congregation knows the historical fact that Christ's death on the cross was **outside the gate** (cf. John 19:20).[232]

The AH gives a summary of what Christ's death accomplishes—it will **sanctify through his own blood the people**. **His own blood** parallels the **blood** of the **animals** used in the Day of Atonement ceremony. Thus, the **concerning sin** aspect of the **animals** death/**blood** applies also to Christ's death/**blood**. Concerning the often used **sanctify**, see the extended discussion at Hebrews 10:10. In brief, I take **sanctify** as having been 'set apart' for God's purposes to accomplish the believer's broad salvation (including justification, sanctification, and glorification).

As previously mentioned in this commentary, the phrase 'he offered himself' (Heb. 9:14; cf. Heb. 7:27; 10:12) wonderfully captures that Christ is both priest and victim. In Hebrews 13:11–12 the emphasis is certainly on Christ as the sacrificial *victim*, but 13:12 also includes Christ's activity showing him to be the *priest*. As priest, **Jesus** intentionally **suffered in order to** actively **sanctify**.[233]

---

231. Related to the view that Christ was not a priest while on earth, Vos counters, 'The ἁγιάζειν of the people to which [Heb.] 13:12 refers was certainly a priestly act, and it took place when Jesus suffered outside the gate' ('The Priesthood of Christ in the Epistle to the Hebrews: Second Article,' 597). See extended discussion in the Reflections section following Heb. 5:1–10.

232. Kistemaker adds similar assumptions in Heb. 5:7–8; 10:12; and 12:2 (*Hebrews*, 421).

233. So also Moffatt, *Hebrews*, 235.

13:13–14 *So now let us go to him outside the camp bearing his reproach. For we do not have here a remaining city, but we seek the coming one.*[234]

As noted above, the AH adds another angle to the **outside-the-camp** typology. Since Christ was sacrificed in a place of and underwent **reproach**, this foreshadows that the people of God will also many times experience **reproach** in this life that parallels **his**. See the AH's same use of 'reproach' in Hebrews 10:33 and 11:26 (see extended discussion at Heb. 11:26).

The AH and believers are exhorted, not to run away from difficulties, but **let us go to him outside the camp bearing his reproach**. Here *inside* **the camp** clearly refers metaphorically to something(s) negative. It probably has quite a broad meaning of worldly doctrines and practices.[235] Due to this 'bad' **camp**, believers who are **outside the camp** may experience physical difficulties due to being connected to Christ, be pressured to remain in improper social groups, be encouraged to believe wrong doctrines, etc. Thus, an incentive to continue **bearing** this **reproach** is that Christ himself, who knew no sin, also bore it (cf. Mark 8:34).[236] In addition, these difficulties that come upon the congregants due to their commitment to Christ are termed by the AH, *his* **reproach**.

Another incentive (**for**) to bear these difficulties is that **we do not have here a remaining city, but we seek the coming one**. Recalling the future 'city' referenced in Hebrews 11:10

---

234. The feminine substantival participle **the coming one** in Heb. 13:14b is clearly grammatically related to the feminine **city** in Heb. 13:14a. Thus most translations insert 'city' in 13:14b.

235. Van Mastricht comments about the gratitude we should offer God, 'He, by choosing us, separated us from the world, in turn we should separate ourselves for him by separating ourselves from the world (John 15:19), by not conforming ourselves to it (Rom. 12:2), [and] *by coming out of it (Rev. 18:4; Heb. 13:13)*' (*Theoretical-Practical Theology*, 3:72–73, emphasis mine).

236. The notes from the Geneva Bible: 1602 Edition remark, 'The godly followers of Christ must as it were go out of the world bearing his cross' (folio 115, updated spelling).

and 11:16 (cf. Heb. 12:22), the AH reminds the congregants that their ultimate destiny is the **coming** city, by which the **remaining city** (this world) will pale in comparison.[237] Thus, the sting of the current **reproach** is put into perspective.

Note that the exhortation **let us go to him** has, as it were, both vertical and horizontal dimensions. Vertically, we are to go 'up' to Christ concerning our 'down here' **reproach**.[238] On the horizontal plane, we are to live 'now' realizing that a 'future' **city** exists, which is similar to those in Hebrews 11 who lived realizing that a 'future' **city** exists.

13:15–16 *Therefore,*[239] *through him let us offer up a sacrifice of praise continually to God, that is, [the] fruit of lips confessing*[240] *his name. And do not neglect the doing-good and sharing, for God is being pleased with such as these sacrifices.*

Hebrews 13:15–16 relates to the OT peace offering (Lev. 3:1–17; 7:11–18). First some background on this offering:[241] The peace offering,[242] also called the thanksgiving offering, is so

---

237. Some argue that here with the use of **city** that the AH is intentionally alluding to the contrast between the present Jerusalem implicitly referred to by 'outside the gate' (Heb. 13:12) with the 'heavenly Jerusalem' (Heb. 12:22). The present Jerusalem stands for all that should be rejected (e.g., Bruce, *Hebrews*, 381). Based on Rome being called the 'eternal city,' Jason A. Whitlark argues that **the remaining city** is an intentional and veiled critique of imperial Rome ('"Here We Do Not Have a City That Remains": A Figured Critique of Roman Imperial Propaganda in Hebrews 13:14,' *JBL* 131 [2012]: 161–79). I am not convinced by either of these proposals, even though I weakly argue that the congregation is in or near Rome (see Introductory Matters chapter).

238. Ellingworth adds that the 'link ... [is] worship,' as shown in Heb. 13:15 (*Hebrews*, 717). Using my words, we worship 'down here' the God who is 'up there.' Also, this worship produces 'down here' good works (Heb. 13:16).

239. A few early Greek manuscripts omit **therefore**. The majority of the UBS committee argues it is original but only with a 'C' rating (Metzger, *TCGNT*², 605). All major English translations include it except for the NJB.

240. Grammatically in Greek, **confessing** is related to **lips**.

241. For an excellent summary, see Richard E. Averbeck, 'שָׁלֵם,' NIDOTTE, 4:135–43.

242. The NIV translates 'peace offering' as 'fellowship offering.'

called because it assumes that sin has been forgiven, resulting in 'peace' between God and worshiper, and 'peace' also between God and the worshiper's family and friends. By bringing the sacrificial offerings, the worshiper 'thanks' God for his spiritual and material blessings. The peace/thanksgiving offering also involves a communal meal with the worshiper's family and friends. The meal comes from portions of the sacrificial animal and loaves. The peace/thanksgiving offering has two additional subset types, vow and freewill (Lev. 7:16). In the OT, the thanksgiving (תודה) offering is consistently translated in the LXX as the 'praise' (αἴνεσις) offering (e.g., Lev. 7:12, 13, 15; 2 Chr. 29:31; Pss. 50:14, 23; 107:22).

Continuing from 'we have an altar' (Heb. 13:10), the AH now uses the typology of the peace/thanksgiving offering.[243] That he is referring to the thanksgiving offering is confirmed by (1) the expression **sacrifice of praise** (αἴνεσις) itself, (2) the two exhortations related to verbally praising God (Heb. 13:15) and sharing material goods (Heb. 13:16) match well with the Levitical thanksgiving offering, and (3) the verbal and conceptual connections to the thanksgiving offering referred to in Psalm 50:14.[244]

The first exhortation is **let us offer up a sacrifice of praise continually to God, that is, the fruit of lips confessing his name**. The Levitical thanksgiving offering included offering a sacrificial animal and loaves along with praising/thanking God. The AH typologically understands that, although physical animals are no longer to be sacrificed on a physical

---

243. So also, e.g., Owen, *Hebrews*, 23:454; Brown, *Hebrews*, 705; Bruce, *Hebrews*, 383; and Lane, *Hebrews 9–13*, 552.

244. Seeing the connections to Ps. 50:14, so also Bruce, *Hebrews*, 383; Hughes, *Hebrews*, 584; Lane, *Hebrews 9–13*, 549; Koester, *Hebrews*, 571–72; and Schreiner, *Hebrews*, 423. Some see an allusion to Hos. 14:2 due to 'calves of lips' from LXX, e.g., Owen, *Hebrews*, 23:456–57; and Moffatt, *Hebrews*, 236. Adam W. Day sees the primary allusion to Ps. 69 primarily based on the 'reproach' connection ('Bearing the Reproach of Christ: The Background of Psalm 68 (LXX) in Hebrews 13:9–16,' *Presbyterion* 44 [2018]: 126–41). Many commentators see no specific OT allusions, e.g., Guthrie, 'Hebrews,' 993. Both **confessing your name** and **fruit of lips** are in Pss. Sol. 15:2–3, although the context is not a thanksgiving offering.

altar, the requirement to **offer up a** verbal **sacrifice of praise** remains because 'we have an altar.'²⁴⁵ This typological thanksgiving offering is **through him** (cf. Heb. 7:25), that is, Christ, as opposed to the OT priests.²⁴⁶ I assume that the **confessing his name** primarily refers to the congregation's corporate worship services, but, of course, it could relate to many other situations.

The AH is also quoting/alluding to a portion of Psalm 50:14, 'Offer to God a sacrifice of thanksgiving and complete your vows to the Most High.' The wording 'to God a sacrifice of thanksgiving' matches very closely to **a sacrifice of praise continually to God.**²⁴⁷ In Psalm 50, Asaph corrects (or mocks) the understanding that God needs the animal sacrifices because he is hungry. No, he has 'the cattle on a thousand hills' (Ps. 50:10). As to levels of importance, thanking God, calling upon him, and being morally ethical are more important than sacrificing an animal.²⁴⁸ One thrust of Psalm 50 is that the ceremonial requirement for burning portions of animal sacrifices for thanksgiving offerings was a secondary level of importance. This dovetails with the AH typological understanding that this ceremonial aspect no longer applies once Christ, the true priest, has come.

The second exhortation is **do not neglect the doing-good and sharing, for God is being pleased with such as these**

---

245. In 1QS IX, 4–5, The Qumran community is encouraged to 'atone' for their sins. Their works of 'prayer' and 'perfection of way' are their sacrifices. The 'perfection of way' is explicitly termed a 'free-will offering,' i.e., a thanksgiving offering.

246. Using similar language, Clement comments, 'we confess [praise] you through the high priest [Christ]' (1 Clem. 61:3).

247. For the partial quote, the Hebrew matches exactly with the LXX given that the Hebrew 'thanksgiving' is consistently translated as 'praise' in the LXX. The Heb. 13:15 partial quote matches the LXX excepting a different order of **to God** and the addition of **continually**.

248. This point is also made elsewhere in the OT, e.g., Pss. 40:6 // Heb. 10:5; 51:15–17; Eccl. 5:1; Mic. 6:6–8; Hos. 6:6; cf. 2 En. 45:3; and Augustine, *City of God* 10.4–6. Philo, as expected, connects various aspects of sacrificial offerings to good doctrines and morals (e.g., *On the Special Laws* 1.201, 252, 272, 277, 287–90).

sacrifices. The AH is typologically connecting the communal aspect of the thanksgiving offering, in which the worshiper shares a meal with his family and friends,[249] to the general spiritual and, especially, material **doing-good and sharing**.[250] This the congregants should do primarily among themselves, and I assume, as appropriate, secondarily with others outside the church. This **doing-good and sharing** recalls conceptually Hebrews 13:1–3; 6:10; 10:24–25, and 10:32–34.

The motivation is that **God is being pleased**[251] by these actions. This is a different motivation than those in Hebrews 13:13–14, but, of course, it fits well with them. Possibly, the AH is explicitly making this point to confirm that animal sacrifices are no longer required as some in the congregants' orbit would have been making.

WCF 19.3, while discussing 'ceremonial laws that are now abrogated' in the one-to-one (my term) sense, very perceptively notes that these ceremonial laws also do include 'divers instructions of moral duties.' It references 1 Corinthians 5:7; 2 Corinthians 6:17; and Jude 23. Hebrews 13:15–16 is another example. The AH typologically used aspects of the thanksgiving offering for these two exhortations, that is, the ceremonial thanksgiving offering includes 'instructions of moral duties.'

13:17 *Be persuaded by and yield to your leaders, for they are watching over your souls as [they will be] giving an account, in order that they may do this with joy and not groaning, for this is unprofitable for you.*

---

249. Deut. 12:12 implies that offerings ought to be shared with the (poor) Levite, including implicitly portions of the vow offering. The Feast of Weeks sacrifices are also to include the disadvantaged (Deut. 16:11; cf. Deut. 14:29).

250. The noun **sharing** (κοινωνία) has a broad semantic range that does include aiding others materially (Rom. 12:13; 2 Cor. 8:4; Gal. 6:6; Phlm 6). In addition to me, those noting that **sharing** here is related to material goods include Owen, *Hebrews*, 23:459; Lane, *Hebrews 9–13*, 552; and Ellingworth, *Hebrews*, 721.

251. For references of the verb 'to please' (εὐαρεστέω) and its cognates, see Heb. 10:5, 8; 11:5–6; 13:16; and 13:21.

The AH ends this section of exhortations with a double exhortation to **be persuaded by** (obey) and **yield** (submit) **to your** current **leaders**. Previously in Hebrews 13:7, he exhorted the congregation concerning their recently deceased 'leaders'. Here and in 13:24 the AH references their current **leaders**. The language strongly implies that these current **leaders** are commendable.[252]

One incentive (first **for**) to follow the **leaders** is that they have the congregation's best interests at heart. One evidence of this is that their ecclesiastical office requires, among other things, that they will **give an account** to God (cf. Heb. 4:13; 9:27; 10:30–31; 12:23) of the manner by which they were **watching over** the congregants' **souls**. Since the **leader('s)** function is important and intended for each of the congregant's spiritual good, the congregant ought to act **with joy** in his manner of **be(ing) persuaded by and yield(ing)** (first **this**). To state the obvious (second **for**), **groaning** makes it harder for a **leader** to shepherd, which is ultimately **unprofitable** for the congregant.[253] Although this exhortation is not to the **leaders**, by implication, these **leaders** and all subsequent ones reading this text realize the gravity of their office.

Reflections

'Jesus Christ is the same yesterday, today, and forever' (Heb. 13:8) is a glorious creedal-type statement. As noted in the exegetical section above, this 'creed' emphasizes two major realities about Christ's person. (1) He is eternal and immutable, which are related truths. In this regard, the divine nature of Christ is highlighted. And (2) his mediatorial office and activity applies to both OT and NT believers.

---

252. So also Moffatt, *Hebrews*, 240; Bruce, *Hebrews*, 385; and Hughes, *Hebrews*, 585.

253. Referencing Heb. 13:17, the Belgic Confession 31 comments, 'Everyone ought to esteem ministers of God's Word and elders of the Church very highly for their work's sake, and be at peace with them without murmuring, strife, or contention.' For creeds also referencing Heb. 13:17, see WCF 20.4; WLC 127; Catechism of the Catholic Church §1269; Bohemian Confession 9 (*Reformed Confessions of the 16th and 17th Centuries*, 1:317); and Apology of the Augsburg Confession 28.

How have systematic theologians and creeds throughout Christian history used Hebrews 13:8 to support/proof-text various doctrines? Heartwarmingly, at least for me who has a high view of traditional Reformed systematic theologians and most creeds, the two emphases just mentioned are the same two doctrines for which Hebrews 13:8 is primarily referenced. Some used Hebrews 13:8 for both, and some for just one of the two.

Jesus Christ is eternal and immutable.
Hebrews 13:8 is used often in a straightforward manner by the Church Fathers and Reformed theologians to show the eternality and/or immutability of Christ's divine person, often noting the connection to 'same' in Psalm 102:27 // Hebrews 1:12.[254] Adding a nuance are Athanasius and Alexander of Alexandria. They use Hebrews 13:8 to stress that when the eternal Logos took human nature, his person did not change fundamentally.[255] Letham adds the twist that God's immutability is not to be understood as 'static' for he 'is a *living* God (Mal. 3:6; Heb. 13:8).'[256]

Jesus Christ's mediatorial office and activity applies to both OT and NT believers.
If Christ is the mediator of the 'eternal covenant' (Heb. 13:21) and he does not change, then he effected salvation for believers

---

254. So, e.g., Ambrose, *Of the Christian Faith* 5.23–25 (*NPNF*², 10:287); Turretin, *Institutes of Elenctic Theology*, 1:287; Shedd, *Dogmatic Theology*, 241, 262, 623; Dabney, *Systematic Theology*, 191; Hodge, *Systematic Theology*, 1:390; A. A. Hodge, *Outlines of Theology*, 172; Bavinck, *Reformed Dogmatics*, 4:709; Vos, *Reformed Dogmatics*, 1:61; Berkhof, *Systematic Theology*, 94; Frame, *The Doctrine of God*, 568; Swain, *The Trinity: An Introduction*, 79, 81; and Documents of the Debrecen Synod, Concerning God (*Reformed Confessions of the 16th and 17th Centuries*, 3:22).

255. Athanasius, *Deposition of Arius* 3 (*NPNF*², 4:70); *Four Discourses Against the Arians* 1.36, 48; 2.10 (*NPNF*², 4:327; 4:334; 4:353, respectively); and Alexander of Alexandria, *Epistles on the Arian Heresy* 2.3 (*ANF*, 6:298).

256. Letham, *Systematic Theology*, 165, his emphasis.

in both the OT and NT. That Christ is the mediator in all ages is a point often made by Reformed theologians and creeds using Hebrews 13:8.[257] Many times, the emphasis in context is Christ's work in the OT. The Westminster divines make the point well:

> Although the work of redemption was not actually wrought by Christ, till after his incarnation, yet the efficacy, and benefits thereof, were communicated unto the elect in all ages successively from the beginning of the world, in and by those promises, types, and sacrifices, wherein he was revealed and signified to be the Seed of the woman, which should bruise the serpent's head, and the Lamb slain from the beginning of the world, *being yesterday and to-day the same and for ever*.[258]

Bavinck adds that Hebrews 13:8 also supports the Covenant of Redemption (*Pactum Salutis*), the Trinitarian agreement in eternity related to our salvation. 'For there is but one mediator between God and humankind, who is the same yesterday and today and forever, who was chosen as Mediator from eternity.' He goes on to note that 'the covenant of grace revealed in time does not land in the air but rests on an eternal, unchanging foundation.'[259]

Vos, although not referencing Hebrews 13:8 per se, notes that redemptive history and revelation unfold progressively, not with 'external accretion,' but with 'internal expansion, an organic unfolding within.' This is naturally required by the 'soteriological purpose' of revelation. This soteriological purpose must be 'essentially the same in all periods' and

---

257. WCF 7.6; 8.6; 11.6; Beza's Confession 26 (*Reformed Confessions of the 16th and 17th Centuries*, 2:279); Confession of Tarcal and Torda 26 (*Reformed Confessions of the 16th and 17th Centuries*, 2:701); Formula Consensus Helvetica 24 (*Reformed Confessions of the 16th and 17th Centuries*, 4:529); Ames, *The Marrow of Theology* 18.9; Turretin, *Institutes of Elenctic Theology*, 2:195, 2:371, 3:28; Vos, *Reformed Dogmatics*, 2:124; Bavinck, *Reformed Dogmatics*, 3:434; Berkhof, *Systematic Theology*, 279; and Frame, *Systematic Theology*, 375–76.

258. WCF 8.6, emphasis mine.

259. Bavinck, *Reformed Dogmatics*, 3:214–15.

the Gospel 'must have been present from the outset ... So dispensation grows out of dispensation, and the newest is but the fully expanded flower of the oldest.' Vos then brings his comments to head, 'Hence, from the beginning all redeeming acts of God aim at the creation and introduction of this new organic principle, *which is none other than Christ.*'[260]

Yes! 'Jesus Christ is the same yesterday, today, and forever.'

Closing (13:18–25)

Hebrews 13:18–25 is quite similar to a typical closing of a Pauline letter. Pauline closings usually have a peace benediction, various greetings, and a grace benediction. All of the Pauline closings do not have all three of these elements, but when they do, it is in this order (1 Thess. 5:23–28; 2 Thess. 3:16–18; 2 Cor. 13:11–14). Pauline closings several times also include brief exhortations (e.g., 1 Cor. 16:13; 1 Thess. 5:25), travel comments (e.g., 1 Cor. 16:12; Eph. 6:22; 2 Tim. 5:21; Phlm. 22), and an autograph (1 Cor. 16:21; Gal. 6:11; Col. 4:18; 2 Thess. 3:17; Phlm. 19) interspersed within the three elements above.[261]

Hebrews 13:18–25 has the order of a peace benediction (13:20–21), then greetings (13:24), and then a grace benediction (13:25). Interspersed within these three are two exhortations (13:18–19, 22) and a travel-plan comment (13:23). I assume,

---

260. Geerhardus Vos, 'The Idea of Biblical Theology,' in *Redemptive History and Biblical Interpretation: The Shorter Writings of Geerhardus Vos*, ed. Richard B. Gaffin, Jr. (Phillipsburg: P&R, 1980), 1–24, esp. 11–12, my emphasis.

261. For a thorough discussion of the Pauline closings, see Jeffrey A. D. Weima, *Neglected Endings: The Significance of the Pauline Letter Closings*, JSNTSup 101 (Sheffield: Sheffield Academic Press, 1994), 28–76; and his more recent, *Paul the Ancient Letter Writer: An Introduction to Epistolary Analysis* (Grand Rapids: Baker, 2016), 165–204. Broadly speaking, Pauline closings are typical of his letters in his day. For a helpful summary of the typical Greco-Roman letter format as it relates to Paul, see David E. Aune, *The New Testament in its Literary Environment*, LEC 8 (Philadelphia: Westminster, 1987), 152–82; For a more general discussion of Greco-Roman letters, see Stanley K. Stowers, *Letter Writing in Greco-Roman Antiquity*, LEC 5 (Philadelphia: Westminster, 1986).

as I do for Pauline letters that do not have specific autograph language, that the AH actually wrote the greeting. This would be evident to an original reader because it would be in a different handwriting than an amanuensis (cf. Gal. 6:11; 2 Thess. 3:17). If not in a different handwriting, I assume that the AH added his signature at the end of the letter.

This close parallel to a Pauline closing is understandable. Given that both the AH and the congregation are closely connected to Timothy (Heb. 13:23), and that the AH and the congregation are closely connected (Heb. 13:19), and that Timothy is closely connected to Paul; it is not unusual that the AH's closing format would match Paul's.[262] The Timothy comment and the matching format are very strong evidences that the AH is part of the Pauline circle (see discussion in Introductory Matters)

13:18–19 *Pray for us; for we are persuaded that we have a good conscience, desiring to behave well in all [situations]. And even more I exhort [you] to do this in order that I might be restored to you quickly.*

In Hebrews 13:18–19, the AH uses both a first person singular (**I**) and first person plural (**us, we**) (cf. 1 Thess. 2:18). Is the plural just a literary or epistolary plural simply meaning "I"?[263] In Hebrews, excepting OT quotes, the explicit first person singular is used in 11:32, here, and 13:22 (twice). Elsewhere in Hebrews, '*we* are speaking' type constructions are used in 2:5; 5:11; 6:3, 9, 11, and 8:1.[264] These *we* verses could

---

262. Some critical scholars see Heb. 13:22–25 as added later by someone other than the AH to ostensibly indicate the Pauline authorship of Hebrews, e.g., Steyn, 'The Ending of Hebrews reconsidered,' 252–53; and Grässer, *Hebräer*, 3:409–10.

263. Commentators are split with more probably opting for **we** as a literary plural. Favoring a literary plural are, e.g., Owen, *Hebrews*, 23:469; Bruce, *Hebrews*, 386 n. 107; Attridge, *Hebrews*, 402; and Johnson, *Hebrews*, 352. Favoring **we** as the AH and others with him are, e.g., Lenski, *Hebrews and James*, 429; Lane, *Hebrews 9–13*, 556; and Kleinig, *Hebrews*, 713.

264. Heb. 8:1 is a plural participle as opposed to a first person plural finite verb.

easily mean either (1) the AH only or (2) the AH primarily but include those few in his ministerial circle with him who are agreeing to what he is saying.

Here in Hebrews 13:18–19, it does make sense to see the **I** and **us/we** distinction as intentional. The AH asks the church to **pray for us**,[265] the AH and his ministerial circle, because (**for**) they do act appropriately as ministers.[266] (The assumption is that among the many things to pray for, praying for ministers is a good thing due to their influence in Christ's church.) I take this request to be for general prayers relevant to ministerial duties. In addition to these general prayers, **even more I exhort you to do this** (i.e., pray) **in order that I might be restored to you quickly.** The AH now explicitly moves to first person singular because his request is specific to himself. He wants to return again to the congregation and location where he had previously been (cf. Heb. 13:23). Given my view of Hebrews 13:18–19, I then register a weak vote for the other *we* verses, at least potentially, minimally including his ministerial circle when he says 'we are speaking' (i.e., option two above).

All agree that **restored** refers to the AH's **desir[e]** to return to a congregation where he had previously lived among them and been a part of it in some capacity.[267] He was to be **restored** in the sense that his friendship and joy of fellowship would be renewed after an absence. This shows some type of 'intimate association' with the church.[268] Commentators, however, admit they have little evidence to distinguish whether the AH

---

265. Note Paul's first-person-plural prayer requests at the end of some of his letters (Col. 4:3; 1 Thess. 5:25; 2 Thess. 3:1; cf. Rom. 15:30).

266. In Heb. 13:7, 'conduct' (ἀναστροφή) is a cognate of **to behave** (ἀναστρέφω). Both contexts relate to ministerial leaders.

267. So also, e.g., Gouge, *Hebrews*, 1110; Brown, *Hebrews*, 713; and Koester, *Hebrews*, 573. Clearly Heb. 5:11–12; 6:9–12; and 10:32–34 confirm that the AH 'was able to recall for them their earlier experiences and efforts' (Johnson, *Hebrews*, 354). This knowledge was not necessarily obtained when the AH was living with the community, but it would have certainly been one way to do it.

268. Cockerill's phrase (*Hebrews*, 714).

ENDING EXHORTATIONS AND CLOSING (13:1–25)   557

was previously there as a member of the church, or a member who became a leader, or was sent to the church as part of the Pauline circle to lead the church. I prefer the latter. Why? It seems that Timothy (Heb. 13:23) and AH are in similar situations. Given this, it would be more likely that they were both sent there as part of Paul's circle rather than that they both just happened to be living in the congregation's city and both became members of the same church.

The congregation and the AH clearly know each other personally. Hence, this letter is not originally anonymous![269]

13:20–21 *Now*[270] *may the God of peace, the one who brought up from the dead [ones][271] the great shepherd of the sheep, by the blood of [the] eternal covenant, our Lord Jesus, prepare[272] you with everything good[273] to do his will, doing in us[274] [what] is pleasing before him, through Jesus Christ, to whom be glory forever and ever.[275] Amen.*

---

269. Lane also makes this obvious point (*Hebrews 9–13*, 558).

270. Benedictions often begin with δέ (e.g., Rom. 15:33;1 Thess. 5:23; 2 Thess. 3:16). Hence, here δέ is not specifically referring to another prayer after Heb. 13:18, which would have been translated as 'and.' Instead, I translated as **now** to show the beginning of a benediction. So also many English translations (e.g., KJV; NIV; ESV).

271. Note that the substantival adjective **dead** is plural in Greek. Hence, Christ is raised from among the **dead ones**. This same plural is also in the received Greek text of the Apostle's Creed (Schaff, *Creeds of Christendom*, 2:45). I assume that the English 'dead' in the translation of the Creed is being used as a collective substantival adjective, and thus should be understood as 'the dead ones.'

272. **Prepare** is in the optative mood; this is common in benedictions (e.g., Rom. 15:5–6, 13; 1 Thess. 3:11–13; 5:23–24; 2 Thess. 2:16–17; 3:5).

273. I did not include 'work' even though the majority of Greek manuscripts do include it. Metzger argues that 'work,' which is omitted in a few important early manuscripts, was added as 'an obvious homiletic gloss' (*TCGNT*[2], 605). As to English translations, the KJV and NKJV include 'work,' although the vast majority of major English translations do not (e.g., RSV, NASB, ESV, CSB17, CEB).

274. The Greek manuscripts are split between **us** and 'you' plural. Most English translations have **us** (e.g., NASB, NIV, NRSV,CEB), while a few have 'you' (KJV, NAB, RSV). See Metzger, *TCGNT*[2], 606.

275. Although some early Greek manuscripts omit **and ever** (τῶν αἰώνων), it is appropriate given this grand benediction to have the double **forever and ever**. It is easy to see how a copyist could skip the second **ever**

Hebrews 13:20–21 is a grand peace benediction. Benedictions are a specialized type of prayer offered by God's authorized representative, in which the representative asks God to bless his people. Often a benediction is included in liturgical contexts. The Aaronic benediction/blessing in Numbers 6:22–27 is the primary example; and, in the tradition of that text, virtually all the NT letters end with a benediction(s).[276] These NT letters, including Hebrews, were written to be read, among other settings, at worship services (cf. 1 Thess 5:27; Col. 4:16). Thus confirming the connection to the Aaronic benediction.[277]

In Paul, aspects of the various elements of letter closings 'echo and reinforce key concerns addressed earlier in the body of the letter.'[278] In this benediction, connections to all of Hebrews includes forgiveness of sins (**God of peace**, cf. Heb. 7:2), Christ is now alive and exalted (**brought up from the dead**), blood related to covenants (**blood of the eternal covenant**, e.g., Heb. 9:18, 20; 10:29; 12:24), God's will (**his will**, e.g., Heb. 10:7; 10:36), perseverance (**doing in us what is pleasing before him**, cf. Heb. 2:1; 4:11; 6:12; 10:22, 39; 12:1), not to mention Christ (!) (**our Lord Jesus, Jesus Christ, to him be glory**, cf. Heb. 1:3; 3:1; 12:2). Given that this is a benediction, which is expected to have formulaic elements that may or not

---

in the phrase τοὺς αἰῶνας τῶν αἰώνων. See discussion in Metzger with which I disagree where the committee sees this as a difficult decision (*TCGNT*², 606–7). All major English translations include **and ever**.

276. There are also some benedictions in the middle of NT letters, e.g., 1 Thess. 3:11–12; 2 Thess. 2:16–17; Rom. 15:5–6, 13.

277. For various discussions of NT benedictions (or 'wish prayers'), see Robert Jewett, 'The Form and Function of the Homiletic Benediction,' *AThR* 51 (1969): 18–34; Gordon P. Wiles, *Paul's Intercessory Prayers: The Significance of the Intercessory Prayer Passages in the Letters of Paul*, SNTSMS 24 (Cambridge: CUP, 1974), 45–71; Weima, *Neglected Endings*, 77–95; and William R. Osborne, *Divine Blessing and the Fullness of Life in the Presence of God*, Short Studies in Biblical Theology (Wheaton: Crossway, 2020), 107–38. The classic study on the verb 'to bless' is by Mitchell, *The Meaning of* BRK *'To Bless' in the Old Testament*. Some of the above paragraph is taken from Cara, *1 & 2 Thessalonians*, 94.

278. Weima, *Paul the Ancient Letter Writer*, 165.

ENDING EXHORTATIONS AND CLOSING (13:1–25) 559

be tightly related to the book of Hebrews, some quasi-unique elements are expected.[279] These include **shepherd**, an explicit reference to the resurrection (**brought up from the dead**), the exact expression **Lord Jesus** is only here in Hebrews, the exact expression **Jesus Christ** is only in Hebrews three times (Heb. 10:10; 13:8; 13:21).

This benediction has multiple subset phrases. The grammatical 'skeleton' of this benediction is: **May God ... prepare you ... to do his will**. At one level, **will** refers to all of God's revealed will (cf. Deut. 29:29), but given the context of the letter, it certainly includes the requirement to *persevere* in loving God through Christ.[280] Also note that this benediction includes both God's activity and the believer's (cf. Phil. 2:12–13).[281] God **prepare[s]**, and a believer is **to do**. Of course, these two activities are not at the same level. If a believer is able to do any good work, it is solely because God enabled him to do it.[282]

The benediction begins with **the God of peace**. Due to the soteriological aspects of the benediction, I take **peace** in the sense of God bringing forgiveness and a change of heart to those who were formerly at enmity with him.[283] The exact phrase **peace of God** occurs several times in Paul (Rom. 15:33; 16:20; Phil. 4:9; 1 Thess. 5:23), although never in the OT and only once in extant Second Temple Judaism literature (T. Dan 5:2). This is probably another result of the AH having been within the Pauline circle.[284]

---

279. So also Cockerill, *Hebrews*, 714.

280. So also WLC 79, which references Heb. 13:20–21, '[God's] decree and covenant to give them perseverance.'

281. So also Lenski, *Hebrews and James*, 495; and Hughes, *Hebrews*, 590.

282. Referencing Heb. 13:21, Somerset Confession 18 states, '[Christ] makes us both willing and able to honor him' (*Reformed Confessions of the 16th and 17th Centuries*, 4:449).

283. So also, e.g., Owen, *Hebrews*, 23:472; Hughes, *Hebrews*, 589; and Koester, *Hebrews*, 579. *Contra* those who, based on Heb. 12:14, take **peace** as harmony among formerly disharmonious church members, e.g., Bruce, *Hebrews*, 387.

284. So also Johnson, *Hebrews*, 354.

Christ's bodily resurrection is only here *explicitly* referred to within this letter in the phrase **brought up from the dead**.[285] Much has been made of the 'absence' of the resurrection in Hebrews by some critical scholars. I respond that given the explicit death of Christ in Hebrews, every time Christ's ascension or his eternal priesthood are mentioned, his resurrection is strongly implied. This is especially true because it is here explicitly stated confirming all of the strongly implicit references. Further, all early Christian churches emphasized Christ's resurrection. Thus the AH and the congregants would have naturally assumed it.[286]

The Father (**God**) is here said to be the agent of Christ's resurrection (e.g., Acts 2:32; 1 Cor. 15:15). Other Scriptures state that Christ raised himself (e.g., Matt. 20:19; 1 Thess. 4:14; John 10:18; Heb. 9:14[287]), and that Christ was raised by the Holy Spirit (e.g., Rom. 1:4; 8:6). Thus the whole Trinity was involved in Christ's resurrection.[288]

---

285. The Greek verb behind **brought up** is ἀνάγω. Only here and Rom. 10:7 is this verb used to refer to Christ's resurrection in the NT. The most common verb is ἐγείρω (e.g., Matt. 28:6; Luke 24:34; John 21:14; Acts 3:15; Rom. 4:24; 1 Cor. 15:4; 2 Tim. 2:8; 1 Pet. 1:21), and ἀνίστημι is the second most common verb (e.g., Mark 9:9; Luke 24:46; John 20:7; Acts 2:32; 1 Thess. 4:14). I am not sure what to make of this unusual usage.

286. For an excellent summary of scholarly views on this 'riddle of Hebrew's silence' (his terminology) concerning the resurrection, see Moffitt, *Atonement and the Logic of Resurrection in the Epistle of Hebrews*, 1–43. Although there is much in Moffitt that I disagree with concerning the atonement and Christ's priesthood, I do agree with many, but not all, of his arguments showing the AH's 'affirmation of Jesus' bodily resurrection unifies and drives the high-priestly Christology and the soteriology of his homily' (p. 299, emphasis removed). For a discussion with similar views as mine, see Schreiner, *Hebrews*, 471–74; and Beale, *A New Testament Biblical Theology*, 317–22.

287. This would be my view as I interpret 'spirit' as referring to Christ's divine nature. Others see 'spirit' as referring to the Holy Spirit. See my discussion at Heb. 9:13–14.

288. This Trinitarian involvement is as an aspect of 'perichoresis', that is, the mutual indwelling of the three persons in the one being. This applies both to the being of God and his work. As Swain notes, 'the mutual relations between the persons of the Trinity exhibit themselves within God's indivisible external works ... all God's external works are indivisible works of the one God,' although each person has a 'distinct mode of acting'

Christ is given the epithet **the great shepherd of the sheep**. The adjective **great** recalls 'the *great* high priest' (Heb. 4:14) and 'the *great* priest' (Heb. 10:21). The phrase **shepherd of the sheep**, although not used elsewhere in Hebrews, does have significant biblical connections that relate to Hebrews. It is used in the OT to describe the function of both the Davidic king (e.g., 2 Sam. 5:2; Ps. 78:71–72; Ezek. 34:23; 37:23; Zech. 13:7) and God himself (e.g., Ps. 23:1; Isa. 40:11; Jer. 31:10; Ezek. 34:11–19).[289] First Peter 2:25 and 5:4 emphasize Christ as the shepherd king. John 10 highlights the priestly aspect of shepherd; 'the good shepherd lays down his life for the sheep' (John 10:11). Following the final Passover meal with his disciples, Christ, quoting from Zechariah 13:7, informs them that God the Father 'will strike the shepherd' and after that Christ will 'be raised' (Matt. 26:31–32 // Mark 14:27–28). Yes, these biblical themes match well to Hebrews. Christ, for his people/sheep, is both the kingly Son and the died/raised Priest. He is both God and man.[290]

In the phrase **by the blood of the eternal covenant**, **blood** clearly refers to Christ's death (e.g., Heb. 9:14; 10:19) and the **eternal covenant** is another name for the new covenant.[291]

(*The Trinity: An Introduction*, 109–10). Commenting on this verse, Aquinas notes that Christ 'rose by the one power of God, Father, Son, and Holy Spirit' (*Hebrews*, 308). For a discussion of perichoresis and the three persons involvement in the resurrection of Christ, see Kelly, *Systematic Theology*, 2:487–89.

289. For a useful summary discussion of 'shepherd' in the OT, see Louis Jonker, "רעה," *NIDOTTE*, 3:1138–43. Some see the AH intentionally referring to Isa. 63:11 due to linguistic connections of 'brought up' (עלה; ἀναβιβάζω) and 'shepherd of the sheep,' and assuming Christ is the greater 'Moses' (e.g., Beale, *A New Testament Biblical Theology*, 321–22; Bruce, *Hebrews*, 388; Lane, *Hebrews 9–13*, 561; and Kleinig, *Hebrews*, 724). These connections are too tenuous for me.

290. Cockerill stresses that **great shepherd of the sheep** especially emphasizes 'the eternal deity of the Son' due to the Ps. 23:1 connection (*Hebrews*, 716–17).

291. In Hebrews, this covenant is referred to as 'better' (7:22; 8:6), 'second' (8:7; 10:9), 'eternal' (13:20), 'new'/καινός (8:8, 13; 9:15), and 'new'/ νέος (12:24). In Hebrews, the adjective 'eternal' modifies 'salvation' (5:9), 'redemption' (9:12), 'inheritance' (9:15), and 'covenant' (13:20).

Exactly what this phrase is supporting (**by**) is less clear. I take this phrase as a summary of the plan of salvation (**eternal covenant**) highlighting the core aspect (Christ's **blood**) (cf. Heb. 9:20). Thus, this phrase would functionally apply to any aspect of the Triune God's work for his people's salvation. Hence, in context, this phrase relates to the whole benediction.

As part of the new covenant, God **prepare[s] you with everything good**. For true believers, God produces internal change and provides outward means for all types of good works, including final perseverance. This **prepar[ing]** by **God the Father** is **through** the instrumental work of **Jesus Christ**, both in his estates of humiliation and exaltation.[292]

There is a doxology added to the end of this benediction, **to whom be glory forever and ever**. Does **whom** refer to God the Father or Christ?[293] Second Peter 3:18 is a benediction followed by a doxology to Christ; and Jude 25 is a benediction followed by a doxology to God the Father. Here, the argument for God the Father relies on 'praise to God' in Hebrews 13:15. I disagree and argue for Christ. In Hebrews, there is an emphasis on relating **glory** to Christ (Heb. 1:3; 2:7, 9; 3:3). In addition, **to whom** follows directly after **Jesus Christ**. Further, the emphasis on Christ's divinity is consistent with this doxology, as one expects a doxology to a divine being. Finally, 'praise to God' in Hebrews 13:15 is contextually too far from the benediction to be determinative.

13:22 *And I exhort you, brothers, bear the word of exhortation, for indeed I have written*[294] *to you with few [words].*

---

292. Referencing this benediction, WCF 17.2 comments that the 'perseverance of the saints depends ... upon the efficacy of the merit and intercession of Jesus Christ.'

293. Commentators are split. Those favoring God the Father include Bruce, *Hebrews*, 389; Lane, *Hebrews 9–13*, 559; and Schreiner, *Hebrews*, 430; favoring Christ include Aquinas, *Hebrews*, 310; Calvin, *Hebrews and 1 & 2 Peter*, 215; Owen, *Hebrews*, 23:480; Attridge, *Hebrews*, 407–8; and Kleinig, *Hebrews*, 733.

294. The Greek behind **I have written** is the aorist (past) tense. The writer

Ending Exhortations and Closing (13:1–25)

In Hebrews 13:22–24, following the benediction, the AH adds (**and**) several more closing exhortations with no conjunctions between them.

Using some rhetoric with **exhort** (παρακαλέω) and **exhortation** (παράκλησις), and warmly referring to the congregation as **brothers**, the AH lightly presses them to consider the message of this letter (**bear the word of exhortation**). One reason (**for**) is that the letter is not that long (**indeed I have written to you with few words**). Possibly, he intends a finer point, that the letter is not long relative to the grandness and importance of the topic.[295]

The AH refers to his letter as a **word of exhortation**. In one sense, all Christian letters and sermons could be called an **exhortation** (cf. Acts 13:15; 1 Tim. 4:13). Given the emphasis on persevering, however, terming this letter an **exhortation** is especially appropriate.[296] Hebrews is certainly a letter, but it is a letter that has more sermon or homiletic aspects relative to those aspects in other NT letters.[297]

13:23 *Know [that] our brother Timothy, having been released, with whom I shall see you if he comes quickly.*

Timothy is the well-known companion of Paul (e.g., Acts 16:1–5; Col. 1:1; 1 Tim. 1:2; 2 Tim. 4:9).[298] The AH

---

assumes the position of the reader who would be looking back in time to when the writer wrote. This use of the aorist is commonly called an 'epistolary aorist.' See Robertson, *A Grammar of the Greek New Testament*, 845–6.

295. So also Owen, *Hebrews*, 23:482–83; Brown, *Hebrews*, 726; and Lenski, *Hebrews*, 497. *Contra* Lane who sees this as 'simply a polite literary convention' similar to 1 Pet. 5:12, Ign. *Rom.* 8:2; Ign. *Pol.* 7:3; and Barn. 1:5 (*Hebrews 9–13*, 568).

296. So also Cockerill, *Hebrews*, 719. Concerning the semantic range of this word group, see discussion at Heb. 6:18.

297. Concerning **word of exhortation**, Hughes well says, 'In view ... of the epistolary conclusion, this composition may be described as both homiletic and epistolary; and there is nothing unusual in this, for the main purpose of the letters of the New Testament is homiletic and hortatory' (*Hebrews*, 592).

298. For a historical summary of Timothy's life that takes both Acts and the Pauline letters as historically accurate, see G. F. Hawthorne, 'Timothy,'

is planning on visiting the congregation (**I shall see you**). He adds that **if he** (**Timothy**) **comes quickly** to the AH's current location, then the AH and **Timothy** will travel and arrive together at the congregation.[299] If not, the AH will come by himself. This upcoming visit is another incentive for the congregation to take the 'word of exhortation' with appropriate seriousness.[300]

More specifically, the AH is informing (**know**) the congregation that the possibility exists that **Timothy** may get to the AH's location **quickly** because recently he has **been released**. It appears that the congregation knew about **Timothy['s]** former situation but did not know he had been recently **released** from it.

But from what was he **released**? The verb **released** (ἀπολύω) is quite generic.[301] Possible options might include being **released** from prison, house arrest, a legal charge, a ministry-job responsibility, or a family responsibility. In Acts and Paul's letters, **Timothy** was never in legal trouble, although his mentor, Paul, obviously was. However, since Hebrews was almost certainly written after Paul's death, it is at least possible that **Timothy** was in legal difficulty after Paul died. I opt, however, for **Timothy** being **released** from a ministry-job responsibility.[302] This eliminates my having to rely on assumed legal difficulties, and none of the prison language in Hebrews 10:34 and 13:3 is used here. Thus, the congregation knew that **Timothy** was sent to a certain church to perform

---

ISBE, 4:857–58; and F. F. Bruce, *The Pauline Circle*, Biblical Classics Library (Carlisle, UK: Paternoster, 1995), 29–34. Eusebius records that Timothy was the first bishop in Ephesus (*Church History* 3.4.6 [*NPNF*², 1:136]).

299. I am assuming that **Timothy** is in a city much closer to the AH than to the congregation. So also Bruce, *Hebrews*, 390; and Lane, *Hebrews 9–13*, 569.

300. So also Koester, *Hebrews*, 583.

301. LSJ, 208–9. This verb does not occur elsewhere in Hebrews.

302. I am in the minority here. Most opt for prison or some type of legal difficulty, e.g., Owen, *Hebrews*, 23:483; Gouge, *Hebrews*, 1123; Lane, *Hebrews 9–13*, 569; and Allen, *Hebrews*, 630.

Ending Exhortations and Closing (13:1–25)

a specific task, and now the AH is informing them this task is completed.

The AH refers to **Timothy** as **our brother**. In the previous verse, the AH has referred to the congregation as 'brothers.' Both **(our)** the congregation and the AH know **Timothy** and have a positive view of him. When combined with Hebrews 13:19, one concludes that both **Timothy** and the AH had lived and ministered as leaders among the congregation, possibly at the same time.

13:24–25 *Greet all your leaders and all the saints. The ones from Italy greet you. May grace be with all of you.*

I assume the letter was delivered to one or a group of the **leaders**. Then the letter was to be read to the entire church presumably during a worship service (cf. 1 Thess. 5:27; Col. 4:16). Thus, although the AH uses the second-person plural imperative **greet**, I take this as meaning that the AH requests **greet** *for me* everyone, both **your leaders** (cf. Heb. 13:17) **and all the saints**; or more clearly, 'I give my greetings to everyone.'[303] **Saints** generally refers to all believers (cf. Heb. 3:1; 6:10), and here it implies the remainder of the congregation beyond the **leaders**.

As all acknowledge, the sentence **the ones from Italy greet you** is ambiguous—of course, to the original congregation, there would have been no ambiguity. Grammatically with no context, it could equally mean (1) **the ones from Italy** who currently live in Italy or (2) **the ones from Italy** who lived in Italy for a significant time but are now living outside of Italy in the city that the AH is currently located.[304] Option two is

---

303. So also Lenski, *Hebrews and James*, 499; and Hughes, *Hebrews*, 593. Speaking specifically about Paul, Weima similarly considers that his second-person greetings 'function virtually as a surrogate for a first-person greeting' (*Paul the Ancient Letter Writer*, 184).

304. The same grammatical expression **the ones from** (οἱ ἀπό) is used in Acts matching to both of these options. Acts 17:13 refers to Jewish Thessalonians who still lived in Thessalonica (option # 1), and Acts 21:27 refers to Jewish Asians who were in Jerusalem (option # 2).

more likely in context. If the AH was writing from Rome, or somewhere else in Italy, he probably would have included 'all' as in '*all* those with me here in the congregation in Rome send you greetings.'[305] But since he did not use 'all' and only selected a portion of the larger congregation at his location for an additional greeting, this confirms that **the ones from Italy** are those from Italy who are now living in the AH's location. But why only have an additional greeting from the Italians? This is due to the congregation receiving the letter being in Italy. Most likely, there were personal connections between the Italians in the two congregations. In sum, the AH is located outside of Italy and writing to a congregation in Italy, probably in Rome.[306] See Introductory Matters chapter.

As typical in the Pauline letters, the AH ends with a grace benediction, **may grace be with all of you.**[307] This is an appropriate way to end a Christian letter and a worship service.

The AH uses **grace** in a variety of ways. He speaks of the 'grace of God' (Heb. 2:9; 12:15), 'the throne of grace' (Heb. 4:16), and the Holy 'Spirit of grace' (Heb. 10:29). He notes that in difficulties believers may find/be-strengthened by 'grace' (Heb. 4:16; 13:9). Connecting to two large emphases in Hebrews, it is only by **grace** that a believer's sins are forgiven, and only by **grace** that one perseveres.

---

305. So also many modern commentators, e.g., Bruce, *Hebrews*, 391; Koester, *Hebrews*, 581; and Schreiner, *Hebrews*, 431–32. *Contra* Aquinas, *Hebrews*, 310; Calvin, *Hebrews and 1 & 2 Peter*, 216; and Spicq, *Hébreux*, 2:439.

306. A variety of subscriptions have been added to the letter (see Metzger, *TCGNT*², 607). One included in the Textus Receptus reads, 'Written to the Hebrews from Italy through [delivered by] Timothy.' This subscription was included in the original KJV. Many complain about this subscription being obviously wrong because Heb. 13:22 does not indicate that Timothy is the letter carrier. So Owen, 23:485; Gouge, *Hebrews*, 1128; and Brown, *Hebrews*, 728. The Westminster Annotations comment, 'Doubtless this subscription was added by some ignorant person, because we find it expressly said, that Timothy was not yet come unto him, verse 23' (*Annotations Upon All the Books of the Old and New Testament*, 3rd ed. [London: Tyler, 1657], *loc. cit.*).

307. In the Greek, this grace benediction matches word-for-word to Titus 3:15.

Reflections

The liturgy of a typical Christian worship service includes a benediction, which is at the end or very near the end of the service. These benedictions are intended to be emotionally uplifting. Both the minister declaring it and the congregation hearing it should enjoy the experience. After all, a benediction is God's authorized representative declaring, based on God's word, the promise of God's blessings.

Possibly, the three most well-known benedictions used in Christian worship services are Numbers 6:24–26, 2 Corinthians 13:14, and Hebrews 13:20–21. Each of them has their own precious promises. The Hebrews 13:20–21 benediction (with the short doxology attached) promises that God will equip us to do his will, while also making statements about Christ that have emotional punch.

It is appropriate to end this commentary with a benediction!

> Now the God of peace, that brought again from the dead our Lord Jesus, that great shepherd of the sheep, through the blood of the everlasting covenant, make you perfect in every good work to do his will, working in you that which is well pleasing in his sight, through Jesus Christ; to whom be glory for ever and ever. Amen. (KJV)

Bibliography

Allen, David L. 'Constructing "Janus-Faced" Exhortations: The Use of the Old Testament Narratives in Heb 13:1–8.' *Bib* 89 (2008): 401–9.

———. *Hebrews*. NAC 35. Nashville: B&H, 2010.

———. *Lukan Authorship of Hebrews*. NAC Studies in Bible & Theology. Nashville, B&H Academic, 2010.

Allen, Leslie C. *Psalms 101–150*. WBC 21. Waco: Word, 1983.

Allen, R. Michael. *The Christ's Faith: A Dogmatic Account*. T & T Clark Studies in Systematic Theology. Edinburgh: T & T Clark, 2012.

———. *Justification and the Gospel: Understanding the Contexts and Controversies*. Grand Rapids: Baker, 2013.

———. '"From the time he took on the form of a servant": The Christ's Pilgrimage of Faith.' *International Journal of Systematic Theology* 16 (2014): 4-24.

———. "Christ," Pages 451–66 in *Companion to the Doctrine of Sin*. Edited by Keith Johnson and David Lauber. Edinburgh: Bloomsbury T&T Clark, 2016.

———. *Sanctification*. New Studies in Dogmatics. Grand Rapids: Zondervan, 2017.

Allison, D. C., Jr, 'Melchizedek.' Pages 729–30 in *DLNT*.

Ames, William. *The Marrow of Theology*. Durham: Labyrinth, 1983 (1629).

Anderson, F. I. '2 (Slavonic Apocalypse of) Enoch.' Pages

1:94–97 in *OTP*.

Annotations Upon All the Books of the Old and New Testament. 3rd ed. London: Tyler, 1657.

Ante-Nicene Fathers. Edited by A. Cleveland Coxe. 10 vols. Grand Rapids: Eerdmans, 1993.

Aquinas, Thomas. *Commentary on the Epistle to the Hebrews*. Translated by Chrysostom Baer. South Bend: St. Augustine, 2006.

———. *Summa Theologiae*. Translated by Laurence Shapcote. Edited by John Mortensen and Enrique Alarcón. Vols. 13–20. Lander, WY: Aquinas Institute, 2012.

ARP Psalter with Bible Songs, The. Pittsburgh, Crown & Covenant, 2011.

Attridge, Harold W. '"Heard Because of His Reverence" [Heb 5:7].' *JBL* 98 (1979): 90–93.

———. *A Commentary on the Epistle to the Hebrews*. Hermeneia. Philadelphia: Fortress, 1989.

Aune, David E. *The New Testament in its Literary Environment*. LEC 8. Philadelphia: Westminster, 1987.

Averbeck, Richard E. 'שָׁלֵם.' Pages 4:135–43 in *NIDOTTE*.

Babylonian Talmud, The: A Translation and Commentary. Translated and edited by Jacob Neusner. 22 vols. Peabody, MA: Hendrickson, 2005.

Bahnsen, Greg L. *Van Til's Apologetic*. Phillipsburg: P&R, 1998.

Bannerman, James. *The Church of Christ: A Treatise on the Nature, Powers, Ordinances, Discipline, and Government of the Christian Church*. Carlisle: Banner of Truth, 2015 (1869).

Barrett, C. K. 'The Eschatology of the Epistle of Hebrews.' Pages 363–93 in *The Background of the New Testament and Its Theology*. Edited by W. D. Davies and D. Daube. Cambridge, CUP, 1956.

Barrett, Matthew. *God's Word Alone: The Authority of Scripture: What the Reformers Taught ... and Why It Still Matters*. Five Solas. Grand Rapids: Zondervan, 2016.

Barton, S. C. 'Hospitality.' Pages 501–7 in *DLNT*.

Bateman, Herbert W, IV. 'The First-Century Messianic Uses of the OT: Heb. 1:5–13 and 4QFlor 1.1–19.' *JETS* 38 (1995): 11–27.

Bauckham, Richard. 'Monotheism and Christology in Hebrews 1.' Pages 167–85 in *Early Christianity in Context*. Edited by John M. G. Barclay. JSNTSup 263. NY: T&T Clark, 2004.

———. 'The Divinity of Jesus Christ in the Epistle to the Hebrews' Pages 15–36 in *The Epistle to the Hebrews and Christian Theology*. Edited by Richard Bauckham, Daniel R. Driver, Trevor A. Hart, and Nathan MacDonald. Grand Rapids: Eerdmans, 2009.

Bauer, Walter, A. F. Arndt, F. W. Gingrich, F. W. Danker, eds. *A Greek-English Lexicon of the New Testament and other Early Christian Literature*. 3rd ed. Chicago: University of Chicago Press, 2000.

Baugh, S. M. 'The Cloud of Witnesses in Hebrews 11.' *WTJ* 68 (2006): 113–22.

Bavinck, Herman. *Reformed Dogmatics*. Edited by John Bolt. Translated by John Vriend. 4 vols. Grand Rapids: Baker Academic, 2003–2008 (2nd ed. 1906–1911).

Beale, G. K. *The Book of Revelation: A Commentary on the Greek Text*. NIGTC. Grand Rapids: Eerdmans, 1999.

———. *A New Testament Biblical Theology: The Unfolding of the Old Testament in the New*. Grand Rapids: Baker Academic, 2011.

Beckwith, Rodger T. and Wilfrid Scott. *The Christian Sunday: A Biblical and Historical Study*. Grand Rapids: Baker, 1980.

Belcher, Richard P., Jr. *The Messiah and the Psalms: Preaching Christ from all the Psalms*. Ross-shire: Mentor, 2006.

———. *Prophet, Priest, and King: The Roles of Christ in the Bible and Our Roles Today*. Phillipsburg: P&R, 2016.

Bennett, Arthur, ed. *The Valley of Vision: A Collection of Puritan Prayers & Devotions*. Carlisle: Banner of Truth, 1975.

Berkhof, Louis. *Systematic Theology*. 4th ed. Grand Rapids:

Eerdmans, 1941.
Berkouwer, G. C. *The Person of Christ*. Translated by John Vriend. Studies in Dogmatics. Grand Rapids: Eerdmans, 1954.

———. *Faith and Perseverance*. Translated by Robert D. Knudsen, Studies in Dogmatics Grand Rapids: Eerdmans, 1958.

———. *The Work of Christ*. Studies in Dogmatics. Grand Rapids: Eerdmans, 1965.

———. *Sin*. Studies in Dogmatics. Grand Rapids: Eerdmans, 1971.

Bible Songs. Due West: ARP Board of Publication, 1931.

Bierma, Lyle D. with et al., ed. *An Introduction to the Heidelberg Catechism: Sources, History and Theology: With a Translation of the Smaller and Larger Catechisms of Zacharias Ursinus*. Texts and Studies in Reformation and Post-Reformation Thought. Grand Rapids: Baker, 2005.

Black, David Allen. 'Hebrews 1:1–4: A Study in Discourse Analysis.' *WTJ* 49 (1987): 175–94.

———. 'A Note on the Structure of Hebrews 12:1–2.' *Bib* 68 (1987): 543–51.

Blass, F., A. Debrunner, and Robert W. Funk. *A Greek Grammar of the New Testament and Other Early Christian Literature*. Chicago: University of Chicago, 1961.

Blomberg, Craig. 'Better Things in this Case: The Superiority of Today's New International Version in Hebrews.' *BT* 55 (2004): 310–18.

Bloesch, Donald G. *Jesus Christ: Savior & Lord*. Christian Foundations. Downers Grove: InterVarsity, 1997.

Boettner, Loraine. *The Reformed Doctrine of Predestination*. Phillipsburg: Presbyterian and Reformed, 1932.

Boring, M. Eugene. *An Introduction to the New Testament: History, Literature, Theology*. Louisville, Westminster John Knox, 2012.

Bousset, Wilhelm. *Kyrios Christos: A History of the Belief in Christ from the Beginnings of Christianity to Irenaeus*. Translated by John E. Steely. Waco: Baylor University Press, 2013 (1913).

Brakel, Wilhelmus à. *The Christian's Reasonable Service*. Translated by Bartel Elshout. Edited by Joel R. Beeke. 4 vols. Grand Rapids: Reformation Heritage, 1992–1995 (1702).

Brawley, Robert L. 'Discourse Structure and the Unseen in Hebrews 2:8 and 11:1: A Neglected Aspect of the Context.' *CBQ* 55 (1993): 81–98.

Bright, John. *A History of Israel*. 3rd ed. Philadelphia: Westminster, 1981.

Bromiley, G. W., ed. *The International Standard Bible Encyclopedia*. 4 vols. Grand Rapids: Eerdmans, 1979–1988.

Book of Common Worship: Approved by the General Assembly of the Presbyterian Church in the United States of America, The. Philadelphia: General Assembly Board of Publication, 1946.

Brooks, James A. and Carlton L. Winbery. *Syntax of New Testament Greek*. Lanham, MD: University Press of America, 1970.

Brown, John. *Hebrews*. Geneva. Carlisle: Banner of Truth, 1961 (1862).

Bruce, F. F. *The Epistle to the Hebrews*. 2nd ed. NICNT. Grand Rapids: Eerdmans, 1990.

———. *The Pauline Circle*. Biblical Classics Library. Carlisle, UK: Paternoster, 1995.

———. 'Habakkuk.' Pages 2:831–96 in *The Minor Prophets: An Exegetical and Expository Commentary*. Edited by Thomas Edward McComiskey. 3 vols. Grand Rapids: Baker, 1992–8.

Bruce, Robert. *Preaching Without Fear or Favour: Previously Unpublished Sermons on Hebrews 11*. Translated and edited by David Searle. Ross-shire: Christian Heritage, 2019.

Brueggemann, Walter. *First and Second Samuel*. Interpretation. Louisville: John Knox, 1990.

Buchanan, James. *The Doctrine of Justification: An Outline of its History in the Church and of its Exposition from Scripture*. Carlisle: Banner of Truth, 1961 (1867).

Burton, Ernest DeWitt. *Syntax of the Moods and Tenses in New Testament Greek*. 3rd ed. Eugene: Wipf and Stock, 2003 (1900).

Buswell, James Oliver. *A Systematic Theology of the Christian Religion*. 2 vols. Grand Rapids: Zondervan, 1962.

Calvert-Koyzis, N. 'Abraham,' Pages 1–6 in *DLNT*.

Calvin, John. *Institutes of the Christian Religion*. Edited by John T. McNeill. Translated by Ford Lewis Battles. 2 vols. Library of Christian Classics 20. Philadelphia: Westminster, 1960.

———. *The Epistle of Paul the Apostle to the Hebrews and the First and Second Epistles of St Peter*. Translated by William B. Johnson. Edited by David W. and Thomas F. Torrance. Calvin's Commentaries 12. Grand Rapids: Eerdmans, 1963.

———. *Commentary on the Book of Joshua*. Translated by Henry Beveridge. Calvin's Commentaries 4. Grand Rapids: Baker, 1996.

———. *Commentary on the Book of Psalms*. Translated by James Anderson. Calvin's Commentaries 4–6. Grand Rapids: Baker, 1996.

———. *Commentary on the Book of the Prophet Isaiah*. Translated by William Pringle. 4 vols. Calvin's Commentaries 7–8. Grand Rapids: Baker, 1996.

Cara, Robert J. *1 & 2 Thessalonians*. EP Study Commentary. Webster, NY: EP, 2009.

———. 'The Use of the Old Testament in the New Testament: Trusting the New Testament's Hermeneutics.' Pages 593–602 in *A Biblical-Theological Introduction to the New Testament: The Gospel Realized*. Edited by Michael J. Kruger. Wheaton; Crossway, 2016).

———. *Cracking the Foundation of the New Perspective on Paul: Covenantal Nomism versus Reformed Covenantal Theology*. Reformed Exegetical and Doctrinal Studies. Ross-shire: Mentor, 2017.

_____. 'Psalms Applied to Both Christ and Christians: Psalms 8, 22, 34, 118 and Romans 15:3 // Psalm 69:9.' Pages 97–111in *Redeeming the Life of the Mind: Essays in Honor of Vern Poythress*. Edited by Wayne Grudem, John Frame, and John Hughes. Wheaton: Crossway, 2017.

_____. 'Covenant in Hebrews.' Pages 247–66 in *Covenant Theology: Biblical, Historical, and Theological Perspectives*. Edited by Guy P. Waters, J. Nicholas Reid, and John R. Muether. Wheaton: Crossway, 2020.

Cartledge, T. W. 'שׁבע,' Pages 4:32–34 in *NIDOTTE*.

Chan, Alan Kam-Yau. *Melchizedek Passages in the Bible: A Case Study for Inner-Biblical and Inter-Biblical Interpretation*. Berlin: De Gruyter Open, 2016.

Childs, Brevard S. *Isaiah*, OTL. Louisville: Westminster, 2001.

Cockerill, Gareth Lee. *The Epistle of Hebrews*. NICNT. Grand Rapids: Eerdmans, 2012.

_____. 'Hebrews 12:18–24: Apocalyptic Typology or Platonic Dualism.' *TynBul* 69 (2018): 225–39.

Compton, Jared. 'The origin of ΣΩMA in Heb 10:5: Another Look at a Recent Proposal.' *TJ* 32ns (2011): 19–29.

_____. *Psalm 110 and the Logic of Hebrews*. LNTS 537. London: T&T Clark, 2015.

Constitution and Standards of the Associate-Reformed Church in North-America, The. New York: T. & J. Sword's: 1799.

Cortez, Felix H. 'From the Most Holy Place: The Period of Heb 9:6–10 and Day of Atonement as a Metaphor of Transition.' *JBL* 125 [2006]: 527–47.

Craigie, Peter C. *Deuteronomy*. NICOT. Grand Rapids: Eerdmans, 1976.

_____. *Psalms 1–50*. WBC 19. Waco: Word, 1983.

Crowe, Brandon D. 'Reading Psalm 40 Messianically.' *RF&P* 2:2 (2017): 31–44.

_____. 'Son and Priest, Then and Now: Christology and Redemptive History in Hebrews in light of the History of Interpretation.' *WTJ* 84 (2022): 19–38.

Croy, N. Clayton. *Endurance in Suffering: Hebrews 12.1–13 in Its Rhetorical, Religious, and Philosophical Context*. SNTSMS 98. Cambridge: CUP, 1998.

Culver, Robert D. 'דִּין.' Page 188 in *TWOT*.

Currid, John D. *A Study Commentary on Genesis 1:1–25:18*. EP Study Commentary. Darlington, England: Evangelical Press, 2003.

———. *A Study Commentary on Deuteronomy*. EP Study Commentary. Darlington: Evangelical Press, 2006.

———. *A Study Commentary on Exodus*, 2 vols. EP Study Commentary. Darlington: Evangelical Press, 2000–2001.

———. *The Case for Biblical Archaeology: Uncovering the Historical Record of God's Old Testament People*. Phillipsburg: P&R, 2020.

Dabney, Robert L. *Systematic Theology*. Carlisle: Banner of Truth 1985 (1878).

Dahl, N. A. 'A New and Living Way: The Approach to God According to Hebrews 10:19–25.' *Int* 5 (1951): 401–12.

Dahood, Mitchell. *Psalms III: 101–150: Introduction, Translation, and Notes*. AB 17A. Garden City: Doubleday, 1970.

D'Angelo, Mary Rose. *Moses in the Letter of Hebrews*. SBLDS 42. Missoula: Scholars, 1979.

Davis, Philip A., Jr. *The Place of Paideia in Hebrews' Moral Thought*. WUNT 2/475. Tübingen: Mohr Siebeck, 2018.

Day, Adam W. 'Bearing the Reproach of Christ: The Background of Psalm 68 (LXX) in Hebrews 13:9–16.' *Presbyterion* 44 (2018): 126–41.

Delitzsch, F. *Isaiah*. Translated by James Martin. 2 vols. Volume 7 of Commentary on the Old Testament in Ten Volumes. Grand Rapids: Eerdmans, 1985.

Denzinger, Heinrich. *Compendium of Creeds, Definitions, and Declarations on Matters of Faith and Morals*. Edited by Robert Fastiggi and Anne Englund Nash. 43rd ed. San Francisco: Ignatius, 2012.

deSilva, David A. *Perseverance in Gratitude: A Socio-Rhetorical Commentary on the Epistle 'to the Hebrews.'* Grand Rapids: Eerdmans, 2000.

Dickson, David. *A Short Explanation of the Epistle to the Hebrews.* Birmingham, AL: Solid Ground Christian, 2005 (1635).

———. *Truth's Victory over Error: A Commentary on the Westminster Confession of Faith.* Translated and edited by John R. DeWitt. Carlisle: Banner of Truth, 2007 (1684).

Dillard, Raymond B. and Tremper Longman III. *An Introduction to the Old Testament.* Grand Rapids: Zondervan, 1994.

du Toit, Andrie. 'Τὰ πρὸς τὸν θεόν in Romans and Hebrews: Towards Understanding an Enigmatic Phrase.' *ZNW* 101 (2010): 241–51.

Ebert, Daniel J. IV. 'The Chiastic Structure of the Prologue to Hebrews.' *TJ* 13 ns (1992): 163–79.

Eisenbaum, Pamela Michelle. *The Jewish Heroes of Christian History: Hebrews 11 in Literary Context*, SBLDS 156. Atlanta: Scholars, 1997.

Ellingworth, Paul. *The Epistle to the Hebrews: A Commentary on the Greek Text.* NIGTC. Grand Rapids: Eerdmans, 1993.

Emmrich, Martin. 'Pneuma in Hebrews: Prophet and Interpreter.' *WTJ* 63 (2002): 55–71.

———. '"Amtscharisma": Through the Eternal Spirit (Hebrews 9:14).' *BBR* 12 (2002): 17–32.

Enns, Peter E. 'Creation and Re-Creation: Psalm 95 and its Interpretation in Hebrews 3:1-4:13.' *WTJ* 55 (1993): 255–80.

Evans, Craig A. and Stanley E. Porter, eds. *Dictionary of New Testament Background.* Downers Grove, IL: InterVarsity, 2000.

Fairbairn, Patrick. *The Typology of Scripture.* 2 vols. Grand Rapids: Zondervan, n.d.

Fanning, Buist M. 'A Classical Reformed View.' Pages 172–219 in *Four Views on the Warning Passages in Hebrews.* Edited by Herbert W. Bateman IV. Grand Rapids: Kregel Academic & Professional, 2007.

Ferguson, Everett. *Backgrounds of Early Christianity*. 3rd. ed. Grand Rapids: Eerdmans, 2003.

Fesko, J. V. *The Trinity and the Covenant of Redemption*. Ross-shire: Mentor, 2016.

Filson, F. V. *'Yesterday': a Study of Hebrews in Light of Chapter 13*. London: SCM, 1967.

Fisher, James. *The Assembly's Shorter Catechism Explained by Way of Question and Answer*. Totton: Berith, 1998 (1765).

Fitzmyer, Joseph A. 'Melchizedek in the MT, LXX, and the NT.' *Bib* 81 (2000): 63–69.

Flannery, Austin, ed. *Vatican Council II: The Conciliar and Post Conciliar Documents*. Revised ed. Vatican Collection 1. Northport, NY: Costello, 1992.

Frame, John M. *The Doctrine of God*. Phillipsburg: P&R, 2002.

_____. *The Doctrine of the Christian Life*. Phillipsburg: P&R, 2008.

_____. *The Doctrine of the Word of God*. Phillipsburg: P&R, 2010.

_____. *Systematic Theology: An Introduction to Christian Belief*. Phillipsburg: P&R, 2013.

Freedman, David Noel. *The Anchor Bible Dictionary*. 6 vols. New York: Doubleday, 1992.

Friedman, Richard Elliott. 'Tabernacle.' Pages 6:292–300 in *ABD*.

Gaffin, Richard B. Jr., 'A Sabbath Rest Still Awaits the People of God.' Pages 33–51 in *Pressing toward the Mark: Essays Commemorating Fifty Years of the Orthodox Presbyterian Church*. Edited by Charles G. Dennison and Richard C. Gamble. Philadelphia: Committee for the Historian of the Orthodox Presbyterian Church, 1986.

_____. 'Systematic Theology and Hermeneutics.' Pages 39–51 in *Seeing Christ in All of Scripture: Hermeneutics at Westminster Theological Seminary*. Edited by Peter A. Lillback. Philadelphia: Westminster Seminary Press, 2016.

Gardiner, Frederic. 'On διαθήκη in Heb. ix. 16, 17.' *JBL* 5 (1885): 8–19.

Geneva Bible, The: The Annotated New Testament 1602 Edition, With Introductory Essays. Edited by Gerald T. Sheppard. Cleveland: Pilgrim, 1989.

Gurtner, Daniel M. 'LXX Syntax and the Identity of the NT Veil.' *NovT* 47 (2005): 344–53.

Gesenius' Hebrew Grammar. Edited by E. Kautzsch. Translated by A. E. Cowley. 2nd ed. Oxford: Clarendon, 1910.

Girardeau, John L. *The Federal Theology: Its Import and Its Regulative Influence*. Greenville: Reformed Academic, 1994 (1881).

Gleason, Randall C. 'The Eschatology of the Warning in Hebrews 10:26–31.' *TynBul* 53 (2002): 97–120.

Glombita, Otto. 'Erwägungen zum kunstvollen Ansatz der Paraenese im Brief an die Hebräer 10:19–25.' *NovT* 9 (1967): 132–50.

Goppelt, Leonhard. *Typos: The Typological Interpretation of the Old Testament in the New*. Translated by Donald H. Madvig. Eugene: Wipf and Stock, 2002 (1939).

Goswell, Gregory. 'Finding a Home for the Letter of Hebrews.' *JETS* 59 (2016): 747–60,

Gouge, William. *Commentary on Hebrews: Exegetical and Expository*. 2 vols. Birmingham: AL: Solid Ground Christian, 2005 (1655).

Granerod, Gard. 'Melchizedek in Hebrews 7.' *Bib* 90 (2009): 188–202.

Grässer, Erich. *An die Hebräer*. 3 vols. EKKNT 17. Zurich: Benziger, 1990–1997.

Griffiths, Jonathan I. *Hebrews and Divine Speech*, LNTS 507. London: T. & T. Clark, 2014.

Grudem, Wayne. *Systematic Theology: An Introduction to Biblical Doctrine*. Grand Rapids: Zondervan, 1994.

———. 'Perseverance of the Saints: A Case Study from Hebrews 6:4–6 and the Other Warning Passages in Hebrews.' Pages 1:133–82 in *The Grace of God, The Bondage of the Will*. Edited by Thomas R. Schreiner and Bruce A.

Ware. 2 vols. Grand Rapids: Baker, 1995.

Gudorf, Michael E. 'Through a Classical Lens: Hebrews 2:16.' *JBL* 119 [2000]: 105–8.

Gurtner, Daniel M. 'LXX Syntax and the Identity of the NT Veil.' *NovT* 47 (2005): 344–53.

Guthrie, Donald. *New Testament Introduction*. 3rd ed. Downers Grove, IL: Inter-Varsity, 1971.

Guthrie, George H. 'Hebrews.' Pages 919–95 in *Commentary on the New Testament Use of the Old Testament*. Edited by G. K. Beale and D. A. Carson. Grand Rapids: Baker, 2007.

Guthrie, George H. and Russell D. Quinn. 'A Discourse Analysis of the Use of Psalm 8:4–6 in Hebrews 2:5–9.' *JETS* 49 (2006): 235–46.

Hagner, Donald A. 'The Son of God as Unique High Priest: The Christology of the Epistle of Hebrews.' Pages 247–67 in *Contours of Christology in the New Testament*. Edited by Richard N. Longenecker, MNTS 7. Grand Rapids: Eerdmans, 2005.

Hahn. Scott W. 'A Broken Covenant and the Curse of Death: A Study of Hebrews 9:15–22.' *CBQ* 66 (2004): 416–36.

Harris, R. Laird, Gleason L. Archer, Jr., and Bruce K. Waltke, eds. *Theological Wordbook of the Old Testament*. Chicago: Moody, 1980.

Hartley, Donald E. 'Heb 11:6—A Reassessment of the Translation "God Exists."' *TJ* ns 27 (2006): 289–307.

Hartog, Paul A. 'The Text of Hebrews 2:9 in Its Patristic Reception.' *BSac* 171 (2014): 52–71.

Hawthorne, G. F. 'Timothy.' Pages 4:857–58 in *ISBE*.

Hawthorne, Gerald F. and Ralph P. Martin, eds. *Dictionary of Paul and His Letters*. Downers Grove, IL: InterVarsity, 1993.

Hay, David M. *Glory at the Right Hand: Psalm 110 in Early Christianity*. SBLMS 18. Atlanta: SBL, 1989.

Heen, Erik M. Heen and Philip D. W. Krey, eds. *Hebrews*. ACCS NT 10. Downers Grove: InterVarsity, 2005.

Hengel, Martin. *Studies in Early Christology*. Edinburgh: T&T Clark, 1995.

Hickling, C. J. A. 'John and Hebrews: The Background of Hebrews 2:10–18.' *NTS* 29 (1983): 112–16.

Hill, Craig Allen. 'The Use of Perfection Language in Hebrews 5:14 and 6:1 and the Contextual Interpretation of 5:11–6:3.' *JETS* 57 (2014): 727–42.

Hodge, A. A. *Outlines of Theology*. London: Banner of Truth, 1972 (1879).

Hodge, Charles. *Systematic Theology*. 3 vols. Grand Rapids: Eerdmans, 1982 (1871–1873).

———. *Exegetical Lectures and Sermons on the Epistle of Hebrews*. Edited and introduced by William VanDoodewaard. Carlisle: Banner of Truth, 2019.

Hollinger. Zoe. 'Rethinking the Translation of τρέχωμεν τὸν ... ἀγῶνα in Hebrews 12:1 in Light of Ancient Graeco-Roman Literature.' *BT* 70 (2019): 94–111.

Horton, Fred L., Jr. *The Melchizedek Tradition: A Critical Examination of the Sources to the Fifth Century A.D. and in the Epistle of Hebrews*. SNTSMS 30. Cambridge: CUP, 1976.

Huddlestun, John R. 'Red Sea,' Pages 5:633–42 in *ABD*.

Hughes, J. J. 'Hebrews IX 15ff and Galatians III 15ff: A Study in Covenant Practice and Procedure.' *NovT* 21 (1979): 27–96.

Hughes, Philip Edgecumbe. *Paul's Second Epistle to the Corinthians: The English Text with Introduction, Exposition and Notes*. NICNT. Grand Rapids: Eerdmans, 1962.

———. *A Commentary on the Epistle to the Hebrews*. Grand Rapids: Eerdmans, 1977.

Hurst, L. D. *The Epistle to the Hebrews: Its Background of Thought*. SNTSMS 65. Cambridge: CUP, 1990.

Hurtado, L. W. 'Lord.' Pages 560–69 in *DPL*.

———. 'Christology.' Pages 170–84 *DLNT*.

Jacob, Irene and Walter Jacob, 'Flora.' Pages 2:803–17 in *ABD*.

Jamieson, R. B. 'Hebrews 9:23: Cult Inauguration, Yom Kippur and the Cleansing of the Heavenly Tabernacle.' *NTS* 62 [2016]: 569–87.

———. 'When and Where Did Jesus Offer Himself? A

Taxonomy of Recent Scholarship on Hebrews.' *CurBR* 15 (2017): 338–68.

———. *Jesus' Death and Heavenly Offering in Hebrews*, SNTSMS 172. Cambridge: CUP, 2019.

———. *The Paradox of Sonship: Christology in the Epistle to the Hebrews*. Downers Grove: IVP Academic, 2021.

Jennings, Mark A. 'The Veil and the High Priestly Robes of the Incarnation: Understanding the Context of Heb 10:20.' *PRSt* 37 (2010): 85–97.

Jensen, Matthew D. 'Some Unpersuasive Glosses: The Meaning of ἀπείθεια, ἀπειθέω, ἀπειθής in the New Testament.' *JBL* 138 (2019): 391–412.

Jeremias, Joachim. 'Hebräer 10:20: τοῦτ' ἔστιν τῆς σαρκός αὐτοῦ,' *ZNW* 62 (1971): 131.

Jewett, Robert. 'The Form and Function of the Homiletic Benediction.' *AThR* 51 (1969): 18–34.

Jobes, Karen H. 'Rhetorical Achievement in the Hebrews 10 "Misquote" of Psalm 40.' *Bib* 72 (1991): 387–96.

Jonker, Louis. 'רעה.' Pages 3:1138–43 in *NIDOTTE*.

Johnson, Luke Timothy. *Hebrews: A Commentary*. NTL. Louisville: Westminster John Knox, 2006.

Joslin, Barry C. 'Can Hebrews be Structured? An Assessment of Eight Approaches.' *CBR* 6 (2007): 99–129.

———. 'Christ Bore the Sins of Many: Substitution and the Atonement in Hebrews,' *SBJT* 11 (2007): 74–103.

Joüon, P. and T. Muraoka. *A Grammar of Biblical Hebrew*. 2nd ed., Subsidia Biblica 27. Rome: G&BP, 2016.

Käsemann, Ernst. *The Wandering People of God: An Investigation of the Letter of Hebrews*. Translated by Roy A. Harrisville and Irving L. Sandberg. Minneapolis: Augsburg, 1984 (1957).

Keil, C. F. and F. Delitzsch. *Biblical Commentary on the Books of Samuel*. Translated by James Martin. Volume 2 of Commentary on the Old Testament in Ten Volumes. Grand Rapids: Eerdmans, 1985.

Keener, C. S. 'Milk.' Pages 707–9 in *DNTB*.

Kees, Jason P. 'Having our Hearts Sprinkled Clean: The Influence of Ezekiel 36:25–26 on Hebrews 10:22.' *WTJ* 83 (2021): 237–50.

Kelly, Douglas F. *The Beauty of Christ: A Trinitarian Vision. Volume 2 of Systematic Theology: Grounded in Holy Scripture and Understood in the Light of the Church*. Ross-shire: Mentor, 2014.

Kennedy, Charles A. 'Early Christians and The Anchor.' *BA* 38 (1975): 115–24.

Kidner, Derek. *Psalms 73–150: A Commentary on Books III-V of the Psalms*. TOTC. Downers Grove: Inter-Varsity, 1975.

Kim, Kyu Seop. Better than the Blood of Abel? Some Remakes on Abel in Hebrews 12:24.' *TynBul* 67 [2016]: 127–36.

Kistemaker, Simon J. *Exposition of the Epistle to the Hebrews*. NTC. Grand Rapids: Baker, 1984.

⸺⸺⸺. 'Atonement in Hebrews.' Pages 163–75 in *The Glory of the Atonement: Biblical, Historical & Practical Perspectives: Essays in Honor of Roger Nicole*. Edited by Charles E. Hill and Frank A. James III. Downers Grove: InterVarsity, 2004.

⸺⸺⸺. *The Psalm Citations in the Epistle of Hebrews*. Eugene: Wipf & Stock, 2010 (1961).

Kleinig, John W. ConcC. Saint Louis: Concordia Publishing House, 2017.

Kline, Meredith G. *Treaty of the Great King: The Covenant Structure of Deuteronomy: Studies and Commentary*. Grand Rapids: Eerdmans, 1963.

⸺⸺⸺. *By Oath Consigned: A Reinterpretation of the Covenant Signs of Circumcision and Baptism*. Grand Rapids: Eerdmans, 1968.

⸺⸺⸺. *Kingdom Prologue*. np: Kline, 1989.

Knapp, Henry M. 'Jephthah's Daughter in English Post-Reformation Exegesis.' *WTJ* 80 (2018): 279–97.

Koehler, Ludwig and Walter Baumgartner. *The Hebrew and Aramaic Lexicon of the Old Testament*. Translated by M. E. J. Richardson. Leiden: Brill, 2001.

Koenig, John. 'Hospitality.' Pages 3:299–301 in *ABD*.

Köstenberger, Andreas J. 'Jesus, the Mediator of a "Better Covenant": Comparatives in the Book of Hebrews.' *Faith & Mission* 21 (2004): 30–49.

Koester, Craig R. *Hebrews*. AB 36. NY: Doubleday, 2001.

Kruger, Michael J. *Canon Revisited: Establishing the Origins and Authority of the New Testament Books*. Wheaton: Crossway, 2012.

Laansma, Jon. *'I Will Give You Rest': The Rest Motif in the New Testament with Special Reference to Mt 11 and Heb 3-4*. WUNT 2:98. Tübingen: Mohr Siebeck, 1997.

Lane, William L. *Hebrews 1–8*. WBC 47a. Dallas: Word, 1991.

———. *Hebrews 9–13*. WBC 47b. Dallas: Word, 1991.

Lawson, Roderick. *The Shorter Catechism: With Explanatory Notes and Review Questions*. Ross-shire; Christian Heritage, 2017.

LeFebvre, Michael. *Singing the Songs of Jesus: Revisiting the Psalms*. Ross-shire: Christian Focus, 2010.

Lehne, Susanne. *The New Covenant in Hebrews*. JSNTSup 44. Sheffield: Sheffield Academic Press, 1990.

Leithart, Peter J. 'Womb of the World: Baptism and the Priesthood of the New Covenant in Hebrews 10.19–22.' *JSNT* 78 (2000): 49–65.

Lenski, R. C. H. *The Interpretation of the Epistle to the Hebrews and the Epistle to James*. Minneapolis: Augsburg, 1966.

Letham, Robert. *Systematic Theology*. Wheaton: Crossway, 2019.

Levenson, Jon D. 'Zion Traditions,' Pages 6:1098–102 in *ABD*.

Lewis, T. W. '"... And If He Shrinks Back" [Heb. X. 38b].' *NTS* 22 [1975]: 88–94.

Liddell, Henry George, Robert Scott, and Henry Stuart Jones, compilers. *A Greek-English Lexicon*. 9th ed. Oxford: Clarendon, 1996.

Lincoln, Andrew T. 'Sabbath, Rest, and Eschatology in the New Testament.' Pages 197–220 in *From Sabbath to Lord's*

Day: A Biblical, Historical, and Theological Investigation. Edited by D. A. Carson. Eugene: Wipf and Stock, 1999.

———. *Hebrews: A Guide*. London: T & T Clark/Continuum, 2006.

Lindars, Barnabas. *The Theology of the Letter to the Hebrews*. NTT. Cambridge: CUP, 1991.

Longenecker, Richard N. *Biblical Exegesis in the Apostolic Period*. Biblical and Theological Classics Library. Carlisle, UK: Paternoster, 1995.

Longman, Tremper, III. *Proverbs*. Baker Commentary on the Old Testament Wisdom and Psalms. Grand Rapids: Baker, 2006.

———. *Psalms: An Introduction and Commentary*. Vols. 15–16. TOTC. Downers Grove: IVP Academic, 2014.

Lotz, W, M. G. Kyle, and C. E. Armerding. 'Ark of the Covenant.' Pages 1:291–94 in *ISBE*.

Lust, J., E. Eynikel, and K. Hauspie, eds. *Greek-English Lexicon of the Septuagint*. Stuttgart: Deutsche Bibelgesellschaft, 1992, 1996.

Luther, Martin. *Lectures on Genesis: Chapters 45–50*. Translated by Paul D. Pahl. Volume 8 of Luther's Works. Edited by Jaroslav Pelikan. Saint Louis: Concordia, 1966.

MacDonald, Nathan. 'By Faith Moses.' Pages 374–82 in *The Epistle to the Hebrews and Christian Theology*. Edited by Richard Bauckham, Daniel R. Driver, Trevor A. Hart, and Nathan MacDonald. Grand Rapids: Eerdmans, 2009.

MacLeod, David J. 'The Cleaning of the True Tabernacle.' BSac 152 (1995): 60–71.

Macleod, Donald. *The Person of Christ*. Contours of Christian Theology. Downers Grove: InterVarsity, 1998.

Marshall, I. Howard. *New Testament Theology: Many Witnesses, One Gospel*. Downers Grove: InterVarsity, 2004.

Martin, Ralph P. and Peter H. Davids, eds. *Dictionary of the Later New Testament & Its Developments*. Downers Grove, IL: InterVarsity, 1997.

Matera, Frank J. 'The Theology of the Epistle to the Hebrews,' Pages 189–208 in *Reading the Epistle to the Hebrews: A Resource for Students*. Edited by Eric F. Mason and Kevin B. McCruden. Resources for Biblical Study 66. Atlanta: Society of Biblical Literature, 2011.

Mathewson, Dave. 'Reading Heb 6:4–6 in Light of the Old Testament.' *WTJ* 61 (1999): 209–25.

Mayes, A. D. H. *Deuteronomy*. NCBC. Grand Rapids: Eerdmans, 1979.

McAffee, Matthew. 'Covenant and the Warnings of Hebrews: The Blessing and the Curse.' *JETS* 57 (2014): 537–53.

McCarthy, Dennis J. *Treaty and Covenant*. New ed. AnBib 21a. Rome: Biblical Institute, 1981.

McConville, J. G. *Deuteronomy*. AOTC 5. Downers Grove: InterVarsity, 2002.

McGrath, John J. *Through the Eternal Spirit: An Historical Study of the Exegesis of Hebrews 9:13–14*. Rome: Pontificio Universitas Gregoriana, 1961.

McKnight, Scot. 'The Warning Passages of Hebrews: A Formal Analysis and Theological Conclusions.' *TJ* 13 (1992): 21–59.

Meier, John P. 'Structure and Theology in Heb. 1, 1–14.' *Bib* 66 (1985): 168–89.

_____. 'Symmetry and Theology in the Old Testament Citations of Heb. 1,5–14.' *Bib* 66 (1985): 504–33.

Mekhilta De-Rabbi Ishmael: A Critical Edition, Based on the Manuscripts and Early Editions, with an English Translation, Introduction, and Notes. Edited and translated by Jacob Z. Lauterbach. Introduction by David Stern. Philadelphia: Jewish Publication Society, 2004.

Merrill, E. 'יסר.' Pages 2:479–82 in *NIDOTTE*.

Metzger, Bruce M. *A Textual Commentary on the Greek New Testament*, 2nd ed. New York: New York, United Bible Society, 1994.

_____. *Lexical Aids for Students of New Testament Greek*. New edition. Princeton: Theological Book Agency, 1995.

Michaels, J. Ramsey. *1 Peter*. WBC 49. Waco: Word, 1988.
Mishnah, The: A New Translation. Translated by Jacob Neusner. New Haven: Yale University Press, 1988.
Mitchell, Alan C. *Hebrews*. SP 13. Collegeville: Liturgical, 2007.
Miller, Samuel. *The Utility and Importance of Creeds and Confessions*. Princeton: Borrenstein, 1824.
Mitchell, Christopher Wright. *The Meaning of BRK 'To Bless' in the Old Testament*. SBLDS 95 Atlanta: Scholars, 1987.
Moffatt, James. *A Critical and Exegetical Commentary on the Epistle to the Hebrews*. ICC. Edinburgh: T. & T. Clark, 1979 (1924).
Moffitt, David M. *Atonement and the Logic of Resurrection in the Epistle of Hebrews*. NovTSup 141. Leiden: Brill, 2011.
⸻. 'Jesus' Heavenly Sacrifice in Early Christian Reception of Hebrews: A Survey.' *JTS* 68 (2017): 46–71.
⸻. *Rethinking the Atonement: New Perspectives on Jesus's Death, Resurrection, and Ascension*. Grand Rapids: Baker, 2022.
Moore, Nicholas J. 'Jesus as "The One who Entered his Rest": The Christological Reading of Hebrews 4:10.' *JSNT* 36 (2014): 383–400.
Morris, Leon. *The Cross in the New Testament*. Biblical and Theological Classics Library Carlisle, UK; Paternoster, 1995.
Morrison, Michael D. *Who Needs a New Covenant?: Rhetorical Function of the Covenant Motif in the Argument of Hebrews*, PTMS. Eugene, OR: Pickwick, 2008.
Moule, C. F. D. *An Idiom Book of New Testament Greek*. 2nd ed. Cambridge: CUP, 1959.
Moulton, James Hope. *Prolegomena*. 3rd ed.. Volume 1 of *A Grammar of New Testament Greek*. Edinburgh: T & T Clark, 1908.
Moulton, J. H. and W. F. Howard. *Accidence and Word-Formation*. Volume 2 of *A Grammar of New Testament Greek*. Edinburgh: T&T Clark, 1929.

Muller, Richard A. *Post-Reformation Reformed Dogmatics: The Rise and Development of Reformed Orthodoxy, ca. 1520 to ca. 1725*. 2nd ed. 4 vols. Grand Rapids: Baker, 2003.

Muraoka, T. *A Syntax of Septuagint Greek*. Leuven: Peeters, 2016.

Murray, John. *Redemption Accomplished and Applied*. Grand Rapids: Eerdmans, 1955.

———. *Principles of Conduct: Aspects of Biblical Ethics*. Grand Rapids: Eerdmans, 1957.

———. "The Attestation of Scripture." Pages 1–54 in *The Infallible Word*. Edited by Paul Woolley. 3rd rev. ed. Philadelphia: Presbyterian and Reformed, 1967.

———. *Collected Writings of John Murray*. 4 vols. Carlisle: Banner of Truth, 1976–1982.

———. 'The Heavenly, Priestly Activity of Christ,' Pages 1:44–58 in *Collected Writings of John Murray*.

———. 'Trichotomy.' Pages 2:23–33 in *Collected Writings of John Murray*.

———. 'Definitive Sanctification.' Pages 2:277–84 in *Collected Writings of John Murray*.

———. *The Covenant of Grace: A Biblico-Theological Study*. Phillipsburg: Presbyterian and Reformed, 1988.

Murray, Scott R. 'The Concept of διαθήκη in the Letter to the Hebrews.' *CTQ* 66 (2002): 41–60.

Nässelqvist, Dan. 'Stylistic Levels in Hebrews 1:1–4 and John 1:1–18.' *JSNT* 35 (2012): 31–53.

Nicene and Post-Nicene Fathers. First Series. Edited by Philip Schaff. 14 vols. Grand Rapids: Eerdmans, 1994.

Nicene and Post-Nicene Fathers. Second Series. Edited by Philip Schaff and Henry Wace. 14 vols. Grand Rapids: Eerdmans, 1991.

Nicole, Roger R. 'C. H. Dodd and the Doctrine of Propitiation.' *WTJ* 17 (1955): 117–57.

———. 'Some Comments on Hebrews 6:4–6 and the Doctrine of the Perseverance of God with the Saints.' Pages 355–64 in *Current Issues in Biblical and Patristic Interpretation: Studies in Honor of Merrill C. Tenney Presented by His Former Students*. Edited by Gerald F. Hawthorne. Grand Rapids: Eerdmans, 1975.

Old Testament Pseudepigrapha. Edited by J. H. Charlesworth. 2 vols. Garden City, NY: Doubleday, 1983, 1985.

Orlov, Andrei A. 'The Heir of Righteousness and the King of Righteousness: The Priestly Noachic Polemics in 2 Enoch and the Epistle of Hebrews.' *JTS* ns 58 (2007): 45–66.

Osborne, Grant R. 'A Classical Arminian View,' Pages 86–128 in *Four Views of the Warning Passages in Hebrews*. Edited by Herbert W. Bateman IV. Grand Rapids: Kregel Academic & Professional, 2007.

Osborne, William R. *Divine Blessing and the Fullness of Life in the Presence of God*. Short Studies in Biblical Theology. Wheaton: Crossway, 2020.

Ounsworth, Richard. *Joshua Typology in the New Testament*. WUNT 2/328. Tübingen: Mohr Siebeck, 2012.

Owen, John. *The Death of Death in the Death of Christ with an Introductory Essay by J. I. Packer*. Carlisle: Banner of Truth, 1959 (1648).

———. *An Exposition of the Epistle to the Hebrews*. Volumes 17–23 of The Works of John Owen. Edited by William H. Goold. Carlisle: Banner of Truth, 1991.

Pate, Brian. 'Who is Speaking? The Use of Isaiah 8:17–18 in Hebrews 2:13 as a Case Study for Applying the Speech of Key OT Figures to Christ.' *JETS* 59 (2016): 731–45.

Pearson, Birger A. 'Melchizedek (NHC IX, 1).' Page 4:688 in *ABD*.

Pearson, B. W. R. 'Gymnasia and Baths.' Pages 435–36 in *DNTB*.

Perkins, William. *Commentary on Hebrews 11*. Volume 3 of *The Works of William Perkins*. Edited by Randall J. Pederson and Ryan M. Hurd. Grand Rapids: Reformation Heritage, 2017 (1607).

Peterson, David. 'The Prophecy of the New Covenant in the Argument of Hebrews.' *RTR* 38 (1979): 74–81.

———. *Hebrews and Perfection: An Examination of the Concept of Perfection in the 'Epistle to the Hebrews.'* Cambridge: CUP, 1982.

Phillips, Richard D. *Hebrews*. Reformed Expository Commentary. Phillipsburg: P&R, 2006.

Philo. *The Works of Philo: Complete and Unabridged*. Translated by C. D. Yonge. New edition. Peabody, MA: Hendrickson, 1993.

Pink, Arthur W. *An Exposition of Hebrews*. Grand Rapids: Baker, 1954.

———. *The Divine Covenants*. Grand Rapids: Baker, 1973.

Plumer, William S. *Psalms: A Critical and Expository Commentary with Doctrinal and Practical Remarks*. Carlisle: Banner of Truth, 1975 (1867).

Poythress, Vern Sheridan. 'Divine Meaning of Scripture.' *WTJ* 48 (1986): 241–79.

———. *The Shadow of Christ in the Law of Moses*. Phillipsburg: P&R, 1991.

Pratt, Richard L., Jr. *1 and 2 Chronicles*. Ross-shire: Mentor, 1998.

———. 'Infant Baptism in the New Covenant.' Pages 156–74 in *The Case for Covenantal Infant Baptism*. Edited by Gregg Strawbridge (Phillipsburg: P&R, 2003).

Proctor, John. 'Judgement or Vindication? Deuteronomy 32 in Hebrews 10:30.' *TynBul* 55 (2004): 65–80.

Ralphs, Alfred. *Septuaginta*. Edited by Robert Hanhart. Revised ed. 2 vols. Stuttgart: Deutsche Bibelgesellschaft, 2006.

Rapske, Brian. *The Book of Acts and Paul in Roman Prison*. Volume 3 of *The Book of Acts in Its First Century Setting*. Grand Rapids: Eerdmans, 1994.

Reformed Confessions of the 16th and 17th Centuries in English Translation. Compiled with introductions by James T.

Dennison, Jr. 4 vols. Grand Rapids: Reformation Heritage, 2008–2014.

Reid, D. G. 'Satan, Devil.' Pages 862–67 in *DPL*.

Rhee, Victor. 'The Role of Chiasm for Understanding Christology in Hebrews 1:1–14.' *JBL* 131 (2012): 341–62.

———. 'Christology in Hebrews 1:5–14: The Three Stages of Christ's Existence.' *JETS* 59 (2016): 717–29.

Rhodes, Enroll F. and Liana Lupas, eds. *The Translators to the Reader: The Original Preface of the King James Version of 1611 Revisited*. New York: American Bible Society, 1997.

Ribbens, Benjamin J. 'Ascension and Atonement: The Significance of Post-Reformation, Reformed Responses to Socinians for Contemporary Atonement Debates in Hebrews.' *WTJ* 80 (2018): 1–23.

Richard, Guy M. 'Covenant of Redemption.' Pages 43–62 in *An Introduction to Covenant Theology*. Edited by Guy P. Waters, J. Nicholas Reid, and John R. Muether. Wheaton: Crossway, 2020.

Ridderbos, J. *Isaiah*. trans. John Vriend, BSC. Grand Rapids: Regency/Zondervan, 1985.

Robertson, A. T. *A Grammar of the Greek New Testament in the Light of Historical Research*. 4th ed. Nashville: Broadman, 1934.

Robertson, O. Palmer. *The Christ of the Covenants*. Phillipsburg: Presbyterian and Reformed, 1980.

———. *The Books of Nahum, Habakkuk, and Zephaniah*. NICOT. Grand Rapids: Eerdmans, 1990.

———. *God's People in the Wilderness: The Church in Hebrews*. Ross-shire: Mentor, 2009.

Runge, Steven E. *Discourse Grammar of the Greek New Testament: A Practical Introduction for Teaching and Exegesis*. Peabody: Hendrickson, 2010.

Schaff, Philip, ed. *The Creeds of Christendom: With History and Critical Notes*. Revised by David S. Schaff. 6th ed. 3 vols. Grand Rapids: Baker, 1931.

Schenck, Kenneth. 'Hebrews as the Re-presentation of a Story: A Narrative Approach to Hebrews.' Pages 171–88 in *Reading the Epistle of Hebrews: A Resource for Students*. Edited by Eric F. Mason and Kevin B. McCruden. Resources for Biblical Study 66. Atlanta: Society of Biblical Literature, 2011.

Schmitt, Mary. 'Restructuring Views on Law in Hebrews 7:12.' *JBL* 128 (2009): 189–201.

Scholer, John M. *Proleptic Priests: Priesthood in the Epistle of Hebrews*. JSNTSup 49. Sheffield: Sheffield Academic Press, 1991.

Schreiner, Thomas R. *New Testament Theology: Magnifying God in Christ*. Grand Rapids: Baker, 2008.

———. *Commentary on Hebrews*. Biblical Theology for Christian Proclamation. Nashville: Homan Reference, 2015.

Scott, J. Julius, Jr., 'ARCHĒGOS in the Salvation History of the Epistle to the Hebrews.' *JETS* 29 (1986): 47–54.

Shedd, William G. T. *Dogmatic Theology*. Edited by Alan W. Gomes. 3rd ed. Phillipsburg: P&R, 2003 (1888–1894).

Silva, Moisés. 'Perfection and Eschatology in Hebrews,' *WTJ* 39 (1976): 60–71.

———, ed. *New International Dictionary of New Testament Theology and Exegesis*. 5 vols. Grand Rapids: Zondervan, 2014.

Smeaton, George. *The Doctrine of the Holy Spirit*. Carlisle: Banner of Truth, 2016 [1889].

Smillie, Gene R. '"The One Who Is Speaking" In Hebrews 12:25.' *TynBul* 55 (2004): 275–94.

Smyth, Herbert Weir. *Greek Grammar*. Revised by Gordon M. Messing. Revised ed. Cambridge, Harvard University Press, 1956 (1920).

Spellman, Ched. 'The Drama of Discipline: Toward an Intertextual Profile of PAIDEIA in Hebrews 12.' *JETS* 59 (2016): 487–506.

Spicq, C. *L'Épître aux Hébreux*. 2 vols. Ebib. Paris: Gabalda, 1952–1953.

Stedman, Ray C. *Hebrews*. IVPNTC. Downers Grove: InterVarsity, 1992.
Stewart, R. A. 'The Sinless High-Priest.' *NTS* 14 (1967): 126–35.
Steyn, Gert J. 'The Ending of Hebrews Reconsidered.' *ZNW* 103 (2012): 235–53.
Stibbs, Alan M. *So Great Salvation: The Meaning and Message of the Letter to the Hebrews*. Exeter: Paternoster, 1970.
Strack, H. L. and P. Billerbeck. *Kommentar zum Neuen Testament aus Talmud und Midrasch*. 4 vols. Munich: Bech'sche, 1922–1928.
Strecker, Georg. *Theology of the New Testament*. Translated by M. Eugene Boring. Louisville: Westminster John Knox, 2000.
Stewart, Alexander E. 'The Temporary Messianic Kingdom in Second Temple Judaism and the Delay of the Parousia: Psalm 110:1 and the Development of Early Christian Inaugurated Eschatology.' *JETS* 59 (2016): 255–70.
Strong, John T. 'Zion: Theology of,' Pages 4:1314–21 in *NIDOTTE*.
Stowers, Stanley K. *Letter Writing in Greco-Roman Antiquity*. LEC 5. Philadelphia: Westminster, 1986.
Swain, Scott R. 'Covenant of Redemption.' Pages 107–25 in *Christian Dogmatics: Reformed Theology for the Church Catholic*. Edited by Michael Allen and Scott R. Swain. Grand Rapids: Baker, 2016.
_____. 'New Covenant Theologies,' Pages 551–69 in *Covenant Theology: Biblical, Historical, and Theological Perspectives*. Edited by Guy P. Waters, J. Nicholas Reid, and John R. Muether. Wheaton: Crossway, 2020.
_____. *The Trinity: An Introduction*. Short Studies in Systematic Theology. Wheaton: Crossway, 2020.
Swetnam, James. 'A Suggested Interpretation of Hebrews 9:15–18.' *CBQ* 27 (1965): 373–90.
_____. 'Jesus as Λόγος in Hebrews 4,12–13.' *Bib* 62 (1981): 214–24.

———. *Jesus and Isaac: A Study of the Epistle of Hebrews in the Light of the Aqedah*. AnBib 94. Rome: Biblical Institute, 1981.

———. 'Hebrews 10:30–31: A Suggestion.' *Bib* 75 (1994): 388–94.

———. ''Εξ ἑνὸς in Hebrews 2,11.' *Bib* 88 (2007): 517–25.

———. 'ὁ ἀπόστολος in Hebrews 3,1.' *Bib* 89 (2008): 252–62.

Terrien, Samuel. *The Psalms: Strophic Structure and Theological Commentary*. ECC. Grand Rapids: Eerdmans, 2003.

Thelemann, Otto. *An Aid to the Heidelberg Catechism*. Translated by M. Peters. Grand Rapids: Douma, 1959 (1892).

Thiessen, Henry Clarence. *Introductory Lectures in Systematic Theology*. Grand Rapids: Eerdmans, 1949.

Thomas, Matthew J. 'Origen on Paul's Authorship of Hebrews.' *NTS* 65 (2019): 598–609.

Thompson, J. A. *Deuteronomy: An Introduction and Commentary*, TOTC. London: Inter-Varsity, 1974.

Thompson, James W. 'Hebrews 9 and Sacrifice.' *JBL* 98 [1979]: 567–78.

———. *The Beginnings of Christian Philosophy: The Epistle to the Hebrews*. CBQMS 13 Washington: Catholic Biblical Association, 1982.

———. *Hebrews*. Paideia. Grand Rapids: Baker Academic, 2008.

———. 'What Has Middle Platonism to Do with Hebrews?.' Pages 31–52 in *Reading the Epistle to the Hebrews: A Resource for Students*. Edited by Eric F. Mason and Kevin B. McCruden. Resources for Biblical Study 66. Atlanta: Society of Biblical Literature, 2011.

Thornwell, James Henley. 'Sincerity.' Pages 2:519–42 in *The Collected Writings of James Henley Thornwell*. 4 vols. Carlisle: Banner of Truth, 1974.

Tipton, Lane. G. *The Trinitarian Theology of Cornelius Van Til*. Libertyville, IL: Reformed Forum, 2022.

Tollefsen, Christopher O. *Lying and Christian Ethics*. New Studies in Christian Ethics Cambridge: CUP, 2014.

Tosefta, The: Translated from the Hebrew with a New Introduction. Translated by Jacob Neusner. Peabody, MA: Hendrickson, 2002.

Treier, Daniel J. "Speech Acts, Hearing Hearts, and Other Senses." Pages 337–50 in *The Epistle to the Hebrews and Christian Theology.* Edited by Richard Bauckham, Daniel R. Driver, Trevor A. Hart, and Nathan MacDonald. Grand Rapids: Eerdmans, 2009.

Trueman, Carl R. *The Creedal Imperative.* Wheaton: Crossway, 2012.

Turner, Nigel. *Syntax.* Volume 3 of *A Grammar of New Testament Greek.* Edinburgh: T&T Clark, 1963.

Turretin, Francis. *Institutes of Elenctic Theology.* Translated by George Musgrave Giger. Edited by James T. Dennison, Jr. 3 vols. Phillipsburg: P&R, 1992-1997 (1679–1685).

Ursinus, Zacharias. *The Commentary of Dr. Zacharias Ursinus on the Heidelberg Catechism.* Translated by G. W. Williard. Phillipsburg: Presbyterian and Reformed, 1985 (1852 reprint of 1591 original).

Ussher, James. *The Body of Divinity: Or, The Sum and Substance of Christian Religion.* Edited by Michael Nevarr. Birmingham, AL: Solid Ground Christian, 2007 (1648).

Vanhoye, Albert. *Old Testament Priests and the New Priest.* Translated by J. Bernard Orchard Petersham, MA: St. Bede's, 1986.

———. *Structure and Message of the Epistle of Hebrews.* Subsidia Biblica 12. Rome: Editrice Pontificio Istituto Biblico, 1989.

Vandergriff, Kenneth A. 'Διαθήκη καινή: New Covenant as Jewish Apocalypticism in Hebrews 8.' *CBQ* 79 (2017): 97–110.

Van de Weyer, Robert, ed. and compiler. *The First English Prayer Book.* Harrisburg: Morehouse, 1999.

van der Woude, A. '11Q Melchizedek and the New Testament.' *NTS* 12 (1966): 301–26.

VanGemeren, Willem A. *Interpreting the Prophetic Word: An*

Introduction to the Prophetic Literature of the Old Testament. Grand Rapids: Academic, 1990.

———. 'Psalms,' Pages 5:1–880 in *The Expositor's Bible Commentary*. Edited by Frank E. Gaebelein, 12 vols. Grand Rapids: Zondervan, 1991.

———, ed. *New International Dictionary of Old Testament Theology & Exegesis*. 5 vols. Grand Rapids: Zondervan, 1997.

van Genderen, J. and W. H. Velema. *Concise Reformed Dogmatics*. Translated by Gerrit Bilkes and Ed M. van der Mass. Phillipsburg, P&R, 2008.

Van Mastricht, Petrus. *Theoretical-Practical Theology*. Translated by Todd M. Rester. Edited by Joel R. Beeke. 7 vols. Grand Rapids: Reformation Heritage, 2018– (1698–1699).

Van Til, Cornelius. *The Defense of the Faith*. 3rd ed. Philadelphia: Presbyterian and Reformed, 1967.

———. *An Introduction to Systematic Theology*. Phillipsburg: Presbyterian and Reformed, 1974.

Vermes, Geza. *The Complete Dead Sea Scrolls in English*. Revised ed. New York: Penguin, 2004.

Vos, Geerhardus. 'The Priesthood of Christ in the Epistle to the Hebrews' [first article]. *PTR* 5 (1907): 423–47.

———. 'The Priesthood of Christ in the Epistle to the Hebrews,' [second article]. *PTR* 5 (1907): 579–604.

———. *The Teaching of the Epistle to the Hebrews*. Phillipsburg: P&R, 1956.

———. *Biblical Theology: Old and New Testaments*. Carlisle: Banner of Truth, 1975 (1948).

———. 'The Idea of Biblical Theology.' Pages 1–24 in *Redemptive History and Biblical Interpretation: The Shorter Writings of Geerhardus Vos*. Edited by Richard B. Gaffin, Jr. Phillipsburg: P&R, 1980.

———. *The Pauline Eschatology*. Phillipsburg: P&R, 1986 (1930).

———. 'The Eternal Christ.' Pages 197–208 in *Grace and Glory: Sermons Preached in the Chapel of Princeton Theological*

Seminary. Carlisle: Banner of Truth, 1994 (1922).

———. *Reformed Dogmatics*. Translated and edited by Richard B. Gaffin, Jr. 5 vols. Bellingham: Lexham, 2012–2016.

Walker, Peter. 'Jerusalem in Hebrews 13:9–14 and the Dating of the Epistle.' *TynBul* 45 (1994): 39–71.

Wallace, Daniel B. *Greek Grammar Beyond the Basics: An Exegetical Syntax of the New Testament*. Grand Rapids: Zondervan, 1996.

Waltke, Bruce K.'נפשׁ.' Pages 587–91 in *TWOT*.

———. 'Cain and His Offering.' *WTJ* 48 (1986): 363–72.

———. *The Book of Proverbs: Chapters 1–15*. NICOT. Grand Rapids: Eerdmans, 2004.

———. *An Old Testament Theology: An Exegetical, Canonical, and Thematic Approach*. Grand Rapids: Zondervan, 2007.

Warfield, B. B. *The Inspiration and Authority of the Bible*. Edited by Samuel G. Craig. Phillipsburg: Presbyterian and Reformed, 1948.

———. 'Spiritual Culture in the Seminary.' Pages 2:468–96 in *Selected Shorter Writings of Benjamin B. Warfield*. Edited by John E. Meeter. 2 vols. Phillipsburg: P&R, 1970, 1973.

———. 'Redeemer and Redemption.' Pages 325–50 in *The Person and Work of Christ*. Edited by Samuel G. Craig. Philadelphia: P&R, 1970.

———. 'The New Testament Terminology of Redemption,' Pages 429–78 in *The Person and Work of Christ*. Edited by Samuel G. Craig. Philadelphia: P&R, 1970.

Watson, D. F. 'Rhetoric, Rhetorical Criticism.' Pages 1041–51 in *DLNT*.

Webster, John. 'One Who is Son: Theological Reflections on the Exordium to the Epistle of Hebrews.' Pages 69–94 in *The Epistle to the Hebrews and Christian Theology*. Edited by Richard Bauckham, Daniel R. Driver, Trevor A. Hart, and Nathan MacDonald. Grand Rapids: Eerdmans, 2009.

Wedderburn, A. J. M. 'The "Letter" to the Hebrews and Its Thirteenth Chapter.' *NTS* 50 (2004): 390–405.

Weima, Jeffrey A. D. *Neglected Endings: The Significance of the Pauline Letter Closings*. JSNTSup 101. Sheffield: Sheffield Academic Press, 1994.

―――. *Paul the Ancient Letter Writer: An Introduction to Epistolary Analysis*. Grand Rapids: Baker, 2016.

Weiser, Artur. *Psalms: A Commentary*. Translated by Herbert Hartwell. OTL. Philadelphia: Westminster, 1962.

Weiss, Herold. 'Sabbatismos in the Epistle of Hebrews.' *CBQ* 58 (1996): 674–89.

Westcott, B. B. *The Epistle to the Hebrews*. Grand Rapids: Eerdmans, 1980 (1892).

Westminster Confession of Faith. Glasgow: Free Presbyterian Publications, 1994.

Wenham, Gordon J. *The Book of Leviticus*. NICOT. Grand Rapids: Eerdmans, 1979.

―――. *Genesis 1–15*, WBC 1. Waco: Word, 1987.

Whitaker, William. *A Disputation on Holy Scripture Against the Papists, Especially Bellarmine and Stapleton*. Translated by William Fitzgerald. Parker Society. Eugene, OR: Wipf & Stock, 2004 (1588).

Whitfield, Bryan J. 'The Three Joshuas of Hebrews 3 and 4,' *Perspectives in Religious Studies* 37 (2010): 21–35.

Whitlark, James A. '"Here We Do Not Have a City That Remains": A Figured Critique of Roman Imperial Propaganda in Hebrews 13:14.' *JBL* 131 (2012): 161–79.

Wiles, Gordon P. *Paul's Intercessory Prayers: The Significance of the Intercessory Prayer Passages in the Letters of Paul*. SNTSMS 24. Cambridge: CUP, 1974.

Wilkins, M. J. 'Milk, Solid Food.' Pages 736–38 in *DLNT*.

Williams, Clarence Russel. 'A Word-Study of Hebrews 13.' *JBL* 30 (1911): 129–36.

Wilson, Andrew J. 'Hebrews 3:6B and 3:14 Revisited.' *TynBul* 62 (2011): 247–67.

Witsius, Herman. *The Economy of the Covenants between God and Man: Comprehending a Complete Body of Divinity*. 2 vols. Phillipsburg; P&R, 1990 (1693).

Wray, Judith Hoch. *Rest as a Theological Metaphor in the Epistle of Hebrews and the Gospel of Truth: Early Christian Homiletics of Rest.* SBLDS 166. Atlanta: Scholars Press, 1998.

Wright, N. T. *The New Testament and the People of God.* Minneapolis: Fortress, 1992.

Young, Edward J. *The Book of Isaiah: The English Text, with Introduction, Exposition, and Notes.* 3 vols. NICOT. Grand Rapids: Eerdmans, 1965–1972.

Young, Norman. H. 'ΤΟΥΤ' ΕΣΤΙΝ ΤΗΣ ΣΑΡΚΟΣ ΑΥΤΟΥ (Heb. 10:20): Apposition, Dependent or Explicative?.' *NTS* 20 (1973): 100–4.

_____. 'The Gospel According to Hebrews 9.' *NTS* 27 (1981): 198–210.

Young, Richard A. *Intermediate New Testament Greek: A Linguistic and Exegetical Approach.* B&H: Nashville, 1994.

Zerwick, Maximillian. *Biblical Greek: Illustrated by Examples.* Translated by Joseph Smith. Rome: Scripta Pontificii Instituti Biblici, 1963.

Zerwick, Maximillian and Mary Grosvenor. *A Grammatical Analysis of the Greek New Testament.* 2 vols. Rome: Biblical Institute, 1974, 1979.

Scripture Index

Genesis
1, ... 35
1:1, ... 280, 415, 424, 514
1:1-2, ... 30, 267
1:1-2:3, ... 133
1:11, ... 200, 430
1:26, ... 347
1:28, ... 81
2, ... 114
2:2, ...132, 138, 140, 144, 146
2:2-3, ... 143
2:7, ... 490
2:8, ... 199
2:17, ... 343
2:24, ... 530
3, ... 91
3:15, ... 92, 431
3:18, ... 200
3:24, ... 307
4:1-10, ... 416–417
4:4, ... 10, 418, 507
4:10, ... 418, 509
5:18-24, ... 419
5:26, ... 93
5:28-29, ... 225
5:29, ... 142
6:2, ... 78
6:8-9, ... 422
6:13-18, ... 421
7:1, ... 422
7:4, ... 421
8:20, ... 422
8:22,................................. 284
9:9, ... 430
11:30, ... 429
12–50, ... 443
12:1, ... 127, 426
12:1-4, ... 210
12:2, ... 237, 429
12:2-3, ... 7, 213
12:2-4, ... 215
12:5, ... 427
12:7, ... 210, 426
13:14-15, ... 426
13:14-17, ... 213
14:17-20, ... 236
14:18, ... 232
14:18-19, ... 227
14:18-20, ... 223, 225–226
.... 228–230, 233, 242, 266
14:20, ... 231
15:5, ... 433
15:5-21, ... 213
15:6, ... 425
15:7-17, ... 333
15:7-21, ... 211
15:12-21, ... 210
15:18, ... 127
16:15, ... 439
17:1-14, ... 210
17:2-14, ... 213
17:5, ... 230
17:7, ... 291
17:8, ... 427
17:15-21, ... 429
17:17, ... 215, 429
18:12, ... 427
18:14, ... 429, 439
18:18-22, ... 231
18:25, ... 507
19:1-3, ... 528
21:1-3, ... 429
21:5, ... 215
21:12, ... 213
21:22-23, ... 211
22:1, ... 210
22:1-19, ... 210, 438
22:5, ... 439
22:15-18, ... 213
22:16-17, ... 209, 213, 217
22:17, ... 214, 215, 237, 433
23:4, ... 427, 435
24:7, ... 211, 213
25:29-34, ... 498
25:31-34, ... 492
26:2-3, ... 435
26:3, ... 211, 427
26:4, ... 433
27, ... 499
27:27, ... 237
27:27-29, ... 440
27:30-40, ... 492
27:39-40, ... 441
27:41, ... 500
28:3-4, ... 441, 499
28:15, ... 62, 533
31:50, ... 211
32:12, ... 433
33, ... 499
43:8-9, ... 254
47:7, ... 237
47:9, ... 427, 435
47:29-48, ... 22, 441
47:31, ... 442
48:3-4, ... 441
48:9, ... 237
48:21, ... 442
49:15, ... 119
49:29–50:14, ... 441
50:24-25, ... 442
50:26, ... 442

Exodus
1, ... 447
1:15-21, ... 457
1:22, ... 452
1:8-22, ... 444
2-14, ... 444
2:2, ... 445
2:11-15, ... 448
2:14-15, ... 449
3:2-3, ... 449
3:6, ... 15, 437
3:12, ... 102
3:14, ... 420
3:20, ... 183
4:22, ... 50, 507, 508
6:7, ... 291, 292
6:8, ... 211

601

6:20, ... 445	.... 277–279, 280	4:3, ... 262, 263
7:1–13:18, ... 449	26:1-14, ... 298	4:3-12, ... 165
11:4-7, ... 450	26:2, ... 298	4:5, ... 173
12:1-8, ... 338	26:8, ... 297	4:18-20, ... 337
12:1-28, ... 450	26:15-25, ... 298	4:24, ... 335
12:5, ... 324	26:30, ... 279	5:13, ... 337
12:12, ... 78	26:31-35, ... 220	5:14-18, ... 311
12:22, ... 335	26:33, ... 306	6:30, ... 543
12:23, ... 450	27:3, ... 300, 304	7:1-6, ... 543
12:43-51, ... 338	27:8, ... 279	7:6, ... 542
13:1-3, ... 450	27:20-21, ... 310	7:11-18, ... 542, 547
13:2, ... 50	28:1, ... 162, 165, 250	7:12-16, ... 548
13:18, ... 449	28:36, ... 261	8-9, ... 249
13:19, ... 442	29, ... 249	8:15, ... 19, 30, 336
14:1-3, ... 451	29:4, ... 313	9:5, ... 159
14:3, ... 452	29:9, 29, ... 173	9:7, ... 159, 165
14:10, ... 452	29:38-42, ... 263, 310	14:4-7, ... 335
14:15, ... 452	29:45, ... 291	15:8, 16, ... 313
14:30, ... 442	30:1-3, ... 204	15:16, ... 430
15:1-12, ... 451	30:1-10, ... 300	16, ... 154, 163, 221,
16:7,10, ... 31	30:6, ... 299, 305, 307	..................................310, 314
16:33-34, ... 307	30:7-8, ... 305, 310	16:1-14, ... 341
16:35, ... 196	30:8, ... 301	16:2, ... 220
17:1-7, ... 119, 125	30:34, ... 303	16:6, ... 17, 24, 165, 262, 263
19:1, ... 324	30:34-38, ... 301	16:12-13, ... 301, 303, 304
19:12-13, ... 506	31:13, ... 143, 292	16:14-20, ... 336
19:16–20:21, ... 504, 506	31:18, ... 279	16:17, ... 305
19:18, ... 513	32, ... 278, 505, 506	16:21, ... 164, 311
20:1–23:32, ... 278	32:13, ... 211	16:27-28, ... 543
20:3, ... 78	32:32, ... 507	16:32, ... 173
20:4-6, ... 517	33:14, ... 139	16:34, ... 263
20:8-11, ... 133	33:21-23, ... 449	17:11, ... 336-337
20:11, ... 144	34, ... 99	19:22, ... 337
20:12, ... 210	34:6, ... 95	20:10, ... 531
20:14, ... 530	34:6-7, ... 519	20:24, ... 183
20:15, ... 532	34:14, ... 517	21:6, ... 260–261
20:19, ... 505	34:29-35, ... 105	21:10, ... 162, 173
21:14, ... 386	35:30–40:33, ... 278	21:18-20, ... 261
22:10-11, ... 211	36:8-38, ... 298	21:21, ... 159
24:1-8, ... 278	37:1-2, ... 307	23:26-32, ... 263
24:3-8, ... 333, 335, 338	37:6, ... 307	24:1-4, ... 310
24:8, ... 336, 507	37:7-9, ... 307	24:5-9, ... 310
24:9-18, ... 278	37:25-29, ... 300	24:10-16, ... 545
24:17, ... 518	38:3, ... 300	
25-31, ... 278, 279	39:30, ... 261	**Numbers**
25:9, ... 279	40:5, ... 26, 305	3:3, ... 173
25:10, ... 279	40:9, ... 336, 340	3:10, ... 165
25:10-11, ... 307	40:18-19, ... 298	6:22-27, ... 231, 238, 558
25:16, 21, ... 308	40:20, ... 308	6:24-26, ... 567
25:17, ... 307	40:26, ... 299	7:1, ... 336
25:18-20, ... 307	40:27, ... 301	8:4, ... 279
25:22, ... 307		8:6, ... 162
25:24, ... 299	**Leviticus**	8:7, ... 313
25:29, ... 36, 304	1:10, ... 335	8:10, ... 190
25:30, ... 310	1:3, ... 324	12:7, ... 104, 107, 108, 374
25:31, ... 299	3:1-17, ... 547	12:11, ... 311
25:31-39, ... 279	4:1, ... 543	13:1, ... 16, 457
25:40, ... 272–273,	4:2, ... 13, 311	13:2-3, ... 136

Scripture Index

13:25–14:38, ... 119, 125
14:1, ... 378
14:8, ... 183
14:11, ... 122, 126
14:22-23, ... 119
14:28, ... 211
14:29, ... 32, 126
14:30-31, ... 126
16:22, ... 489, 490
17:8-10, ... 308
18:8, ... 165
18:8-10, ... 543
18:21-32, ... 231
19, ... 317, 323
19:2, ... 324
19:2-4, ... 323
19:3, ... 545
19:4-6, ... 336
19:6, 51, ... 335
19:9, ... 322
19:11, ... 323
19:12, ... 19, 375
20:1-13, ... 119, 125
20:8-11, ... 308
20:12, ... 127
24:4, ... 16, 180
26:59, ... 445
26:65, ... 145
27:16, ... 489, 490
28:3-8, ... 263
29:7-11, ... 263
31:23, ... 322
32:12-13, ... 135
35:30, ... 386

Deuteronomy
1:8, ... 211
4:9-14, ... 505, 506
4:10, ... 507
4:15-24, ... 517
4:16, ... 279
5:8-10, ... 517
5:15, ... 144
5:18, ... 530
5:19, ... 532
5:22-27, ... 505, 506
5:24, ... 31
6:10, ... 50
7:8-9, ... 12, 211
8:5, ... 482
8:10, ... 237
8:18, ... 211
9:3, ... 518
9:13-21, ... 505, 506
10:3, ... 307
10:5, ... 308
11:2, ... 482
11:8-17, ... 199

12:6-7, ... 19, 231
12:9-10, ... 119
13:8, ... 386
14:29, ... 231
17:2-7, ... 385–386
18:1-8, ... 231
18:15-19, ... 102
19:13, ... 386
21:5, ... 231
21:15-17, ... 499
21:16-17, ... 50
21:22-23, ... 476
22:20-25, ... 531
27:3, ... 183
27:15-26, ... 199
28:2, ... 200
29:6, ... 292
29:12-14, ... 211
29:16-28, ... 497
29:18, ... 492
29:23-27, ... 200
29:27, ... 378
29:29, ... 559
31:6, 8, ... 533
31:27-29, ... 388
32:2, ... 200
32:1-43, ... 388
32:35-36, ... 383
32:40, ... 211
32:43, ... 41, 43, 47, 48,
 .... 49, 50, 51

Joshua
1:1, ... 455
1:1-3, ... 135
1:5, ... 525, 533–534
1:6, ... 427
1:13, ... 119
2, ... 453, 455
2:1, ... 457
2:1-7, ... 455
2:3, ... 456
2:8-21, ... 454
5:1-9, ... 452
5:6, ... 183
6, ... 455
6:2, 7, ... 453
6:20-25, ... 454
6:25, ... 455
8:3-8, ... 457
10:24, ... 62
16–17, ... 441
23:10-11, ... 453
24:1-13, ... 410
24:32, ... 442

Judges
6:11–8:32, ... 460

6:15-18, ... 462
10:6-12, ... 460
10:6–12:7, ... 468
11:24, ... 427
11:29-40, ... 468
11:30-31, ... 468
11:37, ... 469
13:1–16:31, ... 460
13:3-5, ... 528
14:5-6, ... 462
16:21, ... 93
16:23-31, ... 462
20:2, ... 139
20:27, ... 307

Ruth
1:16-17, ... 454
4:29, ... 455

1 Samuel
1:12-20, ... 462
2:4, ... 462
3:20, ... 460
4:4, ... 307
4:11–6:21, ... 308
7:1-3, ... 308
7:15, ... 460
10:1, ... 55
12:6, ... 103
14:24, ... 311
14:45, ... 139
15:17, ... 55
15:22, ... 353
15:29, ... 219
16:1-5, ... 457
17:28, ... 121
17:34-36, ... 462
17:41-49, ... 462
20:13, ... 211

2 Samuel
5:2, ... 561
5:7, ... 510
7:1-3, ... 46
7:12, ... 462
7:12-14, ... 243
7:14, ... 41, 43, 44, 45, 47,
 .... 54, 250
12:7, ... 55
14:13, ... 139
14:22, ... 237
21:3, ... 237
22:26, ... 173
23:5, ... 45

1 Kings
1:47, ... 237
1:48, ... 237

5:3, ... 62	**Esther**	50:14, ... 23, 548, 549
6:20-22, ... 305	10:3, ... 139	51:7, ... 335
8:1, ... 232, 510		51:16-17, ... 353
8:9, ... 308	**Job**	68:5, ... 507
8:27, ... 271, 280	1-2, ... 91	68:8, ... 513
8:56, ... 119, 139	1:6, ... 43	69:28, ... 507
17:8-24, ... 462	2:1, ... 43	69:9, ... 534
18:13, ... 463	5:20, ... 171	72:15, ... 237
19:2-18, ... 461	7:17, ... 76	72:7, ... 54, 232
21:13, ... 465	9:33, ... 282	76:2, ... 232
	24:15-25, ... 531	78, ... 410
2 Kings	25:6, ... 76	78:13, ... 451
4:8-37, ... 462	28:24, ... 150	78:70-72, ... 243
6:31-7:2, ... 461	38:7, ... 43	78:71-72, ... 561
9:3, ... 55		80:1, ... 307
11:12, ... 44	**Psalms**	82:1-2, ... 225
11:17, ... 291	1:3, ... 199	82:6, ... 78
19:31, ... 510	2, ... 43	84:10, ... 448
	2:6, ... 510	86:8, ... 78
1 Chronicles	2:7, ... 41, 43, 166, 167,	86:15, ... 95
5:1-2, ... 499	.... 175, 250	87:1-3, ... 511
13:10, ... 165	2:8, ... 29, 44	87:2, ... 510
17:13, ... 41, 46	5:10, ... 223	89:3, ... 211
22:10, ... 45	6:20, ... 223	89:3-4, ... 45, 54
22:19, ... 297	7:7-8, ... 225	89:20, ... 55
23:13, ... 165	8, ... 74, 76, 79, 534	89:27, ... 29, 50
28:6, ... 45	8:4, ... 73	89:29, ... 46
28:9, ... 150	8:4-6, ... 71–72, 75	90:1-2, ... 59
28:11, ... 279	8:5, ... 78	90:5-6, ... 76
28:11-12, ... 279	8:6, ... 60, 81	91:11-12, ... 64
28:20, ... 533	12:6, ... 180	95, ... 114, 116–118, 123,
29:15, ... 435	18:30, ... 180	.... 135, 146
29:20, ... 237	22, ... 534	95:1, ... 138
	22:1, ... 10, 24, 55, 88	95:7, ... 122
2 Chronicles	22:22, ... 82, 86	95:7-8, ... 134
1:8, ... 45	22:24, ... 170	95:7-11, ... 113, 120, 121, 146
5:10, ... 308	23:1, ... 561	95:8, ... 125
8:16, ... 173	29:1, ... 43	95:9, ... 140
16:9, ... 311	33:13, ... 150	95:10, ... 164
21:3, ... 50, 499	33:19, ... 171	95:11, ... 126, 130, 133
22:11, ... 244	33:6, ... 35, 415	97:7, ... 47, 48, 49, 51
24:20-21, ... 465	34, ... 534	99:1, ... 307
26:16-21, ... 168, 243	34:14, ... 492, 494	100:3, ... 292
29:31, ... 548	34:15, ... 171	100:4, ... 285
30:9, ... 95	36:9, ... 31	102, ... 59
31:2-12, ... 231	39:12, ... 435	102:23-24, ... 58
	40, ... 352, 354	102:25-27, ... 41, 56, 57, 65
Nehemiah	40:20-21, ... 150	102:27, ... 552
6:16, ... 173	40:6-8, ... 250, 346, 351,	103:1, ... 237
9:6-31, ... 410	.... 353, 355	103:8-13, ... 482
9:7-8, ... 427	45, ... 54	103:13, ... 491
9:11, ... 451	45:6-7, ... 41, 53	103:20-21, ... 52, 63
9:17, ... 95	45:7, ... 56	104:1-2, ... 31
9:22-25, ... 462	48:2, ... 510	104:4, ... 41, 52, 63
9:26, ... 463	50:3, ... 518	104:5-6, ... 59
10:32-39, ... 231	50:5, ... 333	105, ... 410
12:44, ... 231	50:8-15, ... 353	105:9-11, ... 426
	50:10, ... 549	105:19, ... 180

Scripture Index

106, ... 410
106:9-12, ... 451
106:20, ... 279
106:27, ... 432
107:11, ... 180
107:22, ... 548
109:31, ... 171
110:1, ... 41, 60, 63, 74, 81,
.... 167, 168, 227, 274,
.... 361, 476
110:2, ... 232
110:4, ... 60, 162, 166, 167,
.... 168, 175, 212, 221, 223
.... 225–226, 227–230,
.... 233–235, 240–242,
.... 245–246, 248–249,
.... 250, 256, 266, 274, 362
118:6, ... 525, 533–534
118:22-26, ... 534
119:82, ... 180
119:97, ... 294
119:110, ... 176, 164
122:2, ... 507
123:2, ... 62
125:1, ... 510
132:8, ... 307
132:11-12, ... 45, 54
132:13, ... 510
132:14, ... 119
133:1, ... 526
133:3, ... 510
135, ... 410
136, ... 410
136:13-15, ... 451
138:2, ... 180
140:2, ... 121
144:3, ... 76
145:13, ... 54
145:8, ... 95
147:12, ... 232

Proverbs
1:2, 7, ... 486
3:4-5, ... 485
3:11-12, ... 480, 485, 486–487
4:20-27, ... 493–494
4:26, ... 492
5:15-23, ... 531
6:23, ... 486
8:10, ... 486
13:24, ... 485, 486
15:29, ... 171
16:8, ... 448
17:18, ... 254
22:26, ... 254
23:13, ... 486
26:23, ... 121
27:17, ... 378

Ecclesiastes
5:10, ... 532
12:7, ... 490

Isaiah
1:10-13, ... 353
1:11, ... 417
4:3, ... 507
5:1-7, ... 199
5:24, ... 180
7:14, ... 45
8:17-18, ... 82, 86, 87, 88, 89
8:18, ... 510
9:6-7, ... 45, 232
9:7, ... 54
11:1, ... 45
26:11, ... 384, 385
26:20, ... 393, 398, 401–402
28:13, ... 180
28:16, ... 510
30:27, ... 180
33:5, ... 510
33:14, ... 518
34:8, ... 510
35:1-10, ... 493
35:3, ... 492
37:16, ... 307
40:9, ... 232
40:11, ... 561
40:19, ... 347
42:1, ... 325
44:4, ... 67
44:6, ... 539
45:3, ... 292
45:23, ... 211
48:16, ... 102
49:8, ... 122
50:2, ... 451
50:9, ... 58, 59
51:2, ... 433
51:6, ... 16, 58, 59
51:10, ... 451
51:17, ... 80
51:23, ... 62
52:8-9, ... 510
52:13–53:12, ... 345
53, ... 317
53:6, ... 164
53:12, ... 259, 345
55:10-11, ... 146, 200
60:1, ... 31
62:11, ... 510
63:12, ... 451
66:1, ... 272, 280
66:22, ... 59

Jeremiah
3:16-17, ... 307

3:17, ... 121
7:8-10, ... 288
7:21-26, ... 284, 353
7:23, ... 291
8:19, ... 288
9:24, ... 292
11:1-8, ... 284
16:12, ... 122
16:14-15, ... 284
17:21-23, ... 288
20:7-10, ... 464
22:8-9, ... 284
23:5, ... 45, 243
23:5-6, ... 284
23:7-8, ... 284
24:7, ... 284, 290, 291
25:11-12, ... 284
29:10, ... 284
30:9, ... 284
30:22, ... 284
31, ... 282, 356, 359–366
31:2, ... 126
31:6-7, ... 510
31:9, ... 507
31:10, ... 561
31:31, ... 507
31:31-34, ... 273, 283–295
31:32, ... 284, 285
31:33, ... 284
31:35, ... 284
32:22, ... 183
32:39-40, ... 284
33:14-18, ... 274
33:14-22, ... 45
33:15-17, ... 21-22, 284
33:20-21, ... 284
33:21, ... 284
34:15-20, ... 211
34:17-20, ... 333
37:15, ... 464
38:6, ... 464
44:23, ... 93
46:18, ... 211
50:5, ... 284

Lamentations
2:20, ... 84

Ezekiel
8:12, ... 150
10:19, ... 307
11:22, ... 307
14:13, ... 197
14:14, ... 421, 422
15:8, ... 197
18:24, ... 197
20:5-29, ... 410
20:6, ... 183

20:12, ... 143
20:27, ... 197
22:4, ... 197
23:14, ... 347
34:23, ... 561
34:23-24, ... 45
36:25-27, ... 190, 376
37:23, ... 561
45:15-17, ... 163
46:11, ... 507
46:13-15, ... 263

Daniel
1:2, ... 62
3:1, ... 347
3:16-18, ... 446
3:23-27, ... 461
6:22, ... 461
7:13, ... 81
7:14, ... 54

Hosea
4:15, ... 311
6:4, ... 441
6:6, ... 353
13:14, ... 171

Joel
1:15, ... 380
2:13, ... 95
3:16-17, ... 510

Amos
5:21-23, ... 353
6:8, ... 211

Micah
4:2-3, ... 510
5:2, ... 45

Habakkuk
1:12-17, ... 403
1:5-11, ... 402
2:3-4, ... 393, 398–399,
.... 401, 402–403
2:4, ... 400, 404–405,
.... 410
2:6-20, ... 403
3:1-19, ... 403

Zephaniah
3:16, ... 510

Haggai
2:1-9, ... 514
2:6, ... 513
2:20-23, ... 514

Zechariah
3:1-2, ... 91
3:6-7, ... 374
6:12-13, ... 231, 232, 274
6:13, ... 168
8:3, ... 275
9:9, ... 232, 510
9:10, ... 232
12:1, ... 490
12:10, ... 337
13:7, ... 561

Malachi
2:11, ... 297
3:6, ... 219

Matthew
1:3, 6, ... 244
1:5, ... 455
2:11, ... 303
3:16, ... 325
3:17, ... 43
5:7, ... 95
5:9, ... 494
5:11-12, ... 463
5:16, ... 31
5:31-32, ... 530
6:12, ... 349
6:19, ... 396
7:22-23, ... 196
8:20, ... 81
10:1, ... 64
10:3, ... 455
10:28, ... 464
11:29, ... 139
11:3, ... 131, 399
13:1-23, ... 195
13:20-21, ... 196
13:32, ... 430
14:23, ... 170
14:31, ... 93
15:19, ... 122
16:28, ... 80
17:5, ... 43
19:1-12, ... 530
20:19, ... 337, 465, 560
20:22, ... 80
20:28, ... 319
21:5, 9, ... 399
21:9, ... 534
21:16, ... 76, 77
21:42, ... 534
22:20, ... 347
23:34, ... 463
23:37, ... 465
23:39, ... 399, 534
24:37-38, ... 421
25:34, 41, ... 437

26:28, ... 326, 336
26:31-32, ... 561
26:36-44, ... 170
26:45, ... 477
27:29, ... 337
27:34, ... 196
27:46, ... 170
27:51, ... 306, 373
28:20, ... 62

Mark
1:14, ... 69
1:35, ... 170
3:14, ... 103
3:18, ... 455
3:28-29, ... 196
4:1-20, ... 195
8:34, ... 546
9:1, ... 80
10:27, ... 439
10:34, ... 337, 465
10:38-39, ... 80
10:45, ... 63, 81
10:48, ... 319
11:9-10, ... 534
12:10-11, ... 534
14:24, ... 336
14:27-28, ... 561
14:32-39, ... 170
15:13, ... 198
15:17, ... 337
15:38, ... 373

Luke
1:1-4, ... 24
1:5, ... 244
1:5-6, ... 422
1:8-10, ... 305
1:11, ... 299
1:32, ... 45
1:35, ... 325
1:55, ... 430
1:72-73, ... 211
2:14, ... 261
2:32, ... 31
2:52, ... 172
3:22, ... 43
3:31-33, ... 244
3:36, ... 225
4:18-21, ... 69
8:4-15, ... 195
9:27, ... 80
9:29, ... 31
10:20, ... 507
10:25-37, ... 205
11:47, ... 463
11:50, ... 342
11:51, ... 465

13:34, ... 170	14:3, ... 437	8:7, ... 64
13:35, ... 534	14:9, ... 31	8:17, ... 190
14:24, ... 80	14:26, ... 250	9:3, ... 31
16:9-18, ... 532	15:1-11, ... 199	9:27, ... 93
16:15, ... 150	15:26, ... 251	12:10, ... 285
17:26-27, ... 421	16:6-7, ... 283	13:3, ... 190
18:32-33, ... 465	16:7, ... 251	13:15, ... 17, 563
19:10, ... 81	16:8-11, ... 146	13:22-23, ... 46
19:38, ... 534	17, ... 259, 354	13:33, ... 43
20:9-18, ... 199	17:1-26, ... 170	13:48, ... 507
20:15, ... 545	17:9, ... 176	14:7, ... 130
20:20, ... 93	17:20, ... 176	15:39, ... 378
20:38, ... 427	17:24, ... 496	16:1-5, ... 563
22:7-8, ... 338	19:1, ... 337	17:16, ... 378
22:20, ... 270, 336, 507	19:2-5, ... 337	17:28, ... 185
22:32, ... 259	19:29, ... 335	17:30, ... 329
22:39-45, ... 170	19:30, ... 317	18:21, ... 190
23:4, ... 157	19:34, ... 326	19:5-6, ... 190
23:18-25, ... 477	20:17, ... 55	20:28, ... 318, 326, 496
23:32, ... 267	20:25-27, ... 267	22:11, ... 31
23:34, ... 259	21:43-44, ... 119	
23:45, ... 373	21:44, ... 135	**Romans**
23:46, ... 170	22:4, ... 135	1:3, ... 46
24:27, ... 44, 136		1:3-4, ... 45
24:46, ... 36	**Acts**	1:4, ... 560
	1:9-10, ... 154	1:15, ... 130
John	2:22, ... 70	1:17, ... 400
1:1, ... 147	2:23, ... 477	1:18-20, ... 344
1:3, 10, ... 30, 65, 267	2:23-24, ... 36	1:18-32, ... 404
1:18, ... 450	2:26, ... 477	1:20, ... 420, 450
3:5, ... 190	2:30, ... 45, 211	1:23, ... 347
3:13-14, ... 81	2:32, ... 560	2:14-16, ... 344
3:34, ... 102, 325	2:36, ... 103	3:2, ... 180
4:21, ... 131	3:15, ... 84	3:25, ... 317, 318, 326,
5:17, ... 140	3:22-26, ... 102	... 329, 507
5:45, ... 100	4:11, ... 534	4:4, ... 397
6:29, ... 102	4:18-19, ... 446	4:13, ... 29, 330, 423
6:37, ... 89	4:25, ... 44	4:16, ... 330
6:68, 69, ... 154	4:25-26, ... 43	5:9, ... 318
7:18, ... 157	5:27-29, ... 446	5:12-14, ... 343
7:39, ... 250	5:30-31, ... 36	5:12-21, ... 81
7:42, ... 46	5:31, ... 84	5:19, ... 171
8:12, ... 31, 315	6:6, ... 190	6–8, ... 400
8:14, ... 131	7, ... 410	6:1-14, ... 357
8:50, ... 166	7:5, ... 210, 426	6:3, ... 189
8:52, ... 80	7:15-16, ... 442	8:5, 14, ... 491
9:4, ... 122	7:19-22, ... 445	8:6, ... 560
9:5, ... 31	7:21, ... 547	8:9, ... 357
10:11, ... 561	7:26, ... 451	8:11, ... 325
10:17-18, ... 356	7:30, ... 449	8:15-16, ... 209
10:18, ... 560	7:38, ... 99, 147, 180	8:17, ... 330
10:28-29, ... 195	7:44, ... 251, 279	8:28, ... 202
10:34, 37, ... 337	7:52, ... 463	8:29, ... 85, 347
11:35, ... 170	7:53, ... 36	8:34, ... 259
12:13, ... 399, 534	7:55, ... 496	9:1-5, ... 526
12:35, ... 122	7:56, ... 81	9:6, ... 195
12:46, ... 31	7:58, ... 545	9:33, ... 88
13:35, ... 205	7:59, ... 465	10:17, ... 130

11:3, ... 463
11:11, ... 196
11:11-24, ... 199
11:22, ... 519
11:26, ... 510
12:1, ... 516
12:10, ... 526
12:18, ... 494
13:9, ... 532
14:19, ... 494
14:23, ... 420
15:3, ... 166, 534
15:14, ... 203
15:33, ... 559
16:1, ... 527
16:20, ... 559

1 Corinthians
1:17, ... 130
2:3, ... 517
2:8, ... 248, 477
2:9, ... 437
3:2, ... 184, 185
4:19, ... 191
5:1–6:11, ... 532
5:6, ... 498
5:7, ... 451, 550
6:9-20, ... 531
7:1-16, ... 530
7:15, ... 527
8:6, ... 30, 65
9:7, ... 184
9:24-26, ... 483
10:1-13, ... 125
10:5, ... 126, 452
10:6, 11, ... 145
10:16, ... 326
11:19, ... 195
11:25, ... 270, 336,
.... 387, 507
13:5, ... 378
14:24-25, ... 148
15:8, ... 70
15:15, ... 560
15:21-22, 42-49, ... 81
15:22, ... 343
15:24-27, ... 81
15:24-28, ... 61
15:27, ... 77, 79
15:28, ... 29
15:50, ... 169
16:5, ... 131
16:7, ... 190
16:12, ... 554
16:13, ... 554
16:21, ... 554

2 Corinthians

1:20, ... 316
2:14-16, ... 146
2:16, ... 368
3:6, ... 507
3:7, 13, ... 105
4:4, ... 91, 347
4:4, 6, ... 31
4:9, ... 431
4:17-18, ... 464
5:8, ... 399, 507
5:21, ... 157
6:2, ... 122
6:10, ... 396
6:17, ... 550
6:18, ... 47
7:1, ... 495
7:10, ... 501
7:15, ... 517
12:12, ... 70
13:4, ... 36
13:11-14, ... 554
13:14, ... 567

Galatians
1:1, ... 70
1:4, ... 91
1:6-10, ... 186
2:20, ... 161, 267
3:7-9, ... 434
3:8, ... 130
3:11, ... 400
3:13, ... 476, 545
3:15, ... 285
3:16, ... 210
3:19, ... 36, 99
3:26, ... 491
4:4, ... 343
4:5, ... 491
4:7, ... 330
4:21-31, ... 433
4:26, ... 507
5, ... 400
5:9, ... 498
6:9, ... 477
6:10, ... 108, 205
6:11, ... 554-555

Ephesians
1:5, ... 491
1:7, ... 326
1:10-11, ... 202
1:18, ... 195
1:20-22, ... 81
1:22, ... 77
2:2, ... 91
2:13, ... 326
2:19, ... 108
4-6, ... 524

4:8-10, ... 251
5:2, ... 267
5:3-5, ... 532
5:22-33, ... 530
6:2, ... 210
6:5, ... 517
6:22, ... 554

Philippians
1:1, ... 496
1:21, ... 399, 464, 507
2:6, ... 166
2:6-11, ... 36
2:6-8, ... 171
2:9-11, ... 29
2:12, ... 517
2:12-13, ... 559
3:20, ... 435, 507
4:3, ... 507
4:9, ... 559

Colossians
1:1, ... 563
1:4, ... 205
1:4-5, ... 380
1:13, ... 91
1:15, ... 347, 450
1:15, 18, ... 50
1:16-17, ... 30, 65
1:20, ... 318, 326, 507
2:2, ... 206
3:5, ... 532
3:10, ... 347
4:16, ... 558
4:18, ... 554

1 Thessalonians
1:5, ... 206
1:10, ... 344
2:18, ... 555
4-5, ... 524
4:3, ... 357, 495, 530
4:3-7, ... 532
4:4, ... 535
4:9, ... 526
4:14, ... 560
5:2, ... 380
5:15, ... 205
5:23, ... 559
5:23-28, ... 554
5:24, ... 377
5:25, ... 554
5:27, ... 558

2 Thessalonians
1:3, ... 205
1:10, ... 399
3:13, ... 477

Scripture Index

3:16-18, ... 554
3:17, ... 554–555

1 Timothy
1:2, ... 563
1:10, ... 532
1:13, ... 211
1:17, ... 420, 450
2:5, ... 161, 163, 282, 507
2:6, ... 319
3:2, ... 496
4:1, ... 64
4:3, ... 530
4:13, ... 563
4:14, ... 190
5:22, ... 190
6:12, ... 93
6:16, ... 450

2 Timothy
1:9-10, ... 202
2:8, ... 46
2:22, ... 494
3:12, ... 487
4:9, ... 563
5:21, ... 554

Titus
1:2, ... 219, 377
1:7, ... 496
1:12, ... 185
2:12, ... 298
3:5, ... 190

Philemon
18-19, ... 254
19, ... 554
22, ... 554

James
1:2, ... 396
1:2-4, ... 487
1:14-15, ... 156
1:17, ... 219
2:15, ... 527
2:24, ... 418
2:25, ... 455
4:12, ... 171
4:13-17, ... 190
5:16, ... 171

1 Peter
1:11, ... 36
1:15-16, ... 488
1:18, ... 319
1:19, ... 157, 317, 326, 507
1:22, ... 526
1:22-25, ... 184

1:23, ... 147
2:2, ... 184
2:5, ... 108
2:6, ... 510
2:7, ... 534
2:8, ... 88
2:11, ... 435
2:17, ... 526
2:21-22, ... 477
2:25, ... 164, 496, 561
3:1-7, ... 530
3:11, ... 494
3:20-21, ... 421
3:21, ... 376
4:6, ... 130
4:11, ... 180
4:13, ... 36
5:2, ... 496
5:4, ... 561

2 Peter
1:7, ... 526
2:5, ... 421, 422
3:5, ... 415
3:14-18, ... 524
3:16, ... 179
3:18, ... 562
3:8-10, ... 380, 399

1 John, ... 18
[yes, a reference to the
entire book]
1:1-4, ... 24
1:7, ... 318, 326
2:2, ... 315
2:19, ... 195
3:5, ... 157
3:12, ... 91, 418
3:14, ... 205
3:16, ... 317
3:24, ... 283
4:9, ... 102
4:20, ... 450, 526
5:16, ... 196
5:19, ... 91

Jude
5, ... 126, 127
5-16, ... 410
23, ... 550
25, ... 562

Revelation
1:4, ... 539
1:5, ... 318, 377, 507
1:8, ... 399
1:13, ... 81
2:2-3, ... 474

2:3, ... 477
2:17, ... 307
2:27, ... 43
3:1, ... 195
3:10, ... 474
3:12, ... 507
3:19, ... 486
4:5, ... 31
4:11, ... 65, 267
5:5, ... 243
5:9, ... 326
8:3, 5, ... 302
11:15, ... 91
11:19, ... 307
12:5, ... 43
12:9, ... 91
12:17, ... 431
13:10, ... 474
14:1, ... 510
14:12, ... 474
14:13, ... 142, 507
14:14, ... 81
18:13, ... 303
19:13, ... 147
19:15, ... 43
20:12, ... 150
21:2, ... 437, 507
21:3, ... 291
21:7, ... 47
21:10, ... 507
21:23, ... 31
21:24, ... 31
21:27, ... 507
22:13, ... 475, 539
22:20, ... 399

Extra-Biblical Sources

m. Abot / Avot
1:12, ... 494

Apostolic Constitutions
7.37, ... 410
8.12, ... 410

Apology of Aristides 406

Barnabas
8:4, ... 323

2 Baruch
4:6, ... 271

1 Clement
17, ... 410
47:5, ... 527
59:4, ... 406

Dead Sea Scrolls
.... 224–225

1QM War Scroll
XII 4-5, ... 78
XV 4, ... 78

11QMelch Melchizedek
.... 228
II 25, ... 78
II, 10-13, ... 225
II, 7-8, ... 225

1QS Rule of the Community
III, 1-12, ... 323

4Q44, Deuteronomy
.... 47, 48

1 Enoch
14:15-20, ... 271

2 Enoch 228
24:2, ... 423
25:1, ... 423
39:8, ... 391
71-72, ... 225

Epistle of Barnabas ... 183
6:8-19, ... 184

Epistle to Diognetus
5-6, ... 443

4 Ezra
6:26, ... 80
7:106-110, ... 410
7:119, ... 188

Josephus
Jewish Antiquities
1.180-181, ... 227
16.125, ... 378
4.78-81, ... 323

Lucian of Samosata
The Passing of Peregrinus
§§1, 11-13, ... 406

1 Maccabees
2:1-60, ... 410
2:59-60, ... 461
10:28, ... 254
13:39, ... 311

2 Maccabees
2:29, ... 431
6-7, ... 463
6:26, ... 391
7:28, ... 423
7:31, ... 391

4 Maccabees
5:24, ... 420

6-7, ... 463
16:16-23, ... 410

Martyrdom and Ascension of Isaiah
5:1-6, ... 466

Mekilita Shirata
10, ... 271

Nag Hammadi Codex
IX, 1, ... 227–228

Nag Hammadi Library
.... 224

b. Nedarim
32b, ... 227–228

Ode
2, ... 47

m. Parah
3:1, ... 323
6:1-11:9, ... 323

Philo
Allegorical Interpretation
3:79-83, ... 226
3.96, ... 347–348
On the Life of Abraham
235, ... 226
On the Life of Moses
1.158, ... 538
On the Migration of Abraham
12, ... 348
17, ... 442
On the Preliminary Studies
99, ... 226

611

Psalms of Solomon
17:7, ... 432

Psalms Targum 228

Shepherd of Hermas
Vision 1.1.6, ... 423

Sirach
4:11, ... 93
15:17-20, ... 531
23:2, ... 311
23:18-23, ... 531
29:15-19, ... 254
44-50, ... 410
44:17-18, ... 421
45:1-5, ... 100
49:15, ... 442
50:19, ... 173
51:19, ... 311

m. Tamid
6:2, ... 301

Testament of Dan
5:2, ... 559

Testament of Judah
18.2, ... 532

Testament of Moses
3:9, ... 211

Testament of Reuben
1.6, ... 531

Targum Jerusalem 227

Targum Onkelos 227

Targum Pseudo-Jonathan
.... 227

Tertullian
To the Martyrs, ... 406

Tobit
3:3, ... 311

Wisdom of Solomon
3:1-4, ... 463
3:13, 16, ... 531
8:15-16, ... 147
9.8, ... 271
10:18-19, ... 451
10:4, ... 421
14:24, ... 531

b. Yoma / Kippurim
52b-53b, ... 303

m. Yoma / Kippurim
3:8, ... 165
4:2, ... 165, 263
4:4, ... 303
5:1, ... 301, 303
6:2, ... 165

t. Yoma / Kippurim
2:1, ... 165
2:14, ... 303

Creeds and Confessions Index

Belgic Confession, ... 7
7, ... 64n
8, ... 33n
10, ... 33n, 235
12, ... 106n
17-18, ... 244n
18, ... 82n, 158n
19 235
21, ... 34, 316n, 362n
23, ... 423n
24, ... 420n
26, ... 259n, 375n
31, ... 166n, 551n
34, ... 189n
35, ... 106n
37, ... 390n, 397n
161, ... 420n

Canons of Dort
1, ... 219n
1,5, ... 208n
3-4, ... 150n
5, ... 199n
5:9-10, ... 208

Catechism of the Catholic Church
128, ... 347n
241-242, ... 33n
296-298, ... 424n
303, ... 150
331, ... 64n
366, ... 490n
367, ... 148n
592, ... 329n
598, ... 193n
612, ... 158n
614, ... 357n
655, ... 193n
679, ... 193n
971, ... 538n
1013, ... 345n
1085, ... 316n

1165, ... 123n
1182, ... 543n
1216, ... 195n
1269, ... 551n
1544, ... 261n, 362n
1578, ... 166n
1601-1666, ... 530n
2100, ... 316n
2178, ... 379n
2683, ... 473n, 538n
2778, ... 108n

Chalcedon Creed ... 34, 158

Confession of the Evangelical Church (Germany) 283

Council of Trent
.... 7, 193, 204n, 247n,
.... 316n, 387n, 530n

Fourth Lateran Council
.... 424

French Confession
.... 7, 64n, 82n, 158n,
.... 166n, 244n, 316n, 357n

Heidelberg Catechism
.... 520
1, ... 92n
20, ... 405n
21, ... 208n, 362n
26, ... 424
27, ... 35
28, ... 490n
31, ... 250n
31-32, ... 39
32, ... 56n
35, ... 158n
36, ... 82n
37, ... 172n

40, ... 82n
46, ... 154, 316n
49, ... 341n
50, ... 61n
63, ... 204n, 397n
80, ... 316n, 357n
101, ... 217n
103, ... 141
108, ... 530n

Irish Articles 7

London Confession
.... 7, 122n, 217n, 362n

Nicene Creed 30n, 31,
.... 34, 65, 97

Sandomierz Consensus ..
.... 7, 64n

Second Helvetic Confession, ...7, 64n, 82n,
.... 111n, 147n, 158n,
.... 397n, 411n, 531n

Swiss Brethren Confession of Hesse .. 150

Ten Theses of Berne .. 111

Waldensian Confession .
.... 147n, 359, 362n,
.... 379n, 538

Westminster Confession of Faith
1.2, ... 7, 147n, 175
1.4-5, ... 214n, 364n
1.5, ... 117n
1.6, ... 390, xviii
2.2, ... 150
3.1, ... 218n

613

4.1, ... 30n, 424	35, ... 290n	27-28, ... 36
5.1, ... 35	37, ...97n, 158n, 261n	29, ... 317n
6.1, ... 127n	38, ... 316n, 326n	30, ... 259n
6.6, ... 127n	39, ...82n, 94n	37, ... 508n
7.2, ... 127n	40, ... 153	80, ... 532n
7.4, ... 329n, 331n	42, ... 38n, 175	86, ... 405n
7.6, ... 290n, 553n	43, ... 117n	89, ... 117n, 147n
8, ... 82n	43-45, ... 38n	90, ... 130n
8.2, ... 155n, 158n	44, ... 316n	
8.3, ... 166n, 256n, 261	45, ... 397n	
8.4, ... 341n, 357n	48, ... 39	
8.5, .. 317n, 326n, 329n, 362n	52, ... 39, 92n, 155n	
8.6, ... 329, 538n, 553n	53, ... 221n	
8.7, ... 316n, 326n, 540	54, ... 61n	
8.8, ... 117n, 259n, 317n	55, ... 259n, 316n, 341n	
10, ... 202	57, ... 316	
10.4, ... 192n, 196	59, ... 317n	
11.3, ... 357n	68, ... 192n	
11.5, ... 491	71, ... 256n, 357n	
11.6, ... 553n	72, ... 127n, 405n	
12, ... 64n, 492	74, ... 491	
13.1, ... 495	77, ... 185	
14.1, ... 405n	78, ... 473n	
14.2, ... 185, 414n, 435	79, ... 258n, 559n	
14.3, ... 475	80, ... 206n, 208	
16.6, ... 204n, 397n	83, ... 390n	
16.7, ... 420n	84, ... 344n	
17.2, ... 562	85, ... 39	
17.4, ... 166n	86, ... 508n	
18.2, ... 206n, 208, 219n	105, ... 122n	
18.3, ... 208n	106, ... 150	
19.3, ... 316n, 347n, 550	127, ... 488n, 538n, 551n	
19.6, ... 397n	129, ... 238n	
20.1, ... 159n, 290n, 317n	130, ... 488n	
20.4, ... 317n, 551n	139, ... 530n	
21.3, ... 517n	144, ... 203n	
21.5, ... 130n, 379n	147, ... 532n	
22.2, ... 217n	151, ... 68n, 387n, 512n	
22.4, ... 469n	152, ... 329n, 337n	
22.7, ... 469n	155, ... 147n	
23.3, ... 166n	159, ... 185	
24.3, ... 530n	160, ... 130n	
25.1-2, ... 195	174, ... 338	
26.2, ... 379n		
28.3, ... 313n	**Westminster Shorter**	
32.1, ... 496, 508n	**Catechism**	
	6, ... 37	
Westminster Larger	9, ... 424	
Catechism	11, ... 35	
4, ... 147n	12, ... 127n	
7, ... 150, 326n	14, ... 127n	
15, ... 424	20, ... 252n	
18, ... 35	22, ... 82n, 94n, 158n, 261n	
19, ... 64n	23, ... 175, 512n	
20-21, ... 127n	24, ... 117n	
24, ... 127n	24-26, ... 38n	
31, ... 252n	25, ... 82n, 264n, 316n	
34, ... 316n, 347n	27, ... 172n	

Subject and Select Author Index

Abel, ... 411, 416–420, 503, ... 507–509
Abraham, ... 93, 207, ... 209–210, 214–216, ... 227, 229, 250, 425–433, ... 436–439, 443, 524
access, ... 372–374
Adam, ... 76, 342–343
Adam, second, ... 81
adoption, ... 422
Alexander of Alexandria, ... 552
allegory, ... 226
altar of incense, ... 300–306
anchor, ... 220–222
angels, ... 36–37, 41–97, ... 507, 528
anointing, ... 53, 55
apocalyptic, Jewish, ... 15, 271
Apollinarianism, ... 97
Apollos, ... 6
apostasy, ... 67, 121–123, ... 191–202, 385–388, ... 400–401, 404–405, ... 512–513, 519
Aqedah, ... 438
Aquinas, Thomas, ... 83, 101, ... 120, 155, 393, 424, 478
archetype, ... 273–283, 297
Arianism, ... 103
Ark of the Covenant, ... 159–160, 306–308, ... 341–342
Associate Reformed Presbyterian Church, ... 511
assurance, ... 206–208, ... 257–258, 375, 381, ... 392–393, 412–413
Athanasius, ... 5, 552
atonement, ... 262–265, ... 311–313, 316–317, ... 327, 329, 333–334,

.... 337, 343, 344–345, ... 356, 372
audience of book, ... 9–12
Augustine, ... 3, 5, 424, 456
authorship, ... 2–9
awe, ... 516–517

balm, ... 393
baptism, ... 188–190, ... 313–314
Barak, ... 459–460
Barnabas, ... 4
begotten, ... 44–45, 167
benedictions, ... 231, ... 554–555, 558–559, ... 565–567
birthright, ... 498–499
bitterness, ... 497–498
blemish, ... 323–324
blessing, ... 440–441
blood of Christ, ... 315ff
blood of covenant, ... 387–388
brothers, ... 86–89

Cain, ... 417–418
calling, priestly, ... 165–166
Calvin, John, ... 6, 31, 36, 63, ... 105, 124, 149, ... 166, 201, 204–205, ... 277, 293, 320, 338, ... 394, 412, 491, 519, 529
Canaan, ... 427, 435, ... 441–442
canonicity, ... 1, 7
Carthage, Third Synod, ... 5
catena, ... 41–42, 51
censer, ... 300–307
chiastic structure, ... 25
Chrysostom, John, ... 5, 80, ... 92, 245, 348, 393, 422
church, invisible, ... 195
church, visible, ... 195

Claudius, ... 13
Clement of Alexandria, ... 3
Clement of Rome, ... 4–5
confession of faith, ... 102–103, 377
confidence, ... 397–398
contentment, ... 531–532
covenant, ... 1, 28, 210, ... 249–252, 332, 497, ... 502-503
covenant, Abrahamic, ... 127, ... 212–216, 253, 330
covenant, Davidic, ... 250, ... 253–256, 284, 330
covenant, eternal, ... 552–553
covenant, Mosaic, ... 253, ... 281–282, 285–286, ... 288, 290, 327, 336, ... 338, 387
covenant, new, ... 16, 281, ... 283–295, 321, 327, ... 328–329, 338, 355, ... 365–367, 387, 561–562
covenant, Noahic, ... 284
covenant, old, ... 367, ... 502–503
covenant of redemption, ... 251–252, 266, 479, 553
creation, ... 24, 35, 58, ... 132–134, 140, 414–416, ... 489–490, 539
creation ex nihilo, ... 409
creeds, ... 416, 423–424
cross, ... 110–111
cross, ... 476
Cyprian, ... 193

Daniel, ... 461–462
date of book, ... 12–14
David (king), ... 243, ... 352–353, 459–462, 533
Day of Atonement, ... 154, ... 262–264, 295, 301,

615

......303–305, 310–311,
......316, 318, 341, 347,
......360, 524, 536, 543–545
Day of Jubilee, ...225
Day of the Lord, ...380
Dead Sea Scrolls, ...11
death, ...90–91, 343
discipline, ...1, 480ff
dominion, ...77
doxology, ...562
duplex gratia, ...293

efficient cause, ...83
Egypt, ...444, 448–449
Elijah, ...461–462
Elisha, ...461–462
endurance, ...21, 471ff
enemies of God, ...61–62
Enoch, ...411, 416, 419–420
entrance
  See access
Ephraim, ...441
Esau, ...440–441, 498–501
eschatology, ...56–57, 74,
......................115, 131, 271
eternal security, ...257–258
Eusebius, ...38
exhortations, ...20–21, 370ff,
..................................525ff
exodus (from Egypt), ...442,
......................448– 451–452
expiation, ...292–293
eyewitnesses of Christ,
....70

faith, ...380, 405, 446, 449,
............................452, 458
definition, ...412–414
faithfulness,......107, 109, 537
false teachings, ...541–542
fear of God, ...129–130
fellowship of believers,
................378–379, 383–384
final cause, ...83
fire, ...384–385, 516–519
firstborn, ...49–50, 508
food, spiritual, ...178–186
foods (ceremonial),
..............................541–543
forerunner, ...374
forgiveness, ...326,
........................337, 355
foundation, ...431–432

genealogy, ...233–235
Gideon, ...459–460
glorification (believers),
................65, 69, 84, 203

God
  attributes, ... 34
  faithfulness, ... 377,
 532–533
  Father of spirits,
  488–489
  fatherhood, ...491–492
  glory, ... 30–31
  immutability, ... 218–219
  name, ... 76
  omniscience, ...149–150
  providence, ...532–533
  substance, ... 32–34
  transcendence, ... 489
  grace, ... 422
  gratitude, ... 516, 520–521
  great salvation, ... 71
Gregory of Nazianzus,
  .... 97, 297

heaven, ... 412–413,
  507–508
heavenly city, ... 428,
  .... 436–437, 507, 546–547
heirs, ... 37, 422, 439
high priests, ...99, 101–102,
  .... 162–165, 248–250,
  260–267
holiness, ... 488, 494–496
Holy of Holies, ... 220–221,
  .... 295–296, 305–306,
  .... 309–310, 312, 318,
  .... 320–321, 371–373, 544
Holy Place, ... 295–296,
  .... 299–300, 304,
  309–310
Holy Spirit, ...117, 214, 326,
  363–365
homily, ... 17–19
hope, ... 108–109, 206–208,
  .... 219, 247, 376–377,
  .... 380–382, 397–398,
  .... 402, 412
hospitality, ... 527–529
house, ... 104–109

idolatry, ... 497
imprint, ... 32–34
inheritance, ... 49, 119, 207,
  .... 330, 332, 338,
  .... 413, 422, 426–427,
  436–441
Irenaeus, ... 423
Isaac, ... 425–426, 429–430,
  .... 434–437, 439–441
Isaiah, ... 466
Israel, ... 451–453
Jacob, ... 425–426, 435–436,

...... 440–442, 499, 533
Jephthah, ... 459–460,
  468–469
Jeremiah, ... 461, 464, 465
Jerome, ... 5
Jerusalem, ... 11, 57, 226,
  .... 232, 507, 545
Jesus Christ
  ascension, ...24, 29, 45,
  ..... 61, 74, 154, 316, 318
  benefits, ... 80, 540
  creator, ... 38, 56, 65
  divine nature, ... 45,
  .... 55–56, 234–235, 239,
  .... 246, 325–326,
  539–540
  eternality, ... 56,
  .... 245–246, 256–257,
  .... 539, 551–552
  exaltation,.......... 36–37,
  .... 45, 49–50, 72–73,
  .... 79–80, 261–262,
  .... 274, 283
  example, ... 474–479
  glory, ... 67, 105–106
  human nature, ... 95,
  .... 170–171, 244
  humiliation, ... 78–79,
  .... 81, 172, 246
  immutability, ...57, 59,
  .... 538–541, 551–552
  impeccability, .. 156–157
  incarnation, ...81–83,
  .... 90–91, 169–170
  intercession, ... 175–176,
  .... 257–259, 317, 341
  kingship, ... 51–54
  love of, ... 476
  mediator, ... 540,
  552–553
  moral perfection,
  264–267
  name, ... 37–38, 43, 56
  nature, ... 32
  obedience, ... 169–173
  offices, ... 274, 330
  omnipotence, ... 60
  perfecter, ... 474–475
  perfection, ... 173–174,
  354
  preexistence,.... 45, 56,
  .... 234–235, 343
  prophet, ... 69–70
  redeemer, ... 38, 65,
  474–479
  resurrection, ...24, 171,
  316
  second coming, ... 29,

Subject and Select Author Index   617

.... 380, 399
session, ... 61–62,
.... 360–361, 474–475
Son of Man, ... 81
Sonship, ... 16, 27,
.... 42–43, 46–47, 153
suffering, ... 171–172,
.... 337
sympathy, ... 155, 159
threefold offices,
.... 38–39
two natures, ... 1
work, ... 269
Jewish Christians, ... 9
Joseph, ... 425–426, 440–442
Josephus, ... 297
Joshua, ... 37, 135–136,
.... 454, 457, 533
Judah (tribe), ... 243–244
judges, ... 459–461, 468–469
judgment, ... 344–346,
.... 384–385, 389–390,
.... 401–403, 507, 514–515,
.... 518–519
justification, ... 65, 69, 185,
.... 203, 292–293, 338,
.... 358, 366

Lamech, ... 225
law, ceremonial, ...542–543
law, moral, ... 294–295
law, Mosaic, ... 68, 266,
.... 347, 385
law, priestly, ... 242–243,
.... 245, 276, 281, 288
leaders, ... 537–538
Levi (tribe), ... 243
Lord's Supper, ... 336–338
love, ... 380–382
love, brotherly, ... 526–527
Luther, Martin, ... 6
lying, ... 455–458

Manasseh, ... 441
marriage, ... 530–531,
.... 534–536
maturity, ... 178–187, 190
means of grace, ... 196
mediator, ... 16,
.... 255–256, 328
Melchizedek, ... 1, 19,
.... 21, 162, 166,
.... 168–169, 173–174,
.... 177, 179, 209, 220–221,
...............................223ff, 285
mercy, ... 519
Messiah, ... 16, 81
ministers/servants, ... 51–52

Moffitt, David M., ... 175n,
.... 176n, 276n, 311n, 316,
.... 318n, 322n, 340n, 343n,
.... 356n, 371n, 508n, 560n
Moses, ... 37, 99–111,
.... 278–279, 335, 444–452,
.... 503, 505–506
Mount Sinai, ... 278,
.... 502–507, 513
Mount Zion, ... 502–503,
.... 506–507, 509–511
Muratorian Canon, ... 4

Naboth, ... 465
Neronian persecution,
.... 13–14
new heavens/new earth,
.... 74, 114, 138–139, 183,
.... 204, 206–207, 216,
.... 219–220, 241, 292,
.... 320, 330, 343, 396–398,
.... 412, 421–422, 428, 435,
.... 437, 443, 468, 472, 488,
.... 491, 508–509, 515, 534
Nir, ... 225–226
Noah, ... 225–226, 411,
.... 421–422, 479
Noahic flood, ... 226
non-canonical literature, .
.... 224–229
Novatian controversy, .. 193

oaths, ... 210–211, 216–218,
.... 249–256, 266
offerings, ... 416–418
Origen, ... 2, 4
outline of book, ... 19–22
outside the camp, .. 544–546
overseeing, ... 496–497
Owen, John, ... 6, 59, 62, 92,
.... 156, 163–164,
.... 244, 245, 257, 291, 349,
.... 367–368
pactum salutis
    See covenant of
    redemption
paideia, ... 1, 480–483, 485
pardon, ... 292–293
partakers, ... 123–124
Passover, ... 338, 449–451
Paul, ... 2–9, 12–13, 70, 123,
.... 125, 145, 184, 380–381,
.... 400, 423, 434, 517, 535,
.... 554–555, 557–559,
.... 563–564, 566
peace, ... 494, 559
peace offering, ... 547–548
Pentecost, ... 69–70

perfection, ... 241, 509
perseverance, ... 21, 116–117,
.... 393, 398, 562
perseverance of the saints,
.... 490
Philo, ... 15, 184
Platonism, ... 15, 270–271,
.... 384, 503
postscript, ... 523–524
praise, ... 548–549
prayer, ... 159
priesthood, Levitical, ...223,
.... 229, 238, 241–243,
.... 247, 260–267
priestly blessing, ... 231,
.... 237–238
priestly lineage, ... 242–243
priests, Levitical, ...37, 168,
.... 173
prisoners, ... 395–396,
.... 405–407, 529
promises, ... 204, 215–216,
.... 282, 333, 397, 413, 434,
.... 441, 462, 467
prophets, ... 37, 66–67,
.... 459–460, 463
propitiation, ... 96
providence, ... 35
psalmody, ... 511
purification, ... 35, 313,
.... 322–323, 326, 335,
.... 339–340, 357, 375–376
purpose of the book,
.... 16–17

Qumran community, ...323

Rabbinic Judaism, ... 15
rabbinical literature,
.... 224–225
race (athletics), ... 473–474,
.... 492–494, 501–502
radiance, ... 30–31
Rahab, ... 444, 453–458
redemption, ...28, 35, 316,
.... 319, 349, 354, 508
redemptive-historical
hermeneutic,
.... 23, 28
reincarnation, ... 345
repentance, ...188–190, 192,
.... 194–197, 202, 500–501
reproach, ... 447–448
rest, ... 113–150
resurrection, ...36, 438–440,
.... 462, 464, 560
revelation, ...24, 26, 28
reverence, ... 516–517

rewards, ... 397, 420–421
rhetoric, ... 17–19
right hand of God, ... 61–62,
.... 160
righteousness, ... 422–423,
.... 491
Rome, ... 11
royal wedding Psalms,
.... 53

Sabbath, ... 114, 133,
.... 137–138, 141,
.... 143–144, 468
sacrifices, ... 35, 163, 438
sacrifices, Levitical, ... 10,
.... 322, 324, 335,
.... 350–351, 451
Samson, ... 459–460, 462
Samuel, ... 459–461
sanctification, ... 65, 69,
.... 84–85, 185, 203, 293,
.... 357–358, 362–363, 366,
.... 377–378, 545
Sarah, ... 425–426, 428–430,
.... 432–433, 436
Second Temple Judaism,
.... 1, 15, 100, 228, 232,
.... 481–482
seed (descendants), ... 46,
.... 93–94, 432–434
shadows, ... 272–283,
.... 347–348, 467–468
shaking, ... 515
shepherd, Great, ... 561
sin, ... 483–484
sin, original, ... 157–158
sin, unpardonable,
.... 386–387
slavery, ... 92
sluggish, ... 178–180
Song of Moses, ... 49,
.... 388–390
sons, ... 484–486
sonship (believers), ... 84
sprinkling, ... 335–336,
.... 450–451, 507
suffering, ... 85, 393–396,
..... 463, 464, 465–466, 486–487
surety, ... 254–256, 259

tabernacle, ... 272–273,
.... 278–281, 295–299,
.... 306–314, 317, 336, 340
tabernacle, heavenly,
.... 272–273, 275, 278–281,
.... 296, 373
teaching/instruction,
.... 291–292

temptation, ... 156–157,
.... 483–484
Tertullian, ... 3–4
testament, ... 331–332
thanksgiving, ... 548–549
theophanies, ... 31
throne, ... 54
Timothy, ... 2–3, 8, 16, 17,
.... 555, 557, 563–565
tithes, ... 231, 236, 238
traducianism, ... 489–490
Trinity, ... 32, 58, 250
typology, ... 16, 195, 299,
.... 317, 320, 324, 339, 440

unbelief, ... 121–123,
.... 130, 134
union with Christ, .. 47, 124

veil of Temple, ... 371–374

warning passages,
.... 66, 382ff
weakness, ... 164–165
wilderness generation,
.... 119, 125–127, 145,
.... 195, 290, 411, 454
witnesses, ... 363–364,
.... 385–386, 471–480
word of God, ... 144–150,
.... 415
word of God (spoken),
.... 415
works righteousness,
.... 346
works, good, ... 377–378,
.... 550
worship, ... 50, 379,
.... 516–517

Zechariah, ... 465

Christian Focus Publications

Our mission statement –

STAYING FAITHFUL

In dependence upon God we seek to impact the world through literature faithful to His infallible Word, the Bible. Our aim is to ensure that the Lord Jesus Christ is presented as the only hope to obtain forgiveness of sin, live a useful life and look forward to heaven with Him.

Our books are published in four imprints:

CHRISTIAN FOCUS

Popular works including biographies, commentaries, basic doctrine and Christian living.

CHRISTIAN HERITAGE

Books representing some of the best material from the rich heritage of the church.

MENTOR

Books written at a level suitable for Bible College and seminary students, pastors, and other serious readers. The imprint includes commentaries, doctrinal studies, examination of current issues and church history.

CF4•K

Children's books for quality Bible teaching and for all age groups: Sunday school curriculum, puzzle and activity books; personal and family devotional titles, biographies and inspirational stories – because you are never too young to know Jesus!

Christian Focus Publications Ltd,
Geanies House, Fearn, Ross-shire,
IV20 1TW, Scotland, United Kingdom.
www.christianfocus.com